Fatima the Spectacular

A New and Very Different Study
of the Events of 1917

Expanded Edition

Bernard F. Kohout

Leonine Publishers
Phoenix, Arizona

Published by Leonine Publishers LLC
Phoenix, Arizona, USA

ISBN-13: 978-1-942190-30-1

Library of Congress Control Number: 2017932340

Printed in the United States of America
10 9 8 7 6 5 4 3 (revised June 2017)

Visit us online at www.leoninepublishers.com
For more information: info@leoninepublishers.com

ACKNOWLEDGEMENTS

I would like primarily to thank my wife, who put up with me during the long years which I spent researching and writing this book. I also thank Father Luciano Cristino, director of the Fatima archives at the time I was there, for his permission to use the archives. I further thank his assistant, Teresa Neto, for her help in locating documents in the files and for offering me space to work there. I thank my computer "gurus," Byron Keadle and Emile Dumas, for their frequent help in solving computer problems. I also thank my friends, Merle Ormond (now deceased) and Richard Grove, for reading earlier drafts of this book and suggesting changes. Finally, I thank my artists for the drawing of Our Lady of Fatima (Vicki Ebbers) and for the front and back covers of the book (Mary Kelly).

A picture of Our Lady of Fatima as described by the three young shepherds. They said she was about fifteen or sixteen years old, which is much younger than she is usually depicted.

CONTENTS

A photograph of the three shepherds who told of six apparitions of a beautiful and radiant "Lady" from heaven and of the Lady's promise of a miracle on October 13, 1917. From left to right, they are Lucia (age ten), Francisco (age eight), and Jacinta (age seven).

FOREWORD

This book resulted from my effort to improve my Catholic Faith. Like many modern Catholics and other orthodox Christians, I found it difficult to accept some of the mysteries of the Faith, especially the Eucharist. The Church has always advanced miracles as important support for its teachings. The early Church was able to cite the miracles of Christ and His apostles and offer witnesses who had seen these miracles. Unfortunately, we can no longer do this. Nor do we have adequate testimony for the many miracles claimed by the Church for the Middle Ages. There is, however, solid testimony for some of the miracles which are claimed for modern times.

After a short study, I decided that the "sun dance" which occurred at Fatima on October 13, 1917, was the most important of modern miracles. I presumed that the event had been adequately studied and reported, and that I would need only to read the best of available books to convince myself of the miraculous nature of the "sun dance." I was wrong, perhaps because I am too skeptical, although I do not come from Missouri. A skeptic would expect to find firm evidence of exactly what was seen on October 13, derived from testimony given in 1917 or 1918, with the names of witnesses and the text of newspaper articles. The statements of many witnesses and articles would seem essential.

However, until 1999 no book on Fatima used more than a few of the available articles from the press for the early years after the "sun dance." Until 1960 no author gave extensive witness testimony, and even this testimony is meager in comparison with what became available later. Since 1992 a much larger amount of witness testimony—letters and other written statements, and newspaper articles, all from 1917 and 1918—has become easily available in Portuguese, from books published by the Fatima archives. Much of this new material is published for the first time in English in this book.

Fortunately, I discovered the availability of these books and have devoted over five years to the study of them. Translation of the significant documents which had not yet been translated was relatively easy. Whereas, analysis of the material to obtain the best possible picture of what was noted by the crowd on October 13 was a difficult and time-consuming task. A small share of the material was directly contradictory. Much more involved variant versions or implied contradictions. Many sources were vague on important points or were grossly incomplete. Some presented difficult problems which had to be solved.

I am now able to present a reasonably firm and detailed picture of the phenomena noted by the crowd on October 13, of the apparitions which were reported by the three young Fatima shepherds, and to explain the contradictions, omissions and other problems reasonably well.

Most books on Fatima make little or no effort to consider the possibility that the phenomena of the "sun dance" have natural explanations. In this book I devote much space to this possibility. I offer a firm, natural explanation for only one of the phenomena. For the rest I present explanations which are plausible. I do not deny the possibility that the phenomena were entirely supernatural. One possibility is a stupendous vision seen by thousands of people, but not by all. A second possibility is real, but supernatural, physical phenomena. The latter possibility has mind-boggling implications, as I explain later.

In writing this book I have tried to consider all the pertinent evidence, whether or not it is favorable to the miraculous nature of the Fatima events. Presenting and analyzing this evidence has required much space, not only for the text but also for very numerous footnotes to enable skeptical readers to review the pertinent material and approve or disapprove of my conclusions. I expect that many readers will not want to read the more lengthy details. Therefore, in reporting and discussing aspects of the sun dance and the apparitions which require much detail, I have given summaries of these aspects in standard print and present the details in smaller print.

For Catholic readers I note that my natural explanations are not harmful to the Faith. Each explanation is a rare, natural phenomenon and the combination of rarities for all the phenomena makes an extreme rarity, a one-in-a-million chance. This allows the conclusion that the "sun dance," occurring at the time a miracle had been forecast in advance, was truly miraculous.

Finally, in this book I ask why this spectacular miracle occurred in our time and why a miracle was forecast in advance for this day and place. My answer is that the threat to the Faith is greater in our day than at any time since the early days of the Church.

The last half of this book consists of translations of documents— newspaper articles, letters, depositions, etc.—which I consider to be the most important evidence for studying the Fatima events.

CHAPTER 1

INTRODUCTION

The events which occurred at Fatima, Portugal, in 1917, are among the most spectacular of the twentieth century. For some Christians they represent the greatest miracle since the time of Christ. Even for skeptics the events, whatever their cause, merit the term spectacular. Strangely, they were little known outside of Portugal and Spain for many years and were almost unknown in the U.S. until after World War II.

Briefly, the Fatima events are these: on May 13, 1917, three very young shepherds—Lucia dos Santos, aged ten, Francisco and Jacinta Marto, aged nine and seven—reportedly saw an apparition, a radiant lady, "all light"; these children (often call the "seers") said the Lady asked them to return each month to the same place for six months; they reported on July 13 that the Lady promised to perform a miracle on October 13; after the purported apparitions on the thirteenth of June, July, August, and September some of those who were at the site claimed to have noted strange atmospheric phenomena; the reports of these claims caused large and growing crowds to gather there each month; on October 13 an enormous crowd (most estimates are from 30,000 to 60,000), drawn by these reports and the prediction of a miracle, gathered there; they witnessed a spectacular event that is often called a "sun dance." Believers called it a miracle. The crowd believed it to be real, but skeptics soon claimed that it was some form of mass hallucination. The seers said that the Lady asked them and others to pray, sacrifice, and reform their lives.

The testimony of a great many witnesses to the "sun dance" has been published recently. There are considerable variations in this testimony. Opponents claim that these variations show the non-miraculous nature of the "sun dance." Supporters say that variations are to be expected in the testimony of many witnesses to an unusual and unexpected event, and they find a strong concordance on basic elements of the "sun dance." As stated previously, until 1992 only a small fraction of this testimony was published, and until 1999 even less was available in English.[1] However, various earlier authors have given their own versions of the "sun dance," presumably based on some of this testimony, and in some cases supplemented by testimony of witnesses interviewed by them but not put into print. Many authors used a fairly detailed account of the "sun dance" by a witness, that of a lawyer, Jose Garrett. I use it and the authors' versions to provide a fairly brief and standard version of the "sun dance."

On October 13 it rained steadily and quite heavily before the hour of the expected apparition and miracle—at noon by the sun. The rain stopped approximately at noon, and the young shepherds seemed to go into ecstasy (the moment of the purported apparition). Some minutes later the oldest shepherd cried out: "Look at the sun," which had just broken through the clouds. Oddly, the huge crowd could stare at the sun without discomfort, even though at times it seemed to be free of clouds. Then the sun, a pearly gray, began to move back and forth in a zigzag fashion, it "danced." And it twirled rapidly on its axis. After a few minutes the "sun dance" stopped, and the sun became too bright to stare at. Then it became gray and repeated its dance, still with a spin. After a few minutes it stopped its dance and became gray once more. Shortly, it resumed its dance a third time, still with the spin. Next a large share of the crowd, apparently not all, had the impression that the sun, still spinning, detached itself from the sky and headed toward them, causing great terror to the crowd. Then the sun seemed to zigzag back to its regular place in the sky. After this the sun sent out colored rays of light on the crowd and the landscape, one color after

---

[1] *God and the Sun at Fatima*, (Stanley L. Jaki, Real View Books, Royal Oak, Michigan, 1999) presents much of the new testimony. I present this testimony, and much unpublished testimony, plus my analysis of it, later in this book.

another. Then many people in the crowd noticed that their clothes, which had been soaked ten or fifteen minutes before, were entirely dry. The "sun dance" was seen not only at the apparition site but also by many inhabitants of a village some eight or ten miles away.

The sun dance itself was truly spectacular. But the facts that it was seen by an enormous crowd, and that a miracle had been forecast for this date (and presumably for this place) three months in advance, make it much more spectacular. As such it was unique in history, whether it was a miracle, a hoax, a mass hallucination, an unheard-of natural event, an optical illusion, a UFO, or anything else. It merits and has received world attention.

A few movies and scores or hundreds of books, plus many magazine and newspaper articles, have been devoted to the events at Fatima. A few were critical, but most were favorable to the claim of miracles for these events. The major aim of most of the favorable writings was to urge readers to respond to the call of the Blessed Virgin by praying, sacrificing, and reforming their lives. As such they devoted relatively little space to the task of proving that the events at Fatima were truly miraculous, although they were convincing to most of their readers, practicing Catholics, and other sincere Christians. Some writers devoted much space to Fatima as God's answer to the challenge of communism. However, as far as I know, none discussed Fatima as God's major answer to all challenges to the Faith, challenges which had arisen or greatly increased in recent centuries and had become acute by the twentieth century. It is from this viewpoint, as God's answer to the modern challenges to the Faith, that I intend to present the Fatima events. I intend to ignore largely the call of Fatima, the call to prayer, sacrifice and reform. This aspect has already been well covered in previous books and articles on Fatima.

If the events at Fatima were, in fact, miraculous and if they are the greatest miracle since the time of Christ and the apostles, a natural question is why did God work this great miracle at this time and why did he promise in advance to perform it. In the gospels Jesus refuses to perform miracles to convince His skeptics; and it is virtually unheard of that a great miracle be predicted in advance. Why the great miracle and the advance notice?

One answer was given by the seers; the Lady promised a miracle to convince people that she was appearing there; and Lucia, the surviving seer, later said that the Virgin tied the Fatima events to the threat of communism. The Blue Army[2] and many other Christians tend to view Fatima as God's answer to the challenges of communism.

It might be much more. If the sun dance was truly miraculous, it could be God's major answer to the skepticism and unbelief of modern times. Certainly many of the spectators at Fatima felt that the skeptics there could no longer maintain their unbelief, not only in the apparitions but also in the God of Christianity. Fatima could also be God's major answer to the threat posed by materialism in our times.

I should add that other spectacular events, which are claimed as miracles in modern times, such as the one at Guadalupe in Mexico, beginning in 1531, or at Zeitun in Egypt in 1968-1971, may also be viewed as major answers to the skepticism of modern times. In this book, however, I am concerned only with the Fatima events. I intend to be complete, scholarly, and as unbiased as possible for a committed Christian.

My basic conclusions are strong—that Fatima is the most spectacular miracle since the early days of Christianity and that modern threats and challenges are the greatest since then. To reach these conclusions I have examined both earlier and modern challenges and threats to the Faith and earlier claims of miracles, as well as modern ones. I did not make this an exhaustive study. Christian history is very long and reported miracles number in the thousands. I have studied only a few histories and a dozen books on miracles. The histories surely report all the serious challenges and threats to the Faith. Presumably they and the books on miracles give the most important and spectacular miracles that are claimed by the Church. It will take only about twenty pages to describe the challenges and miracles. It will take much longer to support convincingly (for profound skeptics) my conclusion that the events at Fatima were truly miraculous.

I must now define my understanding of a spectacular miracle. Throughout history there have been many claims of spectacular

---

[2] The Blue Army is an organization devoted to the spread of devotion to Our Lady of Fatima and the fulfillment of her requests.

miracles. Many are preposterous. Others are plausible, but lack adequate evidence to support them. I am reluctant to accept as great or spectacular a purported miracle that is astounding but lacks the needed evidence to convince reasonable people. For me a miracle can be classed as great and spectacular only if it is reasonably well documented.

I must also note that in reviewing the history of Christianity, I devote over a dozen pages to the periods of greatest danger and bleakest prospects, but only a few paragraphs to the periods of progress and success. This will surely create the impression that Christianity was continually in danger of extinction from external threats, internal division, and moral decay. I now note that such an impression is wrong.

Next, I must note that I use the term "Christianity" in a restricted sense. I exclude the very liberal sects that deny the divinity of Jesus and the virginity of His mother. I agree that these sects are often very Christian in their activities, and note that they are much less threatened by the twentieth century challenges than the traditional sects.

Further, I note that throughout this book I often fail to use qualifiers, which sound practice would require. Thus I often say "apparition" instead of "purported apparition" or "seers" instead of "the children who claim to be seers" or "the Lady" instead of "the supposed vision," etc. I do this to save space and to make the text more readable. I hope my readers will understand that qualifiers are implied, when appropriate.

Also, I note that the sun dance and all the apparitions except one occurred at a natural basin called the Cova da Iria, located a few miles from Fatima. However, the events which occurred there are usually said to have occurred at the nearest town, Fatima, and I continue to do the same. Thus, I say "the Fatima sun dance" rather than "the Cova da Iria sun dance." And I often say "the Cova" rather than "the Cova da Iria." I use the term "pro-Fatima" to mean "favoring the Fatima events as miraculous." "Anti-Fatima" means the opposite. Finally, I sometimes say simply "Fatima" to refer to the sun dance or even to the sun dance and the apparitions.

Lastly, I note that in this book I use parentheses in three ways. One is to enclose statements which I have added to clarify a quotation or to simplify the reading of a statement which I am making. A second is to provide the gist of a text which I am quoting. In such cases I say "Gist" and then give the gisted text. The third is to indicate that the parentheses were given in the text which I am citing. I Indicate this by the use of double parentheses signs.

CHAPTER II

SOURCES AND DOCUMENTATION

Completeness of Sources. Since this book is intended primarily for skeptical readers—Catholics, other Christians, and non-believers—it is important that I use all available sources, whether or not they reflect favorably on Fatima. I have tried to do this and have not consciously ignored any significant material unfavorable to Fatima. I cannot, however, claim that I have found all the available material, especially that from newspapers. I would have liked, as a minimum, to read all the issues from October 13 to December 31, 1917, for the major newspapers of Lisbon and the newspapers of cities near Fatima. Constraints of time, plus my imperfect knowledge of Portuguese, made this impractical, if not impossible. However, I understand that the staff at the Fatima archives has done this. I use this archives as my major source.

In view of the importance attributed to Fatima in later years, one would expect that nearly all the Portuguese press had published much about Fatima in 1917. However, many newspapers then published little or nothing about the sun dance. (See *Fatima os Seus Problemas*, pp 297, 298.) Undoubtedly this was due in part to the anti-Church attitude of many newspapers, but was also due to the fantastic nature of the sun dance. Many editors would not believe in a "sun dance" and were unwilling to give it any publicity.

Original Sources. The few witnesses to the apparitions and sun dance at Fatima who are still living are in their nineties. They can no longer provide reliable testimony to what happened in 1917. Thus the only worthwhile source of witness testimony are written ones—

newspaper articles, letters, recorded interviews, depositions, and other written matter. In recent years this material has been gathered, in the original or in copies, into the Fatima archives. Its directors have attempted to gather all material, whether favorable or unfavorable.

Published Material. Most of the documents which give original testimony have now been published by the current director, with much useful editing and footnoting, and with careful reproduction of the original text—*Documentacao Critica de Fatima*, Vol. I, II, and parts 1 and 2 of Vol. III (1992-2004). These four books provide not only all of the material for 1917-1918 found in other books, but much which was not previously published. They are the major sources for this book.

The number of documents in these four books is enormous—about 1,000. A large majority provide no significant information on the sun dance or the apparitions. Most of the remaining documents, which are the important ones, were not available in English until 1999 (in Father Stanley Jaki's book). Many are published herein for the first time in English. However, it is much beyond the scope of this book to translate all the documents in these four books—some 2000 pages.

The Annex. For future scholars and readers who wish to question my statements and conclusions, I present, in the Annex, translations of all the documents which I consider to be important for this study, whether or not they were previously published in English. For each document I cite the original source—a newspaper article, letter, deposition, etc. I also give the pages in *Documentacao Critica* or other published books where the texts of these documents are found. In the relatively few cases where the original document is missing and only a copy is available, I indicate this with the translation. I assign a number to each document and refer to it by this number when citing it in the body of this book. Often I also cite books in English which provide a translation of the given document.

Part I of the Annex has translations of all the important documents except those which relate chiefly to the six apparitions. It is mainly concerned with the sun dance but also gives some information on the phenomena which were said to have occurred at the earlier apparitions. It further gives some information on the seers, their families, and even on the apparitions. Part II gives the interviews of the seers by four priests, plus the later statements of the oldest seer, Lucia, and testimony given to the Diocesan Inquiry Board in 1923 and 1924. It is the major source of information on the apparitions, but gives almost nothing on the sun dance.

Bibliography. I also give a bibliography of the books on Fatima which I have studied and which may be useful to future researchers. When citing them in the text of this book or in footnotes, I give only the name of the book and the pertinent page or pages. Readers may find the author's name, the date, and the name of the publisher in the bibliography. I also give a list of other books which are pertinent to this study of the Fatima events.

Reliability of the Fatima Archives. While the directors and staff of the Fatima archives might be suspected of bias and an unwillingness to keep documents unfavorable to Fatima, the material which I found in the Fatima files makes this suspicion seem very weak. The archives contain many documents—newspaper articles, letters, diaries, and books—which supporters of Fatima would wish to ignore. I use many of them in this book. I feel sure that it is the policy of the archives director to accept any material which relates to the 1917 events.

Reliability of Clergy. Since both the directors of the Fatima archives and the interviewers of the seers (those whose interviews have been kept and published and provide much detail) are priests, it seems appropriate to make some comments on their trustworthiness. Firstly, I have read no claim by Fatima opponents that these priests were not honorable and worthy priests. Secondly, for many generations most priests have led honorable lives. Admittedly, they are human and some have fallen to temptations of the flesh or the bottle. But a large majority have led worthy lives. There is thus little reason to suspect the directors of the Fatima archives or the interviewers of the seers of basic dishonesty. One may logically suspect subconscious bias, but an attempt to create favorable evidence or to suppress the unfavorable is unlikely.

Sourcing. For part of this book I made no effort to provide sources for my statements. I offer only a list of books which I used to obtain information on Christian history and on miracles. (See my bibliography.) I do not think that sourcing is necessary to prove that several times in the past the future of Christianity looked black. And since hundreds of miracles were reported in the books on miracles which I read, providing detailed sourcing for each is well beyond the time or space I wanted to give to this effort. For the Fatima events, however, I have attempted to give sources for all of my statements, except where I am clearly summarizing or presenting well known and unquestioned facts or uncontested conclusions.

Source Abbreviations. To shorten the space needed for sourcing, I am using the following abbreviations:

Documentacao Critica de Fatima, Volume I	Doc Crit I
Documentacao Critica de Fatima, Volume II	Doc Crit II
Documentacao Critica de Fatima, Volume III	Doc Crit III
Novos Documentos de Fatima	Nov Doc
Fatima in Lucia's Own Words	Lucia's Memoirs
Fatima from the Beginning, Fr. John De Marchi	De Marchi
Fatima in the Light of History, Costa Brochado	Brochado
God and the Sun at Fatima, Fr. Stanley Jaki	Jaki
My Annex, Part I	Annex or Annex I
My Annex, Part II	Annex II
Enquete Sur Une Imposture, Gerard de Sede	De Sede
Fatima Demascarada, Joao Ilharco	Ilharco

Types and Dates of Documents. The documents in the Annex include press articles, letters, depositions, and other written material. When referring to several or many of them, I usually call them sources rather than documents. Sources from 1917 are clearly the most reliable, and therefore the most important. A large majority of the sources in my Annex are from 1917. Most of the rest are from 1918, 1919, or the official Diocesan Inquiry from 1923. I use them as my primary sources in studying the apparitions and the sun dance. I have also studied all later sources, of which I am aware, and make occasional use of them in this book; most of them are available in English or French; they are cited in footnotes when I use them.

Primary and Secondary Sources. Sound practice requires that I cite primary sources, rather than secondary ones. However, I have decided to make one important exception to this practice. When citing sources which are found in the Annex, I cite the document number assigned to the given source in the Annex, rather than the source itself. (Example: Annex I #16.) I do this for the convenience of readers who wish to review the translation of the original text and decide for themselves if my statements are sound. Obviously, it is easier for a reader to turn to the given item in the Annex than to search for this item, usually in Portuguese, in another book or in the Fatima archives. Any reader who prefers to examine the Portuguese text can do so, since I cite the original source in the Annex.

Incompleteness of Data. Despite the large number of documents which are now available on the apparitions and the sun dance, many details remain unknown or uncertain. For example, for the last apparition we have conflicting statements by Jacinta on when World War I would end, which were not resolved before her death in 1920. (See pages 50-51.) We have no firm information on how long the apparent fall of the sun lasted. (See page 159.) Many other details are missing or unclear. It is a tragedy that very thorough interviews of many witnesses were not done and recorded in 1917 and 1918.

In view of the importance of the sun dance and its spectacular nature, one must wonder why neither friend nor foe of the Church made a thorough interview of the witnesses soon after the sun dance in order to determine its details. No firm explanation can be given, but it seems likely that friends were fully convinced that the sun dance was miraculous and saw no need to get the details of each phenomenon of this dance. Foes, it would seem, were firmly convinced that the reports of a sun dance were fantastic and ridiculous and did not merit any search for details. The failure of the formal Diocesan Inquiry to get needed details was clearly due to the greater interest of the inquiry leader in miraculous cures associated with Our Lady of Fatima. He apparently wished to make Fatima into a second Lourdes. (See page 67-68.)

CHAPTER III

THE APPARITIONS

Although this book is concerned chiefly with the "sun dance" of October 13, 1917, I cannot ignore entirely the events which preceded it and led up to it. The believability of the "sun dance," as a miracle, depends in part on the believability of the apparitions. God surely would not perform a great miracle which would seem to give His support to false claims of apparitions. I described the apparitions very briefly earlier and now must describe them, and the phenomena which were said to accompany them, in greater detail, as they were reported by the seers and eye-witnesses.

Sources, Footnotes. The description of the apparitions themselves obviously comes from the seers. In the latter part of 1917, the seers were interviewed by many people and gave accounts of the apparitions to many of them. Some brief accounts of the apparitions, and the phenomena said to accompany them, are available from such interviews and from second-hand and hearsay accounts. I give them in Part I of the Annex, documents #1-15, #21, #32, #42, #43, #49, #51, #55, #58, #64-66, #68, #68A, #69, #72, #76, #77, #79-84, #92, #95-100, #105, and in document #15 of Part II of the Annex.

The only detailed accounts of the apparitions which were recorded and have survived are those of four priests, and later accounts of Lucia. My descriptions of the apparitions of the Lady were derived chiefly from the interviews of these priests with the seers in 1917. The interviews by the seers' pastor, Father Ferreira, were made soon after each apparition. Those of the other priests were made between

September 23 and November 3, 1917. All of these detailed accounts are given in Part II of the Annex.

However, I also use a written account of the apparitions, made by Lucia in 1922, and her testimony to the Diocesan Inquiry Board in 1924. I use single brackets and italics to indicate that I am using one or both of these sources. Further, I use statements made by Lucia in her memoirs in 1937-1941, and indicate such use by double brackets and italics. I make significant use of these later sources only when I have no 1917 source.

Following standard practice, I use footnotes to show the source or sources for the statements which I make. In order to minimize the number of footnotes, I do not give footnotes for each statement or paragraph concerning each apparition. Instead, I footnote all the sources for the given apparition after I have described the apparition in full. Admittedly, this makes it more difficult for readers to verify each statement. However, in the chapters on the sun dance, which I consider to be the most important, I provide much more precise footnotes.

1915 Apparitions. The earliest "apparitions" were reported for 1915. They were said to be a white form of a human or an angel, seen at a considerable distance, which did not move or talk. Skeptics would suspect it to be a cloud formation. Lucia, the oldest seer, then eight years old, was said to have seen it, along with two or three friends, in early 1915. Later these friends confirmed to two writers on Fatima that they had witnessed the "figure" with Lucia.

Some time after this, the same "figure" was seen by Lucia, who was with two boys, one of whom later told a Fatima author that he had seen nothing. A third time in 1915, Lucia saw the same "figure" while with her cousin Joao, who said he saw nothing. When the village learned of the girls' report of having seen a "figure," perhaps an angel, Lucia was roundly upbraided by her mother and mocked by others in her village.[1]

---

[1] Annex II #9C and #12B, Lucia's Memoirs, pp 59-60, 160, 161; *Fatima Joie Intime,* pp 28, 29; De Marchi, p 45

The failure of Lucia's companions to see the "apparition" at the latter two of these events is both puzzling and disturbing. It brings up the possibility that Lucia was inventing these apparitions or was seeing many cloud formations to have the form of an angel. This would have serious implications for her later reports of apparitions.

However, there is a different possibility. It is that the first "apparition" was a very unusual cloud formation which closely resembled the form of a human or an angel; further, at the second and third occasions Lucia noticed a cloud which only vaguely resembled an angel, but (influenced by the first "apparition") she saw it as the "angel" which she presumed she saw the first time. Her companions of course saw no angel in such a cloud formation. If true, this explanation eliminates the conclusion that Lucia was deliberately inventing apparitions.

There remains the possibility that what Lucia and the two other girls saw was a divine vision or apparition. Even if unlikely, the possibility exists that God was accustoming Lucia slowly to her role as the chief visionary in 1917. If so, Lucia alone was gifted with a vision on the second and third occasions. While it may seem strange that such preparation of Lucia began two years before the 1917 apparitions, it can be said that these visions (or angel-shaped clouds) were followed by very different apparitions in 1916, according to Lucia's memoirs.

1916 Apparitions. [[*In 1916 three more apparitions were said to have occurred. All three supposedly were witnessed by Lucia and her two cousins (the seers). In these apparitions the seers were said to see an angel, transparent and more brilliant than crystal, who spoke to them, asked them to pray and make sacrifices, and taught them two prayers. The two girls saw and heard the angel, but the boy only saw it. Afterward the girls told him what the angel had said. At the first apparition the angel said he was the Angel of Peace. At the second he said he was the Guardian Angel of Portugal. Lucia declared that the same angel appeared in all three apparitions and that he was the same as the "figure" she had seen in 1915.*]][2] I note again that the statements enclosed in double brackets come from Lucia's memoirs, written in 1937-1941.

[[*At the third apparition the angel appeared with a chalice in his hand and a host suspended above it, dripping blood into the chalice. Leaving the chalice suspended in the air, the angel knelt and prayed with the seers. Then he rose, took the chalice and host in his hands, gave the host to Lucia and the contents of the chalice to Jacinta and Francisco, saying: "Take and drink the body and blood of Christ."*]][3] The seers kept the 1916 apparitions secret. They were first revealed to the public in 1937-1941 by Lucia, in her memoirs. Francisco and Jacinta were dead at this time and could not be consulted. These late revelations by Lucia caused much controversy and some doubt, which I will discuss later. (See Chapter V, Later Apparitions)

May 13, 1917. The first apparition of the "Lady" occurred on May 13, 1917. It was a clear day and the children—Lucia, Francisco, and Jacinta—were watching the flock and playing. Suddenly they saw a flash of lightning. Fearing bad weather, they gathered the flock and moved a short distance downhill. Then they saw a second flash and also an extremely beautiful young lady, dressed in white and surrounded by, or emitting, a very bright light, standing over a holm oak bush. The children were frightened, but the Lady said: "Don't fear. I will not hurt you." Lucia asked: "Where are you from?" (She always used the respectful "your Ladyship" for "you.") The Lady replied: "I am from heaven." Lucia asked: "What have you come into the world to do?" "I have come to ask you to come here for 6 months and at the end of 6 months I will tell you what I want. [[*Afterward I will return a seventh time*]]." "Can you tell me if the war will last a long time or if it will end soon?" "I cannot tell you yet, while I have not told you what I want." Lucia then asked if they would go to heaven and the Lady said they would, but Francisco would have to say many rosaries. Lucia asked if two dead friends were in heaven and the Lady said that one was in heaven and the other in purgatory.

[[*Then the Lady asked the children if they would accept sufferings, in reparation for the sins and the conversion of sinners, and Lucia replied yes. The Lady said they would suffer much, but God's grace would comfort them. On saying this the Lady "opened her hands for the first time, communicating to us a light so intense that it streamed from her hand, its rays penetrating our heart and the innermost depths of our souls, making us see ourselves in God, who was that light, more clearly than we see ourselves*

---

[3] Lucia's Memoirs, pp 61-65, 161-164

*in the best of mirrors." The children then fell on their knees and prayed
a prayer the angel had taught them. After a few moments the Lady spoke
again: "Pray the rosary every day in order to obtain peace for the world
and the end of the war."*]]

Then the Lady rose in the air, disappearing in the east. Lucia and
Jacinta saw and heard the Lady. Francisco only saw her. Only Lucia
talked to the Lady.

Lucia remembered the scolding and derision she had suffered earlier when her mother heard of the "figure" in 1915, and thus got the
two other seers to agree to tell no one of this first apparition of the
Lady. But Jacinta was unable to keep the news to herself and told her
family. (She did not, however, tell of their coming sufferings or of the
intense light.) The news quickly spread and Lucia was again harshly
treated by her mother and derided by her siblings.[4]

June 13, 1917. A crowd of some forty or fifty people assembled
at the Cova da Iria on June 13. The seers had been urged by their parents to go to the fiesta of St. Anthony in Fatima, but they resisted this
temptation and went to the Cova. The apparition occurred between
noon and 2:00 p.m. They said the rosary with the crowd, Lucia saw
the flash of lightning, and the Lady arrived from the east.

Lucia asked: "What do you want of me?"

The Lady replied; "I want you to return each 13ᵗʰ, *[to pray the
rosary]* and to learn to read, so that I can tell you what I want." *[Lucia
asked the Lady to cure some specified sick and bring conversion to some
sinners, and the Lady said that they would be cured within a year.]* or
[[*she asked the cure of a lame person, and the Lady said he would be cured
if he was converted.*]] [[*Lucia then asked the Lady to take them to heaven.
The Lady said: "Yes, I will take Jacinta and Francisco soon, but you are
to stay here some time longer. Jesus wishes to use you to make me known
and loved. He wants to establish in the world devotion to my Immaculate
Heart." Lucia said: "Am I to stay here alone?" The Lady answered: "No,
my daughter. Are you suffering a great deal? Don't lose heart. I will never
forsake you. My Immaculate Heart will be your refuge and the way that
I will lead you to God." Then the Lady opened her hands and again the*

---

[4] Annex II #1A, #1C, #1E, #1F, #1G, #8D, #9E, #9G, #13 A, #13B; Also Annex I #6,
#51, #58, #64, #68, #69

rays of immense light appeared and they felt themselves immersed in God. Jacinta and Francisco seemed to be in that part of the light which rose to heaven, and Lucia in the part that poured on the earth. In front of the palm of the Lady's right hand was a heart encircled by thorns, which the seers understood was Mary's Immaculate Heart, outraged by sin.]] At the end of the apparition the Lady rose in the air and disappeared in the east.[5]

In an interview with Father Antonio Alves in September 1917, Lucia said the Lady told them a secret at this apparition, which they were to reveal to no one. But in her fourth memoir, in 1941, Lucia said: "Our Lady did not tell us to keep it secret, but we were moved to do so by God."[6] In any case, the seers said nothing about the "immense light" nor about Lucia's mission to spread devotion to the Immaculate Heart of Mary.

At the Diocesan Inquiry one witness, Ignacio Antonio Marques, said in 1922 that he noticed the weather darken, he saw a cloud of dust, and heard a subterranean groan at the apparition site. At the same inquiry in 1923, Maria Carrera said she heard a hiss, like a rocket, and saw smoke rise to the east. But at the same inquiry another witness said she had been at the Cova almost every month and saw nothing unusual.

In view of the small crowd, it is not surprising that written accounts from only two witnesses are available. (They are discussed in the section "The Phenomena," in Chapter IV.)

July 13, 1917. Although these are the only statements of phenomena available from witnesses for June 13, it is likely that others reported that strange phenomena occurred then, since on July 13 a large crowd, estimated in the press at 800 to 2,000 or simply in the "thousands," gathered at the Cova da Iria. It seems unlikely that a crowd of this size would have come unless they had heard of some phenomena which would seem to confirm the seers' claim of an apparition.

---

[5] Annex II #2A, #2B, #2C, #2D, #2E, #2G, #9B, #12A, 13A; *O Mundo*, 19 October 1917

[6] Annex II 2D, #2G

Again the children arrived at the Cova near 11:30 a.m. and led the crowd in the rosary. Shortly after, the seers saw the flash of lightning and asked the crowd to move back. Then the Lady appeared over the holm oak. Lucia asked: "What do you want of me [*today*]?" The Lady replied: I want you to return on the 13th. [*"Do you want to learn a prayer?" Lucia answered: "Yes, we do." The Lady said: "It is the following: Oh my Jesus, pardon us, save us from the fires of hell, and lead all souls to heaven, especially those most in need of it."*]

The Lady added more: "Pray the rosary to Our Lady of the Rosary for the end of the war, for only she can help." Then Lucia asked the Lady to make a miracle so that all would believe (that she was appearing there.) The Lady said she would do so three months from then.

Lucia then asked the Lady for the conversion of two people and the cure of one [or several] people. The Lady promised conversions and improvement within a year. [[*She then asked them to pray and make sacrifices.*]]

[*At this apparition the Lady also told them a secret.*] Lucia told it, or part of it, in her fourth memoir:

[[*"The Lady again opened her arms, as she had done the past two months. The rays of light seemed to penetrate the earth, and we saw, as it were, a sea of fire. Plunged in this fire were demons and souls in human form, like transparent, burning embers, all blackened or burnished brown, floating about in the conflagration, now raised into the air by the flames that issued from within themselves, together with great clouds of smoke, now falling back on every side, like sparks in huge fires, without weight or equilibrium, amid shrieks and groans of pain and despair, which horrified us and made us tremble with fear. ((It must have been this sight which made me cry out, as people said they heard me.[7])) The demons could be distinguished by their terrifying and repelling likeness to frightful and*

---

[7] One source confirms that she cried out. Annex II #15E

unknown animals, black and transparent, like burning coals.[8] *Terrified and as if to plead for succor, we looked up to Our Lady, who said to us so kindly and so sadly:*

'You have seen hell, where poor sinners go. To save them, God wishes to establish in the world devotion to my Immaculate Heart. If what I say to you is done, many souls will be saved and there will be peace. The war is going to end; but if people do not cease to offend God, a worse war will break out during the pontificate of Pius XI. When you see a night illuminated by an unknown light, know that this is the great sign given you by God that he is about to punish the world for its crimes by means of war, famine and persecution of the Church and of the Holy Father.'

'To prevent this, I shall come to ask for consecration of Russia to my Immaculate Heart, and the communion of reparation on the First Saturdays. If my requests are heeded, Russia will be converted, and there will be peace; if not she will spread her errors throughout the world, causing wars and persecutions of the Church. The good will be martyred, the Holy Father will have to suffer, and various nations will be annihilated. In the end my Immaculate Heart will triumph. The Holy Father will consecrate Russia to me and it will be converted, and a period of peace will be granted to the world. In Portugal the dogma of Faith will always be preserved, etc. ...[9] *Do not tell this to anybody. Francisco, yes you may tell him."]]*

Then Lucia asked: "Is there anything more you want of me?" The Lady said: "No I don't want anything more today." Then the Lady rose in the air and disappeared in the east. Lucia said to the people: "Look

---

[8] Lucia did not report this vision of hell in her interviews with the priests in 1917, nor in her first report on the apparitions in 1922, nor in her testimony to the Diocesan Inquiry Commission in 1924. This strongly suggests that the seers considered it part of the Lady's secret. However, a woman with whom Lucia and Jacinta spent eight days in late September or early October 1917, stated in 1968 that: "They told me what most impressed them was the vision of hell. According to what they told me, if it had lasted another minute we would have died." *Ocho Dias com os Videntes da Cova da Iria*, p 39

[9] Following usual practice, I use dots to indicate that I have skipped a portion of the text which I am citing. However, occasionally dots exist in the text. I use bold dots to show this, as I do here.

there to see where she is going." In November 1917, Lucia told Father Lacerda that this apparition lasted "only a little."[10]

With the large increase in the crowd, we have more eye-witness reports which give details of the July 13 event—three newspaper reports and nine letters or depositions. Six merely confirm much of the seers' 1917 testimony on this apparition, including the request for a miracle, and Lucia's 1922 report of a secret. One newspaper gives nothing of value except an estimate of the number of people there. Two newspaper reports say the seers seemed to be in ecstasy.[11] Seven sources report unusual phenomena. (See the section "The Phenomena," in Chapter IV, for details on the phenomena.)

Comments on Witness Testimony. Now it is appropriate for me to state my method of handling the available testimony for this and later apparitions. With many witnesses, variations inevitably exist in their testimony. There are far too many witnesses for me to quote each one. Instead, I have examined all the testimony, produced my own version of each apparition and the phenomena which accompanied them, and cited all my sources. Occasionally, outright contradictions occur in the testimony, but in a large majority of cases the variations represent additions or omissions from one witness to another. Not being able to question the witnesses about these variations (since all of them are dead) I was forced to examine all the testimony and compare each with the others to determine, as well as possible, the most likely account of the phenomena which occurred with each apparition. This involved considering the reliability of each testimony—its date, its bias, its consistency with other testimony, its overall plausibility, etc. In doing this, I have naturally preferred the earliest testimony and that which appeared in the press or other public documents. Where variations occur on a given point, and both or several versions seem reasonable, I often give both or all versions, using statements like "one or several" or putting one version in parenthesis. I have, however, tended to ignore testimony which seems improbable, and that which is given by only one witness. I have tried to avoid long citations from

---

[10] Annex II #3A, #3C, #3E, #3F, #3G, #8D, #9E, #12B, #13B, #15E; Annex I #1, #2, #3, #81, #82, #83, #96, #98

[11] Annex I #1, #2, #3, #21, #81, #82, #83, #96, #97, #98, #100; Annex II #9B; De Marchi, pp 35, 76; Nov Doc, p 24

witnesses, hoping that those who wish to question my conclusions from the available testimony will examine this testimony in my Annex or search the written sources which I cite.

August 13, 1917. On August 13 a much larger crowd—estimated at four or five thousand—gathered at the Cova da Iria. Thus this time we have seventeen sources which give some details on the happenings. However, the seers were abducted and no apparition is reported for this day. When the crowd learned of the abduction many decided to stay until solar noon to see if the Lady would appear anyhow. Again a number of unusual phenomena were reported by some in the crowd and some said they saw none. (See pages 58-60 for details.)

The Abduction. The abduction was carried out by trickery by Arturo Santos, the head of the district in which Fatima was located. He was a foe of the Church but faked an interest in witnessing the apparition and insisted on taking the seers to the site by carriage. Instead he took them to Vila Nova de Ourem, where he kept them in his house for two days. Friends and foes of Fatima agree that his wife treated the seers kindly and let them play with her boys part of the time. But there are major disagreements on other points. It is worth discussing in some detail because Fatima supporters say that the seers' deportment, resisting threats and bribes, is strong evidence that the seers were truthful in telling of the apparitions.

Lucia's Version. The pro-Fatima version is largely based on the July 1924 testimony of Lucia to the Diocesan Inquiry Board.

She said: "(*Gist– Santos took them to Ourem.*) *He interrogated them at the district building, then took them to his house, shut them up in a room with two well-dressed men, it was almost night when they left the room and the wife of the district head fed them bread and cheese. He said he would let them see fireworks and made other promises if they would tell him the secret. ... The next day an elderly lady interrogated them about the secret, and afterwards they went to the district building where they were again interrogated and offered money to tell him the secret. He took them to jail, threatening to leave them there if they did not talk. They returned to the district building and since they persisted in saying nothing, he threatened to have them boiled in oil."*

"*He put them outside on a bench and ordered a servant to heat up the oil. He called Jacinta, saying she was the first to be fried. She went promptly, without saying good-bye. They interrogated her and then put her in a room which seemed to be in the jail."*

"*Then they called Francisco, (said) that she (Jacinta) was fried; that he would have the same fate if he did not talk; they had him put in the same room. They called Lucia, questioned her about the secret, (said) the other two were already fried and she would have the same fate if she did not talk. Although she thought this was the end, she was not afraid. Then they had her join the other two, saying it would not be long before they were fried."*

"After asking them if they chose to be burned, they took them to the home of the district head and they stayed that night in the same room. The next day they went to the district building and were interrogated morning and afternoon. They stayed there that night, and the next day they were taken to the (Fatima) rectory."[12]

Santos' Version. The anti-Fatima version is presented by Arturo Santos. In an article published on July 20, 1951, in *A Republica*, he says: "*(Gist— I took the seers to my house) where they were treated as if they were my family for the two days they were there. The Fatima children played with my sons and other children for two days, being visited by enough persons, some of (upper) society. What is false, very false, is that I threatened or intimidated the children or held them prisoner or incommunicado, or that they suffered the least bit of pressure or violence, as can be testified by all serious and honest people of the whole country, of all political and religious beliefs."*

In another document, undated but believed to be from 1955, he says: "*... the children ... were treated like my own sons ... dozens of people wanted to talk to the children. I refused because there were too many. (Gist— But I let one woman see them.) In the afternoon of that day, Dr. Antonio de Oliveira, and others whom I can't recall, were there, with the militia commander, to talk with the children, and these (children) entertained themselves on the porch with my sons and other children. It is false that the children were interrogated at the district building, as it is false that they were threatened or put in prison, or even were incommunicado."*[13] It is strange that Santos waited until 1951 to publish his denial, since in 1931 the local bishop reported the threat of burning in oil as part of his widely read official approval of devotion to Our Lady of Fatima.[14]

Other Evidence. There is some evidence to support both of these contrasting versions. In a letter of October 31, Isabel Melo describes the seers' treatment, clearly based on what she had heard. She says they were asked: "a <u>thousand questions</u> to trap them. They are threatened with <u>prison</u> and <u>they torment</u> them in every way." Father Manuel Formigao, in his written analysis of the seers' emotional stability, said to be from late 1917, says: "(Gist— Seers' ages were 10, 9, and 7.) How could they maintain their affirmations, despite <u>threats</u> made to them ... and the <u>imprisonment</u> they suffered. The district head ... trying by <u>threat and terror</u> to force them to retract." Dr. Luis Vasconcellos, in a deposition of December 30, 1917, reported his interview with the seers and said: "A woman said to be her (Lucia's) aunt helped sometimes on some questions and made various remarks about a secret. .... which they had and would tell to no one although they already had made various seductive offers and even had threatened (to put them in) a well or <u>burn them</u>, if they did

---

[12] Doc Crit II, pp 129, 130; Annex II #4F
[13] Doc Crit I, pp 374, 381, 382
[14] Doc Crit II, p 273

not reveal it." Lucia, in her first written report about the apparitions, in 1922, said: "And thus we arrived at Ourem. He closed us in a room, promised not to let us leave there until we told the secret. And thus three days passed; we were threatened with various punishments and promised some gold pieces." Finally, a pro-Fatima author said another priest, Manuel Perreira da Silva, said he talked to the seers behind the bars of a window."[15]

But other evidence shows that the seers played openly with other children. A pro-Fatima author says: "Antonio do Reis, born 1904, was a seminary student in Ourem on August 13. He had been a playmate of Francisco. He visited the seers at the house of the district head. He played with the seers in the morning; he stayed only twenty minutes, as he had to go to exams. The children knew they had been abducted, but not that they were prisoners." Another pro-Fatima author says: "Near 10 o'clock on the 14th the children, on their way from the house of the district head to the district building, meet Father Luis de Andrade e Silva. He listens as the children tell him all that had happened and comforts them." Lucia's mother and a pro-Fatima author said that on the 13th Francisco's half-brother and some other boys went to Ourem and saw the seers playing on the Santos' porch.[16] Finally, Lucia reported threats, but not that of burning in oil, in her first written report on the apparitions in 1922, nor did she reveal it to the hostess with whom she spent eight days in late September or early October 1917. This hostess also noted that she told the girls that they might be burned in a barrel of tar, clearly meaning that the seers faced this threat if no miracle occurred on October 13.[17]

The two versions are not quite as contradictory as they appear at first glance. Lucia's version does not exclude the possibility that they were treated kindly and played with other children. Santos' version does not deny interrogations at his home nor attempts to bribe the children, and the "talks" by the militia chief, the doctor and others could well have been interrogations. Still the contradictions are sharp. Lucia's account suggests that they were held rather tightly prisoner and not allowed freedom to play or associate with others. This suggestion seems clearly wrong and may not have been intended. But Santos' outright denial of any threats, which is the major contradiction, is hard to believe, as is his overall tenor, suggesting that there were no harsh interrogations or bribes. He was strongly anti-clerical, and he

---

[15] Doc Crit I, pp 187, 188; Annex I #69, #92; Annex II #4F; *Fatima 1917-1968*, p 224

[16] Annex II #15; *Rediscovering Fatima*, pp 84, 85; *The Sun Danced at Fatima*, J. A. Pelletier, pp 87, 88; De Marchi, p 100

[17] Annex II #4E; *Ocho Dias com as Videntes da Cova da Iria*, da Cruz, pp 28, 29

was under pressure from the press and probably from his anti-clerical superiors, to squelch the activity at Fatima.[18] It is almost beyond belief that he did not use the occasion of the abduction to question the seers separately and extensively, trying to find contradictions, or that he used no bribes or threats. If Santos had conceded use of interrogations, bribes and lesser threats, but denied the harsh story of boiling in oil, his denial would be more credible. As it is, Lucia's version seems much more credible.

Critics might say that it is strange that Lucia seemingly did not report the threat of burning in oil before 1924. However, before 1924 we have very few reports on the treatment of the seers by Santos, and they are very short and vague.[19] Clearly our sources had little interest in the seers' treatment by Santos. Dr. Vasconcellos' stated in December 1917 that Lucia or her aunt said that someone (surely Santos) had threatened to burn them. This suggests strongly that the seers told their parents of the threat of burning oil upon their return home in August 1917.

August 19 Apparition. On August 19, Lucia, Francisco, and his brother Joao were pasturing their flock in a place called Valinhos. Lucia had a premonition of an apparition, the "air was disturbed" or [[*she saw a flash of lightning*]] and she bribed Joao to go get Jacinta. [*When she arrived they saw a lightning flash.*] Then the Lady appeared over an oak bush. Father Ferreira's notes of his interview with Lucia on August 21 have Lucia say that she saw the Lady appear from the east. His edited version of the interview, Lucia's first written account of the apparitions and her testimony to the Diocesan Inquiry Board all omit this, and Lucia later explains that she never really saw the Lady come, but rather saw the flash and knew that she was coming.

Lucia asked the Lady what she wanted, and the Lady said that they should return to the Cova da Iria [*on the remaining 13ths*]. At the request of the woman who was keeping the money which people were leaving at the apparition site, Lucia asked the Lady what was to be done with it, and the Lady replied that the seers with two or three

---

[18] Annex I #1; De Marchi, pp , 95-99; Brochado, pp 82, 83, 108
[19] Annex I #69, #92; Annex II #4E, #8D; Doc Crit I, pp 187, 188

other children were to carry it in litters on the Feast of the Rosary or to the Church of the Rosary and use it for Our Lady of the Rosary.

The Lady also said that if they had not abducted them, or because they had abducted them, the miracle would be better known. (It is not clear whether the seers made these contradictory statements in interviews with different people or if their statements were misunderstood. In any case, the abduction brought more publicity and people to Fatima, which surely made the miracle better known.)

The Lady further said that St. Joseph was to come with the Child Jesus to bless the people of the world or to bring peace, Our Lady of the Rosary was to come with an angel on each side, [and Our Lady of Sorrows and] Our Lord were to come to give peace to the world. These are clearly referring to the visions which the seers said they saw on October 13, while the people were seeing the "sun dance." (It would seem that the seers did not recall well who was to bring peace and who was to bless the world.)

Lucia also asked the Lady for cures of some unspecified sick people who had asked her to intercede to the Lady for them. The Lady said some would get better or be converted within a year. [Lucia again asked the Lady for a miracle, and the Lady said that on the last month she would make a sign in the sun so all would believe.] The Lady then rose in the air and disappeared [to the east].[20]

September 13. The crowd for the September 13 apparition was again much bigger. Four sources give estimates of 15,000 to 20,000.[21] And more testimony is available. Six newspaper articles provide some details, plus nineteen letters, depositions, etc. As before, the information on the apparition itself is derived chiefly from interviews of the seers by the priests and from Lucia's written statements.

The seers arrived at the usual time—near mid-day. They prayed the rosary with the crowd, according to one source, or [this day they did not have time for it.] The seers saw the lightning flash and the Lady appeared from the east over the holm oak. She said: "I want to tell you to keep praying the rosary always, that she lessen the war, that the war is coming to an end (or that it come to an end); on the last day

---

[20] Annex II #4A, #4C, #4D, #4E, #4F, #4G, #12B; Also Annex I #32, #51, #58, #95
[21] Annex I #14, #51, #58, #105

St. Joseph, or St. Joseph with the Child Jesus is to come to give peace to the world, and Our Lord to bless the world, and that you come here on October 13." Lucia again asked for cures and conversions for many persons (again unspecified) and the Lady promised help for some but not others "because Our Lord does not want to believe in them." Lucia said that the people wanted to build a chapel there and the Lady replied that they should use half of the money they had collected for Our Lady of the Rosary and the other half for the chapel. Lucia offered the Lady two letters and a vial of perfume, and the Lady said they were of no use in heaven. [*For the third time Lucia asked for a miracle so that all would believe, because they were saying that she should be imprisoned or burned.*]

Then the Lady rose to the east, as on all the other months. Lucia told the people: "Look there if you want to see her."[22]

Once more there were many people who said that they saw unusual phenomena and many who said they saw none. (See pages 55-56 and 60-63 for details.)

The Threats. As October 13 approached Lucia's family and the townspeople began to worry what would happen if the promised miracle did not occur. Murder or bombing was feared. Among the many thousands of people who were expected, many having traveled long hours or days, at least a few might be so incensed, if a miracle did not occur, that they would try to harm the seers or their family. Lucia reported rumors of bomb threats in her memoirs. Her sister said that their family was very worried and begged her to admit she was lying about the apparition. But Lucia (and presumably the other two seers) showed no fear. In 1923 Lucia's mother reported threats on the seers' lives, and in 1917 another lady reported that a man at the apparition site had a knife and intended to kill the children if nothing happened.[23]

October 13. For this event I will discuss the apparition at once and will discuss the "sun dance" later. Testimony on both is very numerous.

---

[22] Annex II #5A, #5C, #5E, #5F, #5G, #12B; also Annex I #12, #13
[23] De Marchi, pp 127, 128, 133; Annex II #6G, #9E, #15D; Annex I #38, #92

The Crowd. On October 13 a crowd most commonly estimated at 30,000 to 60,000 assembled at the apparition site, despite a steady rain that became heavy later in the morning.[24] With this tremendous crowd we have many sources giving details on what the seers did and what they reported that the Lady said. The interviews of the seers by the priests is still the major source of information on the apparition and on the visions which followed,[25] but the other sources not only give confirmation of the priests information, but provide a few more details.

The Apparition. Near noon the seers arrived at the apparition site. With the help of a very large man, Dr. Mendes, they were able to push their way through the crowd to the oak bush. They prayed the rosary. Before or after, Lucia ordered the people to close their umbrellas. Despite the rain, the people obeyed and the rain gradually or quickly subsided. Lucia saw the flash and said: "Be quiet! Our Lady is coming." Then the Lady appeared, or Lucia saw the Lady descend, over the oak bush. Lucia told the people again: "Be quiet! Our Lady is coming. Look, Look!" Many in the crowd knelt. The children saw the Lady wrapped in a nearly blinding light, as before. Their faces were transfigured.[26]

Lucia asked the Lady: "What do you want of me?" The Lady replied: "I want to tell people to amend their lives and not offend our Lord anymore, for He is already much offended, to pray the rosary to Our Lady every day, to build a chapel here to Our Lady of the Rosary (Lucia was not sure whether she said this or said: 'I am Our Lady of the Rosary. Build a chapel here.') The war is ending this very day, expect the return of your soldiers very soon." (Defenders of Fatima say that the seers misquoted the Lady in reporting this "false prophecy" of the end of the war. See pages 44-52 for explanations of this false "promise.")

Lucia then said: "I have many (unspecified) petitions for cures and conversions. Will you grant them all?" The Lady replied: "I will

---

[24] Annex I #28, #35, etc. Both the crowd size and the rain are reported in so many 1917 sources that I see no need to cite more of them.

[25] Annex II #6A, #6B, #6D-G, #10A-C, #11A-D, #12B, #12D, #13B

[26] Annex I #16, #18, #20, #22, #25, #27, #28, #37, #44, #47, #49, #58, #71, #77, #90, #93; Annex II #6A

grant some, others not." Finally, Lucia asked: "Do you want anything more of me?" The Lady answered: "I want nothing more now." And then the Lady left. Lucia saw her rising high in the sky until she disappeared.[27]

At this moment, more or less, the sun broke through the clouds. Lucia said: "Look at the sun," or "The Lady said, 'Look at the sun.'" Then, while the people were seeing the "sun dance," the seers saw visions of the Virgin, St. Joseph, and Jesus in the sky near the sun.[28] After the visions, which Lucia said were short, the seers saw the sun spinning. Francisco and Jacinta also said they saw various colors on the sun.[29]

The Visions Near the Sun. The information on the visions comes mainly from the 1917 interviews of the seers by the priests, from Lucia's first written statement on the apparitions, in 1922, from her testimony to the Diocesan Inquiry Board, in 1924, and from Lucia's fourth memoir, in 1941. As before, I use single brackets for the 1922 and 1924 sources, and double brackets for the 1941.

All three seers saw the first vision. Lucia alone saw a second, and apparently a third, vision. None of the visions was said to speak. All were seen in the sky, near the pale sun. The first vision was that of St. Joseph, seen only from the waist up, the Child Jesus and the Blessed Virgin. St. Joseph was dressed in red or white. He was holding the Child in his arm, or the Child was standing beside his side. The Child was dressed in red and was about one or two years old. They were on the left [or right] side of the sun. St. Joseph [and the Child] blessed the people. The Virgin was to the right [or left] of the sun. She was dressed in red or white, with a blue cape. She was identified by the seers as Our Lady of the Rosary. The Lady had a shine [which blinded them]; St. Joseph [also did] or did not. They disappeared and all was yellow.

The second (or 2nd and 3rd) vision consisted of Our Lord and the Blessed Virgin. Both had a [great] yellow shine, and were on the right of the sun. Our Lord was dressed in white [or red] and had a small

---

[27] Same sources as footnote 25, plus: Annex I #18-20, #22, #23, #25-28, #31, #32, #34, #38, #39, #42, #43, #47, #49, #54, #55, #57, #58, #64-66, #69, #71, #72, #77, #78, #84, #-85, #89, #95, #96

[28] Annex II #6A, B, E-G; Annex I #26

[29] Annex II #10A, #11C, #11D

beard; Lucia did not see His hair or hands. He blessed the people. The Virgin appeared as Our Lady of Sorrows. She was in white [*or blue*], with a blue [*or purple*] mantle. They disappeared, [*and Lucia did not see them again up to now*—1922]. This last sentence, from Lucia's 1922 statement, seems to say that there was no third vision. And no third vision was reported by Lucia in her interview with her pastor on October 16. But a third is reported by Lucia in her fourth memoir, 1941. Further, in her interview with Father Formigao on October 13, she said: "First I saw Our Lady of the Rosary, St. Joseph and the Child, then Our Lord, then Our Lady of Sorrows, and lastly the Lady who seemed to be Our Lady of Carmel." Also, to the Diocesan Inquiry Board Lucia said that it seems she saw another figure, which seemed to be Our Lady of Carmel; she didn't see her face; she was always wrapped in light.[30]

Perhaps I should note now, as a partial explanation for the variations in the seers' descriptions of the visions, that many of the variations (those in brackets) come from much later testimony of Lucia, when her memory of the apparitions was likely to be weaker. I also note that the seers were constantly besieged for interviews, both before and after the sixth apparition. Many of the letter-writers in my Annex say that they or their friends interviewed the children. One said that Lucia was worn out with visitors and questionings, which began at daybreak and ended far into the night. And one of the priests, in his notes on his interview, stated that visitors were coming to see the seers at all hours of the day and that Lucia was near exhaustion.[31] But despite this stress, and despite their tender age, the seers' accounts of the visions are consistent in major points: the first vision was St. Joseph, the Child and the Virgin; St. Joseph blessed the people; the second (or 2nd and 3rd) vision was Our Lord and the Lady; Our Lord blessed the people. A last vision may have been Our Lady of Carmel.

---

[30] Same sources as footnote #25, plus: Annex I #18, #58, #64, #66, #72, #92
[31] Annex II #11A; Annex I #22, #24, #32, #33, #43, #51, #58, #64, #65, #66, #72, #85, #91, #92

CHAPTER IV

ANALYSIS OF THE APPARITIONS

Although the believability of the apparitions depends chiefly on the believability of the "sun dance" as a miracle, nonetheless other factors must be considered and analyzed. In doing so, I begin by examining the arguments of the opponents of Fatima.

Hoax. Many of these opponents have claimed that the apparitions were a hoax. Most, however, gave no details about why they were claiming them to be a hoax. Some said merely that they were a plot by Jesuits or unspecified priests or were money-making schemes. Only one detailed hoax has been suggested. I will examine it soon. But first I will discuss the most obvious choices for perpetrators of a hoax.

The Seers. No opponent has claimed that the seers were the perpetrators. Their tender age and their lack of education make this claim seem highly unlikely. One opponent said that the children could not have invented the apparitions, that an unlettered child could not have attained easily the ideas she gave out.[1] He probably referred to the unusual features of the purported apparitions, such as their regular monthly occurrence, the promise of a miracle, and the fact that one seer saw, heard and talked, another only saw and heard, and that a third only saw. The facts that the seers came from a pious family, and that Lucia was known to be pious, further argues that the seers were unlikely plotters or participants in a hoax.[2]

---

[1] Annex I #6
[2] *The Whole Truth About Fatima*, pp 23-42; Annex I #32, #43, #66; Annex II #8D, #13A, #14B

The Parents. No opponent has claimed that the parents of the seers were instigators or participants in a hoax. Presumably the reason is that Lucia's mother and both parents of Francisco and Jacinta were known to be pious Christians. It could be added that they made no effort, then or later, to profit substantially from the apparitions. They remained simple peasants, living from the fruits of their labor.[3]

The Pastor. Finally, no opponent has claimed that the pastor of the Fatima church was involved in a hoax. This is probably because he is known to have been highly skeptical of the seers' story about the apparitions, and because he was respected but not well liked by the seers or their families. He was even suspected by the local population of having collaborated in the abduction of the children.[4]

Father Faustino Ferreira. The first detailed claim of a hoax, as far as I have been able to ascertain, was advanced by Joao Ilharco in 1971, and some improvements of the same claim were offered by Gerard de Sede in 1977. They offer the following scenario:

> Four priests were talking together in 1914. One, Father Manuel Ferreira, the pastor of Fatima, is quoted as saying that nothing happened in his parish, it was poor, the people were unhappy and lacking in initiative. Father Bennvenuto de Sousa then remarked: "There is a way to enrich your parish quickly—an apparition like La Salette or Lourdes." Father Ferreira replied: "You're right, especially because the situation is favorable." This conversation was reported by another of the priests, who was present, and it became known in Lisbon. The authors do not claim that any of these priests took any part in any hoax, but only that they floated the idea.[5]

> The only participant named in the purported hoax is Father Faustino Jose Jacinto Ferreira, pastor of the nearby parish of Olival. He was not a relative of Father Manuel Ferreira, pastor of Fatima. It is not stated whether he concocted the hoax or only was the one chosen to execute it, nor whether the parents and pastor of the seers were participants. It is implied, but not stated that he hired two or three people to perform the critical first "apparition."[6] But first, in 1915, Lucia was tested as a good choice for the main seer, and was properly frightened by the ghostly figure.[7]

(Presumably they also implied that this figure was made and used by

---

[3] *The Whole Truth About Fatima*, pp 23-42; Annex I #22, #43, #51, #64, #66, #95

[4] *The Whole Truth About Fatima*, pp 132, 133, 221, 231, 232; Doc Crit I, pp 293-296; Doc Crit III 57-59, 72-74

[5] *Fatima, Enquete sur une Imposture*, Gerard de Sede, pp 88, 89

[6] *Fatima Demascarada*, Joao Ilharco, pp 97, 105-107; De Sede, pp 104-105

[7] De Sede, p 98

the hoaxters.) No explanation is given for the two-year delay between the "test" and the "hoax."

Details of the Hoax. The hoax, as proposed by Ilharco and De Sede, contained gaps. Acting as the devil's advocate, I have filled in these gaps, placing my contributions in double parentheses. The details of the hoax are as follows.

The Cova da Iria was chosen because it was remote and unpopulated ((and perhaps because it was a natural amphitheater, suited for viewing by large crowds)). Sunday noon was chosen as the time for the first apparition because most people would be at church or home, not working the fields in the Cova.[8] ((One or two operatives were hiding behind bushes there. They waited until the children reached the pre-planned location on the hillside.))

Another operative on a nearby hillside then emerged briefly with a mirror and flashed sunlight on the seers. ((As expected, this frightened them and they started down the hill. As they neared the bottom, the operative again flashed sunlight on the seers and on a nearby holm oak, where a woman, and perhaps a man, were hidden.)) A statue of the Virgin, about one meter in size, was raised over the holm oak by him or her. ((The remote operative continued to flash light over the statue and the children, partially blinding them, and they thus saw the statue as a shining vision, not recognizing it to be a statue.)) Francisco had gone to retrieve strays and saw only the end of the event.[9]

((Lucia, the oldest and leader, spoke up. Jacinta listened quietly. As planned, the woman, playing the Lady, told the girls to return at the same time each month, thus assuring a gradually increasing crowd.))[10] And the "Lady" told the girls that in the future ((they would not see or hear her, although she would be there and hear them.)) The "Lady's" answers and message would be given to the girls by Father Faustino Ferreira, and this fact was a secret which they must not reveal to anyone or they would go to hell.[11] ((Presumably the "Lady" also told them to follow Father's instructions to the letter. At the end of the apparition the woman or man lowered the statue, creating the impression that the "Lady" had disappeared.))

((Before the rest of the "apparitions," Father Ferreira told Lucia what the Lady would say. Presumably they were given questions to ask and told to wait some time for the "Lady" to answer. Also, presumably a hidden operative continued to shine a light briefly over the holm oak and the seers, creating the impression that the Lady was there, unseen. He may also have flashed a light at the end to signal her departure. The children then related the messages given to them by Father Ferreira as actually being given by the Lady, presumably believing that she had been over

---

[8] Ilharco, p 18; De Sede, p 99
[9] De Sede, p 104; Ilharco, pp 102, 103
[10] De Sede, p 109
[11] Ilharco, pp 105, 106

the holm oak. The failure of the crowds to see the flash or the hidden operative is not discussed. Further, despite the rain, no explanation is made by Ilharco and de Sede for the flash reported by Lucia just before the October 13 apparition. They admit that there are holes in their version of the hoax. Perhaps some future Fatima opponent will theorize that the sun came out very briefly on October 13 and Lucia confused that with the expected flash. Finally, an explanation had to be found for the prediction of a miracle, clearly a daring move on the part of the hoaxters.))

((Since the hoaxters could not have foreseen the weather and the "sun dance," they had to have some other plan for a miracle on October 13. This plan was to have Lucia say in advance that St. Joseph and the Child Jesus would appear on October 13. They would be seen only by those worthy of it. They relied on the principle of self-hallucination to produce a few hundred, among the many thousands, who would claim that they saw St. Joseph and the Child.[12] Actually a few of the crowd did make this claim, but it was overshadowed by the sun dance.[13]))

This claim of a hoax would not merit the attention I have given it if the authors could not have produced any evidence to support it. However, they did produce some such evidence, using only what supported their claim and ignoring contrary evidence.

Evidence of a Hoax. Some aspects of their claim require no evidence. The Cova da Iria was a remote spot and especially likely to be deserted at noon on Sunday. The flashes reported by Lucia could have come from a mirror. Father Faustino Ferreira was known to be a friend and advisor of the seers. However, the strongest evidence cited by De Sede and Ilharco were statements about the Lady which were ascribed to the seers: she was a pretty doll; she was about 1.1 meters (3'8") tall; she was always serious, never smiled, did not move her lips. This would seem to be more a statue than a vision.[14] The seers claimed there was a shine around the Lady's head, or around her, which could be due to the reflected light of a mirror.[15] There were many contradictions in the seers' testimony about the visions, which would seem to weaken the claim of a real apparition. (I discuss this issue later.) And the seers quoted the Lady as saying that World War I would end that day, October 13, 1917, rather than on November 11, 1918. Surely the Virgin, if real, would make no such mistake. (I also discuss this later.)

Contrary Evidence. While this evidence seems strong, offhand, the contrary evidence is much stronger. Thus, Father Faustino Ferreira was a friend and advisor, but not until after the apparitions.[16] Moreover, it is highly unlikely that any outside priest could come several times to the tiny village where the seers lived (to train the

---

[12] Ilharco, pp 130, 131
[13] Annex #51, #61I
[14] Ilharco, p 99; De Sede, pp 101, 102; Annex II #7A, #13A, #14B; Annex I #1
[15] Ilharco, p 100; Annex II #1D, 1F; Doc Crit II, pp 73, 94, 98, 105
[16] *Fatima 1917-1968*, pp 228, 229; *Toute la Verite sur Fatima*, p 55

children for their part in the hoax) without being noticed. Nor is it likely that Lucia, or all the seers, traveled to Olival (Father Ferreira's parish) before each apparition, given her (or their) tender age. Finally, in either case, the seers' parents would have to know of the arrangement, and were unlikely to have cooperated in any such hoax, given their pious Christianity. In short, Father Faustino Ferreira can be eliminated as a hoaxter.

There is also strong contrary evidence on the Lady's height. Thus the pastor's unedited and his edited notes on his first interview with Lucia in May, and his unedited notes for June have her say that the Lady was of medium height. However, his edited notes, not tied to any specific apparition, have Lucia say that the Lady was little more than a meter tall. His unedited notes have Jacinta say in July that the Lady was "small," the size of "Albina" (a girl of sixteen) and at an unspecified date that she was of regular height. In the October 11 interview with Father Formigao, Lucia said the Lady seemed to be about 15 years old. In 1923 a witness said he had heard a similar statement of Lucia from her mother on September 13, 1917. A girl of fifteen or sixteen is rarely only one meter tall. It should be noted that the statement that the Lady was a pretty doll, which appeared in the newspaper *O Seculo* on July 23, was clearly second-hand or perhaps third or fourth-hand, and thus possibly distorted. A statement that the Lady was 1.1 meters tall came from the unedited notes of Father Lacerda's interview with Jacinta, but follows her statement that the Lady was equal to a twelve-year-old girl. In his published notes he says that, according to Lucia, the Lady was the height of a twelve-year-old girl and might be 1.1 meters.[17] It seems likely that the improbable estimate of height came from Jacinta, a seven-year-old, and I note that even a twelve-year-old girl is unlikely to be only 1.1 meters (3'8"). Finally, Jacinta told a woman interviewer that the Lady was about her (the woman's) height.[18]

Admittedly, the Lady was described by the seers as always serious and not smiling, and Francisco once said he did not see her move her lips. But in 1923 his mother said that he saw the Lady move her lips. And the pastor, in his unedited notes of the second apparition has Lucia say that every time the Lady talked she unfolded her hands, while in edited notes of an unspecified interview he has Lucia say that every time the Lady talked she separated her hands more or less to the distance of her shoulders, and in his unedited notes on the third apparition he has Jacinta say that the Lady opened her hands when she talked to Lucia. Finally, Francisco is quoted by Father Formigao as saying that at the last apparition the Lady pointed to the sun.[19] Statues are not known to move their arms and point.

Lastly, if a hoaxter lifted a statue for the seers to see at the first apparition, it follows that he or she lowered it at the end of the apparition, causing the feet to

---

[17] Annex II #1B, #2A, #3A, #7B, #9E (question 18), #13A (question 2), #14B, (second part), #15G; Annex I #1

[18] Annex I #64

[19] Annex II #2A, #3A, #7A, #11C, #15C

disappear first, followed by the body and head. But Lucia told Father Alves on September 27 that at the first apparition the Lady disappeared slowly, beginning with her head, then her body and then her feet. And she told Fathers Formigao and Lacerda the same thing, apparently referring to the last apparition, October 13.[20] No statements that the feet disappeared first appear in the priests' reports nor in other accounts of interviews with the seers.

In summary it can be said that the claim of a hoax does not stand up. The seers were too young to have concocted it. They and their parents were pious Christians, who would not have taken part in a hoax. A detailed claim of a hoax was offered only fifty-four years after the apparitions. This claim is supported by some evidence, but ignores other evidence which is much stronger. The purported mastermind became a friend of the seers only after 1917. Evidence suggesting that the Lady was a statue is countered by statements of the seers that she opened her arms when she talked. Statements of the seers that she was like a doll are answered by more and stronger statements that she was the size of a woman. Other claims of contradictory and false statements by the seers are discussed in the next paragraphs.

Contradictions in the seers' testimony. To support the theory of a hoax, and to weaken the validity of the seers' claims of apparitions, opponents of Fatima cite a number of contradictions in the seers' statements about the apparitions. Most are minor, but a few are fairly significant.

Before discussing these contradictions, I must note some important considerations concerning them. First, a great many details on the apparitions were told by the seers to the priests and others. Thus, Fathers Formigao and Lacerda asked Lucia some 225 questions, Jacinta some 135, and Francisco about 75. Father Manuel Ferreira, the seers' pastor, does not give his questions in his notes, but only the seers' statements, which cover some eight pages.[21] Inevitably, in them, in the five long interrogations with Father Formigao, and the single interrogations of Fathers Alves and Lacerda, plus the three later statements of Lucia, some contradictions occurred.

---

[20] Annex II #10A, #1C, #13B
[21] Annex II #1A, #2A, #3A, #4A, #5A, #6A, #7A, #7B, #7C, and most of Annex II #8 through #14

Secondly, the seers were ten, nine, and seven years old. Their ability to remember all the details of each apparition, especially when asked about them weeks or months afterward, was less than perfect. There is no evidence nor even a hint that the seers had any copies of any of their interviews with the priests, which they might have used to refresh their memories. Also, their tender age may have caused them to misunderstand a few questions. Finally, they were extremely exhausted after the endless rounds of interviews following the October 13 event.[22] This may have caused them to answer questions quickly and without much thought, hoping to end each session as quickly as possible.

Thirdly, in the many times that the seers reported on the apparitions, they often attributed to the Lady words which had more or the less the same meaning. The same can be said of their description of the Lady. And they often omitted or added a statement of the Lady from one interview to another. I do not consider such variations to be contradictions.

I do not intend to discuss in detail each of the minor contradictions. I note, however, that contradictions occur frequently between statements made by Lucia in 1922, 1924 or 1941 and those made in 1917 statements. Lapses in memory over many years are normal. Some readers may wish to scan or skip this discussion of minor contradictions. I will, of course, discuss in detail the more serious contradictions. But first I must state that the various accounts of the apparitions and the detailed descriptions of the Lady are largely in agreement.[23]

MINOR CONTRADICTIONS

First Apparition

The Lady said only: *Come here* **for six months** or she said come **here** **on the 13th** **for six months**. The latter is less well attested, and was contradicted by Lucia

---

[22] Annex II #11A

[23] To document this broad statement, I would need to cite almost all of Part II of my Annex and many items in Part I. Readers anxious to check my statement need to read through Part II, plus the documents in Part I cited on page 13.

on October 19. In any case, the seers clearly understood that they were to come to there on the thirteenth at the same time as the first apparition.[24]

Second Apparition

You (singular) or *you (plural) are to learn to read.*[25] This subtlety in grammar was probably overlooked by the seers, leading to a minor contradiction.

The Lady's answer to the requests for conversions and cures: **They will be cured within a year;** *or* **If, he is converted, he will be healed.**[26] At most apparitions Lucia asked for cures and conversions. It is likely that, in interviews made weeks or months after these apparitions, the seers confused answers made at one apparition with those made at another and thus contradicted themselves or each other. Also, it is likely that Lucia in 1941 and even in 1922 made errors in reporting details of the apparitions.

She told them a secret.[27] Lucia told this to Father Alves on September 17, 1917, and Jacinta said something similar on October 11. No other sources report this, which suggests that no secret was given. However, in 1941 Lucia revealed a June statement of the Lady about the devotion to her Sacred Heart, which in July she asked to be kept secret. Perhaps the seers failed to mention the June secret to most interviewers. But an alternate explanation is possible, namely that Jacinta and Lucia (or Father Alves) erred in ascribing a secret to the June apparition. None is reported by Father Alves for the July apparition, when a much greater secret was revealed, according to Lucia's memoirs. Further, Father Alves has Lucia quote the Lady as saying, in June, that Our Lady of Sorrows and Our Lady of the Rosary was to appear in October, which elsewhere is ascribed to the August apparition. Father Alves' interview occurred in late September, three months after the June apparition. It is not at all unlikely, it seems to me, that both Lucia (or Father Alves) and Jacinta mixed up the months and ascribed to the June apparition statements which occurred in July and August, and that Lucia's memory was wrong on this point in 1941.

Third Apparition

Again there are **variations in the details of Lucia's requests for cures and conversions**, and in the Lady's answers.[28] The comment made for the second apparition applies here also.

---

[24] Annex II #1A, #1C, #1E, 9E, #9G, #9H, #11B, #12B, #12D, #12D, #13A, #13B, #14B, #14E, Annex I #64
[25] Annex II #2A, #2C, #8D
[26] Annex II #2E, #2F, #2G
[27] Annex II #2C, #2G, #3G, #9G
[28] Annex II #3A, #3E, #12B

Fourth Apparition

If they had not abducted you, or **because they abducted you** *the miracle would be better known.*[29] It may be that the use of the negative conditional confused Lucia and caused her to give contradictory answers.

St. Joseph would come with the Child Jesus to **give peace to the world** or **to bless the world.**[30] This conflict between Lucia's report to Father Ferreira in 1917 and her statement to the Diocesan Inquiry Board in 1924 may have been due to her weaker memory in 1924, seven years after the apparition. Also "to give peace" may refer to the inner peace that comers from a firm faith. In this sense, "to give peace" and "to bless" are not very different.

Variations in the Lady's reply for requests for cures occur.[31] My previous comment applies.

Fifth Apparition

St. Joseph and the Child would come **to give peace to the world** or to **bless the world.**[32] Once again Lucia's 1917 statements conflict with those made years later and may be due to faulty memory over time; or peace may refer to inner peace, as stated above.

Sixth Apparition

The Lady **said nothing** *about another apparition* or she said "**today was the last time**" or *she said afterwards* she will return a seventh time.[33] The reference to the seventh apparition occurs only in Lucia's 1941 memoir. It may be one more error over time. Jacinta's statement that *today would be the last time* may be a seven-year-old child's invention, due to her firm belief that the sixth would be the last time; it is found only in this statement.

First Vision in the Sun

St. Joseph and the Child Jesus appeared **to the left** or **to the right** *of the sun.*[34] Only Lucia's 1922 statement says "to the right." It may be one more lapse in memory at a later date.

---

[29] Annex II #4A, #4C, #12B, #14C; Annex I #32
[30] Annex II #4A, #4F
[31] Annex II #4C, #4E, #4F, #4G
[32] Annex II #5A, #5C, #5E, #5G
[33] Annex II #1G, #10A, #10B
[34] Annex II #6A, #6E, #11C, #12E

St. Joseph **held** *in his arm the Child, who held St. Joseph around the neck* or *the Child* **stood** *at St. Joseph's side.*[35] This is a clash in the testimony of Lucia against Jacinta and Francisco at the same interview. It is a minor detail.

St. Joseph was dressed in **red** or **white**.[36] Lucia's statement of October 16 conflicts with Jacinta's and her statement of October 19. It is another minor detail.

St. Joseph alone or **the Child alone** or **St. Joseph and the Child** *blessed the people.*[37] The latter two are reported only in Lucia's 1924 and 1941 statements. The 1917 statements say only that St. Joseph blessed the world.

The Child was **about one** or **about two** *years old.*[38] It is not surprising that Lucia or Jacinta, at their tender age, was wrong about the approximate age of the Child.

The Lady was on **the** **right** or **left** *of the sun.*[39] Lucia's 1922 statement clashes with Lucia's and Jacinta's 1917 testimony. Again I suspect that the 1922 statement was in error.

The Lady was dressed **in red with a white mantle** or **in white with a blue mantle**.[40] Here Lucia's testimony to her pastor clashes with her testimony and that of Jacinta and Francisco on October 19 and Lucia's later statements. It seems reasonable to assume that Lucia's testimony to her pastor was wrong. Perhaps she confused the Lady's clothing at the first vision with that of Our Lord in the second.

Second Vision in the Sun

Lucia **saw** or **did not see** *Our Lord blessing the people. A bright light accompanied the vision.*[41] The bright light may have affected Lucia's vision and she may not have seen the blessing, and may not have mentioned it on one occasion, but on another occasion she may have assumed that it happened, and said so.

The Lady was dressed in **purple** (Our Lady of Sorrows) or **in white, with a blue mantle**.[42] Only on October 16 did Lucia describe the Lady's dress as *white with a blue mantle*. It seems quite likely that she confused the Lady's dress at the first vision with that of the second.

The second vision was **Our Lord** alone or **Our Lord and Our Lady**.[43] In her interrogation by Father Formigao on October 13, Lucia seemed clearly to indicate that there were four visions, with the second being Our Lord alone, and the third Our Lady of Sorrows alone. But in her interview with her pastor on October 16 and her statements in 1922, 1924, and 1941, she indicates only three visions, with the

---

[35] Annex II #6A, #6F, #10A, #10B, #10C
[36] Annex II #6A, #12B, #12C
[37] Annex II #6A, #6B, #6E, #6F, #6G, #11D, #11E
[38] Annex II #10A, #10B .
[39] Annex II #6A, #6B, #6E, #11C
[40] Annex II #6A, #6B, #6E, #6F, #6G, #11C, #12B, #12C
[41] Annex II #6F, #6G, #10A, #11B
[42] Annex II #6A, #6E, #6F, #6G, #10A
[43] Annex II #6A, #6E, #6F, #6G, #10A

second being both Our Lord and Our Lady. The contradiction may be due to faulty memory of Lucia, under stress.

The Lady's Dress

The Lady wore a dress or jacket and skirt.[44] Both Lucia and Jacinta gave these seemingly contradictory statements. But the contradiction may be more apparent than real. The seers may have been using the Portuguese word for dress, *vestido*, in a broad sense meaning "clothing." If so, the contradiction disappears.

The lady's skirt reached only to her knees or a little below them.[45] This is to us only a minor detail, but may have been a cause of scandal in 1917.

The Lady's mantle was or was not gold-trimmed.[46] Only one of the many sources seems to say that the Lady's mantle was not trimmed in gold.

The Lady was about three and a half feet tall or was average size for a young woman. I have already discussed this contradiction on page 20. I might add that small children are not usually good at estimating a person's height.

FAIRLY IMPORTANT CONTRADICTIONS

The **seers saw** or **did not see** the Lady come down from the sky. This is a fairly significant contradiction because the apparitions become more spectacular if the seers saw the Lady come down onto the oak bush. (Many sources say that the seers saw her depart and none deny it.) Nineteen sources say or seem to say that the seers simply saw her appear on the oak bush.[47] However, eight say or seem to say that the seers saw her come down.[48] Thus, for the October 13 apparition Lucia told her pastor that she saw the Lady come through the air, for the September 13 apparition she strongly implied it to him, and for June 13 she vaguely suggested it to him. But on September 27 Lucia told Father Formigao: "I didn't see her come from anywhere. She appears over the oak bush.[49]

---

[44] Annex II #1A, #2A, #3A, #7A, , #8B, #8C, #8D, #9I
[45] Annex II #2A, #3A, #8D, #10A
[46] Annex II #1A, #1F, #2A, #3A, #7A, #7B, #8D, #13A, #13B, #14B
[47] Annex II #1A, #1C, #1E, #1F, #1G, #2E, #2F, #2G, #3E, #3F, #3G, #4B, #4E, #4F, #4G, #5G, #6F, #6G, #8D
[48] Annex II #2A, #2B, #4A, #5A, #5B, #6A, #6B, 8D
[49] Annex II #2A, #A, #6A, #8D

Lucia provided an explanation for the contradictions in her fourth memoir, where she says: "The flashes were not really lightning, but the reflected rays of a light that was approaching. It was because we saw the light that sometimes we said we saw Our Lady coming. But properly speaking, we only perceived Our Lady in that light when she was already on the oak bush. The fact that we did not know how to explain this, and that we wished to avoid questions, caused us to say sometimes that we saw her coming and other times that we did not. When we said we saw her coming we were referring to the approach of the light, which was after all herself. And when we said we did not see her coming, we were referring to the fact that we really saw Our Lady only when she was on the holm oak."[50]

This statement provides a plausible explanation for the contradictions in the seers' testimony. Certainly, on seeing the flash they felt sure that the Lady was coming, and they may have said, incorrectly, that they saw her instead of saying only that they saw the flash. The many earlier references to the light refer to it as a flash (I counted twenty-two references in my Annex) and Lucia even refers to the flash several times in her memoirs.[51] The evidence thus strongly suggests that the seers did not see the Lady approaching, but saw only a flash.

Perhaps I should allow for the possibility that, at the last apparition, the seers actually saw the Lady come down from the sky. Lucia's October statement said that she saw her <u>descend through the air</u> in October. This follows her September 27 statement that she does not see the Lady come.[52] Thus it is possible, if not likely, that at the last apparition Lucia saw an approaching light and the Lady in it, and that for the other months the seers saw only the flash.

If so, there remains as a firm contradiction, only Francisco's September 27 statement that he saw the Lady come down, after which he added that she always comes quickly.[53] This error (assuming it to be an error), may have been due to faulty memory, a subconscious desire to make the apparitions seem more spectacular, or an assumption that the Lady was in the light.

---

[50] Annex II #1G.
[51] Annex II #1A, #2A, etc. Also #3G, #5G, #6G
[52] Annex II #6A, #8D
[53] Annex II #8B

Lucia **did** *or* **did not** say that she had seen the Lady the year before (in 1916). This "contradiction" is important because it suggests that Lucia was inventing apparitions of the Lady. The "contradiction" is clearly based on a misunderstanding between Father Lacerda and Lucia in his October 19 interrogation. The details are:

Question 12- "What did you do after seeing the Lady?" "They saw, but she said nothing. She had seen it *the other year and told her mother and she scolded her. The first time was at the place called Estrumeiras."* This comes from the unedited notes of Father Lacerda.

From his edited notes, published in *O Mensageiro* on November 15, we have a different version: *"What did you do after seeing and talking with the Lady?" "I said nothing. Last year I had seen the same Lady in a place called Estrumeiras, and I said it to my mother, who scolded me a lot and wanted to beat me a lot. It was Jacinta who talked."*[54]

It is clear that Lucia, in her first statement, was referring to her silence after the May 13, 1917, apparition and Jacinta's revealing it. Her statement about the "other year" obviously was intended as an explanation for her silence in May and clearly refers to the incidents with the "white forms" in 1915, when her mother treated her harshly when she learned of the incidents. Unfortunately, Lucia said she had seen it, meaning that she had seen the white form the "other year." And since Father Lacerda had asked about the Lady, he naturally assumed that it referred to the Lady, and said so in his edited version of the question and answer. He changed Lucia's "other year" to "last year," probably because Lucia's mother had told him, wrongly, that "last year" another image had appeared.[55] This clear explanation of the "contradiction" as a misunderstanding was not available until 1982, nor published before 1992, since prior to then the original notes lay undiscovered among the effects of Father Lacerda.

Prior to this time, the "contradiction" was used as an important argument against Fatima by its opponents.[56] However, either deliberately or unknowingly, these opponents ignored Lucia's reply (on September 27, 1917) to Father Formigao's question: Is it true that the

---

[54] Annex II #13B, #14B

[55] Annex #II #13B

[56] De Sede, pp 102, 104

Lady appeared to you last year? Lucia replied: "She never appeared to me last year ((nor before May of this year)). I never said this to anyone because it is not true."[57] This reply strongly supports the above explanation of this "contradiction."

If the people do not cease to offend God, **a worse war will break out during the pontificate of Pius XI**.[58] This statement, from Lucia's memoirs, is said to be a contradiction of history. For the West, World War II broke out in 1939, with the invasion of Poland, when Pius XII was pope. But it can be argued that the war began in 1937, in Pius XI's pontificate, with the invasion of China by the eastern member of the Axis, Japan; that the second phase began in 1939, with the attack on Poland; that the third phase began in 1940, with the invasion of Russia; and that the final phase began in 1941, with the attack on Pearl Harbor. We have here no clear contradiction.

THE MOST IMPORTANT CONTRADICTION

The most important contradiction, by far, is the statements ascribed to the Lady concerning the end of the war. For the October apparition the Lady is quoted: "*The war* **is ending today** or **is ending soon** or **is coming to an end**." The first two alternatives are a contradiction with history, since World War I did not end until November 11, 1918, or thirteen months after October 13, 1917. The third is vague. The first alternative (today) is the best attested and the third is the least, as I will soon show. Further, the Lady is said to have added that the Portuguese soldiers would return very soon or soon. October 13, 1917, is six months before the Portuguese government decided, in April 1918, to withdraw its troops from the war. This does not seem to be "soon." If the Lady reported by the seers was really the Mother of God, it must be assumed that she would make no error of history. Pro-Fatima authors accept that the seers made an error in this regard and offer explanations.[59]

---

[57] Annex II #8D
[58] Annex II #3G
[59] *Fatima Way of Peace,* pp 27-72; *The Whole Truth About Fatima,* pp 307-320

This error is one of major importance. It is undoubtedly one reason why the diocese took so long (thirteen years) to approve devotion to the Lady of Fatima. And it also helps to explain why the Fatima story was unknown to most Catholics until after World War II. It requires a detailed examination of the facts and possible explanations.

I note first that there appear to be only three possible explanations: that the seers were part of a hoax, an explanation I have already rejected; or that they were victims of a hallucination, a possibility which I will soon discuss, and which is not tenable, in my view; or that the seers misunderstood the statements of the Lady concerning the end of the war and return of the soldiers. It is the third possibility which I will now examine.

I begin with the background. The seers, along with most of the people in Europe, were greatly concerned with the fate of family members fighting in the Great War. Jacinta had a brother there. Thus the third question which Lucia reported for the first apparition is; "Can you tell me if the war will last long or will end soon." At the third apparition Lucia quoted the Lady as saying: "… Pray the rosary to Our Lady of the Rosary, to quiet the war, for only she can help."

At the fourth apparition Lucia gives us: "If they had not (Gist– abducted) you, the miracle would be better known. St. Joseph was to come with the Child Jesus to give peace to the world and Our Lord to bless the world." This August statement seems to say that the Lord intended to bring a quick end to the war, but that in punishment for the evil action of abducting the seers He would not do so. If so, Lucia, only ten years old, may have failed to connect the phrase "was to come to give peace" with the previous phrase: "If they had not abducted you," and thought that the Lady was saying unconditionally that the Lord or St. Joseph would come on October 13 to bring peace.[60] However, there is another explanation that seems equally good or better. The phrase "to give peace" may refer to the inner peace which comes from freedom of the cares of the world.

At the fifth apparition Lucia gives us: "I want to tell you to keep praying the rosary to Our Lady of the Rosary that she lessen the war, that the war is coming to an end. On the last day St. Joseph (or St. Joseph with the Child Jesus) is to come to give peace to the world and Our Lord to bless the people. In the unedited version of Lucia's report to her pastor, the word "war" is followed by a comma, while in the edited version it is followed by a semi-colon. The underlined phrase "the war is coming to an end" is strange and may not be correct. The Lady, if she was from heaven, would surely know that the war was not coming to an end, unless this means "coming to an end in a year or so." Moreover, in Portuguese the verb "is"

---

[60] Annex II #1A, #3A, #4A, #4C, #4E, #5A, #5C, #8D

requires only a small change (*esta* to *estaje*) to make better sense in context. With this change the sentence becomes "… pray that she lessen the war, that the war come to an end." Nonetheless, it seems clear that Lucia understood the Lady to say that the war "is coming to an end," whether or not she understood her correctly. Further, the statement that St. Joseph was to bring peace and that our Lord was only to bless the world, seems strange, unless the peace that St. Joseph was to bring was an inner peace, not an end to the war.

Nonetheless, it seems clear that, after the fourth and fifth apparitions, the seers expected (or at least half-expected) that the miracle, which had been promised for October 13, would be the sudden end of the war on that day. The information about the Lady's statements at the fourth and fifth apparition comes from interviews of Lucia by her pastor soon after the apparitions.

The facts. We have much more information on what the Lady was understood to have said in October. It is clear that Lucia understood her to have said that the war was ending then, on October 13. The details are long, but are important in understanding the explanations for "Lucia's error."

The earliest information comes from the interview of the seers by Father Formigao in the evening of October 13. Lucia was first. Question: "What did she (the Lady) say?" Answer: "She said people should amend their lives, not offend Our Lord, … that the war is ending today and that we should expect our soldiers back shortly." His interview of Jacinta on the same day has: Question: "What did the Lady say?" Answer: "She said we should pray the rosary to Our Lady every day and the war is ending today.[61]

The interview of Lucia by Father Ferreira on October 16 has: Lucia: "What do you want of me?" The Lady: "I want to tell you not to offend the Lord anymore, to pray the rosary to Our Lady, to build a chapel … , the war is ending this very day, expect your military back very soon."[62]

The interview of Lucia by Father Formigao on October 19 has: Question: "On the 13th did Our Lady say that the war was ending on that same day? What were the words she used?" Answer: "She spoke thus: The war is ending, even today. Expect the return of your soldiers very shortly." Question: "But the war is still going on! … The newspapers report that there have been battles after the 13th. How can you explain this, if Our Lady said that the war was ending that day?" Answer: "I don't know. I only know I heard her say that the war was ending on the 13th. I know no more."[63]

---

[61] Annex II #10A, #10B
[62] Annex II #6A
[63] Annex II #11B

The interview of Jacinta by Father Formigao on the same day gives a very different response: Question: "What did the Lady say this last time?" Answer: "She said: I come here to tell you not to offend the Lord, …. that if the people amend their ways, the war would end, if they did not the world would end. Lucia heard better than I what the Lady said." Question: "Did the Lady say the war would end that day or shortly?" Answer: "The Lady said the war would end when she arrived in heaven." Question: "But the war has not ended." Answer: "I think it will on Sunday."[64]

Lucia's interview by Father Formigao on November 2 has: Question: "What did the Lady say in October?" Answer: (Gist– Don't offend God, build a chapel, say the rosary.) A question about cures and conversions follows. Question: "She didn't say anything more? Answer: "She said the war was ending today, and to expect our military very soon." Question: "She didn't say the war would end when she got to heaven?" Answer: "I don't recall if she said it was when she got to heaven."[65]

The interview of Jacinta by Father Formigao on November 2 has: Question: "What did the Lady say in October?" Answer: "(Gist– Don't offend God, say the rosary), that we could expect our soldiers back very soon, and that the war would end that day."[66]

The interview of Lucia on October 19 by Father Lacerda has: Question: "What did the Lady say the … 6th time?" Answer: " … the 6th time (Gist– Don't offend God, pray the rosary, build a chapel), that the war was ending that very day, and we can expect the return of our soldiers very soon."[67]

A statement was added by Father Alves to his report on his interview with the seers on September 17. It is not clear whether the statement was based on a later interview of the seers or on what he had read. His statement says: "She said that she was the Lady of the Rosary, that the war was ending that day, that our soldiers would return shortly, (Gist– to build a chapel and to amend their ways.)"[68]

On October 15 Maria Francisca d'Assis reported in a letter about her visit to Fatima on October 13: " … Dr. Joao do Val with the Saraivas went to talk to her (Lucia or Jacinta). She answered all the questions … and said that Our Lady asked men to … be better, that her dear Son was angry, that the war would end soon and the Portuguese soldiers would return to their land."[69]

On October 16 Maria Stokler Parente wrote, in a letter: "Yesterday we went to see the seers. Lucia …. announced for now—the seer said today—the end of the war and that our soldiers will return shortly.[70]

---

[64] Annex II #11D
[65] Annex II #12B
[66] Annex II #12D
[67] Annex II #13B
[68] Annex II #6D
[69] Annex I #22
[70] Annex I #32

A statement of Joaquim Tovares, dated only "October 1917" tells of his visit to the seers' home after the "sun dance." He says: "... she (Lucia or Jacinta) said ... that the Lady ... told her: 'that she was Our Lady of the Rosary, that the war was <u>ending</u> and to expect the return of our soldiers shortly.'"[71]

A letter of October 27 from Maria de Jesus d'Oriol Pena Rapozo describes her visit with the seers a few days earlier. She says: "What she (Lucia) does confirm is that Our Lady said to her that the war was going to end <u>that day</u>, when she returned to heaven, and that the soldiers would return very soon to their families."[72]

A letter of October 17 from Eugenia de Melo Breyner da Camara describes her visit to Fatima on October 13. She says: "My Adelaide, who managed to speak to the little girl, heard her say that Our Lady had told her that she was the Lady of the Rosary, (Gist– build a chapel, don't offend God), that the war was to end <u>soon</u>, and they could expect the soldiers to return shortly."[73]

The deposition of Father Francisco Bras das Neves to the Ourem Inquiry on December 27 says that he interviewed the two girls (Lucia and Jacinta) on October 20: "Lucia affirmed to him that Our Lady had appeared on October 13 and promised that the war would end <u>on that same day</u>." Further, he declared that he met her (presumably Lucia) again on December 8 and noted to her that the war did not end on the designated day nor up to that date, and she responded that maybe she was mistaken, since her companion Jacinta had said that the Lady, said in her turn that the war would end, yes, but <u>if the people reformed</u>.[74]

The deposition of Luis Antonio Vieira de Magalhaes e Vasconcellos to the Ourem Inquiry on December 30 says that he returned to Fatima some weeks after October 13 to talk to the seers. "She (Lucia) described the apparition of the Virgin in a way that is well known to all—that the Virgin said to them 'that we have offended God much and must amend our ways, that we should build a chapel to Our Lady of the Rosary, that the war would end <u>shortly</u>.'"[75]

Next we have the testimony of those who attended the apparition on October 13 and heard the message which Lucia shouted out to the crowd repeatedly as she was carried home on the shoulders of a very large man, Dr. Carlos de Azevedo Mendes. Most of the statements do not say whether they heard Lucia themselves, and thus some of them may have gotten the message only as it was passed by word of mouth through the crowd. It would seem likely that Lucia, in repeating the message, did not always use the same words. Thus she may have said both "the war is ending today" and "the war is ending soon." To the mind of a ten-year-old, this may not have seemed a significant difference in the joyous news.

---

[71] Annex I #58
[72] Annex I #66
[73] Annex I #65
[74] Annex I #91
[75] Annex I #92

A letter of the same Dr. Mendes, written in late October or early November 1917 (judging by its statement that an inquiry of the Fatima event by the Church was underway) says: "At the end I took the oldest child on my shoulders ... she ... cried out to everyone around that they should do penance, for that is what the Lady wanted. It is certain that she also said that the Lady affirmed that the war would end on that day, and it still continues ..."[76]

Space does not allow me to quote the testimony of those who heard Lucia shout, or who learned what she said by word of mouth from the crowd. There are some twenty statements from such people in letters, newspapers, diaries, etc. I note only that they vary considerably about when the war was to end. Thus seven indicate that the war was ending on October 13th—"today," "that day," "the 13th," "the same day" or "the war had ended." Nine indicate the war was ending "soon" or "shortly." Four say only that the war was "ending." One says "today or soon," another "in these days," another "the nearness of the end of the war," and one "this year." It is obviously impossible to know if these variations were due to Lucia, to the crowd as it passed the message on, or to those who provided the testimony. Most important, it would seem, is that sixteen say "today" or "soon" or an equivalent, and only five are vague. It would seem that most people in the crowd received the impression that the war was ending then or quite soon.[77]

One final source of information is statements of Lucia and others after 1917. They tend, consciously or sub-consciously, to offer explanations for the seers' error in 1917. Lucia, in her 1922 statement, says: "Now I understood that she spoke thusly: 'When I arrive in heaven, the war will end today.' But my cousin Jacinta said she had spoken in this manner: 'If the world reforms, the war will end today.'" In her 1924 testimony Lucia said: "It seems to me that she spoke further in this manner: 'Convert, the war will end today, expect your soldiers back shortly.' My cousin told me at home that the Lady spoke thusly: 'Convert, so that the war ends within a year.' As I was thinking about the requests that I wanted to make to the Lady, I did not pay attention well." In her fourth memoir Lucia merely says: "The war is going to end, and the soldiers will return soon."[78]

Strangely, Dr. Mendes, who carried Lucia on his shoulders told Canon Barthas in 1948, that he heard Lucia say: "If men will be converted, the war will end." In 1954 he was shown a copy of his 1917 letter, where he said "It is certain that she also said that the war would end on that day." He recognized it as his and initialed the copy, even though it contradicted his 1948 testimony.[79]

---

[76] Annex I #20
[77] Annex I #17, #18, #25-#28, #31, #32, #34, #36, #38, #39, #43, #47, #49, #54, #71, #77, #78, #95
[78] Annex II #6E. #6F, #6G
[79] *Fatima 1917-1968*, p 139; *Fatima Way of Peace*, p 64

Explanations. A pro-Fatima source offers an explanation for the seers' error. It is short, but has serious drawbacks. I quote:

On May 18, 1941, in a letter to her confessor, … Lucia explains: "On the subject of the war I remember Our Lady expressing herself in this way: 'The war will end and the soldiers will come home soon.'" This is in fact the formula she retains in her memoirs. "But" she continues, "what perhaps prevented me from giving full attention at the moment was my concern to remember the requests I had been asked to present. … that is why I was slightly distracted." Right after the great miracle the enthusiastic witnesses harried the seers again with innumerable questions. …

There is no question that, in the enthusiasm of the great miracle, the seers were assailed with questions on the precise end of the war. There is an additional proof in a recollection of Sister Lucia, which she reports to her confessor (on 18 May 1941): "I did not say" she explains: "the war is over." I said: "the war will end." And when I was asked "When, today?" to free myself from so many questions, and without attaching great importance to it, or reflecting at all on what Our Lady had said, I answered "Yes, today." This gives us a good insight into the psychological causes of Lucia's error: during the apparition her attention was distracted by her concern for all the requests to be passed on; and right after (that), there were continuous questions on the date of the end of the war, suggesting the erroneous response of an immediate peace. Finally, on the evening of October 13, in her extreme fatigue, Lucia was convinced Our Lady had announced that the war would end that very day.[80]

This explanation has the Lady say to Lucia only: "The war will end," which is vague and almost pointless (no one would assume the war would go on forever). It does not explain the sentence or phrase which followed, according to all sources—the soldiers will return soon or very soon. Since the Portuguese soldiers returned in April 1918, "soon" was six months.

I offer another explanation which is longer, but seems to be better. It begins by noting the intense desire of Lucia and all her family and friends for an end to the war. Jacinta had a brother at the front. Wishful thinking on Lucia's part may have caused her to misinterpret the Lady's words at the apparitions in August and September. A clear indi-

---

[80] *The Whole Truth About Fatima*, pp 311-314

cation of the seers' thinking is given by a lady with whom Lucia and Jacinta stayed in late September 1917. When asked what the seers had said about the war, she replied: "They always said the Lady said it was coming to an end."[81] It would seem that the seers had interpreted both the August and September statements of the Lady to mean that the war would end quickly.

But was not that the meaning of the statements at the fifth apparition? I have already suggested that the Lady did not state simply that "the war is coming to an end" but rather said "pray ... that the war come to an end." Further, the Lady's statement that "St. Joseph is to come (on October 13) to give peace to the world" may not refer to the end of the war, as the seers clearly thought. It should be noted that the Lady is quoted as saying that St. Joseph would give peace but Our Lord was to "bless the people." Certainly it seems strange that St. Joseph was to bring an end to World War I but that Our Lord was merely to bless the people. This suggests very strongly that the peace that St. Joseph was to bring was the interior peace that comes from belief in the mercy and goodness of God. Some support for this conclusion is derived from Lucia's statement to her pastor on October 16 that she saw St. Joseph making signs of the cross to the people on October 13, and Jacinta's statement to Father Formigao on October 19 that Lucia said St. Joseph was giving peace.[82] Nonetheless, it is clear that the seers mis-interpreted the Lady's words and expected that the promised miracle would be the end of the war. (See pages 44-45.)

If we assume that the Lady's statements for August and September did not necessarily mean an end to the war on October 13, we still need an explanation for the statement about the end of the war which was ascribed to the Lady by the seers after the October 13 apparition.

I note first a factor affecting the seers' testimony about the October 13 apparition—their extreme fatigue. It was caused by the constant questioning of the seers by the many visitors, each of whom wanted to hear the seers' story of the apparitions. Both Lucia herself and at least two other sources indicate this, and the statement of Father Formigao is especially telling. He notes that they seemed to be

---

[81] *Ocho Dias com as Videntes da Fatima*, p 42
[82] Annex II #5A, #6A, #11E

answering mechanically and voices fear that their health would suffer if the questionings continue.[83]

We can reasonably assume that Lucia was not only fatigued during the October 13 apparition, but also worried about presenting to the Lady the many requests for healings and other favors which she had received. She said this to the Diocesan Inquiry Board in 1924 and in the epilogue to her confessor (both statements underlined on pages 48 and 49). A major misunderstanding may have occurred with only a short lapse in attention. If we assume that the Lady said something like: "If the people amend their ways the war would end, even today, and the soldiers would return soon" and that Lucia missed only the first short phrase (If the people amend their ways) she would have received the false impression that the war was ending on that very day. Even if Lucia realized that she had been distracted, she would have believed that the Lady had said that the war was ending that day. It was what she had expected. Furthering this explanation is the statement of Lucia to Father Formigao on October 19: "The war was ending even today."

This explanation is in line with Jacinta's statement to Father Formigao on October 19 "if the people amend their ways, the war will end, if they do not, the world would end. Lucia heard better than I what the Lady said." Father Formigao then asked if the war would end then or shortly. Jacinta replied: "The Lady said that the war would end when she arrived in heaven." This explanation assumes that Jacinta was not distracted at that moment of the apparition, and that she heard the Lady's conditional statement on the end of the war. It further assumes that Lucia and Jacinta discussed the apparition during the afternoon of October 13 and Lucia convinced Jacinta that the Lady said unconditionally that the war would end that day, which is what Jacinta told Father Formigao that evening and also on November 2. That Jacinta deferred to Lucia's memory is seen by her underlined statement to Father Formigao on October 19. A final implication is that on October 19 Jacinta had temporarily forgotten that Lucia's recollection was different from hers and gave her own recollection, but gave a different answer when Father Formigao pressed her again on

---

[83] Annex I #66; Annex II #8E, #11A, #14B

the same subject. It is clear that the younger Jacinta gave in easily to her older cousin.[84]

This explanation is given some further support by a statement of Jacinta to Father Lacerda, also on October 19. When asked what the Lady said at each apparition, Jacinta said: "The last time—Lucia asked what she wanted and she said—that the war was ending on the 13th, when she arrived in heaven, that if the people did not want to amend their ways, the world would end. If they <u>did not want</u> to, the war would end."[85] The "did not want" which I underlined is clearly an error (of Father Lacerda or Jacinta), since the context clearly indicates that it should read, "If they <u>did</u> want to, the war would end." This is what she told Father Formigao on October 19. Here Jacinta gives both an unconditional end of the war (which may reflect Lucia's memory) and a conditional one (which may reflect her own memory.)

Finally, we have the word of Father Neves, who talked with Lucia on December 17 and has her say that she may have been wrong, since Jacinta had said that the war would end, yes, but if the people reformed. There is thus fairly good evidence that Lucia missed part of the Lady's statement on the war on October 13, and Jacinta did not.[86]

Critics might ask if it is likely that Lucia was so concentrated on the requests for cures which she had received that she was temporarily distracted from what the Lady was saying and thus did not hear a critical statement of the Lady. Offhand one would suspect that Lucia would be so entranced by the Lady and what she was saying that she missed nothing of what she said.

However, this was the sixth appearance of the Lady. Lucia was likely to be at least slightly less entranced than she was at the first apparition. Moreover, among the many requests for cures which she had received, several surely came for people of her village and nearby villages, people she knew and cared for. At the August and September appearances she had merely asked the Lady for help for "some people" or "some cures." Surely a number of the local people had asked Lucia if she had remembered their requests and Lucia had said no, not

---

[84] Annex II #11D, #10C, #12D
[85] Annex II #13A
[86] Annex II #91

specifically. They must have begged Lucia to remember these requests specifically at the October apparition. It thus is believable that Lucia was most anxious to make these requests and thus missed the critical statement, "If the people amend their ways."[87]

Admittedly, both explanations require assumptions that are not provable and thus are not as strong as we would like. But some such explanation must be assumed to be correct unless we accept the theory of a hoax or a hallucination. I have already noted the weakness of the claim of a hoax, and now will discuss the possibility of a hallucination.

Hallucination. The explanation that the apparitions were a hallucination was occasionally offered by opponents of Fatima.[88] I already have noted that it is rather unlikely that all three seers would have the same hallucination. And it further seems unlikely that one, Francisco, would have the hallucination that he only sees the Lady, while the other two see and hear her.

Beyond this, the only thing that can be said is that the seers seemed to be normal, healthy and active children, spending much time outdoors. Father Formigao, soon after his long interviews with the seers, wrote a long psychological analysis of them, saying that they were quiet, perfectly healthy, well-balanced, not intense or pensive, worry-free, and outgoing. Both he and Dr. Mendes say that the children enjoyed playing games. Father Formigao stated that a doctor had carefully examined the children and said they showed not the least signs of hysteria. Admittedly, both men were strongly pro-Fatima. A pro-Fatima author tells us that during the seers' captivity at the administrator's house in August, Dr. Antonio Rodrigues de Oliveira attended some of the interrogations of the seers and examined them himself, presumably with the purpose of finding them unstable and likely to have hallucinations; and the author says that his findings were never made public, presumably because they were not helpful to the anti-Fatima cause. A woman who visited the children on October 19 said that she found them to be robust, serious, frank and healthy, showed no symptoms of nervousness, and the medium in which they were living seemed to be little appropriate for hallucinations of this

---

[87] Annex II #4C, #4E, #4F, #4G, #5A. #5G
[88] Annex I #7, #76

kind. Finally, a man living near the Cova da Iria said in 1923 that he had seen Jacinta and Lucia at the time of the apparitions and found them to be perfectly normal.[89] Obviously the strongest evidence that the seers were not hallucinating in telling of the apparitions is that a miracle which the Lady had promised occurred at the predicted time, and at the place it was expected.

Finally we have the word of Father Neves who talked with Lucia on December 17 and has her say that she may have been wrong, since Jacinta had said that the war would end, yes, but if the people reformed. There is thus fairly good evidence that Lucia missed part of the Lady' statement on the war on October 13, and Jacinta did not.

THE PHENOMENA

As noted earlier, unusual phenomena were reported by part of the crowd at the second through the fifth apparitions. Naturally, the number of written sources, which are available to study, increases with the growth of the crowds. It is important to study these reports. Critics of Fatima might say that one or more of the phenomena of the sun dance were individual hallucinations, which were caused by the knowledge of the previous phenomena. Also, some Fatima authors have created the impression that some of the earlier phenomena were miraculous.

Non-see-ers. It must be noted first that the available testimony does not suggest that only a tiny fraction of those attending the apparitions claimed that they saw nothing. The testimony, although not precise, suggests strongly that the "non-see-ers" were many more than a handful.

On August 13 a seminarian, at Fatima at this time, talked with many witnesses returning from the Cova immediately after the event and reported that some said that they heard and saw mysterious signs, while others said they saw nothing. One person, reporting hearsay, said no one saw anything, but at noon a supernatural presence was felt.

---

[89] Annex I #51; Annex II #15E; Doc Crit I, pp 189, 190; *The Whole Truth About Fatima*, pp 225, 226

One witness, a supporter of Fatima, said almost all saw extraordinary signs. An anti-Fatima newspaper cited a woman who said that she saw nothing extraordinary. Offhand, one would suspect that those who said they saw nothing implied that they heard no thunder and felt no decrease in the sun's heat, but this clearly was not true for one woman, who reported a noise that made people think they were dying but said that she saw nothing. Nor was it the case for a man who said they all saw nothing, clearly meaning only that nobody saw the Lady.[90]

Again in September there were a number of persons who said they saw nothing unusual. In this group were prominent supporters of Fatima, including three of the four parents of the seers and the lawyer Mendes. A man wrote in his diary that many local people went to Fatima on September 13 and they saw nothing. Also, a man told the Diocesan Inquiry Board that some people saw a star, but he and others saw nothing. A lawyer reported that some said that they saw nothing, others that they saw a star, and still others gave fantastic descriptions. A newspaper reported that many saw nothing except that the sun darkened a bit and the air cooled. And a doctor who was there on September 13 reported, at a much later date, that the lessening of the sun was the most noted phenomenon, but he did not see it. One man said he saw nothing except the dimming of the sun, which he did not find unusual. The bishop's unofficial observer, Father Formigao, said that he scarcely noted the dimming of the sun and found it not worthy of comment.[91] This may also have been true for others who said that they saw nothing.

We do not know the percentage of people who said they saw nothing unusual for any of these months. However, a pro-Fatima author stated that it seems that in September the proportion of "non-see-ers" was about one third of the total.[92] It would thus appear that we cannot explain the existence of "non-see-ers" in July, August, and September by the theory that a few witnesses can be expected to contradict the

---

[90] Annex I #4, #69, #51; Annex II #9B, #15F; Doc Crit III, pp 111-113
[91] Annex I #9, #20, #92, #105; Annex II #15C, #15G; O Debate, 20 September, Doc Crit III, pp 112, 113; Doc Crit II, p 69; De Marchi, p 111; Fatima 1917-1968, p 358; A Guarda, 13 September 1919, Doc Crit III, part 2, p 128; Toute la Verite, p 281
[92] Toute la Verite, p 279, citing Fatima 1917-1968, p 148

basic evidence of the vast majority at any event witnessed by thousands of people. An explanation is needed.

I note first three possible explanations—hallucination, fabrication, and selective vision. I am reluctant to accept any of them. First, there were many who reported the same phenomena; if it was due to hallucination, then we have mass hallucination, which I have already indicated to be an unsupported theory. Next, it seems unlikely that those who reported the phenomena simply invented them, since many of them were sincere, practicing Christians, who were unlikely to be lying. And finally, it would be surprising if the phenomena were visions created by God for a part of the people, but not all; such selective visions seems unlikely (I have never read of it in Catholic literature on miracles); further, many of the "non-see-ers" were very worthy persons, the mother of Jacinta, for example. There are several other explanations for some or all of the phenomena. I discuss them as I report specific phenomena, or at the end.

June. We have little information about the June phenomena. One witness, Ignacio Antonio Marques, said in 1922: "As a disbeliever, I want to deny what I am seeing, but looking in the atmosphere I see that everything is cloudy. It seems that opposite air currents are meeting there and raising a cloud of dust. The weather darkens and I seem to hear a subterranean groan."[93] At the Diocesan Inquiry, in 1923, Maria Carreira said that she heard a hiss, like a rocket, at the end of the apparition and saw a smoke cloud rise to the east.[94] But at the same Inquiry another witness said he had been at the Cova almost every month on the 13th and saw nothing.[95]

July. For July seven sources gave some information on the phenomena. Two newspapers and one written statement reported a noise like thunder. One of the newspapers called it like a clap of thunder, the second said like an echo of thunder, and the statement likened it to the start of thunder. The same statement and a deposition to the Fatima parish board of inquiry in 1922 indicated that the heat, which was great until then, lost its force or began to diminish. The

---

[93] Annex I #100
[94] Annex II #15F
[95] Annex II, #15E

same deposition reported that over the holm oak a little cloud formed, which rose to the east. Also, the same statement indicated that a little fog was seen. Also, Ignacio Marques, who reported phenomena in June, said that the same phenomena occurred in July.[96] In the 1940s Jacinta's father told a Fatima author that he saw a grayish cloud over the apparition site on July 13 and the sun's heat diminished.[97] A man from Fatima told Father Formigao, the bishop's unofficial observer, that a cloud lowered over the oak bush, although there was no dust in the air, and the people heard a noise, implying that it was an unusual one.[98]

In view of the paucity of information, I am reluctant to make any strong conclusions for the June and July phenomena. I note, however, that each of these phenomena was also reported for August and/or September by some sources.

August. Much more information is available for August—seventeen sources. The most widely reported was a noise, apparently a loud noise. Eight sources report thunder, a boom, a noise, an explosion or a loud whisper, including three which specify that it was near the site.[99] Two sources specifically call the sound thunder.[100] Two sources said they saw lightning[101] and five said that the people began to flee, suggesting the fear produced by an unexpected stroke of lightning.[102] Others refer to the sound as an enormous whisper, as a noise, as a strong, unexplained boom, as two explosions like a bomb or shot, as a boom, or as a sound that drove the people crazy.[103] However, one witness said he did not hear a boom.[104]

Before analyzing this and the other phenomena I must repeat that a considerable share of the crowd stated that they saw nothing unusual. This suggests strongly that no unusual phenomena occurred and that the people who reported them were inventing them or hallucinating.

---

[96] Annex I #1, #2, #21, #97, #100, #15E
[97] De Marchi, p 76
[98] Annex II #9A, #9B
[99] Annex I #4, #32, #51, #79, #97, #99; Annex II #15B, #15F
[100] Annex I #4, #32
[101] Annex I #4, #7
[102] Annex I #4, #7, #79, #97, #99
[103] Annex #51, #79, #97, #99, #15B, #15F
[104] Annex #15E

However, for the month of August it is likely that many people, (like Joel Magno[105]) left the Cova as soon as they learned of the kidnapping of the seers and thus failed to see or hear anything unusual.

The five sources which tell of a noise like thunder in July and August suggest quite strongly that such a noise actually occurred. In August the crowd surely felt that the noise showed God's anger at the kidnapping of the seers. One possible explanation, an apparently supernatural one, is that the noise was caused by a nearby stroke of lightning "out of the blue." This is clearly a weather freak, but not an impossibility. I myself witnessed one in upper-middle New York State; the lightning struck near me (I could smell the ozone) and I scarcely noticed the flash because the thunder was so terrifyingly loud. (I cannot recall if there were no clouds in the sky, or if there were only no storm clouds.) However, the lightning could not have struck the Cova itself, since such a terrifying stroke would surely have been reported by all seventeen of our sources on the August phenomena. It is possible that some of the "non-see-ers" heard the loud noise but assumed that it was thunder and not something unusual.

A natural explanation is that the noise was caused by a nearby explosion set off by someone who hoped to gain financially from the development of Fatima as a major Catholic shrine. The two references to the noise as a "boom" and the single reference to it as an explosion fit this explanation. It would explain the single description of the noise as a loud whisper, which frightened the crowd. The low-pitched sound of dynamite, exploded at some distance, might have been considered by this source as a "loud whisper." The one man who said that he heard no boom may simply have been distracted and thus failed to hear it.

Another phenomenon was also reported by a fairly large number of people—color on the clouds, the sun, or the ground. Colored clouds were reported by six sources. Four indicated that the clouds took on various colors, one saying rainbow colors and another giving the colors red, rose, blue, and anise.[106] A fifth reported a blue and white cloud, which descended, then shortly rose and disappeared. A

---

[105] Annex #4
[106] Annex #80, #97, #99, #100

sixth reported a lacy cloud, rosy in places, which briefly covered the sun; it also reported yellow spots on the ground. All six reports may give different aspects of color on the sun. However, the first four are dated well after the sun dance of October 13 and resemble a color phenomenon of the sun dance. Thus, the first four may be wrongly reporting for August 13 the color phenomenon which was noted as part of the sun dance. If so, we have only two reports of color for August 13, neither of which is very impressive.

Five sources report a smoke, fog, dust, or cloud near the oak bush. They vary greatly in details. One simply said it was a fog. A second reported that some said it was fog around the oak bush, but to him it seemed more like smoke from an incense burner. A third said a cloud came over the oak bush and there was no dust in the air. The fourth said that he heard it said many times that a little smoke showed up. Finally, a man said it was a whirlwind which covered 300 people with dust.[107] His testimony is doubtful, since he reports a number of fanciful phenomena. These sources could be referring to smoke from an incense burner or from some chemical source. This may be the same phenomenon as that noted as a smoke column on October 13 by eight sources. (See pages 85 and 86.) If this phenomenon was merely the burning of incense, it may not have been considered unusual by the "non-see-ers."

Two sources report a great or a rapid lowering of the temperature, a relatively unspectacular phenomenon which may have been overlooked by most witnesses, including the "non-see-ers," in view of the loud noise reported by many witnesses.[108] Finally, some rather fantastic phenomena were claimed. Two sources said that stars were seen in the sky (at mid-day). A military cadet reported a number of fanciful phenomena, previously mentioned, namely that the ground shook, the rocks turned color and all saw arches, garlands, and flowers in the sky.[109] It is likely that none of these fantastic phenomena actually occurred.

September. For September there are fifteen reports of phenomena from early sources (1917–1919) and four more from later sources, in addition to the reports of "non-see-ers," which have already been

---

[107] Annex #7, #8, #51; Annex II #9B, #15E
[108] Annex #8, #51
[109] Annex #8, #21, #7

discussed. The phenomena can be grouped into four categories—lessening of the sunlight, appearance of white objects in the sky—birds, white flowers or snowflakes—the appearance of a bright globe—and colors on the sun and clouds.

The most important, from the viewpoint of believability, are the reports of a sudden lessening of the sunlight and a cooling of the air. Seven sources tell of this phenomenon, only two of which say it was sudden; however, four sources say it was a beautiful day, suggesting that the cooling was unexpected.[110] Two of these four indicate that the darkening was slight.[111] Two others say it was like a little eclipse and one simply says that the sun was eclipsed.[112] One says it darkened to the point of seeing the moon and stars, while two others say only that stars were seen.[113] The latter are clearly a gross exaggeration; if stars had actually been visible, it would have been nearly dark and all witnesses should surely have reported this startling occurrence. The comparison with an eclipse suggests that the darkening was somewhat more than slight. In any case, a sudden lessening of sunlight and cooling of the air is believable and may not have been considered significant by the "non-see-ers."

The second phenomena is a white object or objects in the sky. It is also called a star or something like it. One person said that near the sun he saw something like a white star, going "in the same direction," which then went up and disappeared; a second said that many people saw a star or something like a flake of white cotton cross the sky from east to west and disappear; a third has only that some people said they saw nothing, others saw a star; a fourth said that he saw something like white flowers, which other people considered to be stars; a fifth said that there were people who said that they saw a star.[114]

Still others said the object was white birds, white flowers, or even snowflakes. One witness said that some people said they saw a dove, others that they saw stars running and swallows with them, while

---

[110] Annex #10, #32, #51, #58, #100, #105; *A Guarda*, 13 September 1919, Doc Crit III, part 2, p 128
[111] Annex #105, *A Guarda*, 13 September 1919; Doc Crit III, part 2, p 128
[112] Annex #32, #51, #58
[113] Annex I #21, #97, #100
[114] Annex I #13, #51, #92, #97; Annex II #15G

even others saw flowers falling. A second said that an indescribable something, seemingly white flowers, passed over the holm oak, but others saw the same thing but thought they were stars. A third said that there was seen, way above, and cutting through the air from east to west, some very small white bodies which some say are doves, but he said they were not birds.[115] Clearly these objects were not firmly identified. A very tentative explanation is that a flock of white birds passed overhead and flew lower to look at the large crowd. The great variation in details makes it impossible to determine the nature of this phenomenon and to explain why it was not seen by all the people at the apparition.

The third category is a bright oval-shaped object which moved across the Cova and seemed to some to disappear near the holm oak. One witness saw an oval of brilliant, live color, a little larger than an egg, with the larger part hanging below, which made a straight line in the firmament. A second said that twice he saw something like a soap bubble, which he lost sight of a dozen meters above the holm oak. A lady, in a deposition in 1923, said she saw a star, a globe, not entirely round, like an egg, very beautiful, rainbow-colored, with a tail one and a half meters long, which went by very rapidly near the holm oak and disappeared near the ground. A much later report, published in the most widely read book on Fatima, comes from a priest who said that he saw a luminous globe move from east to west, gliding slowly through space; suddenly the globe, with its extraordinary light, disappeared; a child nearby saw it appear again; all around saw the same thing; he thought that it was Our Lady's means of transport. A 1980 book reports the testimony of another priest who saw, about a meter above the earth, a sort of luminous globe, which soon began to descend and from the horizon went up again toward the sun. He said everyone but one saw it,[116] clearly meaning that everyone around him saw it.

This is a widely known phenomenon, and thus an important one to discuss. It might have been the transport of Our Lady, which is an

---

[115] Annex I #21, #97, #100
[116] Annex I #10; Doc Crit III, part 2, p 127; Annex I #80; Annex II #15F; De Marchi, pp 112, 113; *Rediscovering Fatima*, p 83

impression held by many Catholics. However, there is another explanation, which fits well the testimony of the witnesses. A parent from the Fatima area, having no baby-sitter, brought his child with him to the Cova, along with a pail of water, some soap, and a straw. The child amused itself by blowing bubbles, one or two of which turned out to be very big, and an air current blew them up and across a considerable distance before they burst. In one case a number of small bubbles trailed after the big one. If the globe was a soap bubble, obviously it was seen only by people nearby and not by most of the people in the large area of the Cova, which is the size of a major football stadium.

Finally, this month, as in August, there were people who reported a color phenomenon. One said that the atmosphere was yellow, a second that some people saw rosy clouds, here and there, a third saw yellow spots on the ground, a fourth saw rainbow colors on the sun, and a fifth saw a blue mark on a dark cloud. The report of rainbow colors on the sun was second-hand and was made after October 13. Thus it may falsely attribute to September the color phenomenon of October 13.[117] The yellow spots may be due to sun blinding. The remaining items are rather insignificant, especially since each is reported only once.

Summary and Conclusions. Before reviewing and analyzing the individual phenomena, I must repeat that a considerable share of the crowd at the August (and perhaps at the June and July) apparitions said that they saw nothing unusual. This suggests strongly that nothing unusual occurred. However, there are some reasons for thinking that at least one or two of the reported phenomena actually occurred.

A review of the phenomena reported for July through September shows that for most months there are one or two phenomena which were reported only once, for example, a blue mark on a cloud. They are either doubtful or insignificant. Also, there are several phenomena that are fantastic and clearly did not occur, for example the rocks changing color or stars showing in the sky. These phenomena, it must be assumed, were imaginary.

The five sources which tell of thunder for July and August, and of the fright that the noise caused to the crowd, and those which used

---

[117] Annex I #10, #32, #51, #58, #80

other terms for the noise, suggest strongly that this noise occurred. It could scarcely have been a freak stroke of lightning, out of the blue, since such an unusual event would surely have been reported by many of the crowd. However, it may have been an explosion set off nearby by someone hoping to develop Fatima as a major shrine. Many of those who failed to report a noise may have left the Cova as soon as they heard that the seers had been kidnapped and thus failed to hear the noise. Others may have felt it was nothing unusual.

In July, August, and September part of the crowd noticed a decrease in the sun's heat at the time of the apparitions. A few thought it was sudden, implying that it was unusual. Some said it was a large decrease while others said it was slight. Since a fairly large number of people reported this phenomenon, it seems quite likely that it occurred. If so, those who said they saw nothing (and implied that they felt nothing) unusual, did not notice this phenomenon or thought it was insignificant. Not unreasonably, believers view this phenomenon as the work of God.

A number of sources reported rainbow colors on the clouds for August and September. They were made considerably after October 13. There is thus some reason to suspect that they erroneously ascribe to August or September the phenomenon seen on October 13. If so, this explains why this phenomenon was not noted by the "non-see-ers" and many other sources.

There are reports of dust, cloud, fog or smoke at the Cova at the time of the apparitions. They vary greatly in details, which suggests that no such phenomenon may have occurred. Other explanations are the use of an incense burner or chemicals to produce the phenomenon.

In short, it is impossible to say if any of the phenomena were the work of God. However, if the sun dance of October 13 was truly a spectacular miracle of God, one may wonder if He did not wish to have a large crowd to see it. It may well be that the earlier phenomena, even if of human origin and ignoble purpose, were intended by God to bring a large crowd to the Cova on October 13.

It may be argued that the phenomena at the apparitions from June to September were neither unusual nor spectacular, and that this weakens the credibility of the phenomena of the sun dance as miracles. This is a very weak argument, even if we concede that the earlier phenomena were not unusual or spectacular. There is no doubt that the phenomena of the sun dance were both spectacular and unusual, as will be shown in the chapters on the sun dance.

Behavior of the Seers. A final factor in considering whether the apparitions were genuine is the behavior of the seers during the apparitions and throughout their lives. I have already indicated some features of their behavior. I noted that both the seers and their families were devout Christians, and that neither they nor their parents profited significantly from the apparitions. (See pages 31-32.) I also noted that the seers resisted the threats of their captors in August, that Lucia resisted the threats of her mother and the ridicule of her family after the May apparition, and the worries for her safety and even her life if no miracle occurred on October 13. (See pages 17 and 22-25.)

I could add that Lucia's mother continued to threaten and punish her daughter about the apparitions long after May, that Francsico and Jacinta lived a devout life at home until their early deaths, that Lucia lived a devout life at home until June 1921 and then lived a devout life in an open convent and later in a cloister. This is well reported in many books on Fatima.

The seers' behavior before and during the apparitions is also pertinent. Lucia led the saying of the rosary immediately before the apparitions (see page 19), and they appeared to be transfigured or in ecstasy during the apparitions,[118] Lucia spoke (seemingly to the Lady) and then waited for a time, as if waiting for a response,[119] and the seers looked at the sky in the east at the end of the apparitions and told the crowd to look where they were looking, where the Lady was going.[120]

Finally, I must note that many persons interviewed the seers before the sun dance and revealed their impressions, all of which were favorable. Four indicated that they did not think that the seers were lying.[121] Six said that the seers never contradicted themselves or each other.[122]

---

[118] Annex I #2, #42, #69, #84, #97, #98, #100
[119] Annex I #3, #82, #96, #97, #98, #100
[120] Annex I #82, #84, #96, #97, #100; Annex II #3A, #5A, #5B, #6A and #6B; See also pages 11, 15, 17
[121] Annex I #10, #12A, #21, #51, #66, #72 and Annex II #8E, #15E
[122] Annex I #20, #31, #39, #65, #70; Annex II #7B

Of course, each is indicating only that he or she did not notice any contradictions, and, as I have already indicated, there were a number of contradictions, as would be expected from small children who were asked hundreds of questions.

Summing up, it can be said that the evidence on the seers' behavior, both in 1917 and later, provides considerable support for the claim that the apparitions were genuine.

SUMMARY

In summary, I find that the apparitions were clearly not a hoax, as stated by many Fatima opponents. The possibility that the seers were victims of a hallucination seems weak, since there were three of them and they appeared to be normal, healthy children. Their accounts of the apparitions were reasonably consistent, but contained many variations and conflicts, as might be expected from very young children when reporting on the apparitions many times in the latter part of 1917 and in much later years. And the seers' behavior fits well with their reports of apparitions. Lucia clearly erred in stating that the Lady had said that World War I would end on October 13, 1917. Her concern about the many requests for help from the Lady may have distracted Lucia for a moment. There may have been genuine, unusual atmospheric phenomena which accompanied the second, third, fourth, and fifth apparitions, but the evidence for this is not very strong. Some of the phenomena which are claimed may be invention, exaggeration, or some form of individual hallucination. A few may have been contrived by well-meaning zealots or by local individuals, who hoped to gain financially from the development of Fatima as a major shrine.

THE SLOWNESS OF CHURCH APPROVAL

I have not yet considered an objection to the apparitions, which also applies to the sun dance, namely that the Church (in the person of the local bishop) took a very long time after the apparitions before beginning a formal inquiry into them, and then took an even longer time to complete its investigation. The formal inquiry was begun in 1922 and completed in 1930. The investigations and approval of the apparitions at La Salette and Lourdes were much quicker—five years or less.[123] Why, if there was a plausible case for the Fatima apparitions and the sun dance, did the Church take so long to investigate and approve?

The answers are many: 1) World War I was underway and commanded the attention of the Church as well as of all the people; 2) the Portuguese government was strongly anti-Church, and had forbidden the teaching of religion in the schools and had exiled some clergy; thus the hierarchy hesitated to do anything which might provoke further actions against it; 3) since the apparitions at Lourdes, many highly questionable apparitions had been claimed; 4) the almost incredible nature of some phenomena claimed by some witnesses at the August and September apparitions at Fatima, countered by many other witnesses who said they saw nothing unusual, caused much of the clergy and hierarchy to be highly skeptical of Fatima prior to October 13; and the almost incredible nature of the sun dance increased their skepticism;[124] 5) Lucia's "false prophecy" (see pages 46-54) and Coelho's article reporting a second sun dance on October 14[125] caused further skepticism among the clergy; 6) on January 17, 1918, the pope re-established the diocese of Leiria, in which Fatima is located, and the bishop of Lisbon (in whose diocese Fatima was located in 1917), was unwilling to appoint an inquiry commission, preferring to allow the new bishop of Leiria to name his own people;[126] 7) the new bishop of Leiria was not named and installed until August 1920 and required some time to review the Fatima events and to choose the members of a commission;[127] 8) the work of writing up the testimony and the conclusions of the Inquiry Commission was given to Father Manuel Nunes Formigao, who had many other duties and was slow to write up

[123] *Enquete sur Les Apparitions de la Vierge*, pp 180, 185, 196, 200, 201
[124] Doc Crit II, p 10; *Fatima 1917-1968*, pp 216-231, 255-257, 262-264
[125] Annex I #34
[126] Doc Crit II, p 5; *Fatima 1917-1968*, p 255
[127] Doc Crit II, p 5

the results,[128] which were very voluminous;[129] and 9) Father Formigao clearly viewed Fatima as another Lourdes and devoted much time to investigating seventeen cures which were associated with Fatima.[130]

In view of these various explanations, the long delay in investigating and approving Fatima is understandable. In any case, while it may be said that the delay was caused, in part, by the clergy and hierarchy, their very skepticism suggests that the Church inquiry was not begun with a bias in favor of approving Fatima. And the long delay, chiefly due to Father Formigao, clearly did not reflect his skepticism about the apparitions. In this period he published three books and a magazine devoted to Fatima. He was, in fact, one of its strongest supporters.

THE LADY'S UNKNOWN LIGHT AND THE GREAT AURORA

As told in Lucia's memoirs, the Lady said on July 13, 1917: "If people do not stop offending God a worse war will break out during the Pontificate of Pius XI. When you see a night illuminated by an unknown light note that this is the great sign given you by God that he is about to punish the world for its crimes by means of war...."

This statement by the Lady has received little attention in most books on Fatima. The Lady may have been referring to the great aurora which occurred in 1937 and was seen over much of the United States and Northern Europe. It consisted of brilliant, multi-colored flashes, like continuous lightning, which lasted for many minutes, perhaps fifteen. This may have been the Lady's warning that World War II was about to occur.

---

[128] Doc Crit II, p 9
[129] The final version is given in Doc Crit II, pp 64, 258, 279-372
[130] Doc Crit II, pp 279-372

CHAPTER V

LATER APPARITIONS

After the sun dance, the seers continued to live at home and were freely available for interviews. However, within two or three years Francisco and Jacinta died, victims of the Spanish flu. Only Lucia survived. For four years she lived at home, went to school, and was interviewed by many of the thousands of pilgrims who came to Fatima. In 1921 she entered a convent school and in 1925 she became a nun.[1] In 1927 she reported further apparitions. They are of concern for this book because they might reflect on the reliability of Lucia and thus on the reliability of the 1917 apparitions. It scarcely needs to be added that if the 1917 apparitions were false, then the miraculous nature of the sun dance is greatly in doubt.

In 1921, at the urging of the bishop, Lucia's mother agreed to have Lucia enrolled in the convent school of the Sisters of St. Dorothy, in Vilar, near Porto, under an assumed name.[2] She remained incognito and for years the interviews stopped. She became a nun of this order in 1925.[3] In a letter of 1927 to her confessor, Lucia reported that on December 10, 1925, at the convent in Pontevedra, the Virgin Mary and the Child Jesus appeared to her. The Virgin held in her hand her Immaculate Heart, surrounded by thorns. She told Lucia that the thorns were caused by the sins of mankind, asked Lucia to console

---

[1] Doc Crit I, pp 145-147; *Fatima in Lucia's Own Words*, p 167; *Fatima Joie Intime, Evenement Mondiale*, pp 144, 148, 149

[2] *Fatima Joie Intime*, pp 143, 145

[3] Ibid., pp 147-149

her and to tell everyone this message: if, on the first Saturday of five consecutive months, they go to confession, receive Communion, say a rosary, and meditate on the mysteries of the rosary for fifteen minutes, she would help them at the hour of their death with the graces needed for their salvation. This devotion came to be known as the First Saturday devotion. Lucia told her convent superior and her confessor of this apparition. The latter told Lucia to put the apparition in writing, but did nothing at this time to promote the devotion.[4]

In the same letter of 1927, Lucia wrote to her confessor that the Child Jesus had again appeared to her on February 15, 1926, in a courtyard, and admonished her for not spreading the First Saturday devotion.[5] In June 1930, Lucia told her confessor that on May 29, 1930, in a chapel at Tuy, while in prayer near midnight, she heard the interior voice of Our Lord, who explained to her why He wanted a First Saturday devotion of five months, as opposed to nine (for the First Friday devotion, which had existed for many years).[6]

Finally, Lucia reported another apparition that occurred on June 13, 1929, in a chapel at Tuy. Near midnight, the chapel was lighted by a supernatural light, and Lucia saw on the altar a cross of light which reached to the ceiling. With a brighter light there appeared on the upper part of the cross the face and torso of a man, and a dove of equal light on his chest. Nailed to the cross was the body of another man. A little above his waist was a chalice and large host onto which fell drops of blood from the cheek and chest of the Crucified. Under the right arm of the cross was Our Lady with her Immaculate Heart, surrounded by thorns and flames, in her hand. Under the left arm of the cross were the words: "Grace and Mercy." Then Our Lady said: "The time has come when God asks the Pope, in union with all the bishops of the world, to consecrate Russia to my Immaculate Heart, promising to save it by this means." She added that there were so many condemned souls that she had come to ask reparation.[7]

---

[4] Ibid., p 153, 154; Nov Doc, p 120
[5] *Fatima Joie Intime*, pp 154, 155; this same event was reported by Lucia in an undated letter, Nov Doc, pp 115, 116
[6] *Fatima Joie Intime*, pp 158, 159; Nov Doc, pp 123, 124
[7] Ibid., p 198, 199, citing *Documentos de Fatima*, pp 463-465.

In May 1930, Lucia wrote to her confessor that God promised to end the persecution in Russia: if the pope would make a solemn, public act of reparation and consecration of Russia to the Sacred Hearts of Jesus and Mary; and if he would order the Catholic bishops to do the same; and if the pope would approve and recommend the First Saturday devotion.[8]

These later revelations of Lucia, including the portions of the 1916 and 1917 apparitions which Lucia revealed only in the late 1930s (those enclosed in double brackets in my report on the apparitions), made the earlier apparitions much more spectacular and presented important new messages. Specifically, the new revelations about the apparitions were: the apparitions of the angel in 1916; the intense light from the Virgin's hand, which caused the seers to "see themselves in God" at the first two apparitions in 1917; the vision, in June 1917, of the Heart of Mary, surrounded by thorns and her request for a new devotion to her Immaculate Heart (the First Saturdays); in July 1917, the vision of Hell, the threat of communism, the "unusual light" as a sign of the next terrible war (WWII), the devotion of the First Saturdays, and the prediction of the defeat of Soviet communism. These July additions to the 1917 apparitions were not entirely surprising, since the seers had said that the Lady had then told them a secret, which they were not to reveal. These additions were clearly part of that secret.

Most informed Catholics accepted these revelations, but very serious objections to these later revelations were raised by a prominent theologian, the Jesuit Father Edouard Dhanis, a professor at Louvain and later at the Gregorian University in Rome, and a consultant of the pope's Congregation for the Doctrine of the Faith. His objections were seconded by many other prominent clergy, notably Cardinal Journet and Fathers Rouquette, Fesquet, and Laurentin. Their published articles doubted that the three very young seers would have maintained silence on these major aspects of the 1916 and 1917 apparitions at the time and for years later; they suspected that Lucia (the only source for these later revelations) was inventing them, although not consciously.[9]

---

[8] Ibid., page 199
[9] *The Whole Truth About Fatima*, pp 389-393, 432; See also Jaki, pp 268, 277, 305

While Father Dhanis did not question the reality of the apparitions or the miraculous nature of the sun dance, he minimized them.

Although these Churchmen raised some other objections to the later revelations of Lucia (the flames of hell are not real, but the damned do suffer), the major objection raised by them is the silence of the three seers on these revelations in 1917 and succeeding years. Such very young children (9, 8, and 6 in 1916) would not have kept silence about the angel's appearance in 1916, especially after the awe-inspiring chalice in mid-air and their miraculous reception of the Eucharist. Similarly hard to believe is the seers' failure to report the intense light coming from the hand of the Lady in May, June, and July 1917, and their failure to tell of the Virgin's heart with thorns and her statement about the devotion to her Immaculate Heart in June.

If these revelations are true, how can one explain this strange silence? Lucia offered two explanations: they were inwardly inspired to keep them secret; and she was afraid of the angry reaction she would have received from her mother, as occurred in 1915 and again in May 1917; and she convinced the others to keep quiet.[10]

The seers' strange silence is surely difficult for skeptics to believe, but Catholics (and *probably* some other Christians) can readily accept Lucia's explanation that it was due to divine inspiration. Even skeptics might accept it as a theoretical possibility, but they would surely ask why one should accept this possibility rather than the alternative— that the revelations were not true, especially in view of the startling aspects of some details of Lucia's later revelation. An answer is offered by a pro-Fatima author—the sun dance confirms the authenticity of the apparitions, and God would never choose, as His voice to the people, a seer who would later deceive the world so greatly by reporting false visions and false demands for spiritual devotions.[11]

Non-Catholics undoubtedly view some details of the new revelations as bizarre—the chalice suspended in the air, with the drops of blood, the two men on the cross, and the open heart with thorns around it. Skeptical Catholics probably agree. Undoubtedly these

---

[10] Lucia's Memoirs, pp 32, 33, 115, 116, 128, 129, 131, 132, 167, 168; *The Whole Truth About Fatima*, p 97
[11] *The Whole Truth About Fatima*, pp 414, 415

features make it more difficult for many to accept Lucia's new revelations as true. However, I find the explanation of the above-cited pro-Fatima author to be reasonably convincing. But this problem adds greater importance to the major topic of this book—the sun dance of October 13, 1917. If it was a true and spectacular miracle, then one can accept the later revelations as true, despite the long silence of the seers. If it was not, then all the revelations and the apparitions may be seriously questioned.

I have made only a short study of these later apparitions and a very brief analysis of them. The doubts about these later apparitions, which I have stated here, may be unjustified. A thorough and scholarly study of them is clearly needed.

Pro-Fatima sources cite not only the sun dance, but also the healings, as evidence of the reality of the apparitions. The local bishop, in approving devotion to Our Lady of Fatima, placed great reliance on the healings attributed to her and gave less emphasis to the sun dance as evidence of this reality. He gave much documentation on the healings. Considerable material has been published on Fatima healings, but little in English, to the best of my knowledge. I have made no effort to study healings associated with Fatima, and little effort to study the broader topic of healings as miracles. In my mind this is an important, complex, and difficult matter. I hope that future scholars will make this effort.

CHAPTER VI

THE SUN DANCE — INTRODUCTION

An analysis of the sun dance consists of two parts: deciding what happened and deciding what explanations can be found for these happenings. Unfortunately, the information on what happened is incomplete and in some cases is contradictory. Further, the best explanations, or at least the best I have found (other than purely supernatural ones), involve natural phenomena that are rare and for which little has been published in the likely sources of information. The analysis of the sun dance thus has become a difficult and interesting research project. My conclusions, both the firm ones and the tentative ones, may not be correct. But I have provided, in Part I of the Annex, the best available testimony on the sun dance, which perhaps my readers and future researchers will examine and reach better or firmer conclusions.

I begin my analysis of the sun dance with a short presentation of the positions advanced by skeptics and opponents of Fatima.

Hallucination. By far the most common explanation of the sun dance which was offered by opponents is that it was a case of mass hallucination. See Chart I.

In most cases the Portuguese word for hallucination was *sugestao*. In five articles the more specific words *sugestao colectiva* (mass hallucination) were used. I believe that "mass hallucination" better represents the meaning intended by the writers than the more literal "suggestion." In view of the popularity of the idea of mass hallucination in 1917, it seems likely that even when only *sugestao* was used, the writer implied mass hallucination.[1]

The theory of mass hallucination was much in vogue in 1917. It was advanced by Gustave Le Bon in his book *The Psychology of Crowds*. It is cited by a Catholic witness to the sun dance and by a Catholic journal, which was later quoted by a Fatima opponent. His work and its influence deserve careful study. *The Whole Truth About Fatima* gives us the following:

> In reading the historical article of H. F. Ellenberger, in an authoritative work (*Psychoses Collectives*), in *Encyclopdie Medico-Chirurigical*, (1967) we learn that the principle source of the myth of collective hallucination ... is the work of Gustave Le Bon, *The Psychology of Crowds*, published in 1896. This work ... enjoyed an immense success. ... If we are to believe him, collective hallucinations are ... quite common. "The observations made by crowds simply represent the illusion of an individual who, by way of contagion, has planted a suggestion in others." ... in these ten pages ... Le Bon has found only one example which has the appearance of being convincing. The example has become a classic ... for good reason: that it is the only one that exists. Here it is:

> "The frigate *La Belle Poule* was cruising at sea, looking for the warship *Le Berceau*, from which it had been separated in a violent storm. It was broad daylight under a bright sun. Suddenly the lookout signals that a small craft is in distress. The crew looked over to the spot pointed out and everybody, both officers and sailors, clearly perceive a raft full of people, towed by some small boats with distress signals on them. *However, it was only a collective hallucination.*

> Admiral Defosses equipped a small boat to assist the castaways. As they approached, the sailors and officers saw 'a crowd of men waving, extending their hands, and they heard the dull and confused noise of a great number of voices.'

> When the small boast arrived, they found only some branches covered with leaves. Before such palpable evidence, the hallucination vanished. In this example we see clearly the mechanism of collective hallucination in action, just as we have described it."

> Analyzing this example, Ellenberger has no difficulty showing that in no way does it confirm Le Bon's thesis. Indeed, the latter was careful to cleverly isolate the fact which he reported from its whole context, which makes it perfectly understandable:

---

[1] Annex #42, #48, #76, #78, #88

1. The crew, which was afflicted with malaria, was in a state of great physical exhaustion.

2. The sailors feared that the warship, which had disappeared after a hurricane, had sunk, leaving 300 victims.

3. For a whole month while the search was going on, the crew was in a state of anxiety, and the thought of those who had disappeared had become a veritable obsession with them.

4. The warm air was stirring on the horizon, and the sea currents were carrying "a mass of large trees" ((not a few branches!)).

5. The sailor on the lookout, in the face of intense illumination, perceived objects whose nature he could not distinguish and cried out: "Disabled craft in sight!" And this was the point of departure for the illusion, which was easily understandable, and gradually spread to the whole crew.

We should speak rather of a "mirage," or if the term collective hallucination must be retained, its nature should be specified more clearly and the definite causes ... pointed out: physical exhaustion, mental depression, a dominant preoccupation, which over the course of a month had become an obsession, and finally the sensorial factors which favored the creation of an illusion."[2]

Another author, who was less biased in favor of Fatima (he favored a UFO as an explanation for the sun dance) quotes two Brazilian parapsychologists as saying, in 1971 and 1976, that mass hallucination, except for mass hypnosis, does not exist, although one concedes that it might be possible for three or four persons."[3] A pro–Fatima author writes: "in the monumental treatise (in 1973) on hallucination by the great specialist Henry Ey (1,543 pages) not a single chapter deals with this subject."[4] The *Encyclopedia of Psychology* devotes approximately a full page to hallucinations, but makes no mention of mass hallucination.[5] The *Handbook of Parapsychology* has a small section on "Survival after Bodily Death." It says 26 cases were noted when two or more

---

[2] *The Whole Truth About Fatima*, pp 367, 368, 369
[3] *Fatima: o que se Passou em 1917*, p 68, 69
[4] *The Whole Truth About Fatima*, pp 348, 378
[5] *Encyclopedia of Psychology*, Volume II, Second Edition, John Wiley & Sons, pp 101, 102

people see the same phantasmal figure.[6] It gives nothing on mass hallucination. In short, mass hallucination is an unlikely explanation for the sun dance.

The concept that the phenomena of the sun dance were mass hallucinations might seem more plausible if the phenomena were known and expected by the crowd. However, with the exception of the rainbow colors, none of these phenomena was expected nor were even heard of by the crowd. The spin and fall of the sun were not only unknown phenomena, but were scarcely imaginable to the simple folk at Fatima.

No Fatima critic has suggested the possibility of mass hypnosis, which is a plausible explanation for the sun dance. Undoubtedly this is because the closest approach to a hypnotic act was Lucia's words: "Look at the sun." This could be hypnotic only if followed by other commands, such as: "You now see the sun spinning," etc., which were not given. Mass hypnosis, as a possible explanation, therefore can be rejected.

Further, none of the critics who called the sun dance a hallucination has stated or suggested that the thousands who witnessed the sun dance were all victims of some strange form of individual hallucination. Individual hallucination, of course, exists. But it is very unlikely that a large majority of the crowd at Fatima were simultaneously victims of a similar individual hallucination. In short, both mass hallucination and individual hallucination are unlikely explanations for the sun dance. Finally, this possible explanation can be entirely eliminated when we consider that the phenomena of the sun dance were noted at the same time in locations near Fatima. (See the section "Remote Sightings," in Chapter X.)

Non-see-ers. Strangely, the opponents of Fatima have given very little attention to a fact that would seem to support their argument that the sun dance was a hallucination of some kind. There were people at the Cova da Iria on October 13 who claimed that they saw nothing unusual. I refer to them as "non-see-ers." This is an important factor that I must discuss in detail.

---

[6] *Handbook of Parapsychology*, Benjamin B. Woolman, editor, Mc Farland & Co., Jefferson, NC: 1977, p 602

Four press reports indicate or imply that some or many people saw nothing unusual.

O Primeiro de Janeiro on October 16 reported: "A great number (of the crowd), if not a majority, maintain that they saw miraculous signs in the sky."[7] The writer of this article does not give any reason for his implication that many people saw nothing. He cites no sources nor does he imply that he himself was at the Cova on October 13.

A long anonymous letter, from an agnostic, published in *O Portugal* (an anti-Church journal) on October 17 says that the writer was at the Cova on October 13 and "It was (only) on reading (the article) in *O Seculo* that I learned of the miracles that occurred (at Fatima), only on reading *O Seculo* that I learned that the sun had danced."[8] If indeed the writer of this letter was at the Cova on October 13 and saw nothing, he could not have failed to hear from others that they had seen the sun dance. This clearly suggests that the writer of this letter was not at Fatima and merely invented his story to help the anti-Fatima cause.

A Republica, (another anti-Church journal) on October 17 reported: "There are those who saw it (the sun) ... shake and turn on itself ... among the thousands of people who were there, an immense number saw nothing." It then implies that those who saw strange phenomena were victims of mass hallucination.[9] This writer also does not tell us the basis for his statement about non-see-ers and fails to cite any sources or say that he was at Fatima on October 13.

Finally, on November 11, *A Aurora* (still another anti-Church journal), said: "An old man with a long name, erect and bearded, voiced the creed as a solemn profession of faith. A lady deplored with extraordinary fear, <u>the blindness of the curious, who had seen nothing</u>, of the few who still dared to keep their hat on in view of the evidence of a stupendous miracle." This writer was clearly paraphrasing two sentences in the *O Seculo* article of October 15, but the phrase which I have underlined is not included in the *O Seculo* article. This writer was clearly, and falsely, implying that this phrase was in the *O Seculo* article. The *O Seculo* article is given as document #28 in the Index. The *Aurora* article is #78.

Other press reports present a different picture. Most significant is an article in the anti-clerical journal *A Razao* on May 30, 1918. It attacks the apparitions, citing the "false prophecy," and it ridicules the sun dance as a miracle. But it says, "<u>It is uncontestable that the sun suffered some kind of alteration ((facts cannot be questioned)). It was observed not only at Fatima, but also at many other points in the</u>

---

[7] Annex #36
[8] Annex #41
[9] Annex #42

country." See document #109 of the Annex for more details. I have added the underlining to emphasize the importance of the statement.

On October 15, 1917, *O Seculo*, whose reporter stayed at the Cova for at least a half an hour after the sun dance, stated: "People then began to ask each other ... what they had seen. The majority declare that they had seen the trembling and dancing of the sun; others ... that the sun whirled on itself like a giant fireworks wheel ... some say they saw it change colors ..."[10] The reporter implies that he merely overheard these remarks, but more probably he also asked many people what they had seen. It was clearly his duty as a reporter. He makes no mention of non-see-ers, which strongly implies that he had heard of none.

On October 18, *A Lucta*, an anti-clerical newspaper, said: "But all my informants swear that they saw extraordinary things in the sun, which does not disturb my personal criticism. I know well that people ... prefer ... the passing pleasure of legendary images to harsh contact with bitter realities."[11] *A Republica*, in contrast with its article of October 17 (cited above), reported on October 26: "The great majority of all those people saw. The visual impression varies. Some saw a luminous incomparable phenomenon ..."[12]

Many press reports present strong, but indirect, evidence that the non-see-ers were few.

The *Diario de Noticias* reporter presents an unfavorable picture of the events at Fatima. He says that thousands fell to the ground and some say they saw the sun descend to the horizon. He devotes three paragraphs to the sun dance, indicating that it was a case of hallucination. But he fails to claim that anyone saw nothing.[13] He fails to say that he queried members of the crowd, but as a reporter who spent a day's travel for this assignment, he certainly interviewed members of the crowd before he left. It would seem that he, as well as the *O Seculo* reporter, heard no one say that they saw nothing unusual, and that they could not cite themselves as non-see-ers.

Besides the articles already cited, the anti-religious press published a very large number of articles on Fatima in 1917 after the sun dance. I include eleven of them in my Annex.[14] None of these makes any mention of any non-see-ers. I also examined a great many other articles on Fatima in neutral or anti-Fatima newspapers; none mentioned non-see-ers except one article which merely repeated the article of

---

[10] Annex #28
[11] Annex #46
[12] Annex #63
[13] Annex #27
[14] Annex #24, #29, #40, #41, #42, #45, #62, #63, #76, #78, #88

October 16 in *O Primeiro de Janeiro*, cited above. See Chart I. Many of these journals were dedicated foes of the Church. They probably knew of the claims of non-see-ers published in at least one of the four journals which I cited above. Their failure to echo these earlier reports of non-see-ers strongly implies that they believed that the Portuguese public had rejected these claims as largely or entirely unfounded. Significant is a long pamphlet of the Civil Register and Association of Free Thinkers, published in December 19, 1917, which explains the sun dance as a hoax or a hallucination, but fails to mention any non-see-ers.[15]

Further evidence that there were very few non-see-ers is found in letters and other written testimony made soon after the sun dance.

A letter of October 15 describes the sun dance and then adds: "I interviewed various people about what happened and all told me like what I had seen." He later says: "All were indignant with the free-thinkers, and 100,000 people are witnesses of a miracle that nobody can deny."[16] Another letter of October 15 is particularly emphatic. It says: "And all … 30,000 people there, according to estimates made, people (who) were far apart from one another, all, I repeat, in those short moments saw the same phenomenon."[17] A letter of October 16 is also quite strong: "There were 50,000 people there, respectful and devout. Men in the thousands. None saw Our Lady except the three children, but what all saw was the golden light on all the people during the stay of Our Lady on earth."[18] A statement of October 20 by a man who arrived too late for the sun dance says he interviewed people there and all said they had seen the sun dance.[19] A letter of October 21 describes the sun dance and says: "Everyone saw, about 100,000."[20] A deposition by another witness on December 30 says that his brother and other people he met said they saw the sun dance too, varying a little in their accounts.[21] Another deposition of December 30 says: "Of the thousands of people who saw the movement of the sun … as far as I know, none doubted the veracity of the phenomena…"[22] A newspaper article said: " …a tremendous wave of faith … passed over the vast majority of the crowd."[23]

---

[15] Annex #88
[16] Annex #25
[17] Annex #30
[18] Annex #31
[19] Annex #51
[20] Annex #55
[21] Annex #92
[22] Annex #93
[23] Annex #34

Later interviews of witnesses by two pro-Fatima authors also supports the conclusion that there were very few non-see-ers.

Father De Marchi, author of the best-known book on Fatima, whose interviews were made in the 1940s, states: "Up to the present we have not met a single person, among the many we have interviewed, who has not confirmed this phenomenon."[24] And John Haffert states: "All testify to having seen something inexplicable. There is not a single exception to this among all the persons questioned in our 1960 survey."[25] He further names nine witnesses to the sun dance whom he asked if they had heard of any non-see-ers, and all said no.[26] But he had earlier said: "In the rather thorough investigation made for this book, ... only two persons thought they had not seen a miracle."[27] He does not explain the apparent contradiction, but possibly means that two persons had seen unusual phenomena, but did not think them to be miraculous.

However, it would be wrong to say there were no non-see-ers. A diary and two letters tell of specific people who were there and said they saw nothing unusual. The diary of Manuel Brites says that he saw nothing but the darkening of the sun for about fifteen minutes. The letters were from Leonore Manuel and Izabel de Melo.[28] Both were clearly strong believers, while Brites appears to have been at least a nominal Catholic. Thus these three people do not seem to be biased against religion or the Church.

Another non-see-er was Maria Oriol Pena, whose letter tells us: "... when I saw the tremendous agitation, ... I fell upon my knees and could not see anything more." This probably means that she kept her eyes on the ground, although she does not say so. And a letter from Dr. Nascimento e Sousa says that after the sun dance he interviewed others, and only one person said he saw nothing.[29] A letter of October 21 also merits mention. It says: "the people ... who had their eyes open (saw); those who had them closed saw nothing, and maybe there were those who saw and said they did not, in order not to give honor to the Mother of Heaven." The writer clearly implies that at least a few people said they saw nothing.[30]

There is also a little later testimony of non-see-ers.

---

[24] De Marchi, p 136, footnote 2
[25] *Meet the Witnesses*, p 111
[26] Ibid., pp 80, 82, 86-95, 101, 122, 123, 124
[27] Ibid., pp 92, 100, footnote #2
[28] Annex #17, #33, #69
[29] Annex #43, #70
[30] Annex #21

A book of 1950 mentions two women who were at Fatima on October 13, 1917, and saw nothing extraordinary, although a companion saw "all the phenomena." And a young woman, aged nineteen on October 13, 1917, later said she saw nothing "of the beautiful colors" described by others, that she was only aware that she was going to die. Nearby her, she said, two persons fainted.[31]

Reviewing all the above, it seems very probable that a large majority of the people at the Cova da Iria on October 13 claimed that they saw some extraordinary phenomena. The early press reports claiming or implying the contrary, with one possible exception, were clearly biased against Fatima, and their writers apparently were not at Fatima on October 13 (even the letter writer whose presence there is questionable) and they did not cite anyone who was there. The failure of unfriendly newspapers to pursue the topic in later issues suggests further that the public had accepted that nearly all the people at Fatima on October 13 had seen very unusual phenomena. And the articles in *A Razao, O Seculo, A Lucta,* and *Diario de Noticias,* plus many letters written soon after October 13 and the later testimony reported by pro-Fatima authors lead to the conclusion that a great majority of the crowd at the Cova on October 13 thought that they saw some very unusual things. However, the 1917 testimony of three pro-Fatima sources and of two later sources clearly indicates that at least a few in that vast crowd reported that they saw nothing unusual. Explanations for "non-see-ers" depend on explanations for some of the phenomena of the sun dance and thus are given later. See chapter XII, pages 206-210.

Psychic Phenomena. Another author, D. Scott Rogo, a believer in psychic phenomena, claims that the sun dance was a psychic phenomenon resulting from the ardent desire of the majority of the crowd to see a miracle. He insists that it was a real phenomenon, not a hallucination, but does not explain how the movement of the sun was real, or if it was not, how this psychic phenomenon differs from mass hallucination.[32]

UFOs. Another explanation for the sun dance is offered by a supporter of UFOs. Not surprisingly he suggests that the dancing sun

---

[31] *Message of Fatima,* p 82; *Toute la Verite sur Fatima,* p 354, citing the 1958 book of Abbey Richard, *The Queen with Hands Joined,* p 99; see also Jaki, pp 232, 245
[32] *Miracles,* D. Scott Rogo, pp 229-231, 235, 236

was actually a flying saucer or some such vehicle from outer space.[33] I view this explanation as highly unlikely for three reasons. One is that the existence of UFOs is not yet firmly established. The second is the great unlikelihood that a UFO, if such a vehicle exists, would appear at this time, but never be seen again by a crowd of similar size. The third reason is that if a UFO was there and created the phenomena seen by the crowd, it would be most unlikely that it would choose to descend from (and depart into) the exact location in the sky where the sun was at that time. I say this because I have found no sources (with one minor exception) which state or imply that the object which they saw was not in the normal position for the sun at that day and hour.

The minor exception is the book by Rogo, cited above, which says: "… judging by the descriptions which we have, the disk was at the wrong elevation and azimuth to have been the sun. The object seems to have been an immense UFO-like silver disk." He does not say which descriptions caused him to make this judgment, and I have found no sources which lead me to agree with him.

Two sources clearly indicate that the dancing object was the sun.[34] Jose Garrett is especially convincing: "This phenomenon, except for two brief interruptions, when the fierce sun … forced us to look away, must have lasted about ten minutes. This pearly disk had a vertiginous movement." He clearly implies that the pearly disk was the sun.[35] Moreover, if the dancing object was not in the right place to be the sun, this fact would surely have been noted by many people at the sight and would have been reported by the anti-Fatima press. It was not.

Other Explanations. Since hallucinations, psychic phenomena, and UFOs seem to be unsatisfactory explanations for the sun dance, we are left with four possibilities: an optical illusion; unusual meteorological phenomena; a fully supernatural miracle, (an event entirely outside the laws of nature); or some combination of these three. It is also theoretically possible that all who claimed to see unusual phenomena were simply inventing their accounts, but such mass prevarication is beyond belief.

---

[33] *Fatima: o que se Passou em 1917*, pp 205-225
[34] Annex I #71, #90
[35] Annex I #90

Many or most Fatima supporters view the sun dance as a fully supernatural miracle. I see no reason to reject this as a theoretical explanation. If God exists, it is within His power to suspend the laws of nature and perform fantastic supernatural phenomena. This explanation does not necessarily demand that God made the sun fall or jump around in the sky, since He could have simply created this impression in the minds of the crowd. To avoid repetition, I note now that each of the phenomena might be purely supernatural. I do not intend to repeat this possible explanation as I discuss each phenomenon.

However, I am reluctant to accept a supernatural explanation, if reasonable natural explanations for the sun dance can be found. In saying this I am following the great St. Augustine, who said: "A miracle should never be proclaimed when a natural explanation is possible."[36] In recent times, two books have been published by pro-Fatima authors which raise the possibility that some or all of the phenomena of the sun dance were unusual meteorological occurrences. Neither says that they clearly were such occurrences, nor even that they probably were. And neither views any of the phenomena of the sun dance as an optical illusion.[37]

Both of these authors present much more of the written testimony of people who attended the sun dance than is found in other books on Fatima, but both fail to give much other important testimony, recently published in Portuguese, and which I have translated and include in my Annex.

The Column of Smoke. This phenomenon appears to have occurred before the sun dance and is reported by only a few of the many who have left us testimony on the events of October 13 at the Cova da Iria. Only eight of the seventy in my Annex. Another mentions a fog, which may refer to the same phenomena.

Two give no details on the location of the column of smoke which rose up at the Cova. Six indicate that the smoke was at or near the oak bush, where the seers were. Eight sources refer to it as smoke, but most say smoke or something else. These "something else" include incense (3 times), cigar smoke (2 times), bonfire (2 times), cloud (2 times) and mist (once). One describes it as a slender bluish smoke column and one calls it transparent white smoke. Two indicate that the column of

---

[36] Jaki, p 65
[37] Jaki, pp 346-350, 357, 369; *O Fenomeno Solar*, 13 October 1917, pp 36-56

smoke appeared and disappeared three times, and another indicated several times. Two tell us that there was no fire near the oak bush, and in view of the rain it would seem unlikely that there was any fire. Smoke from incense burning is a possibility, although no source mentions it.[38]

Despite the fact that most of the witnesses to the sun dance do not mention the smoke column, I feel quite sure that it occurred. My reason is that most people may have seen it but considered it unimportant, and may even have forgotten it, after the spectacular sun dance. Fatima supporters clearly consider the smoke column to be miraculous. I would not deny it, but note that it is the only phenomenon reported for October 13 which has a hoax as a possible explanation. A pro-Fatima witness who reported the smoke and considered it to be important, Professor Goncalo Almeida Garrett, on September 29, 1918, offered three possible natural explanations: evaporation (a mist), incomplete combustion (bonfire), or a chemical reaction, like that of two gases.[39] Only the latter two produce the impression of smoke.

Since a bonfire is untenable as an explanation, in view of the rain, the only natural explanations which can be offered are incense or a chemical reaction. The incense burner also seems rather unlikely, in the rainy conditions, and we have testimony that no burning was noted.[40] A chemical reaction remains as a possibility. Presumably this reaction, if it occurred, would have been designed to create the false impression of a miraculous smoke column. The perpetrator of such a hoax would surely have been someone hoping to gain financially from the development of Fatima as a major shrine—perhaps a local merchant—or someone acting from a distorted sense of piety, a fanatic who decided that there would be at least one miraculous sign on October 13.

The perpetrators of such a hoax would surely have had to hide their actions from the eyes of those around them and to choose a chemical reaction with little smell or noise. Two or three people, co-conspirators, would have had to stand in front of the individual exposing or mixing the chemicals, and all would have had to keep the

---

[38] Annex I #16, #23, #65, #72, #89, #90, #94, #96, #97
[39] Doc Crit III, part 2, p 51; Annex I #89
[40] Annex I #90, #97

secret to their deathbed. This seems an unlikely explanation for the column of smoke, but not an impossible one.

A somewhat similar phenomenon was also reported by a few witnesses at the July and August apparitions as a fog, dust, cloud or pillar of smoke. (See pages 57 and 60.) I end the discussion of this phenomenon by noting that it is a relatively unimportant one, and is not a part of the sun dance itself.

The rest of this book is devoted to presenting and analyzing the available data about the sun dance, in order to establish, as far as possible, what was said to have been seen by the majority of the people, to presenting possible natural explanations, and to presenting evidence on the rarity of the meteorological and optical phenomena or other natural causes, which are offered as explanations for the sun dance; I also discuss why God performed this great miracle at this time.

STATISTICS, VARIATIONS IN TESTIMONY, WEATHER

The Sources. I begin my discussion of the sun dance by noting that there is a plethora of testimony on it, some of which is contradictory or confusing. One critic has noted that "it was impossible to extract the facts from the mass of tales which have been handed down."[41] This impression may be obtained from a perfunctory examination of the testimony, but a thorough study of the available testimony and of related factors gives a different result. The testimony on some phenomena is quite consistent, while that on others, especially the color phenomenon, contains many variations, and seems confusing. It requires a very thorough study.

I must first discuss the available information on the sun dance. Some of it is found in earlier books on Fatima and is derived from interviews or statements which were made many years after 1917, or which are simply undated. I occasionally use such testimony and cite the source. However, such testimony, which may be accurate and

---

[41] *The Evidence for Visions of the Virgin Mary*, McClure, p 78

reliable, is not as valuable as earlier testimony. Over time, memories of the details of the sun dance may have become weak and may have been influenced by what was read and heard about it. For this reason, I have included very little testimony after 1917 in Part I of the Annex, where testimony on the sun dance is given. Only nine documents are later, five of which are from 1918 or 1919. My study of the sun dance is based almost entirely on the documents in Part I of the Annex.

In Part I of the Annex, 110 documents are dated on October 13, 1917, or later. Among these, 75 provide significant information on the sun dance,[42] including four which are more or less duplicates of information provided by the same person in other documents.[43] There are thus 71 unique sources. From here on, I will consider that these 71 or 74 documents are my only sources, in providing statistics, and I will count each of the four duplicate sources only once. The remaining documents, among the 110, give testimony on the seers, the apparitions, on the "column of smoke," and/or indications that a miracle or alleged miracle occurred on October 13, with no details on it.

It may be noted that most of the testimony in the 71 documents come from witnesses who were believers, or from skeptics who became believers in the apparitions on October 13. This is to be expected, since believers or Catholic skeptics were more likely to have come to Fatima on October 13 and to have written about it to friends. But there are, among the 71 sources, 18 documents from neutral or unfriendly sources.[44]

Among the 71 sources many give a very incomplete account of the sun dance. Undoubtedly many writers of letters and newspaper articles reported only what they considered to be important. Some thirty sources are very brief—only a line or two on the sun dance. Of

---

[42] Annex #16-20, #22, #23, #25-32, #34, #37, #39, #42-44, #46, #47, #49-52, #54-59, #61, #61B-61M, #62, #63, #65, #68-74, #77, #78, #85, #86, #89, #90, #92, #93, #95-97, #100, #101, #102, #103, #104, #107, #108, #109

[43] Annex #16 and #37, #44 and #86, #49 and #73, #58 and #85. Annex #28 and #68, and Annex #101 and #102, are also by the same persons, but are quite different in content.

[44] Annex #24, #27, #28, #29, #40-42, #45, #46, #54, #57, #62, #63, #68, #76, #78, #88, #109

these about three fourths have only one line.[45] Only nineteen are fairly long—seven lines or more—and may be fairly complete accounts.[46] A precise count of the number of lines on the sun dance in each document is difficult because significant data is often interspersed with insignificant data, giving several partial lines and requiring a judgment on what is significant. In counting the number of lines on the sun dance, (underlined in Part I of the Annex) I exclude redundancies, descriptions of the smoke columns, and most statements on the muted sun.

One type of source merits special mention. It consists of the inquiries made by priests at the request of the bishop. In 1917 one was made by the dean of Porto de Mos, one in 1918 by the Fatima pastor, and one in 1923-1924 by the Diocesan Inquiry Board. Strangely, it would appear (judging by the written documents published by these priests) that the inquiries consisted solely in recording the statements made by the witnesses that appeared before them, and in showing the recordings to the witnesses for approval or correction. No effort was made, it would seem, to elicit further details from the witnesses nor to reconcile discrepancies among the witness accounts and the accounts which had appeared in the Portuguese press. In short, it seems that these priests did very little to help the Church, as well as authors writing about Fatima, to determine exactly what happened at the Cova da Iria on October 13, 1917. Apparently they felt this was not needed.

Variations in Testimony. If so, I cannot agree. There are many variations in the statements on some features of the phenomena. Most are not very significant and can be ignored. But there remain many that are fairly important or very important. They require discussion and explanation. I therefore present the details of such variations and offer explanations or possible explanations as I discuss each phenomenon.

Common Factors Related to Variations in Testimony. Many factors related to the variations in testimony are common to all the phenomena. One is simply poor memory. It is a well-known fact that

---

[45] Annex #17, #20, #29-32, #42, #43, #51, #54, #56, #57, #61C-61M, #62, #63, #74, #78, #97, #104, #107, #108, #109

[46] Annex #25, #28, #44, #46, #49, #50, #55, #58, #59, #61, #65, #71-73, #77, #89, #90, #102, #103.

witnesses to a given event—a car accident, for example—usually give different accounts of the event, often very different. Variations include conflicts, additions, and omissions, in comparing one account with another. A second factor is the elements of excitement, fatigue, and fear. These elements did not affect all witnesses at Fatima equally. Many believers were highly excited by the prospect of a miracle. Others were highly skeptical and less excited. Some were tired by their long journey and hours of standing in the cold and rain. Others arrived later and were sheltered in cars or carriages. Some were by nature easily frightened, others were not. Certainly those who had the impression that the sun was falling on the earth were greatly frightened. Even those who felt that the sun was merely zig-zagging in the sky were likely to feel some fear. And this fear was likely to have been increased by the cries for God's mercy and help from the Virgin, heard by many witnesses. (See pages 157-158.)

A third factor is astonishment at the spectacular and unexpected nature of the event. Certainly in the eyes and mind of the beholder, the colors, the fall of the sun, and its rapid spin on its axis were spectacular. Phenomena (except color) reported at the earlier apparitions were in no way similar to this. And these phenomena had no precedent in the history of the Church. Many of the witnesses were clearly transfixed with awe at what seemed to be an awesome display of God's power.[47] Surprise, awe, and fear were likely to have caused many witnesses to recall some phenomena much more vividly than others, to forget some and to recall incorrectly some details of the phenomena, such as the colors or the order in which the colors occurred.

In addition to these psychological factors, there is an important physical factor which may have resulted in different impressions of the phenomena, namely the considerable distance that separated people in various parts of this natural amphitheater. A few witnesses indicated that they were on the road, about 100 meters (more than the length of a football field) above and away from the seers, who were at the center of the amphitheater. One said he was 200 meters away.[48] Others were

---

[47] Annex #16, #23, #25, #26, #27, #28, #43, #44, #46, #50, #55, #65, #71, #76, #90, #92
[48] Annex #28, #32, #44, #90, #92

near the seers and some were surely on the slope opposite the slope on which the road was located. One source indicated that the people were in a circle of one kilometer, which surely was an exaggeration.[49] However, it is clear that many people were a full 100 meters from others, and 200 meters is not at all unlikely for those who were on opposite sides of this large bowl. Remembering the heavy weather which preceded the sun dance, it is reasonable to suspect that very low clouds passed before the sun during the sun dance, giving different degrees of cloud cover to people in different parts of the Cova da Iria.

Another factor is the nature of the documents we possess. Some were formal and intended for publication or Church inquiries. I presume that most of these writers were careful in reporting their testimony. But many of the documents, being letters to friends or family, were informal and the writers, in recounting their testimony, did not necessarily use care in recounting details and may easily have omitted one or more phenomena. At least a few may have had a natural tendency to exaggerate. Further, some of the sources were second-hand testimony.

One more factor, or at least a possible factor, is that some of the witnesses may have looked only at the sun during the sun dance, while others stared at the sun part of the time, and at the people at other times. And, as I have already indicated, a few witnesses stared only at the ground and people; fear of staring at the sun was clearly a reason. No sources say that they stared only at the sun, but it would not be surprising if some found the amazing phenomena of the sun to be so riveting that they did not look elsewhere during the sun dance. This latter possibility is more likely if the sun dance lasted only a few minutes, rather than eight or ten minutes, as estimated by some sources. This factor could account for the fact that some witnesses only reported color on the sun, while others only reported color on the ground and people.

Yet another factor, probably not a very important one, is optical illusion caused by staring at the bright sun. At Fatima this appears to have affected four witnesses, who reported seeing spots or stains

---

[49] Annex #25

on the people or landscape.[50] No other mentions of spots occur, and thus it appears that most of the people who reported color were not victims of the kind of optical illusion caused by staring at the bright sun, namely spots before their eyes.

However, there is the possibility that staring at the muted sun causes another kind of optical illusion. A German meteorologist claimed (in about 1950) that staring at the muted sun for about one minute creates the impression that the sun is spinning very rapidly, but is largely covered by a dark-blue disk.[51] He does not claim that any other color was caused by staring at the dull sun, nor any impression that the sun is falling or moving in the sky. I discuss this much more thoroughly when I discuss the phenomenon of the spinning of the sun. But the possibility that the spinning sun was an optical illusion (although it was not mentioned as a possible explanation for the spinning sun by Fatima authors until 1999) suggests that other phenomena at Fatima must be investigated as possible optical illusions.

The Weather. In view of the possibility that some of the phenomena of the sun dance were meteorological ones, I must say something about the weather which preceded and accompanied the sun dance. It was rainy, windy, and cold.

One source says that the weather at Fatima on the 13th was rainy and cold, contrary to the previous days.[52] Another source suggests that the weather on October 12 was nice. This same source, a woman who traveled by mule cart from Rodrigos to Fatima (some 20 miles) reported that at night it became cloudy, and from about midnight to 2:00 a.m. of the 13th there was a violent thunder storm, with rain being light by dawn.[53] Three other sources indicate that it rained during the night.[54]

In early morning of the 13th the rain obviously stopped for an hour or two, or perhaps three, since five sources tell us that it began to rain in early morning or mid-morning.[55] It gradually increased[56] and became torrential.[57] The sky became

[50] Annex #46, #50, #92, #42?
[51] Jaki, p 303; on page 332, Jaki says that this German was a professor of physics and astronomy.
[52] Annex #44
[53] Annex #16
[54] Annex #25, #50, #61
[55] Annex #20, #27, #28, #92, #95
[56] Annex #32, #47, #85, #95
[57] Annex #20, #49, #52, #55, #58, #67, #73, #86, #92

very heavy, with dark clouds, and remained heavy until nearly noon, sun time.[58] The wind became strong and the rain soaked all but those in excellent shelter, mostly those in cars and carriages.[59] The weather was cool, and with the wind and rain the crowd shivered.[60] The rain continued steadily until about 11:30 or 12:00, sun time. It then decreased gradually and stopped shortly before the sun dance.[61] Four sources seem to say the sky was heavy until the sun dance,[62] but two say that the sky became lighter before then.[63] No sources indicate any lightning or thunder in the entire morning, and thus it is clear that there was none.

Clouds During the Sun Dance. It is important to note the evidence that clouds existed in front of the sun and around it during and after the sun dance. Clouds are important in explaining the color phenomena, the lateral movement of the sun, and its spin. One book on Fatima indicates that the sky was clear of clouds during the sun dance.[64] This is false, as Father Jaki has clearly indicated in his book on Fatima.[65] Many of the sources in my Annex speak of clouds on or around the sun during the sun dance or right after it.[66] The false impression that the sky was free of clouds during the sun dance may have been due to the eight reports that the sun was free of clouds, but yet could be stared at (see pages 99-101). However, three of these eight clearly showed that clouds remained in the sky near the sun. One said the sun was "between the clouds," another has it in "a corona of such (colored) clouds," and the third puts it in "patches of clear sky."[67] The well-known Jose Garrett gives a long report on the clouds. See Document #90.

Cirrus Clouds. Garrett creates the impression that the heavy, lower clouds disappeared and only light, wispy cirrus clouds remained. He writes: "It was about 2:00. The sun, a few minutes before, had broken through the ... clouds ... (Gist– The sun was a lively pearl color, with sharp edges.) The arch of the sky was mottled with light,

---

[58] Annex #23, #32, #42, #67, #69, #71, #72, #85, #90, #92
[59] Annex #23, #28, #29, #34, #58, #67, #77, #90, #95
[60] Annex #25, #44, #49, #50, #58, #95
[61] Annex #16, #23, #25, #32, #37, #44, #50, #71-73, #90, #92
[62] Annex #23, #61, #90, #92
[63] Annex #50, #71
[64] *Fatima 1917-1968*, pp 131, 132
[65] Jaki, pp 55, 72, 73, 91, 92, 106, 134, 135, 140, 152, 223, 224, 257
[66] Annex #16, #25, #37, #39, #50, #55, #58, #65, #69, #72, #77, #92, #95
[67] Annex #16, #55, #90

cirrus clouds, having slits of blue coming through here and there, but sometimes the sun stood out in patches of clear sky. The clouds passed lightly from west to east, and did not obscure the light of the sun, ((which did not hurt)), giving the impression of passing behind it. … but sometimes these flecks, which came as white, seemed to take on tones of pink or diaphanous blue as they passed before the sun." His statement that the clouds passed "lightly" seems to mean "quickly." If so, his identification of the clouds as cirrus is probably wrong, since cirrus clouds are usually at a very high altitude and their movement does not normally seem quick to viewers on the ground.

Garrett makes no mention of any other clouds after this, but he states that it became dark during the period when purple color was noted on the people.[68] This implies clouds heavier than cirrus. Garrett may have seen the sun in patches of blue sky, but if so, all the clouds around the sun surely were not cirrus. His report is by far the longest and most detailed one on the sun dance and the clouds, and it is not surprising that it influenced some Fatima authors to assume that the heavy clouds had disappeared very rapidly and were gone during the sun dance.

The impression of a clear sky is made, but much less strongly, by the other well-known report on the sun dance, that of Avelino de Almeida, who wrote in *O Seculo*: "… the Lady had spoken again and the sky, still obscure, begins all the sudden to clear above us." He then describes the sun dance, as seen by him and others. Then he adds: "It is almost 3:00 in the afternoon. The sky is swept clear of clouds."[69] While this remark does not indicate or imply that at the time of the sun dance (near 2:00) the sky was clear of clouds, it nonetheless creates an impression that the heavy clouds disappeared quickly.

However, many other sources indicate that clouds existed in the sky during the sun dance. None tell their type. Most do not even say whether they were light or heavy, nor high or low. One source indicates that after the sun dance the clouds disappeared gradually.[70] One source refers to dark clouds, another says that their density was variable, and two tell of billows of very light clouds.[71] Six sources say that

---

[68] Annex #90
[69] Annex #28
[70] Annex #61
[71] Annex #25, #34, #49, #55

the clouds were diaphanous or that a veiled light was seen.[72] Three sources indicate that there were still clouds on or around the sun after the sun dance[73] and three others suggest the same thing.[74] Two sources say or seem to say that clouds briefly hid the sun during the dance.[75]

In short, it seems entirely unlikely that no clouds or only cirrus clouds were seen during the sun dance. Perhaps only cirrus clouds were noted fairly soon after the sun dance and Garrett, writing two months after the sun dance, wrongly recalled the time when they were seen. Or, perhaps, toward the end of the sun dance, part of the sky was clear of lower clouds, but some remained around and over the sun, allowing its silvery form to be seen through them, and cirrus clouds passed behind them, creating the impression that the cirrus clouds passed behind the sun, as stated by Garrett.

The existence of very light wispy clouds during the sun dance is firmly established. Presumably heavier clouds existed at a higher altitude and at times covered the sun, but allowed its silvery form to be seen through them. While this is not stated, it is reasonable, in view of the rain, which stopped shortly before the sun dance.

I must note that here and elsewhere in this study, when I say that clouds were near the sun, I obviously mean that they were near the image of the sun, not near the sun itself.

The Timing of the Sun Dance. It would be most spectacular if we could say that the Lady predicted a miracle at an exact time on October 13, and that the sun dance began exactly at that minute. However, the evidence does not permit us to be this precise. The Lady clearly predicted that the miracle would occur on October 13, as stated by the seers, but she did not specify the time, as can be seen in the chapter on the apparitions (see pages 19 and 27). However, both the public and the seers expected the miracle to occur near noon, sun time. The previous five apparitions had occurred at about noon. In a limited sense, then, the miracle was predicted for about noon on October 13.

The evidence is very strong that the sun dance began between 10 and 33 minutes after noon, sun time.

---

[72] Annex #34, #37, #50, #58, #90, #92
[73] Annex #50, #69, #95
[74] Annex #16, #65, #77
[75] Annex #16, #25

Fourteen sources indicate this in one way or another.[76] Offhand, much of the testimony seems contradictory, but it is cleared up when we consider the three kinds of time which were in use in Portugal in the summer of 1917. The peasants and some of the upper class clung to solar time. Much of the upper class had accepted Greenwich standard time, which had been in use for only six years and was 37 minutes earlier than solar time. But some, probably most of the upper class, used the official "war time," decreed only the previous year, and which was one hour and 37 minutes earlier than solar time. For them solar noon occurred at 1:37.

Five sources indicate that they consulted watches or car clocks to determine the time of the start of the sun dance. Two indicate that it began at 2:10 (33 minutes after solar noon).[77] Two others give 1:00, clearly meaning 1:00 standard time, or 23 minutes after solar time.[78] A fifth, apparently using a watch or clock has the sun dance start soon after 1:45 or about ten minutes after solar noon.[79] Other sources which give the time of the sun dance do not indicate that they used a watch or clock and thus provide less firm and precise evidence.

Since four of the five sources indicate that the start of the dance was between 23 and 33 minutes after solar noon, this is the likely time. Perhaps the watch of the fifth was slow, or his "soon after" meant 15 minutes or more rather than five or ten.

A List of the Phenomena. The major phenomena are: the colors, the spin of the sun, and the fall of the sun. The minor phenomena are: the "stare-ability" of the sun, its zig-zag movement in the sky, and the great heat. "Stare-ability" refers to the ability of the crowd to stare at the sun in the clear blue sky without any harm or pain to the eye.

Start and Sequence of Phenomena. None of the sources in the Annex, nor any other which I have read, indicate how long it was after the muted sun appeared that the first unusual phenomenon began. The famous letter of Jose Almeida Garrett stated that: "It was remarkable that over a long time one could fix one's eyes on this day star," but does not say nor imply that this "long time" preceded the next phenomenon.[80] This statement might be pertinent if we could say that each phenomenon was ended before the next began, but this we cannot say.

---

[76] Annex #23, #31, #32, #34, #39, #44, #46, #47, #55, #70, #72, #90, #92, #103
[77] Annex #44, #47
[78] Annex #32, #92
[79] Annex #34
[80] Annex #90

It is difficult, if not impossible, to determine the order in which the rest of the phenomena appeared, after the silvery sun came out. Unfortunately, none of the sources tell us that they are describing the phenomena in sequence, although some of them appear to be doing so. Also unfortunately, there is great variation in the sequence in which the phenomena are reported in available sources. I have therefore decided, arbitrarily, to begin with "stare-ability" and the color phenomena, for which I offer a common explanation, and then discuss the spinning of the sun, its fall, its zig-zag movement, and finally the unusual heat.

THE MUTED SUN AND STARE-ABILITY

The Muted Sun. The first phenomenon of the sun dance itself was the breakout of the sun through the clouds and its silvery color. It would seem an unimportant one. Everyone has seen the sun appear silvery through fairly heavy clouds. But this phenomenon at Fatima on October 13 is important because eight witnesses, and pro-Fatima books, indicate that the sun was free of clouds at times and yet could be stared at without discomfort.[81] Thus the phenomenon deserves some detailed discussion.

Thirty documents provide some information on the muted sun. Nine, or possibly eleven, of them indicate that the sun came out bright before it became muted.[82] Two of these nine specified that clouds covered the sun again before it became silvery.[83] The descriptions of the color of the muted sun vary considerably. Fifteen or sixteen sources call it dull silver or like a silver plate.[84] Six called it white.[85] One said it was blue-silver and two that it was pearl-colored.[86] Two said it was like the

---

[81] Annex #16, #23, #28, #44, #50, #59, #90, #92; *The Whole Truth About Fatima*, p 346; *Fatima: The Great Sign*, p 61
[82] Annex #27?, #32, #46?, #47, #49, #58, #61, #65, #71, #90, #96
[83] Annex #65, #71
[84] Annex #23, #27, #28, #39, #50, #51, #56, #58, #59, #61, #68, #69?, #77, #78, #93, #95
[85] Annex #19, #37, #59, #65, #95, #101
[86] Annex #49, #50, #90

moon.[87] Three indicated that it was luminous or shiny.[88] Many of these sources also said that it could be stared at without discomfort. Three others said the same.[89] And many of the rest, which did not specify that the sun could be stared at comfortably, implied this, since they could not have described its color, its spin or its fall unless they were able to stare at it easily.

Almost all sources describe the muted sun very briefly, using only a phrase or a short sentence. One, however, uses ten lines and is perhaps significant. Jose Garrett says that the sun was not a dull silver color, "It was lighter, more alive … having something of the luster of a pearl." He adds that it was not spherical, like the moon. He also says that this is not a poetic description. He clearly implies that this was a most unusual kind of muted sun.[90]

From all of this I conclude: that the sun probably appeared briefly at full strength, but this fact was deemed unimportant and was omitted by most people in reporting on the event; that it next appeared as a muted sun, which seemed silvery, white or pearly at times; and that all could stare at it with ease.

The question arises whether the sun stayed muted by clouds during the entire sun dance. Most sources suggest that it did, since they do not report any interruption of the sun dance. However, Jose Garrett reported that twice during the sun dance the sun became briefly too bright to stare at. He implies that the bright sun interrupted the apparent spin and fall of the sun, which occurred three times.[91] No other sources report a similar bright sun interrupting the sun dance. However, two sources report a bright sun, but without saying that it was too bright to stare at. One said that the sun became yellow, then celestial blue "followed by a very intense shine, like a spring of bright lights" and by the spin and fall of the sun. The other source said that the sun seemed to head toward the earth, "accompanied at times by an extraordinary bright shine."[92] Twelve sources say or suggest that the phenomena of the sun dance were interrupted and repeated one or more times, but none except Jose Garrett (and perhaps these other two sources) say or imply that the interruptions were due to an overly

---

[87] Annex #16, #25
[88] Annex #39, #90, #72
[89] Annex #61K, #61L, #70
[90] Annex #90
[91] Annex #90
[92] Annex #71, #93

bright sun.[93] In view of this evidence, it would seem quite likely that the sun dance was interrupted for a brief time by a very bright sun only in a small part of the Cova da Iria. Perhaps in an adjacent area the sun may have been lightly muted, causing onlookers to note a brief bright shine, without forcing them to look away. In other parts of the Cova the sun apparently was muted during the entire sun dance. In still other parts the muting may have been interrupted briefly by heavy clouds over the sun.

Stare-ability. More significant than these brief interruptions of the sun dance is the claim that at times the sun was free of clouds and yet could be stared at with ease. This phenomenon has not been greatly emphasized or studied in Fatima literature. But as an apparently miraculous feature of the sun dance it deserves attention. Eight sources seem to say that the sun was free of clouds and could be stared at comfortably.[94] Only one states that this was remarkable.[95] Sixteen others vaguely suggest that the sun was free of clouds by saying that one could stare at it with ease.[96] It would scarcely be worth saying this if the sun was muted by clouds.

The earliest of the eight sources are two letters of October 13. One says: "The sun appears between the clouds, but with no shine." The other says: "the sun, which ... (had been) ... covered with dense black clouds, since from 8:00 ... the rain had not stopped a moment, ... suddenly showed itself free of clouds, at its zenith, the rain stops, the sun is like a dull silver plate and it is possible to stare at it without the least effort."[97] The next source was the important article in *O Seculo* on October 15: " ...the immense crowd turns toward the sun, which appears free from clouds and at its zenith. It looks like a dull silver plate and it is possible to stare at it without the least effort. It does not burn or blind. One would say that an eclipse was taking place."[98] This is an especially strong statement. Clearly this reporter indicated that

---

[93] Annex #39, #59, #61, #61H, #61G, #69, #71, #72, #89, #90, #95, #103
[94] Annex #16, #23, #28, #44, #55, #59, #90, #92
[95] Annex #90
[96] Annex #25, #39, #44, #52, #54, #57, #61K, #61L, #68A, #69, #70, #72, #73, #89, #96, #101
[97] Annex #16, #23
[98] Annex #28

the muted sun was free of clouds and yet could be stared at. His statement that it was like an eclipse suggests strongly that he could stare at the open sun for more than one second or two.

The fourth source, a letter of October 18, merely says: "...thousands of terrified eyes saw the sun in the clear blue, visible to all without the intensity of the rays hurting the retina or bothering their vision."[99] The fifth source, a letter of October 21, says: " .... until 2:00 or mid-day, solar, the moment when the clouds separated to the sides, leaving the sun open, and immediately there began to pass before the sun billows of very light clouds .... I also saw in the open space and around (it) a marvelous corona of such clouds in various colors."[100]

The sixth source, a letter from a priest published in *A Liberdade* on October 23, says: "... the sun ... moved the clouds away fairly rapidly ... giving us the opportunity to observe a phenomenon that seemed extraordinary to all. The sun, now without clouds, did not send rays on the earth, but seemed wrapped in pale-colored flames. Suddenly it lost all this light or flames and seemed to us a dull silver plate." He then reports the spin and fall briefly and says, "One could stare at it indefinitely without bothering one's sight."[101]

The seventh source, the famous letter of Dr. Jose Garrett of about December 18, says: "I turned to the magnet that was drawing all eyes and I could see it like a disk with a clean-cut rim, ... but which did not hurt the eyes ... It looked like glazed mother-of-pearl ... The arch of the sky was mottled with light cirrus clouds, having slits of blue here and there, but sometimes the sun stood out in patches of clear sky. The clouds passed lightly from west to east and did not obscure the light of the sun ((which did not hurt)) ... It was remarkable that over a long time one could fix one's eyes on this day-star [the sun] ... without any pain or blinding of the retina."[102] This testimony clearly implies that he could stare at the open sun for more than one or two seconds.

The last source, a deposition of December 30, says: "... at first I saw only that the clouds, moving lightly left the sun in the open. Sud-

---

[99] Annex #44
[100] Annex #55
[101] Annex #59
[102] Annex #90

denly I saw an intensely rose-colored edge around the sun, that looked like a dull silver plate ... Diaphanous, vaporous clouds went by, a little purple, a little orange."[103]

It would thus seem that all eight of these sources indicate (and the other sixteen witnesses hint) that they could stare at the sun with no discomfort, while the sun was free from clouds. Admittedly, the last one tells of light, diaphanous clouds passing by, but nonetheless seems to say that at times the sun was free of clouds. It would also seem that they could stare at the open sun for several seconds and possibly many seconds.

Possible Explanations. Possible explanations are: that an air lens (a phenomenon discussed in detail on pages 113-115) weakened the sunlight and permitted the crowd to stare at the sun in the open sky; or that these sources did not mean to say what their statements seem to say; or that a small cloud, not much larger than the image of the sun, covered the sun and perhaps a small area around it, allowing the sun to be seen as muted (silvery) and the area around it as blue sky. The latter explanation, a very doubtful one, is discussed in detail on pages 111-112.

The Air Lens. The air lens explanation needs some discussion. Normal sunlight has a large frequency range, contains all the colors of the rainbow, and is unbearably bright. The full range of any color (for example, green from bluish green to yellowish green) would have a fairly large frequency range and may be too bright to stare at. However, a very precise shade of a given color would have a very small frequency range and be much less bright, perhaps weak enough to be stared at comfortably. There is some evidence that the viewers at Fatima saw such a precise shade when looking at the sun. It is clear that only one color was seen at a time, it is quite probable that a given color was seen over the entire Cova, there are a few indications that the colors changed slowly from one to another. (See page 127.) If so, the shade of the given color changed almost imperceptibly over the length of the Cova and each viewer, when looking at the sun, was seeing the precise shade of the given color for his spot at that moment. When looking at the people or landscape, he saw a much larger range

<hr/>

[103] Annex #92

of shades. In essence, the air lens was acting like an enormous crystal, producing a rainbow of colors over the Cova, one after another.

Why So Few Sources. We might ask why only eight (or 23) of the 71 sources which report on the sun dance mention (or suggest) that the sun was in the clear and yet could be stared at comfortably. Possible explanations are that many sources were brief and incomplete, and that other phenomena seemed more important. It is also possible that this phenomenon was not seen all over the Cova because of variations in cloud cover. Summing up, I would say that the evidence is reasonably strong that this unusual phenomenon was real.

CHAPTER VII

THE COLOR PHENOMENA

Types. Three types of color were said to have been noted at Fatima. One is colored flames on the sun. It is not firmly established. A second phenomenon is all colors of the rainbow on the sun, clouds, and ground, possibly caused by an air lens. The third is silver, white, black or a very dark color on the sun, possibly part of an optical illusion that the sun was spinning. This chapter is concerned only with the first two types. The third will be discussed in the chapters on the spinning and falling sun.

Real or Not. A great many witnesses to the sun dance reported that they saw unusual color phenomena. Some reported color on or around the sun; others reported that color was seen, or also seen, on the clouds on the ground, on the people or on the horizon. The reports vary greatly and it is difficult to determine firmly all the details of the color phenomena. However, the reports of color phenomena are so many (fifty[1] of the seventy-one sources which give data on the sun dance) that it seems highly unlikely that all were mere inventions or were due to some form of individual hallucination. Further, fifteen of the twenty sources which give nothing on the color phenomena, give only one or two lines on the entire sun dance, and thus seem to

---

[1] Annex #16, #18, #19, #22, #23, #25, #26, #28, #31, #37, #39, #42, #43, #44, #46, #47, #49, #50, #51, #55, #59, #61B-G, #61I, #61J, #61L, #63, #65, #68, #70, #71, #72, #73, #74, #77, #89, #90, #92, #93, #95-97, #101, #102, #103, #107

be incomplete reports on it.[2] The remaining sources are also fairly short and possibly incomplete.[3]

Non-see-ers. I should note that among the fifty witnesses who gave some report on the color phenomena, a few gave reports that were more or less negative. Two indicated that others said they saw various colors, but that they personally saw only yellow. One of these two did not seem to doubt that other colors were seen. He said: "What happened on that occasion? .... A solar phenomenon with more or less a display of colors, don't doubt this. I saw only a very pronounced yellow and it seemed to me that I saw a black color below the solar disk, but I don't guarantee this." The second appears somewhat doubtful of the other colors. He said: "the sun's rays showed yellow, green, blue and purple, according to what they say, but I saw only the yellow color."[4] A third noted that some people said they saw various colors on the sun, but he saw only snow white, then dark gray.[5] A fourth said many saw extraordinary colors, but she was so excited that she fell on her knees and saw nothing.[6] A fifth said that she saw electric blue after the sky cleared, but added that the colors others reported—red, yellow, and purple—were caused by staring at the sun.[7]

Thus, the third clearly denies seeing any of the rainbow colors and the fifth implies it; the first two reported only yellow. The fourth may have been so frightened that she did not dare to look up. The one clear and the one implied denial and the two or three weak or partial denials (plus, the two or three who saw no unusual phenomena, previously discussed) cast only a weak shadow of doubt on the reality of color phenomena. And this shadow is further weakened by the reports that people in nearby towns also saw color phenomena on this day and at about the same time. (See the section "Remote Sightings," in Chapter X.)

---

[2] Annex #17, #20, #29, #30, #32, #54, #56, #57, #61H, #61K, #61M, #62, #78, #104, #108
[3] Annex #27, #52, #69
[4] Annex #70, #93
[5] Annex #19
[6] Annex #43
[7] Annex #61

Further, two sources seem to indicate that the color was not an optical illusion caused by staring at the sun because they did not stare at it. One says that he saw the crowd as pink, then blue and yellow, adding that he didn't want to look at the sun to avoid optical illusion, and further said: "But in front of me was a woman with a white felt hat that served me as a mirror." He concluded: "I heard laments at my side … and they said the sun was spinning like a firewheel," which further suggests that he did not look at the sun.[8] The other source simply said: "With eyes fixed on the oak bush …. without deliberately looking at the sun, I noticed that while the people were shouting loudly … about what they saw in the sun, the people as well as the trees and everything in sight took on different colors."[9]

If the color phenomena, or at least the rainbow colors, were real, as seems very likely, an explanation is needed for these five "non-seeers." One may assume that the fourth source kept her eyes on the ground and thus saw nothing. Three explanations are available for the other four.

The first explanation is that two of the sources may have stared at the sun during most of the dance and looked around only near the end and thus saw only the yellow color. There is considerable evidence that yellow was the last color seen (see pages 120-121). The third and fifth sources may have stared at the sun during the entire sun dance and thus saw none of the rainbow colors.

A second possible explanation is that: 1) in all or most of the Cova da Iria the color phenomenon followed the spin of the sun, and 2) most onlookers suffered a temporary eye injury from staring at the muted sun, which resulted in the optical illusion of the spin of the sun. As I indicate later, this illusion is the most probable natural explanation for the spin of the sun. If so, it is likely that this injury prevented them from seeing colors (other than the white, silver or blackish color on the spinning sun) while the injury lasted and that the injury was more severe in some people than in others. Therefore, it is reasonable to conclude that the two sources which reported seeing

[8] Annex #47
[9] Annex #97

only yellow[10] were more seriously affected by the eye injury than most onlookers and recovered only when the color phenomenon was almost over, during the yellow phase. And it is further reasonable to conclude that the two who saw no color[11] were even more seriously affected by eye injury and recovered only after the color phenomenon was over.

Some support for this conclusion comes from one of the four "non-see-ers," who said that the sun spun and seemed to fall, accompanied at times by an extraordinary bright shine and an intense heat.[12] Only one other source uses similar language and thus appears to have been similarly affected by the sun. It says the muted sun had a yellow color, changed to sky blue, followed by a very intense shine and the spin and fall of the sun.[13] No other source says or implies that the spin was accompanied by an intense shine.

A third possible explanation for "non-see-ers" is that the color covered all the Cova except the upper edge of the southern side and that the people there stared southward away from the Cova and toward the sun, which is in the south in mid-October at noon. These people may have turned to the side to ask their neighbors what they had seen, but unless they turned fully around toward the Cova they would not have seen the colors.

Variations in Testimony-Related Factors. The reports on the color phenomena vary greatly and they are the most difficult phenomena to analyze. In view of the many variations it is important to consider the possible causes. In addition to the common factors related to all phenomena (previously discussed on pages 89-92), a few more specific ones must now be considered. One is the difference in the condition of the eyes of the spectators. A fair number were surely color blind to a lesser or greater degree. A few surely had cataracts or other eye ailments. Cataracts make bright colors appear dull—red will appear as pink, for example. Cataracts also make one very sensitive to bright light and easily blinded by such light. Another factor is the use or non-use of sunglasses, and the darkness of the given sunglasses. Certainly the majority of the spectators, peasants, were too poor to

---

[10] Annex #70, #93
[11] Annex #19, #61
[12] Annex #93
[13] Annex #71

have sunglasses. But virtually all of them were illiterate, while those who wrote about the sun dance (and thus became our sources) were middle class or wealthy and fairly likely to own sunglasses. Obviously the sunglasses modified the brightness of the colors.

Color on Sun, Clouds, Ground. Color is reported on the sun, around the sun, on the clouds, on the people and landscape (which I refer to as color on the ground), and on the horizon. Many reports are quite detailed but most are short and give little detail. Thirty one (or possibly thirty-three) sources report color on or around the sun.[14] Twenty five indicate color on the ground.[15] Some sources report color on the clouds or sky, or merely report colored rays. At least fifteen, and possibly sixteen, sources indicate that one or more of the colors seen on or around the sun were also seen on the ground.[16]

We might ask why, if the color phenomena were real, only fifteen (or possibly as many as sixteen) sources out of fifty report color both on the ground and on or around the sun. A number of explanations, taken together, provide an answer: 1) many sources were very brief (see pages 87-88) and clearly were an incomplete account of the sun dance; 2) some of the crowd were fearful of staring at the sun and stared only at the people and landscape (see page 101), and others probably were transfixed by the sun dance and stared only at the sun and sky; 3) the color phenomena may have been fairly brief, and some witnesses may have stared at the ground and people only before (or after) the color phenomena occurred; 4) differences in cloud cover may have caused the color phenomena to be weaker or even non-existent in some parts of the Cova da Iria; and 5) the spin and fall of the sun may have been considered more spectacular and thus may have limited reporting on the colors, not only in the brief reports but even in some sources of medium length. None of the sources which

---

[14] Annex #19, #22, #23, #25, #28, #34, #39, #42, #44, #46, #49, #55, #58, #59, #61B, #61E, #61F, #61G, #61I, #61J, #61L, #65, #68, #71, #73, #74?, #77, #89, #92, #95, #96? #102, #103

[15] Annex #16, #18, #22, #23, #25, #26, #31, #39, #44, #46, #47, #50, #55, #58, #61B, #61C, #61E, #71, #72, #89, #90, #92, #96, #97, #101

[16] Annex #22, #23, #25, #39, #44, #46, #55, #58, #61B, #61E, #71, #73, #89, #92, #96, #102?

only report color on or around the sun say or imply that no color was seen on the ground, and vice-versa.

Color On or Around the Sun. Among the thirty-one (possibly thirty-three) sources mentioned above, four are vague about whether the color was on or around the sun.[17] Eighteen (possibly nineteen) say, or seem to say, that the color was on the sun;[18] and eleven say, or seem to say, that the color was around the sun.[19] Two say both on and around the sun.[20] The fact that there are only two such reports, out of thirty-two, is explained, in part, by the brevity of most reports, the more spectacular nature of the spin and the fall of the sun, the variations in cloud cover, and the informal nature of many reports.

Color Around the Sun. The color around the sun can be divided into three categories—colored flames, a colored edge or ring around the sun, and a colored circle of clouds around the sun, at an unspecified distance from it.

COLORED FLAMES

The phenomenon of colored flames is reported by only a few sources. Therefore, we must wonder whether this phenomenon actually occurred. But all sources which say "flame" appear to be believable. Four were published in the press soon after the sun dance, two within a week. They come from a prominent Catholic layman, a newspaper editor or reporter (using oral reports and letters as his source) and three others who appear to be prominent citizens. They have received little attention in Fatima literature, perhaps because they are so few. Assuming the flames to be real, a possible explanation for the few number of reports on them is that they were seen in only a limited area of the Cova which had favorable cloud cover.

---

[17] Annex #44, #59, #61J, #77
[18] Annex #19, #22, #23, #25, #28, #42, #46, #49, #58, #61E, #61G, #61L, #68, #71, #73, #74?, #89, #95, #102
[19] Annex #25, #34, #39, #55, #58, #61B, #61F, #61I, #65, #92, #103
[20] Annex #25, #58

Despite a great deal of study, I have found no good explanation for this possible phenomenon, nor any sound reason for ignoring it, except that it appears to be a relatively unimportant phenomenon. I therefore offer a fairly long discussion of it, which many readers may want to skip or scan. I hope that some, however, will not only read it carefully but also will find a good explanation for it.

The color reported to be on or around the sun is called flames in at least four and possibly six cases.[21] Two clearly indicate that the flames surrounded the sun.[22] A third is less clear. It says that the sun was "wrapped" in flames. A fourth says that a bright red flame or cloud covered the sun, and a fifth (a much later one) says that the sun began to rotate upon itself, pouring out shafts of flame of various colors; three said it looked like a saw of a sawmill. [23] (Two other sources may also refer to this same phenomenon. One refers to an intensely rose-colored edge around the sun, and the other to yellow-reddish color around it.)[24] Another reports a flame, but does not say it was colored.[25]

The much later (1952) source, attributed to a Catholic priest, which says clearly that colored flames surrounded the spinning sun, is questionable because in 1931 the same priest published an account of the sun dance, which mentioned the spin but failed to mention the colored flames.[26]

One of the six sources is tentative in that it reports a cloud or flame of brilliant red, which covered the sun.[27] Since this is the only source which says that the flames were on the sun, it is likely that the flames, if real, surrounded the sun. If so, it is likely that this source meant to indicate that the cloud or flame was around the sun when he said that it covered it. It is possible that this cloud or flame was the same phenomenon that elsewhere was reported as red color. However, among the many reports on color, there are only two mentions of red color on the sun (both very questionable mentions), and one mention of bright pink. (See pages 141 and 127.)

Among the other sources, one is long and appears to be a complete report of what was seen by Father Cruz Curado. He says that the sun came out, was wrapped in pale flames, lost its flame and became dull silver, spun rapidly, seemed to fall, flamed again in rose color, perhaps a minute passed, again the flames disappeared and the sun was white and spinning, then the sun, which danced around, was wrapped in blue flames, followed by a loss of light and another spin. Then the

[21] Annex I #34, #58, #59, #77?, #102?
[22] Annex I #34, #58
[23] Annex I #59, #77, #102
[24] Annex I #61B, #92
[25] Annex #52
[26] Annex I #102, #101
[27] Annex #77

phenomena ended.[28] To me, the term "wrapped in" seems to say that the flames surrounded the solar disk, but it might mean that they covered it. Three (or five) other sources clearly say that the flames were around the sun.

Father Curado's report is the only one that indicates clearly that the flames preceded the silvery sun, which seems wrong in that so many sources indicate that the silvery sun was the first phenomenon. A fairly likely explanation is that the first appearance of the dull sun was an item of no importance to Father Curado and he eliminated it. Or perhaps he simply forgot it. He also makes no mention of color on the sun or on the ground. It is hard to believe that he failed to see such colors, if they actually occurred all over the Cova. Perhaps he was so entranced by the phenomena of the flames, the spin and the fall that he failed to report other colors or had forgotten them, or perhaps the color was not seen all over the Cova.

Father Curado is also unique in that he is the only one who tells us clearly that the flames occurred three times. However, two other sources (among the six which report flames) are vague on this point. One says that the sun passed through various aspects, <u>sometimes</u> seeming to be surrounded by flames, <u>at other times</u> to be a silver disk, etc.[29] The second source says the sun was <u>at times</u> surrounded by reddish flames, <u>at other times</u> with a ring of yellow or violet, <u>at other</u> times, etc.[30] The remaining sources (among the six) mention only a single occurrence of the flames. Two are fairly long and seem to be full reports on the sun dance. The third is also quite long but is disjointed and is less clearly a full report.[31] It would seem that the flames, if real, were seen two or three times in one part of the Cova, but were seen only once in another part.

Father Curado's report says that once the flames lasted "perhaps a minute," but gives no clues to the length of time the flames lasted on the other two occasions. None of the other sources give any clue to this length of time.

One variation between Father Curado's report and the others concerns the color of the flames. The color is called reddish by one source, and scarlet or brilliant red by two others.[32] Two do not give color. Father Curado, however, reports the color once as pale pink and once as blue. A fairly good explanation is available. Father Curado may have had cataracts in his eyes and thus saw as pink what others saw as red. Cataracts cause such an effect. Or he may have worn very dark sunglasses. His single reference to blue flames remains unexplained.

Father Curado clearly says that the flames preceded and followed the spin of the sun, and did not occur during the spin.[33] The 1952 source clearly says that flames accompanied the spin; however, this source seems to equate the flames to the sparks,

---

[28] Annex #59
[29] Annex #52
[30] Annex #34, #58
[31] Annex #58, #77
[32] Annex I #34, #58, #77
[33] Annex #59

which were said to accompany the spin of the sun (see pages 138-139).[34] The other sources on flames are less clear on this point. However, the other three firm sources suggest that the flames preceded the spin. A tentative conclusion is that the flames, if real, did not accompany the spin of the sun.

In summary, at least four, and possibly as many as eight sources refer to the flames. All but one, or possibly two, indicate that the flames were around the sun. One suggests that the flames may have lasted two or three minutes and the others provide no clue to their length of time. Three describe the flames as bright red, but one calls it pink or blue. One source reports three occurrences of the flames and two others are vague on this point; they may refer to two or three occurrences of flames; the others mention only a single occurrence. Finally, it seems quite likely that the flames, if real, did not accompany the spin of the sun.

Possible Explanations. If we accept the flames as a reality, some explanation for them is needed. One explanation is individual hallucination, which I cannot entirely reject, but which I am reluctant to accept, since the sources reporting the flames seem sound and reliable. Another is that the flames were an optical illusion, due to staring at the sun. However, this is not a normal result of staring at the bright sun, and I know of no evidence that such an illusion is caused by staring at the muted sun. One more explanation, that the flames were pure invention, is highly unlikely in view of the nature of the sources.

Yet another explanation is that the flames were the same phenomenon as the sparks which were reported to be seen around the spinning sun. (See pages 138-139.) This explanation fits well with the 1952 report that flames were like sparks, but clashes with Father Curado's account, which clearly and strongly separates the flames from the spin. It also clashes with the evidence that flames were red, since the sparks (often described as like a fireworks wheel) are normally viewed as silvery, white, or light yellow.

Two more explanations can be offered. One is that an air lens (which is described in detail on the next page) covered the sun in such a way as to enable a few viewers to look at the sun without harm to their eyes and to see the flames normally seen during an eclipse of the sun. Since I have read nothing about an air lens above ground level, I cannot say whether it may cause such flames to be noted.

The second explanation is quite fantastic—that a small, thick cloud covered the sun and mimicked the effect of a full eclipse of the sun, allowing the corona (the flames) of the sun to be visible. This, I presume, is a theoretical possibility. Heavy clouds often block the sun entirely, as does the moon during an eclipse. But it is utterly fantastic that a small, thick cloud be fairly round and large enough to mute or block the sun entirely, but yet be small enough for the sun's corona to be visible. If this cloud was not entirely round, which seems more likely, the witnesses would see flames only around a portion of the solar disk, but would assume that the flames circle the entire disk, and might report it as such. If this explanation were true, it

---

[34] Annex #103

would then seem likely that this phenomenon was noted in only a limited part of the Cova da Iria, (to account for the fact that only a few sources report flames), and that in other parts of the Cova the thick cloud completely covered the sun or that it did not cover the bright sun completely enough to allow the onlookers to stare at the sun's corona, because the partially covered sun was too bright.

Support of these two explanations is offered by the fact that the predominant color of the flames was red, as indicated above. Flames are usually described as yellow or orange, not red. But red flames and semi-darkness are features of an eclipse. Further support is also offered by the several reports which note or suggest semi-darkness or that the situation seemed to be like an eclipse.[35] The important journal *O Seculo* said, on October 15: "One would say an eclipse was taking place." (See #28.) For a description of an eclipse, I quote from the *Encyclopedia Americana* 2001, Volume 9, page 584:

> A rapid approach of the moon's umbra and the increasing darkness of the sky prepare observers for the moment when total eclipse begins. At that moment a relative darkness begins, somewhat like a night when the full moon is shining. .... At the moment of total eclipse the brilliant red chromosphere appears around the moon's dark disk. It is interrupted, here and there, by more or less extended high red flames. These flames are *prominences* that penetrate the silvery corona; the corona, in turn, spreads to a long distance its long streamers, curved at the poles.

Some further support for these explanations are the reports that at Fatima the sun was free of clouds, but could be stared at without discomfort, as already noted (see pages 99-100). In order to note the red flames around the edge of the sun, obviously the sky must be free of clouds around it. It thus may be said that in three respects—red flames, semi-darkness, and open sky around the muted sun—a number of reports on the sun dance resemble an eclipse.

However, the longest and most detailed report on flames, that of Father Curado, presents a major objection to the fantastic explanation. As stated above, Father Curado indicates that the flames occurred three times and that at least once the flames lasted "perhaps a minute." Therefore, for this explanation to be correct, the small dark cloud over the sun must have appeared three times and once it must have stayed over the sun for a considerable time. A short, single occurrence of such a phenomenon that resembles an eclipse is already fantastic. Three occurrences, with one being quite long, is much more fantastic.

Since one of these explanations is fantastic and the other involves an unknown weather phenomenon, I would prefer another explanation. Unfortunately, I can find no other.

---

[35] Annex #17, #18, #28, #61, #61B

RAINBOW COLORS

Possible Explanations. Before discussing the rainbow colors which were noted at Fatima, it might be useful to describe three meteorological phenomena which might explain these colors. The first two are unlikely explanations, but have been discussed in earlier books on Fatima.

HALOS. One is called a halo. It is described as follows: "The refraction of light rays by ice crystals produces halos around light sources. When one looks at a moon or sun through a thin cloud containing hexagonal-shaped (ice) crystals, a bright ring with a radius about 22 degrees (as measured by the observer) appears around the moon or sun. A cloud producing rectangular crystals produces a ring that is about twice as large in diameter. The various wave lengths are refracted differently, so that the halo may appear varicolored, with red on the inside and blue on the outside."[36]

CORONAS. A second phenomenon is called a corona, and is distinct from the solar corona seen during an eclipse, which was described earlier. This atmospheric corona is described as follows: "Corona—in meteorology a sequence of colored rings observed around the sun or moon when the bodies are viewed through clouds composed of water droplets. The colors range through the spectrum from a blue inner ring to a red outer ring." The same source also stated: "Water Droplets—the colored rings or corona <u>closely centered</u> around the sun are produced by diffraction of light by small spherical droplets."[37] A second source gives two pictures of coronas, and shows no appreciable space between the sun and the inner ring of the corona.[38]

AIR LENSES. Air lenses are also called atmospheric lenses. They are the only natural explanation which I have found for the rainbow colors at Fatima. Unfortunately, they are less well-known and/or less frequently observed. I say this because I have found very little to be written about them in the several books and several articles or chapters on atmospheric phenomena which I have examined. I found much on halos, coronas, and other atmospheric phenomena. Two Fatima authors (Fathers Jaki and Amorim) vaguely hinted that air lenses were the cause of some of the phenomena noted at Fatima. Neither purports to be an authority on meteorology or air lenses, and both appear

---

[36] *Encyclopedia Americana* 1999, Vol II, p 630
[37] Ibid., Vol VII, pp 88, 114, 115
[38] *Weather,* Time-Life, 1996, p 258, various authors; this article was authored by Richard Whitaker

to have relied heavily on a statement of professor D. H. Menzel of Harvard, an astronomer. He is quoted as saying:

Sometimes we forget that air is like glass in some respects. It is usually transparent in small thicknesses, but in large thicknesses, and where irregularities are present, it can give appreciable distortions. A few miles of air can give as great or greater distortion than a few inches of irregular glass can produce. The air, then, proves to be a lens of a sort, usually a bad lens, but occasionally very effective.[39]

Father Jaki also quotes a 1950 book which cites the opinion of another astronomer who said that the explanation (presumably for the color phenomena) should be sought not in astronomy but in meteorology. He said: "Given layers of air of different temperature, I do not see why they should not produce the same effect as a series of lenses and thus account for the observed result."[40]

Two articles by authorities in the field of meteorology confirm that air lenses exist and that they cause mirages and color at sunset.

One says:

Acting as a lens …. The atmosphere produces mirages by refraction. …. The index of refraction of air depends on the density of the air and the amount of moisture in it. The contribution of moisture to phenomena involving light, however, is so small that it can be ignored. The density of the air depends on its temperature and pressure. Since most of the mirages we shall discuss are caused by shallow layers of air, over which the change in pressure is slight, we can pretend that the index of refraction depends only on the temperature. A high temperature corresponds to a low density and a low index of refraction. The stronger the temperature gradient (the greater the change of temperature with distance) … the greater the amount of refractive bending of the light. If the temperature of the air is the same everywhere, the light will travel in a straight line. The nature of the atmospheric lens, and therefore of the mirage images it produces, thus depends on the way the temperature varies in the atmosphere, primarily with height. (Gist– A mirage is more likely when a person on land views an object near a large, enclosed body of water, since the temperature of the air over the water varies from that over the nearby land.) …. Towering, the term given to an image when it is magnified, occurs when the temperature

---

[39] *Flying Saucers*, D. H. Menzel, Harvard Press, Cambridge, MA, 1953, pp 206, 207
[40] Jaki, pp 232, 245

gradient and the temperature increase together. .... Such conditions are to be found over enclosed bodies of water in the early morning and also over sun-heated ground later in the day.[41]

A second author says:
At the same temperature and same level, moist air weighs less than dry air. (Keep in mind that we are referring to water vapor—a gas—and not suspended droplets). ... Moist air is less dense than dry air. .... When the sun is 4 degrees above the horizon, sunlight must pass through an atmosphere 12 times thicker than when the sun is directly overhead. (Gist– This causes various colored sunsets, depending on whether the air is clear or hazy.) ... Atmospheric mirages are created by light passing through and being refracted by air lenses of different densities.[42]

Finally, Keith L. Seitter, Deputy Executive Director of the American Meteorological Society told me by telephone on October 16, 2002, that air lenses exist at altitudes above ground level, that they occur during very rapid changes of temperature, that they may cause the sun's image to be displaced, that they <u>may</u> cause some color separation, that the air lenses are very hard to notice, that they are the cause of some colors seen at sunset, and that he does not know where I might find written information on air lenses.

From all of the above, I conclude: 1) that air lenses exist at ground level and at higher altitudes; 2) that they may cause the sun's image to be moved from its true position; 3) that they may cause the sun's image to be magnified; and 4) that they <u>may</u> diffuse the sunlight into its component colors. Thus an air lens <u>may</u> provide an explanation for the colors noted at Fatima and also for its apparent fall. The weather at Fatima may have favored the formation of an air lens, since there is some evidence of a rapid change from cool to warm weather. Further, to the extent that water vapor in the air lens is a factor in color diffusion, the weather at Fatima was favorable, in view of the rainy weather.

If, in fact, an air lens can cause the color dispersion of sunlight, which apparently occurred at Fatima, it raises the question of whether the human eye can view such dispersed rays for any length of time without feeling pain. The answer would appear to be yes, since many

---

[41] *Atmospheric Phenomena*, various authors, W.H. Freeman & Co., circa 1980. Article by Alistair B. Fraser and William H. March.

[42] *Meteorology Today*, Donald Ahrens, West Publishing Co., St. Paul, MN, pp 28, 29, 130, 135

people reported seeing color on the sun and none said that looking at the colored sun bothered their eyes. I have already discussed this possibility (see pages 99-100), noting that the color seen at any given moment may be only a small segment of visible light and thus much weaker.

As I explain later, neither halos nor coronas can account for the color phenomena at Fatima. An air lens is thus the only explanation I have found for the rainbow colors.

Color Around the Sun, Other Than Flames. Eight sources report color around the sun, other than colored flames.[43] Three are brief. Two say merely that the sun was surrounded by various colors;[44] the third says that the sun had a ring of yellow or bright violet around it.[45] Others say that the color was on clouds around the sun. All may refer to a ring or circle of colored clouds.

"Circle" of Colored Clouds. In three or four cases the color appears to have been seen on a circle of clouds around the sun. One source indicated that the clouds separated to the sides, leaving the sun in the open, then billows of light clouds—gold, purple, and red—began to pass before it. It fell and spun. Further, she says, she saw in the open space around the sun a marvelous corona of such clouds in various delicate colors, and the people became the color of the clouds.[46]

The second source reported a silvery disk over the sun, its spin and fall, and then a beautiful cloud which surrounded it, "now rose–colored, now yellow, now purple, which colored the faces of the bystanders."[47]

The third source says that in the cloud-covered sky a circle opened up, in which the silvery sun appeared, the circle than took on successively the colors blue, red, yellow, and green and all objects took on the same color. This source has dubious features. He says when "Our Lady went up to heaven," which is clearly conjecture, since he could not know when or if Our Lady rose to heaven. Further, he exaggerates

---

[43] Annex I #25, #34, #39, #55, #61B, #61F, #61I, #92
[44] Annex I #61F, #61I
[45] Annex I #34
[46] Annex #55
[47] Annex #39

the size and area of the crowd, the time it took to disperse, and offers phenomena which has little support from other witnesses.[48]

The fourth source may also refer to colored clouds around the sun. It reports a silvery sun, its spin and fall, and then "a beautiful cloud, now fire-colored, now purple, now rose, now golden, appeared and disappeared successively" reflecting the colors not only on the people but also on all that basin. This source does not say whether or not the cloud was around the sun, but otherwise it is quite similar to the other three.

Another source tells of a yellow-reddish color around the sun, which was reflected on the crowd and the horizon.[49] He could easily be referring to colored clouds around the sun, since in the other sources the colors were said to be reflected on the ground. Or, as previously stated, the reddish color may be the same as the red flames reported by other sources. The three brief sources, which merely report color around the sun, may also be referring to colored clouds. Only one of the eight sources on color around the sun appears not to refer to colored clouds and his reference to colored spots suggests that he was blinded by the sun and that his testimony about an intensely rose-colored edge around the sun[50] is an illusion.

Summing up, we may note that four sources refer to colored clouds, one specified that there was open space between the sun and clouds, and three say that the crowd or landscape took on the same color as the clouds. Three of the four sources report the color on the clouds to be after the fall and spin. The fourth, the dubious one, puts it before, and also says that it lasted one minute. Three brief sources may also refer to colored clouds around the sun. Presumably the clouds were never a perfect circle and even a rough circle may not have lasted very long. See pages 121-122, for more on colored clouds, which were not necessarily around the sun.

Offhand, we might wonder if this circle of colored clouds was actually a halo or corona. But neither halo nor corona has its color appear one after another, nor are their colors so strong that they reflect

---

[48] Annex #25
[49] Annex #61B
[50] Annex I #92

on the people and landscape. It thus appears that a halo or corona can be eliminated as a possible explanation for the colors around the sun.

While it may be that a number of clouds briefly formed a circle around the sun and took on its color, there is another explanation. It is that the air lens (which I assume diffused the sunlight into its component colors) was above a thin cloud and caused colored rays to pierce the cloud and pass on to the people, seeming to leave a circular hole in the cloud; part of the cloud, at the edge of this hole, took on the color of the rays. The fact that only three or four sources firmly report this ring of colored clouds may be due to its short duration; also, many sources may have felt that it was less important than color on the sun or ground and the other phenomena, such as the spin and fall of the sun.

Other "Colors" Around the Sun. Two sources give other reports of "color" around the sun. They refer to a disk or edge around the sun, but both quite probably refer to a golden or silvery edge around the sun, which is seen as part of the optical illusion of the spinning sun. (See pages 139, 146-150). One of the two tells of a gold edge of the sun around a spinning, black disk, which clearly fits this illusion.[51] This gold edge is clearly a different phenomenon from the yellow color in the many reports on rainbow colors.

The second source reported first a bright sun, then the sun seen as a "dull silver globe, with a purple disk surrounding it, very dark, as when eclipses are not quite total" and then a rapid spin of the sun.[52] However, a disk could not surround the sun, as a ring could. It thus seems clear that this lady meant to say that the very dark purple disk covered the dull silver globe, and did not mean to say that it surrounded it. A dark purple disk around the sun would certainly not be like a nearly total eclipse, but such a disk over the sun would be. Thus this second source also can be said to fit the description of the optical illusion of the spinning sun, and we can only surmise that a silvery ring (the edge of the dull silver globe) appeared around the dark disk, as part of this optical illusion.

---

[51] Annex #65
[52] Annex #61

Color on the Sun. As stated before (pages 107-108), eighteen or nineteen sources say, or seem to say, that color was seen on the sun. Of these, seven or eight are brief or vague. They report only "various" or "different" colors, or simply say that colors were seen on the sun.[53] Another report mentions no specific color, but otherwise is important. It is the report by the editor of the major Lisbon daily *O Seculo,* who was at Fatima on October 13 and later said that the sun danced a wild dance, "that a great number of people imagined to be a serpentine dance, so beautiful and glowing [were] the colors that covered the sun one after another."[54]

Many sources indicate that one or more specific colors were seen on the sun. Three (or possibly five) tell only of one color.[55] Another reported a bright red flame covering the sun, but may have meant to say it was around the sun.[56] (See page 109.) Seven sources report two or more colors.[57]

Among the sources which report only one color, two may (or may not) tell of a red color on the spinning or falling sun.[58] (See page 141.) Another reports a "rotary movement of the sun that showed a dark green color."[59] These three reports may refer to color as part of the optical illusion of the spinning sun which I mentioned earlier. The fourth source reports only blue, but later says that yellow was seen on the ground, which would seem to indicate that yellow was also seen on the sun.[60] The fifth source indicates that several colors were seen, but specifies only a vivid rose.[61] Quite likely, both of these latter sources saw several colors, but specified only one.

Thus, if we assume that there were three separate color phenomena—colored flames, rainbow colors, and a silver, gold, or very dark color associated with the optical illusion of the spinning sun—only

---

[53] Annex #19, #25, #28, #42, #44?, #61E, #61G, #61L
[54] Annex #68
[55] Annex #71, #73, #74, #90?, #102?
[56] Annex #77
[57] Annex #22, #23, #46, #49, #58, #89, #95
[58] Annex #90, #102
[59] Annex #74
[60] Annex #71
[61] Annex #73

two of these five reports fall clearly into the category of rainbow colors while three are tied to the spin or fall of the sun.

However, all of the seven reports which show two or more specific colors fall into the category of rainbow colors. They report the colors green, blue, yellow, purple, and orange, but most sources give only two or three of these colors. Yellow is mentioned in six reports. No sequence is noted, except that yellow appears last three times and one man said firmly that it was last. It appears that most witnesses did not remember the sequence well or were unconcerned which color appeared first, second, etc. Further, the nine sources which report "various" or "different" colors, surely refer to rainbow colors. Thus it seems likely that most of the witnesses who report a rainbow color or colors actually saw two or more colors and even that most of the people saw two or more colors.

I offer no explanation for the rainbow colors except the one already proposed—that an air lens caused the sunlight to be diffused into the colors of the rainbow. As discussed before (see pages 100 and 101) the diffused light, one color after another, may have been much weaker than full sunlight and thus the sun could be stared at and rainbow colors could be seen on it. The air lens could account not only for the colors noted on the sun, but also for colors on the clouds and on the ground. I have already offered possible explanations for the phenomenon of flames and I suggest explanations for the dark colors in the chapter on the spin of the sun.

Color on the Ground. Color on the ground is indicated in various ways—on the landscape, on the crowd or the people, on their faces, their clothes, and on "objects." All clearly refer to rainbow colors. Twenty-five sources indicate color on the ground,[62] including fifteen (and possibly sixteen) which also reported color on or around the sun,[63] two which also reported color on the clouds,[64] two that also reported color in the atmosphere,[65] and one that also reported color in

---

[62] Annex #16, #18, #22, #23, #25, #26, #31, #39, #44, #46, #47, #50, #55, #58, #61B, #61C, #61E, #71, #72, #89, #90, #92, #96, #97, #101

[63] Annex #22, #23, #25, #39, #44, #46, #55, #58, #61B, #61E, #71, #73, #89, #96, #92, #102?

[64] Annex #39, #72

[65] Annex #16, #90

the sun's rays.[66] Among the twenty-six, five are vague about the color, saying only "various colors," etc.[67] In the rest, yellow or golden again predominates, being mentioned fifteen times.[68] Next is red or pink, which is mentioned seven times,[69] and blue six times.[70] The other colors occur even less frequently.

In the twelve sources which mention more than one color,[71] no sequence of color predominates, except that yellow or golden is mentioned last in five cases.[72] Moreover, yellow is the only color mentioned in four sources.[73] More significant is that two say "finally" yellow or golden, one of which says that this color lasted longer than the others.[74] There is little doubt that yellow was the last color seen. The lack of sequence in the reports which give two or more colors is not surprising or troublesome. Clearly many witnesses did not remember the sequence and many sources were simply unconcerned with sequence.

Colored Clouds. Nine, or possibly ten, sources said that they saw colored clouds during the sun dance. They can be placed in three categories—clouds in front of the sun, clouds around the sun, and clouds whose location, in relation to the sun, is not specified. Five sources report colored clouds in front of the sun.[75] Three or four sources mention clouds (or a cloud) which surrounded the sun, already discussed in detail. (See pages 116 and 117.) Two sources are less specific about the cloud location.[76] Three describe the clouds as very light or diaphanous.[77] One woman said that the sun sent out "billows of smoke" of the color seen on the sun, apparently referring to diaphanous clouds.[78]

---

[66] Annex #50
[67] Annex #26, #46, #55, #61C, #61E, #97
[68] Annex #16, #18, #22, #23, #25, #31, #39, #44, #47, #50, #58, #72, #90, #96, #101
[69] Annex #16, #25, #39, #47, #61D, #96, #101
[70] Annex #16, #25, #47, #50, #61D, #101
[71] Annex #16, #23, #25, #39, #44, #47, #50, #61D, #72, #89, #90, #96
[72] Annex #16, #47, #50, #72, #90
[73] Annex #18, #22, #31, #71
[74] Annex #16, #58
[75] Annex #55, #58, #65, #90, #103
[76] Annex #37, #72
[77] Annex #55, #37, #92
[78] Annex #49

The colors reported by these sources vary considerably—rose, yellow, and purple, in one case, gold, purple, and carnation in another, etc.

The two less specific sources merit some detailed discussion. One noted that the clouds parted, the white sun appeared, and a very transparent cloud passed, the clouds turned purple, blue, and green. The second said that a beautiful cloud of several colors appeared and disappeared, reflecting these colors on the people. The first allows the implication that the colored clouds were transparent or diaphanous, and the second the implication that at times the sun seemed to be free of clouds.[79]

One source mentions colored clouds both in front and around the sun. She says that billows of very light colored clouds passed before the sun, then that the sun seemed to fall and spin, it became white, and she saw also in the open space around the sun a marvelous corona of colored clouds. She adds that the people became the color of the clouds and that the sunlight seemed to be filtered, like light through colored glass.[80]

In explanation, the variations in specific colors mentioned by the various sources can be ascribed to imperfect memory and also to variations in peoples' perception of color, as well as to differences in location of witnesses throughout the Cova da Iria. I note next that in view of the weather which preceded the sun dance, it would seem most likely that, in addition to the cirrus clouds reported by one source, light clouds passed in front of the sun at lower levels, diaphanous clouds through which the sun could be seen and which might seem to some onlookers as billows of smoke. If, in fact, diffused rays did appear on such diaphanous clouds, it is reasonable to infer that these clouds weakened the color and brightness of the rays, and that this weaker color was projected on the people and landscape. This is in accord with the fairly numerous indications of diffused or pale light seen on the landscape and people. (See page 127.)

Color on the Horizon and Sky. Ten sources report color on the horizon, most of which add other features. Three short ones provide only a statement of colors seen—yellow-reddish, blue and red, and

---

[79] Annex #37, #72
[80] Annex #55

"different" colors.[81] Other colors noted on the horizon were: yellow, orangish-red, and pink. One merely says "luminous."

On the horizon, "focals," beams, or arcs were reported and were said to be equidistant, one from another, in three sources. One of the three says that the horizon was yellow, with a series of arcs, equal in size and equidistant from one another. Another reports an orange-reddish horizon, with beams of pale light placed at an equal distance (apart). Later this same source describes the beams as oval-shaped. The third source says that the horizon was marked by luminous "focals," equal in size and distance from one another, like "burns," but in the yellow color seen at sunset. Yet another source, apparently referring to the same phenomenon, says that around the valley some stains of the three preferred colors followed each other with the greatest symmetry. A fifth source tells of a veil of pink behind every mountain or behind every crest.[82] One man, who may have stared too long at the bright sun, reports yellow spots on the horizon, the landscape, and the people.[83]

None of the sources give any clue to the duration of these beams, arcs, "focals" or stains, and the fact that they were reported by only three (or four) sources, among seventy-one, suggests they were brief. It may be that a somewhat orange color was noted on the horizon, but not distinctly so, and that some saw the color as being on the red or yellow side of orange. I know of no natural explanation for these beams, and would be inclined to accept them as imagination or eye damage, (especially the yellow spots), except for the several references to equidistance. It seems rather unlikely that three sources would have invented this odd feature.

The horizon is technically only the line where the land meets the sky. However, when we talk of the horizon we usually mean not only this line but also the sky immediately above it. Thus those who reported color on the horizon were surely referring to a small area above the horizon. Next, remembering that the weather just before the sun dance had been rainy, it is very possible that clouds blocked

---

[81] Annex #61B, #61C, #61D
[82] Annex #39, #44, #49, #72, #55, #86
[83] Annex #92

out the blue sky at the horizon above the Cova da Iria. If so, it is reasonable to presume that these clouds were struck by colored rays from the sun and thus this false horizon appeared colored to the onlookers. Presumably this feature of the sun dance, if it occurred, was not very striking or did not last very long, since only ten sources mention it.

Four sources tell of a colored atmosphere or sky. One said the atmosphere was tinged with the colors of the rainbow. Another said the atmosphere and objects nearby were clothed in bright yellow. A third source, clearly second-hand, said the heavens were filled with indefinite colorations. Jose Garrett said that there were changes in the color of the atmosphere, objects near him, and the sky and atmosphere took on a purple color. Further he said that the atmosphere, although purple, remained transparent to the edge of the horizon, which he could see clearly. Later he said that everything turned yellow, as if a topaz had been vaporized in the air.[84]

Since only two sources mentioned a colored sky, it seems highly unlikely that much of the sky was colored. If much was colored, it would certainly have been spectacular and have been reported by many persons. Further, the atmosphere is transparent and cannot appear to be colored. Thus it is very possible that the sources were simply wrong in reporting a colored atmosphere; perhaps they were describing color on the horizon or on the clouds.

Colored Rays. As indicated above, color has been reported on clouds, and colored rays of light were also said to have been seen. Four sources reported colored rays—one gives blue and yellow rays, another red, yellow, and purple, a third yellow, green, blue, and purple, and a fourth yellow, scarlet, and green.[85] But, as noted above, three sources say that no rays were seen.

Fairly good explanations for these seeming conflicts can be offered. The differences in color may be due to faulty memory related to the excitement, awe, and fear at that event, and to indifference about color sequence. Two explanations are available for the conflict between those who reported colored rays and those who said they saw none. One is that none of the witnesses actually saw rays; instead the

---

[84] Annex #16, #58, #63. #90
[85] Annex #50, #51, #93, #96

four witnesses who said they saw rays actually only saw color on the people and the landscape, and assumed that they were due to colored rays. The second is that these four witnesses saw colored rays in the sky falling earthward at a considerable distance from them, and the other witnesses, not looking in that direction, saw none. It would seem unlikely that witnesses could have seen colored rays that fell in the area near them. As we know, the sun's rays, as they fall around us, are not visible as shafts or beams of light. We are conscious only of the colors we see on the objects around us, as far as we can see. But on occasion, especially near sunset, we see beams of light in the sky, which we could easily call rays, and which seem to be falling at a place quite distant from us. The fact that only four sources reported seeing colored rays suggests that most people did not note such a phenomenon for one of the reasons just cited.

Summary on Color at Locations. In summarizing the preceding information on the location of the rainbow colors, it can be said that color was noted by many people on the sun, around it, on the clouds and on the ground. Although only a minority of sources say that the colors were noted both on the sun and the ground, it seems likely that most people saw the colors, or at least one of the colors (yellow) in both places. I now proceed to a discussion of details of the rainbow colors without reference to location.

Succession, Repetition. I first note a facet of the rainbow color phenomenon that appears to be firm. Two or more colors did not appear simultaneously, but rather, one color followed another. Sixteen reports say this in one way or another, saying that the colors appeared in succession, or that one appeared and then another, or that the sun changed colors, etc.[86] Only one source, a very late one, suggests the contrary.[87] None of the reports say that any color was repeated, which strongly suggests that each color occurred only once.

Duration of Colors. There is very little other evidence on the duration of the rainbow colors. One source reported no phenomena except rainbow colors and said he did not stare at the sun (and thus

---

[86] Annex #16, #22, #23, #25, #28, #34, #39, #49, #58, #59, #61G, #68, #72, #89, #90, #95
[87] Annex #102

implies that he did not see the spin or fall), and he adds that "this," presumably the colors, lasted some twenty minutes. While his time is clearly too long, he strongly implies that colors lasted throughout the sun dance.[88] The dubious source, mentioned previously, indicated that the colored circle (of clouds) and the color on the ground, which accompanied it, lasted one minute and indicated that it preceded the spin and fall of the sun.[89] Four other sources are vague but indicate that the colors lasted for some time. One describes the blue color, and indicates that it faded slowly and then yellow followed. Another source says that the yellow color lasted longer than the other rainbow colors, suggesting that it also faded only slowly. Another source has a short illegible section, but may say that the yellow color lasted some thirty seconds after he first saw it. Finally, Jose Garrett says that he saw the purple color, feared eye injury and thus turned away, covered his eyes, then opened them and still saw purple.[90] A weak hint that the colors lasted throughout the entire dance can also be derived from the information on the sequence of the phenomena. (See pages 128-129.)

If so, we might ask why no sources clearly state that colors were seen during the spin and fall of the sun. An answer is that the spin and the fall, were optical illusions due to staring at the muted sun, which may cause a temporary eye injury, preventing them from seeing the colors.

All this evidence allows no precise conclusions about the duration. However, the rainbow colors probably lasted for a few minutes or longer and were probably seen by most people after the other main phenomena.

Only two sources provide clues to how long each color lasted. One indicates that the purple color lasted a considerable time.[91] The second says that the color on the ground changed slowly from blue to yellow.[92] However, the evidence that the rainbow colors lasted for a few minutes or longer suggests that each color lasted for a considerable time.

---

[88] Annex #47
[89] Annex #25
[90] Annex #50, #58, #90, #71
[91] Annex #90
[92] Annex #50

Speed of Change of Color. Very little information is given on the speed of change from one color to another. One witness said that the light changed slowly from blue to yellow, while a newspaper article, clearly second-hand, said that the landscape was modified by sharp changes in color.[93] This is a clear conflict. The former version seems more likely because of the very few mentions of the speed of change. A sudden change would have been spectacular and is likely to have been mentioned by many sources. A gradual change would not.

Brightness of Color. In most cases the brightness of color is not indicated. But it is occasionally stated directly or suggested. The color of the flames on or around the sun was thrice called red, once being bright red, and once it was said to be pale pink.[94] The rim or edge around the sun was once called intense pink.[95] The color on the sun is once called bright pink, once bright yellow, and once vivid purple and emerald green.[96] But twice the yellow color is called pale or ghostly, pale purple is cited three times and "other pale tones" are once reported.[97] A possible explanation for these variations in brightness of the color on the sun is suggested by the source which reported pale purple, then green (presumably pale) seen through diaphanous clouds, then sharp and completely green (presumably bright) after the passing of the clouds, and finally bright yellow.[98]

The color seen on the ground was frequently described as pale in one way or another. Pale, ghostly or dark yellow is indicated in four sources.[99] Pale blue and pale purple are also reported, and unspecified pale colors are cited in one source.[100] However, a bright color is indicated for the yellow in one source, and for pink in another.[101] Again these variations may be due to variations in cloud cover.

Color is reported not only on the sun and ground, but also on the clouds and sky. This color, if real, must have come from the sun, but

---

[93] Annex #46, #50
[94] Annex #58, #77, #59, #34
[95] Annex #92
[96] Annex #49, #58, #95
[97] Annex #22, #34, #46, #58
[98] Annex #58
[99] Annex #22, #47, #50, #90
[100] Annex #50, #90, #55
[101] Annex #58, #49

two sources indicate that they saw no rays of the sun.[102] Five sources, however, indicate that they saw rays or beams of light.[103] One clearly indicates the rays to be pale, since she describes them as seeming to come through colored glass, but another calls the rays (yellow, scarlet, green) bright.[104]

The brightness of the color reported on the clouds is not always given. But diaphanous clouds of pink and blue are mentioned once, as are diaphanous clouds of purple and orange, presumably meaning light-colored clouds in both cases.[105]

The source which stated that a colored cloud appeared and disappeared is in accord with other reports of intermittent clouds[106] and with the weather which preceded the sun dance. It is also in accord with the sources which reported bright colors on the people and landscape, the brighter colors appearing when the sun was free of clouds.

The color on the clouds can scarcely have been spectacular, since it was reported only by nine or ten of the seventy-one sources on the sun dance. Reasonable assumptions are that they seemed pale from the ground, that they occurred for only a short time, that they were considered unimportant, and/or that they were forgotten by most sources.

Sequence and Timing. As I noted earlier, the evidence on the sequence of the sun dance phenomena is weak. However, it can be said that the colored flames, if they were real, preceded the other phenomena. The rainbow colors, on the other hand, are hard to place in sequence with the other major phenomena.

Only one source states this sequence. Jose Garrett stated that the colors did not occur at the beginning of the sun dance and he rather thought they occurred at the end.[107] A few sources appear to give the phenomena in sequence ("then," "next") but most merely suggest sequence by the order in which the phenomena are reported.

---

[102] Annex #49, #59
[103] Annex #44, #50, #51, #93, #96
[104] Annex #50, #96
[105] Annex #90, #92
[106] Annex #58, #90
[107] Annex #90

Three sources seem to indicate that the rainbow colors preceded the spin and fall of the sun.[108] Eleven sources, not counting Garrett, seem to say that the colors came after them.[109] Of these, four sources report only yellow or gold color.[110] Further, two sources seem to indicate color before and after the spin and fall.[111] Finally, five sources suggest that the colors may have occurred during the spin and fall of the sun, as well as before or after these phenomena.[112] Only one appears to say firmly that the colors occurred during the spin.[113] Some other sources on colors were clearly not reporting the phenomena in sequence and have no value in studying sequence. Particularly puzzling is the testimony of one woman, who seems to say quite firmly in one document that the colors preceded the other phenomena, but in a later document that the colors were after the other phenomena.[114]

Overall, the evidence that the rainbow colors were seen after the spin and fall of the sun is stronger. But, considering the three sources which favor an earlier occurrence, plus the two which favor both early and late occurrences, it seems quite possible that the colors also preceded the other major phenomena. And there is even some reason to think that colors occurred also during the spin and fall of the sun. Remembering the large area covered by the crowd, it is possible that the colors were seen before the other phenomena only in a limited area of the Cova da Iria.

There remains the possibility that rainbow colors were seen throughout the sun dance, at least in some parts of the Cova da Iria. As stated previously, one source reported no phenomena except rainbow colors and said he did not stare at the sun (and thus implies that he did not see the spin or fall), and he adds that "this," presumably the colors, lasted some twenty minutes. While his time is clearly too long, he strongly implies that colors lasted throughout the sun dance.[115]

---

[108] Annex #16, #37, #49, #96
[109] Annex #18, #23, #39, #50, #58, #72, #73, #77, #89, #93, #95
[110] Annex #18, #70, #77, #93
[111] Annex #44, #71
[112] Annex #39, #44, #49, #55, #95
[113] Annex #44
[114] Annex #49, #73
[115] Annex #47

Area Covered by Each Color. It is reasonably clear that each color, as it appeared, was seen over the entire Cova or over almost all of it. No sources say the contrary. Jose Garrett said that he saw purple on nearby objects and further afield to the horizon.[116] Another witness said a yellowish red was seen on the people and landscape.[117] A third said the fields and crowd were bright pink.[118] Yet another said that the sun changed to a bright yellow, which it passed to the earth, the atmosphere, and the objects nearby.[119] Two others indicate that yellow was seen on the people and landscape.[120]

Darkness During the Sun Dance. One more factor which concerns colors is the statements about darkness during the sun dance. Jose Garrett stated that during the colors, "I noticed that everything around me was becoming darkened." He then said he saw everything to be amethyst in color. He then kept looking at the sun and then noticed that the atmosphere had become brighter and everything had a yellow damask color. Another source reports the spin of the sun and then says, "All was semi-dark and the features of everyone was yellowish." A third source reported a yellow-reddish color on the horizon and people, with a weakening of light at the same time. A fourth source merely says: "What was seen of the apparition was the sun getting dark for a quarter of an hour." And the *O Seculo* report of October 15 said that "one would say that an eclipse was taking place."[121]

An impression of darkness may have been caused by an air lens, which dispersed the sunlight so that the onlookers saw only a small segment of the frequency range of visible sunlight. (See page 101.) Such a segment probably would have been much weaker than normal sunlight and perhaps weak enough to create the impression of semi-darkness, especially if the brightness were further weakened by intervening clouds.

---

[116] Annex #90
[117] Annex #61B
[118] Annex #49
[119] Annex #85
[120] Annex #50, #71
[121] Annex #17, #18, #28, #61B, #90

SUMMARY AND CONCLUSIONS

The existence of a color phenomenon at Fatima is firm. Nearly all reports, except some very short ones, tell of colors. The rainbow phenomenon—the appearance of one rainbow color after another—is also firm. A large majority of the reports on color concern this phenomenon. Only a few reports deal solely with the phenomenon of colored flames, and such a phenomenon may not have occurred. One report, and perhaps a few others, concern a silver or yellow rim around the edge of the sun, which is part of the presumed optical illusion of the spinning sun, and should not be viewed as part of the rainbow color phenomenon.

There are a great many variations in the reports on the rainbow phenomenon. Some tell only of color on the sun, others only of color on the ground, a number tell of colored clouds or a colored horizon, and some tell of color on two or all of these locations, often with varying details. The sequence of colors varies greatly in sources which report two or more colors, and the brightness of colors also varies. And the sequence of the color phenomena, in relation to other phenomena, also varies greatly.

There are, however, many convincing explanations for these variations. Some apply to all of the sun dance phenomena: witnesses generally vary greatly in describing an event, especially an unusual and frightening one; awe and fear may have affected their ability to remember correctly what they had seen; low clouds may have caused people in one part of the Cova da Iria to have different cloud cover from people in another part, and thus to have seen the phenomena differently; many sources were short and clearly incomplete; some witnesses stared only at the people and landscape, fearing sun blindness, while others may have been so fascinated that they stared only at the sun. Other explanations apply only to the color phenomena: color blindness and other eye ailments may have affected some witnesses and some surely wore sunglasses, while others did not.

Despite these variations, some strong statements can be made about the rainbow colors. They were reported by such a large share of the crowd that there is no reasonable doubt that such a phenomenon occurred, especially since colors were also said to have been seen at the nearby village of Alburitel at about the same time. The colors occurred one after another, and each lasted an appreciable amount of time before the next color was seen. The phenomenon clearly lasted at least a minute, probably two or more, and may have lasted for much or all of the sun dance.

I can offer only one natural explanation for the phenomenon of rainbow colors. This is that an air lens existed between the sun and the crowd at Fatima, that it diffused the sunlight into its component colors, that this air lens was above some or all of the clouds, and that it colored these clouds as well as the people and the landscape. Further, when the people looked at the sun, they saw it to be the same color as they were seeing on the landscape and people. Differences in cloud cover caused the colors to appear bright at times and pale at other times.

Little is published about air lenses in books and articles on meteorological phenomena, where one would expect to find them described. I would like to have more on them. However, the information I have acquired (from one oral source) indicates that air lenses exist in the upper air and <u>may</u> cause sunlight to be diffused into its component colors. If, in fact, the color phenomenon at Fatima was due to an air lens, then this lens clearly diffused the sunlight into bands, so that only one color appeared at a time to the viewers at Fatima.

An unanswered question is how an air lens could diffuse light into its component colors. As indicated earlier (see pages 113-116) an air lens is a body of air that is different in temperature, density, and moisture from the air that surrounds it. The term "lens" implies a flat shape, like glass. But little is known about air lenses above ground level. Thus it may be that an "air lens" at higher altitudes may not be lens-shaped and should not be called a lens. This allows for the possibility that a large and distinct body of air (an "air lens" or whatever it may be called) may take the shape of an enormous crystal, like that of a chandelier. If so, it is reasonable to assume that the body of air diffused light into broad bands of its component colors, as was seen at Fatima.

Ice crystals and water globules are also known to diffuse light into its component colors, causing rainbows, halos, and coronas. Perhaps they may also exist in an air lens at such a concentration and shape as to create the broad bands of color noted at Fatima.

Neither of these explanations seems particularly likely to me. However, since the color phenomenon seems to be firm, some natural explanation for it must be viewed as a strong possibility.

There remains one possibility which I am reluctant to accept, but which logic requires that I mention. I noted earlier (see page 84-85) that the phenomena of the sun dance might be a combination of natural and supernatural ones. As I show later, the possibility that the spin, fall, and lateral movements of the sun were real but supernatural, represents miracles of such fantastic proportions that they boggle the mind and cause us to prefer other explanations. The same is not true for the rainbow color phenomenon. It is less than mind-boggling to assume that God supernaturally diffused the sunlight at Fatima into its component colors, but did not do so for other parts of the earth. Nonetheless, I prefer to believe that God achieved the color phenomenon by natural means, such as an air lens.

Colored flames were also reported by a few sources in the media, and they seem reliable. No reasonable explanation for such flames is known to me, and thus these flames may be the same phenomenon as the rainbow colors, but viewed differently by a few people. Or they may be the same as the sparks said to have been seen around the spinning sun. However, the witnesses speak firmly of flames, and they may be a separate phenomenon. If so, the only explanation I can offer is the fantastic one that a small thick cloud, nearly round, covered the sun but not its corona, and allowed the flames of the corona to be seen by a small share of the crowd, and the rest of the crowd did not see the corona, perhaps because a cloud of this shape was seen only in a small part of the Cova.

CHAPTER VIII

THE SPIN OF THE SUN

The rapid spinning of the sun on its axis is one of the most spectacular phenomena reported by most witnesses to the October 13 sun dance. Many sources state that the spin was rapid or very rapid. Some say "vertiginous."[1] None state or imply that it was not rapid. And, like the color phenomena, it would appear to have been seen by almost all witnesses who report on the sun dance. Of the seventy-one unique sources which give significant data on the sun dance, forty-nine report the spin of the sun, including two whose wording was not clear and certain.[2] Twenty-one fail to mention the spin, but none say or imply that they did not see it. However, a 1923 source, not counted in these statistics, said he saw the color phenomenon but did not see the spin.[3] Perhaps he feared the sun and did not look at it, like one other witness.[4]

Among the twenty-one sources which do not report any spin of the sun, fourteen are very brief.[5] Ten give about one line on the sun dance and the other four give two. The one-liners are clearly incomplete reports on the sun dance. For example, one says only: "We all

---

[1] Annex #16, #18, #19, #23, #26, #27?, #30, #34, #44, #49, #52, #54, #55, #58, #59, #61, #71, #90, #96

[2] Annex #16, #18, #19, #23, #26-28, #30, #34, #39, #42, #44, #47, #49, #50, #51, #52, #54-56, #58, #59, #61, #61B-61D, #61F-61H, #61J-61M, #62, #65, #69, #71, #72, #74, #77?, #78?, #89, #90, #93, #96, #101, #102, #103, #107

[3] Annex II #15G

[4] Annex #47

[5] Annex #17, #20, #29, #31, #32, #43, #57, #61E, #61I, #63, #97, #100, #104, #108

saw the sun dancing and taking on appearances which had never been seen before." A second says: "What surprises us is … that the sun … dances like a mad dancer in a wild country dance." A third says: "… at 2:00 exactly the sun appeared, taking on the most extraordinary lights." A fourth gives no information on the sun dance except an exact time for its start.[6]

One of the four two-liners said he did not look at the sun; thus he could not have seen it spin; the second said it "danced," the third said it was "oscillating in a rapidity of movement." The fourth states that "they say" that the sun had a terrible heat and it "came forth in a mad dance."[7] The "dancing" and "rapid oscillation" are vague terms but could refer to the spin of the sun. Thus the only clear "non-see-er" of the spin, among the four, is the one who did not look at the sun.

Among the seven longer sources, one is only three lines long and is a second-hand report;[8] another is also only four lines long and mentions "unusual gymnastics of the sun,"[9] a third is a report, strange in other respects, which mentions clouds spinning around the sun;[10] the fourth twice mentions seeing yellow spots, suggesting that he had become sun blind.[11] Except for the man who appears to have been sun blinded, none of these four appear to be clear "non-see-ers" of the spin of the sun.

The remaining three sources are fairly long (several lines), and are pro-Fatima; they are the only ones, among the twenty-one sources, in which we would clearly expect to find a reference to the spin of the sun, but do not find it.[12] The failure of these few sources, among seventy, to mention the spin of the sun would not seem to be very significant. The spin of the sun was thus a phenomenon noted by a large majority of the crowd at Fatima. It was also said to be seen at the nearby village of Alburitel at the same time. (See page 175.)

---

[6] Annex #20, #29, #31, #32
[7] Annex #97, #57, #107, #108
[8] Annex #22
[9] Annex #46
[10] Annex #25
[11] Annex #92
[12] Annex #70, #68, #95

Non-see-ers. However, an explanation is needed for the three sources which are longer and may be "non-see-ers" of the spin of the sun. One seems particularly important. Avelino Almeida, editor of *O Seculo,* gave his eyewitness account, without telling of the spin. Earlier he had also given what appeared to be his eyewitness account, again without telling of the spin.[13] This certainly suggests he had not noted the spin of the sun.

The second source, which also seems important, is a multi-page pamphlet by a pro-Fatima witness, in which one would expect to find a complete account of the sun dance. The author reports the heat and color phenomena and twice mentions the fall of the sun.[14] This suggests that she had not noted the spin. But if the spin and fall were part of a single optical illusion, as I propose later, this source surely noted the rapid spin but failed to report it.

The third source said it would be hard to give a description of the sun dance, but suggested that he would try to do so. He said that the sun trembled and that a color phenomenon occurred, but that he personally saw only a pronounced yellow, and perhaps a black color below the sun.[15] His description of the sun dance is fairly short and thus his omission of the spin is less significant. It is, of course, possible that "trembled" meant spin.

Possibly Almeida and the others had seen the spin and simply failed to mention it. Almeida was clearly expected by his superiors to downplay and ridicule the event. But the spin of the sun was surely a very spectacular phenomenon. It seems unlikely that a reporter (even one under pressure to be negative) would have failed to mention the spin in his eyewitness account, if he had seen it. Recalling also the few who said they saw no phenomena at all, it seems clear that there were "non-see-ers" of the spin of the sun among the crowd at Fatima, but that they were a very small share of the crowd. An explanation is needed.

If the spin of the sun was an optical illusion caused by a temporary eye injury due to staring at the muted sun (a possibility which I shall

---

[13] Annex #28, #68
[14] Annex #95
[15] Annex #70

soon note), then it is possible that Almeida and the few other sources were less susceptible to this eye injury (or perhaps had particularly effective sunglasses) and thus failed to have this optical illusion. It is further possible that Almeida and the others turned more frequently to talk to his neighbors and friends and to observe the crowd, thus staring at the muted sun for shorter periods, lessening the likelihood of eye injury and thus of having the optical illusion.

Sparks From the Spinning Sun. Some sources report the spinning of the sun, but give no details. Most, however, provide at least a little detail. Undoubtedly the most common detail is that the spinning sun resembled a fireworks pinwheel. This, I presume, refers to the circular device which I remember from my youth, which had something like firecrackers on its exterior, and which was pinned to a tree or post at night and ignited, causing it to spin very rapidly and to send out a stream of sparks as it spun.

Eight sources specifically call the spinning sun a fireworks wheel.[16] Nine others merely call it a firewheel.[17] There is little doubt that all were referring to the same kind of fireworks display.

It would seem that all references to the firewheel or fireworks wheel indicate not only that the sun seemed to be spinning rapidly, but also to be sending out a trail of sparks. However, only one source specifically reports seeing sparks. This source said that "the sun thrice showed a rotary movement on its periphery, flashing sparks of light from its edge, like the well-known fireworks wheel."[18] None of the many sources which mention the spin, without likening it to a firewheel, say that sparks were seen. None, however, deny it.

There are, in addition, three other sources which may be referring to sparks. One says: "This host (the sun) changed into a black disk surrounded by a round gold circle, and this black disk began to spin around on itself... throwing out, from time to time, luminous rays, or to put it better, (flashes of) lightning."[19] A much later source says that the firewheel "began to rotate on itself with great velocity, pouring out

---

[16] Annex #28, #54, #61, #61C, #61F, #61L, #69, #89
[17] Annex #19, #26, #44, #61G, #61H, #61J, #61K, #61M, #102
[18] Annex #89
[19] Annex #65

shafts of flame of various colors."[20] A 1926 source, apparently based on notes made in 1917, says: "The sun's disk lost its brilliance, turned black; a band of the color of fire began to rotate now in this, now in that direction in front of the sun. Surrounding the sun, along all its circumference, an enormous splendor, also the color of fire, a splendor full of majesty and of great dimensions, appeared to many thousands of observers."[21] Finally, I note that three of the fourteen sources which describe later sun dances report sparks, strong radiations or flames around the spinning sun (those for October 11, 1946, October 13, 1998, and unspecified dates in 1987-2001; see chapter XI.)

Since, among the forty-nine sources which mention the spinning sun, only one clearly speaks of the sparks and three others may refer to them, perhaps no sparks were actually seen, despite the many references to a firewheel, which implies sparks. Maybe all or most viewers seemed to see the sun spinning rapidly, not sending out sparks, but merely saw a bright edge around the spinning sun, which vaguely resembled a fireworks pinwheel, with which they were familiar, and they knew no better way to describe this unusual phenomenon.

Color of the Spinning Sun. Relatively few of the forty-nine sources which tell of the spinning sun tell us clearly what color it was. A large number suggest or imply colors by reporting the colors immediately before or after they say that the sun was spinning. The colors which were reported vary greatly. They fall into three categories; 1) white, silvery, gray, pearly or luminous; 2) black or other dark color; and 3) one or more of the rainbow colors.

The first category represents various shades of the muted sun. For it we have the most numerous statements. Jose Garrett said: "This pearly disk had a vertiginous movement. It was not the sparkling of a (star). It spun on itself with a crazy velocity." The reporter of *Diario de Noticias* said: "the sun appeared, the color of dull silver, with a circular movement." A 1931 source said: "Looking like a snowball revolving on itself ...." Another said: "the silvery sun, ... shrouded in the same grayish lightness of gauze, was seen to rotate and turn ...." Father Curado reported the sun to be wrapped in flames and then

---

[20] Annex #102
[21] Annex #103

said: "Suddenly it lost all this light or flames and seemed to us a dull silver plate, as *O Seculo* has properly said. It took on a rapid and visible rotary movement, seeming even to come close to earth." He then said that the sun was again wrapped in flames, perhaps a minute passed "and again it lost its light and flames, becoming again the plate, now very white, with the same very rapid movement of rotation."[22]

Other sources indicate that the muted sun was silvery or yellow, but was luminous or shiny. One said: "They all ... saw a disk silvery and luminous (Gist– but easy to stare at, like a mirror) which stood out or superimposed itself on the sun and began to descend with a rotating movement." Another said: "... a luminous disk the size of a big host (Gist– which one could stare at like the moon) seemed to detach itself from the sun ((or got in front of it)), lowering visibly, with a continuous rotation, and after a stop, repeated itself." A third said: "The sun-globe, like a silver disk, turned on an imaginary axis and at this moment seemed to descend ... toward the earth accompanied at times by an extraordinary bright shine." A fourth said: "It takes on the appearance of the moon, all yellow, but without sending out light, it changes to a celestial blue, followed by a very intense shine, like a spring of bright lights. Next it takes on a very rapid circular movement and approaches the earth." One more source may refer to a luminous or shiny sun. It says the sun was a silvery disk with no rays and the sun "takes on its natural color and begins to turn vertiginously." Presumably its natural color was yellow and luminous or shiny.[23] Finally, one source merely indicates a muted color for the spinning sun. It says the sun became bright, took on various colors "and then lost its shine and color (Gist– being easy to stare at) and took on a rapid rotating movement."[24]

Six other sources suggest or imply that the spinning sun was white, silvery or golden, by mentioning the spin before or after they tell of a muted sun.[25] Presumably, if the sun had changed to a very dark or rainbow color before or after spinning, they would have mentioned it.

---

[22] Annex #90, #27, #101, #50, #59
[23] Annex #39, #72, #93, #71, #73
[24] Annex #96
[25] Annex #23, #27, #51, #55, #69, #89

The second category is a dark sun. Two sources clearly said that the spinning sun was black. One said: "Suddenly the completely black sun seems to loosen itself from the sky and seems to turn on itself very rapidly." The second said: "... and the black disk ... began to spin around on itself." A third reported: "... the rotary movement of the sun, that showed a dark green color." The fourth said the sun "turned black; a band of the color of fire began to rotate, now in this, now in that direction in front of the sun." A fifth source appears to report a very dark purple disk over the sun and then a rapid spin of the sun, as explained previously (see page 118).[26] All of these sources seem to be describing the optical illusion reported by Professor Stokl, soon to be discussed in detail.

The third category is rainbow colors. Only one source seems to say quite clearly that the spinning sun had a rainbow color. It says the sun was: "crowned by various colors, in a movement of rapid rotation."[27]

Thirteen others suggest or imply rainbow colors for the spinning sun by mentioning the colors before or after telling of the spinning sun.[28] However, five of these were witnesses at the Porto de Mos Inquiry and their statements were so short that I wonder if they were merely reporting two phenomena without intending to say that they occurred together. Further, in four of the remaining cases the report of the spin of the sun was sandwiched between a reference to the muted sun and to rainbow colors[29] and thus may indicate that the sun was white or silvery rather than rainbow-colored.

Two other sources offer very weak evidence that the spinning sun was red. Jose Garrett first calls it pearly, as stated above, and then says: "The sun, keeping its speed of rotation, loosened itself from the firmament and advanced (*sanguinio*—blood red or terrifying) upon the earth, threatening to crush us with its huge fiery weight." Considering the context, he probably meant "terrifying" rather than "blood red." The other, a young boy at the time, reported in 1952: "It was rather

---

[26] Annex #16, #65, #74, #103, #61
[27] Annex #44
[28] Annex #23, #49, #51, #55, #61B-D, #61F, #61G, #61J, #61L, #72, #93
[29] Annex #23, #51, #72, #93

like a firewheel, very large and reddish," but in 1931 he said the spinning sun was white.[30]

Summing up, it can be said that many sources give strong evidence that the spinning sun had a color of the muted sun. However, a fairly large number saw a black or dark color, and there is even the possibility that others saw a rainbow color.

I know of no explanation for these variations except that the phenomenon of the spinning sun was an optical illusion (as I soon discuss in detail) and that the apparent color of the spinning sun during this illusion may vary considerably, depending on such factors as the meteorological conditions, the health of each individual's eyes, and the use or non-use of sun glasses.

Duration of the Spin. It would appear that the spin of the sun lasted quite long. One source says eight to ten minutes, more or less.[31] Another source says the sun spun, with some intermissions, for eight to ten minutes.[32] One more seems to say it lasted some minutes.[33] Jose Garrett said the dance was about ten minutes, interrupted by two short intermissions.[34] Father Curado reported three occurrences of the spin and said that one lasted "perhaps a minute."[35] No other source gives an indication of the length of the spin. However, at another sun dance, in 1998, the spin of the sun was said to have occurred three times and to have lasted some ten to fifteen minutes. (See chapter XI.) No sources indicate or even suggest that the spin of the sun was very short. Thus it seems likely that for most of the crowd it lasted several minutes or more.

Several Occurrences of the Spinning Sun. Most sources report only one occurrence of the spinning sun and other phenomena. Eight however, indicate two or three (or several) occurrences.[36] Five others imply or suggest several occurrences.[37] Most sources, as stated earlier, give only a few lines on the sun dance, and for these it is not surpris-

---

[30] Annex #90, #102, #101
[31] Annex #89
[32] Annex #18
[33] Annex #69
[34] Annex #90
[35] Annex #59
[36] Annex #39, #59, #61, #61H, #69, #71, #72, #89
[37] Annex #18, #61G, #77, #90, #103

ing that they fail to mention several occurrences, even if they were noted by these sources. They may well have judged the phenomena themselves as more important than the fact that they were repeated. However, eighteen sources are somewhat longer (four to ten lines), but fail to mention several occurrences,[38] plus another which reported on the sun dance at the same time in the nearby village of Alburitel.[39] This large number of sources which seem to report only one occurrence of the phenomena, as opposed to the eight (or thirteen) which report several occurrences, poses a problem. Were the eight (or thirteen) wrong, or were the others simply incomplete, or is there another explanation?

One explanation is that variations in cloud cover at the Cova da Iria caused some onlookers to see only one long set of phenomena, while others saw two or three shorter sets, interrupted by heavier cloud cover. Specifically, in some parts of the Cova, a dark cloud may have temporarily blotted out the sun and stopped the apparent spin, then passed by, allowing the muted sun to be seen again, followed by a repeat of the spin. Or, in some parts of the Cova, the clouds over the sun may have temporarily cleared away, leaving the sun too bright to be stared at, followed by more clouds which muted the sun and by a repeat of the spin. Elsewhere in the Cova the sun may have been visible but muted for the entire sun dance, leaving the impression of a single spin of the sun.

Another possible explanation is that some of the onlookers rested their eyes for a short while after first seeing the phenomena, or looked at the people and landscape, and then stared at the sun a second time, and even a third, seeing first the silvery sun and then the spin, as before. If the spin lasted several minutes, as stated above, surely many of the viewers would have rested their eyes or turned and discussed with their neighbors what they were seeing. Other viewers may have stared continuously.

A third explanation, which seems unlikely, is that all eighteen of the fairly long reports, which mention only one occurrence of the sun

---

[38] Annex #16, #23, #25, #28, #44, #46, #47, #49, #50, #52, #55, #58, #65, #70, #73, #92, #93, #96
[39] Annex #101

dance, were simply incomplete. This explanation is more believable for the ten sources with only four or five lines on the sun dance.[40] It is not very surprising that some of the eighteen mentioned no re-occurrences of the phenomena, assuming they had noted such re-occurrences. Fear and awe may have caused some to forget the re-occurrences and some may have felt that the phenomena themselves were all that mattered. But it seems rather unlikely that all eighteen, plus the many shorter sources, would have failed to make any mention of re-occurrences, if they had noted them. It thus appears that many people noted only one occurrence, but at least a few noted two or more occurrences.

Delay in the Appearance of the Spinning Sun. Next I note that a German meteorologist, Professor Stokl, has stated that staring at a muted sun <u>for about a minute</u> creates the optical illusion that the sun is largely covered by a dark disk, that only its perimeter is visible and that it seems to be spinning very rapidly. (See page 148.) Thus it seems important to find out if the crowd stared at the muted sun for about a minute before the start of the spin at Fatima. Unfortunately, none of the sources, which report the spin of the sun, tell how long the muted sun was seen before the start of the spin or of any other phenomena. A full minute, however, is a long time, if one simply stands and stares at the sun, waiting for something to happen. (Readers are invited to check this for themselves.) One would expect that at least a few sources would mention such a long delay. Thus the failure of all sources to mention any delay suggests that few onlookers noted any long delay. A few seconds, perhaps ten or fifteen, seems quite likely.

Spinning Disk in Front of Sun. Two sources indicate that the spinning object which they saw was not the sun, but a spinning disk which superimposed itself over the sun. One source called the disk white and the other luminous. Both also say that the disk seemed to fall toward the earth and that the spin and fall occurred two times.[41] A third source, which does not mention the spinning sun, says that a white form detached itself from the sun and descended toward the earth "a third time," apparently meaning that this form, presumably

---

[40] Annex #16, #23, #44, #47, #52, #65, #70, #92, #93, #96
[41] Annex #39, #72

a disk, covered the sun and descended three times.[42] Presumably this phenomenon was the same as that which was much more frequently reported as the spinning and falling sun. Once again a possible explanation for the variations is that the spin was an optical illusion, which varies depending on such factors as the meteorological conditions, the health of each person's eyes and the use or non-use of sunglasses.

Spinning Edge or Center. Most sources indicate that the sun seemed to spin, presumably meaning the entire form of the sun. However, one source indicates that an inner black circle (clearly meaning a disk) rotated, and two say that the periphery spun.[43] A possible explanation is that the single source had a false impression.

Spin and Fall Together. Many sources say, or seem to say, that the spin and fall of the sun occurred together. Of these, six clearly indicate that the spin and fall occurred together.[44] Nine others appear to say the same thing by telling of one immediately after the other.[45] No sources deny this. The evidence is thus quite strong that the sun seemed to spin during its apparent fall toward earth.

One source, Jose Garrett, tells us that the sun first spun for an unspecified period of time and then kept spinning, but also seemed to fall.[46] Two other sources seem to say the same.[47] With only these few sources as evidence, we might suspect that they were simply wrong in saying that the spin came first and then the spin and fall together. But there are strong reasons for thinking that they were right. Most other sources which report both the spin and the fall tell first of the spin and then the fall, which might indicate that the spin preceded and then accompanied the fall.[48] Only four report the fall and then the spin.[49] A second reason is the strong evidence that the spin lasted for several minutes (see page 142) and the fairly strong evidence that the fall was much shorter—only seconds instead of minutes. (See page 159.) If

---

[42] Annex #95
[43] Annex #65, #89, #103
[44] Annex #16, #39, #72, #90, #93, #96
[45] Annex #16, #28, #52, #58, #59, #61C, #61G, #61M, #69, #71, #96
[46] Annex #90
[47] Annex #49, #86
[48] Annex #23, #27, #28, #49, #51, #52, #58, #59, #61C, #61D, #61H, #61M, #69, #71, #101, #102
[49] Annex #19, #61G, #61L, #72

the spin came first and then the spin and fall together, why do so few report this detail? The answer would seem to be that this detail seemed unimportant to most people reporting on the sun dance.

Summary. A large majority of the people at Fatima on October 13 noted a rapid spinning of the sun. Many sources liken the spinning sun to a firewheel, implying a trail of sparks, but only one specifically mentions sparks, which leaves some doubt that the others imply them. Most reports on the spinning sun do not compare it to a firewheel. Most sources mention only one occurrence of the spin, but at least eight, perhaps as many as thirteen, indicate two or three or several occurrences. Most sources do not tell the color of the spinning sun, but a dozen indicate, or seem to say, that it was silvery, white or light colored, while at least four, and maybe seven, say it was black or dark. Two or three say the spin was accompanied by a great shine. Almost all sources say that the spinning object was the sun, but two or three sources say it was a white or silvery object which detached itself from the sun.

The duration of the spin is seldom indicated, but the available sources suggest that it was quite long—probably several minutes or more. Finally, many sources seem to indicate that the spin and fall occurred at the same time. One witness says that the spin preceded and then accompanied the fall, and some others suggest it. No sources report any delay between the first viewing of the silver sun, or other colors on the sun, and the start of the phenomenon of the spin, which suggests that no long delay occurred.

Despite the fairly large number of variations in details of the spin, there are reasonable explanations for them. The variations on the occurrences—one or several spins—have several possible explanations; they are: variations in cloud cover in various parts of the Cova da Iria, interruptions from staring at the sun to talk with neighbors, and incomplete reporting. The variations in color of the spinning sun may represent normal variations on this illusion due to different conditions of the eyes of the viewers, their use or non-use of sunglasses, and variations in cloud cover in the Cova. These factors may also account for the fact that a few witnesses said that they saw a disk in front of the spinning sun (or saw the disk itself spin) while most witnesses said that they saw the entire sun to be spinning.

Basic Conclusion. As stated earlier, the rapid spin of the sun at Fatima, if real, is mind-boggling. Whether the spin was a real spin has not been discussed in books on Fatima, as far as I know. However, the fast spin noted at Fatima was clearly not the normal spin of the sun, since the sun requires twenty-seven days for a single revolution and thus is turning too slowly to be noted by the human eye.[50] A rapid spin is surely one revolution per second, or perhaps one in two seconds. If the spin noted at Fatima was real and rapid (one revolution per second) the speed of the sun was increased by 2,332,800 times.

Thus I conclude that the spin of the sun was an illusion, probably an optical illusion. My reasons are: 1) the spin was not the normal spin of the sun, which is too slow to be noticeable to the human eye; 2) I am reluctant to accept that God speeded up the sun's spin millions or hundreds of thousands of times to make it noticeable as a rapid spin at Fatima but not at any of the world's observatories; 3) I am also reluctant to accept the spin as a supernatural vision, seen by some people at Fatima, but not by all; 4) there are too may reports of the spin to make hallucination or invention believable; this phenomenon was entirely unknown by the crowd at Fatima, and it seems impossible that a large majority of them would have had the same unexpected hallucination; 5) I know of no purely meteorological explanation; and 6) an optical illusion also accounts for the spin of the sun reported by many witnesses at later dates, assuming that at least one or two of them were not hallucinations, imaginations, or inventions.

I must now qualify my statement that I know of no purely meteorological explanation for the spin of the sun. Father Jaki has offered the following idea, which he insists is not an explanation:

An air lens formed in the cloudy sky about five hundred meters above the ground. The air lens contained ice crystals that can refract the rays of the sun into the main colors of the rainbow. Then the two streams of air, blowing from different angles at the air lens, could have put it into a circular motion, exactly as this happens when a tornado is formed.[51]

---

[50] *Encyclopedia Americana* 2002, Vol 26, page 12
[51] *The Sun's Miracle, or of Something Else*, pp 25, 26

This concept, if not an explanation, is intriguing. Perhaps Father Jaki hesitates to call it an explanation because so little is known about air lenses and we cannot say whether two streams of air blowing on an air lens at different angles would cause it to spin rapidly or to dissipate. There is also the thought that the air lens, if spinning rapidly, would cause the diffused colors to change from one to another very rapidly, which is contrary to the evidence of a slow rate of change in the colors. (See page 125-126.) Therefore, following Father Jaki's lead, I have decided not to consider this idea as one possible explanation for the spin of the sun. Obviously, I agree with his concept that an air lens could have caused the rainbow colors at Fatima. Father Jaki is a distinguished theologian and man of science. He is a professor at Seton Hall University and is the author of 30 books and 100 articles. His statements deserve serious consideration.

A specific explanation for the spin is suggested by a report of a German meteorologist. However, there are major variations between the details of the spin, reported as an optical illusion by professor Karl J. Stokl, and the details of the spin reported by many sources at Fatima. Further, in books on meteorology (see my bibliography) I have found no other meteorologist and no expert in the field of optical illusion who reports this illusion. I must thus give Stokl's description of the illusion and make some comments about it to facilitate comparison of it with Fatima.

Professor Stokl's Spin. He said:

> When the sun is high in the sky it is dangerous to look at it even for a few seconds. When the sun is not so high, namely when a veil of clouds, or humidity and dust dominate more and more in the atmosphere and dampen the sunlight, one can, for several minutes, look at the sun without damaging the eye. The following subjective effects may arise ((I made that experiment myself several times)): after almost a minute ((the time varies according to the condition of the atmosphere and the momentary condition of the eyes)) one thinks to see a dark blue disk in front of the sun ((this is already a sign of the highly excited state of the retina)). According to my experience and also according to the communications of many

observations of the phenomenon of July 13, 1944,[52] this dark blue disk is somewhat smaller than the solar disk, so that the edge of the disk stands out as a ring beyond that dark blue disk. Then one has right away the impression that the solar disk rotates with great speed in one or the other direction. This I have experienced often enough. All this is a subjective appearance that has nothing to do with the external world.[53]

It should be noted that Professor Stokl implies, but does not state, that the illusion he describes occurs when the sun is "not so high," perhaps toward sunrise or sunset.

He does not state the color of the outer ring (the visible part of the solar disk), but he said earlier that the sun was muted. This clearly implies a sun, whose color was white, silvery or light gold, prior to the spin, and thus suggests that the spinning ring seen around the dark-blue disk was white, silvery or light gold.

He states that he noted the illusion "several times," presumably meaning on several occasions, not several times on one occasion. This suggests that other meteorologists are likely to have seen this illusion at least once in their career. I have, however, not read of any other meteorologist who reported such an illusion.

He does not state that the illusion occurred every time he looked at the muted sun for about a minute, but probably he would have (and surely he should have) said that sometimes the illusion does not occur, if on occasion he failed to note it.

He does not state that the illusion occurred more than once on any of the times he saw it, nor that the spin was accompanied by an apparent fall of the sun, by sparks, by color phenomena or by extraordinary heat. Since he was reporting to the local Catholic bishop, who was investigating Fatima-like events, he would scarcely have failed to mention such Fatima-like phenomena, if he had noticed them. This suggests that his illusion was limited to a single occurrence of a rapid spin of the image of the sun behind a dark-blue disk, much after midday.

---

[52] In Germany. See page 108 for details.

[53] Jaki, p 303; on page 332, Jaki says that this German was a professor of physics and astronomy.

He does not state how long the illusion lasted, but his statement that one can stare at the sun for several minutes hints that the spin lasted for a few minutes or longer.

He gives no information on the weather at the time of the spins.

He does not give the dates or the location for his observation of this illusion, but context suggests a date between July 1944 and March 1952, and a location somewhere in Germany.

He implies, but does not state, that the spin of the sun seen by him was not at a site of a purported apparition of the Blessed Virgin or other religious site.

Comparison of Details. Readers with good memories may already have noted the many differences in detail between the spin of the sun at Fatima and the optical illusion reported by professor Stokl. Nonetheless, I think it worthwhile to record them:

The spin at Fatima was accompanied by an apparent fall of the sun, by color phenomena and by a lateral movement of the sun in the sky. None of these phenomena were reported by Professor Stokl.

Professor Stokl's illusion began after he had stared at the muted sun about a minute; no precise information on this point is available for the spin at Fatima, but it seems likely that the spin began with less delay.

The Fatima spin began near noon, solar time. Stokl's spin apparently began much later, perhaps toward sunset.

The largest number of the Fatima sources which indicate or suggest the color of the spinning sun give it a light color. Stokl's disk was dark.

Stokl's illusion included a dark disk which imposed itself in front of the sun, whose outer rim seemed to spin rapidly. At Fatima only a few reported a disk over the sun and they said it was light in color.

Finally, none of the Fatima reports are similar to Stokl's illusion in all points—a minute's delay, a dark colored disk, a disk in front of the sun, and the rapid spin of the sun's periphery. But seven sources resemble the Stokl illusion in two points, one of them being the rapid spin.[54] Four of the seven further mentioned a dark color for the spinning sun,[55] three (and apparently four) report a disk in front of the sun,[56] and one a rapid spin of the periphery,[57] which suggests that a disk covered all but the periphery.

Analysis and Explanations. I think that the optical illusion of professor Stokl is genuine. I suspect, however, that he noted this illusion on one day only, not several days, as implied by his statement. I see no reason to question his competence, and several witnesses at Fatima and at later sun dances report details that are similar to those of Stokl. Offhand, the many differences in detail between the Stokl's spin and the spin at Fatima strongly suggest that they are not the same phenomenon. They may well be two different illusions, with some similarities.

Nonetheless, the similarity of the rapidly spinning sun at Fatima to Stokl's rapidly spinning rim of the sun is striking, as is the fact that seven Fatima sources have one other detail in common with Stokl. This, and the fact that both spins appear to have lasted several minutes or more, suggests that they are the same phenomenon. If so, we need explanations for the many differences in detail.

A number of explanations are available for the differences. One is the weather. Stokl does not tell us about the weather during his illusions, but his statement that one could stare at the sun for several minutes without harming one's eyes implies stable cloud conditions—a dull and formless blanket of clouds over the whole sky. At Fatima the cloud conditions were not stable, and movement of lower clouds in front of the muted sun very probably account for the impression of lateral movement of the sun in the sky (the dance itself), as I later indicate (see page 168). And if a blanket of clouds covered the sky at Stokl's site, no great heat is to be expected. But at Fatima the weather changed rapidly from wet, cold, and windy to dry and sunny, causing great heat or the impression of great heat to be noted.

The color phenomenon at Fatima also has an explanation, that of an air lens. Since Stokl makes no mention of a color phenomenon, it is reasonable to conclude that no air lens existed at the site or sites of his observations. Thus three differences in detail between the spin at Fatima and that of Stokl have believable explanations.

---

[54] Annex #16, #39, #61, #65, #72, #89, #103
[55] Annex #16, #61, #65, #103
[56] Annex #16, #39, #61, #72
[57] Annex #89

There remain three apparent differences for which only tentative explanations can be offered—the color of the spinning sun or disk, the delay in the start-up of the spin, and existence or non-existence of a dark disk in front of the sun. I say "apparent differences" because the testimony on these three details at Fatima is inconsistent and/or vague. (See pages 139 and 144.)

Several factors may help to account for these differences between Fatima and Stokl. Weather again is one. Variations in cloud cover, cited above, may have affected one or more of these differences. Also the sun dance at Fatima occurred at noon, while the optical event of Stokl probably occurred much later, perhaps at sunset, when the light must travel through many times as much atmosphere, than it does at noon.[58] Unfortunately we have too little information about this optical illusion to say if these two factors really account for the differences under consideration.

Differences in eye conditions are a possible explanation for two of these differences. We know nothing about the condition of the eyes of Stokl (nor if he wore sunglasses) and we can only assume that the many witnesses at Fatima varied greatly in the condition of their eyes. Thus it is possible that Stokl's eyes were more resistant to the illusion of spinning (or that he wore sunglasses) and thus he required more time of staring before the illusion began. A few of the witnesses at Fatima may also have had eyes that were especially resistant to the optical illusion, or wore dark sun glasses, and thus had an illusion similar to Stokl, while most may have had weaker eyes and no sun glasses, and required less time for the illusion to begin. A longer stare may also have caused the impression of a dark disk in front of the sun, while a shorter may not have. I repeat that we know very little about this optical illusion and can only speculate about how differences in eye conditions affect different viewers.

Another possible explanation for two of these differences concerns the air lens which presumably existed at Fatima and which possibly did not exist at the site of Stokl's spins. I have suggested that the refracted light might have been weak enough to allow the Fatima onlookers to stare at the sun with ease. If so, the cause of the muted sun there was different from the cause at Stokl's site. This difference may have caused a shorter delay for the start-up of the phenomenon at Fatima and may have caused the color of the spinning sun to be light, as opposed to the dark color for Stokl's illusion. Again, we lack needed knowledge about this illusion and about the air lens to make anything more than a speculative guess.

Because both Stokl and Fatima sources report a rapid spin of the sun, because I find believable reasons for the three differences in detail between the spin at Fatima and that of Stokl, have speculative explanations for three other differences, and because I find no good alternate explanation, it seems rather likely that they are the same illusion.

---

[58] *Meteorology Today*, Donald C. Ahrens, West Publishing Co., St. Paul, MN

However, I note again that they may be two different illusions, with some similarities.

Stokl's strong implication that his sun dance may be seen any time that one looks at the muted sun for about one minute is clearly wrong. If it were right, the phenomenon would surely be well known. It seems that some additional atmospheric condition is needed for the sun dance. One possibility is the air lens, which I have already offered as an explanation for the color phenomenon. It may be that looking at the muted sun through this lens, or even looking at the open sun through it, may cause the illusion of the spin and fall of the sun.

I end this chapter by repeating my basic conclusion: 1) the spin was not the normal spin of the sun; 2) I am reluctant to assume that God gave the spin as a vision to some of the crowd but not all; 3) it is mind-boggling to assume that God increased the speed of the sun by a million times to make it visible to the human eye as a rapid spin; 4) many individual hallucinations of a spin of the sun is most unlikely, since this rapid spin was a phenomenon which was unheard of and had never been imagined by most of the crowd; and 5) books on meteorology offer no meteorological explanation. An illusion is thus the only reasonable explanation and an optical illusion is the only natural illusion of which I am aware. I emphasize that the illusion which occurred at Fatima on October 13, 1917, was unknown at the time and I concede that it may never have occurred since then, despite the many pilgrims who have reported sun dances since October 1917.

There remains the possibility, which I am reluctant to accept, that God merely created this illusion in the minds of the vast majority of the people at Fatima, but not in all.

CHAPTER IX

THE FALL OF THE SUN

The "fall" of the sun toward the earth on October 13 was not noted anywhere on the planet except at Fatima. A real fall would have caused disastrous consequences. While in theory God could cause the sun to fall, to be noted only at Fatima, and to cause no unusual effects on the planet, such a fantastic miracle has not been suggested by any supporter of Fatima. The "fall" was clearly an apparent fall, not a real one.

However, a very large number of people, probably a large majority, had the impression that the sun was detached from the sky and headed toward the earth. Of the seventy-one sources which give significant data on the sun dance, thirty-four make some mention of the fall.[1] Three more make statements which suggest it.[2] Since twenty others were very brief—only a line or two[3]—it can be said that a large majority of the sources which reported on the sun dance in some detail included a mention of the fall of the sun. Nonetheless, the apparent fall of the sun was reported somewhat less frequently than its rapid spinning and probably was noted by fewer people.

Color of the Falling Sun. Relatively few of the sources which tell of the falling sun reveal its color. In view of the evidence, previously

---

[1] Annex #16, #19, #22, #23, #25, #27, #28, #34, #39, #49, #51, #52, #55, #57, #58, #59, #61C, #61D, #61G, #61H, #61L, #61M, #62, #69, #71, #72, #78, #86, #90, #93, #95, #96, #101, #102, #103

[2] Annex #18, #77, #107

[3] Annex #17, #20, #29, #30, #32, #42, #43, #54, #56, #57, #61E, #61F, #61I, #61J, #61K, #63, #74, #97, #104, #108

cited, that the apparent fall of the sun was accompanied by a rapid spin (see page 145), we might presume that the colors reported to be seen on the falling sun were the same as those seen on the spinning sun. If so, the evidence advanced earlier for the color of the spinning sun would seem to say that most people saw the falling sun as light in color—silvery, white, or pearly. However, it seems wise to examine the evidence for the falling sun.

Dark Color. Only two of the four references to a dark color on the spinning sun, indicate also that it was falling,[4] and no other sources report the falling sun as dark colored. One other source mentions a snow white, then a dark-gray sun, without a clear indication that either color was seen during the fall or spin of the sun.

Specifically, it says: "I saw the sun descend ... causing uncomfortable heat. I saw it turn rapidly, like a little firewheel. ... There are those who say they saw the sun with various colors. I saw snow white, then dark gray."[5] We might thus say that we have two clear references to a dark color on the falling sun and one possible reference.

Silvery Color. Four sources say that the falling sun was silvery or white,[6] and two others suggest it.[7] Two others mention the fall of the sun immediately before or after they describe it as silvery, which may indicate that they saw it as silvery.[8] Another reports that a luminous, silvery disk detached itself from the sun and seemed to fall toward the earth.[9] Another called the falling sun a luminous disk, at which one could stare, while two more said it had a very intense shine.[10] One says that the falling sun was muted, presumably silvery, white, or light yellow.[11]

Rainbow Colors. Five other sources suggest that the color of the falling sun was one of the rainbow colors by reporting the fall of the sun (or the spin and fall) immediately before or after reporting the

---

[4] Annex #16, #61, #65, #103
[5] Annex #19
[6] Annex #59, #93, #95, #101
[7] Annex #23, #51
[8] Annex #25, #69
[9] Annex #39
[10] Annex #72, #71, #93
[11] Annex #96

rainbow color.[12] None, however, clearly indicates that the color of the falling sun was a rainbow color.

Once again, as with the spinning sun, the available evidence indicates that most of those who noted the apparent fall of the sun had the impression that the sun was light-colored—silvery or white and perhaps shiny. Here again it would seem much more likely that the many who failed to tell the color of the falling sun saw it as silvery or white, since they were less likely to report a continuation of the silvery or white color of the muted sun than to report a change to a dark or rainbow color.

Several Occurrences. For this phenomenon also most sources tell of only one occurrence. However, five sources tell of two, three or several occurrences.[13] A sixth suggests three,[14] and another five suggest several occurrences.[15] This is, of course, only an implied contradiction, since no sources deny that two or three occurrences were noted. The explanations offered for this implied contradiction are the same as those offered for the several occurrences of the spinning sun (see pages 142-144). Briefly, many reports were short and apparently did not give full details; variations in cloud cover may have caused some onlookers to see only one longer fall, while others may have seen two or three shorter ones; and some spectators may have looked away for a while, discussed the event with neighbors and then looked back at the sun, gaining the impression that the spin and fall occurred a second or third time.

Crowd Terror. Further evidence that a great many people seemed to note the fall of the sun are the many reports of crowd terror.[16] A number specified that the crowd feared the end of the world[17] or that they would be burned up[18] or that they prayed for mercy and forgiveness.[19] Although most reports do not mention crowd terror, and two

---

[12] Annex #25, #49, #61G, #61L, #86
[13] Annex #39, #71, #72, #95, #69
[14] Annex #59
[15] Annex #18, #61G, #61H, #77, #90
[16] Annex #16, #22, #23, #27, #49, #59, #61, #71, #90, #101, #102
[17] Annex #22, #101, #102
[18] Annex #71
[19] Annex #16, #23, #49, #59

witnesses state that they personally felt no fear[20] there is little doubt that a large share of the crowd was terrified. This is evident from the statements, such as: "Everyone imagined it was the end of the world," and "Many people, thinking that the sun would hurl itself upon the earth, broke out in loud cries," and "The crowd, kneeling in the mud, yelled in distress."[21] Probably the sources which did not mention crowd terror felt that it was not important enough to mention.

Description of the Fall. Descriptions of the fall vary considerably in details, as is to be expected. Thirteen sources recognized that the sun did not actually fall, by saying that it seemed to fall or created that impression.[22] Most sources give few details. They merely say that the sun fell or lowered itself or descended or approached the earth or neared it. A number said that it seemed to loosen or detach itself from the sky or left its orbit.[23] Only one source indicated the speed of the fall, saying it was brusque and rapid.[24] A second said that the sun lowered "visibly," a statement that hints that the fall was neither long nor rapid.[25]

Few tell us if the fall was direct. A much later report noted that the sun descended in a zig-zag at Alburitel, near Fatima, on October 13.[26] A second-hand source said the sun fell in a curved line, with small circles imposed on it.[27] And the above mentioned source, which describes the fall as "brusque" seems to hint at a jagged fall, rather than a direct one. All the rest merely note that the sun fell, or seemed to fall, creating the impression that the sun fell in a straight line.

A number of sources indicate in one way or another that the sun seemed to approach close to the earth. One said it seemed to be some 500 or 600 meters away.[28] Another told that it approached to the height of the clouds.[29] Others said that it seemed to near the earth

---

[20] Annex #90, #92
[21] Annex #22, #27, #59
[22] Annex #16, #22, #23, #25, #34, #51, #52, #55, #58, #59, #72, #77, #95
[23] Annex #16, #27, #34, #52, #72, #90, #95
[24] Annex #23
[25] Annex #72
[26] Annex #101
[27] Annex #39
[28] Annex #71
[29] Annex #18

or come close, that they feared it would burn the earth, or that it menaced the earth.[30] A news reporter, clearly biased against Fatima, stated that some witnesses said that the sun descended to the horizon, which would not seem frightening, but he also said that many people thought that the sun would hurl itself upon the earth.[31] Moreover, the impression of a near approach is clearly indicated by the many sources which expressed terror. Jose Garrett gives his vivid impression: "The sun, keeping its speed of rotation ... advanced terrifying (or blood-red) upon the earth, threatening to crush it with its huge, fiery weight."[32]

Duration of the Fall. Most sources give no clue to how long the sun seemed to fall. None say or imply that it was a long time. A few suggest that it was fairly short. Jose Garrett, cited above, suggests that it lasted only a short time—perhaps ten or twenty seconds—"They were seconds of terrifying impression." A girl reported the fall and the crowd terror, her own stunned reaction, and then said: "it all passes in a moment." A third source said the uproar was greater at "the moment the sun descended."[33]

One very late source says that the sun stayed over the Alburitel church tower for two or three minutes.[34] No other sources say whether or not the sun seemed to stay at its low position for any length of time before returning to its usual position, and thus we have no worthwhile information on this point.

Return of the Sun. Strangely, only a few sources tell us that the sun, after its fall, climbed back up in the sky. Five sources say it in various terms (it ascended and descended, it resumed its place, it turned again to the sun, it rose with a fiery cloud).[35] Two sources say the fall and spin stopped and started again, without saying that the sun ascended, or was covered with clouds, or anything else.[36] In view of the weather, one might suspect that in some parts of the Cova clouds

---

[30] Annex #23, #59, #28, #71, #90, #101
[31] Annex #27
[32] Annex #90
[33] Annex #90, #16, #49
[34] Annex #102
[35] Annex #25, #69, #71, #95, #101
[36] Annex #39, #72

covered the sun, ending the phenomenon of the fall and spin of the sun, rather than an apparent return to its normal position. However, only two sources seem to say that the phenomenon ended in this way.[37]

Falling Disk. I noted earlier (see page 145) that a few sources said that the spinning object was not the sun, but a disk that superimposed itself on the sun. These same sources say that the disk seemed to detach itself from the sun and fall toward the earth. All the rest indicate, or seem to indicate, that the falling object was the sun. A possible explanation for this variation is that the spin and fall were a single optical illusion, which varies depending on such factors as the meteorological conditions, the health of each person's eyes, and the use or non-use of sunglasses.

Fall and Heat. Five sources which report the fall of the sun also indicate that the fall was accompanied by a great (uncomfortable, suffocating, strong, exceptional, intense) heat.[38] Two others also mention heat, without calling it great.[39] Three others suggest great heat by saying they feared the earth would be burned up.[40] Another said the sun spun rapidly, put out puffs of heat like one gets upon opening an oven, and seemed to near the earth; in this case the tie-in of the heat with the fall is not fully clear.[41] The many other sources which refer to the fall of the sun do not mention heat. Thus, despite these strong statements on great heat, there remains the possibility that the heat was not unusual, but only seemed very great because of the contrast with the very chilly weather which immediately preceded the sun dance, or because of the great heat expected from the falling sun. See also the section "Extraordinary Heat," pages 169-172.

Rising Clouds. There exists the possibility that the impression of a falling sun was an optical illusion caused by a rapid rising of clouds around the sun. Technically, this illusion is called induced movement. A common example of this illusion is the impression that one's train is moving when in fact it is standing still in a railroad station and the train next to it is moving. Two sources speak of rising clouds

---

[37] Annex #16, #77
[38] Annex #19, #22, #34, #52, #93
[39] Annex #61B, #61D
[40] Annex #28, #71, #90
[41] Annex #23

during the sun dance. One notes the impression of a falling sun and then says: "But it all passes in a moment. The sun is again covered by clouds, a cloud which seems to rise." The other source, which I previously noted was somewhat unreliable, said: "...a dark cloud formed around the sun .... and seemed to descend on us. Then .... the cloud, which now seemed a fire, rose again with the sun."[42] No other source speaks of rising clouds, which weakens this possible explanation for the falling sun.

Increased Size. Another explanation for the apparently falling sun is that a gradual increase in the brightness of the muted sun caused an apparent increase in its size. An anti-Fatima book, reporting on a 1956 sun dance said: "When the thickness of the clouds lessened, the sun shone more brightly, creating the impression that it increased in size, as would be said of an object that neared the earth." (See chapter XI.) However, only two Fatima sources mention that the sun's size seemed to increase. One said it: "seemed to swell and want to head for or talk to the earth." The other, a very late one, said: "the sun detached itself from its orbit, advancing toward the earth and assuming gradually greater proportions."[43] This explanation, also, is weakened by the fact that the increase in brightness would have to be steady for many seconds, in order to cause the fright noted at Fatima. It does not seem to be a very likely explanation.

Another explanation for an increase in size of the sun is the phenomenon called towering, which magnifies the image being seen, and is caused by an air lens in cases "where the temperature gradient and the temperature increase together."[44] I lack the technical knowledge to make any conclusion about the likelihood of this explanation.

Temperature Inversion. It has been suggested that a temperature inversion may explain the impression that the sun was falling. Unfortunately, we know nothing of the air temperature above ground level at Fatima on October 13, 1917. However, it is possible that a layer of warm air existed beneath a layer of cold air and that the warm air

---

[42] Annex #16, #25

[43] Annex #77, #103

[44] *Atmospheric Phenomena*, David K. Lynch, Freeman & Co., (date unknown), page 87, gives articles from Scientific American. The given article was by Alistair Fraser and Wm. H. March, both at Penn State University.

suddenly found a break in the cold air layer and rose rapidly upward. If so, clouds which existed in the layer of warm air may also have risen, and this may have caused the optical illusion of induced movement of the sun, an illusion discussed briefly above.

Other Weather Conditions. Perhaps there are other weather conditions which could have caused the apparent fall of the sun, as well as the unusual heat which is said to have accompanied it. I am aware of none, but wonder if wind shear might be such a condition. I understand it to be a strong wind which blows perpendicular to the ground, rather than parallel to it, as most winds. Perhaps such a wind existed at Fatima on October 13 and caused clouds around the sun to move rapidly upward, creating the illusion of a fall of the sun (induced movement).

Stokl's Illusion. Finally, it is possible that the optical illusion noted by Professor Stokl, the illusion of a rapidly spinning sun caused by staring at a muted sun, may also cause the illusion that the sun is falling, in some cases. The fact that they were often reported together supports this conclusion. Stokl did not mention any fall of the sun in connection with this illusion. However, I noted previously that the spin at Fatima varied considerably from the spin reported by Stokl, and yet seemed quite likely to be the same illusion. If so, it may well be that the illusion of a spinning sun is accompanied, in some cases, by an illusion of a falling sun. It may also be that for some people, with stronger or weaker eyes, the illusion of the spin of the sun is not followed by the illusion of the falling sun. (Again I note that little is known about this illusion.)

Summary and Conclusions. There is little doubt that most of the people at Fatima on October 13 had the impression that the sun was falling. The number of sources which mention it is impressive, and those which fail to mention it are mostly short. However, the somewhat fewer number of sources which mention the fall seems to indicate that not all those who noted the spin of the sun also had the impression that it was falling. The fall was clearly an apparent one rather than a real one. Details on the fall are weak. It may have been fairly short, only seconds instead of minutes. But it lasted long enough to cause great terror among the crowd.

Several explanations for the fall of the sun can be made, all quite tentative. One is that a change in cloud cover caused the sun to brighten and appear to grow in size. A second possibility is the phenomenon called towering. Another is that a temperature inversion caused the clouds around the sun to rise quite rapidly. All might create the illusion of a falling sun. Or the illusion of a falling sun may accompany the illusion of a spinning sun, caused by staring at the muted sun. While none of these explanations seems strong, the falling sun was most probably an optical illusion and one of these four explanations seems likely to be correct. I show in chapter XII why the last explanation is the most likely.

CHAPTER X

OTHER PHENOMENA

The Dance Itself. Throughout this book I use "sun dance" to mean all of the phenomena which were reported for October 13 at Fatima, except the column of smoke. However, the term was also used in a much more limited sense to describe an apparent movement of the sun reported by as many as twenty-two sources.[1] The movement they refer to was a lateral movement in the sky, a movement different from the apparent fall of the sun and also different from the normal trajectory of the sun, which is too slow to be noticeable by the human eye. This apparent movement was given various terms or descriptions—dance, turn-about, brusque movements, shake, tremble, wander, zig-zag. Of these twenty-two sources, ten are vague and it is not certain that the terms they use refer to the lateral movement.[2] For example, the term "dance" is sometimes vague and may refer to the lateral movement or to all the phenomena of the sun dance. There are thus only twelve firm sources. Many of the twelve are short and provide little information on the lateral movements. However, six sources provide more details.

One of these is Avelino de Almeida, editor of *O Seculo*, probably the most influential and widely read newspaper in Portugal. He was at Fatima on October 13 and describes the "dance" thusly: "the sun trembled, it made brusque, unprecedented movements, outside

---

[1] Annex #20, #22, #23, #25, #28 and 68, #29, #42, #46, #49 #50, #51, #57, #59, #61B, #61K, #62, #68 A, #70, #77, #78, #92, #101, #102, #108
[2] Annex #20, #22, #23, #29, #42. #51, #57, #62, #77, #108

all cosmic laws, the sun 'danced,' according to the typical expression of the peasants. .... People then began to ask each other ... what they had seen. The majority declare that they had seen the trembling and dancing of the sun." Later, in a weekly magazine published by *O Seculo*, Almeida wrote: "At the hour forecast in advance the rain stopped, ... and the sun ... appeared at full zenith and began to dance in a violent and compulsive movement that a great number of persons imagined to be a serpentine dance, so beautiful and glowing (were) the colors ... (Gist– of the sun)."[3]

On October 18 the newspaper *A Lucta* reported that the sun "was shaken by irregular, distorted movements, it trembled, it trembled and remained quiet." On October 31 a lawyer said, in a letter, that the sun and the clouds which surrounded it trembled hesitatingly, as if to obey a superior will.[4]

A fourth source is Ana Maria da Camara, who describes this phenomenon in a statement of November 3 and in a letter of October 19. On November 3, she wrote: "The uproar is immense at the moment the sun descends, a movement which I see distinctly, as well as a movement to the right or left, or vice versa, but at the usual altitude of the sun. These two latter movements were very much less noticeable than the descending movement and I cannot be sure that they followed immediately after it."[5]

A fifth source, Father Curado, described the colored flames, then the spin and fall of the sun, a repetition of the flames and the spin, and then says: "Even a third time the sun, which seemed to have brusque, shaky movements, was wrapped in blue flames ... followed by a loss of light and rotary movement of the sun. The phenomenon was over."[6]

A sixth source says: "the rays of the sun were tinged, successively blue, yellow and purple (and) at the same time some trembling and unknown movements were seen on that star (the sun)."[7]

---

[3]
[4] Annex #46, #70
[5] Annex #73, #49
[6] Annex #59
[7] Annex #68A

It may be noted that none of these sources indicate that the lateral movement occurred during the spin or fall of the sun, but three associate it with the color phenomenon.

Dance Is Not Spin. One might wonder if the words "dance," "shake," "tremble," etc. refer to the apparent spin of the sun, rather than to a lateral or zig-zag movement. However, the reference in the fourth source, above, to movements to the right or left make it clear that she was not referring to the rapid spin of the sun. Other terms used to describe this movement—tremble, shake, wander—also are descriptive of a back-and-forth or a zig-zag movement, but not of a rapid spin.[8] Moreover, several sources indicated that the sun shook <u>and</u> spun, or it rotated <u>and</u> wandered, or it danced <u>and</u> turned, seemingly indicating that the spin was a separate movement from the shaking, wandering, or dancing.[9] It thus can be said firmly that the sun seemed to many onlookers to spin <u>and</u> to move about in the sky. This movement was surely an apparent movement and not an actual movement, since even a tiny change in the sun's trajectory would have been noted and reported by many observatories.

Scope and Length of "Dance." No sources tell us whether the "dance" movements were long or short, nor how long they lasted. However the terms "tremble" and "shake," which were used six times, suggest only short movements in one direction and another, rather than long ones.[10] Only the term "wander," used only once, suggests a fairly long movement in one direction and another.[11] And, as noted previously, da Camara called the movement "very much less pronounced." One source said the sun "trembled hesitatingly," which scarcely would have been said of long movements in one direction or another. There is one further suggestion that these apparent movements were neither long in distance nor in time. Only twenty-two (or less) of the seventy-one sources which report on the sun phenomena tell of the apparent movement of the sun. Surely, if the sun seemed to make long movements in one direction and another, or if the movements lasted for a considerable length of time, they would have seemed more spectacular

---

[8] Annex #28, #42, #50, #61K, #70
[9] Annex #42, #50, #62
[10] Annex #28, #42, #46, #61K, #70, #78
[11] Annex #50

and would have been reported by more witnesses. It thus seems likely that the "dancing" movements were short and brief, and that they were less spectacular than the color phenomena, the spin of the sun, and the fall of the sun.

Optical Illusion. A firm natural explanation for this phenomenon is an optical illusion similar to that which is often noted on moonlit nights with small clouds over and around the moon. When these clouds move quite rapidly, it often seems that the moon, rather than the clouds, is moving back and forth a short distance. This is another example of the illusion of induced movement.[12] This kind of optical illusion may also be seen for the sun, but much less frequently. It cannot be observed with a bright sun and small clouds, since we are unable to stare at the bright sun as we stare at the bright moon.

However, if a fairly high, but broad cloud mutes the sun, and if lower, small clouds move fairly rapidly around and across the muted image of the sun, they may create the illusion that this image is moving in the sky. While in theory such a juxtaposition of upper and lower clouds and the image of the sun might last for a considerable time, it seems unlikely that clouds moving fairly rapidly would remain for very long in the necessary location.

Further, it is not unlikely that unfavorable movement of clouds caused this illusion at Fatima to cease and then favorable movement caused it to reoccur. Such breaks and repetitions might well have caused the viewers to describe the movements as a "dance." Supporting this explanation for the lateral movement at Fatima is the letter which says that the sun, and the clouds which surrounded it, trembled.

I should further add that my own experience indicates that this illusion may not have been noted by all who looked at the sun at this time. On one occasion on a cloudy night a friend said to me: "Look! The moon seems to be moving in the sky." I looked and could only see clouds moving around the moon. But I continued to look and after a short time I also had the same impression of movement of the moon.

The foregoing discussion offers a firm explanation that the "dancing" movement noted at Fatima on October 13 was an optical illusion of brief duration, with the shaded sun appearing to move a rather

---

[12] *Encyclopedia Americana*, Deluxe Library Edition, 1999, Vol 14, p 784

short distance back and forth. If so, it may not have been seen by all the crowd. Some may have looked and not seen the illusion, as I suggest above, and others may have stopped looking at this time to talk of the phenomena with their neighbors or to watch the crowd. And such a phenomenon would probably have seemed less spectacular than the other major phenomena—the colors, the spin of the sun and its fall, and thus be reported by fewer people. These three factors would explain why the "dancing" movement was reported only by a minority of the seventy-one reports on the phenomena of that day.

I scarcely need to note that that it would require a spectacular change in the laws of nature for the sun to dance back and forth in the sky and be visible as a dancing movement to the crowd at Fatima. The sun is 193 million miles from us. To be visible to us as changes in its course would certainly require it to travel at enormous speeds. And to reverse its course several or many times would surely cause enormous damage to the sun, unless God worked a spectacular miracle to avoid the damage. And for such a "dance" to be noted only at Fatima would require another spectacular change in the laws of nature.

EXTRAORDINARY HEAT

The last of the Fatima phenomena, and probably the least important, is extraordinary heat, which was said by some sources to have occurred during the sun dance. As noted earlier, five sources indicated great heat at the time of the fall of the sun, and two others reported heat, but not necessarily unusual heat (see page 160). One source implies that the heat came at the start of the dance; she said that the heat was like entering a green house.[13] The rest of the seventy-one sources on the sun dance make no mention of heat, although none suggest or imply that the cold continued or that the sun's heat was merely normal.

One might suspect that an impression of great heat was made on the cold and wet crowd by the sudden appearance of the bright sun, which was reported by nine sources (see page 97). One of these

---

[13] Annex #95

nine indicated (and another suggested) that it stayed bright for a few minutes,[14] probably long enough to create the impression of great heat on the shivering crowd. However, none of the nine sources associates great heat with the bright sun; and, as noted above, others associate it with the fall of the sun, when it was no longer bright. They clearly imply that the great heat was unusual. There remains the possibility that many in the crowd merely assumed that the falling sun would bring great heat.

We might further speculate that the failure of most sources to mention the unusual heat would seem to indicate that no such heat was noticed by them. But since most of these sources were brief, and the other phenomena—especially the color, and the spin and the fall of the sun—were surely viewed as more spectacular, the failure of these sources to mention the heat does not seem to be very significant. Thus the possibility that the apparent fall of the sun was accompanied by an unusual increase in heat is fairly strong but is not at all firm.

Drying Clothes. A phenomenon associated with the unusual heat by some authors is the unusually fast drying of the wet clothes of the crowd. Two men reported that during the sun dance their clothes dried exceptionally fast, as one might expect from a period of intense heat. One man said: "… although moments before I was soaking wet, I noticed that I was now dry. Is this a miracle? I do not think so. What I believe is that the same (thing) happened to others."[15] Another man, clearly reporting only what he had heard, said: "the sun, they say, came out … with a great heat, which in a few minutes dried the soaking clothes (of the people)."[16]

Four women indicated that their clothes did not dry quickly. One said: "(After the sun dance) we head toward Fatima … When we arrive our clothes are still half dry." Another woman said: "I had a big shaggy coat. … Since this coat served as a sponge, (the rain) passed through my skin and my clothing … from head to toe. In the car (after the sun dance) I took off my coat so my body and clothes would dry." A third said that when they got back to Ourem they were lent clothes to

---

[14] Annex #49, #90
[15] Annex #47
[16] Annex #108

replace the wet ones.[17] And the fourth woman said: "I returned home covered with mud and water, but happy."[18]

It might be argued that the failure of almost all the 1917 sources to tell of any unusually rapid drying is a strong indication that no such phenomenon occurred, or that it occurred to only a small portion of the crowd. However, surely most of the crowd talked excitedly with their friends and neighbors for many minutes after the sun dance, comparing impressions. Thus they may have failed to notice the condition of their clothes for ten or fifteen minutes. By this time, with the sun shining brightly, the complete dryness of their clothing, if it occurred, may not have seemed highly unusual and worthy of comment.

All of this suggests that the supposed drying of clothing is not worthy of further comment. However, this phenomenon is reported in major books on Fatima and thus should not be ignored.[19] These authors perhaps had testimony from people who were at Fatima on October 13, but probably relied chiefly on a statement in a 1937 book of Jose Marques da Cruz. He states: "After the miracle ((although it seems unbelievable)) all felt well, with dry clothes, which caused them greatly to admire (it). Dozens and dozens of people, whom we have known since childhood, of absolute probity, and who were there, assured us of this with maximum frankness and sincerity."[20]

This statement implies that da Cruz made a major effort to study this question, and that all whom he interviewed said that their clothes dried unusually quickly. However, he does not state this. Nor does his phrase "after the miracle" indicate that the drying was noted immediately after the sun dance, although the statement that the drying was admired implies this. Further, da Cruz' statement appears as a footnote in a short poetic work which praises the Virgin of Fatima and makes no pretensions of being scholarly or unbiased. Nonetheless, his strong statement lends considerable support to the claim that clothes dried abnormally fast at Fatima on October 13.

---

[17] Annex #16, #33, #95
[18] Annex #104
[19] De Marchi, p 141; *Fatima 1917-1968*, p 133; *Fatima: The Great Sign*, p 52
[20] *A Virgem de Fatima*, Comp. Melhoramentos, Sao Paolo, 1937, p 29, footnote 1

Two other late sources also tell of very rapid drying of their clothes. In 1967, Dr. Pereira Gens said: "(Gist– The sun danced, stopped, and danced again.) I now feel my suit almost dry, while it was soaked only a few minutes ago." Gens was chief of Service of the Sick at Fatima in 1967.[21] In a TV interview in 1960, Dominic Reis described the sun dance and said: "As soon as the sun went back in the right place, the wind started to blow real hard, but the trees didn't move at all. The wind was blow, blow and in a few minutes the ground was dry as this floor here. Even our clothes had dried." Only one other source, also a late one, says that the ground was dry.[22]

Although this late testimony, especially from pro-Fatima sources, is of doubtful value, it cannot be entirely ignored. But the four 1917 sources which indicate that their clothes did not dry quickly are strong evidence that the clothes of some of the crowd did not dry quickly.

A simple explanation is available for the apparent contradiction on this phenomenon—some types of clothing dry much quicker than others, coarse wool dries faster than fine cotton, and a heavy, shaggy cotton coat dries slower than a light wool sweater. Most of the men at Fatima on October 13 undoubtedly wore wool suits, appropriate for a festive occasion in mid-October 1917, in a mountainous region. (As noted above, men reported the rapid drying.) Many of the women surely wore heavy cotton dresses. (And it was women who reported the slow drying.) Additionally, many women knelt in the mud and were mud-covered to their knees, as stated by one source.[23] Such mud-covered clothing would surely dry slower than clean clothes. It thus is quite likely, recalling the fairly strong possibility of exceptional heat at this time, that those wearing wool noted that their clothes dried very quickly, while those in heavy cotton, and with muddy skirts, did not.

Summing up, it seems probable that the clothes of some of the crowd at Fatima on October 13 dried very rapidly, presumably the woolen ones. But it is impossible, from the available evidence, to say whether or not the drying was unusually fast. As a relatively minor feature, it would have received less attention from the crowd at Fatima,

---

[21] *Fatima 1917-1968*, pp 357-358
[22] *Meet the Witnesses*, p 32; *Fatima: The Great Sign*, p 52
[23] Annex #58

in their reporting on the events of the day, and from those who later studied the Fatima phenomena.

Duration of the Sun Dance. It is important to determine the length of the sun dance for several reasons. A short period would increase the likelihood that the rapid drying of clothes was unusual and weaken the likelihood of two or three repetitions of the phenomena; a long period would make the sun dance more sensational.

For analyzing the rapid drying of clothes it would seem wise also to note the length of time between the stopping of the rain and the start of the sun dance. Several sources indicate that this time was in the order of ten minutes. One places the end of the rain at about 2:00 p.m. on his car clock and the start of the sun dance at about 2:10.[24] Another source says the rain stopped a bit before 2:00 and still another has the sun dance begin at 2:10.[25] Two sources indicate that a few minutes passed during this period.[26] Another says that the sun dance began "moments later."[27] But one woman noted that in this period one and one half rosaries (or twenty to thirty minutes) were said, but previously this same woman had suggested a much shorter period.[28] In view of all the other testimony the implication of twenty or thirty minutes can be ignored. Ten minutes seems quite likely.

None of the available sources say that they timed the sun dance on their watch or clock. Many estimates of its length were made. Three sources said ten minutes.[29] Another said eight or ten minutes.[30] One heard talk of four minutes, but said it seemed much longer to him.[31] Yet another said five minutes, at most.[32] Two others said fifteen and twenty minutes.[33] A few used vague terms, all suggesting a short period—short moments, some minutes, not seconds but perhaps

[24] Annex #44
[25] Annex #47, #72
[26] Annex #49, #90
[27] Annex #72
[28] Annex #73, #49
[29] Annex #22, #23, #101
[30] Annex #89
[31] Annex #49
[32] Annex #96
[33] Annex #25, #47

minutes, few minutes.[34] With only two of the thirteen sources suggesting more than ten minutes, it is most likely that the sun dance lasted no more than ten minutes, while four or five minutes also seems possible. It thus can be said with reasonable confidence that the time from the stopping of the rain until the end of the sun dance was fifteen to twenty minutes, a short time to dry clothes.

REMOTE SIGHTINGS

A sun dance on October 13 was reported to be seen not only in the Cova da Iria, but also in towns nearby and in more remote locations. Five sources of 1917 indicate this. A letter of October 14 says: "Do you know that here in Granja (100 miles from Fatima) there were persons who saw the rotation of the sun and a rose-colored cloud passing in front of the sun?"[35] In a letter of October 16, a lady said that she and another lady (or perhaps two) saw a sun dance after they had traveled "some kilometers" on their way back to Lisbon from Fatima on October 13.[36] (See page 182 for more details.) A long letter of October 27 tells of the reactions of some persons to the sun dance, and then adds: "The signs were seen in the surroundings of Leiria (sixteen miles NW of Fatima), Batalha (about fifteen miles NW of Fatima), etc. In Leiria everybody believes."[37] In a newspaper article of November 8, Father Jose Ferreira de Lacerda comments on the sun dance and then says: "How is hallucination possible in persons of such diverse categories and even more in persons who, not having gone to Fatima, witnessed the event at Leiria at that hour?"[38] And a short letter of November 24 to the seer Lucia from a witness to the sun dance says: "Here in Torres Novas (twenty miles SE of Fatima) at the same hour something was also seen in the sun, but by the description that they make to me it cannot compare."[39]

---

[34] Annex #30, #69, #92, #93
[35] Annex I #24A
[36] Annex I #33
[37] Annex I #64
[38] Annex II #14A
[39] Annex I #87

An article in an anti-Fatima journal on May 30, 1918, is very strong. It says: "It is uncontestable that the sun suffered some kind of alteration ((facts cannot be questioned)). It was observed not only at Fatima but also at many points of the country."[40] The phrase in parentheses was given in the article.

A number of later sources also tell of sightings of a sun dance on October 13 in remote locations. The most important and best known is a statement of a missionary priest, published in 1931, which describes in detail the spin and fall of the sun and the color phenomenon. He says that in 1917 he was a nine-year-old student in Alburitel, a village about eight miles from Fatima, and that the sun dance was witnessed by him and an unspecified number of other people of Alburitel at about noon on October 13.[41] His brother, who also became a priest, at an even later date said that he saw the sun dance and was so frightened that he hid under his mother's skirt.[42] And the daughter of the Alburitel teacher, who became a nun, reported much later that some twenty townspeople saw the event and she gave details on the event at Alburitel which she had heard later. She was a four-year-old in 1917 and apparently did not see the dance herself.[43]

A vague statement on remote sightings was made in 1930 by the local bishop, in his official approval of devotion to Fatima: "The phenomenon … was witnessed … even by individuals at kilometers of distance, which destroys any explanation of collective illusion."[44]

Two remote sightings were reported by John Haffert in his 1961 book on Fatima. They were based on his interviews with witnesses, which apparently took place in 1960. One was Albano Barros, a building contractor in New Jersey, but who was twelve years old in 1917, and who said he saw the sun fall in Minde, about eight kilometers from Fatima. The other was Guilhermina Lopes da Silva, residing in Leiria, and who was in Leiria in 1917. She said that she and two men

---

[40] Annex I #109
[41] Annex I #101; Jaki, p 209
[42] *Fatima: as Suas Provas, os Seus Problemas*, pp 228, 231; *Fatima Joie Intime*, p 96; *The Sun Danced at Fatima*, J. A. Pelletier, p 163
[43] Brochado, pp 57-59. The distances from Fatima to Granja, Torres Novas, and Leiria are found on page 60 of Brochado. The estimated distance from Batalha to Fatima is mine, derived from a map of the area. *Fatima Joie Intime*, p 5
[44] Nov Doc, pp 96, 97

working for her saw a great red flash in the sky at noon.[45] She clearly meant the Fatima sun dance.

Finally, I can cite the testimony that I obtained on one of my visits to Fatima (in 1998 or 1999) from Amelia (Pereira?), the lady in charge of the kitchen at the Fatima hotel of the Blue Army. She said that her mother saw the sun dance in her home town of Vale Tacao and that it was also seen in other towns near Fatima—Atouguia, Sao Memede, and Santa Catarina.

A questionable claim of having seen the sun dance at S. Pedro de Muel (twenty-four miles east of Fatima, on the Atlantic) was made in 1935 by the poet Afonso Lopes Vieira to fellow poet Marques da Cruz. It is questionable because Vieira wrote letters to the bishop some time after the Fatima sun dance and a letter in 1928 to Father Formigao, the priest in charge of the Fatima Inquiry Board, in all of which he strangely failed to mention that he had seen the sun dance, a matter of much concern to the bishop and to Father Formigao.[46] However, in about 1970, his widow told John Haffert that she had seen the sun dance with her husband.[47]

Four of these indicate that the remote sun dance occurred at the time of the Fatima sun dance, but they probably meant at about the same time.[48] They were not at Fatima for the sun dance, and they probably had heard only the approximate time of the Fatima sun dance. Also, they may not have noted the precise time of the sun dance which they saw. All but one of the remaining sources simply do not tell us the hour when their sun dance occurred.

This one is the lady who reported that she saw the sun dance after she had left the Cova and had traveled "some kilometers" on her way back to the Lisbon area.[49] In view of the enormous crowd which exited on foot and in carriages, and which surely clogged the only available road, a double lane, for a mile or more, this later sighting of a sun dance surely was noted at least fifteen minutes after the sun dance at the Cova and may have been seen much later. This suggests that

---

[45] *Meet the Witnesses*, pp 66, 67
[46] Jaki, pp 202, 203
[47] *Meet the Witnesses*, p 65
[48] Annex I #87, #101; Annex II #14A; *Meet the Witnesses*, pp 66, 67
[49] Annex I #33

the sun dance noted at many places near Fatima and "at many points in the country" did not occur at the same time as at Fatima. One might suspect that the movement of clouds or other meteorological phenomena caused the sun dance to move from place to place. It is even possible that this movement was slow and reached the Lisbon area (ninety miles away) early on the fourteenth, where it perhaps was seen by the noted Catholic, Pinto Coelho, who lived near Lisbon. In the major newspaper *A Ordem*, he reported seeing the sun dance at Fatima on the thirteenth and again on the fourteenth at an unspecified place and hour. (See page 182 for more details.)

Summary and Conclusions. Admittedly, much of this testimony on remote sun dances is vague or second-hand, and most of the witnesses were strong supporters of Fatima. However, the number of witnesses is quite large, which in itself suggests that on October 13 some people in the remote locations saw phenomena similar to that which was seen at Fatima. This testimony on remote sightings weakens the already weak claim of mass hallucination and also weakens the doubts about the reality of the sun dance which were raised by the testimony of two or three "non-see-ers." It thus must be studied in some detail.

Doubters might say that these people invented or imagined these sun dances after hearing what happened at Fatima. But this could not be said for the unfriendly source which reported "alterations" in the sun in many points of the country. It was clearly conceding something which it would have preferred to deny. In using the term "alterations" rather than "phenomena," the journal was clearly attempting to minimize the sun dance.

Another important source is the lady who reported seeing a sun dance after traveling "some kilometers" from Fatima after the sun dance there. From the text of her letter it seems that she was a firm Catholic and thus unlikely to be deliberately lying. Moreover, in this same letter, this same lady had said that at Fatima she had not seen the sun dance, as others around her did. It seems most unlikely that she would have invented a story about a later sun dance, simply because she had not seen the one at Fatima. An easier and more likely prevarication would have been to say simply that she saw the sun dance at Fatima with the others. Hallucination is also unlikely, since two persons, and perhaps three, saw this remote sun dance.

A third important source is the priest who reported seeing a sun dance at about noon in Alburitel. It seems unlikely that a man of God, who had given up the joys of sex and was serving as a missionary in Asia would be lying. Since his account was not published until 1931, some details might be wrong, but he could scarcely have simply imagined the entire sun dance. Furthermore, he added that a number of his fellow townsmen also saw the sun dance. Therefore, he would have risked exposure by his townsmen, if his account were an invention. Hallucination is eliminated, if a number of people saw the sun dance at Alburitel.

It seems unnecessary to study all the other sources of reports of remote sun dances, except to reiterate that it seems unlikely that all would be prevaricating.

There remains a possibility which, as far as I know, has not been considered, the possibility that the miracle forecast by the Lady of Fatima was not limited to Fatima, but referred to the "many points in the country" where a sun dance was noted. In this regard, I should note that the Lady said that the miracle would occur on October 13, but did not say that it would occur at Fatima,[50] although this was assumed to be its only location by everyone. If in fact the Lady had forecast a miracle at many locations, assuming that a sun dance actually occurred at the "remote" locations where it was said to have occurred, this would make the miracle much more spectacular.

An obvious question is whether the sun dance at each location was a separate occurrence or were all connected and thus was a single occurrence of great size. In essence, assuming that the Lord did not produce purely supernatural miracles at many locations, did meteorological conditions, which caused the sun dance, show up simultaneously at many locations or did the conditions move from one site to another? The latter alternative seems very plausible. Specifically, it is plausible that the conditions were blown by a mild wind from one town to another. If so, one would expect that the locations occurred in a fairly straight line, and that the atmospheric conditions moved from west to east, in view of the prevailing winds. This fits quite well with the reported sun dances near Fatima. Thus these conditions may have

---

[50] Annex II #3A, #3G, #4F, #4G, #5E, #5F, #5G

been blown from Leiria and Batalha or even from San Pedro de Muel on the east to Alburitel, to Fatima, to a point west of Fatima (where the lady saw the sun dance "some kilometers" from Fatima) and then to Torres Novas. By the time the conditions reached Torres Novas they may have weakened considerably (at Torres Novas the sun dance "could not compare" with that at Fatima) and shortly after broken up entirely. In this case, the sun dance may have moved about thirty-five miles (from Leiria to Torres Novas) or about sixty miles (from San Pedro to Torres Novas.) A more spectacular (and less likely) assumption is that the wind changed at Torres Novas and blew the atmospheric conditions south and also somewhat east, and thus reached the Lisbon area early Sunday morning, where it seems a sun dance was seen by Pinto Coelho.

The alternative possibility—that the sun dance seen at each of these locations was a separate occurrence—cannot be discarded, in view of our small knowledge of sun dances. But it seems a less likely alternative.

Yet one more possibility exists—that the conditions which caused the sun dance occurred at a high altitude and were stable, but covered a wide area, so that the sightings at Leiria, Alburitel, Fatima, and Torres Novas occurred at the same time, and that they were not seen again on this day. If so, these conditions apparently covered a very large area—thirty miles or more in one direction. This possibility is weakened by the report of the lady who said she saw a sun dance after the one at Fatima was over, when she had traveled "some kilometers" from there, probably fifteen minutes later, or more.

All of these possibilities are conjectures, and deserve consideration in future studies of the Fatima events. However, it seems quite certain that phenomena like those at Fatima were observed at other points in the country on the same day, October 13.

Critics might wonder if those who reported remote sightings had heard of the sun dance at Fatima and were merely imagining their remote sightings. This would seem unlikely for the sightings at Leiria, Torres Novas, and Alburitel, which were said to have occurred at about the same time as the Fatima sun dance. In view of their distance from the Cova and the likelihood of a traffic jam, people at these locations probably did not hear of the Fatima sun dance until two hours or more after the event. If so, it is most unlikely that the people in these remote sites invented or imagined unheard-of phenomena which were like those at Fatima before they heard of the Fatima event.

WHY NO PHOTOGRAPHS

The question has been raised: why are there no photographs of the sun dance? Juda Ruah, a prominent photographer for the major journal *O Seculo*, was there and published ten photographs of the crowd and site in a magazine on October 29, 1917.[51] Why did he show no pictures of the movement or spin of the sun and none of color on the sun or the crowd? These questions would not have been asked in 1917 or even in the 1920s. People then knew the limitations of the available cameras. But for modern readers it may be worthwhile to answer these questions.

One answer is that Ruah clearly did not have a motion picture camera. Such cameras were in their infancy, and were expensive and bulky. Still cameras, of course, could not show movement. Further, still cameras produced blurred pictures when photographing objects in motion. Thus Ruah surely would not have tried to photograph the sun when it seemed to be moving, spinning or falling. A second answer is that color cameras had not yet been invented and Ruah's black-and-white camera could not show the color phenomena.

THE INDEX

For readers who may wish to make a study of the sun dance, I include at the end of this book a detailed index to the sections in each of the chapters which deal with specific aspects of the sun dance.

---

[51] *Ilustracao Portuguesa*, 29 Oct, Doc Crit III, pp 167-184; Jaki, pp 26, 100,101

CHAPTER XI

OTHER SUN DANCES

Some Fatima authors state or imply that the sun dance at Fatima on October 13, 1917, was unique in history. Certainly it is true that these phenomena were unknown to the thousands who witnessed them, except that most of the crowd may have heard of colored clouds in August and September and may have heard of rainbow colors on the sun and yellow spots on the ground, which had been reported by a few at the previous apparitions. But the other phenomena—the dancing, the spin, the fall, the "stareability," and the rainbow colors on the ground—were entirely unknown to the crowd. This is not to say that such phenomena had never been noted before October 13. Perhaps they had. But if so, they had gotten little publicity. None of the sun dance phenomena were reported in the books on atmospheric phenomena in my bibliography, except the dancing, the back and forth movement of the sun.

However, reports of Fatima-like phenomena have been made frequently since October 13, 1917, mostly in association with Fatima or other devotional sites of the Blessed Virgin. I am sure they will continue to occur. Many, if not most, surely are the product of an overly excited or unstable imagination (individual hallucinations) or a wish to attract attention. A few may be outright fakes. Perhaps some are supernatural. Skeptics may view these many later reports as evidence that the Fatima sun dance was a hallucination or a fairly common natural phenomenon. Believers may find in them further actions of grace by the Blessed Virgin. In either case, a review of these later sun dances seems necessary for a full analysis of the Fatima sun dance.

13 October 1917. The first Fatima-like sun dance was seen within a few hours of the sun dance at Fatima. It was seen by one (and apparently two) of the "non-see-ers" of the Fatima event itself, as they returned by car and were "some kilometers" from Fatima. Leonore Salema Manoel, in a letter of sixteen, reported seeing a silvery sun, then different colors on it, and the spin and fall of the sun. She said the phenomena lasted some long moments.[1] This phenomena may have been merely a later occurrence of the one noted shortly earlier at Fatima.

14 October 1917. An occurrence of a sun dance on Sunday, October 14, was reported by a well-known Catholic leader, Pinto Coelho, in the major Catholic newspaper *A Ordem*, on October 16. He said: "We could see the sun half overcast with clouds, as on Saturday. And sincerely, we saw the same succession of colors, the same rotary movement, etc." He suggested that a sun dance was not a rare event and he openly questioned the miraculous nature of the sun dance of October 13.[2] This article surely retarded the acceptance of devotion to Our Lady of Fatima by the Church. A number of priests supported his skepticism in the press.[3] Coelho does not state where "we" saw this second sun dance or how many people saw it. However, he went to Fatima by car with his family,[4] which makes it seem likely that he returned to his home near Lisbon (only ninety miles from Fatima) or stopped somewhere on the way for the night. An article in the Catholic weekly of Leiria of October 25 says that he saw this second sun dance in Cascaes, near Lisbon, but has parentheses around "Cascaes," suggesting that this may have been only an assumption.[5]

20 October 1917. A letter of December 3 from professor Goncalo Garrett to Father Formigao reports: "The bishop of Portalegre and Mrs. Maria de Jesus Raposo relate that, being in Torres Novas (a town near Fatima) with others on October 20 (a Saturday) at an unstated time they saw the rotary movement of the sun and change of colors. The same lady states that these manifestations in the sun

---

[1] Annex #33
[2] Annex #34
[3] Jaki, pp 61, 62, 88, 89, 112, 113, 117
[4] Annex #33
[5] Annex #106

were very different from those in Fatima and did not have the same greatness as those on October 13." Later in this letter he says: "Up to now nobody has seen the fiery rotation of the sun, and now everyone is seeing them many days and times. A lot of this is imagination."[6]

2 February 1918. Jacinto Lopes told the Fatima parish inquiry that he had seen the sun dance on October 13 and that on the feast of the Purification on February 2, 1918, about 3:00 in the afternoon, while at the same site (the Cova da Iria), he noted in the sun the same signs as those on October 13, and that he had not noted them the many other times when he was there. Before this, he had said that on October 13 he had seen yellow, scarlet, and green colors on the sun and ground, as well as the spin and fall of the sun.[7] He clearly implied that he had seen these colors, the spin and fall on February 2.

13 May 1920. Another letter to Father Formigao, this one from G. F. dos Santos, reports that on May 13, 1918, he brought a statue of Our Lady of Fatima to the chapel at the Cova da Iria at 3:30 and placed it on a table there. At the same moment the people shouted and asked pardon, since they were seeing the same solar phenomenon as on October 13, 1917; the phenomenon remained while the people said a rosary (about 15 minutes). During this time the statue took on a golden hue, and candles which he lit took on red and rose color, rather than their natural color.[8]

13 October 1922. A solar miracle on October 13, 1922, is reported by "V. M.," probably a typographical error for "V. de M." the pseudonym used by Father Formigao. He says that, during Mass some women called out to the celebrant (apparently Father Formigao himself) to look at the sun. He did not, thinking it was hallucination or imagination. But the cries got much louder and he asked the people to be quiet. Finally, he looked and saw the same phenomenon as on October 13, 1917, "though with less intensity and for a shorter time and without the luminous explosions of that day." Afterward, the celebrant checked with prominent friends, many of whom confirmed his impressions, but others denied it, most being those who had not

---

[6] Annex #89
[7] Annex #96
[8] Nov Doc, p 91

looked at the sun. A few days later a reporter of *A Epoca,* who was at Fatima on October 13, 1922, stated that some souls claimed to have seen indescribable phenomena, which he attributed to mass hallucination.[9]

13 August 1924. A sun dance was reported for August 13, 1924, by the Fatima press. It states that fifteen people were riding from Leria to Fatima in a truck, and near 8:00 they saw for about a half an hour the phenomena, usually seen on the 13ths, but less intense than on October 13, 1917. It adds: "It is noteworthy that this year the phenomena occur in the morning, especially since May and were seen at the Cova."[10] This statement implies that there were many other sightings of a sun dance at Fatima after October 13, 1917.

13 October 1925. A sun dance on October 13, 1925, was reported by the historian Joao Ameal in two long articles in a Porto newspaper on October 17 and 20, 1925, and repeated in the Fatima press on December 1925 and January 1926. Ameal describes his trip to Fatima, says he tried to avoid self-hallucination, and tells that the sky was covered that morning. At 12:10 the statue of Our Lady passed between the crowd, which was in ecstasy. The sun came out, he stared at it and it did not hurt his eyes. It seemed that there was a "strange tremor" in the sun. He checked, and to his surprise the picture (or vision—*visao*) cleared up. "The sun became a fine circle, a kind of gold ring, and in the center it turned into a dark sphere in rapid rotation. For some minutes, impressed and overwhelmed, I verified the exactness of this strange occurrence." He checked with his friend and others and all said they saw the same thing.[11] One might wonder whether only Ameal and a few others, among the several hundred thousand who were there, saw this sun dance. This is the only report of a sun dance in the three issues of Father Formigao's monthly newspaper, which followed October 13, 1925 (November, December, and January).[12] Surely, if all or most of that vast crowd had seen the sun

---

[9] Jaki, pp 168-170, citing *Voz de Fatima* #2, 13 November 1922; *A Epoca,* Nov 14-17 (exact date not given), 1922

[10] Jaki, pp 173, 174, citing *Voz de Fatima* #22, 13 September 1924

[11] *Voz de Fatima* #39, 13 December 1925, and #40, 13 January 1926

[12] Jaki, pp 184, 185; *Voz de Fatima* #38, #39, #40 of 13 November, 13 December 1925, and 13 January 1926

dance, it would have been reported in the November issue and would have received great coverage. Since Ameal states that "the sun came out," perhaps it was very cloudy and the sun was visible only in a small portion of the Cova da Iria and thus only a small share of the crowd saw the sun dance.

11 October 1946. Next is a report of a sun dance on October 11, 1946. It has many disturbing similarities to the sun dance on October 13, 1917, with a very different outcome. It is of major concern and must be discussed in some detail. All of my information is derived from a long section of an intensely anti-Fatima book, found in the Fatima archives.[13]

Amelia Fontes, an illiterate woman of twenty-two years, residing in Vilar Chao, Portugal, was sick in May 1945 and thought to be dying. She called for a priest and received the last rites. The next day she revealed to him that the Virgin had appeared to her. The priest suggested that the woman ask the Virgin to cure her, and on the following two days she was cured. She then revealed that the Virgin had appeared to her six years earlier, foretold her illness, and demanded secrecy.

Two weeks later her father noted that she seemed to be in ecstasy, presumed it was the Virgin, and was about to leave, when his daughter said: "Father, come and see, an angel is putting down flowers for me." He saw no angel, but did see marvelous flowers that were forming a pyramid. The father called in his neighbors to see the miraculous flowers. A journalist reported that after two months the flowers had not faded, and a Coimbra University professor learned that the flowers were tiny orchids, unknown in the region. Perhaps they were hidden in small pots. Orchids bloom for long periods of time, and thus the flowers may not have been "miraculous."

Unspecified "miracles" followed, but the priest, Father Hubert Flores, asked Amelia to request an incontrovertible miracle of the Virgin. Two days later a clear figure of a cross appeared on her head, and later a similar stigmata appeared on her hands. Thousands of people began to visit her and were charmed by her naïve and angelic air. Many "cures" were reported in some detail in the press, which

---

[13] *Fatima Demascarada*, pp 143-154

compared her case with that of Fatima. Over 100,00 visitors were said to have seen her.

Amelia reported that on October 11, 1946, the Virgin would make some important revelations. Thus, by 7:00 in the morning a crowd estimated at 30,000 to 40,000 gathered with the young woman at an unspecified site. At this time a sun dance occurred which received extensive press coverage. A press article said that nearly all saw the sun dance, it spun, gave off sparks, took on varied colors, and did not hurt the eyes.

It then gave more details: "Using the accounts of people we can sum up the happenings. It must have been 7:00. Suddenly the electrified people turned their eyes to the sun. Something extraordinary was happening. The sun, having in its center a bluish disk, according to some, a silver color, according to others, set up two rotary movements, to the right and to the left. Around in a bigger circle the sun radiated live light, in changing colors, surrounded by a yellow aureole."

Another newspaper article gave the testimony of "some eyewitnesses." "On the sun was seen a green disk, sharp, illuminated, and around the sun could be seen strong radiations. There was the impression that the sun turned on itself. But it did not blind the sight." No sources reported a fall of the sun, great heat, or color on the ground and people.

No further sun dance is reported at Vilar Chao, but it is said that the pilgrimages to Amelia's place continued, presumably with more cures. However, after five years she was induced to go to a hospital in Coimbra for a serious examination. There it was discovered that her stigmata were false, being produced by a cross dipped in a red liquid. Nothing more was stated about her fate, but presumably the pilgrimages stopped and her apparitions were considered to be fakes. A later book gives a list of apparitions of the Blessed Virgin and says that the apparitions at Vilar Chao in 1946 were arranged with the connivance of a doctor and a priest (and) the family. The book does not say whether this "connivance" was merely presumed or was known to have happened.[14]

---

[14] *Sintese Critica de Fatima: Ineidencias e Repercussoes*, p 23

The information on these events is quite incomplete. We are given very little information on the apparitions, not even the number of them nor where they occurred. Nor are we told why the large crowd assembled so early at the unspecified site on October 11. Presumably it was because "important revelations" were predicted. We are not told whether the weather was cloudy, as at Fatima, nor if the crowd was led to expect a sun dance. Of course, the crowd knew of the sun dance at Fatima. And we are not told if the seer or her family benefited financially from her visitors. Further, none of the reports came from newspapers in Vilar Chao. This seems strange if "nearly all" the people saw the spectacular phenomena. Perhaps many did not.

It is possible, but not likely, that the apparitions, the miraculous flowers and the cures, which preceded the "stigmata" were supernatural. It is conceivable (but unlikely) that Amelia was devout and sincere prior to the "stigmata." But it is not possible that the sun dance was also supernatural. The Lord would surely not perform a miracle for such an unworthy person. We must thus find another explanation for this sun dance. Perhaps her backers had heard that the spinning sun was noted most often at sunrise or sunset and were hoping for a cloudy or hazy sunrise. Offhand, I can think of no other reason for such an early hour for the event. And perhaps Amelia had gotten her followers to assemble at this time on several occasions and this time the conditions were ideal for the illusion of the spinning sun. The crowd may well have had this illusion. A few may have seen the color of the sunrise and wrongly associated it with the spinning sun, knowing that color on or around the sun had been noted at Fatima. No fall of the sun nor any color on the landscape was reported. Thus this "sun dance" may have been merely an occurrence of the illusion of a spinning sun. Or it may have been simply individual hallucinations by many people who were aware of the phenomena of the sun dance at Fatima.

May 1948. Another sun dance which appears to be important occurred on May 23, 1948, at Gimigliano (Ascoli Piceno), Italy. It is said that apparitions of Our Lady occurred to a thirteen-year-old girl there on May 17, 18, 20, 22, and 23, and that on May 23, 120,000 people were there, "in addition to the miracle of the sun." My source provides no further information, but this statement suggests that all or most of the crowd saw the sun dance. However, this event has received little publicity outside of Italy (and perhaps not even there), and I wonder if the number of people who claimed to see a sun dance was actually rather small.[15]

7 April 1950. The miracle of the sun was said to have been repeated on April 7, 1950, at Necedah, Wisconsin, five or six times from morning until mid-day at the gesture and cry of a nine-year-old boy, who was said to have seen apparitions of the Blessed Virgin. Presumably it was witnessed by crowds, but this is not stated in my only source on this sun dance.[16] Again I would like more details.

July 1950. On three days in July 1950, a sun dance is said to have occurred at different places in Sri-Lanka (formerly Ceylon), when the Traveling Virgin (a statue of the Virgin of Fatima) came there. Specifically, it is said to have occurred in Negombo on July 11, where it was seen by many hundreds of people, and at Wattala two days later, outside of churches in Colombo, Pettah, and Kochikade on the next day or two and finally at the racetrack in Colombo, the capital, before a large crowd on July 15. The crowd was there to bid farewell to the Traveling Virgin.

I wrote to the archbishop of Colombo, asking for more details. Strangely, the archbishop, through an aide, replied that there was no mention of these miracles in the Catholic and secular press.[17] I therefore must give more details on these seemingly important sun dances. All of my information on these dances comes from three sources.

One is the *Voz de Fatima* (Voice of Fatima) #337, October 13, 1950, giving a letter of July 17, 1950, from John Rajapakse at Negombo. In it he says:

> When the Traveling Virgin came to Negombo on the 11th of this month, many hundreds of people saw the sun spin for more than an hour in the afternoon/evening (tarde). From time to time the sun gave out various colors, blue, white, with yellow predominating. One of my servants, a Buddhist, said she saw the figure of Our Lady on the sun while it spun. But we Catholics only saw the sun spinning, and once it descended.

> Two days later the same thing happened in Wattala. This time the *Ceylon Observer* (a Buddhist journal) publicized it on the first page. The reporter

---

[15] *Sintese Critica de Fatima: Ineidencias e Repercussoes*, p 23
[16] *Sintese Critica de Fatima: Ineidencias e Repercussoes*, p 23
[17] Letter of the Catholic Information Center of the diocese to me, dated 9 May 1999

himself had seen the miracle, as well as the noted Catholic priest, Father Nicholas Pereira. Since then many Hindus, Buddhists and Catholics said they had seen the sun spin when they were outside the churches in Colombo, Pettah, and Kochchikade, and also during the final meeting at the playing field of Colombo. I can point out Hindu businessmen who will testify to this phenomenon of the "sun dance" during the visit of the Traveling Virgin. The Buddhist journals call the statue the "miraculous statue."

P.S. The *Ceylon Daily News* of today gives the letters of some who saw the sun dance during the farewell ceremonies.

John Rajapakse

The text in *Voz de Fatima* was in Portuguese, presumably a translation of the letter, which probably was in English, the (or an) official language of Ceylon.

This was the only source of information on the Sri Lanka sun dances which I had found when I wrote to the archbishop. Later, in the Fatima archives, I found two other sources.

One is the *Messenger*, a Catholic English-language journal, apparently in Melbourne, Australia. In it we read:

> After that (India) it (the statue) went to Ceylon and at Colombo some of the wonderful spectacle of Fatima seems to have been repeated … The *Melbourne Advocate* recently quoted a letter from Mrs. Sellar, a Ceylonese lady, wife of the resident doctor in Marawila. Mrs. Sellar wrote: "The last farewell was at the racecourse. Thousands flocked there to get the final blessing. … from about 5:15 to 5:45 the sun revolved and threw many hues, from pink to gold. I saw it with my own eyes and it was most frightful and beautiful. Thousands and thousands of eyes were focused on the sun. It was like a huge host, turning around."

> An account of the phenomenon was given in the Colombo press, which gave rise to some controversial correspondence, from which we select two letters of eyewitnesses.

> Sir: With reference to Mudaliyar D. B. J.B. Opatha's letter, appearing in your paper today, please allow me to say that the same spectacle appeared at 5:15 last Saturday at the race course—not only to a few hundred, as at Wattala, but to the mammoth crowd assembled there to bid farewell to Our Lady's statue. What I saw there will be confirmed by hundreds and thousands there; the sun started turning like a disc; then it was radiating colors of yellow, blue and purple.

When I looked at the crowd immediately afterwards, they looked colored. I asked a number of people around me to verify the phenomenon, thinking I might be mistaken. They all saw the same thing.

Yours, etc., Norbert Rodrigo.

Sir: I read Mudilyar Opatha's letter in your paper of today's date, and on Saturday, the fifteenth at the race course the strange phenomenon was visible again, lasting for about fifteen to twenty minutes. I certainly saw the sun rotating, vigourously throwing out beautiful colors. I wonder too if others had witnessed it.

Yours, etc., E. F. Kelaart.

Since reading the above, I have had handed to me by Rev. T Lees, S.J., of St. Patrick's College, Melbourne, a letter received by his mother from her sister, who is a Little Sister of the Poor in Colombo. Sister Agnes writes:

We have had further news of the farewell to the Pilgrim Virgin's statue at Colombo. A phenomenon was seen in the morning and evening for two days. Everyone of our sisters at Colombo saw it at least twice. The sun revolved and whirled rapidly around, changed color several times and could be looked at for long intervals with the naked eye. It lasted for about two hours each time. Sometimes a cloud would appear the same color as the sun, that is to say pale blue, pink, mauve, green or yellow, and would reflect the same color on the earth, tinting persons, houses, trees and objects into the same delicate shade. No doubt Our Lady wanted the people of Colombo to know she was pleased with the wonderful reception she received everywhere during her stay on the island; of course newspapers say it was not a miracle, but it could happen through certain disturbances in the elements.[18]

The second source is the book *As Brancas Pombas da Paz*. It quotes a journal *Voz* or *A Voz* in Goa. It is not from the August issue of *Voz de Fatima*. The book says: With a date of 5 Aug, 1950, the *Voz* publishes the following:

"Goa, 4 (Aug) One more extraordinary fact, among so many that have amazed the crowds of the faithful was noted (during) the passage of the Traveling Virgin of Fatima through the streets of the world. When the statue was transported from Wattala to Mutival, in Colombo, the faithful which accompanied it, some hundreds, including Father Nicholas Pereira, pastor of Wattala, saw the sun become blue and turn slowly on itself. This noteworthy phenomenon was reported with great empha-

---

[18] *The Messenger*, 2 October 1950, pp 636-638

sis by the Indian press, including the *Goa Mail, Undentichen Neketr* and *Ave Maria*, and the correspondent in Wattala of the *Ceylon Observer*, after saying that, etc."[19]

These sources say that articles on the sun dance appeared in the Colombo and Indian press during and after the visit of the Traveling Virgin's statue. Yet the archbishop's aide said she was unable to find anything, and even offered to get copies of the *Catholic Messenger* for me, if I wanted them. This would seem to show that the aide glanced through the *Catholic Messenger*. It is clear that there was a *Catholic Messenger* in Colombo and a *Messenger* in Melbourne. After finding these later sources I wrote several more letters to the archbishop's aide, who is also the editor of the *Catholic Messenger*, asking for the text of the articles in the Colombo press. They have produced no results. One would expect that the archbishop and his aide would be very well aware of the 1950 sun dance, if it was really seen by a large majority of the people, as at Fatima. Nonetheless, the testimony cited above cannot be ignored. An answer to this puzzle is badly needed.

Until this answer is found, there is some reason to believe that one or more of these sun dances in Ceylon/Sri Lanka were real, despite the negative report of the archbishop's aide. Also, I note that the fall of the sun is mentioned only once and may not be a feature of these sun dances.

13 October 1950. A sun dance, seen by thousands of people was said to have occurred in Bogota, Columbia, on October 13, 1950. In this case also I received a letter from the archbishop that seems to deny the sun dance. Specifically, the archbishop wrote: "In the archives of the archdiocese we have found nothing that refers to this phenomenon, the people who at this time took part in the reception and the peregrination of the statue of the Virgin of Fatima affirm that no such phenomenon of the sun occurred." I thus must give the available information in detail.

In the Spanish version of *Voz de Fatima* #58, November 13, 1950, the following is given, under the heading, "Did the Miracle of the Sun Repeat Itself in Bogota?"

Bogota, 13 October. Thousands of people who accompanied the statue of the Virgin of Fatima, in a procession begun under a heavy rain, noted that

---

[19] *As Brancas Pombas da Paz*, p 95.

the sun modified its appearance and changed its color, being first silver, and afterwards purple, gray and rose. At the same time a dark-colored spot appeared and disappeared continually in the center of the sun, while the faithful knelt in the streets. ...

This appears to be a telegram from a priest or other person with the Traveling Virgin, but no signature is given. In view of the negative report of the archbishop, this "sun dance" at Bogota must be considered questionable.

October–November 1950. Cardinal Tedeschini reported in a speech that Pope Pius XII saw repetitions of the Fatima miracle in the Vatican gardens at 4:00 in the afternoon on October 30 and 31, on November 1 and on the octave of November 1 (November 7 or November 8), 1950. The only detail that was reported was that the sun was surrounded by a halo and that the pope could stare at it. On November 1 the bodily assumption of the Blessed Virgin into heaven was formally declared to be Church dogma, a major event in the Church. Cardinal Tedeschini's speech was reported in the Vatican journal *L Osservatore Romano*.[20]

11 October 1954. At about 6:00 p.m. on October 11, 1954, on a pilgrimage coming from Fatima to France, Italy, and Spain, American pilgrims were nearing Salamanca, Spain, in a bus, when a woman and then eleven other passengers noted a sun dance. The rest of the passengers could not see it. The twelve saw the sun rotate on itself, emit rays of various different colors, and then seem to approach the bus like a shot, and then slowly resume its place in the sky, continuing to rotate until it disappeared behind the mountains. This phenomenon was said to have lasted about fifteen minutes. All twelve made depositions, available at the Holy See.[21]

26 December 1956. The previously mentioned author of an intensely anti-Fatima book describes a sun dance seen on December 26, 1956, at about 11:30. From the text it is not clear whether the author saw it or another anti-Fatima author (Guimaraes) saw it. He says that the sky was cloudy, but not uniformly so. The clouds resem-

[20] *Voz de Fatima* #13, November 1951; Jaki, p 299
[21] *Voz de Fatima* #13, November 1955

bled veils of gas of varying thickness, that one could stare at the sun without hurting the eyes. The wind blew the clouds with some speed,

but as it was all covered, the movement could only be seen in front of the sun. One's eyes, however, suffered the illusion that the sun was turning on itself in the direction opposite to the movement of the clouds. …When the thickness of the clouds lessened the sun shone more intensely, creating the impression that it increased in size, as would be said of an object that neared the earth. As a result of this momentary increase in shine, which bothered one's vision, a negative of the sun's image was formed on our retina, which covered the real image, creating the impression of an eclipse.[22]

He does not give a location or say if others saw this sun dance.

This report uses one of the possible explanations for the apparent fall of the sun. (See pages 159-162.) It also is one of the few reports of a sun dance which clearly is not associated with Fatima or religion in some way. It is noteworthy that the author makes no claim of seeing color on the sun or ground, nor does he say that the spin was rapid.

Other Dates. In addition to these sun dances, several more have been reported briefly in *Voz de Fatima* #410, November 13, 1956, but with less detail. They are:

13 May 1922. At 7:00 in the evening, between Vila Nova and Torres Novas, Fatima pilgrims saw: "the same prodigies as on October 13, but less intense."

13 May 1923. No details are given on this sun dance, which was said to be reported in *Voz de Fatima* #9 (presumably dated 13 June 1923).

13 March 1924. In the *Colegio de Regeneracao* (a Catholic high school) in Braga, a sun dance was seen by a priest and a nun.

13 May 1925. A sun dance was seen by a priest and his companions at Fatima, and also in Alcacer do Sol by Luis Antonio Carraca and his family at Herdade de Ervideira and by fifteen men who worked for him.

---

[22] *Fatima Demascarada*, pp 138-141

13 May 1928. A sun dance was seen at the Cova da Iria, as related by Dr. Weiss d' Oliveira on 29 May.

July 13, 1944, and October 9, 1949. Still other sun dances, associated with apparitions were reported by a German journal. Two were said to have occurred on July 13, 1944, at an unspecified location in Germany and on October 9, 1949, at Thurn-Heroldsbach (Franken) in Germany. No details are given. Twenty apparitions, with associated sun dances, between 1931 and 1950, were listed and discussed in four articles by this German journal.[23] Another source reports a sun dance at Heroldsbach in October 1950,[24] which may be an error for October 1949.

Undated, Perhaps 1950. The German journal, above, reported a sun dance, limited to a dark and rapidly spinning disk superimposed on the sun, which was said to have been seen several times by a German meteorologist, probably in the late 1940s or 1950. I give his account of these sightings on pages 148-150.

This presentation of information on other sun dances is not complete, since I have made no major effort to locate more. Many others are known to have been noted by individuals who did not bother to report them, or whose reports to the press were not deemed newsworthy. I say this with confidence, based on my own experience with Fatima pilgrims. In three pilgrimages, I met three couples and one lady who said that they had seen sun dances. None were published by the press. I give their accounts, both as samples of unpublished accounts, and as further evidence on the nature of sun dances.

13 October 1998. Probably the most interesting account is that of Mr. and Mrs. Dan Wittman of Hilton Head, South Carolina. He describes a sun dance at Conyers, Georgia, where apparitions were reported by Nancy Fowler, and where many pilgrims had assembled on October 13, 1998.

At about 5:30 in the evening they walked to the church parking lot; Dan happened to look up and saw a vapor trail, which he followed, looking for the jet plane, and noticed that the vapor trail

---

[23] Jaki, pp 303, 331, citing *Marienerscheinungen Seit Fatima* by G.J. Strangfeld in Der Groosse Entschluz, 7 December 1951, pp 82-85, and 7 January 1952, pp 121-125, and 7 February 1952, pp 148-152, and 7 March 1952, pp 180-181

[24] *Miracle of the God,* last pages of the book

swerved to the right, making a jagged bow of perhaps a mile, and then resumed its course to the west. He says he is sure the jagged semi-circle made by the vapor trail was too tight to have been made by a jet plane. (I include this seemingly unrelated detail because of its possible relation to "air lenses," a possible explanation of sun dance phenomena.)

At this point he heard *ahs* from the 100-200 people in the parking lot, all of whom were looking to the west. Dan moved into the lot to look past the church, and at once he saw the spinning sun, coming at them and getting larger and larger. He called his wife over, and she confirmed what he was seeing. Specifically, he says the sun was covered by a white or light gray disk. The sun appeared to rotate behind this disk, being seen on various sides, but only enough to convey a flashing appearance. He doesn't recall any rays. The disk made it possible to stare right at the sun.

The first time the sun came at them, he adds, was the closest, so much so that he thought of being frightened; the second advance was maybe half as close, and the third less still. Dan cannot say how long the sun dance lasted, but guesses ten to fifteen minutes. After the third retreat they walked behind the church and did not see the sun become normal. It seemed that everyone in the parking lot saw the "miracle." The weather was quite clear, but had small white clouds, high in the sky, with blue coming through here and there. They saw no color phenomena.

This is a most interesting account because it is more detailed than any other of the "other sun dances" that I have read about, because of the "bow" of the vapor trail, and because it provides a possible explanation for the "fireworks wheel" reported by so many at Fatima on October 13, 1917. It is also interesting that they saw no color phenomena.

Unspecified Dates, 1987-2001. Charles and Dorothy Martin, of Belmont, South Carolina, said that they had seen the sun dance many times at Conyers, Georgia, and Cold Springs, Kentucky. They did not give me dates. The weather was sunny (at least for some of the dances). They saw the sun dance almost as soon as they looked at it. It was dark, almost black in the center. They could look at it for a long time, and it kept spinning and sending off sparks of light. Sometimes the sun dance occurred on sunny days. Many others saw the sun dance, but not all saw it at the same time they did. They also said they had seen other light phenomena at one site or the other. Apparitions of the Blessed Mother have been reported at both sites.

Unspecified Dates after 1981. Debbie and Melissa Malarcher, of Greer, South Carolina, reported that they saw unusual phenomena at Medjugorje, Bosnia. One said she saw colors but no spin, and the other said she saw a spin but no colors. Both said that not everyone saw these phenomena at the same time. Mrs. Betty Jean Purdy, of Hilton Head, South Carolina, reported seeing the sun spin many times at Medjugorje. Apparitions of the Blessed Mother have been reported at this site, which were not offically accepted by the Church, but the Vatican continues to investigate. The information is presented here to give additional context.

In view of the fact that seven pilgrims, among the 200–250 on my three pilgrimages, said that they saw the sun dance, it seems certain that, among the millions of pilgrims to Fatima and other pilgrimage sites, thousands claim to have seen a sun dance. Probably many claimed to have seen a sun dance on October 13, the same day of the year as at Fatima in 1917.

Secular Sun Dances. There remains the possibility that sun dances have occurred in circumstances unrelated to Fatima or any religious context. I have already mentioned one such claim by an opponent of Fatima in an anti-Fatima book and the report of several occurrences of the spinning sun by a German meteorologist, presumably in secular circumstances. Two of the other cases, which I have given, may or may not have been secular. One is the sun dance of October 14, 1917, reported by Coelho. The other is the event of October 20, 1917, seen by the bishop of Port Alegre and others. I know of no other report of a secular sun dance.

Admittedly, my information comes entirely from books and other sources on Fatima. Thus, the possibility exists that other secular sun dances have occurred. However, it seems likely that such sun dances, if actual, are quite rare, since pro-Fatima writings have reported only the few cited above and the anti-Fatima sources give only one example. The rarity of sun dances, as meteorological phenomena, is shown by the fact that none are mentioned in the books on such phenomena that I have examined. (See my bibliography.)

There remains a question concerning the later sun dances. Were any of them miraculous? If a natural explanation exists, perhaps they were not. But if the Fatima sun dance was miraculous, then it is possible that a few later ones also were.

SUMMARY AND CONCLUSIONS

In this chapter I have presented over twenty-eight reports of Fatima-like sun dances. In addition, many more are said to have been seen, but have not been publicized. Many of the reports were vague—fourteen of the twenty-eight which I have presented.[25] Thirteen of the remaining fourteen told of the spinning sun.[26] Two of them said that the spinning sun was dark and two said it was light in color.[27] Three reported something like a fireworks wheel-sparks or a flashing appearance.[28] Six of the thirteen also reported color.[29] Another reported color only.[30] Five of the thirteen said that the sun seemed to fall.[31] These later dances are thus quite similar to that which was seen at Fatima on October 13, 1917. Many are vague; and among those which are not, almost all report the spin of the sun, many report color and a lesser number report the fall of the sun. They differ from Fatima in that two of the four which report a color mentioned a dark color on the spinning sun, while at Fatima only a few say it was dark.

---

[25] 2 February 1918, 13 May 1920, 13 October 1921, 13 August 1924, 23 May 1948, 7 April 1950, October-November 1950, 13 May 1922, 13 May 1923, 13 Mar 1924, 13 May 1925, 13 May 1928, 13 July 1944, 9 October 1949; the twenty dances reported by the German journal are not included in these totals, since we have no details on them.

[26] 13 October 1917, 14 October 1917, 20 October 1917, 13 October 1925, 11 October 1946, July 1950?, 11 October 1954, 26 December 1956, 13 October 1998, three unspecified dates in the period 1980-2000.

[27] 13 October 1925 and 1987-2001; 13 October 1917 and 13 October 1998

[28] 11 October 1946, 13 October 1998, 1987-2001

[29] 13 October 1917, 14 October 1917, 20 October 1917, 11 October 1946, July 1950, 11 October 1954

[30] 13 October 1950

[31] 13 October 1917, 11 October 1950, 11 October 1954, 26 December 1956, 13 October 98

Since only a handful of the later sun dances occurred in secular circumstances, I must ask if this is significant. Many Catholics will surely say yes—the Blessed Virgin is repeating and high-lighting the message of Fatima, even if only a few of the many later reports of sun dances are real. Skeptics might wonder if my sources have an unintentional bias in favor of a religious context for sun dances. At present I can make no worthwhile comment on this question. I have not made an exhaustive check for secular sun dances. I have, however, searched for information on optical illusions related to the sun or meteorology in indexes of libraries and have found nothing except items concerning induced movement, which I use to explain the appearance of lateral movement (zig-zagging) of the sun at Fatima. I have myself tried to stare at the muted sun, but have found only a few occasions when I could do this for up to one minute. On other occasions, clouds intervened too quickly or the sun became too bright. On all the occasions, I noted no dark or spinning sun, and of course no falling sun or colors on the sun or ground.

Opponents of Fatima will surely claim that the occurrence of so many reports of sun dances after October 13, 1917, is evidence that both the later sun dances and the one at Fatima were hallucinations. Supporters of Fatima, on the other hand, will surely see the hand of God in some of these later occurrences; very few, however, would claim that all or most of the many later sun dances are real. If they number in the many hundreds or thousands, surely most are hallucinations or inventions. Perhaps some may be divine visions. But if the Fatima sun dance was due to physical phenomena or optical illusions associated with meteorology, there is no reason to deny that it could occur again.

Nonetheless, if many of the later sun dances were hallucinations, I must ask if this is an indication that the Fatima sun dance was also a hallucination. In this regard, an important distinction exists between the Fatima sun dance and all the later ones. At Fatima the phenomena of the sun dance were entirely unknown to the crowd, while at the others the phenomena were known. For most of the later sun dances individual hallucination is a plausible explanation. But it is utterly unreasonable to conclude that the thousands at Fatima had similar individual hallucinations of phenomena unknown to them. And, as I indicated earlier, mass hallucination cannot be accepted.

Next I must consider if the hand of God was at work in any of the later sun dances. I cannot offer worthwhile comment on this. It would require a much more detailed and thorough study of later dances. More study is needed, particularly on the sun dances in Vilar Chao and Sri Lanka.

It is not my intention, in this book, to examine further the problem of other sun dances. I hope that some writer will, in the future, make a much more thorough search for information on other sun dances and then will analyze and report on them adequately. It is my purpose only to use these later sun dances to help understand the Fatima sun dance of October 13, 1917.

CHAPTER XII

THE EVENTS — SUMMARY AND CONCLUSIONS

It is now appropriate to review the previous chapters and to make final analyses and conclusions. For some aspects of the apparitions and the sun dance, I have already presented summaries and conclusions, and I will only briefly repeat them in this chapter. However, a few aspects were left unexplained or partially explained. To these aspects I will devote more space and attention. I begin with the apparitions.

The Apparitions. On May 13, 1917, three very young shepherds reportedly saw a radiant Lady. The children said that the Lady asked them to return to the same place for six months; they reported on July 13 that the Lady promised to perform a miracle on October 13 to show that she was appearing there. The seers said that the Lady asked them to pray the rosary for peace. After the events on the 13th of July, August, and September, some of those present claimed to have seen unusual atmospheric phenomena. These reports caused large crowds to gather there each month. On October 13 an enormous crowd gathered there. After the apparition, the sun dance occurred. The children then said that the Lady asked for a chapel to be built there in her honor, said that the people should reform their lives and pray the rosary, and that World War I was ending that day.

The possibility that the apparitions were merely a hoax can easily be rejected. The tender age of the seers makes this unlikely, as does their piety and the piety of their families. Since they lived in a tiny village any priest or other outsider, coming to train the children for a hoax, would have been noticed by the villagers. Moreover, the local priest was unsympathetic to the seers, and the likelihood that he or other priests orchestrated or accepted a hoax is minimal, since most priests at that time were conscientious men of God. Finally, neither the seers nor their parents benefited financially to any significant degree from the apparitions and their consequences.

The major argument against the apparitions which was advanced by opponents was that the apparitions were hallucinations. Against this it can be said that it is unlikely that three children would have the same hallucination and even less likely that one would "see" the Lady but not "hear" her. Further, the seers were noted to be normal, healthy children and not the kind likely to have hallucinations.

The seers were reasonably consistent in their many retellings of the apparitions and they resisted strong threats to admit that they were lying. The two younger seers did not repudiate their accounts of the apparitions in the rest of their short lives, and Lucia repeated her account of the apparitions many times in the four years that she lived at home, gave three long written accounts later, all confirming the early accounts, and she never retracted them. The two younger seers lived devout lives in the few years after 1917 before their deaths and are considered saints by the Church. Lucia lived a devout life at home, then spent many years in an ordinary convent, and finally entered a cloistered convent, where she died in 2005.

The available testimony indicates that the seers acted as one would expect during an apparition, speaking and waiting for an answer unheard by the crowd, and seeming to be in ecstasy. At the end, as would seem natural as the apparition departed, they looked and pointed to the sky and sometimes told the crowd to look there also.

There were many variations and contradictions on minor details, as the seers recounted the apparitions many times and answered hundreds of questions of their interviewers. This in no way weakens the believability of the apparitions, since such variations and contradictions are to be expected from the three very young seers as they repeated their accounts.

However, one statement was a contradiction of fact, was important, and required detailed study. This was the "false prophecy" that the war would end on that day, October 13, over one year before the actual end. That such a false prophecy would be made by a heavenly being is simply untenable. This implies that Lucia misquoted the Lady or that the apparitions were not genuine. It is reasonable to guess that Lucia misquoted the Lady because: she firmly expected the end of the war to be the miracle predicted by the Lady, and she was distracted during the apparition by the many requests she had been asked to make of the Lady and thus failed to hear properly what the Lady said about the end of the war, and she convinced her much younger cousin that her imperfect recollection of the prediction was the correct one. It seems that we must accept this explanation (or some other one) for the false prophecy, or else reject the apparitions as not genuine despite the considerable evidence to the contrary. However, the strongest evidence that the apparitions were real is the sun dance of October 13, a date when a miracle had been predicted by the Lady well in advance.

The Phenomena at the Second Through Fifth Apparitions. Another item for review is the phenomena which were reported for the second through the fifth apparitions. We have very little information on such phenomena for the second and third apparitions, both of which were viewed by relatively small crowds. But for August 13 and September 13 much more information is available. Many witnesses reported unusual phenomena. And the fact that the crowds had increased greatly at each apparition suggests that unusual phenomena were reported and became well known for the second and third, as well as the fourth and fifth ones. Crowds in such large sizes would surely not have come to a site as remote as Fatima solely because the seers said they had seen a "Lady."

An important feature of the August and September apparitions is that many who were there stated that they saw nothing unusual. For both months, one or two phenomena were reported by many witnesses and might be explained as unusual weather phenomena—a loud noise that may have been freak thunder or a sudden and unexplained decrease in the sun's brightness. The noise heard in July and August may have been caused by an explosion of TNT. A number of other phenomena were reported by only a few people—smoke or dust at the apparition site, a darkening of the sun so that one could see stars, white objects falling from the sky, and a transparent ball or bubble floating through the air over the apparition site, and a change of colors on the sun.

In view of the fact that many onlookers said that they saw nothing unusual, a plausible explanation for the reports of unusual phenomena is that they were illusions, hallucinations, or inventions. However, for both months another explanation is possible and reasonable—that the more widely reported phenomena were real, but were not viewed as unusual by many people, and the other phenomena were exaggerations of natural phenomena, illusions, hallucinations, or outright inventions. Unfortunately, even for August and September the information is fairly slim, which makes it hard to choose between these explanations.

Conclusions. Summing up, it can be said that the evidence (without considering the sun dance) is quite strong that the apparitions were real, despite the false prophecy. The reality of the phenomena reported by many witnesses cannot be firmly denied nor accepted. It is clear, however, that the crowd at Fatima on October 13 expected that the miracle, if it occurred, would be associated with the sun or the atmosphere and would be near noon.

The Phenomena at the Sixth Apparition. The phenomena reported for the sixth apparition are the smoke column and the sun dance. The sun dance, in turn, consists of three major phenomena— the colors, the spin of the sun, and its fall—and three minor phenomena—the muted sun in the clear blue sky, the lateral motion of the sun (the dance itself), and the great heat. The time when the sun dance occurred, not a phenomenon in itself, is nonetheless a major factor in analyzing the apparitions and the sun dance.

The Columns of Smoke. The columns of smoke are a minor phenomenon, which I reported and analyzed only briefly. It preceded the sun dance and was reported only by a few sources. This is not surprising since it was a minor phenomenon and the major phenomena attracted the most attention. The rainy weather makes a fire or incense unlikely sources of the smoke, but a chemical reaction is a viable explanation. If so, it would surely be the work of a hoaxter, hoping to make a profit from pilgrims, or of a misguided religious fanatic. Offhand, it would seem hard for anyone to avoid being seen as they aired or mixed the appropriate chemicals, and thus I am inclined to view this explanation as unlikely, but not highly unlikely. Pro-Fatima authors clearly imply that the columns of smoke were supernatural.

THE SUN DANCE

For the sun dance, I will review possible explanations for each of the phenomena and also discuss their rarity. Clearly, if the phenomena were natural, the sun dance can be miraculous only if their rarity is such that their occurrence at the time a miracle was forecast would seem miraculous.

Supernatural Explanations. God, of course, could have produced the smoke columns and the sun dance in a purely supernatural way. One supernatural way would be that all, or nearly all of the onlookers at Fatima received a similar vision of the smoke columns, the colors, the spin and fall of the sun, and the other phenomena. Another way would be that all the phenomena were real but entirely outside of the laws of nature. That God produced real color phenomena in a super-natural way is not very difficult to accept.

But that the lateral movement of the sun, the spin and fall were supernatural but real occurrences is much harder to accept. For the spin to be real and be noticeable as a rapid spin (one revolution per second), the sun would have to spin one or two million times as fast as it now spins, and the devastating effects of this increase would have to be negated. For the fall of the sun to be real and appear threaten-ing to the crowd would require a major change in the direction of its travel through space and a rapid increase in its speed of travel (which I did not note previously) and again the devastating effects would have to be negated. And for the lateral movement to be real would require that the awesome effects of this change in its orbit would also have to be offset. Finally, one more fantastic miracle would be required so that the incredible phenomena would be seen at Fatima but not be noticed at any of the observatories of the world.

God, I repeat, could perform such fantastic miracles. But they boggle the human mind. I am thus inclined to look for other expla-nations for these phenomena, perhaps also fantastic, but less utterly fantastic.

Arguments of Opponents. Before discussing the other phenomena of the sun dance, I will review the major arguments against the supernatural nature of the sun dance, as a whole. One argument—that the sun dance was simply the movement of a UFO—is highly unlikely. The appearance of UFOs on earth has not yet been proven, nor has an occurrence of a UFO before such a large crowd been clearly shown (I presume it has never occurred), and it would seem most unlikely that a UFO would have appeared at the hour a miracle had been forecast and would appear and leave at the same azimuth as the sun. It has also been suggested that the sun dance was a psychic event, but it can easily be argued that the sun did not spin exceedingly rapidly nor did it fall toward the earth, and thus the psychic event would seem to be a form of mass hallucination. (See pages 83.)

The most common argument against the miraculous nature of the sun dance is that it was simply mass hallucination. This was a concept that received much publicity and support in the early years of the twentieth century, but it has subsequently been rejected by authorities in the field of hallucination. (See pages 75-78.) Further, it is unlikely that a large majority of this crowd had a similar individual hallucination of phenomena previously unknown to them (the spin and fall of the sun). Finally, this argument is eliminated by the reports of sun dances at this time in towns near Fatima. Strangely, the proponents of hallucination did not pursue the strongest argument in its favor—the existence of witnesses at Fatima who said that they saw nothing unusual.

Non-see-ers. It is clear that only a small, probably a very small, proportion of the crowd at Fatima on October 13 failed to note unusual phenomena. Soon after October 13 three articles in anti-Church newspapers suggested that such "non-see-ers" were numerous, but offered no specific support for such claims. Three other press reports of this time imply that all, or at least most, of the people saw startling phenomena. More importantly, the anti-Fatima press printed a great many articles against Fatima in the rest of 1917, but ignored the existence of "non-see-ers." It would seem that it recognized that the public had accepted the idea that everyone at Fatima had noted unusual phenomena. Further, a 1918 article in an anti-Church journal firmly stated that something unusual had happened in the sky. And a great many letters of 1917, as well as later testimony, strongly support the contention that nearly all the crowd at Fatima had the impression of seeing spectacular phenomena. However, three witnesses who seem to be unbiased reported in 1917 that they saw nothing unusual. A 1950 book mentions two more. (See pages 78-83.) I have left for this chapter a detailed discussion of this problem.

We may dismiss the three newspaper articles which report "non-see-ers" as biased and unsubstantiated, but the statements of the three unbiased witnesses clearly indicate that at least a few of the people at the Cova da Iria had no impression of unusual phenomena. I first present their testimony and then discuss it.

One merely says in his diary that he was at Fatima and that he saw nothing unusual except a darkening of the sun that lasted about fifteen minutes. He fails to mention that most people seemed to see some startling phenomena, which raises the possibility that he left the Cova before the sun dance began and thus missed seeing it. This is not unlikely, since he had earlier noted that local people had been at the Cova on September 13 and saw nothing unusual. He was surely skeptical that anything spectacular would happen on October 13.

Since the sun dance began considerably later than expected (about a half hour), this man may have left fifteen or twenty minutes before the sun dance, wanting to avoid the traffic jam that clearly would occur later. He added in his diary that the seers said that the war was ending, which suggests that he stayed until the end of the sun dance. But he also adds that a priest stayed at his house that night, and he may have heard of the statement of the seers from this priest.[1] This leaves the possibility that only two of the three unbiased reports actually represent "non-see-ers" at Fatima.

The other two reports are from "non-see-ers," who clearly stayed for the sun dance. One was from Isabel de Melo, who wrote in a letter that she heard everybody shout "Miracle!" and other praises to God and Mary, that the sun was silvery and began to turn on itself and ascend and descend several times, adding: "That is what people next to me say, and what thousands of people affirm that they saw. Me, I did not see it. I could easily stare at the sun, and was terribly excited to

---

[1] Annex #17, #9

hear everyone shout that they saw extraordinary signs in the sky." She also says: "Two of my female cousins who were next to me were beside themselves and affirm that they saw the sun exactly as a fireworks wheel that turned on itself vertiginously."[2]

The other report was from Leonore Manuel, who said she had moments of sadness because: "at that solemn moment I saw nothing of what others were seeing. I saw then on the sun nothing to justify all the to-do that I saw around me." She gives no details on what the others were seeing. Later that afternoon, this woman reportedly saw a sun dance from her car on her way back from Fatima. Commenting, she asks: "Could it have happened to someone besides me and Geni that they saw nothing there (at the Cova) and then saw something afterwards?" She clearly implies that she and Geni (Eugenia) stayed together at the Cova. Geni is identified as the daughter of Isabel de Melo and thus Leonore and Geni may have been with Geni's mother at the Cova.[3] If so, the three "non-see-ers" were at the same spot in the Cova. This raises the possibility that all of the "non-see-ers" were in this part of the Cova.

It would be helpful if we could say that these three (or five) were the only "non-see-ers" at the Cova da Iria on October 13. If we had only these few among so many thousands, we might simply ignore them as unreliable. But our seventy sources are only a tiny fraction of the thousands of witnesses, and yet three unbiased sources say that they saw nothing.

Admittedly, this small fraction may not be representative. Nonetheless, it seems likely that many saw nothing, perhaps a few hundred. One or two hundred, among tens of thousands, might not have come to the attention of the public or the opponents of Fatima. But hundreds, or dozens or even three "non-see-ers" leads us to ask again if the phenomena at Fatima were actually hallucinations. However, recalling the strong arguments against hallucinations, it still seems that hallucinations must be rejected as an explanation for the "non-see-ers." Other explanations must be looked for.

---

[2] Annex #69
[3] Annex #33

God could have given a vision of the phenomena to most of the onlookers at Fatima, but not all. But such a supernatural explanation for the phenomena should not be accepted if a good natural one is available.

A possible natural explanation for "non-see-ers" is that a considerable number of the crowd failed to see one or two of the phenomena, for one of the reasons, which I next present, and that a much smaller number failed to see any of them, for the same reasons.

A specific possibility is that the non-see-ers were concentrated in a small section of the south side of the Cova da Iria containing a few thousand viewers. It is reasonable to assume that the color phenomenon covered all of the Cova except this section. Spectators on this section necessarily turned away from the Cova and faced south to view the spinning and falling sun, since in October at noon the sun is in the south in northern latitudes. Such people would have seen no color at all unless they turned around fully to look at the people in the Cova, behind them. Most of these, however, may have seen the apparent spin and fall, since it was noticed by almost all of the crowd at the Cova. A small share of them, however, may have had eyes which were resistant to this illusion but looked continually at the sun in the hope of seeing the phenomenon which the others said they were seeing. Thus these few (perhaps as many as one thousand) on the south side may have missed all of the major phenomenon of the sun dance.

There remain two or three minor phenomena. As indicated earlier, one of these, the "dancing" movement of the sun (the lateral movement of the sun in the sky) is hard to notice and may have been quite brief; also, the phenomenon of extreme heat may well not have occurred. The third minor phenomenon, "stare-ability" (the ability to stare at the sun in the open sky) may have been seen only in a part of the Cova, due to variations in cloud cover. Thus, it may well be that a small share of the people on the south side, perhaps only one hundred, failed to see any of the major and minor phenomena and were complete "non-see-ers."

There is another possible explanation for some of those who said they saw nothing at all. The prospect of seeing a great miracle was certainly frightening to some of the onlookers. This fright may have been intense in a few people and caused them to freeze their senses and fail to see what others were seeing. Or fright may have caused them to block from their minds the entire event.

It is thus reasonable to conclude that there may have been a very small share of the people at Fatima on October 13 who failed to see unusual phenomena, and yet the phenomena were "real," that is either physical phenomena or optical illusions due to meteorological conditions. Admittedly, one of these explanation, probably the better one, is very complex and involves assumptions which cannot be proven to be correct or incorrect. Nonetheless, these explanations for "non-seeers" are much stronger than the alternative of mass hallucination.

Clashes in the Explanations for the Phenomena. I am aware of the possibility of clashes between the explanation for one phenomenon and that for another. This is between the illusion of the spin of the sun and the other phenomena. Professor Stokl hinted that this illusion may involve a temporary injury to the eye. He said: "This is already a sign of the highly excited state of the eye." Although this is only a hint, and since there are differences between professor Stokl's illusion and the one at Fatima, nonetheless there remains the possibility that the Fatima illusion involved a temporary injury to the eye during the spin of the sun. Only one of the many mentions of the spin of the sun says that this occurred during the spin, and this is a 1952 report, which is much too late to have much value for this report. I will examine the color phenomena first for such a clash. In considering this possibility, I recall my conclusion that the best explanation for the spin of the sun is an optical illusion similar to the one reported by Professor Stokl, but that the Fatima illusion varied considerably from that of Stokl. One variation concerns the color of the spinning sun, which Stokl saw as dark blue. At Fatima a few witnesses saw the sun as black or a dark color. A much greater number of Fatima sources said or suggested that the spinning sun was silver, white, or light yellow, the color of the muted sun; and there was also some rather weak testimony that the spinning had a rainbow color.

If, in fact, the spinning sun seemed to have various colors, this merely adds another variation between Stokl's illusion and the Fatima illusion. Since so little is known about this illusion, it is possible that the color of the spinning sun varies and may sometimes be black, silver, or one of the rainbow colors. A clash would occur only if black, silver, or rainbow colors were noted on the people and landscape (and perhaps on the clouds) while the onlookers were suffering the illusion of the spinning sun. There are no reports of black, or any colors of the muted sun being seen on the people or the landscape during the spin. But there were some tentative reports of rainbow colors being seen on the people and landscape during the spin. Therefore, I give the details of this potential clash.

I noted previously that about a dozen sources suggested, more or less strongly, that a rainbow color was noted on the sun during its spin (see pages 140 and 141). Eleven of these same sources say or suggest that one or more rainbow colors were also seen on the clouds, the people, or the landscape. Two were very short and it is very doubtful whether the sources intended to say that the colors were seen on the people during the spin.[4] Six others merely report colors after they report the spinning sun and thus offer only weak evidence of a rainbow color on the crowd during the spin.[5] Another source seems not to be reporting events in sequence.[6] The other three sources seem to say that color was seen on the clouds, people, or landscape while the sun was spinning. None, however, clearly say this.

One of the three sources said the sun was "crowned by various colors, in a movement of rapid rotation, (Gist– which seemed a firewheel). The spectators, looking at each other showed a yellow color."[7] While this text does not specifically say that the yellow color occurred during the spin, it strongly suggests it.

The second source, a letter, also suggests it fairly strongly. It says the sun was a blue-silver color and "a bit from here on the sun is tinted green, purple, yellow and blue, but it stayed without rays. It sends out billows of smoke, so to speak, of the color which it shows, but the shape of the disk is perfect and this disk turns with a vertiginous rapidity and at a certain moment the sun descended. Later it appeared more to the right and later more to the left or vice-versa. At a (certain) moment the sun takes on a bright pink color, and behind each mountain there appears something like a veil of the same color."[8]

However, this same source, in a sworn statement, later said:
I see a very light silvery-blue disk, with no rays, that takes on its natural color and begins to turn vertiginously, and then this disk takes on different colors. It sends out from itself something like billows of smoke of the color of which it is tinted, but it keeps its perfectly round form, without rays, and can be stared at perfectly. At a certain moment I see the coloring to be

---

[4] Annex I #61C, #61D
[5] Annex I #23, #44, #51, #55, #72, #93
[6] Annex I #55
[7] Annex I #44
[8] Annex I #49

vivid rose. Behind every peak rises a gauzy veil of the same color. Both the land and crowd reflect it.[9]

The word "then" (which I underlined) clearly seems to say that the color came after the spin of the sun. This statement not only seems to contradict the earlier letter, but probably was more carefully thought out, since the writer swore to it.

The third source says: "the sun, which had uncommon signs, turning on itself, shaking, and he noticed at the same time that around it was a yellow-reddish color, which was reflected on the whole crowd and the horizon."[10] This seems a clear indication that color was seen on the crowd during the spin, although it could mean that color was seen during the "shaking" (the horizontal movement of the sun). Further, this source was an illiterate whose testimony was written up by a scribe and read to the testifier. This makes it less sure that the key phrase "at the same time" was intended by the testifier.

In summary, eleven sources seem to suggest or imply that they saw a rainbow color or colors on the people, landscape, or clouds while the sun was spinning. None are entirely firm on this point and only two (or possibly three) are more than weak suggestions. Therefore, if the spin of the sun was an optical illusion which resulted from a temporary injury to the eye, it would seem very likely that the testimony of these sources is misleading and was not intended to suggest or imply that rainbow colors were noted on the crowd or land during the spin. The likelihood of a clash between the rainbow color phenomenon and the spin of the sun is thus greatly reduced, if not entirely eliminated. The likelihood is further reduced by the fact that fifty sources reported seeing a color phenomena (see page 103). It is very hard to conclude that so many wrongly thought that they saw this phenomenon.

However, the same thing cannot be said of the phenomenon of the falling sun. Six sources clearly say that the sun was spinning as it seemed to fall toward the earth, and nine other sources appear to say the same thing (see page 145). I previously noted four possible explanations for the falling sun, all very tenuous (see page 163). One was that the fall was part of the illusion of the spinning sun. The other three require normal eyesight and would seem to be impossible, if one's eye was temporarily injured from staring at the muted sun. Thus it would seem that the best explanation for the fall of the sun is that it

---

[9] Annex I #73
[10] Annex I #61B

was part of the illusion of the spinning sun. As such, the possibility of a clash would be the same as that for the spinning sun.

The next phenomenon to be considered as a possible clash is the lateral movement of the sun in the sky. Two sources clearly indicate that this movement did not coincide with the spin of the sun. One first describes the spin and the fall and adds: "Later it (the sun) appeared more to the right and later more to the left, or vice-versa." The second tells of two occurrences of flames around the sun, followed by two spins, and then says: "Even a third time the sun which seemed to have brusque, shaky movements, was wrapped in blue flames, which were followed by the loss of light (the blue flame) and the rotary movement of the (sun)."[11] Most other sources provide no information about whether the lateral movement coincided with the spin. However, two sources suggest that the lateral movement may have accompanied the fall, which is known to have occurred while the sun was spinning. One says that the sun seemed to near the earth in "brusque and rapid movements." The second says that the spinning sun suddenly came down in a zig-zag.[12] If the sun was falling and moving laterally back and forth at the same time, this would presumably result in a movement that seemed to be a zig-zag.

Unfortunately, I can offer no explanation for this apparently contradicting testimony, except that part of it was wrong, or at least is misleading. In any case, it is only a possible clash, since we have the two sources which said that the lateral movement did not accompany the spin of the sun. Since there is a firm explanation for the lateral movement, assuming that it was not noted during the spin, I prefer to accept these two sources. However, for this phenomenon, there remains the possibility of a clash.

The other two minor phenomena also have no clear tie-in with the spinning sun. The ability of the crowd to stare at the sun in the open sky was quite strongly indicated by eight sources, as reported in detail earlier (see pages 97-100). None suggest that this sun in the open sky coincided with the spin, except the literary figure, who clearly was writing a work of art rather than a careful detailing of the facts. Her

---

[11] Annex I #49, #59
[12] Annex I #23, #101

statement that the sun "was seen to rotate and wander within the circle of receded clouds"[13] may not have meant that the spinning and wandering occurred together.

Finally, the phenomenon of great heat must be considered. It was reported by six sources, five of which indicate that it occurred during the spin (see pages 169 and 170). And since the sun was spinning during the fall, it follows that the great heat, if real, occurred during the spin and fall. However, this phenomenon would have been <u>felt</u> and not <u>seen</u>, and thus logically could have occurred during a period of temporary injury to the eye.

Reviewing the possibility of clash between the explanations for the spin of the sun and the other phenomena, no clear clash occurs. There appears to be a clash with some explanations for the fall of the sun. However, if other explanations are rejected and the explanation chosen is that the fall is an optical illusion no clash occurs. I now have finished my explanations of clashes between the phenomena. I next give a summary of each of the phenomenon of the sun dance.

The "Dance Itself"—the lateral movement of the sun. The lateral movement of the sun is one of the minor phenomena of the sun dance. It is the only one for which a firm explanation is available. It is mentioned by as many as twenty-two sources, most of which give no worthwhile details. The movements back and forth were probably very short in each direction and were probably quite brief. It was surely much less spectacular than the major phenomena, which accounts for the fact that most sources do not mention it. A few sources, however, give details and leave no doubt that the phenomenon occurred.

The firm natural explanation for this phenomenon is the optical illusion called induced movement. Specifically, higher clouds or an air lens may have caused the sun to be visible but muted in brightness, so that the crowd could stare at it comfortably, and small lower clouds near the sun moved fairly fast, and this cloud movement created the illusion that the sun was moving. This phenomenon was less widely reported than the major phenomena, and it may have lasted only a short period of time, or perhaps it occurred on two or three short periods of time. Being less spectacular and probably much briefer than

---

[13] Annex #50

the major phenomena, it deserves to be called a minor phenomena, although it clearly impressed many onlookers. (See pages 165-169.)

This phenomenon is clearly very rare, since it requires that higher clouds be thin enough to produce a muted sun but not be so thin that the sun is hard to stare at; and it also requires that smaller clouds occur at a lower level in the area of the sun and be moving in such a way as to create the illusion of induced movement. Alternatively, it requires an air lens, also a rarity, to mute the sun above the lower clouds.

The Color Phenomena. The phenomenon of rainbow colors is the only one that can be said to be a firm, real and physical one. It was reported by a large majority of the available sources. However, there are a great many variations in the reporting. A few sources gave reports which were somewhat negative, but there are several explanations for them, in addition to the explanations that are common to all the phenomena. (See pages 89-91, and 106-107.) There is another possible color phenomenon, that of colored flames. Since it was reported by only a few sources it might be that what they saw as flames was what other witnesses saw as sparks around the spinning sun or as rainbow colors. But, the sources of the reports of flames seem sound, and the possibility that the flames were a separate phenomenon cannot be entirely rejected.

The only known explanation for the rainbow colors is an air lens, a meteorological phenomenon which diffused the sunlight into broad bands of its component colors. This explanation seems solid, but suffers from the fact that I have only an oral, and not any written, authoritative source for the ability of an air lens to diffuse light into its component colors. I have no explanation for the colored flames, if they are a distinct phenomenon, except the fantastic one of a small cloud covering the sun and mimicking the effects of an eclipse.

The Spin of the Sun. The spin of the sun is probably the most spectacular of all the phenomena of the sun dance. It was reported by a large majority of the available sources and only one denies it, plus the few who said they saw no phenomena at all. It was undoubtedly an optical illusion, since the real spin of the sun would have to be speeded up by millions (or at least hundreds of thousands) of times in order to be noticeable by the human eye as a rapid spin, and the devastating effects of such a spin would have to be negated; also the ability of observatories to note this change would have to be negated.

There were many unimportant variations in details of the spin, mostly due to incomplete reporting, but there were a number of significant variations—in its color, on whether it occurred once or several times, and on whether or not the sun was covered by a dark object. There are good explanations for these variations and no reasonable doubt that this illusion occurred and was noted by most of the crowd.

Only one natural explanation is known for this phenomenon— that it is an optical illusion due to a temporary injury to the eye caused by staring at the muted sun. My only source for this explanation is a German meteorologist, but his statements are firm and strong. I have no reason to doubt them except that I have found no other source for this illusion in the many books on meteorology which I have read. Nonetheless, this phenomenon was surely an optical illusion, whether or not it was the same as the illusion seen by the German meteorologist.

Fall of the Sun. It seems clear that a considerable majority of the crowd at Fatima on October 13 had the impression that the sun was falling from the sky. Many were terrorized, but some were not. This was clearly an apparent fall. A real fall would have had disastrous effects. We have fewer details on the fall than on the spin, but have similar variations in detail, namely on the color of the falling sun and on the repetition or non-repetition of the fall. The explanations for the variations are similar to those for the spin.

I have already indicated that the only tenable explanation for the fall of the sun is that the fall is part of a combined optical illusion of the spin and fall of the sun. (See pages 172, 173, and 211-214.)

Staring at the Open Sun. A minor phenomenon reported by a limited number of sources was their ability to stare at the sun in the open sky. Despite this limited number, it is quite clear that such a phenomenon occurred. Support for this conclusion comes from the many witnesses who stated that they could stare at the sun and implied that this was unusual, or else they would not have bothered to report it. We are not told how long this phenomenon lasted, but we have firm evidence of clouds covering and uncovering the sun during the sun dance.

Two explanations are offered for this phenomenon. One is that the diffused light of the sun, caused by an air lens, was weak enough to allow the crowd to stare at the sun even when it was not covered by clouds. The other is quite fantastic and is similar to the one offered for colored flames—that a small cloud mimicked the effect of an eclipse, enabling the crowd to stare at the sun in the open sky. The first explanation appears to be much stronger, but needs support from an authority in the field of diffusion of sunlight.

Extraordinary Heat. The final phenomenon is that of extraordinary heat. It was reported by only a few sources, but receives some support from a few men who said that their clothes dried unusually fast after the rain. (A few women indicated that theirs did not.) Despite the very strong statements of these men (for example, heat like an oven opening) there remains a distinct possibility that no unusual heat occurred, and that the sudden appearance of the sun, coming right after the rain and cold, created a false impression of great heat. Also, those who feared the falling sun would burn up the earth may have imagined great heat. I know of no good explanation for this phenomenon, if real. Perhaps a meteorologist can offer one.

RARITY OF THE PHENOMENA

As noted earlier, if the phenomena of the Fatima sun dance were natural, it can be considered miraculous only if they are so rare that their occurrence at the forecasted time and place would seem to be a mathematical impossibility. Thus I must discuss their rarity. That the phenomena are rare cannot be doubted. The mere fact that I have had great difficulty in finding any reference to them is by itself evidence of their rarity. None of the major phenomena of the sun dance are mentioned in the seven books on meteorology which I examined (see my bibliography) including one which was devoted exclusively to atmospheric phenomena. However, since I have so little information, it is difficult to say how rare each of the phenomena is, except one, which can be said to be exceedingly rare.

The Color Phenomenon. This one is the color phenomenon, specifically the rainbow colors. As noted before, this phenomenon, unlike the other major phenomena, could be a supernatural miracle and one which did not boggle the mind. If so, there is no need to discuss its rarity. However, it could also have a natural cause. Available testimony strongly suggests that it was a real meteorological phenomenon, rather than an illusion. Therefore, the fact that such a phenomenon is not mentioned in the seven recent books on meteorology suggests by itself that the color phenomenon is very rare. Meteorology has been a major science for over a century. For purposes of forecasting the weather, meteorologists have long studied weather conditions over much of the world. In the process, they have noted and reported on many unusual meteorological phenomena, such as coronas, halos, sun dogs, and sun pillars. If the color phenomenon was anything but exceedingly rare, it surely would have been known and reported by at least a few meteorologists, and thus would be mentioned in books on meteorology.

A few facts and a little mathematics support the concept that the color phenomenon may be real and yet be unknown to meteorologists. If one assumes that a color phenomenon like that at Fatima occurred a few times in the last century somewhere in the more populated areas of the world (thereby excluding Canada, Australia, Russia, including Siberia, and Antarctica), what are the chances that they occurred in an area with a population of more than a few dozen people? (Occurrences in an area with two dozen people or less might not have become known to meteorologists or have been ignored by them as unreliable.) The area of this portion of the earth is roughly 42,000,000 square miles. The population is highly concentrated. Much of the area is agricultural or forested, and is lightly populated; much is even more sparsely populated (the Rockies and Andes, the jungles of South America and Africa, the Sahara and Gobi deserts).

The area covered by the color phenomenon at Fatima is unknown. If it was one quarter of a square mile (much larger than the Cova da Iria) there are sixteen such areas in a square mile or about 670,000,000 such areas in 42,000,000 square miles. If the area covered by the color phenomenon was one square mile, the figure becomes 42,000,000. Even if the area covered at Fatima was 100 square miles, there remains 420,000 such areas in the more populated areas of the world. There may be 420,000 places on earth with a population of more than a few dozen people, but there clearly are many less than 670,000,000 or even 42,000,000. This suggests that a color phenomenon like that at Fatima could easily have occurred a few times in the last century somewhere in the "more populated" areas and yet have been seen by no one or only by a very few people and be unknown to meteorologists.

None of the other phenomena of the sun dance appear to be purely meteorological, although all involve staring at the sun, and thus have a meteorological element. As such, one would expect that they would be mentioned in books on meteorology, if they were common or even fairly common.

The Lateral Movement of the Sun. The lateral movement of the sun, the "dance itself," is explained as an optical illusion caused by a large upper cloud (or perhaps as an air lens) which muted the sun and further by small lower clouds which moved around the sun's image to create the impression that the sun was moving rather than the clouds. Since this illusion requires a combination of conditions it is surely rare. Even the similar, and much more common, illusion that the moon is moving, rather than clouds around it, is quite rare.

The Spin and Fall of the Sun. The other two major phenomena— the spin and fall of the sun—are best explained as an optical illusion caused by staring at the muted sun. The only source for this phenomenon which I have found is Professor Stokl. His statement suggests that the phenomenon of the spinning sun is quite common. However, this is clearly not the case, since I have found no other reference to it, and until 1999 it was never mentioned as a possible explanation for the spinning sun. My own efforts to confirm this phenomenon by staring at the muted sun for about one minute were a failure. I suspect that some other atmospheric condition, in addition to a muted sun, may be required for this illusion to occur. In any case, it seems to be a rare phenomenon. Clearly, the illusion of a spinning sun is a rare one.

Moreover, the optical illusion of Professor Stokl did not include an illusion of a falling sun. Yet it appears to have been part of the illusion of the spinning sun at Fatima. I can only conclude that the falling sun is not always a part of this illusion. Obviously this suggests that the illusion that the sun is spinning and also is falling occurs less frequently than the single illusion that the sun is spinning. The combination of the two phenomena would appear to be very rare.

I am reluctant to discuss the rarity of the other two minor phenomena—the ability of the crowd to stare at the open sun, and the unusual heat—since neither is firmly established. However, the "stareability" is a fairly firm phenomenon and merits comment. I have found no reference to such a phenomenon in the books on meteorology which suggests that it is also a rare one. If it occurred at Fatima, it adds another layer of rarity to the sun dance.

CONCLUSIONS

Assuming that each of the phenomena at Fatima were rare or very rare, the combination of the rarities of each of the phenomenon certainly suggests that the sun dance was an exceedingly unlikely occurrence. And of course it is much more unlikely that such an occurrence would happen at the time and place that a miracle had been forecast. Conservatively, it can be said that the chance that the phenomena noted at Fatima would occur at the hour forecast is one in a million. In view of such odds, it seems to me that the occurrence can be considered as miraculous.

It has been argued that the fact that many sun dances are said to have occurred after the one at Fatima means that sun dances are not truly a rare occurrence. However, most of the supposed sun dances were said to have happened at the site of an apparition by the Blessed Virgin or in some other religious context. Those who claimed to have seen these sun dances after October 13, 1917, were surely aware of the Fatima sun dance. Most were surely hallucinations, imaginations or inventions, although I will admit the possibility that some were individual visions granted by God and that a few were real but have natural explanations. One or two may be miraculous repetitions of the Fatima event, although this is doubtful. A thorough and scholarly study of these later sun dances needs to be made. But unless and until such studies prove that sun dances are less than one-in-a-million occurrences, I remain convinced that the Fatima event was a very rare and miraculous occurrence, as well as a very spectacular one.

I have now presented what I view as firm evidence that the Fatima sun dance at Fatima on October 13, 1917, was a true miracle—the work of God. However, I note that further research needs to be done to establish even more firmly the miraculous nature of the Fatima sun dance. A thorough and scholarly study of the claims of later sun dances must be made. Further studies of the claims that the sun dance was noted in towns near Fatima on October 13, 1917, should also be done. And studies by meteorologists, experts on optical illusions, and chemists are needed. It is my hope that in the twenty-first century scholars will undertake thorough and complete studies of Fatima and of other modern miracles. I hope such studies will be as thorough and complete as those made in the preceding centuries for Sacred Scripture and Biblical background and history.

The main purpose of this book has now been achieved—to establish with reasonable firmness that the Fatima events of 1917 were truly spectacular and miraculous. I now need to answer the questions posed at the beginning of this book—was Fatima the greatest miracle since the time of Christ; if so, why did God perform this miracle at the start of the twentieth century, and why did He make it more spectacular by promising it three months in advance, thus guaranteeing that it would be seen by tens of thousands of people.

As I stated at the beginning of this book, the answers to these questions may be: that Fatima is truly the greatest miracle since the time of Christ, that the challenges and threats to Christianity in the twentieth century were greater than at any time since the early days of Christianity, and that Fatima is God's strongest answer to these challenges and threats. The rest of this book shows why these conclusions are reasonable.

CHAPTER XIII

EARLIER CHALLENGES
AND MIRACLES

Ours is not the first great challenge to the Faith. There have been many times over the centuries when thoughtful Christians feared that all was lost.

The first challenge occurred right after the crucifixion of Jesus. His disciples feared a similar fate and hid themselves. Peter denied he was a follower of Christ. These frightened men seemed unlikely to spread his gospel. This danger, according to Scripture, was overcome by the miracles of the Resurrection and the descent of the Holy Spirit on the apostles. Christians rightly consider them (and creation) as the most important miracles. But the Resurrection may not have been as spectacular as it is pictured in Christian art. Admittedly, it and the tongues of fire, which are said to have descended on the apostles with the Spirit, seem quite spectacular. But Scripture gives us firmly only about a dozen people who could testify to these two miracles, and to that extent they are less spectacular than the sun dance.[1]

This first threat was followed by another serious one—the danger of becoming merely a sect within Judaism. It is clear from the *Acts of the Apostles* and the epistles that the twelve apostles viewed their mission to be only to the Jews. Gentiles could become followers only by being circumcised and obeying the Mosaic Law, with its extremely

---

[1] Paul's 500 people who saw Christ after the Resurrection (1 Corinthians 15:6) are less firm, in view of the failure of Acts to report this tremendous event.

severe requirements, (little activity on Sunday, no contact with Gentiles or "unclean" persons, no eating of pork or shellfish, etc.). Under these conditions Christianity was unlikely to be accepted by many Gentiles, and Christianity might have become merely a liberal branch of Judaism. *Acts* tells us that this threat was avoided by Peter's dream or vision, followed by the conversion of the Roman centurion, by Paul's miraculous encounter with Christ on the road to Damascus, and his later victory over the Judaizers at the meeting in Jerusalem. These events might be called miraculous, but hardly spectacular. Critics say that Paul merely had a sunstroke, during which he imagined his encounter with Jesus. This threat was overcome only at the expense of the mission to the Jews, most of whom remained faithful to Judaism.

Another danger occurred near the end of the first century AD. Christians expected Christ's return during the lifetime of those who had heard Him preach. Both *Acts* and the epistles make this clear. Christ's failure to return by AD 100 or 110 must have caused many Christians to waver in their faith. History tells us nothing about this problem, neither that it became a crisis nor how it was overcome. But the likelihood that it was overcome by a spectacular miracle is virtually nil. If such a miracle had occurred, it would surely have been remembered and recorded by Christians of that time.

One more serious danger for Christianity at this time was the danger of breaking into competing sects as the Church developed its doctrines. It is clear from the New Testament and early Christian history that Jesus left His followers no full set of doctrines, but only vague teachings on many matters of faith. Questions which had to be answered included: was Jesus truly and eternally divine and if so was he also truly human; was He equal to the Father; was there only one God or two or even three; was the Spirit a separate God or Being and was It equal to the Father and the Son; was there a real or only a symbolic presence of Jesus in the Eucharist; and if Christians sinned grievously, could they be forgiven and by what procedure.

History tells us very little about how these questions were answered. Undoubtedly the apostles played an important part, but we have no details. Many scholars believe that Paul played a major role, and his epistles reveal teachings which are missing or vague in the gospels—original sin and Redemption, among them. But his epistles and other early Christian writings, plus the Nicene Creed, indicate that "prophets" played a major role also. The Creed says that the "Spirit spoke through the prophets." The New Testament also tells us that "false prophets" disturbed the early Church. Serious dissensions did arise. Marcionism was one of them. But by the time of Constantine, the Church had developed its major doctrines and most of the Christian world accepted them. That this happened might be considered miraculous. Christians believe that the Church was guided by the Holy Spirit but do not claim that the Spirit used spectacular miracles in the process.

One more major challenge facing the early Church was developing its organization without splitting into two or more sects. In the New Testament we find no indication that Jesus gave His apostles any detailed instructions on Church organization. Catholics claim that He put Peter in charge, but Paul's epistles show that he claimed considerable independence. We do not know how the Church developed into a hierarchical body, with priests, bishops, and a leading bishop in Rome. Many scholars believe that, in the days of the apostles, Jewish-Christian communities tended to be hierarchical, while Gentile-Christian communities tended to be evangelical, that is to be guided by "prophets," rather than by elders or priests. Again we might consider it miraculous that Christianity avoided falling into two forms of organization (hierarchical and evangelical) and that the various bishops and communities came to accept the bishop of Rome as the head (or at least the leading) bishop. Once more the Church claims that this unity in organization was achieved with the aid of the Holy Spirit, but does not claim it was achieved by obvious and spectacular miracles.

Early Christians faced yet another challenge—the best-known one—persecution. The first severe persecution came from the Jews, supposedly spearheaded by Paul. *Acts* implies that this persecution was weakened or stopped by Paul's miraculous conversion on the road to Damascus, a miracle of major importance, but not a spectacular one. In the next two and a half centuries a number of serious persecutions occurred. The most serious were the "Decian" (AD 250-260) and the "Diocletian" (303-323). Major defections followed, and if either persecution had been continued for a few more years, the results might have been disastrous for Christianity. But the "Decian" was weakened by the early death of Decius and the favorable attitude of his successor Valerian (253-260), who briefly renewed the persecution in 258, until his capture by the Persians. Christians might claim that the death of Decius and the capture of Valerian were the work of God, but they do not claim that they were openly miraculous.

The persecution begun by Diocletian is the best known. It started in AD 303 and was very harsh throughout the Empire, with the possible exception of Gaul, where Constantus is said to have been lax in enforcing it. It was ended in the western part of the Empire in 312 with the victory of Constantine. It was relaxed temporarily in the East in 311, but resumed later and ended only in 323 with Constantine's victory over his last rival. Christian Tradition has long claimed that his crucial victory in the West occurred in a spectacular and miraculous way, namely that Constantine and his army saw a fiery cross in the sky, with the Latin words for "In this sign conquer," that he had his soldiers put this sign on their shields, and that his victory in the crucial battle of Milvian Bridge was the result of this great and spectacular miracle.

If this tradition is true, then the miracle was truly great and spectacular. But modern historians, including Catholics, tend to view this tradition as legendary. They note that the Christian writer, Lactantius, in AD 320 wrote only that Constantine had a vision of Christ, who told him to put the Christian emblem on his army's shields. Not many years later the famous Christian historian Eusebius, who interviewed Constantine and surely got his story from him, reported that Constantine and his army saw the fiery cross and the words in the sky. Either version makes Constantine's victory against a superior force seem miraculous. But the version of Lactantius, and the opinion of modern scholars, suggests strongly that it was not a spectacular miracle. Critics would say that Constantine had a dream or he invented the whole story.

It seems likely that Christianity faced one more challenge in its earliest centuries—acceptance of its doctrines by the highly intelligent. The Church would have scarcely been accepted by leaders and other prominent men, including Constantine, unless it had achieved some acceptance among the more intelligent. Certainly its opponents—

pagan priests and philosophers—attacked the Church with intellectual arguments.

Many of the Church's teachings presented little difficulty to the intelligent of the Empire. This was especially true of the teachings derived from the Old Testament: the existence of only one God; His purely spiritual nature; the gradual creation of the world; Adam and original sin; the Flood and the Tower of Babel; the Promised Race; Moses and the Ten Commandments; the promise of a Redeemer; and the human soul and life after death. These teachings, if not necessarily true, were at least intellectually acceptable and vastly superior to pagan teachings.

But many of the new teachings of Christianity were very difficult to accept intellectually: the Eucharist as the body of Christ; the divinity and humanity of Jesus; the three Persons in God; the doctrine that Jesus, being God, made reparation to God for the sin of Adam; and the virginity of Mary. We do not know how Christians convinced deep thinkers to accept these doctrines. Undoubtedly many were impressed by the piety and charity of Christians and their steadfastness in persecutions. But we might wonder if this was enough to convince them. Logically, Christians should have cited the great miracles of Jesus and the apostles as God's support for their difficult doctrines. Perhaps also, the heavy thinkers were impressed by miracles unknown to us, in the dark period of Christian history in the second and third centuries. One claim of a spectacular miracle in this period has survived.

This is the miracle of the Twelfth Roman Legion. Sometime near AD 170 the Roman Emperor Marcus Aurelius was in deep trouble. Prolonged war in the East and a plague had depleted him of men and money. When Germanic tribes invaded he had to patch together an army that included slaves and gladiators. At first they were successful but then they were surrounded by the Qaudi, who cut off their water supply. Their situation seemed desperate; surrender seemed inevitable. Christian Tradition has it that a large group of Christian soldiers knelt openly, in view of the Quadi, and prayed to God for help. Suddenly it rained and the soldiers caught water in their helmets. Hail and lightning frightened the Quadi, who surrendered on the spot. Christians claimed a great miracle. But Marcus Aurelius gave the credit to Jupiter Pluvius. Perhaps the Christian claim helped to convince some intellectuals. But this event can scarcely be viewed as a great and spectacular miracle, since it has a purely natural explanation—that of a fortuitous storm.

The first three centuries of its existence were clearly critical for Christianity. That the Church overcame all the threats and challenges that I have just cited seems by itself truly miraculous. Offhand, it would seem that the dangers faced by early Christianity were as great or greater than those of the twentieth century. And yet I find no miracle after Pentecost which equals or approaches the miracle of Fatima in "spectacularity," except possibly that of Milvian Bridge, and its spectacular nature is highly doubtful, as I have already noted.

THE MIDDLE AGES

From the time of Constantine to the Renaissance, Christianity remained dominant in Europe. By AD 500 it was the religion of the majority of the people of the Roman Empire and had spread to the barbarian tribes, the Persian Empire, and even farther east. This greatly reduced the danger that Christianity would be wiped out by persecution, but nonetheless over the centuries it faced a number of challenges that seemed critical to many and caused them to fear that the Church was doomed. Thousands of miracles were claimed over this long period and a large number were accepted as authentic by local or regional Church authorities. But few, if any, are so spectacular as to seem to be God's answer to the danger of the time. Moreover, formal procedures to verify these claims did not exist, at least in many cases and places, and adequate documentation is seldom available to verify these claims. Often the earliest reports that have survived are dozens of years after the purported miracles. All this makes it very difficult to distinguish fact from legend. Consequently, most modern scholars tend to view the more spectacular claims as legendary. Even ignoring this, I have as yet found no claims of miracles for this period which equal the Fatima events in "spectacularity."

Serious threats to Christianity occurred in the fourth century and were caused chiefly by the Arian and Donatist heresies. In AD 361-363, the emperor Julian tried to re-establish paganism and favored the heretics to weaken Christianity. His reign was too short to allow him success. Then in 392 Eugenius became emperor and again tried to reinstall paganism. He was defeated in battle by Theodosius, who supported the Church and suppressed the heresies. A miracle is claimed for his victory. One version says he prayed openly for victory, in view of the opposing troops, the day before the battle. Another says that the apostles appeared to him and promised victory. The next day a storm arose at a critical moment and the troops of Eugenius believed the gods were against them and lost courage. Even if not legendary, this could not be called a great and spectacular miracle, given the possibility of a natural event.

The barbarians who overran the Empire in this period were chiefly Arians, and their victories for a while divided Christianity. But being fewer in number and culturally inferior, they gradually adopted orthodox Christianity. I have read of no great miracles associated with this gradual process.

In the seventh century, an even greater danger was posed by the Muslims, who conquered Arabia, Syria, Egypt, all of North Africa, Persia, Spain, and part of Southern France. Had they conquered Europe, Christianity might have been reduced to a minor religion like Zoroastroanism. But they were beaten in the West by Charles Martel at Tours in central France; and in the East the Christian Byzantine Emperors Leo III and Constantine V halted their advances. Once more I have found no great miracle associated with the Christian victories. But in this case all the conquered lands except Spain and southern France were lost permanently to the Muslims, who remain a threat to Christianity today.

However, a fairly spectacular victory is claimed by the Eastern Church for this period. The Persian Empire, still intact, had joined with the barbarian Avars to attack and had Constantinople under siege for ten days. As the center for the Eastern branch of Christianity, its loss would have been disastrous. Then (on August 6, AD 626) the Patriarch Sergius organized a procession through the city and had a statue of the Virgin placed at the city gates. The next day the enemy saw a very beautiful lady come out through the Blachernes gate. With an imposing air and majestic bearing she passed through the enemy camp without fear. This "apparition" caused concern among the enemy, who quarreled about it and eventually lifted the siege. Clearly this event, if not legendary, has a non-miraculous explanation—the lady was a beautiful and brave Christian, perhaps made up to look ethereal.

The next century—AD 750 to 850—was relatively peaceful and Christianity fared well, especially during the long reign of Charlemagne. But the next one—850 to 950—was almost disastrous for the Church. The dynasty of Charlemagne broke up. Feudalism developed rapidly, with constant fighting among feudal lords. Commerce suffered greatly. The disorder was worsened by serious and widespread attacks by the Norsemen, who plundered and ravaged the coasts and up the major rivers of Europe. In Spain the re-conquest of the country from the Muslims met a severe setback. Pagan Magyars took over Hungary. Muslim forces conquered Sicily and Crete, and set up strongholds in southern Italy. Most seriously, in this darkest of the Dark Ages, the Church suffered a very profound moral decay that almost seemed fatal.

The rot at the top was probably the worst. The papacy, having lost its support from the Charlemagne dynasty, was taken over by powerful Roman families and the mobs they controlled. Unworthy popes were elected and lived scandalous lives. Their reigns were often very brief. There were seventeen popes in the period 897-955. One was said to have been poisoned. John XII was named pope at the age of eighteen and lived a very dissolute life. The decay extended to the bottom. Bishops tended to act as civil magistrates rather than clergy. The morals of priests and monks deteriorated, although there were some bright spots.

The Synod of Trosle recorded the despair of the time:

"The cities are depopulated, the monasteries ruined, the country reduced to solitude. As the first men lived without law or fear of God, abandoned to their passion, so now every man does what seems good in his own eyes, despising laws human and divine and the commandments of the Church. The strong oppress the weak; the world is full of violence against the poor and of the plunder of ecclesiastical goods."[2]

In defense of the Church it should be noted: that conditions at the time caused the hierarchy to lessen their attention to spiritual matters; as the civil authority deteriorated they were forced to take over civil duties—to care for the poor, widows and orphans, to administer justice and even to raise armies to defend themselves; also, that the power and wealth of the Church attracted unworthy men to the clergy; not only was the Church the major power, but it had acquired much property through wills and gifts.

Christianity was saved from the threatening disaster partly by its own internal renewal, led by such men as Alfred the Great and movements like that of the Cluny monastery in France. But probably the most important factor was the revival of the Holy Roman Empire under Otto I and his successors. These emperors were largely responsible for the election of worthy popes and the nomination of worthy bishops, although their motives were not entirely spiritual. They clearly hoped to dominate the Church (and use it to help control the diverse people of their empire), a problem which was to be with the Church for centuries.

There may have been major miracles which aided the Church to survive this great trial, but I am aware of only one such claim, and I presume it is poorly attested. Once again the great miracle is claimed by the Eastern Church in the defense of Constantinople. Again barbarian hordes were attacking the city. It is claimed that the faithful at the Blachernes Church there saw a great light above them and several of them saw the Virgin Mary accompanied by St. John the Baptist and the apostles, and that she spread a veil over the people as a sign of her protection. While my source does not say that the city was saved, it is clearly implied, as is the Virgin's role in its defense. It seems likely that whatever records of this event were made in that era were destroyed in 1453, when the Turks captured Constantinople.

The late Middle Ages, from AD 950 to 1300, are generally considered as prosperous years for the Church in the West. However, the

---

[2] *A Concise History of the Catholic Church*, p 220, Thomas Bokentotter, Image Books, Garden City, NY, 1979

Church in the East suffered from attacks by the Turks and Crusaders and from the seizure of most of Russia by the Mongols. The Latin Church engaged in a long struggle to maintain its independence, first against the German emperors and later against the French kings. The Renaissance, which followed, was again a low point for Christianity.

THE RENAISSANCE 1300-1600

The period from 1300 to 1600 is roughly the era of the Renaissance and the start of the Enlightenment. It was again a period of great troubles for Christianity, and again many pious souls feared for its future. The Church in the East suffered greatly. By 1400 the Islamic Turks had conquered most of Turkey and Bulgaria. And Islam maintained its control of the Middle East and North Africa. In 1453 a major Christian disaster occurred—the loss of Constantinople. By 1500 the Turks were in control of Greece and the Balkans. It is true that Christianity survived in Russia, where Ivan the Terrible drove out the Mongols, but Ivan and later tsars dominated the Church and used it to control the people and otherwise serve their goals.

To many, the advance of Islam was terrifying. In Europe in the 1500s it controlled the Balkans, part of south Russia, Bulgaria, Roumania, and Hungary. In Austria it even besieged Vienna. At its peak, under Suleiman the Magnificent (1520-1566) its fleets and raiders also controlled most of the Mediterranean and gained a foothold in Italy. Rivalry between Christian kingdoms weakened papal efforts to resist the Turks. Elsewhere Islam made further advances. Islamic powers ruled a large Persian Empire, almost all of India and Java and a part of black West Africa. Christians could take some consolation from the expulsion of Islam from Spain, the death of Suleiman, and the great naval victory at Lepanto.

In Europe, for other reasons, this period was a very bleak one for Christianity. It saw the rise of nations, with rulers in Spain, France, England, and Central Europe fighting to gain control of the Church in their lands and to gain support and domination of the papacy. The popes, meanwhile, had to contend not only with these rulers, but also against the Italian city-states and the mobs in Rome. Even worse, it had to overcome the corrupting influence of its own power and wealth, which nearly overwhelmed it in this period. And throughout this period it often saw the sad picture of Christian armies of one nation fighting those of another Christian nation. The Hundred Years' War between England and France is one case.

Until this period, it was possible to speak of the Church or Christianity as the same thing. Various heresies had threatened to split Christianity in the past, and the East had never fully accepted Roman authority, but nonetheless Christian unity had survived. But in 1472 ties between the East and West were finally and formally broken. And in several ways the unity and independence of the Church in the West was broken

In the period 1300-1378, it appeared that the Latin Church had become the French Church. It began in 1303 with an unsuccessful attempt by Philip the Fair to kidnap the pope. But in 1305 or 1309 Philip forced the weak pope Clement XIII to move to Avignon, away from the scheming Italian princes and the fickle Roman mobs. The Avignon popes, often dominated by French kings, made the French a large majority among the cardinals, the electors of the pope. The independence and international character of the Church was threatened. Also, the prestige of the Church and its finances were weakened by the richness and splendor of the papal palace and the papal court in Avignon.

Despite the pomp of the papal court, these popes, as a group, were not unworthy. They strove to reform the Church and to stay independent. No spectacular miracle is claimed in their eventual return to Rome. It was facilitated by victories of the papal army and its great general Albernoz, and by the efforts of Saint Catherine of Siena. But the return to Rome was soon followed by a danger greater than the Avignon threat.

This danger is usually referred to as the Great Schism. It began in 1378, largely as a reaction of the Roman mobs to the Avignon years. They warned the cardinals, who assembled to elect a new pope, that they must elect a Roman or at least an Italian. Feeling threatened, they elected the bishop of Bari, as Urban VI. They viewed him as stable and dependable. But he soon acted tyrannical and unstable. He publicly criticized the cardinals in fits of anger. Some historians think he may have been mentally unhinged by his election. The French cardinals, joined by three Italians, declared his election invalid, due to the threats, and elected Robert of Geneva as Clement VII, who chose Avignon as his residence. The nations divided rather evenly between the two. Both sides took up arms and increased taxes to support the effort. Urban's condition worsened. He tortured five cardinals whom he suspected of plotting against him and they died. He died in 1389. Succeeding popes on both sides continued the schism. Christians everywhere were scandalized. Cardinals, bishops, and rulers on both sides tried to mediate. Eventually the cardinals, in despair, called a council at Pisa in 1409. It deposed both popes and elected a new one, who soon died and was replaced by John XXIII.[3] There were thus three claimants to the papacy, all with the support of some rulers. Christianity in the West seemed hopelessly divided.

Once again the great danger was overcome largely through the efforts of the Holy Roman Emperor, in this case Sigismund. He called a second General Council in 1414 and induced John XXIII to legitimize it. It hoped to get all three popes to resign. But John fled and left the council members in dismay. Happily, Sigismund insisted that the Council continue. John, whose financial dealings and nepotism were scandalous, lost his support. The Council deposed him. Gregory XII, the reigning successor of Urban VI, resigned; but Benedict XIII, the Avignon pope, refused to resign, was deposed by the Council and abandoned by most of his supporters. The Council then elected an Italian as Martin V, who got wide support, effectively ending the schism. Once more the triumph of the Latin Church over this great threat is not credited to any great miracle by historians.

In the period 1450-1600 Christianity in the West not only suffered the great break-up of the Reformation, but also lived through a period of great moral decay. Before the break-up, the decay was so great that Christianity could not have survived indefinitely in this condition. And while the Reformation gave great impetus to moral reform, it also resulted in the scandal of Christians killing and torturing each other in the name of religion, and it created a rivalry between

---

[3] He is obviously not considered a true pope by the Church. Another pope took the name John XXIII in 1958.

Catholics and Protestants which lasted into the twentieth century. The antagonism, even hatred, was intense following the Huguenot wars in France and the Thirty Years' War in Germany.

The degradation in the period 1450-1550 is painful for Catholics to contemplate. This is the era of the scandalous Borgia popes and the ambitious Medici popes. Many of the popes, cardinals, and bishops lived scandalous lives. Church offices were regularly sold to the highest bidder. Many popes named relatives as cardinals, often at a very young age. Many bishops had two or more bishoprics but resided in neither and failed to supervise them; much of the lower clergy was also morally corrupt. Even the more worthy popes, living fairly austere personal lives, succumbed to the Renaissance spirit and reigned with great pomp and lavish ceremony. Unfortunately, many popes were more concerned with defending and expanding the Papal States in Italy than with their spiritual duties and devoted Church resources to military efforts. The Church claims no great miracle in its recovery from this disastrous condition. Clearly the Reformation, and the Catholic Counter-Reformation after the Council of Trent, were major factors in the spiritual revival in both Protestant and Catholic countries at the end of this period.

An unfortunate accompaniment of the Christian re-conquest of Spain occurred at this time—the Spanish Inquisition. Originally aimed at the Moors, it was extended to Jews and eventually drove most Jews from Spain. The tortures, deaths, and exiles created a great resentment against Christianity and especially against the Catholic Church among Jews. This undoubtedly hurt the Church as Jews became prominent among intellectuals of the West. Moreover, non-Jewish opponents of Christianity later cited the Inquisition, as well as the moral degradation of the period, as arguments against the Church and Christianity.

Near 1550, Christianity reached its nadir. The Muslims were conquering everywhere. The Great Schism was a recent memory. The Orthodox break was finalized. Catholics and Protestants were everywhere fighting each other. And efforts to bring needed reform to the Catholic Church had failed. But even at this dark moment no great and spectacular miracle is claimed by the Church or Christianity.

Again the fact that Christianity survived and flourished would seem almost miraculous.

THE ENLIGHTENMENT 1600-1800

In the period from 1600 to 1800, Christianity rose somewhat from the depths into which it had fallen in the preceding period. The Austrian and Russian armies defeated the Turks, who lost Hungary, Roumania, and part of the Balkans and South Russia. After 1648 the religious wars between Catholics and Protestants ceased. And Christianity was solidly established in both the Americas and in the Philippines. But the rivalry between Catholics and Protestants continued, the breakup of Protestants into sects continued and European monarchs continued, with some success, their efforts to control the churches in their countries and to get priests who would support them to be named bishops and cardinals. And most seriously, Christianity faced major intellectual challenges to its beliefs.

The intellectual challenge had roots in the late Middle Ages and the Renaissance. Universities were founded then and the study of Greek philosophers became very much in vogue. Aristotle was considered as "the" philosopher. His works, especially as derived from Arabic translations and commentary, clashed with Christian doctrines. His ideas were condemned by some, but others, especially Thomas Aquinas, reacted by accommodating the teachings of Aristotle to Christian doctrine. Modern Catholics tend to think his ideas were quickly accepted by the Church. Quite the opposite is true. A bitter battle ensued between the supporters of Aquinas and his conservative opponents. In 1277 the Bishop of Paris issued a famous condemnation of liberal errors, which was widely accepted. Somewhat later Aquinas' works lost ground to the mystical philosophy of Thomas Ockham. But by 1600 Aquinas' teachings, including the Aristotelian view of the universe, were accepted as gospel. In the struggle with Galileo, Aquinas' supporters became the new conservatives, a stand that Aquinas probably would have rejected.

In 1609, Galileo Galilei, using the recently invented telescope, first noticed and published evidence that Aristotle's earth-centered view of the universe was wrong. He met immediate sharp criticism. In 1615 he published a paper which showed how Genesis could be newly interpreted to permit the concept that the earth revolved around the sun. He met further condemnation, but in 1632 he felt safe in publishing a paper that clearly presented his earth-shaking ideas. He was wrong. In 1633 he was brought to trial by the Church, forced to recant, and silenced on this subject. It was a tragedy for Christianity, which became identified by scholars as the opponent of science and free inquiry. This reputation, supplemented by later Church actions, continued into the twentieth century. It was part of the intellectual challenge which Christianity faced at the time of the Fatima events and still faces.

Defenders have noted that the Church at this time was engrossed with the Reformation, that Tycho Brahe the most famous astronomer of the time, disagreed with Galileo, and that Galileo's claim was not yet proven and his explanations had errors (for one, Galileo taught that the motion of the earth caused our tides). They also note that the Church did not teach that the earth is the center of the universe, although almost all people believed it to be true. The Church does not claim any miracle in thus avoiding erroneous doctrine, but it does cite the continued guidance of the Holy Spirit.

I now note that Christianity no longer faced its challenges as a unit. Protestant reaction to the revolutionary ideas of Galileo is less well known than that of the Catholic Church, but was equally negative, if not more so. A main reason it is less well known is that Protestantism was divided and in some branches was less authoritarian. No Protestant leader could speak for even half of the Protestants. However, Protestants have tended to react in the same way as Catholics to modern intellectual challenges, further deepening the rift between Christianity and the intellectual world. Because Fatima occurred in a very Catholic context, from here on I am chiefly concerned with the challenges faced by the Catholic Church and its reaction to them. I will, however, note a few cases where Protestant reaction was different and significant.

The challenge of Galileo was not the only intellectual challenge faced by Christianity in this period. Another was Biblical criticism, based on Rene Descartes' principle of radical doubt: that inherited or new teachings should be subject to strict logical tests and not accepted until soundly proven. Richard Simon, the founder of modern Biblical criticism, tried to show it was not necessarily harmful to the Faith. He argued that Moses was not necessarily the sole author of the Pentateuch, and was strongly criticized by the French hierarchy. In 1682 his work was put on the *Index*. This and later actions of the Church against Biblical criticism, plus the continued use of the *Index*, were other reasons that scholars viewed Christianity as an enemy of science and learning.

Another major challenge of the Enlightenment was the demand for religious freedom. The demand was not yet strong. The old idea that unity of religion was needed to assure order was still widely held. It was unquestioned by the Orthodox East and the Muslim world. European monarchs had long favored the old idea. In both Catholic and Protestant countries there was an established religion. Christianity thus became identified with religious intolerance. It was a heritage that carried over, at least in Europe, to the time of Fatima. This reputation was clearly harmful in the young United States.

Another challenge of this era was that of freeing Christianity from its close association with the nobility and authoritarian rule. This association proved to be very harmful, at the end of this era, when the leaders of the French Revolution viewed the Church as an enemy and tried to eliminate it. Even though this effort eventually failed, the concept that the Church was the enemy of the lower classes survived and was spread by Napoleon to much of Europe, especially in the cities. Anticlericalism became strong and much of the lower class was lost or became only nominal Christians.

Christianity in this era was also weakened by the continued breakup of Protestantism into sects. In addition to Lutherans, Calvinists, and Episcopalians, from the previous era, there developed strong sects of Methodists, Baptists, Quakers, and others. And with the continued breakup, the possibility of Christian unity grew weaker. This was to make it very hard for Christianity to fight successfully against anti-Christian trends in modern times.

CHAPTER XIV

MODERN CHALLENGES AND MIRACLES 1800-2000

The era before the Fatima events brought enormous new challenges to the Catholic Church and to all Christianity, as well as a continuation of some older threats and problems. They might be summed up as the challenges of the modern world. It was industrialized, urban, and well educated, a world of vastly increased knowledge, with thousands of scholars and scientists, a world with political and religious freedom in some countries and demands for it in many others. It was also a world of great powers, with enormous armies and costly weapons. Finally, it was a world of great wealth and poverty, with governments threatened by new movements: socialism, communism, and anarchy. It was a very different world.

On the surface, Christianity was doing very well. The Muslim challenge substantially decreased as the Turks lost their power in Europe, and European powers replaced Muslims in India and Indonesia. Christian missionaries made great progress in black Africa, and the newly important Americas became solidly Christian. The threat to unity in the Catholic Church from Gallicism and Modernism was overcome and the antagonism between Catholics and Protestants lessened. Thus, in 1917 few Christians realized the enormity of the threats which they would face in the twentieth century. Few would have said that the threats would be the greatest since the early days of the Church. But looking at these threats from the perspective of the twenty-first century, we can see how serious they were and still are.

The industrial revolution was the source of one major challenge to Christianity. It created great wealth and great poverty. People flocked to the cities and horrible slums arose. Low wages and long working hours brought labor unions, socialism, and communism. These conditions presented a problem to the Church, in its traditional role of defender of the poor. For the most part, the Catholic Church and other Christian sects reacted slowly or negatively to the new situation. A few Catholic leaders, such as Bishop Kettler of Germany, recognized the challenge and supported labor unions and state intervention for workers. But only in the English-speaking world, among the major powers, did the Church successfully identify itself with the working class, and even this stand was taken only near the end of this era, largely through the efforts of Cardinals Manning and Gibbons. As late as 1866, conservative American and Canadian bishops tried to get the pope to condemn labor unions, which were largely Catholic in membership. Fortunately for this challenge, the very conservative Pius IX was succeeded by Leo XIII. In 1891 he issued his encyclical *Rerum Novarum*, often called the Magna Carta of the Christian labor movement. But the slowness of the Church in reacting to this challenge facilitated the creation of powerful socialist and communist movements in Europe, with negative attitudes toward Christianity. In Russia the very conservative Orthodox Church failed to ally itself with its small labor movement and disaster struck under Lenin.

The vast increase in knowledge, which began in the previous era with Galileo, was another source of challenge to Christianity in this period. Darwin presented a convincing case for his theory of evolution, geologists found that the earth was millions of years old, anthropologists discovered ancient bones (Cro-Magnon) which were entirely like those of modern humans and which were some 25,000 years old, and astronomers learned that our solar system is a tiny fraction of the universe. This new knowledge was entirely contrary to the understanding of the creation of the world and of man, as derived by Christians from Genesis. It challenged Christianity to re-interpret Genesis, in the light of the new knowledge. Current information has shed new light on these early discoveries and exposed some of them as not entirely accurate.

A similar challenge was presented by Biblical scholars in this era. A detailed study of the Pentateuch convinced many scholars that it was not written by Moses. Linguistic studies convinced experts that the apostle Matthew did not write the gospel attributed to him, although they did not deny that he was a source for it. Scholars further found convincing reasons to believe that the gospels were written long after Christ's death—some thirty-five years for *Mark*, nearly fifty years for two others, and sixty or seventy years for *John*. Some scholars gave even later dates. Most seriously, some scholars found strong arguments for the claim that the important monologues of Jesus in *John* were not spoken by Jesus, but represented the author's interpretation of the message of Jesus. And scholars also noted historical errors in the Old Testament and seeming contradictions in both Testaments. These scholarly studies received wide attention, at least among Protestant and Catholic scholars.

Various parts of the Protestant world reacted differently to these scholarly findings. Some reluctantly accepted them. Others refused and held to a literal interpretation of Genesis and insisted that the Bible was inerrant. At the other extreme, some, such as Albert Schweitzer, accepted them and argued that Jesus was not divine. These liberals did not achieve wide acceptance among the faithful in this era, but their views became known and liberal Protestantism was born. It would grow greatly in the twentieth century.

The Catholic and Orthodox world, being more authoritarian, avoided a similar split at this time. The popes did so by, in effect, putting blinders on its scholars and placing books with liberal theological tendencies on the *Index,* the list of books which Catholics were forbidden to read. Popes in this century sided with conservative Protestants. They insisted that Moses was the author of the Pentateuch and denied Darwin's theory of evolution, but not as infallible teachings. As late as 1909 the Pontifical Biblical Commission insisted on the literal historical accuracy of Genesis, even including the creation of Eve from Adam's rib, although conceding that the days of creation may not have been 24-hour periods. Two major pronouncements attacked modern thought. Pius IX, in his *Syllabus of Errors* in 1864, rejected freedom of religion and seemingly attacked progress and modern civilization. This reaction not only failed to meet the challenge, but furthered the belief among scholars that the Church and Christianity were the enemies of science and knowledge.

In defense of the Church's reaction (and that of conservative Protestantism) I note that these new views of the Bible presented serious threats, little noticed by most of the faithful, and required a careful development of responses to it. Thus, a simple concession that Genesis may not be historically accurate and that the Bible is not entirely error-free would have allowed theologians and the faithful to advance interpretations that clash with essential teachings. Serious splits could have developed (and in the Protestant world did develop). For example, denying the historical accuracy of Genesis could lead many to question the descent of the entire human race from the same parent, and thus to doubt the doctrines of original sin and Redemption.

Another challenge, which the Church faced in this era, was the growing demand for religious and political freedom. The Church and much of Christianity reacted negatively to this demand. With the horrors of the French Revolution in their mind, this reaction is not surprising. In Europe, Catholic and other sects openly favored monarchies. As demand for freedom grew, the pope issued two encyclicals (1832 and 1864) which attacked it. The 1832 document rejected separation of Church and State, denounced liberty of conscience, and called freedom of the press abominable. In Spain, the Inquisition was re-instituted. As mentioned earlier, the *Index* was used to suppress books deemed undesirable. At the end of this era, a broad censorship of statements of theologians and prelates was established.

Besides recollection of the French Revolution, other factors influenced the popes in their reactions: the long history of close ties between Church and State, and especially the entirely unacceptable teaching of the most liberal Catholic theologians, and of several prominent Protestant theologians. While it was logical for the Church to condemn these teachings, it was clearly unfortunate for the Church that it went to extremes in suppressing independent thought. At the end of this age the Church badly needed to change its image as the enemy of freedom.

In Latin America, the Church faced the challenge of replacing European priests with native priest, who were adequately trained. The revolutions in the early part of the century made the task doubly difficult. Many European priests, siding with the mother country, perished or left. Some seminaries closed. A struggle between the mother country and the new governments over the appointment of new bishops left many bishoprics without a bishop. Finally, the anti-clerical attitude of the French Revolution was successfully exported to Latin America, with anti-clericals often controlling the governments there. Later in the century the Church made some progress, but the century ended with a shortage of native priests, a poorly educated faithful, and much anti-clericalism.

In Italy the Church faced the challenge of adjusting to Italian nationalism and met the challenge poorly. Believing that an independent Papal State was necessary for the Church's wellbeing, it resisted Italian nationalism. Its actions probably accounted, in part, for the continued drift of Italians into nominal Catholicism.

In Spain and Portugal, the Church's support of monarchies probably had the same result. In 1910 in Portugal, this stigma, plus failure to support the laboring class, resulted in the overthrow of the monarchy and the installation of an anti-clerical government with a pro-communist bias. Fortunately, it had found no strong leader by 1917 and had been weak and inept in governing. But this could change easily, as Lenin proved in Russia soon after the Fatima events.

Two events occurred in this era which tended to reinforce the Jewish view of the Church as the enemy of Judaism. The lesser was the return of the Jews in Rome to their ghetto by Pius IX. The more important was the pogrom against the Jews in Russia by the tsar. Due to the very close ties of the Orthodox Church with the tsars, and its failure to fight the pogrom, it was clearly tied, in the Jewish mind, with their exile. For Jews it was one more expulsion from a Christian country, with expropriation of land and property. In the next era, individual Jews were to be influential opponents of Christianity.

THE TWENTIETH CENTURY 1917-2000

Christians at the time of the Fatima events were confident of the future of Christianity. It was dominant in the West, and the West controlled most of the world. Moreover, a large percentage of Christians were church-goers and, like the clergy, lived good lives. Few Christians thus could see the problems which were to come. There were to be

serious persecutions—from communist, Nazi, and Islamic governments. There was to be a much greater division of Christianity into
liberal and conservative groups. The intellectual challenge to the Faith
was to continue its growth, as science, knowledge, and education
advanced explosively. And material prosperity was to create a more
materialistic outlook in the West, which was contrary to Christianity.
This outlook, in conjunction with other new factors—birth control
and population growth—led many to abandon traditional Christianity. In examining each of these areas of challenge, I think I can well
establish that in the twentieth century the challenge and threat to
Christianity, or at least to traditional Christianity, was greater than at
any time since the days of Constantine. Some of these challenges did
not affect liberal Christianity and even fostered it.

The challenge of persecution clearly affected much of the world.
The communist threat began in Portugal, where the government in
power since 1910 persecuted the Church. If it had found an effective leader, it might have lasted until World War II or later. It would
have given important aid to the pro-communist government in Spain
against Franco, possibly causing his defeat. And when the Popular
Front took control in France, much of Western Europe would have
been in pro-communist hands. Although this danger of persecution
was avoided in Western Europe, the communist government in the
Soviet Union undertook a major persecution of religion and a major
campaign in favor of atheism. It extended this persecution and propaganda to Eastern Europe after 1945, and it was extended to all of
China in 1950. By the mid-sixties communists had taken over Cuba
and North Vietnam, communist-led revolutions were underway in
Venezuela and other parts of South America, and large communist
parties were threatening to take over the ballot box in France and Italy.
Communism seemed to be on the march everywhere, and the term
"domino effect" was coined by the press to describe the threat posed
by world communism.

At the present time this threat has greatly decreased (and the Blue
Army and other Christians who followed the request of the Virgin at
Fatima surely feel that their prayers were an important factor), but
China is still communist and the Communist Party is still strong in
Russia. Christianity has survived well the long persecution and pro-

paganda in Poland. But it suffered great losses among the people of other former Soviet satellites. It remains for the future to tell us how well Christianity will recover from the half-century of persecution and propaganda in Eastern Europe and the Soviet Union.

I scarcely need to note that the Nazi and Japanese governments aimed to conquer the world and that they were strongly anti-Christian. Had they succeeded, a worldwide persecution of Christianity would surely have followed. Today we tend to forget how close they came to winning. If Hitler had invaded England in 1940 he probably would have won, making a victory over the Soviet Union much more likely. Further, if the Japanese had delayed their attack on Pearl Harbor and the U.S. had remained neutral, the Soviet Union, without our massive aid, may have fallen in 1942. History records other blunders and missed opportunities of theirs.

In this century Islam has strongly recovered from its depths of the nineteenth century. Pro-Islamic governments have replaced the English and French in Egypt, North Africa, and almost all of the Middle East, as well as in Pakistan and Bangladesh; and the government of Indonesia is leaning that way. Further, Islam is making progress in black Africa. And, most importantly, Muslims have become zealous and militant in their faith. They are at present a serious threat to Christianity. Recent years have seen persecution of Christians by Muslims in Africa and Asia.

Although the danger of persecution has been and still is great, Christianity has faced and still faces an equal or greater challenge from other developments. This challenge has several aspects, including the intellectual. Much of the intellectual challenge is a continuation and expansion of nineteenth century ones. These include biological and astronomical discoveries that give Biblical creationists an opportunity to clarify the Genesis account.

Another aspect of the intellectual challenge is modern education, especially college education. I have already noted the existence of an anti-Christian bias among scientists and scholars in the nineteen century. In the first part of the twentieth century the Catholic Church, with its *Index* and its severe censorship of theologians and clergy, and fundamental Protestantism, with the Scopes monkey trial, did much to further this bias among scientists and educators. This bias was probably not greatly harmful to Christianity until the twentieth century. Before then, only a small percentage of the population went to college and thus few were influenced by teachers with this bias. But college-educated people number in the tens or hundreds of millions now. A large majority were educated in secular universities and many were influenced by the anti-Christian (and often agnostic) views of their professors. There are, perhaps, no statistics to prove the existence of this challenge, nor of the number of people affected by it. But there is no doubt that it existed and was strong. The Catholic Church met this challenge in the middle and latter part of this century by abolishing its *Index* and granting its theologians much greater freedom to publish their views. The majority of the Protestant world also granted its scholars much freedom, leaving the fundamentalists as a smaller but vocal minority. At the end of the century, Christianity had greatly reduced the bias against Christianity among intellectuals of all kinds, but during the century it sustained many losses among its faithful because of this bias and the great influence of college professors.

Another, and more difficult, challenge was presented by Biblical scholars. In large part it was based on findings of nineteenth century scholars, which received wider acceptance among Biblical scholars, theologians, and the general public. But it was also based on new findings of science, archaeology and Biblical studies. Due to its importance, I will discuss it in considerable detail.

The Old Testament. In this century Darwin's theory of evolution became accepted not only by scientists but also by most Biblical scholars and most of the public. The finding that beings like ourselves existed at least 25,000 years ago became better known and was also accepted by most Biblical scholars. Scholars also advanced some evidence against the account of Noah and the Ark. These scholars, using only their natural reason, said that its incredible size was beyond their technical capability, many animals (polar bears, for example) did not live in the Middle East, and there is not enough water on the earth (right now) to flood it to the top of Mt. Ararat. They did not account for a "firmament" of water in the sky nor did they account for any miraculous work of God. For these and other reasons most scholars, including many Catholic scholars, came to accept the conclusion that much of Genesis is a "myth," an account that teaches religious truths, but not early history of the earth or of mankind.

Archaeologists and linguists continued their success in reading Egyptian, Babylonian, and other ancient Middle-Eastern languages, and thereby learned much about the ancient Middle East. They found support for the account of Abraham. But, despite much information about that time, they found no Egyptian mention of the plagues or the Jewish exodus. Many scholars concluded, again, without assuming that future scholars might uncover further information, that the plagues were natural events and came on less suddenly than depicted in Genesis. They found a Babylonian creation account which many felt had caused the Jews to devise their creation account. Many orthodox scholars accepted this conclusion, but insisted that the Jews were subconsciously inspired by God in devising their account. Certainly it is vastly superior to the Babylonian version. Archaeologists discovered Babylonian structures, which many believed were the source for the story of the Tower of Babel, and both they and linguists doubted the existence of a single language at this time and the sudden creation of many languages.

Biblical scholars also noted (and looked for) natural explanations for many of the spectacular miracles claimed in the Old Testament. For example, they claimed that the stopping of the Jordan was caused by a landslide, or the destruction of Sennacharib's army was due to a devastating plague. Other miracles were said to be gross exaggerations or simply unbelievable legends. This conclusion could be easily believed by many scholars because they accepted the evidence that the Old Testament, in the form which has survived to our day, was written only after the return of the Jews from the Babylonian captivity, some 1,000 years after Moses and hundreds of years after the events in many of the Old Testament books.

The New Testament. Traditional views of the New Testament were also attacked by Biblical scholars. Many came to accept the concepts of eighteenth and nineteenth century scholars already mentioned—the late date of the writing of the gospels, the uncertainty about their authorship, the claim that Jesus' monologues in *John* were not spoken by Him, etc. And they noted and publicized problems already known by scholars, but not by most other Christians, for centuries—the major differences in the two Nativity accounts and the four post-Resurrection accounts, the fact that only in *Luke* does Jesus tell the apostles to perform the Eucharistic rite, and others.

And they found natural explanations for many of the miracles in the gospels. The healings were psychosomatic, the exorcisms were only recoveries from epileptic seizures, the apparent raising from the dead were recoveries from comas or mis-diagnoses of death. The most important miracles were questioned. The resurrected Jesus was seen only by His followers, and the miracle of the loaves and fishes was only a miracle of generosity—people with food miraculously decided to share it with others.

Many scholars also found other reasons for doubting other accounts in the Old and New Testaments. I omit most of them for the sake of brevity. But I cannot overlook one major problem, that of documentation. Modern scholars, in studying a claim of miracle, demand a full description of the event, the names of witnesses and dates of their testimonies, their signatures on statements of their testimony, doctors' testimonies and signatures, in the case of healings, etc. And solid documentation is also required when quoting an individual. No such documentation is available for miracles in the Old or New Testament, nor for the statements of Christ. Further, scholars note that the long time between events and their being reported in the Bible weakens the believability of Biblical accounts.

Defenders of traditional Christianity offer some rebuttals. They say that the apostles proved by their martyrdom that their testimony on the risen Lord was true, and that neither Jewish nor pagan writings of the first two centuries deny the truth of gospel miracles. However, many scholars find these arguments and others advanced by conservative scholars to be only weak support for the miracles in the Bible. Given the importance of miracles in defense of the Faith, and the weak documentation and late dating of Bible miracles, and the fact that we can document well only modern miracles, these modern miracles, especially Fatima, become an important element in the intellectual defense of the Faith.

I must now note that not all modern Biblical scholars accept the new findings of recent centuries. Fundamentalists and some other traditional scholars do not. But the majority, including many Catholic scholars, has come to accept them. However, Catholics and many others refused to accept the interpretations and conclusions, which the more liberal scholars drew from these new findings. An important example concerns the divinity of Christ. Many orthodox scholars agree that Jesus' outright statements of His divinity in *John* probably were not spoken by Him, but they find other evidence for His divinity, such as His forgiving sins and His performing of miracles on His own. Nevertheless, the new understanding of the Bible caused big problems for Christianity. It became quite widely known, at least among the more educated Christians, who had both the time and money to read the less technical books on the subject. Partly as a result, liberal Protestantism grew greatly in this century. This is particularly true if we class as liberal Protestants the very large number of Christians who seldom go to church, and who accept Jesus and Christianity only weakly, and accept firmly only the existence of God.

Still another challenge of the twentieth century is related to the large increase in college-educated people. A small percentage of them, but still a very large number of people, have been engaged in various kinds of research—in science, psychology, history, military intelligence, and other subjects. Their work requires them to examine old and new material and conclusions, and to analyze them with a very critical eye. They learn to consider all the likely implications of the material they are studying. They tend to bring this same attitude to matters of religion. They would read that Cro-Magnon man lived 20,000 years ago and ask not only how this affects the Biblical account of the creation of Adam and Eve, but also how it affects the Fall and the doctrine of original sin. Or they would read the story of the "sun dance" at Fatima and ask if other "sun dances" had occurred and ask if meteorologists and ophthalmologists or other experts on optical injuries and their effects had been consulted on this subject. They require not only a better defense of the miracles claimed for Fatima, but also of modern miracles as a whole. Unfortunately, most of this huge task has not been done, nor has it been undertaken, as far as I know.

Materialism. The many technological advances of the nineteenth and twentieth centuries have resulted in an enormous increase in wealth in the West. In the U.S. and some other countries, the middle class has become much the largest. And many of the poor were and are optimistic that they would and will rise to the middle class. With this prosperity, the traditional Christian emphasis on the spiritual, with the acceptance of poverty as an ideal, was hard pressed. Materialistic values prevailed with most people. Thus the "blue laws" were repealed and everywhere stores opened on Sunday. The observance of Lenten penance declined. Large families were viewed as a misfortune. Vocations to the priesthood decreased as the degree of sacrifice it involved became greater. Clearly, by the end of the century, materialistic values had increased in importance for most Westerners, now often non-Christian or only nominally Christian, and spiritual values had decreased. Materialism has presented, and still presents, a great challenge to Christianity.

A major challenge to Christianity was presented by the development of birth control devices and pills. It caused an enormous crisis in the Catholic Church and a great problem for all traditional Christian sects. The new devices and pills not only made it possible to control family size quite well, but also to have "safe sex" outside of marriage. Traditional sects continued to condemn sex outside of marriage, but a majority of the youth came to accept it by the end of the century. And the practice of pre-marital sex is certainly one reason why a large share of our youth, who were raised in traditional Christian families, have abandoned traditional sects and become liberal Christians or merely nominal Christians.

Birth control presented an even greater problem for the Catholic Church. By the middle of the 1960s and '70s, large numbers of Catholic families were using birth control and Pope Paul VI decided to have a large-scale study of this problem. He appointed a group of prominent theologians to study it and make recommendations. Presumably they examined the problem in the light of previous Church teachings and pronouncements, and in the light of the "population crisis." This group recommended some relaxation in the Church's teaching on birth control. Despite this, the pope came forth with an encyclical condemning it.

Reaction of Catholics was strong. Most reactions were unfavorable or only weakly supportive. Some priests strongly protested and a few bishops openly or covertly objected. In this period many priests left the priesthood, partly over this issue. More importantly, relatively few priests came out strongly in favor of the encyclical, and a majority of Catholics refused to accept it. It created another gap between Protestants and Catholics, since virtually all Protestants accepted birth control. The materialistic drawbacks of a large family were certainly one reason for its acceptance by both Protestants and Catholics. Birth control remains a major problem for the Church today.

Related to this problem, and probably a part of it, is the world population explosion. The population in the twentieth century grew from some two billion to nearly six billion, and an increase to eight or ten billion is expected by 2050. Some scholars and scientists have been worrying for many years that the world population will soon outrun its resources. Shortages of oil, metals, and water have been forecast. Undoubtedly, some Christian scholars, scientists, and part of the faithful have begun to ask if God's command to expand has been fulfilled and if population growth is no longer required by Him. Most Christians, I fear, would say yes. To the world the Catholic Church seems to say no, despite its permission under grave circumstances of natural birth control (NFP, or what used to be called the "rhythm" method). The inspiration of the Holy Spirit seems to be needed on all these problems of birth control.

The development of seemingly safe and simple methods of abortion has presented one more challenge to traditional Christianity. Largely for materialistic reasons, it has obtained strong support among the people, especially among liberal Christians, nominal Christians, and non-Christians. Even many traditional Christians support it or are neutral toward it. The Catholic Church and some other sects have made major efforts to convince their followers that abortion is a great moral wrong and to overthrow the Supreme Court decision in its favor. They have had, until now, only partial success with their followers and little success with the rest of the people. It remains one more great challenge of the twenty-first century.

Yet one more challenge of the twentieth century was presented by the movies and television. In mid-century they were a moderately good influence, but in the last third of the century they have become a purveyor of values which are very anti-Christian. Specifically, they have come to portray sex before marriage as normal and acceptable behavior, divorce as entirely acceptable, and often portray both nudity and sexually explicit situations. It has had a very negative influence on morality, and traditional Christian sects have not met this challenge with any significant success. Clearly the media could have a very positive effect on morality.

Summary. In its long history, Christianity has suffered several periods when its future looked bleak—during the persecutions of Diocletian, the attacks of the Arabs in the seventh century, the moral decay of the Church in the tenth century, the threat to become a French Church in the fourteenth century, the great Schism, the moral decay in the fifteenth and sixteenth centuries, and the victorious march of the Turks in the sixteenth century.

However, the threats and dangers which orthodox Christianity faced in the twentieth century, and still faces, can well be said to be greater. It faced a great threat from the Nazis and the Japanese, the only one which was overcome. It suffered major losses from world communism, which still represents a serious danger. But more seriously, it has been able to meet only poorly the dangers of materialism; and it has had to meet major intellectual challenges, which it still faces.

MODERN MIRACLES

Miracles. Hopefully, I now have shown that the challenges and dangers faced by Christianity in the twentieth century were greater than at any time since its first three centuries. I have not yet discussed miracles which occurred during and since the Renaissance. I will now do so.

Sources. In recent years many books have been published on miracles as a whole and on broad categories of miracles. I have found and read a very lengthy book on miracles as a whole by a Catholic author, a long book on Eucharistic miracles by the same author, several books on apparitions of the Blessed Mother and on miracles associated with these apparitions by Catholic and non-Catholic authors, a book on miracles as a whole by a researcher of psychic phenomena, apparently non-Catholic, and two older books on miracles as a whole by Catholics.[1]

These books give details of many hundreds, perhaps thousands, of miracles in a dozen or more categories. Some documentation is available for many of them. Many were spectacular, but none were said to have been forecast in advance, and only one was said to have been witnessed by many thousands of people.

That one is the miracle which is said to have occurred at Zeitun, near Cairo, in Egypt, from 1968 to 1971. This supposed miracle was a silent one, like that at Knock in Ireland and some others. It consisted of a luminous figure, presumably the Blessed Virgin, which appeared on top of the roof of an Egyptian Orthodox church and remained there for substantial periods of time on many nights. The figure was said to move at times, and to be that of a woman, but the few photographs available show only a luminous figure that seems to be a robed human being, or at least could be such. Details such as hands and legs were not visible in the photos. The events at Zeitun were seen by hundreds of thousands of Christians and Muslims (perhaps over a million), and except for Fatima and later "sun dances," is the only supposed miracle seen by many thousands of witnesses in recent centuries, as far as I know.

Healings. The most common kind of miracle claimed by Christians surely is healings. At least hundreds and perhaps thousands are well documented. I have no source for this statement, but feel sure that the many beatifications of saints which have occurred over the past five or six centuries, mostly supported by healings, and all carefully researched and documented, would alone support my statement. And a great many others have been claimed by Protestant faith healers and by cures at Catholic shrines, such as Lourdes, many of them well documented. Some were quite spectacular, including a few that were instantaneous or nearly instantaneous. Some may have been "seen" by thousands of witnesses, meaning that thousands were present when

---

[1] Important older books which I have not examined include Alban Butler's 12-volume *Lives of the Saints* and Herbert Thurston's *The Physical Phenomenon of Mysticism*.

the healing occurred, but the number that actually were able to see the person as she or he was healed was surely small, and very few could say that they knew that person's condition before the cure took place. More significantly, perhaps, modern doctors have reported seemingly miraculous cures entirely outside of any religious context. This is one reason why I think that Christianity badly needs serious, detailed, and scholarly studies of modern miracles.

Levitations. Among the most spectacular miracles reported for recent centuries are "levitations" of saintly persons. One source says that levitations have been reported for over 200 saints and holy persons. They are not, however, a feature of twentieth century Catholicism. In some cases, the purported levitation consisted in the raising of the saint a few inches or feet from the ground and remaining there for some time. In one case in the 1600s, involving St. Joseph of Cupertino, he is said to have flown from the congregation's area to the altar and to have been seen by the entire congregation (size unstated). St. Martin de Porres, who died in 1639, was said to have been on a picnic with 30 novices about one and a half miles from their monastery and late for services. They prayed and instantly were back at the monastery. St. Gerard Majella, who died in 1755, is said to have levitated and flown one quarter of a mile, but was seen by only two witnesses.

Bi-locations. Another quite spectacular kind of miracle is called "bi-location." In this kind a given person, invariably a saintly one, is said to have been in two places at the same time. Such miracles, if proven, would certainly be spectacular, especially if corroborated by many witnesses at both places. Bi-locations are claimed for some saints in the earlier part of the modern era. A recent bi-location is claimed for Padre Pio, based on the memory of one witness.

Walking on Water. A number of saints are said to have walked on water, some many times. Probably the most spectacular is claimed for St. Gerard Majella in the 1700s. He is said to have walked on water to save a passenger ship in distress in the bay of Naples, and to have dragged it to shore, a feat seen by the passengers and many on shore. This would be a truly spectacular miracle if there is adequate documentation to separate it from pious legend.

Incorrupt Bodies. The bodies of many saints are said to have failed to decompose for centuries and to be still incorrupt today. Over the years their bodies have been seen by thousands of people. Among them are the bodies of St. Teresa of Avila, who died in 1582, St. Charles Borromeo, died in 1584, St. Catherine of Genoa, 1510, and St. Mary Magdala of Pazzi, 1607.

Guadalupe. Probably the two best known miracles of modern times are those said to have occurred at Lourdes and at Guadalupe. The miracle at Guadalupe, Mexico, occurred in 1531, at the start of the modern era. The Virgin is said to have appeared to a Mexican native, Juan Diego, and asked that a church be built there. The bishop told Juan Diego to ask the Virgin for a sign of her appearance. She is said to have complied by giving him a field of flowers in winter, some of which he gathered in his cloak to show the bishop. When he opened his cloak, the bishop was astonished to see not only the flowers, but also the picture of a woman, which he instantly believed to be that of the Blessed Virgin. The cloak has long been venerated by Mexicans and other Latin Americans, and has not deteriorated despite being made of a local material that usually deteriorated within a few dozen years and despite being exposed to the elements for some 200 years before being enclosed in glass for viewing by modern pilgrims.

Lourdes. The miracles at Lourdes are better known in the U.S. The Virgin appeared to a teenage girl, her priest asked for verification, roses appeared in the winter, and a fountain appeared where the girl dug in the ground at the request of the Virgin. Hundreds or thousands of cures have been claimed for those who dipped in the fountain. There have been, however, tens or hundreds of thousands who have come there seeking a cure.

The above may be an incomplete account of spectacular miracles claimed for the many centuries of Christianity. My study of miracles was far from exhaustive, and I did not even consider undertaking the monumental task of deciding which miracles were adequately documented. Moreover, deciding which is most spectacular is clearly a subjective decision, and readers or scholars may disagree with my opinion that Fatima is the most spectacular miracle since the early ages of the Church. However, it can scarcely be denied that the event at Fatima on October 13, 1917, was very spectacular.

Chapter XV

Fatima as God's Answer

In this very brief chapter, I propose answers to a question not previously mentioned—in what way is Fatima an answer to the challenges and threats of the twentieth century and the third millennium. Many readers will probably feel that the ways are obvious.

The threats are twofold—moral and intellectual. The way that Fatima answers the moral threat is by the message of the Blessed Lady—a call to prayer, sacrifice, and moral reform. This is not a new message. However, it can be said that the spectacular nature of the sun dance gives a unique and powerful emphasis to this message. God considered it so important, so it would seem, that He even took the unique step of predicting it in advance and having thousands of witnesses.

The way that Fatima answers the intellectual challenge and threat is quite obvious. The spectacular nature of the sun dance and the fact that it was predicted three months in advance is strong evidence that God exists. Surely all, or virtually all the skeptics who were at Fatima on October 13, 1917, became convinced of the reality of God. I hope that many other skeptics will learn of the spectacular phenomena of Fatima, will study them, and become convinced that they were performed by God, and will believe in God.

Most Fatima authors, and most of the Christian world, seem to assume that the message of Fatima was addressed only to Catholics. This is clearly false. The message to pray, sacrifice, and reform one's life was addressed to all Christians and even to non-Christians. I hope that many non-Catholic Christians will examine carefully this or other accounts of the Fatima events, will add devotion to Our Lady of Fatima to their devotional life, and will accept and follow the message of Fatima.

I might further note that this tremendous miracle was performed in an orthodox Christian environment. The "Lady" of the apparitions is clearly identified as Mary, the mother of Jesus. The families of the seers were pious Catholics and Portugal was a Catholic nation. However, the Portuguese government was persecuting the Church. In view of these circumstances, the fantastic miracle of the sun dance would seem to show God's support and approval of orthodox Christianity and even of Catholicism.

Chart 1: Press Reports on Fatima

This chart is derived from *Documentacao Critica de Fatima*, Volume III, book 1, and from my Annex, Part 1. It shows the various explanations for the sun dance which were offered by the non-Catholic press of Portugal in 1917. I include all articles after October 13 which referred to Fatima, whether or not they offered an explanation for the sun dance.

Column 1– Document number. The number of the article in *Documentacao Critica*, unless the number is preceded by a number sign (pound sign), which indicates a document in my Annex, Part 1.

Column 2 – The date of the article on Fatima.

Column 3 – The name of the journal in which the article is found. All articles are from 1917.

Column 4 – Bias. The bias of the given journal. *Con* means that the journal was clearly and openly anti-clerical. *Neut* indicates that the journal was not openly biased against the Church; however, many such journals were quite biased against it because of its long time support of the monarchy.

Column 5 – Explanations for the sun dance. Most entries in this column are self-explanatory. *Non-see-er* means that the journal reported that one or more witnesses claimed that they saw nothing. *False Prophecy* means that the journal reported the false prophecy of the end of the war on October 13, 1917, casting doubt on the reality of the apparitions and sun dance miracle. *Derision*, by itself, means that no specific explanation was offered, but the sun dance was treated with derision, skepticism, or disbelief. In some cases, the journal merely cited an explanation offered earlier in another journal. In these cases, I put the explanation in parentheses and give the document number of the other journal. The explanations were often very brief, but occasionally were quite long.

Doc. No.	Date	Journal Name	Bias	Explanations
#24	Oct 14	Jornal-de Leria	Con	Hallucination, Derision
81	Oct 14	Jornal-de Leria	Con	Derision
82	Oct 14	Semana Alcob	Neut	Derision, Hoax
#27	Oct 15	Diario de Notic	Neut	Hallucinations
#29	Oct 15	O Portugal	Con	Derision, Disbelief
#28	Oct 15	O Seculo	Neut	None
96	Oct 16	A Capital	Con	Derision, Hoax
100	Oct 16	O Portugal	Con	Derision, False Prophecy
#36	Oct 16	Primeiro Janeir	Neut	Non-see-er, False Prophecy
102	Oct 16	O Seculo	Neut	None
103	Oct 16	O Seculo	Neut	(Skepticism) Quotes Annex I #34
#40	Oct 17	O Portugal	Con	(Derision, Skepticism) Quotes #34
#41	Oct 17	O Portugal	Con	Non-see-er
#42	Oct 17	A Republica	Con	Non-see-er, Hallucination
#45	Oct 18	Democ do Sol	Con	Hoax
#46	Oct 18	A Lucta	Con	Hallucination
#48	Oct 18	O Seculo	Neut	Hallucination
131	Oct 20	Concelho d Estar	Con	False Prophecy
133	Oct 20	Correio de Extr	Con	Derision
134	Oct 20	Correio de Extr	Con	Derision
136	Oct 20	Gaz de Coimbra	Neut	False Prophecy
141	Oct 20	Marinhense	Con	(Hallucination) Quotes Annex I #24
142	Oct 20	O Mundo	Con	Hoax
144	Oct 20	O Portugal	Con	Skepticism
145	Oct 20	A Republica	Con	Derision
#57	Oct 21	A Defesa	Neut	False prophecy

Doc. No.	Date	Journal Name	Bias	Explanations
148	Oct 20	O Defensor	Con	Derision, Hoax
149	Oct 21	Democ do Sul	Con	Derision
150	Oct 21	Distrit do Guard	Con	False Prophecy
152	Oct 21	Notic de Alcob	Neut	(Non-see-er, False Prophecy) Quotes #36
155	Oct 21	Notic del Norte	Neut	None
#105	Oct 21	Portugal, Mader	Neut	(Hallucination) Quotes Annex I #27
155	Oct 21	Semana Alcob	Neut	Hoax
157	Oct 22	O Mundo	Con	Hoax
160	Oct 23	A Montanha	Con	Derision
161	Oct 23	O Mundo	Con	Hoax
164	Oct 23	O Seculo	Neut	Hoax
167	Oct 24	O Mundo	Con	None
168	Oct 24	O Mundo	Con	Hoax
#60	Oct 24	O Seculo	Neut	None
170	Oct 24	O Seculo	Neut	Derision
173	Oct 25	O Debate	Con	Derision
174	Oct 25	Democ du Sul	Con	Derision
172	Oct 25	O Debate	Con	(Skepticism) Quotes Annex I #34
176	Oct 25	Diario de Notic	Neut	None
183	Oct 25	O Mundo	Con	Derision
185	Oct 25	O Portugal	Con	False Prophecy
#62	Oct 26	O Democrata	Con	False prophecy, Sun Blinding, (Skepticism) Quotes Annex I #34
190	Oct 26	Diario Not Sant	Neut	None
192	Oct 26	O Mundo	Con	Hoax
194	Oct 26	O Portugal	Con	None
#63	Oct 26	A Republica	Con	Hallucination, Hoax
188	Oct 26	O Seculo	Neut	None
201	Oct 27	Correio de Avei	Neut	None

Doc. No.	Date	Journal Name	Bias	Explanations
208	Oct 27	Marinhense	Con	None
209	Oct 27	O Mundo	Con	Hoax
212	Oct 27	O Portugal	Con	Derision
213	Oct 27	Corrieo de Extr	Con	None
218	Oct 28	O Defensor	Con	None
223	Oct 28	A Republica	Con	Derision
226	Oct 28	O Tempo	Neut	Derision, False Prophecy
225	Oct 28	O Seculo	Neut	None
#68	Oct 29	Illust Portug	Neut	None
229	Oct 29	O Portugal	Con	None
230	Oct 29	O Seculo	Neut	None
231	Oct 29	O Seculo	Neut	None
233	Oct 29	O Seculo Comico	Neut	False prophecy
234	Oct 29	O Seculo Comico	Neut	Derision
242	Oct 31	O Portugal	Con	Hoax
246	Nov 1	Eco de S. Pedro	Con	Hoax
251	Nov 2	O Defensor	Con	Hoax
252	Nov 2	O Democrata	Con	Hoax
255	Nov 2	Correio de Extr	Con	None
256	Nov 3	Marinhense	Con	None
265	Nov 4	O Mundo	Con	Hoax
266	Nov 4	O Regional	Neut	Hallucination
267	Nov 4	Trafaria	Neut	Disbelief, Derision
268	Nov 5	O Mundo	Con	Hoax
269	Nov 7	O Mundo	Con	Hoax
#76	Nov 8?	(Pamphlet)	Con	(Hallucination, Hoax, False Prophecy, Skepticism) Quotes Annex I #34
274	Nov 9	O Democrata	Con	Hoax, False prophecy
278	Nov 10	O Mundo	Con	None
#78	Nov 11	A Aurora	Con	Hallucination, False Prophecy
283	Nov 11	O Mundo	Con	Hoax

Doc. No.	Date	Journal Name	Bias	Explanations
284	Nov 12	O Mundo	Con	None
285	Nov 12	O Mundo	Con	Hoax
287	Nov 13	Diario de-Funch	Neut	(Hallucination) Quotes Annex I #27, #28
296	Nov 14	A Republica	Con	Derision, Hoax
299	Nov 15	O Debate	Con	Hoax
302	Nov 15	O Mundo	Con	None
305	Nov 16	Eco de S. Pedro	Con	Hoax
309	Nov 18	O Mundo	Con	Skepticism
317	Nov 22	O Seculo Comico	Neut	Derision
318	Nov 23	O Mundo	Con	Hoax
320	Nov 22	O Debate	Con	None
320	Nov 24	O Mundo	Con	Hoax
321	Nov 25	O Mundo	Con	Hoax
325	Nov 27	O Mundo	Con	Hoax
328	Nov 28	O Mundo	Con	None
331	Nov 30	O Mundo	Con	False prophecy
332	Dec 1	O Mundo	Con	Hoax
#88	Dec 2	(Pamphlet)	Con	Hallucination, Hoax
337	Dec 4	O Mundo	Con	Hoax

BIBLIOGRAPHY

I have given only the English versions of books which were originally published in another language and then translated into English. I have given the name of the publisher of each book, when known. Parentheses and a question mark indicate that the given publisher is presumed to have published this book, on the basis of other books of the given author.

A. CHURCH HISTORY

Bokenkotter, Thomas. *A Concise History of the Catholic Church.* Image Books–Doubleday & Co, Inc., Garden City, NY, 1979.

Hummel, Charles E. *The Galileo Connection: Resolving Conflicts between Science and the Bible.* Intervarsity Press, Downers Grove, IL, 1986.

Johnson, Paul. *A History of Christianity.* Simon & Schuster, New York, NY, 1976.

Latourette, Kenneth Scott. *A History of Christianity*, Vols I, II. Harper & Rowe, New York, 1975.

Mouret, Fernand, and Newton Thompson. *A History of the Catholic Church*, Vols I, II, III. B. Herder Book Co., St. Louis, MO, 1931.

B. MIRACLES

Allegri, Renzi. *Padre Pio, Man of Hope.* Servant Publications, Ann Arbor, MI, 2000.

Aradi, Zsolt. *Book of Miracles.* Longman and Green, New York, 1956.

Chiron, Yves. *Enquete sur les Apparitions de la Vierge.* Perrin-Mame, (no city given), 1995.

Cruz, Joan Carroll. *Eucharistic Miracles.* Tan Books and Publishers, Inc., Rockford IL, 1987.

—————. *Mysteries, Marvels, Miracles in the Lives of the Saints,* Tan Books and Publishers, Inc., Rockford IL, 997.

Franciscan Friars of the Immaculate Heart. *Handbook of Guadalupe.* Park Press, Waite Park, MN, 1997.

Helle, Jean. *Miracles.* David McKay, New York, 1952.

Jaouen, Jean, M.S. *A Grace Called La Salette.* La Salette Publications, Attleboro, MA, 1991.

McClure, Kevin. *The Evidence for Visions of the Virgin Mary.* Aquarian Press, Wellingborough, Northhamptonshire, 1983.

Nolen, William A. *Healing: A Doctor in Search of a Miracle.* Random House, New York, 1974.

Odell, Catherine M. *Those Who Saw Her: Apparitions of Mary.* Our Sunday Visitor, Publishing Division, Huntington, IN, 1986, 1995.

Rogo, D. Scott. *Miracles: A Parascientific Inquiry into Wondrous Phenomena.* Dial Press, New York, 1982.

Smith, Robert D. *Comparative Miracles.* Herder Book Co., St. Louis, MO, 1965.

Zindars-Swartz, Sandra Z. *Encountering Mary.* Princeton Press, Princeton, N J, 1991.

Contrary to usual practice, I list the remaining books in alphabetical order by book title rather than by author. My reason is that these books are sometimes mentioned in footnotes in the main body of this book, and there I give only the book title and the pertinent page number. Thus arranging these two lists in alphabetical order by title makes it easier for anyone to locate the author, date, and publisher, if desired. I place the author's name in bold print to make it easier to find the work of a given author, if desired.

C. APPARITIONS AND SUN DANCES

As Brancas Pombas de Fatima. Marguerita **Caupers de Braganca.** Lisbon, 1951.

As Grandes Maravilhas de Fatima. Fr. Manuel Nunes **Formigao.** Union Grafica, Lisbon, 1927.

A Virgem de Fatima. Jose Marques **da Cruz.** Comp. Melhoramentos de Sao Paolo, Sao Paolo, 1937.

Bij Verschijningen en de Voorseggingen van Fatima. Fr. Edouard **Dhanis,** S.J. Brussels, 1945.

Documentacao Critica de Fatima, Vols I, II, III. Editor-in-chief, Fr. Luciano Coelho **Cristino,** Santuario de Fatima, 1992, 1999, 2002.

Documentos de Fatima. Fr. Antonio Maria **Martins,** S.J. (Livraria Apostolado da Imprensa?), Porto, 1976.

Enquete sur une Imposture. Gerard **de Sede.** Editions–Alain Moreau, Paris, 1977.

Evidence for Visions of the Virgin Mary. Kevin **McClure.** Aquarian Press, Wellingsborough, Northhamptonshire, 1983.

Eyewitness at Fatima. Mabel **Norton.** J.C. Fallon, Dublin, 1950.

Fatima from the Beginning, 9th edition. Fr. Joao **de Marchi.** Ravensgate Press, Still River, MA, 1994.

Fatima Demascarada, 3rd edition. Joao **Ilharco.** (No publisher), Third edition, Coimbra, 1971.

Fatima: The Great Sign. Francis **Johnson.** Tan Books, Rockford IL, 1980.

Fatima, Joie Intime. Fr. Casimir **Barthas.** Fatima Editions, Toulouse, France.

Fatima Joie Intime, Evenement Mondial, 2nd edition. Brother Francois **de Marie dos Anges.** Editions–Contre-Reforme Catholique, Saint-Parres-les-Vaudes, France, 1993.

Fatima in the Light of History. Idolino de Costa **Brochado**. Bruce Publishing Co., Milwaukee, 1955.

Fatima in Lucia's Own Words. Sister Maria **Lucia** of the Immaculate Heart. Ravensgate Press, Cambridge, MA, 1976.

Fatima 1917–1968: Histoire Complete des Apparitions et de leur Suite. Fr. Casimir **Barthas**. Fatima Editions, Toulouse, 1969.

Fatima: o que se Passou em 1917. Fina **d'Armada**. Livraria Betrand, Sarl, Lisbon, 1980.

Fatima: as suas Provas, os seus Problemas. Fr. Sebastiao **Martins dos Reis**. Depositaria Livraria Alpha et Omega, Lisbon, 1953.

Fatima Way of Peace. Fr. Antonio M. **Martins**, S.J. Augustine Publishing Co., Devon, England, 1989.

God and the Sun at Fatima. Fr. Stanley **Jaki**. Realview Books, Royal Oaks, MI, 1999.

Lucia's Fourth Memoir. Published as part of *Fatima in Lucia's Own Words.* Sister Maria **Lucia** of the Immaculate Heart. Ravensgate Press, Cambridge, MA, 1976.

Meet the Witnesses. John **Haffert**. AMI International Press, Fatima, 1961.

Message of Fatima, The. Cyril. C. **Martindale**, S.J. Burns, Oates and Washburn, Ltd, 1950.

Miracles. D. Scott **Rogo**. Dial Press, New York, 1982.

Nossa Senora de Fatima. Luis Gonzaga **de Fonseca**. Porto, 1934.

Novos Documentos de Fatima. Fr. Antonio M. **Martins**, S.J. Livraria Apostolado da Imprensa, Porto, 1984.

O Confronto de Ideologias na Segunda Decada do Seculo XX: A Volta da Fatima. A. **Teixera Fernandes**. (Publisher unknown, See p. 18 of Doc Crit III).

O Fenomeno Solar. An article by Diogo Pacheco **de Amorim** in the Acts of the Marian Congress, Lourdes, 1958, Vol. XII (Rome: Pontificia Academia Mariana Internationalis, 1962) pp. 189–232.

Ocho Dias com as Videntes de Cova da Iria em 1917. Alfredo **de Matos**. (No publisher given), Printed by Grafica de Leiria, Leiria, 1968.

Os Acontecimentos de Fatima. Viscount **de Montelo** (pseudonym of Fr. Manuel Nunes **Formigao**). Guarda, 1923.

Os Episodios Maravilhosos de Fatima. Viscount **de Montelo** (Fr. Manuel N. **Formigao**). Guarda, 1921.

Our Lady of Fatima. William Thomas **Walsh**. Image Books, Doubleday, New York, 1954, 1960.

Rediscovering Fatima. Fr. Robert J. **Fox**. Our Sunday Visitor, Huntington, IN, 1982.

Sintese Critica de Fatima: Ineidencoes e Repercussoes. Fr. Sebastiao **Martins dos Reis**. (Ediciones Salesianas?), Porto, 1968.

Sun Danced at Fatima, The. Fr. J. **Pelletier**. Image Books, Doubleday, 1983.

Sun's Miracle, or of Something Else, The. Stanley L. **Jaki**. Realview Books, Pinckney, MI, 2000.

Toute la Verite sur Fatima. Brother **Michel de la Trinite**. Editions-de la Contre, Reforme Catholique, Saint-Barre-les Vaudes, France, 1983.

Vision of Fatima. Thomas **McGlynn**, O.P. Little, Brown & Co., Boston, 1948.

Whole Truth About Fatima, The, Vol 1. Brother **Michel de la Trinite**, CRC. Immaculate Heart Publications, Buffalo, NY, 1989.

D. METEOROLOGY AND OPTICS

Atmosphere, The. Frederic K. Lutgens and Edward J. Tarbuck. Prentiss Hall Inc., Englewood Cliffs, NJ, 1955.

Atmospheric Phenomena. Editor David K. **Lynch**. (Articles from Scientific American), W. H. Freeman & Co., San Francisco, CA, circa 1980.

Cambridge Guide to Weather. Ross **Reynolds**. Cambridge U. Press, Cambridge.

How the Weather Works. Michael **Allaby**. A Reader's Digest Book, Darling Kimberly Ltd, London, England.

Journal of the Optical Society of America. Special Issue, August, 1979.

Meteorology Today. C. Donald **Ahrens**. West Publishing Co., St. Paul MN, 1988.

Weather. Wm. J. **Burroughs,** Bob **Crowder**, Ted **Robertson**, Eleanor **Valier-Talbot**, Richard **Whittaker**. Nature Co./Time Life Books, (no city), 1996.

Weather and Climate. (No author stated.) Time Life Books, 1966.

ANNEX I

INTRODUCTION

In this Annex to *FATIMA THE SPECTACULAR*, I give translations of documents which concern Fatima and which I find to be important. I assign a number to each document. In many cases I give the "gist" of the text of a given document because that part was not important for my purposes, or because the text is already available in a book in English. In nearly all cases, I did not examine the original Portuguese source—newspaper, letter, etc.— but derived my text from books published by the Fatima archives (Doc Crit I, II, and III) or some other written source, chiefly published books. Thus for virtually all documents in this Annex, I cite both the original Portuguese source and the source from which I derived the text. An example is my first document, taken from the newspaper *O Seculo* of 23 July 1917, given in the original text in *Documentacao Critica de Fatima*, Volume III, and translated in full in *Fatima in the Light of History*, by Brochado. I indicate this as:

Source: *O Seculo*, 23 July 1917, Brochado, pp 81-83; Doc Crit III book 1 pp 34, 35.

In this Annex, I use the abbreviations for my most common sources, as indicated in my chapter "Sources and Documentation." I must note also that in 1917 and for many years after, Portuguese newspapers had very few pages and thus I find no need to cite the page on which the pertinent articles appear. The articles can easily be found despite the lack of a page number, unlike an article in the New York Times.

I divide the Annex into two segments. The first segment is chiefly concerned with the sun dance. It gives the text, or text and gist, of newspapers, letters, etc., which concern the "sun dance" and/or the apparitions. The second segment is chiefly concerned with the apparitions. It gives the text of the interviews of the seers by the priests in 1917, already mentioned, plus the text of Lucia's first written statement on the apparitions, made in

1922, and her testimony to the Diocesan Inquiry Board, made in 1924. It also gives the text of Lucia's testimony on the apparitions from her memoirs, 1937-1941, readily available in English.

Throughout this Annex, I use parentheses for two purposes. I often use gists for the sake of brevity and enclose them in parentheses, preceded by the word "Gist–" Occasionally the Portuguese text contained a word or phrase in parentheses. Of course, I keep the parentheses in my translations. I also use brackets for two purposes. Often I add a word or phrase, not found in the Portuguese text to clarify it or make it more readable. I enclose such additions in brackets. I also use brackets to indicate a comment of mine; an example is: "[Text not given here, since it is given in #3 of this Annex.]" Further, I use dots in two ways. Following usual practice, I use three or four dots in normal print to indicate that I have omitted an unimportant portion of text, and use three or four dots in bold print, if the text itself contained the dots. I have tried to be conservative and gist or omit only text which I consider to be unimportant. However, occasionally I gist a fairly important text if it is readily available in English in another book.

In the first segment (Part I) I give the documents in chronological order. For those of 1917 I cite the month and day, but not the year. I learned of several significant letters or newspaper articles after preparing this Annex, and I include them at the end, out of chronological order. On the first line of each document I give the number I have assigned to that document and its date. For newspaper articles I also give the headline of the given article. For other documents I give a short description of the document.

Document #1 Jul 23   A HEAVENLY EMBASSY

Meia Via—Torres Novas, 21 C—For some time in this locality the rumor has spread insistently that at a certain place in the Serra da Aire [mountains] on the 13th of this month the mother of Jesus Christ appeared to two small children to whom she has appeared several times before at the same place.

Naturally this rumor aroused widespread curiosity in the town of Torres Novas, and its environs, where this place is located. The rumor brought thousands of people to the given spot, some of them [curious] unbelievers, the others pious folk going because of belief and devotion.

… The event caught on so much that in Torres Novas … (Gist– which has lots of vehicles for hire, none of which was available to be rented on the 13th.) Many shops even closed down.

It was about 2:00 when many people on their way back appeared here, most of them religiously inclined, who had gone from here to witness the

miracle which had been forecast. (Gist– They sang hymns and shouted hur-
rahs as they left for home.)

On the following day, out of an irresistible curiosity .... we approached
a woman who, I believe, also was one of the pilgrims by the complete information she could give. We asked her some questions on the subject, and she
replied as follows, with an inflection which allowed her emotions to show:

On the 13ᵗʰ, the appointed day for the apparition of Our Lady, we went
to the indicated place. (Gist– It was crowded.)

The curiosity was general, and at a given moment everyone was silent,
with mouths wide open, searching, looking about as if to hear some voices
which might come from the bowels of the earth. At this point there was
heard a sound similar to the echoing of thunder, and immediately thereafter
the two children, who were near a red oak surrounded by many flowers,
paradisiacs, I think, broke out into a distressed chorus, making epileptic
gestures, and afterward falling into ecstasy. To one of them, who had the
privilege of seeing and hearing the saint, various people put many questions,
to which she replied that she saw a kind of very pretty doll who spoke to her.
She had, she said, a radiance about her head and she called her in a very quiet
and melodious voice to come closer. Among the many things, which she said
to her, the main thing was to announce her reappearance on the 13ᵗʰ of the
next month at the same site, and another appearance to state the reasons
why she had come into the world.

(Gist– After thanking her for her information) I left formulating an
opinion on what I had just heard. The case seems to be extremely ridiculous,
and seriously I would not have believed it if that woman did not merit the
greatest confidence for being sincere and truthful, and if she were not corroborated by others who spoke of it, using the same words and citing the
same happenings. However, it is my opinion that this is a case of a premedi-
tated money-making scheme, the sources of revenue for which exist in the
depths of the Serra in some mineral spring, which some astute person has
recently discovered and who, in the guise of religion, wishes to transform the
Serra de Aire into a miraculous resort like Lourdes.

The authorities already know of the affair, and if they don't, this will
serve as a warning.

Source: *O Seculo*, Lisbon, 23 July, a daily newspaper of the Republican
Party, Brochado, pp 81-83; Doc Crit III book 1 pp 34, 35.

Note: In that era, *O Seculo* was the most widely-read newspaper in the
country; Brochado, p 83. This article was repeated in *O Mensageiro* of 25
July; Doc Crit III book 1 p 37.

#2 Jul 25   FROM NORTH TO SOUTH

In the Serra d'Ayres [mountains], Torres Novas County, on the 13th of this month, thousands of people gathered, with the intention of attending an apparition of Our Lady, which rumor began to spread among the people, without knowing its source. Suddenly a sound like a clap of thunder was heard, immediately after which two female children, full of lively excitement, said they had seen an apparition of Our Lady and were so moved that they fell into ecstasy. In the afternoon the people came down from the mountain, singing hymns to the Virgin.

Source: *A Liberdade*, a Catholic journal, 25 July; Doc Crit III book 1 p 36.

#3 Jul 29   FATIMA—REAL OR SUPPOSED APPARITION ... ILLUSION

This parish, on the 13th of this month, had the most marvelous and moving spectacle that one could imagine.

Would the Queen of Heaven want to make this parish a second Lourdes?!.... Who would merit it?

Nothing is impossible to God and the Virgin Mother.

(Gist– It is impossible to estimate the number of people at this third event on 13 July.)

Everyone there, or at least most of them, were satisfied just to see the way the children acted and talked—questioning ... requesting ... and waiting some time for a response that no one else heard.

This—they say, because I wasn't there—was in the presence of 800 to 1,000, by some estimates, and 1,000 or more than 2,000 by other estimates. (Gist– The people cried, prayed and then they had to take the seers away by car to avoid the crowd.)

It was simply admirable, but for now I say nothing more.

Source: *O Ouriense*, Vila Nova de Ourem, bulletin of the Ourem parish, 29 July; Doc Crit III book 1 p 38.

#4 [August]   JOEL MAGNO LETTER

(Gist– I went by bicycle to the apparition site. Lots of people were there. I met some seminarians and we stayed together the whole time. They were [names seven, including Antonio Pocas]. We stayed a long time in the shade.

The big influx of people came, using all sorts of transport. By mid-day, old time, the hour set for the apparition, there were many thousands at the apparition site. I am not good at calculations, but those who made the minimum estimate talked of 5,000 people.)

The children were already late when Pocas came with the sad news that the administrator had (Gist– kidnapped) the children. Thus this evil and cowardly man betrayed all these people, but in this there seemed to have been some divine intervention, in that the place [Fatima], usually crowded, was deserted, and the only eyewitnesses [to the kidnapping] were the pastor, the priest of Torres Novas and Father Manuel Pocas, who were on the rectory porch, as they themselves told me later. When the people learned [of the kidnapping], they were very mad, and since it was already 3:00 I went to Fatima with some of the seminarians to learn what happened. I was so angry I don't know what I said there. Of course, the priests there called me silly or something like that. ... [Then] some men appeared to tell us that Our Lady had appeared.

I said good bye to the priests and headed up [toward the Cova]. The roads were full of people who were discussing the amazing occurrence. I asked each group what they had seen, and in less time than striking a match, I was surrounded by shouting people, who told me they heard thunder and all fled. Turning then, they saw a blue and white cloud descend, which shortly rose and disappeared. Others said they saw lightning, and there was a little old woman with tears in her eyes, who told us very assuredly that she saw Our Lady. In sum, all were satisfied, and by what I heard from Ourem, the administrator seems to have risked his life in the kidnapping.

In all of this, however, it seems that a major influence on the people was the old [Latin] saying—*quod volumus facile credimus*—(which doesn't mean I dare to doubt them, because sadly I wasn't there) because some deep, educated people, like Mario Murao, Pocas and others told me there was not enough [evidence] on the supernaturalness of this ... not saying that they saw nothing, which other people also told me.

Then I went home. Father Manuel Pocas talked with the children—they are three children, (a boy of ten and two girls of 6 and 8 years), and was charmed. He says he cannot doubt that...

Source: Part of a letter of Father Joel Deus Magno, 23, to Dean Francisco Felix, both at Santarem Seminary; Doc Crit III book 1 pp 41-43.

Note: The beginning and end of this letter are missing. The approximate date and identification of the writer is supplied by the Fatima archives. I presume that the date is based on the text, and the identification is based on a comparison of the handwriting of this letter with that of Joel Magno [#10 of this Annex]. A similar letter, clearly from Magno, and concerning the August apparition, was published in *A Guarda*, 30 August 1919; Doc Crit III book 2 pp 113, 114.

#5 Aug 18   FROM NORTH TO SOUTH

(Gist– Three children say the Virgin Mary appears to them on the 13th of each month at Fatima. The report has spread so widely that on the 13th there came here more than 5,000 people from many counties, using every kind of transport.) The administrator, Artur de Oliveira Santos, with Candido Alho, an official, went to the seers' home in the morning. Among others, some ten priests were there. Santos, under the pretext of having the pastor hear the seers before going to the mountain, convinced the parents to go to the rectory. Afterward the administrator would take the children there … where he wanted to attend the apparition. Thus the administrator was able [instead] to take the children to the administration center precisely at the hour of the Virgin's apparition. The unwary [in Fatima] were thus cheated.

Source: *A Liberdade*, Porto, a Catholic newspaper, 18 Aug; Doc Crit III book 1 p 45.

Note: This pastor published a long denial of any involvement in the children's kidnapping; *O Mensageiro*, 14 Aug; Doc Crit III pp 57-59; *O Ouriense*, 1 Sep; Doc Crit III book 1 pp 72-74.

#6 Aug 19   THE FRAUD OF MIRACLES

How People Are Deceived—What Has Happened at Fatima

Yesterday *O Mundo* referred to what has taken place [at] Fatima … with the *"apparition* of a *saint* who on the 13th of each month deigns to talk with three poor children who humbly watch their sheep at the Cova de Santa Iria in the foothills of the Serra de Aires… The case has become well-known and simple people have heard this tale ecstatically, which in the past would have enchanted them, but [which now] cannot be taken seriously, for the explanation and exploitation are clear. Are we dealing with a case of hallucination of some poor, [pious] children … or with a clerical trick? The authorities have the duty of investigating, and we are sure they will, especially with the administration headed by the dedicated Republican, Arturo de Santos… The matter already looks like a clerical hoax. *O Ouriense* … edited by a priest, has published the following: [Text not given here, since it is given in #3 of this Annex.] As can be seen the clerics already accept as an established fact that the *apparition* was real.

How the hoax began. The start of the clerical exploitation was on May 13. Three children—Lucia, 10 years old, Francisco, 8, and Jacinta, 7, residents of Aljustrel, went to the vast plain of the Cova de Santa Iria to pasture sheep, when a Lady, all dressed in white, according to Lucia, appeared to them. The Lady told the little shepherds that they should learn to read and write, and that she would appear in the same place near an oak tree on the 13th of each month. On the 13th of October she would come down for the last time from heaven to bring peace to the world and end the war. Everyone who did not believe in her work would be punished.

(Gist– Here we have another saintly figure promising good, but threatening harm to all who don't believe. It is like the sick case of St. Dominic of Guzman, whose dream led to the Inquisition.) This apparition, like the other one, preaches hatred. It should be agreed that this is too much for the imagination of children. An unlettered child could not spontaneously have had, nor could have attained easily the ideas she gave out. They were previously prepared to act out this role. (Gist– Moreover, Lucia is very pious.) And she insists on keeping a secret which she can reveal only on Oct 13. The priests have all flocked to this place—and strangely!—all find in the little child traces of the smooth-talking parrot, Bernadette of Lourdes.

More apparitions and hatred of liberals begin to appear. On June 13 the children came again to see the Lady at the same place and time, from noon to 2:00. With the children were some people who saw nothing, yet thought they saw [something]. The priests began to exploit the affair by trying to make people believe that this was a true miracle. Poor women of the people remembered Catechism phrases, and simple children of tender age dreamed that a good angel appeared [to them] to give eternal happiness. (Gist– The sick begged the seers to intercede for them.)

On Aug 13 everyone wanted to attend the apparition. They were preparing to follow the children [to the site]. Then the authorities intervened. The children were taken to Ourem so they could offer no more opportunities for hoaxes. In the field ... holy creatures incited the simple folk, already fanaticized by the perverse work of the Church, to slay the Republicans,[1] Masons and liberals. And the priests sanction these shows of the credulous ... (even when they don't arouse it.) J. V. [Jose Vale]

Source: *O Mundo*, Lisbon, a Republican daily newspaper, 19 Aug 1917, Brochado, pp 108-110; Doc Crit III book 1 pp 49-52.

Note: *O Mundo* was the organ of the national irreligious movement; Brochado, p 105.

---

[1] The Republicans and the Monarchists were the two major political groups then.

#7 Aug 22   MIRACULOUS APPEARANCE

(Gist– The Fatima events are quite well known. We can't anticipate the Church's decision. But for our readers we publish a letter we have received, with small changes in punctuation and spelling.)

Familacao, 14-8-1917
Dear Sir Francisco da Silva Coelho,
(Gist– I wish you good health and ask you to pass this letter to Mrs. Gloria, who wanted very much to hear what happened at Fatima. The account is serious and true. I arrived at the Cova da Iria, heard of the kidnapping and that some people tried to catch up with the administrator but failed. The people who had been there last month said: let's wait, since there are only five minutes until the time of the apparition last time.)

The people were quiet, the weather was clear, when suddenly there was a stroke of lightning over the altar and a whirlwind around the altar, which covered over 300 people with dust. Everyone fled, fell down, cried. The ground cracked, but very strongly, the rocks changed color, and many people began to shout: Look, Look, Our Lady is coming here, see, with a white dress. Those who saw her on the ground were many, but those who saw her in the sky were many more. And over 3,000 did not see more, because when the ground *shook* and the rocks changed color, all who were closer, some fell down, and others genuflected, and I too was so upset that, of all I wanted to see, I saw a little. But what I, and all those who were gasping, saw very well were arches and garlands in the sky on the south side, with flowers of every color. This all the people saw.

And the flowers which covered the altar were admired because it was hot and they kept getting prettier, and they weren't in vases. If the people had much faith [before], they had much more [afterwards]. If the administrator took the children, this did not stop Our Lady from appearing. [In August] Our Lady didn't speak, of course, because there was no one to reply. (Gist– The people said let's go get those persons, the administrator, etc.) I know no more, but on the 13ᵗʰ I'll be back, God willing. The time she appeared was 12:30. Mr. Coelho, please pass this letter to my good friend Alexander Marques. ….. All I say here is true. [More personal matter follows.]
Joao Pereira Novo

Source: *O Mensageiro*, 22 Aug; Doc Crit III part 1 pp 54-56. Much of this letter was published, with unfavorable comments, in *Semana Alcobacense* on 2 Sep; Doc Crit III part 1 pp 79-82.

Note: In 1917, Novo was 42 years old. Familacao is in Cortes parish, Leiria county.

#8 Sep 1   NEW SHOWING

(Gist– On the 13th of each month three children are given a supernatural vision. A lady of extraordinary beauty appears to them in the country in the middle of a cloud at a fixed site. She asks the lad of three (sic) years old to pray the rosary and the two young girls to pray for the country and their family, adding that on 13 Oct she will tell them what she wants. In times of great suffering people are more inclined to accept the supernatural. However, until the Church speaks we cannot comment on this event. But simply as pious believers we offer some parts of a conscientiously written letter of one of our female subscribers. The letter follows.)

(Gist– A description of the site and the people at Fatima on Aug 13 is given.) I don't exaggerate in saying that there were over 4,000 people there. (Gist– They were praying, very devout.) All were waiting for the arrival of the children; but at the time they were due to appear a lad arrived on bicycle, saying that the administrator of Ourem had taken them away. They did not want to believe this. Then I remembered to ask F … to find out if it was true. He returned soon confirming the news.

The administrator, who had been in the house of the seers' family since morning, ordered them [to go] … to the rectory, where he made a new, long and insistent interrogation. The children did not recant, no matter how much he intimidated them, even the young one of 6 years said: "We are not afraid." It's extraordinary, is it not? It is said that they seemed like three little lambs, and without crying or shouting they got into the carriage, where the administrator told them that he himself was going to take them to the [apparition] site. But when he caught them in the carriage, he whipped the horses and … went with them to Villa Nova de Ourem, which was his plan.

However, at the site it seemed nobody could pull himself away. They had been there for hours and were in no hurry to leave. I said to F … now that we're here I'd like to stay until 2:00, which is the end of the solar mid-day. She and the family of C … agreed and we kept sitting on some rocks. And then, my daughter, at 2:00 exact, by my watch, there was a rapid lowering of the temperature, without wind, producing the sensation like an eclipse of the sun, and instantly something like an electric current put the whole crowd in communication, all the men took off their hats, and men and women knelt in an act, spontaneous and well noted. Why did this happen? I can't say. Many people, including my maids, say that they saw a pretty cloud at the foot of the sun and that it disappeared in moments. I saw nothing [of it]. (Gist– I saw nothing, but felt a disturbing impression and many people cried.)

What caused the instantaneous effect? Let the future tell. But it is certain that nobody expected anything. They were discouraged and began to get ready to leave when this happened, as I described it. I looked at the oak bush and saw it was surrounded by a fog, like that which they say was always seen. I had F ... look at it. Was it dust carried along by the momentum of the crowd? Maybe, but at no other point did it happen, and I repeat, there was no wind. It was fresh. A little before, a small man ... had said to me: "Look, senhora, the stars are setting, just like a month ago today." The clouds faded and formed something like a very light web, it is sure, but nothing extraordinary. The sensation which I and all suddenly felt was extraordinary.

Source: *Raio de Luz,* a Catholic magazine, Lisbon, 1 Sep; Doc Crit III book 1 pp 75-78.

Notes: The text of this letter was repeated by *A Ordem* on 20 Oct. See Annex #53. It seems likely that the lady who wrote this letter is the same one who wrote the letter given in #72. See note on #72.

#9 Sep 13   BRITES DIARY

... On this day many people from here went to Fatima to see the miracle of the apparition of Our Lady, but nobody saw anything. .... [No more on Fatima in the diary of 13 Sep.]

Source: Diary of Manuel Pereira Crespo da Costa Brites of Martinela, Leiria county, 13 Sep; Doc Crit III book 1 p 92. See #17 for another entry from his diary.

#10 Sep 17-23   JOEL MAGNO LETTER

As in the past month, I went to Fatima on the 13th, but this time I wasn't expecting to because it wasn't easy and I wasn't tempted to go there. It happened that on the night of the 12th X. arrived here and an enormous truck, which carried 16 people from Benedicta to Fatima, where he wanted to go to be present at the phenomenon that usually occurred there on the 13th of each month from May of this year.

X. spent the night at my house, and on the next morning he invited me to take a place on the vehicle, an invitation I accepted willingly.

(Gist– Crowds had passed through town that night. We took the trip. The roads were filled with pilgrims, whose faith we admired. Their behavior is described in detail.)

It was almost 10:00 when we reached our goal. The crowd, which was already numerous at that hour, approached the apparition site full of respect. The men took off their hats. Almost everyone knelt and prayed with fervor. When we arrived, X. and I headed for the children's home, photographed them and talked with them. This was a scene that impressed me most. I was absolutely enchanted. The angelic simplicity and absolute lack of worry which they showed could not lie. They do not have the timidity expected in peasant children from the fields and mountains in the presence of strangers. They speak as easily with one stranger as with many. Their replies are always the same. They seem adults in the way they express themselves. From the children's house we went to the rectory, where there were, besides the pastor, some friends of mine and of X., with whom we exchanged impressions on the subject of the day. After noon we headed for the apparition site.

Exactly at noon, sun time, the sun began to lose its brilliance. Nobody failed to note this fact, which since May was noted on each 13th of the month. A little after this, the oldest seer ordered those standing around to pray.

(Gist– I was very impressed by the fervor of the crowd.)

It was at this time that many persons saw an oval, of brilliant, live color, with the larger part hanging below, (which) made a long straight line in the firmament. Some saw that phenomenon for a longer, others for a shorter, time. I didn't see it, and was sad about it.

Dr. Figuereido and many persons from here went [to Fatima]. There were many serious persons from here who saw a kind of flowers which came from above and didn't reach the ground. The atmosphere was a yellowish color, perhaps because of the obscuring of the sun. What happened in this quick quarter of an hour never will escape [me], but also is not easy to describe. Later I will tell you some things, so I won't bore you, Father, in this letter. (Gist– Frs. Formigao and Figuereido will better tell you what happened. Excuse me for writing such a long letter). When the sun regained its usual light the children left and the crowd dispersed little by little. (Gist– Estimates of crowd size were 15,000 or 20,000 or more.) It was a beautiful spectacle... [Personal matter follows.]

Joel de Deus Magno

Source: Part of a letter of Fr. Joel Magno to Fr. Francisco M. Felix, 17-23 September; Doc Crit III book 2 pp 99-105.

Note: X. is identified as Father Joaquim Antonio do Carmo. The date of the letter is not given, but can be learned from statements made in it to be between 17 and 23 September. The original text is available only for the last two of its six pages, beginning with "Dr. Figuereido and more people."

The other four pages have been recovered from notes made by Father Formigao, and from edited versions of the letter published by Father Formigao
in *A Guarda*, 13 September 1919, and in his book *As Grandes Maravilhas da
Fatima;* Doc Crit III, book 1, p 99; Doc Crit III, book 2, pp 125-128. In
the *A Guarda* letter, the oval is said to be "little larger than an egg," page 127
of Doc Crit III, book 2.

#11 Sep 22   MIRACULOUS

(Gist– Times are hard. Prices are high. Bread, fish, oil, etc. are in short
supply. Inflation is here. But people spend wildly at fiestas, forgetting tomorrow.)

In a site near Fatima [and] Vila Nova d' Ourem, in our district, a strange
case is occurring. A *saint*, covered with flowers, dressed in a multi-colored
tunic of shiny silk and surrounded by an aureole of light, appeared to some
shepherds. She came down from the ethereal regions, not to forecast the end
of the war nor reveal the winning lottery number. She came to censure the
unbelief, the sins of mortals, who now are not going in so great numbers to
fill the coffers of the churches. (Gist– and of the Jesuits, the nuns.) It is thus
every 13th—a fatal day—they return to such a site to hear these censures
heard by many people.

And thus, on last Friday the number of people who were at Fatima to
see the virgin was calculated at 20,000. (Gist– They came from all over. The
priests should be happy.) [A long section follows, calling the apparitions a
hoax and saying that those guilty should be punished.]

Source: *O Marinhense*, a liberal weekly, Marinha Grande, 22 Sep;
Doc Crit III book 1 pp 114-117.

#11A Sep 17-21?   LETTER OF MARIA DA CAMARA

[The second page of a two-page letter; the first page is missing.]

About the apparition, I heard … that one occurred again on the 13th.
The sisters[2] would very much like to go there in October. Can you imagine
that Ramalho, married with Florida Rafael was there and saw such a cloud
and lightning. He says it was a beautiful day and suddenly the sun began to
redden and to darken and then a cloud descended over the holm oak and
lightning was seen. Only the little ones see Our Lady. This is at mid-day

---

[2] Maria do Carmo de Figueiredo Cabral da Camara and Margarida Maria Cabral da
Camara.

exact. The sisters told this to me when I was ready to go. If I had learned earlier, I would have talked with the man.
[Personal matter follows.]
Maria da Graca

Source: The second page of a letter of Maria da Graca da Sigueira da Figueiro Cabral da Camara to Maria das Necessidades; Doc Crit III book 1 pp 848, 849.
Note: The text suggests that the letter was written between the 17th and the 21st of September; Doc Crit III book 1 p 848, footnote #2. The date of the phenomena cited in the letter is not given, but the reference to the lightning suggests that the date was 13 Aug. July 13 is also possible, but is less likely, since the crowd was much smaller in July. No lightning was reported for the September event.

#12 Sep 29   WHAT THEY ARE SAYING

… That Our Lady has appeared at Fatima and has forecast the end of the war.

Source: *Correio de Extremadura*, Santarem, 29 Sep; Doc Crit III book 1 p 125.

#12A Sep 8   MENDES LETTER

My dear Prazeres,
Soudos 8/9/917
(Gist– I am sorry for not writing yesterday. I wish you had been with me at Fatima. I went there for the sport of it and out of curiosity. Julio went with me. The trip was not short. I got directions, didn't sleep well that night. We went on horseback, starting at 6:00. The area isn't pretty, with rocks and pines. We reached Fatima at 10:00. The church is not very interesting, but the pastor's house is beautiful. People were surprised by two people on horseback. Lots of people were in the church. I went to confession and Communion. The people were devout. After Mass we talked with the vicar. We had breakfast with him and five other priests. I told them why we had come. The children had been there to be interrogated by the priests the evening before. The priests had been impressed.)
(Gist– The vicar sent his servant to take us to the home of the seers. Jacinta's mother received us well. Only Jacinta and Francisco were hers. Lucia was her niece. She gave their ages. She sent someone to get her at Lucia's house. She said she was worried because of the trouble the seers had caused.

She said they were unworthy of the honor of an apparition, especially her brother, Lucia's father. She told me about the kidnapping of the seers. Lucia had gone to bring lunch to her father and Jacinta did not want to come without Lucia. But her sister brought Jacinta home.)

(Gist– Jacinta is very tiny, very babyish. I sat down to be able to see her better and set her on a chest near me. Thus I could observe her at will. The vicar had told me that she is an angel, but I wanted to form my own opinion. I assure you, Prazeres, she is an angel, a very dear one. She would have enchanted you. She had a red handkerchief on her head, old and not very clean, jacket also not very clean and a wide skirt. I would like to describe her well, but I can't.)

The kerchief ... served to emphasize her features. Her eyes are dark and charmingly vivacious, her impression angelic, with a goodness that seduced us, an extraordinary overall [something] that attracted us, I don't know why. She was so shy that we had difficulty hearing the little she said in reply to my questions. She was missing her Lucia. It was no use. After talking and joking with her for some time ... Francisco arrived.

With his cap on his head, a very short jacket ... open to show his shirt, narrow pants, he was, in short, a little man. He has a handsome boyish face, his expression is lively and manly. He answered my questions confidently. Jacinta began to gain confidence. Shortly afterward Lucia arrived. You can't imagine Jacinta's joy when she saw her. She smiled all over, ran to her and never left her. It was a beautiful sight—Lucia on one side, no, in the middle, Francisco on one side and Jacinta on the other, very close and resting her head on her.

Lucia is not impressive to look at. Only her eyes are lively. Her features are vulgar. She is typical of the region. At the beginning she was shy, but I soon put her at ease, and then she replied with no shyness and kept satisfying my curiosity. After convincing myself that my interrogation was complete, I asked them to come with me to say the rosary at the apparition site. If their mother permits it, they'll go. I asked the permission myself. As soon as their mother said yes, Jacinta went to get dressed. (Gist– She dressed well.)

You are anxiously waiting for my impression, aren't you. Well, okay, my girl. As I said, I ... examined the three separately. All said the same thing without the least variation. The main thing they told me, I deduced, is "that the apparition wants to spread devotion to the rosary." The little ones say always that the person who appears to them is the Lady. They don't know who she is. Only after the six times, on Oct 13, will she say who she is and what she wants. The naturalness and simplicity with which they talk and describe what they saw is admirable and impressive.

Lucia sees the Lady, hears and talks with her. Jacinta sees the Lady but doesn't talk to her. Francisco sees, but doesn't hear or talk to her. The difference is interesting, isn't it, Prazeres? But besides interesting, it is even extraordinary. To hear these little ones, see them in their simplicity, examine them overall, impressed us in an extraordinary manner, and leads me to conclude that, in all they say, there exists something supernatural. To be with them moved us very intensely. I am now convinced that [this] is an extraordinary event, beyond our reasoning. I await with great anxiety the next 13th. It is clear that we felt very close to the little ones and lost our sense of time. They have an attraction I can't explain.

One of the most intense impressions of the children is that of the beauty of the Lady. The boy, to show his admiration, said she was very pretty. I showed him a photograph of you and asked: is she prettier? "Much more." The Lady is dressed in white, with gold. She has no blue band, as people have said. If she is Our Lady of Peace ... do you recall what she said at the second apparition? That they should learn to read. Jacinta told me that she was already at A.

While the little ones ate, I talked with the father. They had me eat bread, cheese and grapes! Not to hurt them, I accepted and offered him some cigars in exchange. (Gist– They only know what the children tell them. I think they know little more than I do. After eating we went to the apparition site.)

(Gist– I asked for a leaf from the holm oak and they said there were none left, but Francisco went to get one at home. The girls talked lightly and played the game of "bridges." They argued, but in a most friendly way. Francisco returned with a tiny branch for me. What a joy! I'll give it to you. On the way I became friends with the children. They laughed with me. Jacinta is a dear. Lucia is more reserved but has a strange charm.)

We arrived at the site. Near the road, on a slope is a beautiful spot where you can see very far. (Gist– The holm oak is small. The site has a wall around it, with vases of flowers on it and an arch of greenery.) The three kneel. Lucia, in the middle, begins the rosary. The offering is interesting. It is for the soldiers at war. With what devotion, Prazeres, the rosary is said! I think I never prayed with such attention. (Gist– I took a branch of the flowers for you. They taught me the prayer which the Lady taught them.) "Oh my Jesus, forgive me, keep me from the fires of hell, take all souls to heaven, especially those most in need." How simple. It is interesting that she taught it, but did not ask them to pray it.

I left the children with farewells. It was 6:00. We had left the Prior's house at 4:00! After eating supper, the Prior read to me the interrogation he had made of the children. [Gist– It was late] but I made some rapid notes which I will show you later, dear. But they added nothing to what you already know. Here you have my impressions of my yesterday. What do you make of such a long account?

(Gist– He describes his return home and gives personal matter.)

Your Carlos

Source: A letter of Carlos de Azevedo Mendes, a lawyer at Soudos, Torres Novas county, to his fiancé, Maria Prazeres Courinha; Doc Crit I pp 385-393; De Marchi, pp 245, 246.

#13 Oct 3   LETTER OF MARQUESA DA RIBEIRO GRANDE

[A copy of part of the letter of the Marquesa.]

(Gist– The letter reviews the earlier events very briefly, saying that there were seven apparitions, that the crowds kept growing, and that on Oct 13 Our Lady will appear with St. Joseph and the Child Jesus to bless the crowd and bring an end to the war. People who were there say the crowd in September was 80,000.)

They did not see Our Lady, but thought they saw a star in the middle of the day at 1:00. The little ones say they see and talk with Our Lady. I talked with a priest … who had been there who told me that on the right side of the sun he saw something almost like a star, round and white as the clouds which was going in the same direction, and then went up and disappeared. That was all he saw. (Gist– We'll see what happens on Oct 13. The trip there is hard.)

Oct 3, 1917 M za [Marquesa] de Ribeira

Source: Letter of Luisa de Cunhao e Menezes, the Marquesa da Ribeiro Grande, 74, to an unknown person, 3 Oct; Doc Crit III book 1 pp 133, 134.

Note: This extract was copied onto a single piece of paper, along with an extract of a letter sent to the Marquesa in the latter part of October by Maria Coelho. [Annex #19.] Both extracts are in the same handwriting. This extract was signed by the Marquesa, which suggests that both extracts were made by her. The extracts come from the files of the diocese of Leiria and probably were made soon after the Diocesan Inquiry was formalized on 3 May 1922; Doc Crit III book 1 p 133.

#14 Oct 13   THE MIRACLE OF FATIMA

Vila Nova de Ourem, 11th. On Friday of Ascension Day, this year, some children of this county were walking in Fatima, guarding the flock. While they were praying the rosary, a vision appeared to them, said it was Our Lady, according to what the children said. They have already been at the county headquarters, at the order of the proper authority.

The same vision declared to them that she would appear to them monthly, for six months, on the 13th at this place, which ends the day after tomorrow, on the 13th of this month. For this reason, some thousands of people from all classes of society are coming here with the purpose of attending the conversation of the vision with the innocent children. In the past month the number of people who were here for this purpose was over 20,000.

Source: Diario de Noticias, Lisbon, 13 Oct; Doc Crit III book 1 p 195.

Note: This newspaper was the largest daily newspaper in Portugal; *Fatima: The Great Sign,* p 54.

#15 Oct 13   IN FULL SUPERNATURAL

Thousands Rush to Wild Site near Ourem
to See and Hear the Virgin Mary

Let pious souls not be offended or saddened, and pure, believing hearts not be upset or afraid; we have no intention of being a scandal for those who sincerely hold to their faith, and whom the miraculous still attracts, seduces, bewitches, consoles and fortifies, as has been the case for thousands of years. ...

Whether by satire or argument, nobody intends to ridicule these pious souls. This is only a short article on an event that is not new in the history of Catholicism, but which, to the contrary, has occurred often, under almost the same forms, in different times and countries, and which has always been and always will be judged differently. Some regard it as a message from heaven and a grace; others see in it a sign and proof that the spirit of superstition and fanaticism has planted deep roots, which are difficult, if not impossible, to destroy.

Times of great calamity have always revived and renewed religious ideas and have favored them. And the war, by its scope, offers them the most favorable and fertile soil. We see that confirmed in the life of the trenches and even in the spiritual atmosphere of the belligerent countries. Or are there, perhaps, speculators who profit from this good opportunity to achieve hidden but lucrative plans, and profit-makers, for whom touching and holy simplicity is their primary object of exploitation? We don't want to deny it, because the events show us things [which] are similar over the course of centuries. Nor would we be surprised if tomorrow we discover that the famous apparitions at Fatima had brought especially material gains to lots of people. ...

Basically, of what do these apparitions consist? The Virgin descends the 13th of each month, since May, in the form of a very pretty woman ... to show herself to three children, whom she orders, in a charming voice, to pray and make her presence known to all. She tells believers and non-believers that on Oct 13—that is today—she will tell the true reason for her visits and console with her heavenly apparition those who are in the state of grace.

(Gist– The news has spread over the whole country. Thousands come to Fatima. Many say they see curious happenings. The phenomenology of miracles is always the same. Fatima is like Lourdes, La Salette and others. The apparition always appears to poor, simple children, asking for prayers and homage.)

We don't know if the apparition at Fatima has already asked for the building of a chapel, but for this purpose they have already organized a collection, to which the pilgrims will surely contribute generously.

The miracle takes place between noon and one o'clock, according to those who have been there. But not all have the luck to see the holy figure. The number of the elect seems very small. Despite their efforts many see nothing at all. Those nearest the children are content to hear them speak with an invisible partner. Others, however, at the divinely solemn moment, see stars shining in the sky, even though the sun is at its peak. They hear an underground groaning which announces the presence of the Lady. They claim that the temperature falls and some compare the impressions of that moment with those one gets during an eclipse of the sun.

According to what the children say, the figure of the Virgin appears over an oak bush, surrounded on all sides by a cloud that would seem to be a cloud of dust, as if at that moment dust had been raised by the wind. The mass hallucination, that the supernatural is acting, and that a superhuman force is causing the happenings, is so strong and entrancing that eyes fill with tears, some faces become pale as corpses, men and women prostrate themselves on the ground, chant songs and say the rosary together.

(Gist– We don't know if cures or conversions have already occurred, but it matters little. The word has spread; thousands flock to Fatima from all over each 13th. There is no transportation, nor place to eat or sleep; all are happy, even when nothing amazing happens, except the good behavior of the crowds.)

What will happen today at Fatima? We will soon know. Pious people hope the Virgin will answer them about the end of the war and (Gist– even say) when the peace will be signed.

The local clergy, as well as those in the surroundings, maintain a wise reserve about the events, at least in appearance. It is the custom of the Church. It proclaims loudly that in such circumstances, doubts mean nothing, for doubts also come from the devil. (Gist– But they rejoice over the events since May.) There are even people who, besides a huge church, dream of large hotels, ... souvenir shops and a train [to the site]. Will the dream come true, in which our mystical anxieties and our just commercial aspirations come together and collaborate?

Avelino de Almeida

Source: *O Seculo*, 13 Oct, *Our Lady of Fatima*, Wm. Walsh, pp 139-141; Doc Crit III book 1 pp 196-204.

Note: This article is important both to show the bias of Almeida and the prevailing impression of the five previous apparitions.

#16 Oct 13   BASTO NOTES

[Two blank lines and two lines of poetry are given.]

1917

9:00—Recio station. We are in the best place. It was almost fought over by hand. But we are okay. This has to be ready to go.

We have already passed the tunnel. We are staying in Campolide. The trip will be boring, since we have to stop at all the stations. But since we are not in a hurry, this also will amuse us. The weather could not be better. We are going to have a beautiful day at last. We didn't stop at all the stations.[3]

Arriving at the station of Torres, we go into a carriage (Gist– of some kind) which goes between the station and town. (Gist– She describes the town, a church and statue there.)

After seeing two farms ... we begin our trip to Rodrigo,[4] which for me closed our first day with a gold key. We came on four burros, but gentle ones, which didn't even stumble. ... When we get here it is already night. We eat and go to sleep.

---

[3] Written on 11 Oct.
[4] Rodrigo is a town in Torres Novas county.

Mr. Asumpcao and his Carlos are very nice. And these country ways are for us very nice. (Gist– The animals were noisy and kept them from sleeping.)

We passed the day getting ready for the trip. We were to leave at 11:00 at night, making the trip at night to arrive there in the morning.

During the night the weather begins to be cloudy, and shortly the thunder lets loose. But what thunder! It was past midnight and only thunder is heard and lightning is continual. What to do? It would be desolating not to go. Carlos blesses himself and says with such [weather] he is not going on. He waits and asks Our Lady to stop the thunder. At 2:00 the weather is better. We decide to go on. The night is very dark. They take a mule carriage. They put in some low chairs for us, and with some covers we install ourselves there. On the front bench are Carlos' wife and his daughter-in law. We [I and my sister Rita] and Regina and Amelia are in the back. Carlos takes the mule by the halter and we begin the trip.

From time to time the lightning illuminates the road and the thunder is further away but continuous.

We go like this for over an hour. The roads are awful. The carriage stumbles along. It has the advantage of not letting us sleep. Amelia makes us laugh all the time.

We are already climbing the Serra de Aire. The worst is that the rain returns, and we have little protection, since the water, which falls in buckets, muddies the carriage and wets our blankets.

Carlos for a while gets up and guides the mule. What matters is that he knows the roads very well.

The rain begins to be light. Now it is a drizzle, almost a heavy mist. Since now it is almost light we see trees hit by lightning. Here on the Serra, it must have been frightening. Carlos was right to tell us not to come [earlier]; he knows them [the storms] well.

We have gone a long way on the Serra, which seems to have no end. Now they say we are near Fatima. It is raining a lot. We are already muddy, but (Gist– we don't stop, and get out to help the mules.) We all go on foot except Amelia, who can't walk much.

Finally we arrive at Fatima. It is 9:00. The weather is a little better, but the sky is entirely covered and threatens more rain. Lots of people are arriving from various roads on the Serra. Most are all wet, like us, but all come, I don't know why, because nothing is marked, and only because they say that today Our Lady will talk to Lucia.

The carriage stays in Fatima. We eat something and now go on foot to the Cova da Iria, where they say the apparitions have occurred.

We walk almost an hour. When we arrive at the field—an area fairly large but lower than the road, and where there are only some oak trees— there are plenty of people who are waiting. We will see for what!

It is near noon. They say that the shepherds are going to arrive. I would like to see them. The apparition site is marked off by some poles, so the little ones can be more free from the people, but we can't get close, since there are lots of people. The ground is so soaked that our feet sink in; we are already muddy anyhow. We decide to stay in a place a little higher, but further away. There is movement in the crowd. It is the shepherds who are arriving. Some men open the way. I don't see them well. They go to the site of the poles. It is raining fairly hard.

It starts to be said that Lucia says to close the umbrellas, that Our Lady is coming. But it is raining so much! However, everyone obeys and shuts their umbrellas. And actually, a little after, the rain stops, but we see nothing more. Our eyes look all over. Now a little cloud of smoke seems to grow over the oak at the site of the poles. The sun appears between the clouds, but with no shine; one would say it is the moon and has a cross in the middle. Now, oh marvelous, the atmosphere is tinged with the colors of the rainbow. I see Rita's white felt hat orange-colored, then green, then bluish, then rose,

[A drawing of Our Lady and a moon with a cross appears here.]

and finally golden. It's all golden. What a beautiful thing.

Everybody feels fascinated. A man near us faints on the ground. Suddenly the completely black sun seems to loosen itself from the sky and seems to turn on itself very rapidly. It seems it is going to fall. A cry is heard from all the crowd, which falls on its knees, asking mercy.

I also find myself on my knees on top

[A drawing of the church of Valhelha appears here.]

of a pile of stones without noticing it. But all passes in a moment. The sun is again covered by clouds, a cloud which seems to rise. All are unable to understand what happened, as if stunned. They say Lucia talked with the Lady. We could not get to see the shepherds again. We head toward Fatima, where we get in the carriage and turn toward Rodrigo. The weather is good. We can only see some isolated clouds in the sky and the sun has its natural shine.

When we arrive our clothes are still half dry. Emilia is upset, because they say we could get sick. But no, what we are is very tired. We eat something and go to bed. Tomorrow we head toward Lisbon.

Source: Notes made on a small notebook by Maria Bettina Basto, 19, of Lisbon, on her trip to Fatima, 11-13 Oct; Doc Crit III book 1 pp 186-192.

Note: Most of the short sentences lacked punctuation, which I have supplied. This and the text itself, especially the use of the present tense, creates the impression of being notes made many times during this three-day period. A reasonable assumption is that each paragraph was a separate entry. More information on this trip is given by Basto in Annex #37.

Note: Footnotes #25 and #26 say that Maria Bettina told **us**: "The drawing which I made was what I imagined to be the form of the Lady who was appearing to the shepherds." And, "The [drawing] of the church was made on the 12th, when we visited this church, near Rodrigo." "Us" is clearly the staff of the Fatima archives. Footnote 15 of #55 says that Basto made this statement about the Lady to <u>us</u> in 1978; Doc Crit III book 1 pp 191, 192, 375. Some details of her trip are also given in #55.

#17 13 Oct   BRITES DIARY

I went to Mouta[5] to see the apparition of Our Lady with my sons, and had dinner with Francisco from Boucinhas, in the house of his cousin in Mouta and had lunch at his daughter in Barreira.[6] (Gist– It rained all morning and we made this pilgrimage full of water.) That night Father [Jose da] Silva came to stay in my house. <u>What was seen of the apparition was the sun getting dark for a quarter of an hour.</u> The children said that Our Lady said that the war was ending and she wanted them to build a chapel there.

Source: Diary of Manuel Pereira Crespa da Costa Brites, 13 Oct; Doc Crit III book 1 pp 193, 194. See Annex #9 for an earlier diary entry of his.

#18 Oct 13   FATHER DA SILVA LETTER

Blessed and loved be our most holy Lady.
My dear.
The promised has happened. I am writing from Monte Redondo at 9:30 at night of the 13th. Our Lady gave me a favor. She deigned to give a clear sign of her apparition to the children of Fatima.

At mid-day we were at Fatima. There were more than 90 automobiles, an infinity of carriages of all sizes, shapes and makes, and an enormous crowd of people. [A Latin phrase on people follows.] All were soaked, … but happy.

About noon the children came to the site and started praying the rosary, as usual. When it was finished, the children asked Our Lady if the prom-

---

[5] Refers to the village of Moita Redonda in Fatima parish, near the Cova da Iria.
[6] In Santa Caterina Parish of Leiria county.

ised sign was given. At once the sun appeared, with its edge well defined. It approached as if to the height of the clouds and began turning on itself vertiginously, like a fixed firewheel, with some intermissions, for more than eight minutes. All was semi-dark and the features of everyone were yellowish. They all knelt, even in the mud.

All the time the [people] here and there sang, prayed, etc. All left satisfied. The little ones said that Our Lady of the Rosary appeared. Later, (when the sun made its sign) St. Joseph appeared. The little ones said that this one [St. Joseph] said that today, or soon, the flag of peace would be raised, that [the people] should pray the rosary, that our troops would be there soon, that [the people] should do penance and reform our lives, because if not, the world would end. Oh how it seems to me that Our Lady is still helping [us] with her all-powerful prayers. [Personal matters follow.]

Yours, Father Silva

Source: Typed copy of a letter of Father Manuel Pereira da Silva, 40, pastor of Monte Redondo parish, to Father Antonio Pereira d'Almeida, 13 Oct; Doc Crit III book 1 pp 164-166.

#19 Oct 13?   COELHO LETTER

[Extract of a letter of Mariano P. Coelho to her aunt,
the Marquesa Ribeira Grande.]

I am going to give you my impressions of [what happened] on the 13th of this month at Fatima.

They were the best, ... and I will never forget those delicious moments. I saw immense things. I saw the sun descend on the earth in an extraordinary manner, to the point of causing uncomfortable heat. I saw it turn rapidly, like a firewheel. I saw the sun like a host. There are those who say they saw the sun with various colors. I saw snow white, then dark gray. I saw all this, and what most impressed and consoled [me is] the great manifestation of faith. I talked with the oldest one, who is not pretty, but is very pleasant, shy and modest, and I had to pull the words from her, and at the end of it all—talking to the masses—she seemed like a priest on a pulpit, and with her face transformed.

Source: An extract from an undated letter from Mariana Pinto Coelho to her aunt, the Marquesa de Ribeira .... Grande; Doc Crit III book 1 p 203. The first sentence indicates that this letter was written in October.

Note: The author was the daughter-in-law of the famous Domingo Pinto Coelho. The Marquesa apparently made this extract. See the note in #13. See #34 for Pinto Coelho's article on the 13 Oct event.

#20 Oct 13?[7]   MENDES LETTER

Torres Novas, 1917

.... [The start of this letter is missing.] But let us turn to Fatima. I will try to give you a brief account of my impressions.

From May onward rumors began to circulate that something extraordinary was happening in the region of Fatima. The rumors grew, and I, who heard them with a certain skeptical and even scoffing air, began to feel my curiosity aroused. In the beginning of September ... I went there for an outing on horseback. I spoke to the parish priest and afterwards to the two little girls and to the boy. I interrogated them separately ...

They left on me an extraordinary impression which was truly sensational. I was with them three hours, even going to the site of the holm oak to pray the rosary. I could not discover a single contradiction, however slight; all of them made precisely the same statements. The youngest is eight years old, and all three have the most ingenuous air, combined with a truly primitive culture, as you can imagine among shepherds of our mountains. After leaving them, the parish priest showed me his report and I was amazed to find that it agreed exactly with my inquiry. Everyone who has gone there and interrogated them has arrived at the same conclusion. ....

The 13th arrived and I went to the spot with great eagerness. Such were my dispositions that I went to Communion before going there. ... I sought to get near the children and succeeded. The sun was blazing; I was soaked with perspiration but did not move a foot. The time passed, the children said they had seen the vision, and as for me ... I neither saw nor felt a thing! ... I was disheartened and at that stage classified the whole thing as a hoax! The crush was great. The children were distressed and wept. I took one of them up in my arms. Her timidity was obvious, yet she assured that in October the Lady would come again.

So I would come on that day; once I had begun I would carry my cross to the end ... The 13th of Oct arrived; it was raining. It cleared a bit and off we went. Halfway there, the rain came down in torrents, and it came to such a point that neither mantles nor hats could keep the rain from getting through. But nobody was discouraged. Everyone advanced. The general aspect was impressive and wonderful. There was not one complaint about the rain, but rather respect on the part of all.

---

[7] The date of Oct 13? was given in my source, but with a footnote saying that the letter was surely written in late Oct or early Nov in view of the reference to the inquiry which was underway.

Over 50,000 people were present, and not one had been invited, not one protested. Time was flying and anxiety increased. It was already past the time, when the children cried out—that she was coming. Was it truly an apparition? ... The atmospheric signs, which surely you know about, were they natural? I do not know, but what I can affirm is that precisely at the moment that the little girl said: "Look at the sun, the sign is there of which the Lady had spoken to me," we all saw the sun dancing and taking on appearances which had never been seen before. Were those appearances natural? What does it matter to me? Nobody knew about them ... Nobody knew that they existed and would appear; and yet for six months the children have been saying that there would be a sign which would make everyone believe that, in fact, the Lady had appeared. How beautiful it was to see those thousands of believers on that occasion! ... It is a sight that I shall never forget! At the end I took up around my neck the oldest child, the seer, and how different now was her attitude from the 13th of September! ... Now she seemed to be a messenger bearing some news, because from my arms she gesticulated and cried out to everyone around—that they should do penance, for that is what the Lady wanted. ...

It is certain that she also said that the Lady had affirmed the war would end on that day, and it still continues, but for me the most extraordinary thing of all that I saw was the coincidence of the atmospheric signs with the child's forecast, and afterwards that immense crowd of people in the best and greatest of order, with the most profound respect, and without the least invitation (to be there). Was there a miracle? I await expectantly the Church's pronouncement, all the more so as I have heard it said that they are proceeding to an inquiry. But in my innermost soul I have the sound conviction that in this entire case of Fatima there is something supernatural. I am told that there have been some extraordinary events, miraculous even. What is certain is that it was a happening which had such repercussions, that during days on end it was the subject of conversation in the whole of Portugal.

Here you have my impressions, written in great haste.

It [the copy] matches [the original]

Carlos A. Mendes

Source: A typed [and signed] copy of part of a letter written by Dr. Carlos de Azevedo Mendes, 29, a lawyer in Saudos, Torres Novas county, to a brother of his, *Fatima Way of Peace*, pp 65, 66, and Doc Crit I pp 395-398. The lawyer Mendes read this letter and acknowledged it to be his, even though it contradicted a later statement of his concerning Lucia's words about the end of the war on 25 Nov 1954; Doc Crit I p 398.

Note: See #12A for details of his September visit with the seers.

#21 Oct 13[8]   STATEMENT OF BENTO

1) Near Fatima or Cova da Iria, beside Aljustrel, ... near the asphalt road on the north side.

Events witnessed by me: On June 13 I was there for the first time; I wasn't on time, but talked with the little ones in front of the church. I interrogated them attentively and saw in them what seemed to me impossible to me not to be true. From that time, I was a believer in that the Most Holy Virgin was coming there.

2) I was also there on July 13. At the time of the apparition a little fog [was seen], the sun lost its force, ceasing to produce the heat, which was great until then. And many people said that when the apparition talked, they heard her, but did not perceive what she said. I only heard when Lucia said: "There she goes."

I heard in the air a roar which seemed to be the start of thunder.

3) I was there also on Aug 13. The girls and boy were taken prisoner. There were lots of people. At the very time of the apparition, the stars and sun showed themselves the same as the other times, and [there was] an extraordinary sign in the stars.

On 13 Sep I was also there. The sun and stars made the same picture, and the people looked enthusiastically in the air, some said that they saw stars, others that they saw a dove, others that they saw stars running, and swallows with them. All were enthused. [There were] even others who [said that] they saw flowers falling.

4) On Oct 13 it rained almost all morning. At about the time of the apparition, it stopped raining. What extraordinary things occurred in the sun! Everyone saw it: the people who had their eyes open; those who had them closed saw nothing, and maybe there were those who saw and said they did not, in order not to give honor to the Mother of Heaven; there was (perhaps) an error in regard to the war. The extraordinary happenings that were there are unparalleled.

J d S Bento

Source: Statement of Jacinto de Sousa Bento, Oct? 1917; Doc Crit III book 1 pp 210, 211.

Note: The reference to the error on the war suggests that this statement was written at least a few days after 13 Oct. It was not dated and had no paragraphs. His writing, spelling, and punctuation were poor and it had no

---

[8] The date was annotated by another person.

paragraphs; it has been modified for readability. Bento was from the village of Assentiz. His age is unknown. The occasion for the statement was not given.

#22 Oct 15?   **LETTER OF DE CASTRO**
[THE SARAIVAS]

Oct 1917

My dear grandmother,

I am going to tell you what happened at Fatima. I am simply repeating what the Saraivas said they saw, and which I think is true, for the most part, since everyone confirms it.

(Gist– On Friday, the 12th, at Tomar, we saw the crowds pass, lots of people on all kinds of transport and on foot. No vehicles could be hired.)

Here is what the Saraivas said about the next day:

After 7 hours of train, with a light rain, they arrived at the site of the miracle, soaked. There were lots of people there, calculated at over 50,000. Between noon and one o'clock the little one arrived, with some men who stopped the people from crushing her with an excess of kindness.

Lucia (the little one), when she arrived at the holm oak, where the Lady appears, asked the people to recite the rosary, while she was waiting. Families joined in groups of 8 or 10 and recited the rosary with great devotion. It was a spectacle of medieval faith. I forgot to say that when Lucia arrived the rain stopped immediately.

Suddenly the sun began to have a greenish color, changing successively to light yellow, which made the people look ghostly. Then it made something like a turnabout, a push. It seemed it was going to fall on the earth. Everyone fell on their knees and one heard only cries: "God save us. Jesus. Holy Virgin." At that moment the heat was so great that she almost suffocated. Everyone imagined that it was the end of the world. People cried. This lasted 10 minutes. When they came to their senses after this great emotion, Our Lady was no longer there. Nothing more was seen, but the little one looked at a fixed spot and smiled.

When the little one returned home, Dr. Joao do Vale went with the Saraivas to talk to her. She answered all with the greatest of simplicity and said this: "that Our Lady asked men to make an effort to be better, and that her dear Son was angry, that the war would end soon and the Portuguese soldiers would return to their homes. She asked especially that they pray a lot. If they wished, they should build a chapel there and venerate her as Our Lady of the Rosary."

Asked about Our Lady, she said she was beautiful, had a very white, straight dress (it must be a tunic), was barefoot, and had a blue kerchief on her head, blue and very long blue mantle. Her voice was very pretty and she called the little one by her name—Lucia.

The little one only replies to questions, but with no embarrassment, but before the apparition was very shy.

She said, as before, that the Lady told her a secret that she tells no one, not even her mother. (Gist– A lady tried to bribe her with 1,000 reis, but she refused.)

Lucia is poor, but despite this does not accept money they offer her. It can be seen that she is not a faker. Despite the soaking rain and the long road, no one was sick. This also seems from God.

This is the truth without doubt, because other people have told it to us, and it is always the same. (Gist– Fond wishes.) Francisca d' Assis

Source: A typed copy of a letter from Maria Francisca de Castro, 16, of Quinta da Cima, Tomar county, to her grandmother. Both ladies were countesses. The copy was sent to the Fatima archives by the writer of the letter in August 1967; Doc Crit III book 1 pp 222-225.

Note: The date in Oct is not given. Its envelope is stamped 20 Oct.

#23 Oct 13?   STATEMENT OF CORREIA

I, Maria Luisa Correia, my sister Maria Garrett Correia, my sister-in-law and other friends, who accompanied us, affirm that we were witnesses of what we are going to describe briefly. About 70,000 people awaited the time predicted by the children, the time when Our Lady said the visual prodigy would happen for everyone, who on Oct 13 would be at that holy site.

The old hour is that which the people follow. At a half hour, more or less, by solar time, the sun, which up to this time was covered by dense, black clouds, since from 8:00 in the morning the rain had not stopped a moment, accompanied by a tempestuous wind, [the sun] showed itself suddenly free of clouds, at its zenith, the rain stops, the sun is like a dull silver plate, and it is possible to look at it without the least effort. To the frightened eyes of the people, while the child who addresses the Virgin, orders that the people kneel and uncover their heads, the sun turns on itself in a vertiginous movement, putting out puffs of heat, like a lit-up oven that had been opened, the sun seems to near the earth in brusque and rapid movements, changes color one after another and the landscape becomes yellow, then it becomes purplish, according to the colors covering the sun. This phenomenon lasts about ten minutes, while the crowd knelt, and with hands in prayer, asked for pardon and mercy.

From the place where the Virgin talks with the children there arose a transparent white smoke, which formed something like a little cloud, which covered the area between two small oaks where the children were awaiting the apparition. The oldest child, Lucia—ten years old—asks the Virgin in a loud voice: Who are you? What do you want? The answers are not heard, but when the sun retakes its usual course, the child turns to the crowd, on the shoulders of a man, who holds her in his arms, and repeats the words of the Lady.

["] I am the Lady of the Rosary; I want a chapel built here for me. ["]

She says to the people that they should amend their ways, stop offending God, and says that peace is being made today, and that your soldiers are going to return. The two other children, Jacinta and Francisco, see the Virgin but don't talk to her.

Source: A handwritten statement of Maria Luisa Garrett Correia, not further identified. It is not dated, but said to be from about 13 Oct. The occasion for the statement is not given. It was given to the Bishop of Leiria on 10 Mar 1972, by Hugo Fernandes Azevedo, who received it from a person in Oporto; Doc Crit III book 1 pp 212, 213.

#24 Oct 14   THE LADY OF FATIMA

(Gist– A long article, written by Miguel Pinto de Figueiredo, says that some poor people at Fatima had hallucinations, and complains that the Lady did not help with any of the problems of the world, the war, the loss of the Titanic, or other happenings. It tells us nothing significant about the "sun dance" or other Fatima events.)

Source: *Jornal de Leiria*, Leiria, 14 Oct; Doc Crit III book 1 pp 216-219. This journal was a weekly of the Portuguese Republican Party. The article is the first press report on Fatima.

#24A Oct 14   LETTER OF PROENCA GARRETT

Granja, 1917, 10/14

Esteemed Reverend,

Permit me, while still under the great impression I felt yesterday in that place where I am convinced supernatural things are happening, to claim your Reverence's attention, on my own behalf and that of many devout persons who are greatly interested in the same matter.

I know that your Reverence remained in Fatima until today and must have spoken calmly to the children, and so I come to ask you the favor to tell me what they say about Our Lady's words to them, to be repeated to the people. Did the little girl assert what I heard from her, that Our Lady said the war was to end yesterday? I am afraid this was not said by Our Lady and that someone inspired the little one with this idea, which she somewhat unconsciously repeated. If the war does not end and the child persists in her assertion, it will do a lot of harm to the public because many people will become unbelieving.

I saw the child, but only briefly, and I had no time to ask her if Our Lady had spoken about praying the rosary and if she had said anything else which she wanted done. And did the Lady tell her another secret? And did the other little ones know what the Lady said? And did Our Lady promise to appear more times and give a sign about that? I greatly wish to know this, for there are a great many people who are lamenting that they had not gone there yesterday and they would like to go another time.

Please have patience with my annoying questions, but your Reverence understands them well and that it is not through mere curiosity that I am making all these questions to you. And I will only use what your Reverence will tell me I can repeat. Do you know that here in Granja there were persons who saw the movement of the sun in rotation and a rose-colored cloud passing in front of the sun?

My husband is still ill and sends his compliments to your Reverence. I am, etc. yours,

Maria Joaquina Tavares de Proence Garrett

Source: Letter to Fr. Formigao, *Fatima Way of Peace*, pp 62, 63; Doc Crit III book 1 pp 214, 215.

Note: Mrs. Proenca Garrett, 67, in Granja, was the wife of Professor Goncalo Garrett and thus the mother of Jose Garrett, author of the famous letter on Fatima cited in my introduction (page 2). See #89 and #90 of this Annex; see #90A for information on other letters of Proenca Garrett.

Note: The underlining in this letter was not contained in the original text; Doc Crit III book 1 p 215, footnote 7.

#25 Oct 15   COUTINHO LETTER

15 Oct, 1917

Dear Amadeu,

(Gist– The first part describes his trip and arrival at a rooming house where he had to sleep in the hall, and then describes going to Fatima, and the crowd going there. He left at 4:00 and went 12 kilometers in constant rain. At 9:00, when he arrived, there were already people who had passed the night in the rain. Up until 2:00, when the miracle was supposed to happen, it kept raining and all the people got wet to the bone. He then describes the crowd going there and the Cova da Iria. Despite the lower number given by anti-Catholic newspapers, he and everyone figured the crowd to be at least 100,000 persons from all parts of the country and Spain and France. Despite the rain people sang hymns. The people kept coming until 2:00, when the children arrived.)

The little ones knelt in the mud at a rude altar barely 100 meters away, where I was lucky to be. The circle of people around the children was a kilometer long and wide, with a dense mass of people inside. The rain kept coming until the wet chins of the women chattered. Meanwhile the children ordered the people to close their umbrellas and the rain stopped at once.

In the sky, which was completely covered with clouds, there opened up a circle in which the sun appeared, like a moon on a moonlit day, and next showed a silver aura around [it].

The circle then took on successively the colors blue, red, yellow and green, and at the same time all objects [around] took on that same color. This lasted one minute, after which the sky [presumably meaning the sun] became covered again. At once the occasion when the Lady talked with the children, and for which she came down from heaven [occurred], a dark cloud formed around the sun, which all the people could look at without hurting their eyes, [and which] took on various colors and seemed to descend on us. Then, when Our Lady went up to heaven, the cloud, which now seemed a fire, rose again with the sun, and the cloud began to turn around the sun, while it, still with a silver aura, began to tremble immensely against the blue background of the sky.

You would need to see this dazzling miracle to get an idea of it. And I give you my word of honor that it convinced me that it was a miracle, and I have as witnesses the 100,000 people who were there. I tell you also that when the miracle, which lasted 15 minutes in all, was over, the sun shone as usual, so no one could stare at it for a moment, as you know. At the same time that the phenomenon occurred, pious exclamations came from 100,000 mouths. I thus had, as other people also said, an extraordinary impression, and at the same time a desire to know the impossible. After the miracle, all the people woke, as if from a dream, and the impression passed.

Our Lady told the little ones to have a chapel made at the site, and that the war would soon end and the Portuguese soldiers would return shortly. The man at my side, who did not believe in anything, was converted little by little as the miracle took place. (Gist– People tried to quiz the seers, they left in good order, and no one drank or quarreled.) I interviewed various people about what happened, and all told me like what I had seen. For four to five or six hours only half (the people)—those from the west left by the other road—filed out slowly like on the avenue on a Sunday. (Gist– I made the trip of 22 km to the train station. There must have been 1,000 vehicles in all, since over 100 cars were there from the east. More on his return trip follows.) All were indignant with the free-thinkers, and 100,000 people are witnesses of a miracle that nobody can deny. (Gist– More on his trip follows. He excuses his bad writing, he makes an unfavorable comment on the *O Seculo* article of 15 Oct and asks the recipient to keep the letter.)

Fernando

Source: Letter of 15 Oct from Fernando S Coutinho at Casais, Cartaxo parish, to Amadeu B. Martins; Doc Crit III book 1 pp 226-231.

Note: A statement of Coutinho on the sun dance was published in his book *Parcelas do meu Caminho*, pp 132-137, Lisbon, 1959, and in *Novidades* on 12 May 1967. It has some variations with his letter. In 1917 he and Amadeu were cadets at the Military College; Doc Crit III book 1 p 226; Jaki, pp 317-318.

#26 Oct 15   LETTER OF SAMPAIO

Torres Novas 15-10-917

My dear mother

"Copy of the original"

I am sorry I can't fly there to tell you what happened at Fatima on the 13th. Praise God, all the people marvel at the great power Our Lady showed to men. (Gist– There were over 50,000 people there, coming from all over.) Only in seeing so many people there a disbeliever would be converted. It is said that many people were converted. We are all in admiration. <u>Do you know that at mid-day exactly they saw some colors of the sky fall over the great crowd, then a star</u> came over the oak bush where the little ones were kneeling and an enchanted atmosphere came over all of us who were there. It was noted that the Blessed Virgin was talking to the lucky child called Lucia. That child shouted to the people that Our Lady said the people should look at the sun, and all the people began to exclaim: "Hail to the Virgin of heaven and earth!" All around me people were kneeling on the ground and saying loudly: "Hail to the Virgin of heaven and earth." … and others were looking at the marvels in the sun. <u>Do you know that the sun began to turn rapidly, like a firewheel? And then it stopped, and still without brilliance, so that</u>

all could see better, it stayed in the sight of all in the form of a sacred host. Everyone there was astounded by "such a miracle." After everything had passed, Lucia [said] that Our Lady said that the war was ending and the flags of peace already in sight—(a miracle). But Our Lady also said that all the people should pray the rosary every day and build a church at that site. Do you know, mother, that little Lucia moved in triumph; everyone tried to hear and kiss the children, including me. I found a good spot and was able to see her. Here nobody talks of anything else, they are all in admiration, and soon we will have our soldiers back.

Your loving daughter,

Maria

Source: A copy of a letter of Maria Asuncao Sampaio to her mother, Maria Santana; Doc Crit III book 1 pp 232, 233.

#27 Oct 15   THE MIRACLE OF FATIMA

More than Fifty Thousand People Rush to the Apparition Site

Vila Nova de Ourem, 13th. Despite a light but bothersome rain that began to fall early in the morning, an extraordinary number of people hastened to the parish of Fatima to be present at the remarkable affair of the apparition, which since Ascension Thursday [May 13] has held the attention of the people and has attracted to that site thousands and thousands of pilgrims of all sexes and all classes.

Already the day before, groups of men and women began to go through this town. With complete devotion and faith, singing hymns and praying the rosary, they headed for the place where the "miracle" would be repeated for the last time, according to the statements of the three little shepherds to whom, as they declare, Our Lady deigned to appear several times on the 13th of the month since then [May 13].

In order to give an idea of the number of people, we [hereby] give a listing of those vehicles we were able to count: carriages – 240, bicycles – 135, automobiles – more than 100. These statistics represent only the number of vehicles which returned through the city [Vila Nova de Ourem].

At the hour of the talk [with the Virgin] at 1 P.M., the anxiety was evident.

Although the rain continued to beat down on the crowd, no one left that privileged site. Exactly at that time the three little shepherds, whose names are Lucia, Jacinta and Francisco, arrived at the designated place, immediately falling on their knees under an arch purposely erected there as if it were to serve as an altar.

Hallucination immediately took hold of these thousands of believers and the curious. Since a great number had their umbrellas open, the children ordered them to be closed; and then, according to the testimony of thousands of people, a strange thing [happened]: the sun appeared, the color of dull silver, with a circular movement, as if powered by electricity—according to the expression used by illustrious people who witnessed the event.

And thousands of people, under mass hallucination, and who knows if they were even confused by the very light of the sun, which appeared for the first time that day, fell to the ground, crying and raising upward their hands, instinctively joined.

On their faces was a look of ecstatic rapture that indicated an absolute alienation from life. These simple souls cried and prayed, in the presence of the strange sensation of an event, which was for them, and at that moment, miraculous. There were even those, according to some we heard, who seemed to see the sun abandon its supposed orbit, break through the clouds, and descend to the horizon. The hallucination of these seers spread to others, to whom they explained the phenomenon, and because of this, many people, thinking that the sun would hurl itself upon the earth, broke out in loud cries, imploring the protection of the Virgin.

The "miraculous hour" passed.

The smiling children got up and explained to their anxious listeners that "the Lady" had told them that peace would come shortly and that the return of our brave soldiers, who are fighting heroically in France, would not be long delayed. At the site, postcards, with pictures of the simple children, were sold.

After those anxious moments, the pilgrims returned to their homes, desirous of telling those who did not have the good luck to go to the holy place, what their eyes, and mainly their believing souls, had observed with so much enchantment.

Source: *Diario de Noticias*, page 2, 15 Oct; Jaki, pp 47, 48; *Fatima: The Great Sign*, pp 54, 55; and Doc Crit III book 1 pp 245, 246.

#28 Oct 15 ASTOUNDING THINGS! HOW THE SUN DANCED AT MID-DAY AT FATIMA

The Apparition of the Virgin—In What the Sign from Heaven
Consisted—Many Thousands of People Affirmed That a Miracle
Has Been Performed—War and Peace

[Here appears a photograph of the three children.]

(From our special envoy)

Ourem, 13 Oct

(Gist– He describes his trip to Ourem from the train depot at Chao de Macas, and the people going toward Fatima in great detail. He passed the night in Ourem.)

The sun was rising, but the skies appeared stormy and threatening. Black clouds loomed directly over Fatima. (Gist– He provides more detail on the people and vehicles going to Fatima.)

By ten o'clock the sky became totally overcast, and it was not long before a good rain began. The falling rain, whirled around by a sharp wind, beat on faces, drenched the roadway and soaked to the bone those travelers not provided with umbrellas or any other protection. But nobody got impatient or stopped moving forward, and if some sought shelter under trees, near the walls of farms or in the rare houses to be found at intervals near the road, others continued the march with striking endurance. Some ladies could be seen with their clothes glued to their bodies, as a result of the persistent rain, etching the outline of their forms as if they had just come out of a bath!

* * *

The spot in the hollow of Fatima, where it is said that the Virgin appeared to the little shepherds from the village of Aljustrel, is dominated over an enormous stretch by the road that goes [from Ourem] to Leiria, and along which were parked the vehicles which had carried the pilgrims and spectators there. Someone counted over a hundred cars and a hundred bicycles, and it would be impossible to count the various conveyances which blocked the roadway, one being the bus from Torres Novas, in which people of all social conditions were united as one family.

But the bulk of the pilgrims, the thousands of creatures who came from many leagues around, and who were joined by the faithful from other provinces, from Alentejo and Algarve [in the South] to Minho and Beira [in the North], were gathered around the small holm oak which, according to the little shepherds, the vision had chosen as a pedestal, and which could be considered as the center of an ample circle, on the rim of which other spectators and other devotees are forming. Seen from the road, the spectacle is simply fantastic. Many of the prudent peasants, encamped under enormous umbrellas, accompany the eating of their meager provisions with the spiritual sustenance of sacred hymns and decades of the rosary. None are afraid to dig their feet in the sodden earth in order to have the good fortune of a close-up view of the holm oak, over which a rustic portico had been erected and on which two lanterns were swinging. ... The groups singing the praises of the Virgin alternate, and a hare, which races in fright through a thicket outside, attracts the attention of a half dozen youths who chase it and lay it low with a blow.

And the little shepherds? Lucia, 10 years old, the seer, and her little companions Francisco, 9, and Jacinta, 7, have not yet arrived. Their presence was noted perhaps a half hour before the time indicated for the apparition. They lead the little girls, crowned with wreaths of flowers, to the spot where the portico had been put up. The rain falls incessantly, but nobody lost hope. Carriages with the late arrivers reach the road. Groups of the faithful kneel in the mud and Lucia asks, [even] orders, them to close their umbrellas. The order was transmitted and obeyed at once, with minimum reluctance. There are many people who seem to be in ecstasy; people overcome with emotion, on whose dry lips prayer is paralyzed, people transfixed, with their hands joined together and their eyes moist and protruding, people who seem to feel and touch the supernatural ... The child affirms that the Lady had spoken once again, and the sky, still obscure, begins all of the sudden to clear above us. The rain stops and one can guess that the sun is about to flood the landscape, which the wintry morning had left even sadder. ...

The old time is what counts for this crowd, which the impartial calculations of educated persons, altogether removed from mystical influences, reckon at thirty or forty thousand persons ... The miraculous manifestation, the visible sign forecast is about to take place, many pilgrims assure ... And then they witness a spectacle that is unique and unbelievable for anyone who was not a witness of it. From the road above, where the vehicles were parked, and where many hundreds of people, who had not dared to brave the mud, are congregated, one can see the immense crowd turn toward <u>the sun, which appears free from clouds and at its zenith.</u> It looks like a dull silver plate, and it is possible to stare at it without the least effort. It does not burn or blind. <u>One would say an eclipse was taking place.</u> But at that moment a great shout went up, and one can hear the spectators nearest at hand exclaiming:

"A Miracle, a Miracle! A Marvel, a Marvel!"

Before the astonished eyes of the crowd, whose attitude takes us back to Biblical times, and who, bareheaded, eagerly search the sky, their faces pale with apprehension, <u>the sun trembled, it made brusque, unprecedented movements, outside all cosmic laws—the sun "danced," according to the typical expression of the peasants</u> .... Standing on the running board of the Torres Novas bus is an old man whose appearance in face and figure, gentle and energetic at the same time, reminds one of Paul Deroulede. With his face turned to the sun, he recites the whole Credo in a loud voice. I ask who he is and I am told that he is Senhor Joao Maria Amado de Melo Ramalho da Cunha Vasconcelos. I see him afterward going up to those around him who still have their hats on and vehemently imploring them to uncover before such an extraordinary manifestation of the existence of God. Identical scenes are repeated elsewhere, and at one stage a woman, bathed in tears of distress, and almost suffocating, cries out:

"How terrible. There are even men who do not uncover before such a stupendous miracle."

People then begin to ask each other if they saw and what they had seen. The majority declare that they had seen the trembling and dancing of the sun; others affirm that they saw the smiling face of the very Virgin; they swear that the sun whirled on itself like a giant fireworks wheel, and that it lowered itself almost to the point of burning up the earth with its rays ... Some say they saw it change colors successively.

* * *

It is almost three o'clock in the afternoon. The sky is swept clear of clouds and the sun follows its normal course, with its usual splendor, which no one would dare to stare at openly. And the shepherds? Lucia, the one who spoke with the Virgin, is carried on a man's shoulders from group to group, and announces with dramatic gestures that the war has ended and the soldiers will return ... News like this, however, does not increase the joy of those who hear it. The heavenly sign is everything. There is an intense curiosity to see the two little girls with their wreaths of roses, and some try to kiss the hands of the "little saints," one of whom, Jacinta, is more inclined to collapse than to dance. But the thing for which they had all longed—the sign from heaven—suffices to satisfy them, to root them in their rock-like faith. Traveling vendors offer photographs of the children on post cards, and others showing a soldier of the Portuguese Expeditionary Force, "counting on the aid of their protector for the salvation of their native land," and even an image of the Virgin as being the figure of the vision. This was good business, and undoubtedly more coins entered pockets of the vendors and the alms box for the little shepherds than the extended hands of the lepers and the blind, who elbowed their way through the pilgrims and cast piercing cries in the air.

The dispersal is accomplished rapidly, without any difficulties, without a shadow of disorder, without the needs of any guards to control it. The pilgrims who leave the quickest, hurrying out onto the road, are those who had been first to arrive, on foot and barefooted, with their shoes bundled on their head or hanging from their staffs. Their souls rejoicing in prayer and praise, they go off to carry the good news to their villages, which were not entirely depopulated [that day]. And the priests? Some are present at that place, smiling and taking their stand more with curious spectators than with the pilgrims, avid for heavenly favors. Perhaps one or two do not disguise the satisfaction that is so frequently evident on the faces of the triumphant ...

It remains for the experts to do justice to the macabre sun dance which today, in Fatima, made hosannas burst forth from the breasts of the faithful, and naturally left an impression—according to what trustworthy persons assured me—on the freethinkers and other persons without interests of a religious nature, who hastened to the now famous hollow.

Avelino de Almeida

Source: *O Seculo*, 15 Oct, *Fatima Way of Peace*, pp 44-50; Doc Crit III book 1 pp 237-243. The three dots in the text were supplied by the reporter and do not indicate any skip of text.

Note: In view of the wide readership of this newspaper and the unfavorable article on Fatima by the same reporter on 13 Oct [see Annex #15], this article had a major influence on public acceptance of the apparitions and of the "sun dance" as a miracle. Almeida was an ex-seminarian, but at this time was a strong supporter of the Republican regime and perhaps of its anticlerical attitude. See Father Jaki's book, pages 12-14, for more on Almeida. See #68 for another article of Almeida.

#29 Oct 15   THE SUN DANCES MADLY

The day before yesterday some inspired and fortunate people had the opportunity to see the sun "dance" madly near Vila Nova de Ourem. Thus writes the editor, whom a morning newspaper had expressly sent to the hollow of Fatima, a place chosen by the Virgin Mary to reveal herself to three rustic children with whom, punctually on the 13th, for some months, she has deigned to keep a rendezvous.

What surprises us is not that a dense and noisy crowd ran to the place of the marvel to participate in heavenly revelations—we are already very much used to the manifestations of native credulity—but what in truth surprises us is that the sun, a respectable star, one with its credits firmly established, also takes part in the affair and dances like a mad dancer in a wild country dance, despite its considerable age of thousands of centuries, which, if they have not given it white hair, at least has produced certain indications on its burnished face, which astronomers interpret as a sign of old age. For many years now, the sun has been considered, relative to our planetary system, as a fixed star—the affirmation of which caused some unpleasantness to its discoverer [Galileo]. But now three boorish children have come along and overturned scientific truth. Through their influence in the court of heaven, they caused the sun to dance over the chosen place of Fatima.

Will not this sun dance turn out to be a skillful American-type advertisement for the Russian ballet, which is shortly scheduled for Lisbon?

Source: *O Portugal*, Lisbon, 15 Oct, Brochado, pp 154, 155; Doc Crit III book 1 pp 247, 248.

Note: *O Portugal* was a big daily newspaper, the organ of the Democratic Party, and clearly anti-clerical. This was the first anti-Fatima article in the major Portuguese press; Doc Crit III book 1 p 247.

#30 Oct 15   RAMOS PINTO LETTER

Leiria, 15 Oct, 1917

My dear,

(Gist– I got your letter today and I am sorry that you had not come [to Fatima]. *O Seculo* explains what happened at Fatima. There must have been over 300 vehicles, with perhaps 100 cars. People came from all over. You can tell the people's sentiments from *O Seculo*. The wise can explain the events as they want, but the phenomenon—not foreseen—occurred exactly when predicted by those children.)

The sun rotated vertiginously.

It spun like a "waterwheel," as expressed by a peasant.

And the weather, which was raining and seemed likely to last all day, cleared up precisely at that time. Coincidence? Maybe.

But how can disbelievers explain the fact that the child, seconds before the phenomenon occurred, had said: "Look at the sun. Now is it."

And the phenomenon occurred. And nobody knew what kind of phenomenon would occur. And all, from the closest to the most remote, and you know there were 30,000 people there, according to estimates made, people [who] were very far apart from one another, all, I repeat, in those short moments saw the same phenomenon. For this there was no hallucination.

The phenomenon occurred.

The wise, the disbelievers—let them explain if they can. I limit myself to bowing in the face of such an extraordinary and surprising event.

Good bye, health

Your Joaq.

P.S. There was an inexact statement in *O Seculo*. The child did not say that the war had ended, but that it was ending and our soldiers would return to Portugal shortly.

Source: A letter of 15 Oct from Joaquim Ramos Pinto, age unknown, to his brother Jose Antonio; Doc Crit III book 1 pp 234, 235.

#31 Oct 16   HOLSTEIN LETTER

Quinta da Barao, Carcavelos, 16 Oct

Dear cousin,

I had the good fortune of going to Fatima, with the greatest difficulty to the end, but I conquered all and went. I will never forget!! There were more than 50,000 people there, respectful and devout.

Men in the thousands. None saw Our Lady, except the three children, but what all saw was the golden light on all the people during the stay of Our Lady on earth. Can you imagine, it was raining buckets, but at 2:00 exactly the sun appeared, later taking on the most extraordinary lights possible. Our Lady said she was Our Lady of the Rosary, who came to bring peace, that even this year the war was ending and our soldiers would return soon; that we should build her a chapel there, pray the rosary a lot and reform our lives, because we have greatly offended God!! You can imagine the impression all that made. The three little ones never contradict themselves and are as simple and innocent as can be.

I'll never forget the shout of all those people and the devotion with which they prayed. What is going to happen? There are still many people who doubt, and anything is possible. Time will tell. You can get all the news from Father Francisco, who was there and is very impressed. I am writing on the run, because it is First Communion day ... but I want you to have the news. [Personal matters follow.]

[Your] cousin

Source: Letter of 16 Oct from Adelaide de Sousa Holstein to her cousin, Adelaide de Almeida Vasconcellos; Doc Crit III book 1 pp 251, 252.

Note: The word "lights" may refer to what many others called colors.

#32 Oct 16   STOKLER PARENTE LETTER

Dear Sir,

In fulfilling my promise, here you have my account of the amazing and marvelous spectacle that I had the good fortune to witness. I don't know how it deserves to be treated, and I can't do it. I will try simply to explain the events that have been happening in this region for six months, since the 13th of May. Our Lady appeared, in the parish of Fatima, to some shepherds on the same day of each month. I am sending you pictures *of the children*. The oldest, the main seer, is ten years old, and the youngest is six. The boy,

I think, is eight. They are cousins. The event, which was believed by some, doubted by others, and denied by many, caused the administrator of the county of Vila Nova de Ourem to abduct the children on 13 Aug, taking them to the home of the pastor *days* after having held them prisoners.

On that date there did not fail to be something abnormal in the sky, preceded by one or more thunder claps, which the people heard.

On the 19th Our Lady appeared to the said children *in another place*, telling them that because they were held prisoners, the miracle would be more visible. It was just this way that I heard it expressed. I continue to the 13th of Sep. This time, after the apparition, the children said Our Lady would make a miracle so great that nobody could doubt. Those who were there on the 13th of Sep say that from 12:00 to 1:00, old time, the day *being very beautiful and the sun hot*, the temperature suddenly lowered, making a little eclipse on that star [the sun]. There were people who saw rose clouds, here and there, but they were not believed by all.

The 13th of Oct was awaited with incredible anxiety by believers and unbelievers for very different reasons. Rain came with the morning and it kept increasing, until it was heavy. I cannot describe the appearance which the site presented!

The children had gone to the place at the usual hour, and we, who had remained in the car at a great distance, saw very well when the people knelt, and we guess it must be when the seers announced the apparition of the Virgin. Songs are heard. We look at the sky, and a certain sadness must certainly have taken over the hearts of everyone, because the rain continued incessantly, and no phenomenon showed up. Time moved on, and nothing! However, we looked at the site of the apparition, and there saw that the large crowd still had not left. This was a sign that the seers were still there, and our hope was reborn. Louise Alvaiazere, now *half-doubting*, also said—even now at the site they say that <u>the seer affirmed that it will be 1:00 exact</u>. They look at their watches. <u>It was two minutes before</u>. <u>Suddenly</u>, the rain stops, as if by enchantment, and <u>the sun breaks out *very* brilliantly</u>, and things happen which I will never erase from my memory *even if I live a thousand years*!! It is an indescribable marvel which our eyes see but for me, a believer, and today more than ever, the most marvelous of this marvel consists in its having been forecast by a simple child of ten years; and exactly <u>on the day and hour</u> forecast, the phenomenon amazed us! The wise people will not be able to explain this, but what certainly they will not know, not be able to know, and not want to explain, is the supernatural power that produced it. *Perhaps they will not accept the miracle, but I believe that in their hearts they recognize it, because it cannot be disputed.*

Yesterday, we went to see the seers. Lucia is the only one who talks to Our Lady. She was in church, where she had gone with her mother to hear Mass and go to Communion. She received First Communion when she was seven. She is very short. She said to us—playing with our hands or lorgnette—that Our Lady wants us to pray the rosary every day, to ask pardon for our sins, because Our Lord is much offended, and that we should build her a chapel at the site. She appears as Our Lady of the Rosary. She is dressed in white, without shoes, a white veil on her head and some white beads in her right hand. She announced for now—the seers said today—the end of the war and that our soldiers will return shortly. Our Lady told her a secret which they insisted that she divulge, but she persists in not divulging it. She replied to a man: "Our Lady told me I should not reveal it to anyone, and you, sir, are some one."

On the occasion of the miracle, everyone was crying, and from *almost* every mouth came the anguished cry: "My holy mother, save *our* sons;" "Our Lady, save Portugal!"

(Gist– She comments on Alcobaca's varied faith and need for spiritual help, says the mail is ready to go and asks forgiveness for her imperfections in the letter.)
Alcobaca, 16/10/1917
M.C.S. P.

Source: Letter of Maria de Conceicao Stokler Parente, wife of an officer quartered in Alcobaca, age unknown, to a priest of Porto; Arch Doc #96.

Note: The letter is signed only M.C.S.P. It is virtually identical with a letter published in *A Ordem* on 27 Oct and repeated in *Estrela Oriental* on 1 Nov. In it she says she was in a car at the event; Doc Crit III book 1 pp 503-507. The original letter has apparently been lost, since I translated it from a transcription, which I made earlier at the Fatima archives. The words in italics come from *A Ordem* and were not given in the letter, as originally written.

#33 Oct 16   MANOEL LETTER

Cascaes, 16 Oct
My dear Anna,

I want to communicate with you as the one to whom I turned when I wanted firm information. But I neither know what to tell you, nor can I explain my impressions. Thanks be to God for letting me live until that day. I firmly believe that He is Truth; in that Faith I went there. I had there moments of affliction and disconsolation, which did not result in my not believing; it only caused me great pain! It was when, at that solemn moment, I saw nothing of what others were seeing. I saw then nothing on the sun, I saw nothing to justify all the to-do that I saw around me. But this spectacle, and all that I saw from 10:00 on, was enough to cause me to continue to believe. But it was a struggle, because at the same time I was sad, a sadness which, without my wishing, came to my head, which made an impression on some people.

We got underway and having already gone some kilometers by automobile on the way back, Mariana Ribeiro, who had seen all and had heard the message of the child (I was not close enough to hear the words, but was able to see that she was talking in a very lively fashion, in contrast with what I had seen before, as I will tell you later.) Mariana said to me:[9] Look at the sun, that even now it is not normal. I then looked and saw, I guarantee I saw, and will swear if necessary. The sun had no shine, no color. I could stare at it. A light white cloud was passing. I said—let's see what happens when the cloud passes. It passed and I [could] still stare at it. I saw it pass through different colors, which I can't give with precision—it became green, clearly light green, like salsa green, with a golden ring around it, and turning. Some very long rays seemed to touch the earth, and the sun seemed to be separated from the sky. Then the sky took on pink brightnesses. It changed to yellowish around the sun, and further on, stains here and there. After some long moments, which I can't specify, it became normal, and I could not stare at it again.

Why did I see it there [underway] and did not see it there [at Fatima]? Could it have happened to someone besides me and Geni [Eugenia] that they saw nothing there [at Fatima] and then saw something afterwards, not such as I was seeing, and as I told you in passing, that Mariana was almost ecstatic! I don't know. What I know, what I affirm, is that this happened thusly.

As we [had] arrived early, we went to Aljustrel. We went on foot and it was already raining quite heavily. We saw the little one, we talked with her, asked her some questions, which she was not disposed to answer. However, she smiled at us very simply and nicely. Very insistently she told me, as if she was repeating something already much said, the account of the first apparition, … She said nothing more and we did not insist.

Please tell me who was the man who carried her on his shoulders who repeated what she was saying. They tell me he is a doctor from Torres Novas,

---

[9] What follows seems to be his account of the "sun dance" seen in the car, not that of Mariana.

who was an unbeliever, who went there other times, and after talking with the children, believed. In truth, I am sorry now not to have been closer to the people who were following this more closely. Tell me what you know for sure. But tell me who said and who saw. I don't need these affirmatives for myself. It is for the others who are querying me. For those of good faith … and for others.

Going from here were only us and our companions in the car, who were Mariana Ribeira, Maria do Carmo Albergaria and the little Pereira de Melo Salema. In the other car were the family Pinto Coelhos, and I know from Estoril were the Coruches. All of this was only put in doubt or in exaggerated precaution by Pinto Coelhos, who left until Sunday to write in *A Ordem* that on the next day he saw the <u>same thing</u> on the sun! And he is talking a lot about precautions, as if people did not know that the Church which is always cautious and that we have to await its decisions.

I was sorry not to see. I would so much like to have met people who could tell me more things. We are not lost, Ana, if Our Lady comes to be with us.

Now when I pray I only see before me (Gist– the arch with flowers) and besides that the crowd praying the rosary and singing the litany, only because they believed that Our Lady had been there and was going to be there. Try to write and tell us something. Answer the questions I have made and more than that, if it is <u>sure</u> what you said earlier about the day after the day when there was no apparition because the children were abducted, that the little one said that Our Lady talked to them on the following day. Finally, tell me what you know that is interesting.

Oh how we got wet! I had a big, shaggy coat, which I wore for the cold, but no rain hat. Since this coat served as a sponge the rain passed through it, my clothing and my skin from head to toe. In the car I took off my coat so that my body and clothes would dry. (Gist– More about clothing and shoes and the wind, and nobody getting sick, even though some in the caravan were not in good health.) I am waiting for a letter from you when you have time. [More personal matter is given.]

Leonor[e]

Source: Letter of 16 Oct [from Cascais] of Leonore das Dores Salema Manoel to Ana M. Camara; Doc Crit III book 1 pp 253-256. See Annex #49 for a letter of Ana M. da Camara and #73 for a statement by her.

Note: The letter had few paragraphs and little punctuation. They have been added for ease in reading. "Geni" is identified as the sixteen-year-old daughter of Isabel Brandado de Melo; Doc Crit III book 1 p 254, footnote 14. Isabel also reported seeing nothing. See #69. The underlings were given in the letter. We are not told whether Maria do Carmo and the little Pereira also saw the sun dance on the way back.

#34 Oct 16   THE FATIMA CASE

The leading newspapers have begun to speak of this case with some frequency, and it will therefore be good not to reach a wrong conclusion before considering some ideas that should be presented in cases of this type.

It is clear that as Catholics we accept the full possibility of miracles. God, since He made the laws which rule natural phenomena, can therefore alter or suspend them.

Simply put, a miracle is an exception.

And exceptions are not presumed. They require firm proof.

The Catholic Church has consistently insisted on the matter of proofs before it would agree to establish the miraculous character of any event or series of events.

In Lourdes, for example, the ecstasies of Bernadette were clearly visible on her face; the complete sincerity of the small girl was evident; her recounting of the apparitions was notable for its clarity and uniformity; the bursting forth of the spring was a palpable fact; various extraordinary cures seemed to have confirmed the virtue of the water; Dr. Dozous, a doubting doctor (may the reader pardon us for changing the name), verified the phenomenon of the candle's flame burning for some minutes in contact with the seer's hand without affecting the skin. But the Church was silent and reserved.

It was so silent and reserved, and recommended such reserve to its ministers that it was criticized by some of the impetuous Catholics. The Church consented to the abandonment of this attitude only when—without haste—her multiple inquiries had ended with this conclusion: that natural laws are absolutely insufficient to explain the many established facts. The supernatural character of these events is thus rigorously insisted upon. ...

And what about Fatima? What happened?

Three small shepherds (a boy and two girls) state that a lady of great beauty appeared to them. The visions occurred on the 13th of each month, beginning in May.

The children are simple and little given to chatter. Before the real or pretended visions, they reply to questions with great difficulty. Immediately afterwards they speak with much more firmness and facility, and people worthy of being believed, who heard them on the last 13th, say they affirmed that once more Our Lady had appeared to them that day, recommending that the faithful do penance and pray a lot, that they erect a modest chapel to her on the spot of the apparitions, and promised that peace and the return of the Portuguese soldiers would come shortly.

Coinciding with the apparitions, and as if to corroborate them, those who were there at the place on the 13th of the past months say that extraordinary signs were manifested in the heavens and, above all, on the sun.

In this regard, we can give witness to what happened on Saturday, the 13th because we were there, not as a pilgrim, note that well, but as a curious spectator.

From 11:00 until 1:30 the rain was constant and driven by a strong wind; a frankly rough and disagreeable weather, which the enormous crowd of many thousands of people endured with excellent humor, without shelter other than umbrellas and [their] vehicles, since not even one building was to be found in the vicinity.

1:37 and a half—or noon by solar time—was the time set for the vision, with which it was hoped that the phenomena in the heavens would coincide.

At this moment it kept raining. Minutes later the rain slackened, and at 1:45 it stopped altogether.

The sun, until then hidden, showed itself among the clouds that moved fairly fast. Because their density was variable, the veil which they threw over the sun was more or less diaphanous. Like the crowd, we looked toward the sun with rapt attention, and through the clouds we saw it under new aspects—new for us, mark it well.

At times surrounded by reddish flames, at other times with a ring of yellow or bright violet, at other times seemingly enlivened by a very rapid rotating movement, and at other times even seemingly detaching itself from the sky, approaching the earth and giving forth strong heat ...

Why deny it? The phenomena, which we had never before witnessed, impressed us greatly. Among the crowds a collective psychology established itself. And generally speaking, there passed over the vast majority of the crowd a tremendous wave of faith that was very moving.

One doubt remained with us, however.

Was what we saw in the sun an exceptional thing? Or could it be reproduced in similar circumstances?

Now it was precisely this similarity of circumstances that presented itself to us yesterday [Sunday]. We could see the sun half overcast with clouds, as on Saturday. And sincerely, we saw [on that day] the same succession of colors, the same rotary movement, etc.

(In parentheses, it is our duty to warn readers not to try the same experiment. A physician told us that the pupil of the eye, when exposed to overly strong light of the sun, contracts so [strongly] that sometimes it never dilates again. No more, then about such a great horror.)

Eliminating, then, the only extraordinary fact, what remains?

Right now the statement of the three children and nothing else.

It is very little.

Are the children sincere? We have no reason to doubt it; their humble state is a guarantee of this for us ...

[Paraphrase—We ask proof for the unfavorable accounts of Fatima by those who imply a profit motive to the seers. Do the firmly convinced want us to believe them without proof? Very well. But by the same right we demand from those, who see Jesuit trickery in all of this, the same proofs they demand so strongly from us, rather than dispensing with them by use of slander.]

In sum, we returned from Fatima in the same state of mind in which we went there—in doubt. Was there a miracle? Were there apparitions? It is possible.

But between possibility and reality there is an abyss.

We will therefore continue with an open mind, benevolent, if you wish, but nothing more. And let us be permitted to advise those, who by their position and intelligence can influence others, not to go beyond this limit.

We very well understand, since we share it, the strong desire of those who want it confirmed, that the most holy Virgin, our Patroness and Mother of the sons of this land of Holy Mary, has once more looked upon our country with preference. But ... no imprudence. We do not want to authorize it to be said that we believe in miraculous events without foundation. This is not what the Church demands of us.

In matters of such consequence, let us be sons of prompt and complete obedience.

A. de F. [Well known initials used by Pinto Coelho, 62, a lawyer and a very prominent Catholic. He probably lived in Cascaes, near Lisbon. See #106.]

Source: *A Ordem*, Lisbon, 16 Oct, a Catholic newspaper, Brochado, pp 155-158; Doc Crit III book 1 pp 261-264.

Note: This article was of extreme importance in delaying the acceptance of the "sun dance" as a miracle. It was quoted widely by anti-Fatima newspapers and caused *A Ordem* to receive and publish letters of support and protest, which I have chosen not to include in this Annex. However, two documents [#52 and #56] seem to reflect the caution of Coelho.

#35 Oct 16   THE CASE OF THE DAY

(Gist– Journals of various leanings have reported on Fatima. It is not an unusual case in our day, at the dawn of the 20th century. Already the radicalized France knew [the case of] Bernadette; and some months ago, on the side of the Suajo mountains, in the Minho cliff, terrible but picturesque, there appeared a similar apparition to a mountain shepherd; let's not explore the case. Leave it to those who make fun of the touching simplicity of poor believers, or to those who believe in it more for unconscionable reasons than from profound convictions.)

That which we want to highlight, from the more or less literary and impressive description of the case, which is not unusual from the start of the world, is that some 45,000 to 50,000 creatures clogged the roads to see the radiant and holy light of the apparition, creatures of various social levels. What we want to highlight is the power of this belief, more heroically firm each time since Alfonse Costa. .... said, with a haughty gesture, it would take only two generations to put an end to the religious spirit of a people, who through faith brought civilization to primitive worlds and still believes in the miracle of Ourique, the reason for its [Portugal's] greatness and historic existence.

Source: *A Patria*, a monarchist daily, Oporto, 16 Oct; Doc Crit III book 1 p 266.

#36 Oct 16   POLITICAL NOTES

Lisbon 15(th)

The religious events of Fatima, Vila Nova de Ourem county, are now clad in a most interesting aspect, even from the political point of view. The shepherdess-seer announced the nearness of the end of the war and the return of our soldiers; this filled with happiness the crowd which had assembled there, and which was estimated at between 40,000 and 50,000 people. A great number of them, if not a majority, maintain that they saw miraculous signs in the sky. This mass of people, who came from all parts of the country to assemble on the 13th at Fatima, upon dispersing after having prayed aloud and having assisted at what it classified as a miracle, calls to mind the phrase of those who had proclaimed the end of religion in two generations, and puts in opposition that extraordinary manifestation of faith, whose greatness can only be doubted by those who did not attend it.

Source: *O Primeiro de Janeiro*, a major newspaper in Oporto, 16 Oct, Brochado, p 159; Doc Crit III book 1 p 268.

#37 Oct 17   BASTO LETTER

Bemfica 17 X 917

Dear Fernanda,

(Gist– A long introduction describes the weather at Fatima on Oct 13 and other background information. See Annex #16.)

The shepherdess arrives at mid-day and asks the people to close their umbrellas. At the same instant the rain stops, and we <u>see the clouds part and the sun appear, without brilliance and white, and in the middle a cross like a host. Afterwards the clouds become golden and there is seen to pass a very transparent cloud, the form of Our Lady. The clouds turn blue, purple and green. The sun seems to separate itself from the sky, turn on itself and disappear, only to appear to us later as brilliant as ever.</u> The clouds keep going and it becomes a beautiful afternoon. Isn't it extraordinary? This is the main [story]. I will tell you the details later. [Several personal sentences follow.]

Bettina

Source: Letter of 17 Oct from Maria Bettina Basto at Bemfica, Lisbon, to Fernanda G. Basto-Rosado, her sister; Doc Crit III book 1 p 272.

Note: The letter often omits punctuation and capital letters. I have supplied them for the sake of readability. See also #16, the notes of Maria Bettina Basto for 11-13 October.

#38 Oct 17   PENA RAPOZO LETTER

Carcavalhaes 17/10/1917

My dear friend,

You have nothing to thank me for. ... I am still not back to my normal self from the astonishment in which the stupendous miracle left me, the unexpected marvel which I had the happiness to contemplate, being unworthy of such a grace!

Do you know that this time the Holy Family appeared? And the phenomenon of the sun took place when Our Lady said to the little one: "Tell the people to look at the sun"?! I have not heard that any further apparition has been announced, but I will not resist for long without going to speak with those lucky children. The child replied to a priest, who asked why she was not always looking at the vision, but lowered her eyes: "No, she blinds me!" That was how she explains the brightness and beauty of the Lady.

It is certain that Our Lady has asked that they continue praying the rosary a lot. It seems that she made this recommendation every time. She said that she wanted a chapel there, and that the war would end very soon, which she had already promised the other times. But she also said that after this sign, this warning, the people did not amend their ways, a great punishment would come on Portugal.

An unfortunate man, who went there carrying a knife, saying that if he saw nothing he would kill the children, returned so ill that he could not continue his journey and had to stay here in Riachos (a place just ten minutes away from this), and in the morning he was found dead! All this is frightening and makes one tremble, does it not?

I do not know yet if anyone is charged with taking in the offerings. I saw several people handing in money to the parish priest for the chapel, and if you wish, with the best will in the world, I will accept what you send and ensure it is handed to him.

Our Lady always looked serious, not smiling, and the two little girls, separately, gave this description of the vision, perfectly, in the same form: Our Lady had a white rosary, St. Joseph was to the left, and the Infant between the two.

It all seems a dream to me, and I am afraid I did not value it as I should, did not kiss the children (Gist– as I should have. A land that receives such a grace cannot die.) So it seems to me that everyone recognizes it and bows in acceptance of the truth of such an evident and irrefutable event. [Personal matters follow.]

Very sincerely,
[Your] friendly and grateful
Maria de Jesus d' Oriol Pena Rapozo

Source: A photocopy of a letter of 17 Oct from Maria de Jesus d'Oriol Pena Rapozo, Quinta da Carvalhaes, to Maria Joaquina T. P. Almeida Garrett, *Fatima Way of Peace*, pp 30, 31; Doc Crit III book 1 pp 274, 275. See #39 and #66 for other letters of Pena Rapozo. See #24A and 90A for letters of Almeida Garrett. Rapozo lived in Torres Novas.

#39 Oct 17   DE MELO BREYNER LETTER (PENA RABOZO)

Casa de Mateus 17-X-1917
My dear,
I went yesterday to Urros with Fernando [de Almeida de Albuqurque, Count of Mangualde] and Maria Theresa. On reaching there we met Maria

de Lourdes [de Mendonca Amaral Leitao] on the road, who said to me: "Do you know about Fatima?" I replied that I knew nothing, and then she told me she had received a telegram from Maria de Jesus [d'Oriol Pena Rapozo], saying: "Amazing miracle!" and they were eager to know what happened. (Gist– On the 13th the last apparition and something extraordinary was to happen.)

With that, a letter from her came in the mail for [her mother] Piedade, who began to read it aloud right away. In it she related what she [Rapozo] had witnessed, together with some 40,000 people, which is the number she says had gathered that day. I am going to give you a summary of what she narrates.

She said that it had rained all that morning, but that about 2:00 in the afternoon the sun broke through the clouds, and at that time—which was always the time of the apparitions—she suddenly saw the people, who were nearest the children, turn and look up at the sun. She later learned that the little one had said what Our Lady said to her: "Tell the people to look at the sun."

They all looked and saw a disk, silvery and luminous, but on which one could gaze without the least effort, which she compared to a small mirror, and which stood out, or superimposed itself on the sun and began to descend with a rotating movement, stopping and starting again with the same movement. A beautiful cloud surrounded this disk, now rose-colored, now yellow, now purple, which colored the faces of the bystanders and everything around them and the horizon seemed surrounded by a yellow circle, around which were a series of arcs, all equal in size and equidistant from one another, which she traced out like this.

[At this point in the letter the rough drawing shown below was inserted.]

This phenomenon was witnessed by all the crowd, as some newspapers, as *Diario de Noticias, O Dia* and *A Ordem* have already given an account of eyewitnesses. When the apparition was over, the little ones related that Our Lady had appeared to them with St. Joseph and the Child Jesus on the right, and she said to them that she wanted a little chapel built there, that these apparitions were a proof that she would protect Portugal, but that it was necessary for all to pray and do penance, because otherwise a great chastisement would fall on Portugal. She said that the war would end shortly, but on this point the letter is a bit confused, so I cannot repeat what she said. She also announced that she was Our Lady of the Rosary.

The little one repeated all this in sonorous and measured tones, without showing the least embarrassment, although surrounded by thousands of people. And the smallest, who is [only] six, even when separated from the other, said exactly the same thing, without contradicting herself on any single point. There you have what happened, which perhaps you have already seen written up in the papers.

Each one can draw whatever conclusions he wants. If the apparitions were really true, then the truth will prevail in any case. Even if the celestial phenomena which accompanied the last vision could be explained by science, there remains the remarkable coincidence of their having occurred on that day and exactly at the time which had been predicted long beforehand by these words: that something would happen in October, after which there would be no unbelievers.

Maria de Jesus says that an impious man was converted right there, crying out: "I believe, I believe, I believe!" (Gist– She and her friends regret that they did not go to Fatima, then.)

[Personal matter follows.]

M e M Am

[Abbreviations for "Your mother and best friend."]

Source: Letter from Teresa Francisca de Melo Breyner de Sousa Tavares e Moura, Countess of Vila Real e de Melo at Casa de Mateus, to her son Fernando, *Fatima Way of Peace*, pp 32-34; Doc Crit III book 1 pp 277-280.

Note: See the previous item #38 and also #66, for other letters of Pena Rapozo.

#40 Oct 17   PRUDENCE

Talking to ourselves, we have been surprised that the Catholic newspapers had not given their opinion on the events at Fatima. *A Ordem* now meets our wonderment and speaks of the case with the meticulous care of one who walks barefoot over broken glass. Clearly this attitude did not please its readers, who naturally wanted more enthusiasm and faith. Therefore today *A Ordem* rewrote its opinion, now sheltered by the authorities of the Church.

"*A Ordem* stands with St. Augustine when he said: 'A miracle should never be proclaimed when a natural explanation is possible.'" We ought to do this St. Augustine the justice of considering him a sly person. ... seeing that he foresaw the miracles of Fatima and the dance of the sun. But the Catholic organ is not content with the authority of the bishop of Alexandria, it even goes to the authority of St. Thomas: seeing is believing. Without a repeat of the sun dance *A Ordem* does not consider the case as an official miracle nor the inspired shepherds worthy of entering the calendar as saints of the second class. Now in this matter *A Ordem* has the authority of a veritable *Diario de Governo* ... of heaven.

Source: *O Portugal*, 17 Oct, Brochado, p 161; Doc Crit III book 1 pp 285, 286.

#41 Oct 17   THE MOOR OF MIRACLES

From an assiduous reader, as are all who write to newspapers, we have received the following letter, which we are publishing, thinking we are offering [it] as a worthwhile lesson to those who suffer the vice of curiosity.

Dear editor: I am Portuguese and from Lisbon, two important reasons for the spirit of curiosity which I have, and which, by me, is one of the reasons for living and one of the most noble defects of man. As a curious person, I was at Fatima on the 13th to "testify" to the miracles which might occur and which had been so loudly forecast. There was no more impartial spectator than me. In regards to the existence of God, I neither affirm nor deny it, because if he exists, he is certainly greater and more complex in his essence than my small human intelligence could conceive; and if he does not exist, this is reason enough that I should not weary myself in convincing others of this very thing or the contrary.

Dear editor, I was thus at Fatima, and my impulse of curiosity cost me some money and inconvenience, which I now regret sincerely. Because the truth is that only in reading the article in *O Seculo* did I learn of the miracles that occurred [at Fatima], the names of the inspired children, and even the number of people who awaited a message from heaven. Because my eyes, accustomed to see crowds, did not get the impression of the thousands which the editor of that newspaper reported. We had 50,000 people in France and it seemed to us that the whole country was there in force. It was [only] on reading *O Seculo* that I learned that the sun had "danced" and that Lucia had talked with the Virgin, and that a character named Ramalho, and compared with Paul Deroulede, had recited the Creed, standing on the running board of a bus. It is clear that my curiosity was satisfied and the money I spent was lost, because of all the things reported by *O Seculo* I only observed one and I confirm only it, the request to the men to take off their hats in the face of the evidence of a miracle and the saintliness of the shepherds. It seems that he was a singular type, but familiar with intimidation, like the one addressed to me by one of the believers in these humble Christian terms: "Take off your hat, you no-goodnik."

But I am writing you, sir editor, not to lament the time and money spent, but only to ask that in the columns of your respected newspaper, of which I am an assiduous reader, you insist that the "learned," to whom the editor of *O Seculo* appeals, explain the astronomical phenomena which it is said took place on the 13th of this month at the moor of Fatima. Since I saw nothing there, I would like at least that the observatories and scientific societies of the [proper] specialty, make a pronouncement, to get back my money and not leave the editor of *O Seculo*, Mr. Avelino de Almeida, compromised. He seems to believe enough in science and also a little in the Virgin.

Insist on explanations, sir editor, and if they are given you will have made a valiant service to those who, like me, saw nothing miraculous at Fatima, maybe because we were not in the state of grace. I at least was in the state of ... paying. Believe me, etc.

An assiduous reader

Source: *O Portugal*, 17 Oct; Doc Crit III book 1 pp 287, 288.

#42 Oct 17   SUPERNATURAL

(Gist– The article gives the background, such as the age of the seers and something on the previous apparitions. It says the Lady is said to be luminous and that Lucia's eyes were ecstatic. It has a few errors, such as that only Lucia hears the Divine voice and sees the astral phenomena. It says that it is strange that there were so many people on the moor on Saturday. All wanted to see a miracle in the open, like at Tilly sur Seulles, in Normandy and thought that a great good or bad would come to them.)

But the Virgin appeared to no one but her dear Lucia, because only in the eyes of her dear Lucia did she appear, and because only in the ears of her dear Lucia was she heard.

Yet, it was still raining and the sun hid behind gray clouds. Lucia, on arriving at the site, ordered, with her imperative voice of a ten-year-old child, that those who had umbrellas open should close them, and they did. The time fixed for the apparition was about to come, and then the rain stopped, the dark clouds broke up, and between them the sun appeared discreetly, a little covered, and like about to smile. There are those who saw it upset, to be covered with instantaneous stains, to shake [and] to turn on itself. There were those who said they saw, on the light of the sun, the face of the Virgin to be outlined.

There was this, and among the thousands of people who were there, an immense number saw nothing. But the curious phenomenon of repeated hallucination of the seer Lucia, and the no less curious phenomenon of mass hallucination of the crowd of believers, similar to that which happened at La Salette, at Lourdes and Tilly, does not cease to interest us, like many of these things interested us when we studied them some years ago. Thus, it is possible that we will return to them again.

Meanwhile, it does not surprise us at all that, in the words of Lucia, the Lady announced peace. She ought not to come on earth, the mother of men, for another reason. We think it is very soon, in this case, to confuse the supernatural manifestations of divinity with the immediate profit, which will be taken by certain Catholics, selling post cards with pictures of the shepherds, certainly well-intentioned, and friends of the children.

Source: *A Republica*, Lisbon, an organ of the Evolutionist Party, 17 Oct, Brochado, p 163; Doc Crit III book 1 pp 289, 290.

#43 Oct 18   ORIOL PENA LETTER

18. 9. 17

My very dear aunt,

(Gist– The letter begins with personal matter, and then says that you probably know about the Fatima apparitions, and that at the last one there was supposed to be a miracle. All the hotels were reserved in advance. It was difficult to go there, and crowded all the way. Behavior was excellent. We went in the automobile of aunt Camilia Maldonado.)

The apparition of the Lady was not an article of faith and I confess that I was little believing, but I assure you that I saw, like thousands of persons also, what happened in the sky at the time indicated by the children, a phenomenon so extraordinary that I will never again see anything like it in my life. To describe it in detail would take time, and I leave this for when we see each other. *O Seculo* of the 15th gives a fairly extensive account of it that you have seen, of course. Except for a phrase or two, which shows its origin, it is not badly done. All that he says about what was seen in the sky is absolutely true.

The extraordinary color the sun gave, many persons saw it (one of them being my aunt Camilia). But I cannot describe them, because when I saw the tremendous agitation, I was so impressed that I fell to my knees and could not see anything more. (Gist— The oak bush where the seers say that Our Lady appeared was torn to its roots.)

It seems that Our Lady said she wanted them to build a chapel at the site, that she recommended that they pray the rosary, and she said the war would end on the 13th.

She also told them a secret which human power cannot force them to reveal. They have tried everything: threats, petitions, bribery, and even a person authorized to test them tried to intimidate them by religious scruples. Everything was futile, and they continue to be firm.

My parents and Zinha went also to Fatima yesterday to see them up close and to talk with them. They say they are very pleasant, but not pretty; the smallest one is prettiest. They are very poor and the mother is a saintly woman, who gives a hard time to her husband, a noted drunkard. Neither she nor the pastor wanted to take charge of the offerings, but another little lady has taken charge of this and already has much more than 100,000 [reis].

I don't know if I have been bothering you with all these details ... but I think they would interest you. [More personal matter follows.]

M. Benedita

Source: A letter of 18 Oct from Maria Benedita Oriol Pena at Quinta da S. Venancio, Leiria, to her aunt, Maria Luisa de Santa Marta, in Cascais; Doc Crit III book 1 pp 295-298.

#44 Oct 18   SERRA LETTER

Dear Isabelinha

(Gist— A long introduction is given. He was a disbeliever, invited by Maria de Jesus Pena Rapozo to go by car or truck to Fatima with her. They left Torres Novas at nine o'clock. A miracle had been forecast. They stopped at the Fatima rectory and had breakfast. It was cold, windy and rainy, unlike the previous days, and continued to rain when they arrived at the site. Thousands of people were there. They stopped at the rectory and were fed.)

We were less than 100 meters from the famous oak bush, which seemed to serve as a throne for the celestial vision, and the distance did not stop me from seeing what happened near the oak bush. (Gist— The behavior of the people was admirable.)

The children had just arrived, ignorant and simple, protagonists of the most grandiose and extraordinary spectacle that I ever had the opportunity to see. On the clock of the car the hands marked 2:00. The august moment was arriving, which thousands of people, rich in faith, were awaiting. The rain, which had diminished, then stopped entirely. Then to the north, in a small opening in the sky, I spy the clear blue, cleaning away the leaden clouds.

My spirit, already moved by what I had witnessed, wondered what could happen that rainy morning. From the dark skies might come a *mis-en-scene* of a grandiose spectacle, which could occur. The hand marked 2:05, later 2:10 and on the ground the silence was broken only by the indistinct echoes which repeated the prayers made near the oak bush, while the crowd awaited, in anxious anticipation, the marvelous event which would invigorate their faith. I thought lightly of leaving to avoid the ridicule of my every day friends.

Some pious souls were already afraid that the event so loudly forecast would not happen, when suddenly all that immense crowd was stirred, and, in a brouhaha indicating surprise and fear, raised their heads to the sky, where thousands of terrified eyes saw the sun in the clear blue, visible to all without the intensity of the rays hurting the retina and bothering their vision. [It was] crowned by various colors, in a movement of rapid rotation, which, in the picturesque expression of some people, resembled a firewheel.

The spectators, looking at each other, displayed a yellow color ... and on the orangish-red horizon, wherever their eyes fell, they saw beams of pale light, which seemed to be placed at an equal distance [apart] and reflecting on the earth.

Such was the surprising phenomenon everyone had the opportunity to observe, and which from some brought forth a sincere confession of ardent faith, and from others, from whom the harsh wind of skepticism had taken the flower of faith, it gave a more benevolent outlook.

Some unbelievers were there and even some with signs of atheism, who declared themselves convinced by the power which worked such a prodigy.

Here you have, my dear Isabelinha, what I saw, and with me thousands of people. (Gist– This is a matter which interests the whole country.) Now I will give you my impression.

It cannot be doubted that we were in the presence of a happening that deeply moved the crowd, many not hesitating to call it a miracle.

Was it so? It would be bold to affirm it.

Yet it is certain that in good historical criticism we should not and cannot, in appraising the events, separate them from the circumstances that preceded and accompanied them. I believe and admit that most, if not all of the occurrences observed have a scientific explanation. And it also seems to me that the state of the public spirit, for many and varied reasons, which are based on the hardships of life at present, torn up by difficulties of all kinds, laced with sadness and sorrows, worried about the health of dear ones far away, who run grave risks in the battlefields, is exceedingly propitious to attract tormented souls to the pure regions of the ideal, in search of aid and comfort which they do not find on earth. Whether it be terror, superstition or whatever, what is certain is that there thousands of souls found aid, solace and soothing. And, in the case of Fatima, if we admit that all is explained by natural causes, one circumstance is enough to give it the right of miraculous—it having been forecast to the day and hour six months in advance, and later on the very day.

(Gist– He then notes that Lucia said that the Virgin had appeared and had told them to tell the people to look at the sun, where the sign which had been forecast would occur, and immediately it happened, and he offers further thoughts on the event, followed by personal matter.)

Torres Novas 18-10-17
Joao Lucio

Source: A letter of 18 Oct from Joao M.L. Serra, a postal inspector in Torres Novas, to Isabel Caravalho; Doc Crit III book 1 pp 299-304.

Note: See #86 for his letter, very similar in content, published in *A Ordem* on 21 Nov. See also #38 and #39 for more information on Pena Rapozo. In the vehicle with Serra were the well-known Dr. Formigao and eight or nine others; Doc Crit III book 1 p 300, footnote 4.

#45 Oct 18   THE JESUITS

15/10/17

Near Vila Nova de Ourem, in Fatima there occurred recently an infamous Jesuit hoax, with the fantastic and ridiculous vision of some *little saint*, who remembered, they say, to appear to the children and say things about Portugal.

There are many who are engaged in this hoax, with the criminal assent of the local authorities, who have not decided to put an end to such an infamy, … to which *O Seculo* is currently giving the most helpful publicity with its enormous readership.

The affair is proceeding in the best of worlds and the said *traveling Virgin* continues to let herself be seen only by the children, being careful not to appear to adults, perhaps fearful that some good temptation would cause her to lose her sanctity and reduce her to the natural state of vulgar mortality.

The acting against the law deserves a strong censure by the authorities, who, according to my information, are acquiescing in compromising the law because they are convinced that, with this *apparition,* a new Lourdes can be set up in Fatima, at reduced prices, which would be able, say the Papists, to drain off much money from foreign and national Catholic tourists for the poor of those places, hurting by the competition the well-known Lourdes.

It thus seems, besides a hoax with a conscience, to be the creation of a competing market, with the offer of cheaper miracles.

S. Saboya

Source: *Democracia do Sul,* Evora, a bi-weekly journal of the Portuguese Republican Party, 18 Oct; Doc Crit III book 1 pp 306, 307; *Fatima, a suas Problemas,* p 302; and Jaki, p 76.

#46 Oct 18   YESTERDAY AND TODAY
The Lady of Fatima

(Gist– The first half of this long article describes the crowd going to Fatima in unfavorable terms. It notes that there are lots of people in need— the poor, the sick, etc. It asks: "What mysterious force of hallucination attracted them?" It mentions the hope that the Lady would cure the sick and bring an end to the war. In the middle it describes the Fatima event of 13 Oct as follows.)

What happened in that uncultivated strip of land where the Virgin promised to descend and to talk to the people of Portugal? About 2:00 in the afternoon one of the three children, who was praying near the oak bush, pointed, and the large crowd knelt together. And then the sun, breaking from the clouds, came forth with great brilliance, it was surrounded by a dark circle, took on the paleness of the moon, was at once spotted with fluid blue, with a sad yellow, with other pale tones, it was shaken by irregular, distorted movements, it trembled, it trembled, and remained quiet. With sharp changes of color, the landscape was modified, it lost its sharpness, its firmest features were wrapped in a vague mist.

The women clenched their hands, white with surprise, implored heaven with begging eyes, and had a disturbed attitude of fervor and ecstasy. "Beautiful sun," "What a beautiful thing," "There she comes," were exclamations that arose in a burst of ohs and ahs. ... The miracle limited itself to fantastic changes of the scenery, to unusual gymnastics of the sun, to dazzling pyrotechnics, done in the clouds, to the most exotic refractions of the [sun]light, a more than ethereal miracle, hovering at a certain height, to be seen from afar, as [the city] Braga is seen, and did not dignify itself to descend to the top of the mountain and the oaks. But all my informants swear they saw extraordinary things in the sun, which does not disturb my personal criticism.

I know well that people are poetic and inclined to consoling mirages; they prefer living in the passing pleasure of legendary images to harsh contact with bitter realities. How many tens of miracles are numbered in the Restoration period? How many old tales of pleasure were found ...

Miraculous things were always with our romantic people, from gnomes and vampires, ... to witches, werewolves and sprites, and it is from these old swindles that life is colored and tinged with seduction. Miracles cannot be eliminated, today as yesterday. And when it doesn't exist, it is invented in the literature of a Jules Vernes, Welles and Poe. Nobody gets along without a miracle. Everyone laughs at Fatima, and everyone goes there, some this month, the rest in another. I myself, if it weren't for the after-effects of an illness, would have gone in the company of friends. And why not? It is the medium where we feel better, more charmed, closer to ourselves, where some of us are unrepentant miracle-lovers.

A famous PhD of my country, who was the finest flower of local Jacobism, told me that he yelled like one possessed, hands crossed, white-eyed: "There goes the Virgin. There she goes." And I would not be surprised if the man saw her. He is a businessman, who is a Mason and an atheist, but not considered stupid, and he palmed off paper figures of saints to suckers, and it seems to me he had great luck at Fatima.

Since alongside these face-to-face meetings, like a lackey promoted to chief, there appears, bent over, the wise old one, who was not at Fatima because in his mind the Divinity has not appeared, does not appear, and will not appear. Thus he cuts out with one stroke the heart of the matter. A terrible counselor!

When suddenly I slip out [and] a venerable old man with a big white beard and scintillating spirit jumps out from a corner to ask me: "And then?" "Then ..."

So what! When the sun comes up it is for everyone, therefore ...

And while these commentaries were echoing in my ears, the people of my country, inclined to credulity, to miracles, to apparitions, were returning from Fatima. (Gist– He describes their clothes), for who knows if St. Joseph would bless this perverse world, and that our soldiers would return from war in some near day, full of glory, strong blonds, like idols, and brimming with youth. Amen.

Leiria, Oct 17—Alfredo de Caravalho

Source: *A Lucta*, Lisbon, an organ of the Unionist Party, Oct 18, Brochado, p 163; Doc Crit III book 1 pp 308-312.

#47 Oct 18   THE APPARITIONS OF FATIMA (SILVA LETTER)

We can say nothing more about what happened at Fatima besides what we say in the letter we publish below.

(Gist– Gives the age of the seers.) These seers, simple and ignorant, could not fool the tens of thousands of witnesses, and even so there remains the sun phenomena, which science did not predict and we think will not explain, showing that the Fatima event has something of the extraordinary, which we do not understand.

We hope the Church will speak on this matter, and not wishing to follow in the footsteps of the vicar of Lourdes in the visions of Bernadette, we say that only a divine power could cause what thousands of people witnessed at Fatima on the 13th of this month.

The letter we received follows.

Sir editor: Various people who know me, who know that I am no *Jesuit* or fanatic on religion, have asked what I witnessed and what happened at Fatima. As I was among the *stupid* ones, as some people say, who went there, (Gist– I want to tell my version briefly.)

On the evening before, I stayed at the home of my friend and reporter on the *O Mensageiro*, Antonio Pereira das Neves in Quinta de Sardinha. (Gist– I was well treated.) At 4:00 I headed for Fatima to attend the miraculous apparition, which the little ones said would be the last. (Gist– He gives much detail on the people and vehicles going there.)

The rain began to fall, getting heavier little by little. (Gist– More on the rain, umbrellas and effects of the weather. People sang songs.)

It was 1:00 (official) and all were anxious for the arrival of the children. I was near an enormous oak tree, (Gist– cold and soaked to the bone). Then a rabbit appeared, chased by some persons. (Gist– More on the chase.)

I looked in front and saw a large crowd that accompanied the little ones toward the oak bush where the little ones say the Virgin appeared, an oak bush of which only ten centimeters of trunk remain, since people had taken parts as relics.

One of the children said *Our Lady is already here. Take off your hats and pray.*

The rain stops, and <u>the clouds move with great speed, the brilliant sun comes out</u>, shooting its luminous rays over the people there.

I don't know how, I see everyone take off their hats and kneel. It was 14:10, official.

I hear various prayers to the Virgin and Holy Mother, and I see the faces of the enormous crowd to be strongly pink. Then it changes to blue and at once to a ghostly yellow!! I don't know what this means and I did not want to look at the sun in order not to attribute [it] to an optical illusion.

But in front of me was a Lady with a white felt hat, which served me as a mirror of what happened in the king-star [the sun]. This lasted some twenty minutes. I heard at my side laments and various supplications, and they said the sun was spinning like a firewheel.

A little later the children told what Our Lady said to them—*The war was ending in these days. Our soldiers will return shortly to Portugal. Men must be good to each other, pray the rosary and build a chapel, since I am Our Lady of the Rosary.*

The children are carried in triumph among the crowd, heading for their homes, and the crowd begins to head for their towns, (Gist– convinced that it was worth enduring all that rain and wind).

And I was standing there, looking like a fool, looking at all this without knowing how to explain such an imposing phenomenon.

And if this happens again tomorrow, I would fall down there again, since I do not regret having been present at something I had never witnessed.

What amazes me is that although moments before I was soaking wet, I noticed that I was now dry. Is this a miracle? I do not think so. What I believe is that the same [thing] happened to others.

(Gist– Two or three paragraphs follow, of little importance. He admires the safe, orderly departure of the people. He says that at 16:00 there were few people left and he headed for Moita, where he ate something with his friend Antonio Pereira das Neves and his family. He returned to Quinta da Gardinha, made his farewells and went by bicycle to Leiria.)

Now I ask what occurred of extraordinary in the stars, that the astronomers did not predict? Then did two shepherds take so many thousands of people to a wilderness only to see the sun? Who made the propaganda for this phenomenon? It's a mystery.

Here you have what I saw and what happened. Whoever does not believe me, it does not matter.

Yours, etc.

Carlos Silva

Source: *O Mensageiro*, a Catholic weekly, Leiria, 18 Oct; Doc Crit III book 1 pp 315-318.

#48 Oct 18 THE CASE OF FATIMA

(Gist– The famous astronomer, Federico Oom, was queried by us about the 13 Oct event at Fatima.) The illustrious astronomer had the kindness to give us the following response:

"Had it been a cosmic phenomenon, the astronomical and meteorological observatories would not have failed to register it. And this is precisely what is lacking, the unavoidable registering of all disturbances, however small, in the system of the worlds. You see ..."

We interrupt: "Is it then a phenomenon of psychological nature?"

"Why not? Perhaps, and surely very curiously, the effect of collective hallucination. In any case, it is entirely outside the branch of science that I study ..."

Source: *O Seculo*, 18 Oct; Doc Crit III book 1 p 321; *The Whole Truth About Fatima*, p 345.

#49 Oct 19 DA CAMARA LETTER

Junqueira, Lisbon, 19 Oct 1917

My dear mistress,

(Gist– The first page is background. It tells of sending a book to the bishop of Portalegre. Then she says she is happy she went to Fatima and gives a sentence on its appearance, and then says it is impossible to describe what happened.)

We arrived about 10:00. It rained torrentially, which chilled us to the bone; the crowd was frightening; the newspapers talk of 50,000 people; I do not doubt that there were more. There was no complaint against the bad weather and no foul language. They prayed aloud and sang. About 1:00 I went down from the road toward the field and arrived at the rough little altar, built on the apparition site, but could not get to see the little ones. As soon as they arrived they ordered the people to shut their umbrellas and the rain stopped. The everyday sun broke out from the gray cover that all morning darkened the sky. We keep praying. I ask the time.

Somebody replies it is a little after 1:30. We are, however, at full midday by the sun. A few minutes later I hear something like a gigantic gasping and someone says to me: "Look at the sun." At first I saw nothing, but seconds later I see it [the sun] like a moon, of a blue-silver color, very light, and a bit from here on the sun was tinted green, purple, yellow and blue, but it stayed without rays. It sends out billows of smoke, so to speak, of the color which it shows, but the shape of the disk is perfect and this disk turns with a vertiginous rapidity and at a certain moment the sun descended. Later it appeared more to the right and later more to the left, or vice versa. At a certain moment the sun takes on a bright pink color, and behind each mountain there appears something like a veil of the same color. The fields and crowds reflect it.

There are no words to describe such splendor. I have thought much of the words of the Church: "Who is it that comes shining with the rising [sun]? Is it the people?" The people cry, shout, implore Our Lady and Jesus in the Sacrament. There is a mixture of confidence, joy and fear. I feel like all that we are in the presence of a full supernatural [event]. I can only say, like all the others: "Our Lady, save us." I don't know how long it lasted, but I heard talk of four minutes. It seemed to me much more.

Little Antonia got to see one of the little ones, very ruddy, washed in tears, carried on the shoulders of a man, and later this man, a doctor, repeats the words of the little one: "Our Lady asks us not to offend Our Lord any more and to do penance, promised the end of the war shortly. The mothers should pray and have confidence that our soldiers are about to return. She blesses the people and asks for a chapel there with the title of Our Lady of the Rosary."

(Gist– I want to send you an excellent article from *O Seculo*. It's too bad he suddenly remembered what paper he was writing for and wrote something to their taste.) I can't talk of anything but this. We must pray that Our Lady's visit is accepted as a sure fact.

An astronomer has already said that science can't explain the events and the equipment did not register any solar movement. They are talking here about a collective hallucination, but when we were there, it was by the voice of a child who, in the name of Our Lady, forecast a sign for the 13th, [and] we had no idea what would happen.

At the moment the sun descended the clamor of the crowd was much greater. Then we all saw [it] at the same time, and a man next to me, terrified, exclaimed: "Holy Virgin, save us, we are all dying here. Forgive us our sins." (Gist– A short personal note follows.)

Ana M[aria]

Source: A letter of 19 Oct from Ana Maria da Camara to Sister Margarida Maria de Cunho Castro Marin; Doc Crit III book 1 pp 323-326. See Annex #73 for a statement by da Camara.

Note: On the top of the page is a note saying that this is an account of the great miracle by one of our old students—Ana Maria da Camara.

#50 Oct 19   IMPRESSIONS OF FATIMA

(Gist– In several paragraphs, and in very literary or almost poetic language, the author describes the crowds which had been going to Fatima for days prior to the 13th. She says that a chill and piercing northeast wind was blowing.)

All night long and into early morning a sad, drizzling rain fell. It soaked the fields, saddened the land; dank and cold, it chilled to the bone, with a humid cold, the men, women and children and the beasts who plodded through the muddy road, hurrying toward the hill of the miracle.

The rain kept falling, a soft, unending drizzle.

(Gist– She describes the effect of the rain on the people, the ground, the roads and the women's clothes.)

They went up the hills without stopping, illuminated by faith, anxious for the miracle promised by Our Lady to the pure simple shepherds for the 13th at one o'clock, sun time.

(Gist– More about the pilgrims and the countryside follows.)

The rain began to decrease. And then there was only a veil of very light mist, which was disappearing little by little, and little by little the mountain was clearing up.

A murmur drifting down from the hills reached us. It was a murmur like the distant voice of the sea, lowered to a hush in the silence of the fields. ... It was the religious songs, now becoming clear, intoned by thousands of voices.

On the plateau, covering the hill, filling the valley, [was] what appeared to be an enormous stain, a mass of thousands upon thousands of souls in prayer. Hands upright, eyes in ecstasy, they come with faith in their belief. They came to ask for the miracle of Our Lady, to ask forgiveness of sinners, to ask for a blessing for the hardships of life.

At one o'clock, sun time, the rain stopped. The sky had a certain grayish tint of pearl and a strange clearness filled the gloomy landscape, ... every moment getting gloomier. The sun has something like a veil of transparent gauze to enable us to stare at it [without difficulty]. The grayish tint of mother-of-pearl began changing as if into a shining silver disk, that was breaking out slowly until the clouds separated and the silvery sun, shrouded in the same grayish lightness of gauze, was seen to rotate and turn within the circle of the receded clouds!

The people cried out with one voice, the thousands of creatures of God whom faith had raised up to heaven, fell on their knees upon the muddy ground.

[Then] as if seen through the stained glass windows of a great cathedral, the light became an exquisite blue, spreading its rays upon the people who knelt with outstretched hands. ...

Slowly the blue faded away and now the light seemed to be filtered through yellow stained glass. Yellow stains now were falling upon the faces, the white kerchiefs and the poor dark skirts of coarse wool. They were stains which repeated themselves indefinitely over the lowly holm oaks, the rocks, the hills.

Everyone was weeping and praying, hat in hand, under the grandiose and unique impression of the expected miracle. These were seconds, instants, which seemed hours, so vivid were they.

Clouds passed over the vague and grayish lightness that veiled the sun!

Life returned to the souls in prayer whose life had been suspended for an instant.

The clouds broke up, patches of blue appeared in the sky. The sun, in its impassive serenity, as always, illuminated vaguely the barren fields where Our Lady had brought together, through the mouths of three shepherd children, thousands and thousands of creatures of God.

Quinta do Amparo, on the 13th, on returning from the miracle
Maria Magdalena [Patricio]

Source: *O Dia*, Lisbon, 19 Oct, De Marchi, p 130; *Crusade of Fatima*, pp 90-92, 102, 103; Doc Crit III book 1 pp 329-332.

Note: *O Dia* announced this article two days earlier and called Patricio an author "whose beautiful talent shines in her artistic and literary works ... and who once again honors us with her brilliant collaboration." Doc Crit III book 1 p 281.

Note: *O Dia* was a big daily newspaper; Jaki, p 50. The two mentions of 1:00 may refer to 1:00 standard time, or 2:00 war time, which is the approximate time the miracle was expected and when the sun dance occurred.

#51 Oct?   STATEMENT OF SILVA CONSTANCIO
The Miracle? .... Of Fatima

Having learned at the end of July that there were at Fatima ... three shepherds, who from May on the 13th of each month were favored by a heavenly apparition, we decided to go there in August and for the next two months, since the children said that the apparition was to reveal what was to come in six months. We wanted to gather information to verify what happened, but we were certain that, even if it were true, we would not see the apparition, but we wanted, at least, to see the children, see their attitude during the apparition and talk with them afterwards.

Thus we went there on the 13th of August. We left the house at 9:30. The day was beautiful but not very hot, the temperature even agreeable… (Gist– We were apprehensive. The trip to Fatima took three hours by car.) There was already a large crowd when we arrived. …. We left the car on the road and went some meters to where the crowd was. …

(Gist– We asked if the seers were there. They told us no, the apparition would only come between 12:00 and 1:00 and the children would come about this time. We said it was almost 1:00, the children should already be there. I asked a peasant woman what time do they use. She said that they go by the old time.) While we were waiting, we talked with the people, … and they said that at the indicated time the sun would be covered by light clouds and a fog would envelop the tree on which Our Lady, descending from a cloud, would stand to talk with the children.

(Gist– We met and talked with friends and relatives about what we had learned. Some of the information was extraordinary, other incredible.)

At this time a man appeared and said the children would not come because they had been taken prisoner by the administrator of the county and taken to Ourem. (Gist– The crowd didn't believe him, a lady went by car to check; she returned and said it was true. It looked like the start of a persecution.)

Everyone protested and was mad, but the protest was orderly, and although there were 5,000 or 6,000 people there, nobody thought to fight or revolt. …

Of the people present, many thought about leaving then. But suddenly this cry arises from the people: "Let's stay and wait until the hour, and if this is from heaven, there will be [some kind of] manifestation … since the authorities can do nothing against the power of God and the Virgin."

We admire the faith of the people and keep anxiously awaiting the anticipated hour. … We planned to leave at 2:00, thinking that nothing abnormal would happen, since the children were not there.

But just at this moment we heard an enormous whisper which made us all turn. We were then given a moving manifestation of faith, which we had never witnessed.

(Gist– The people fell to their knees, took off their hats, and prayed, with tears in their eyes.)

Everyone looked at the sky, which was covered by a light cloud, like a very fine lace, in places rose-ish. The sun, which for an instant was entirely hidden, left us lighted by a very exquisite light; yellow stains showed on the ground and on all of us, and a great drop in temperature [occurred], like that during an eclipse of the sun. Someone said: "Look, the fog around the oak bush." We looked, and actually there it was. Was it really a fog? Was it smoke? Was it dust? ... It could be any of these things. But to me it seemed more like smoke, coming from an incense burner, which rose up from the ground in light wisps and dissolved then around the tree.

Some said it was dust, that a light breeze had raised up. But how can one explain that the breeze arose only at that site and that it happened always on the 13th of each month?! ... At this time the sun had regained all its old brilliance. (Gist– A man, an unbeliever, claimed he saw the Virgin. Was it hallucination? We all saw nothing. Much discussion of his claim follows.)

(Gist– I had come to Fatima without much expectations, and came away impressed. I went to the rectory to get information on the children and returned from Fatima convinced that something abnormal was happening there, wondering how something like an eclipse could have happened four times already, as well as the fog that was seen only there. We learned later of the apparition at Valinhos, where the Lady had said that they should pray to Our Lady of the Rosary for an end of the war, and that, since they had been kidnapped, the same signs would not be seen the next month and the miracle would be better known.)

(Gist– On Sep 13 she went back to Fatima from Caldas da Rainha. The morning was beautiful, a clear, hot day, with no breeze. She arrived about 12:00, the crowd was much bigger, estimated at 15,000 to 20,000. It feared another kidnapping. They prayed the rosary and sang.)

(Gist– The children arrived, they prayed the rosary and litany.) Suddenly, with no cloud cover, a difference in temperature was felt and we could feel that the intensity of the sun was decreasing. Yellow stains were seen on the ground, and also on the white blouses which some ladies wore. It was only an instant. Everything passed quickly. The crowd, as in August, fell to the ground, showing their faith.

(Gist– In August not one priest had been there; they did not want it said that they were there to induce hallucination; but in September some were there, discreetly.)

I saw only a light eclipse of the sun, but many people saw a star or rather a tiny white cloud like a little flake of white cotton, that crossed the sky, like a falling star, coming from the east to the west and disappearing in space, as if submerged suddenly! I heard this from more than one person in the same way, without their having been together or heard each other talk. For me, it deserves full credit. A coincidence, this passage of the star or cloud above the oak bush with the time the children said they had seen the Lady!

There were also people who said they had seen two stars and there were some who said they saw three! Would this not be many stars together?! I don't know, but what it seemed to me was that those who said they saw them were convinced that they were telling the truth.

(Gist– They returned to Caldas, and the same thing happened to many people who were there from Caldas. They were also very much impressed, and they talked to other people who hadn't been there and convinced them they should go. She told them that they had seen only a light eclipse of the sun and an extraordinary show of faith.)

(Gist– She said it had rained on the 13th as well as the night before. She gives a long description of their trip to Fatima on Oct 13; her car nearly fell into a ravine, but she got free with the intercession of Our Lady. She arrived a half hour late for the miracle of the sun. But she got around to talk with other people.)

When I arrived at Fatima I tried to exchange impressions with various people I knew. All of them told me the same thing. ... All had seen. But what did they see, I asked. "<u>We saw the sun, as if covered by a silver plate, in a constant rotary movement, sending out red, yellow and purple rays and seeming to loose itself from the sky and approach the earth</u>."

I talked with the people, and they told me the same thing, although in different words. ... They said they [the seers] had seen Our Lady, St. Joseph and the Child Jesus, and what else can I say ... the whole celestial court <u>at the same time that they [the people] had seen the sun dance</u>. I did not believe in such a vision.

It certainly is possible they thought they saw, perhaps hallucination? Our people in general are very ignorant and very credulous, and it would be very easy to convince them that they really saw what they wanted to see. (Gist– This credulity makes it very easy for them to be led by demagogues.)

In the more cultured classes, nobody told me they had seen the celestial apparition, but it is certain that all, famous and non-famous, showed their faith. (Gist– She was much affected by the great faith of the people. Almost all had tears of joy. All were convinced that something supernatural had happened. Again she was unable to talk with the seers, who were surrounded by people.)

(Gist– On Oct 19 she returned to talk with the children.) A priest was with us, who had already at times interrogated them, these interrogations being very interesting. To the contrary of what happened to some people, the children pleased me immensely. They were robust, serious, frank and pleasant, with an open attitude appropriate to their age. They did not flee away from us, but received us pleasantly. We attended a long interrogation made to each child separately. They responded frankly, promptly and with the greatest simplicity. Nonetheless, it can be seen that they don't like to be interrogated …, and only reply because they have to.

(Gist– Then she describes how the children see the vision. Each is different. Lucia sees, hears and talks with the Lady, Jacinta sees and hears her, but does not talk, and Francisco only sees her, and never even sees her move her lips, and he never saw her as well as he did on Oct 13.) (Gist– She interrogated them. On May 13 they heard thunder, the apparition told them to pray the rosary for the end of the war and to return for six months. In June she told them to learn to read, which they could not because there was no teacher.) And now, without anybody having asked for it, it seems that a teacher has been named there for two years … and the children are beginning to go to school, … especially Lucia. (Gist– She then talks about the apparitions in general, says she is sure that the children did not lie and wonders if it could be a nervous hallucination.) Maybe, but the children seem robust and healthy, don't show any symptoms of nervousness, and the medium in which they live seems to be little appropriate for hallucination of this kind.

A hoax, as many say? But why? The parents of the children are not poor (for the medium in which they live), they receive no donations, they refuse firmly whoever offers any, saying they don't need money. Some say there is a woman behind this hoax!! A woman? But what woman? Where is she? Why and how does she do the hoax? I confess I don't see [it], it is beyond my comprehension. In Fatima there is no place to spend money; would it be, rather, a business man there who plans to exploit the event, because it seems to me that a very few made money with the crowd there. Others went further, saying that the work at the church was even paid for by donations given to the children. Evil? Ignorant? Or what? They certainly want to speak badly [of it] and see things which do not exist. The work at the church was already very far along at the first apparition and it continues without needing to resort to a hoax.

(Gist– She then discusses the possibility of hallucination or demonic work, which she rejects, since she has seen the seers, and then says the children describe the Lady as very beautiful, dressed in white with a white rosary, say she said she is from heaven and the children will go to heaven.)

Source: An undated statement of Leonore de Avilar Silva Constancio, age unknown, apparently from Caldas da Rainha`; Doc Crit III book 1 pp 335-347.

Note: The date is later than 19 Oct, based on the above text. The priest who was with them on 19 Oct was clearly Father Formigao. The occasion for this statement is not given.

#52 Oct 20   THE FATIMA CASE

(Gist– The article begins by asking if the apparitions at Fatima are real. Many thousands of people saw the children in ecstasy on the day and hour previously announced, with much anticipation. Were there real phenomena? Thousands of people say yes.)

It was raining torrentially. At the hour forecast for the apparition, the rain stopped, as if obeying the voice of the children, who said they didn't need to keep their umbrellas open.

The sun came out, being like a strange light, able to be stared at like one stares at the full moon. The light passed through various aspects, sometimes seeming that the solar globe was surrounded by a halo of flames, other times like a silver-like metallic disk. It was seen to turn on itself rapidly and gave the impression that it left its orbit, approached the earth, and produced exceptional heat.

This no one of good faith contests. From eyewitnesses we have heard it; and letters coming from the vicinity of Fatima confirm it.

Was this a natural phenomenon that repeats itself under identical conditions? Electric phenomenon, as some contend? We do not know, nor do we think it is up to us to pronounce on such a delicate subject.

Be that as it may, it should be noted that the phenomenon occurred on the day and precise time when miraculous phenomena were predicted, a month in advance, by three raw children, incapable of foreseeing phenomena that no scientist foresaw. It should also be noted that the three children, the oldest of which is ten, interviewed by various people about the apparitions of the Virgin, never contradicted each other, never stopped insisting on the truth of what they say they saw, resisting contrary insinuations, promises of money and even threats.

The power of God is infinite, miracles have occurred, they can occur again.

The ecclesiastical authority must pronounce on this event with that [serious] deliberation always required for cases like this. Until that happens, without doubting that which thousands of people affirm they saw, (because this would be to deny the evidence), we will not say that there was a miracle or was not. We are sons of the Church. Let us submit to that which in this respect might be said by its legitimate representatives. Let us neither be hasty nor drag our feet.

Source: *Beira Baixa*, Castelo Branco, 20 Oct; Doc Crit III book 1 pp 348, 349.

Note: *Beira Baixa* was a Democratic weekly, founded in 1911. Its director was Jose Maria de Proenca de Almeida Garrett; Doc Crit III part 1 p 348. He undoubtedly is the same Jose ... Garrett who wrote a letter for Father Formigao describing what he saw at Fatima. I used it earlier in describing the sun dance [see page 2] and it is quoted in many books on Fatima. See Doc #90.

#53 Oct 20   THE CASE OF FATIMA

About the case of the visions and apparitions at Fatima, which have so impressed the country these last few days, thanks to the Lisbon press we report the words of Dr. Pinto Coelho, published ... by our colleague, *A Ordem*. [See #34.]

For curiosity, and so that our readers may know the facts in more detail, we are going to give also parts of the information published by *O Seculo* and *Diario de Noticias*. For the vision of 13 May (sic) we are giving some interesting information which we found in *Raio de Luz*.

(Excerpts from *O Seculo, Diario de Noticias*, and *Raio de Luz* follow. See Annex #28, #27, and #8.)

Source: *Correio de Beira*, a Catholic journal, Viseu, 20 Oct; Doc Crit III book 1 p 351.

#54 Oct 20   POINTS OF FIRE

(Gist– The article gives a short history of the events at Fatima, and says some people believe them to be miracles and others that the phenomena are natural.)

They say that on the sun, at a fixed time, extraordinary phenomena were seen, such as a very rapid movement of rotation, like a fireworks wheel, which could be seen by the unprotected eye, and which was seen by thousands of people. And some shepherds say they saw Our Lady the Virgin at different times, say that they conversed with her, and she orders them to tell the people to do penance to placate God's wrath, and she will soon give peace to the world. We shall see if the "Star" will laugh at our ingenuousness and credulity.

Don't bother, lady.

We are not credulous nor superstitious. But we believe in the Supernatural, and it doesn't bother us to believe in one more miraculous manifestation of the Divine Goodness in these trying times, through the intercession of Her who is justly called "Our Cause" and "Consolation of the Afflicted."

Too much license is given today to "Star" today and its sectarianism is decadent, and that which prevails in world intellectual circles is the accented tendency, spiritualist and Catholic, onto whose shining platform all the men of science all over the world are falling. …

(Gist– The author then hopes that the "Star" will kneel with her before the God of the Armies.)

Galanta

Source: *Gazeta de Familicao*, a pro-monarchy weekly, Familicao, 20 Oct; Doc Crit III book 1 pp 356, 357.

Note: No explanation is given for "Star." Galanta is unidentified.

#55 Oct 21   LETTER OF MARIA CAMINHA

Sunday, 21 Oct 1917, Lisbon

My very dear Mimi,

Today is 8 days since I returned to Lisbon from Fatima, where I went to see the great miracle. It is impossible to describe what we all saw. Regina went with Emiliana, Rita and Bettina, on the 11th to Rodrigo to stay a few days there. It is near Fatima. It is only 9 hours by carriage. I was invited by Mr. Constanca, and went by auto on Friday the 12th. There we did not even catch sight of them [but] it seemed to me we saw them. Read *O Seculo* of the 15th. All they say is true and there is much more that they don't say because they don't want to and can't ….

(Gist– Since May 15th Our Lady has been appearing to three shepherds.)

It was raining torrentially and all on firm footing settled in until 2:00, or mid-day solar, the moment when the clouds separated to the sides, leaving the sun open, and immediately there began to pass before the sun billows of very light clouds, yellow, with purple, carnation-colored etc. At this the sun seemed to loosen itself and descend suddenly. A moment of fear! At this there began a rotary movement of incredible speed. Suddenly it is the moon, but only for a moment, for [immediately] it becomes a sacred host, with even the cross being visible, as if made with an opaque material, the color of wheat flour, very white.

I also saw in the open space and around [it] a marvelous corona of such clouds in various colors—a spectacle of frightening beauty. You can't imagine the delicacy of the tones. How God looked with care on this earth at that moment. We felt ourselves loved in the extreme.

Everyone saw, about 100,000 people.

The people became the color of the clouds. It was interesting to see [that] the sun, with its light behind, seemed to filter the brightness, as if [coming] through colored glass windows.

All this happened while Our Lady came down and talked to little Lucia. All three children .... see, but only the oldest talks to her. Our Lady was visible to some people. I was not blessed with this grace. I did not need it to believe. Rita and Betina had this luck, and many other persons. Rita saw, in front of the sun, the face, but only the face, of Our Lady and she was ... I don't even know how to say it, she lost the notion of time and cannot describe what she saw, she doesn't know how. Nothing can compare with the beauty and sweetness of that smile. Bettina then was the most blessed of all. Of course she was the one who most needed it. She saw Our Lady of the Rosary, beautiful, descend to us. She disappeared to her just as she approached the earth. She said to Regina, crying and trembling: Don't you see her? It is Our Lady of the Rosary. Don't you see? Many other people saw [her].

There were so many supernatural signs that it was impossible for all to see everything. ... Around the valley chosen for such marvels, as simple ornaments, and with the greatest symmetry, some stains of the three preferred colors followed each other.

The little Lucia said she is Our Lady of the Rosary, that she wants them to build a church there for her and stated that God was much offended by the people and showed His power so they would be converted and saved. If they don't take advantage of this manifestation of His power, he will send a punishment. I did not hear or talk with the girl, but all this seems natural to me. She said much more, but I don't know it all.

The impression was so strong that I think it will remain with me forever. (Gist– They admired the behavior of the crowd, with no police there.) At a certain time when it was raining a lot, the little one told them to close their umbrellas, they closed them, and the rain stopped.

Our Lady told Lucia that St. Joseph came to bless the people and that all believers (present there) were pardoned up to that moment. That site was blessed—people, animals, all. At this time there was a great shine. It is too bad you were not there. What happened is, in my opinion, the most admirable miracle of recent centuries, a miracle seen by believers and unbelievers! [Personal matter follows.]

Maria Caminha

Source: A letter from Maria Caminha, Lisbon, Travesa da Fabrica dos Pentes #7-3 to Maria do Livramento de Vasconcelos de Provenca; Doc Crit III, book 1, pp 372-377.

Note: Most of this letter, edited and very slightly revised, and without the personal matter, was published in *A Guarda*, 12 Jan 1918; See Doc Crit III, book 1, pp 825-828; Jaki, p 151. The persons cited in text are: Regina Ferreira, Emiliana, her servant, Rita and Maria Bettina Basto. See Annex #16, where Bettina does not mention that she and Rita saw the Virgin descend, and Annex #37, where Bettina says only that she saw a cloud in the form of Our Lady.

#56 Oct 20 THE APPARITIONS OF FATIMA

(Gist– All Portugal knows of this case. Three shepherds say they saw Our lady on the 13th of each month. They were taken prisoner and efforts made to get them to deny it, but they refused.)

On the 13th there were 50,000 people at the site and, a strange case, but not outside the laws of nature, the sun, which was covered by clouds which released a downpour of water, <u>uncovered itself at that same time, looking like a dull silver plate and with a circular motion</u> that the crowd called a miracle.

We don't know what the power of hallucination can do to crowds. Our Lady is able to grant the grace of a miracle for the Land of Mary but we can't let ourselves be carried away thoughtlessly by appearances. The case of Fatima is not clear. We can't pronounce for or against it. (Gist– Then it says the Church will go into this with care, says we shouldn't be too enthusiastic and it quotes Pinto Coelho in this regard.)

Source: *A Guarda*, a Catholic weekly, Lisbon, 20 Oct; Doc Crit III book 1 pp 358, 359.

#57 Oct 21 MIRACLE

In the parish of Fatima in our neighboring county of Ourem a little shepherd of 10 years affirmed some months ago that she had seen and talked with Our Lady, whom she saw over an isolated oak bush in the middle of a moor.

Since the child affirmed that the apparition and the nonsense would be repeated on the 13th of each month, the past Saturday more than 40,000 people gathered at this moor to see the miracle.

At the end <u>the pilgrims only saw the sun, … which to some it even seemed that it danced and approached them.</u>

Our Lady only stooped to talk with the little shepherd, telling her, without any [other] person hearing, that the war was ending and our soldiers would return.

(Gist– She need not have come to tell us this. The war has to end and our soldiers to return. We ask the shepherd to ask Our Lady when it will end.)

Source: *A Defesa,* an independent weekly, Pombal, 21 Oct; Doc Crit III book 1 p 378.

#58 Oct 21?   STATEMENT OF TOVARES
The Miracle of Fatima

Thomar, 17 Oct 1917

In the place of Ajustrel, 1 kilometer from Fatima, in Ourem county, reside 3 shepherds, Lucia 10 yrs, Francisco 8, and Jacinta 7. They have declared that, 18 months ago, while all three were walking to pasture their flock in a lonely spot 2 kilometers from their homes, a very pretty lady appeared to them, without saying a word, and that the sheep stayed quiet while they saw the lady, fleeing into a nearby wheat field as soon as she disappeared. They say also that on 13 May she appeared to them again at the same site on an oak bush or a little oak tree between mid-day to 1:00, telling them a secret that they should tell no one, and saying that they should say the rosary daily and be there on the 13th of each month at the same time.

As the event was gradually reported, the crowds at the site grew. On 13 Aug the administrator of the county of Ourem came to the parents of the shepherds, taking them in his carriage to Ourem, avoiding their appearance at the site of the purported apparition, and thinking that thus he would hinder the people from going there. On the contrary, all who intended went there, and said that at the appointed hour they felt a shock and strong commotion and all fell on their knees. A neighbor of the shepherds told us that they said that, after returning from Ourem on 15 Aug, Assumption Day, near their home they saw a stroke of lightning, a sign that preceded the Lady's apparition, and she appeared to them on another oak bush, after Jacinta went to fetch her brother at home, and she said to them to keep coming, come on the 13th of the next months to the original site, and that she had already told them that she would appear for the last time on 13 Oct, a day when many people would be there, including foreigners, and that, as a result of a prodigious sign, many people would be converted.

It is calculated that on 13 Sep there were about 15,000 people there, many of whom said that the sun was eclipsed (it was a beautiful summer day) and there was seen on it a change into the colors of the rainbow, however not very intense. Then we decided to go to Fatima on 13 Oct. Many people from here and elsewhere asked our opinion on the reported events and asked if they should go there on that day. To all we replied that since God is the author of the laws that rule the phenomena of nature, he could easily change or suspend them (to deny this would be equivalent to denying the Divine Omnipotence); and that we did not have the information to affirm or deny the apparition; and that we do not advise them to go or not to go.

We left on the morning of the 13th. We breakfasted in Ourem, with a fine rain falling, which gradually increased. When we arrived in Fatima it was torrential, impelled by a strong wind from the south, miserable weather and a real winter day. There were already many people there, some staying in carriages and others finding cover under umbrellas. We head for the site where they say the Lady appeared to the shepherds. It was already surrounded by many people. With difficulty we got near. They had already put up a kind of trapezoid with a cross high in the middle, and two lighted oil lanterns hung above. Below, on the oak bush, or rather on the trunk, because the branches had already been taken off by pilgrims, was an arch of real flowers and a little altar. At every instant, carriages full of people were arriving, and auto horns were heard. Three hours later the shepherds arrive, the rain having lessened. A little after kneeling and praying over the altar of flowers, they order [the people] to close their umbrellas and almost at once almost all remove their hats. We are some four meters from the shepherds.

The rain stops completely. The clouds, moving rapidly, open clearings, and the sun, sending out rays, appeared with its golden wig and natural color. It passed to a dull silver color, becoming next surrounded by scarlet flames; at a given moment it was animated by a rapid rotary movement, and seemed to loosen itself from the sky and fall onto the earth. It changed to pale purple and [then] showed a green color, which was seen through the diaphanous clouds; the solar disk appeared sharp and completely green after the passing of these [clouds], and finally there followed the bright yellow, which lasted longer and with such intensity that it was seen to pass from the sun to the ground, with the atmosphere and nearby objects being clothed in the same color.

We must say that, although we admit the possibility of some miraculous event, we were, as a result of earlier talks with various persons, skeptical, with a fixed opinion in regard to the changing of the color of the sun. First we looked at the sun and then at the cross and arch of flowers. So that there be no doubt in our mind after such a stupendous phenomenon, we even looked at the sun for some time without noting the least alteration after the end of the yellow color. Some people at our side said they saw a picture form on the sun.

One cannot describe the wave of lively faith which came over that crowd. We never have seen the like of it. A startling spectacle! From among the throng which packed the whole slope, many hands were raised up, clamoring for the Blessed Virgin. On the slope in front and on the road many people were kneeling ... in the cars and ... the carriages. It is impossible to calculate for certain the number of people who were there. But whoever saw a crowd, as we did, on the esplanade at Samoeiro, calculated at 300,000, can't figure this number at less than 100,000. The place had become an enormous mud pit. Many people were completely wet and a large number of ladies had their clothes muddy up to their knees. Nonetheless no one heard a complaint nor was shown the least gesture of unhappiness or frustration. When the shepherds got up, Lucia was carried with great effort on the shoulders [of a man], saying to those around her that they should mend their ways, that the war was ending and that we should expect the return of our brave soldiers shortly, etc.

The exodus begins. It took more than an hour, first that our carriage could clear a path. It was beautiful to see that line of cars, carriages and other vehicles, in number over 500, followed by a whole lot of people. We headed to the house of the shepherds, where we asked them various questions and admired the firmness of their replies. Francisco said he saw the Lady with her hands up, but he didn't hear what she said. Lucia is the one who talked to the Lady, and said she was very pretty and appeared to them barefoot, with dress and mantle of white, her hands up, with a rosary in her hands, which opened when she talked. Jacinta said that she saw the Lady in the same form and heard that which she said to Lucia. We asked her what was on the sun and she said it was St. Joseph giving peace to the world, and that the Lady came down on the oak bush and told her: "That she was Our Lady of the Rosary, that the war was ending and to expect the return of our soldiers shortly, that men must reform and pray the rosary daily so that God would pardon their sins, and that they should make a little chapel at the site where she was talking, according to the wish of the people, whom finally she blessed." I say it is impossible, unparalleled, that the extraordinary phenomenon occurred on the day and hour previously indicated by the shepherds, and it touched the hearts of many unbelievers. We guarantee the truth of what has been said. If they ask us if the Virgin really appeared to the shepherds, in conscience we cannot say yes or no.

For God, however, nothing is impossible. The calm and conviction of Lucia, as she passed through the crowd on the shoulders of Dr. Carlos Mendes and waved her right hand simply and slowly, and kept saying to the people that the Lady said that they should reform and that the war was ending etc., etc., seeing herself in an enormous squeeze, as if in a circle of iron, with everyone trying to get near to her to hear, to kiss and embrace her, without seeming to be the least upset, is a factor in her favor, which cannot be erased from our mind and leaves us amazed. Prudence, however, demands that we keep to the sequence of events. It is the present opinion that, if the Great War ends soon, Fatima will become a second Lourdes, and in place of a simple chapel a sumptuous monument will be built there.

Thomar, October 1917
Joaquim Gregorio Tovares

Source: Statement of Joaquim G. Tovares; Doc Crit I pp 401-406. Tovares was a postal employee at Tomar, 60 years old. No precise date was given, but since the document contains articles from *Liberdade* of 20 and 21 Oct, and since he also dates it in Oct, the precise date is between 21 and 31 Oct; Doc Crit I page 401.

Note: This statement had only two paragraph breaks, and I have added others. His statement, somewhat abbreviated, was published in *Concelho de Macao* on 18 Nov. See #85.

#59 Oct 23   THE CASE OF FATIMA

(Gist– We haven't referred to this event before because we were awaiting the action of the proper ecclesiastical authorities.) From all sides we are getting requests, full of anxious curiosity, asking for details. At the same time we have the testimony of the respected Father Jose Antonio Marques da Cruz Curado, of Pencova, who was in Fatima on the 13th of this month. We are going to publish it, thus breaking our silence, which is no longer justified, since other journals, even Catholic, have reported the case. [The letter follows.]

Since [even] *Liberdade* says nothing on the subject, we are going to tell it as an eyewitness. We arrived at the site four or five minutes before the supposed vision. There were some 40,000 people from all over the country. Somebody showed us the place marked by a flag on a wooden pole saying that the three shepherds were there, awaiting the apparition. Shortly after, the immense crowd took off their hats. Everyone stared at the sky, still covered with clouds, looking for something supernatural, the prodigious sign. It seems that the children had knelt, confirming that the Virgin had appeared once more. Perhaps four minutes had passed when <u>the sun</u>, like a torch, [which] after being lit, makes a shiny circle in the middle of the darkness, [the sun] <u>moved the clouds away fairly rapidly, [clouds] which darkened it,</u>

making also a circle around it, and giving us the opportunity to observe a phenomenon that seemed extraordinary to all.

The sun, now without clouds, did not send rays on the earth, but it seemed wrapped in pale-colored flames. Suddenly it lost all this light or flames, and seemed to us a dull silver plate, as *O Seculo* has properly said. It took on a rapid and very visible rotary movement, seeming even to come close to the earth. One could stare at it indefinitely, without bothering one's sight. A little after, it flamed up again (let's say it that way), then becoming again wrapped in rose-colored flames, and also without sending rays on earth. Perhaps a minute passed, and again it lost its light and flames, becoming again the plate, now very white, with the same very rapid movement of rotation. Even a third time the sun, which seemed to have brusque, shaky movements, was wrapped in blue flames, which was followed by the loss of light and the rotary movement of the plate. The phenomenon was over.

When the sun again had light we could not stare at its luminous rays. The crowd, kneeling in the mud, in tears, yelled in distress, with eyes fixed on the sky and hands joined in prayer. Some clamored for Our Lady to save them; others, confessing their serious sins, asked for pardon. It was truly an impressive scene. We were also impressed with the coincidence of the phenomenon with the time of the vision or the supposed apparition. And this impression rose quickly when the Reverend Cardoso of Portalegre, who during the vision was near the shepherds, told us that the oldest, still kneeling in front of the oak bush, said to all those around her: "Now look at the sun." and the solar phenomenon followed at once. This fits with the reply which she gave me when I asked her if the phenomenon occurred during the vision, she said: "No, the Lady had already disappeared."

(Gist– The crowd left, but many followed the seers to ask questions. They sold postcards and stamps with the seers' picture on them.)

Father Jose Antonio Marquues de Cruz Curado

Source: *A Liberdade*, Porto, 23 Oct; Doc Crit III book 1 pp 401-403; *O Fenomeno Solar*, pp 23, 24.

#60 Oct 24   THE MIRACLE OF FATIMA

(Gist– The altar and oak bush have been stolen from Fatima and are on display in Santarem.)

Source: *O Seculo*, 24 Oct; Doc Crit III book 1 p 425.

Note: This event was reported later by many newspapers. I do not include them in the Annex.

#61 Oct 25   FATIMA

With complete impartiality we think it is our duty on this subject, which continues to interest our readers, to keep reporting the observations which are sent to us, since some are expressed in acceptable language and with the most possible preciseness. An esteemed lady sent us the following correspondence:

I declare, and with me various persons of distinction, with whom I talked, and whose illustrious names I can cite, that we deliberately looked at the sun several times for specific time periods to make sure of the happenings. We saw nothing abnormal after the miraculous phenomenon. That the miracle occurred is true. Thousands of people confirm it, not only simple peasants, but the most illustrious people, who know well the laws of nature, and in a common show of respect, fell on their knees, proclaiming the greatness of the miracle, without the least doubt.

If it concerns any cosmic phenomenon, would not this be predicted and announced by the learned who are concerned with the science of the stars? And with all of this, I did not hear the least mention of this since the month of the Virgin [May], when the extraordinary events began to occur each 13th of the month until now, in the month of the rosary [October], when these miraculous manifestations, previously announced by the little Lucia, ended.

I, modesty aside, who am neither stupid nor ignorant, was there, full of curiosity, but without faith in the apparition, with a soul completely alien to the greatness of the mystery, deaf to the words of the inspired children, who ordered us, in the name of the Lord, to look at the sun. Fearing to damage or lose my sight by this, according to the common thought, I resisted the suggestion; and only after others around me [made] ecstatic exclamations was the curiosity of looking aroused in me. I forgot the fear of losing my sight and I then looked. Blessed be Jesus! I saw! I saw what thousands were contemplating. The rain, which fell all night and all morning—drizzily, persistent and tiresome—[and] completely covered the sky with a gray blanket, suddenly stopped at the time announced by the little shepherds. The clouds began to break up and opened (permit me the comparison) as if it was a theater curtain, to let us see the sun, flashing and playing its luminous rays over the site where the prophetic creatures were in ecstasy. The sun then presented the appearance of a dull silver globe, with a purplish disk surrounding it, very dark, as when eclipses are not entirely total.

Then we saw a marvelous thing. The sun turned rapidly, like a fireworks wheel. This prodigious event repeated itself three consecutive times.

Thus there occurred the prodigy forecast by the little ones so that all would believe in the apparition of Our Lady.

Afterwards the clouds disappeared little by little from the sky, which became clear, serene and blue, to which there is no equal in our beautiful Portugal. I looked around and the appearance and colors of the landscape were the same as one sees over the length of an eclipse—the same unique, bluish light, of this electric blue, special and peculiar to phenomenon of this nature.

In order to show how much I avoided letting myself be suggested, I would further say that the colors—yellow, red and purple—which many people said they saw on lowering their eyes over the landscape or on the headscarves, which tears obliged us to bring to our eyes, were no more than the result of staring at the sun with the naked eye, which always happens in such circumstances.

Over the grandiosity of the spectacle, the beauty of the landscape, the impressiveness of the crowd, the touching effect, which was caused by the devotion in so many believing souls, [who] intoned as a group the Ave, the Creed, the Tantum Ergo, the fervent prayers to the Virgin, Our Lady of the Rosary. ....

Maria Romana

[There follows a rather long discussion on the miraculous or non-miraculous nature of the sun dance, signed by A. de F., the initials used as a pseudonym by Pinto Coelho. See #34.]

Source: *A Ordem*, Lisbon, 25 Oct; Doc Crit III book 1 pp 450-453; Jaki, pp 84,85; *O Fenomeno Solar*, pp 24, 25.

Note: While it may seem strange that this lady [not further identified] and others show an unusual familiarity with the phenomena of an eclipse, it can be explained that a full eclipse occurred in Portugal on 28 May 1900; Doc Crit II p 236, footnote #155.

#61A Oct 25   PORTO DE MOS INQUIRY

On 25 Oct 1917, before the Dean of the Porto de Mos Deanery and me, the scribe, appointed ad hoc, there appeared the witnesses named below.

(signed) Father Joaquim Vieira da Rosa

Joao Gomes Menitra

[The names of 16 witnesses to the events at Fatima on 13 Oct 1917, and the depositions of 12 of them, follow. All swore on the Bible. The scribe signed in the place of the illiterate. The other witnesses signed their depositions.]

Source: Porto de Mos [inquiry board]; Doc Crit I p 201-208.

Note: This inquiry was requested by the bishop of the diocese; Doc Crit I pp 197-201. I have chosen to call the inquiry group a board.

#61B Oct 25   DEPOSITION OF RAMOS MIRA

First Testimony. Antonio do Ramos Mira, married, inhabitant of Reguengo do Fetal parish, an eyewitness of the events which occurred at Fatima on 13 Oct 1917, having sworn on the Bible, said: that he went to the apparition site in a rain, that a quarter hour after it stopped he saw the vast crowd of people, with a great uproar, and almost all kneeling, turned toward the sun, <u>which had uncommon signs, turning on itself, shaking, and he noticed at the same time that around it was a yellow-reddish color, which was reflected on the whole crowd and the horizon, with a weakening of the light at the same time and an increase in temperature.</u> The multitude, even the unbelievers, said that it was a clear miracle. It is known that the children said, six months before, that on that day, time and place there would be a miracle, which drew the crowd of about 40,000 people, who returned home believers. He said no more and signed his deposition.

(signed) Father Joaquim Vieira da Rosa
Antonio dos Ramos Mira

Source: Deposition of Antonio dos Ramos Mira; Doc Crit I p 202.

Note: All the depositions were signed by Father da Rosa, dean of the deanery of Porto da Mos. For brevity, I will omit his signature and that of the witness or scribe for the other depositions.

#61C Oct 25   DEPOSITION OF ANZEBINO MIRA

Second Witness. Anzebino Francisco Mira, married, resident of Reguengo de Fetal parish, eyewitness, etc. ... said: having gone to the apparition site in a rain, the rain stopped between noon and 1:00 and then he saw <u>the sun turning like a fireworks pinwheel and approached the crowd that was there and he saw also different colors on the people and the horizon</u>, and all of this was at the same time as the events on the 13th of the five preceding months. He said no more and signed.

Source: Deposition of Anzebino Mira; Doc Crit I pp 202, 203.

#61D Oct 25   DEPOSITION OF MANUEL CARVALHO

Third witness. Manuel Ribeiro de Caravalho, married, a proprietor, resident of Reguengo de Fetal, … Said: that a quarter hour, more or less, after the rain stopped, he saw <u>the sun turn on itself, approached the people, send out enough heat, and at the same time he saw blue and red color on the horizon</u>. He said no more and signed.

Source: Deposition of Manuel Carvalho, 36 years old; Doc Crit I p 203.

#61E Oct 25   DEPOSITION OF ANTONIO MENITRA

Fourth witness. Antonio Maria Menitra, married, a proprietor, a resident of Reguengo de Fetal … said: that having rained torrentially in the morning, a bit after mid-day the rain stopped and he saw a huge crowd of people, kneeling, looked at the sun, and he <u>looked also and saw different colors on the sun and the people</u>. He said no more and signed.

Source: Deposition of Antonio Menitra; Doc Crit I pp 203, 204.

#61F Oct 25   DEPOSITION OF ROMANO DOS SANTOS

Fifth Witness. Romano dos Santos, married, a resident of Alqueidao da Serra … said: that he heard that all should kneel, that Our Lady was coming, words that he heard from the crowd and that they came from the shepherds, who were far away. When these words were said the crowd knelt, the rain having stopped by then, and looking <u>at the sun he saw it was surrounded by different colors and turning like a fireworks wheel</u>. He heard the uproar of the crowd, saying that it was a clear miracle. He said no more and did not sign his deposition, not knowing how.

Source: Deposition of Romano dos Santos; Doc Crit I p 204.

#61G Oct 25   DEPOSITION OF MARIA VIEIRA DA ROSA

Sixth witness. Maria da Silva Vieira da Rosa, single, adult, inhabitant of Alqueidao da Serra … said: that when the crowd knelt, the rain having stopped a little before, she looked at the sun and <u>saw that it changed into</u>

different colors, coming closer and turning like a pinwheel. She saw this phenomenon three times. The whole crowd, bathed in tears, shouted for Our Lady. She said no more and signed.

Source: Deposition of Maria Vieira da Rosa, 34 years old; Doc Crit I pp 204, 205.

#61H Oct 25   DEPOSITION OF MANUEL JOAO SENIOR

Seventh witness. Manuel Joao Senior, married, resident of Alqueidao da Serra ... said: that [with] a large number of the crowd kneeling, he looked at the sun perfectly without any problem for the sight and not burning, and he saw it turn like a firewheel three times, coming close at the hour indicated by the three shepherds. He said no more and didn't sign, not knowing how.

Source: Deposition of Manuel Joao Senior; Doc Crit I p 205.

Note: A footnote identifies him as Manuel Joao Caravalho, 64 years old, presumably Manuel Senior; Doc Crit I p 205.

#61I Oct 25   DEPOSITION OF ADRIANO DE MATTOS

Eighth witness. Adriano de Mattos, married, resident of Alquidao da Serra, ... said: that he looked at the sun perfectly without it bothering him and he seemed to see Our Lady with the Child Jesus on her left arm and he saw different colors around the said sun. [No statement is made on signing.]

Source: Deposition of Adriano de Mattos, 48 years old; Doc Crit I pp 205, 206.

#61J Oct 25   DEPOSITION OF ANTONIO AMADO

Ninth witness. Antonio Vieira Amado, married, resident of Alqueidao da Serra ... said: that he saw the sun very clearly and within [it] he seemed to see three images, and before the sun various colors, turning like a firewheel, having heard before this that all should kneel, that Our Lady was coming, to which the crowd obeyed, with a loud uproar and shouting for Our Lady. He said no more and signed.

Source: Deposition of Antonio Amado, 28 years old; Doc Crit I p 206.

#61K Oct 25

DEPOSITION OF JOAO VIEIRA GOMES

Tenth witness. Joao Vieira Gomes, married, resident of Alqueidao da Serra … said: that he saw the sun turn like a pinwheel, staring at the sun with no hurt to the organ of sight, it [the sun] shaking and all the crowd shouting for Our Lady. This event was witnessed by all the crowd. And if someone saw nothing, it is because he didn't want to see. He said no more and didn't sign, not knowing how to write.

Source: Deposition of Joao Vieira Gomes, 46 years old; Doc Crit I pp 206, 207.

#61L Oct 25

DEPOSITION OF MANUEL CARAVALHO

Eleventh witness. Manuel Carvalho, married, resident of Alqueidao da Serra … said: that he saw the sun descend, as he understood it, clothe itself in various colors, turning like a fireworks pinwheel, and it could be seen without bothering [his sight]. The witness noticed that, after raining all morning, the rain stopped at the time the children arrived, that [they] said the rosary, and they ordered the crowd to kneel, [a crowd] which numbered 50,000, which shouted for Our Lady. He said no more and signed.

Source: Deposition of Manuel Carvalho, 51 years old; Doc Crit I p 207.
Note: Although three depositions bear the name Manuel Caravalho, each was from a different person, with a different age; Doc Crit I pp 203, 205, 207.

#61M Oct 25

DEPOSITION OF DOMINGOS PEDRO

Twelfth witness. Domingos Pedro, married, resident of Alquiedao da Serra … said: He saw the rain stop, I say the rain, when the children ordered the people to close their umbrellas, and [he saw] the sun turn like a fire-wheel and descend, as it seemed to him. The crowd knelt at the word of the shepherds, who said: "There comes Our Lady," these phenomena occurring continually and at the time indicated six months before. All those who witnessed the event considered it miraculous. He said no more and didn't sign, not knowing how.

Source: Deposition of Domingos Pedro; Doc Crit I pp 207, 208.

Note: The names and residences of four more witnesses are given, along with the statement that they said the same as the twelfth witness, since they were together. Father de Rosa sent these depositions to his bishop with a statement that he had queried more witnesses and all had said the same as these witnesses and therefore he stopped getting more depositions. He added that the faith of some people was weakened by Lucia's statement on the end of the war; Doc Crit I p 208, 209.

#62 Oct 26   THE MIRACLE OF FATIMA

(Gist– This long article begins by saying that Fatima is like Lourdes and nothing new. In time we will learn who has a profit motive in it. The ignorant and some clever persons are making it into a real, non-disputable miracle.)

Some months ago three children, as ignorant and wild as the pine trees and moors where they roamed, began by saying they had seen the Virgin Mary, who despite being mother continued to be virgin in the same way as she conceived by the grace and work of ... the Holy Spirit, an apparition that was repeated with the punctuality of lovers.

(Gist– These rumors kept growing, and the 13th of this month was said to be the date of the last apparition.)

From Aveiro some of the coarse and ignorant people, and a very large number of people who can spice up life by attending all spectacles, all went to Fatima—to see what?

We do not reply. We pass the pulpit to the religious journal *A Ordem,* and the reader [may] appreciate the testimony of an eyewitness. [Then it gives the 16 Oct article of Pinto Coelho and comments on it for several paragraphs. One line is fairly significant: "Seeing the sun dance, turn and descend and rise up—but why? As the logical consequence of slow and fixed staring at the sunlight."]

(Gist– The Lady gave the news to the children that the war was ending soon and our soldiers are returning. The last two paragraphs are unimportant. One mentions the famous appearance of Christ at the field of Ourique.)

Source: *O Democrata,* Aveiro, a radical Republican newspaper, 26 Oct; Doc Crit III book 1 pp 457-459.

#63 Oct 26   CHRONICAL

(Gist– The article notes the failure of Alfonse Costa's statements and efforts, such as the persecutions of the Church. It notes in much detail how the faithful are taught and imbibe the faith from childhood, that the war has made people more religious, and that there are more miracles and seers than ever, after Costa's famous statement.)

This was the case of three shepherds, two girls and a boy, who have announced for some months, on the 13th of each month, that they saw the Virgin Mother of Christ, that she communicates with them and said that on the 13th of Oct at the usual site, ... she would be visible for all the people.

A hoax or hallucination, resulting from ingenuous religious belief. Since 1858, when Bernadette had the vision at Lourdes, the miraculous apparitions have been multiplying, and many elect have affirmed that they received divine communications. For a long time, however, none have had the success of the three shepherds of Ourem.

Local information figures the number of people going there in the tens of thousands, and there were hundreds of carriages and cars bringing the devotees. The day was harsh, a fine rain was falling, constant and disagreeable. But all the crowd remained on firm ground, anxious and expectant. They all closed their umbrellas when the seers ordered it, as they were kneeling under an arch of greenery. And—oh, the power of hallucination! Oh, the incomparable psychology of crowds!—The great majority of all those people saw. The visual impression varies. Some saw a luminous, incomprehensible phenomenon to be produced; the heavens were filled with indefinite colorations; others saw the clouds break apart, and in the space left by them a figure broke forth sharply. They say that only the three elect heard the communication which matched the general preoccupation of all minds—the duration of the war.

We cannot doubt the good faith of so many people, whom we have heard. What this proves is that religious belief still is and will be so vigorously rooted in the spirit of the masses that it has a very strong suggestive power, which comes forth more easily when the spiritual soil is [made] more appropriate by the mystical preparation, by the decoration of the site, by poetry—so fundamentally impressive—of legends, especially sacred legends, and by the innate tendency for the marvelous.

This proves that no law of separation, no abolishment of religion, will tear down beliefs so strongly rooted; that the persecution of the Church and the restriction of rites, invigorates it even more, and you cannot get rid of it simply with a sheet of paper, with a castle of letters .... (Gist– More discussion on the difficulty of uprooting religion follows.)

Max Imo

Source: *A Republica*, 26 Oct; Doc Crit III book 1 pp 470-472.

Note: Alphonse Costa was a former head of the government, who said in a speech to the Legislature that religion would be eliminated in two generations.

#64 Oct 27   LETTER OF (BEATRICE GROJAO)

Mondego 27-10-1917

Dear Joaninha,

Today I received an interesting letter from Beatrice about her trip to Fatima, from which I am going to copy some parts so you and all there can read it, since Beatrice asked me, because she hasn't the time to write to you as she would like. Read it and pass it on. It is worth the effort. (Gist– I believe in the Fatima miracle.) Beatrice says:

(Gist– We went first to the apparition site and saw people praying. Then we went to the pastor's house and told his sister, who told us that she had seen signs on the sun, that we would like to see the seers. Fatima is small. The pastor's house, which is very modest, is the best one. We went on foot to Aljustrel. On the way we met the oldest, who was with a group of people on their way to Ourem. She wanted to keep going. She said that Jacinta would tell us all, and show us the way to the site.) Some women there told us that Jacinta never talks to anyone, (Gist– but we decided to try anyhow).

When we were ready to leave the little Jacinta appeared. … She is seven years old and is a real honey. We stayed there seated on the ground, holding the little one around our neck, in turn. We asked her how the Lady was and how she was dressed. And the little one, without the slightest exhortation, and wanting to explain in live form, stood up and said Our Lady was of her height. (Gist– The Lady's dress was quite long.) She explained later that Our Lady did not wear a veil, but a mantle, which fell from her head, according to the gesture of the little one, to about three or four fingers above the [bottom of the] tunic. She was all in white, without the blue band and she had her hands in prayer. (Gist– Jacinta demonstrated and separating her hands a little, she said when she talks she was like this.) She had on her head a thing of many colors. The oldest gave us the same explanation, and the young boy, whom we met afterwards [did too]. (Gist– She said no one she had seen who was as pretty as the Lady; and the boy said that there was never such a beauty in the world.)

We asked her to describe for us the first apparition. The little girl explained that they were going along, taking care of the sheep, which belonged to Lucia's family, … and suddenly they saw a flash of lightning and were afraid, very afraid. While they were kneeling in prayer they saw the Lady on the oak, and then they saw another flash, the sheep went into the chick peas, and a lady called to them from afar—"Turn these sheep away for me." But the Lady said (the little one tried to make her voice gentler): "Don't turn away the sheep. They are not going to eat anything." And then Lucia asked: "Who are you? What do you want?" and she said: "I am the Mother of Heaven. I want you to come here on this day for six months, and at the end of six months I will tell you what I want. Pray the rosary." Afterward the owner of the chick peas appeared, whom the lady went to call, and he came to complain, because it was very bad, but he didn't complain at all because he saw the chick peas had not been eaten. (Gist– Isn't this marvelous?)

(Gist– Aljustrel is very small, as is Fatima, with a road that ends there, and is little used.) There was no advertising in the newspapers, and in 6 months the news spread everywhere, and despite the rain and lack of transport, some 30,000 people, according to some, and 50,000 according to others gathered there. But returning to what I was saying, the little one talked afterward of the end of the war and the end of the world, if there was not faith. (Don't worry, there's more.)

(Gist– I wonder if the Lady would really have talked of the end of the war or were the seers mistaken, with all the questions asked of them. Our Lady told them a secret and the mothers have not been able to learn it.) According to what they say, the administrator promised them 20,000 reis if they would tell it, but there is no way of getting it out of them. (Gist– More discussion on the secret.) Our Lady on the last day said more—that she was the Virgin of the Rosary, and she wanted the people to build a chapel there—but that is far from the most important; imagine our impression when the little one ... told us that on the last day, the 13th, St. Joseph and the Child Jesus appeared to her!! It was a matter of the Holy Family. Our first impression was doubt and fear. Would all this come tumbling down? But some neighbors who were there told us that the three children had, some times [before], talked about St. Joseph and the Child Jesus. The little one then explained that St. Joseph had come to give peace to the world, and with a hand made the sign of the cross many times, imitating the gesture of bishops when they walk and bless the faithful. She told us that St. Joseph and the Child Jesus were like some of the little saints they had at home. (Gist– Someone offered to go get it, but the little one replied that she also had pictures on the wall. We went there. It was small, but clean.) The mother of the little ones seems to be a peasant, very pleasant and nice. Both she and her husband do not accept money, they fear that someone might suspect they have some kind of profit motive, and then [said] thanks to God, "We are not hungry. We have (according to her expression) enough potatoes for the whole year."

On the 13th somebody put a coin of 500 reis in the hand of one of the children; the child, not knowing what it was for, since it was wrapped in paper, went to take it to her mother, who was upset and asked in a loud voice—Who could be accused of giving the 500 reis. Nobody responded. And the 500 are still there, wrapped in paper, beside the kindling wood. She didn't want to touch it. The money does not belong to her.

They told us more—that the children, one day came home telling us they had seen the Lady of the sky, she replied that they must be dreaming and were not worthy of this. But the little one insisted. She made a description of what she had seen to the mother and she told that which she had already told us on the way. But let's get back to what I was saying. The little one says she has at the house some pictures, but she had not looked at them. She went to a box, and she took out a group of the Holy Family, saying: Do you see? St. Joseph and the Child Jesus were like they are here, but here St. Joseph has his eyes closed and there he had his eyes open. Wanting to see if we could trap them, we said if St. Joseph and the Child are like they are here, Our Lady on the last day should have been like that one [here] with colored veil and mantle. We asked several times. But she always replied that Our Lady was not like the one there, but was in white, with a rosary. We said further that since they were a Holy Family, they should be together, and she always said no. Our Lady was on the oak and St. Joseph and the Child Jesus were near the sun. We tried the same thing with the little boy and he always replied like his sister. It is sure that the six appearances of Our Lady can be confirmed, without necessarily confirming that of the Holy Family.

The oldest, before leaving for Ourem, also told us about St. Joseph and the Child Jesus. However, this is not much spread about, and we ourselves told it only to a few people, since it is much more extraordinary (which I think was not spoken of anywhere on earth). We are afraid it will frighten many "people" and make them not believe.

Can you imagine my fear when yesterday a girl from Alemquer came here and told me that a man from Alemquer had gone to Fatima, very incredulous and the worst of that kind, and returned very impressed and described to all the people the extraordinary things he had seen, and that he affirms that he saw the Child Jesus and St. Joseph. Nobody believes him, the wretch, *because nobody there knows really* that the Holy Family appeared. Would Our Lady have conceded this great grace to this man for his conversion? Emilio Infante and Nazareth were in Fatima on the 13th. Emilio fell on his knees, crying, and said if he knew there would be another apparition he would not fail to be there, even if he had to suffer through as much rain as this time. The signs were seen in the surroundings of Leiria, Batalha, etc. In Leiria everybody believes.

(Gist– I prayed the rosary at the apparition site with the seers and 30 others, and was very much impressed with everyone's devotion.)

Here you have, my dear Joaninha, what Beatrice told me today about her trip to Fatima, and I copied it textually in order not to make errors. (Gist– What a case! I wish I had gone there.)

I am writing in a hurry. ... Pay no attention to how it is, and keep this letter, despite the trouble it caused me to get to the end. It's so great! Show it afterwards to your cousin Guilhermina and send it [afterwards] to Chica, who should be happy to read it. (Gist– Greetings to all.)

Anita

Source: A copy of a letter of 27 Oct from Anita [unidentified] at Mondago, Favios parish, Vila Real county, to Joaninha [unidentified]; Doc Crit III book 1 pp 476-482.

Note: At the bottom, a note apparently added by someone other than the letter-writer, says: "a copy of the letter of a qualified witness" (Mrs. Beatrice Grojao), apparently indicating that the letter given in much detail was from Beatrice Gorjao. A comment added by the Fatima archives says that the letter was from Beatrice Gorjao. Her statement that "in Leria everybody believes" suggests that she lived in Leria.

#65 Oct 27   EUGENIA CAMARA LETTER

Alagoa (Carcavelos) 27 X –917

Dear Maria do Carmo

(Gist– Forgive me for not answering sooner. On returning from Fatima I wanted to write to everybody, but got too busy. I know that the event was already reported in the newspapers, but I will give you what I and uncle Tasco saw, plus what all who were with us told us. The spectacle was imposing and the crowd was moving, not being upset by the rain and mud, with no accident or disorder.) We were unable to get near the holm oak because there was a great crowd of people there already, ever since the evening before, but we were close, although we could not see the little ones' expressions, which I lamented greatly. Shortly before the hour when Our Lady was to appear, the rain stopped suddenly as if by magic and the sun came out, only to be overshadowed after a short while, so that it seemed like a warning. Shortly after, we noticed something which impressed us, which was to see the faces of the people who were in front of us, with shadow on the side of the sun, (which was still covered over) and lit up from the opposite side, that is, from where the holm oak was! [By this] I do not mean that I saw any brightness, for that I did not see.

When we were observing this scene, including a certain smoke or mist to be seen above the heads of the persons near there, we got the impression of choirs intoning on every side, and little by little all were baring their heads. Suddenly the sun came out again, and everyone began to turn (that way) and I heard exclamations. We resisted for a while, but they insisted so much that we looked and saw that we could gaze at the sun without any trouble at all. It was a white disk, that seemed like a host. Suddenly this host changed into a black disk, surrounded by a round gold circle, and this black disk began to spin around on itself, throwing out, from time to time, luminous rays, or to put it better, [flashes of] lightning.

Then it became white again and afterwards it was covered by a golden cloud! You cannot imagine what chills it sent down our spines, what commotion, how the people cried, what were the exclamations!

My Adelaide, who managed to speak to the little girl, heard her say that Our Lady had told her that she was the Lady of the Rosary, that she wanted a chapel built there, that they were to repent because God was already much offended, that the war was to end soon, and that they could expect the soldiers to return shortly! That is all I know! The little girl is ugly, not pleasant, quite ordinary in appearance. But she speaks firmly and never contradicts herself.

[Personal matter follows.]

From your very dear aunt,

Eugenia

Source: A letter of Eugenia de Mello Breyner da Camara, age unknown, at Alagoa, Carcavelos, to her niece, Maria do Carmo, *Fatima Way of Peace*, pp 39-41; Doc Crit III book 1 pp 473-475.

#66 Oct 27   LETTER OF PENA RAPOZO

Carvalhaes 27/10/1917

My good and esteemed friend,

(Gist– I received your letter and picked up your money on the way to Fatima.) I gave it into the hands of the parish priest of Fatima, but not without much protesting on his part. He showed me ... the instructions of ... the Archbishop ... about this matter, and among them, the express injunction that he should not accept donations, and that preferably they should be left with persons recognized as trustworthy, but not with him.

(Gist– I finally left the money with him, and wrote the name of the sender on the outside, saying that he could hand it over to the archbishop, if he wished. Indeed, I am more and more impressed with the simplicity and sincerity of that good priest. I read your letter to him, and he said that in the seer's home is a book with a brief account of the apparition at La Salette.)

The oldest child told me that it was only much later, after Our Lady had appeared, that the story [of La Salette] was related to her. The other little ones know practically nothing about the matter. The mother reads quite a bit; the child goes to school now, and I could not get her to accompany me to the [apparition] site without her mother's permission. .... Lucia is worn out with visitors and questionings, which begin at daybreak and end far into the night. The priest told me that if he himself were tormented with questions like that, he would be out of his mind. He says that it is especially when she sees priests that she wants to run away, for they ply her with questions so repeatedly.

The boy, who is little Jacinta's brother ... made a great impression on me yesterday. He has a very bright appearance, a truly joyful face, and seemed quite at his ease. He confirmed (when we interviewed him alone) that Lucia had said, at the moment of the miracle: Look at the sun! But Lucia insists that she has no recollection [of this], neither of Our Lady having told her, nor of repeating it herself. But it is a fact that is confirmed by other reliable people who were near her. I am of the opinion that the child is distraught as a result of weariness and exhaustion.

What she does confirm is that Our Lady said to her that the war was going to end that day, when she returned to heaven, and that the soldiers would return very soon to their families. She says she is not quite sure if Our Lady said that she was Our Lady of the Rosary, or if she wanted a chapel of Our Lady of the Rosary, but it was one of those things.

(Gist– The seers will not tell the secret to anybody. The boy refused gifts for anything in the world. The father of the boy and little girl is a sincere believer; the priest says that if he errs, it is by exaggeration; but Lucia's father is, in effect, an alcoholic and is not very religious; the child says he prays sometimes, but I think he is not much concerned about this matter.)

(Gist– It is true that people from Santarem stole the holm oak, the arch, bench and lanterns (from the Cova da Iria). It won't help their cause.)

I have just received this information by mail from Laura Avellar, who is a person to be trusted ... who lives there:

The children do not expect Our Lady to appear again. She asked that the rosary be prayed often in reparation to her Son, for He is much offended. Our Lady stood on the holm oak, not on the clouds. She had her hands joined and opened them when speaking (like Our Lady of Grace), and a rosary hung from her hands. When Our Lady disappeared, they looked at the sun, where they saw her with St. Joseph blessing the people, together with the Child Jesus, but only to the waist, and in different colors, which could be explained by the variety of colors that we all saw, although at first sight the explanation of the children might seem strange.

(Gist– I think I have answered all your questions. Personal matter follows.)

(Regards)

Maria de Jesus Oriol Pena Rapozo

Source: A photocopy of a letter of Maria de Jesus d' Oriol Pena Rapozo to Maria J. Tovares de Almeida Garrett, *Fatima Way of Peace*, pp 35-38; Doc Crit III book 1 pp 483-486. See Annex #38 and #39 for other letters of Pena Rapozo. For other letters of Garrett, see #24A, #38, #66, and #90A.

Note: From the text it appears that the interview of the seers was on 26 Oct.

#67 Oct 27   FATIMA

(Gist– The article gives a fairly long description of what happened at La Salette and Lourdes, asks if Fatima will become another Lourdes, and then describes what happened at Fatima. It also says that the Lady of Fatima promised peace and the return of the Portuguese soldiers shortly.)

Heavy clouds covered the sky; there was a very strong wind; water, falling in a downpour, put a note of doubt in the hearts of believers, and in the hearts of the indifferent or atheists [it put] the certainty that they were attending a religious fiasco. The time of the apparition approached, and the clouds separated, the wind calmed down, and the water stopped falling. The children of the vision fell on their knees and began to pray, and the sun began to show up, very different than it always is. *Sometimes it was encircled by red flames, other times with a ring of yellow or light purple, other times seeming to be animated by a very rapid rotary movement, other times even seeming to detach itself from the sky, approach the earth and give off great heat.* The faithful then acknowledged the supernatural, the miracle, unmistakable and palpable, and acclaimed with all the force of their lungs and with all the enthusiasm of their faith, the Immaculate Virgin, the Lady of Fatima, the patron of Portugal. The unbelievers, tortured by doubt, passed on to science the word that it should explain the phenomenon they had seen and should justify the philosophical theories of the atheistic school, always in conflict with the supernatural. (Gist– The article then says they hope that science will talk and the Church will speak its infallible words.)

Source: *Voz de Parocho,* a weekly of several parishes (near) Viseu, 27 Oct; Doc Crit III book 1 pp 513, 514.

Note: The words in italics are clearly taken from Coelho's article in *A Ordem* of 16 Oct. See #34. This article of 27 Oct was reprinted in several other Catholic journals.

#68 Oct 29   THE MIRACLE OF FATIMA

(Gist– After 20 years of silence you write and ask me to tell you in detail what I saw at Fatima, along with the thousands, drawn there more in hope of a miracle than by mere curiosity or fear of a hoax. Some Catholics thought that the promise of a miracle had been fulfilled. Others were far from sure. Your family dragged you there, and your reasoning received a blow. You want the help of an unbiased person like me, since I was there only on an assignment from *O Seculo.* I'm sorry, but what you saw and heard was no different than what I saw. Few were indifferent to this unique spectacle.)

What was it that I heard and that brought me to Fatima? I heard that the Virgin Mary had appeared, after the feast of the Ascension, to three little shepherds who were pasturing their flock, two little girls and a lad. She urged them to pray, and promised to appear there on the holm oak on the 13th of each month until Oct, when she would give them some sign of the power of God and would make revelations. This news was spread all around for many miles, then flew like wild fire from place to place throughout Portugal. The number of pilgrims increased month by month, coming on pilgrimage to this barren spot, so that on 13 Oct some 50,000 people had gathered there, according to the calculations of some impartial individuals. At the previous meetings of the faithful there had not failed to be those who were supposed to have seen strange astronomic and atmospheric occurrences, which they took as direct signs of divine intervention. Some reported sudden lowering of the temperature, the twinkling of stars in the full middle of the day, and beautiful clouds, never seen [before] around the sun. There were those who repeated and proclaimed heatedly that the Lady asked for penance, that a chapel be built on the site, that on 13 Oct she would show, through a proof, noticeable to all, the infinite goodness and power of God. ...

(Gist– He describes in detail the crowds going to Fatima, the rain and mud there and the cold weather.) I saw the multitude densely massed around the little miraculous oak and plucking its branches to keep as relics, or overflowing through the immense moor, traversed and dominated by the road from Leiria, and which now presented the most picturesque and varied gathering of cars and people that thronged it on that never-to-be-forgotten day, [all] awaiting in orderly fashion the supernatural manifestations, without fearing that the wintry weather would do any harm or diminish their splendor or magnificence. ...

I saw that they were not discouraged, their confidence remained alive and ardent, despite the unforeseen difficulties, and that the composure of the crowd, in which peasants were super-abundant, was perfect; [and I saw] that the children, who are said to be the privileged ones, were the objects of the most intense affection of those people, who kneeled, bared their heads and prayed at her [the Lady's] command, at a time when the hour of the "miracle," the "palpable sign" approached, the ardently awaited mystical hour of contact between heaven and earth. ...

And when I could no longer imagine anything more impressive than this noisy but peaceful crowd, animated by the same obsessive idea, and moved by the same powerful anxiety, what further really strange thing did I see on this moor of Fatima? At the hour forecast in advance, the <u>rain stopped; the thick mass of clouds broke apart, and the sun—a dull silver disk—appeared at full zenith and began to dance in a violent and convulsive movement, that a great number of people imagined to be a serpentine dance, so beautiful and glowing [were] the colors which covered the surface of the sun, one after another.</u> ...

A miracle, as the crowd cried out; or a natural phenomenon, as the learned say? It is not important for me to know the answer now, but only to confirm to you what I saw. .... The rest we leave to science and the Church.

Avelino de Almeida

Source: *Ilustracao Portuguesa*, 29 Oct, *Fatima: The Great Sign*, pp 59, 60; Doc Crit III book 1 pp 530-533.

Note: *Ilustracao Portuguesa* was a major Sunday magazine, associated with the paper *O Seculo*; Jaki, p 104.

#68A Oct 30   MARVELOUS CASE

(Gist– Fatima, a small town of 1600 souls, located about 8 kilometers from Vila Nova d' Ourem, has become famous for the apparition that took place there before 50,000 people. We are not going to comment, but only make use of reliable information we have received. We have a letter from a distinguished local gentleman who was one of the numerous witnesses to the event. He went to Fatima by car. More than 500 cars were there on that dark and rainy day.)

He says that, at the time the miracle was expected, <u>the sun appeared for the first time and could be stared at perfectly well by the crowd</u>, [and] <u>that the rays of the sun were tinged successively blue, yellow and purple</u>, [and] <u>that at the same time some trembling and unknown movements were seen on that star [the sun]</u>.

(Gist– That is all he tells us, which is confirmed by various newspapers. The sensational news of what was happening there had been known for a long time.)

On Ascension Day, 13 May, three children—Lucia, 10, Francisco, 9, and Jacinta, 7—were pasturing their sheep in the neighboring region; they had the pious thought of saying the rosary. During this devotion, they declare, a Lady of extreme beauty came and asked them to come there for six months on the same day. The children did this; many other persons also went to the site; their numbers kept growing as the sensational news spread.

On 3 [error for 13] Sept the crowd reached 20,000, who saw nothing unusual, but who carried the sensational news that on 13 Oct, the sixth and last day of scheduled apparitions, a sensational and miraculous event would corroborate the truth of the apparitions reported by those three children.

(Gist– Part of the article about Fatima from *A Ordem* of 16 Oct is given. See #34.)

(Gist– *O Dia* published the report of the famous writer, Maria Magdalena Martel Patricio, a contributor to the woman's page of *Diario Nacional*. A part of her article follows. See #50.)

Avelino d'Almeida, a renegade Catholic, presently belonging to the radical and Jacobin ranks of *O Seculo*, was there as a special envoy of that journal. He published an account of what he saw. From what he wrote we have extracted the following: [A part of his article of 15 Oct follows. See Annex #28.]

(Gist– The interview of the astronomer Frederico Oom is also reported. See Annex #48.)

Source: *A Verdade*, apparently a pro-Catholic newspaper, Angra do Heroisma, the Azores, 30 Oct; Doc Crit III book 1 pp 544-547.

Note: I received this article late and do not include it in my statistics on the sun dance.

#69 Oct 31   LETTER OF IZABEL DE MELO

To Reverend Father Gelase, Capuchin, at Sion [Valais], Switzerland
Espinho, 31 Oct
My reverend Father

(Gist– The first page and part of the second are personal.)

From my arrival in Lisbon, they were talking about the marvelous apparition of Our Lady to the little ones [at Fatima]—two little girls of ten and seven, and a boy of about the same age. These children say that one day, while they were watching their sheep in the mountains they heard something like a clap of thunder and were afraid of a storm; they began to gather the flock to leave. Then they saw a Lady of great beauty who said to them, "Don't fear. I am from heaven. Come to this place the 13th of each month. (It was then the 13th of May.) I will appear to you and in six months, on 13 Oct, I will make a sign so that all will believe in me."

The children told of this and on the 13th of the next month they went to the same site, accompanied already by a lot of people, and at noon they are seen to be transfigured, they are heard to address themselves to a person that no one sees, their lips are seen to move, but what they say is not heard. Only everyone feels that they should kneel and pray. After a few minutes they get up, say that the Holy Virgin is gone and she said that they must pray and do penance. The next month the same scene is repeated, except that there are more people each time.

At last, in September, [error for August] the authorities of the area don't let the children go to the site of the miracle, as everyone calls it. They are kept by the mayor, who asks them a thousand questions to trap them in their response. They are threatened with prison and finally they torment them in every way, but the poor little ones say the same thing as always: "We see a 'Lady.' She tells us to pray, to tell everyone to do penance, and that on 13 Oct everyone will believe." Despite the absence of the children lots of people go to the usual site of the apparition, no one sees anything, but at noon a supernatural presence is felt, which forces them to pray.

(Gist– On 13 Oct, I arranged to go there with my sister, cousins and friends.) There is no train to the village, and from the village to the apparition site is fairly far. Thus we rented a big car and left Lisbon at 2:00 in the morning to be at the site at noon. We traveled all night. At 10:00 we were at the apparition site. There was already an enormous crowd waiting. It is figured that there were more than 50,000 people. (Gist– She describes the people going there.) It was raining heavily, as it seldom does at our place in October, when it is still so pleasant. But nobody complained. We were there in the rain, waiting! One heard a sound like the sea, and it was all the people who prayed aloud and sang hymns.

At last, at noon, we heard a murmur of exclamation. It was the children who arrived, accompanied by the local doctor, who took them under his protection. The pastor and other neighboring priests were not there. The bishop had ordered the clergy not to get involved at all, from fear that the government, which was always ready to persecute religion, would say that the priests were running this affair. No Catholic journal had spoken of the apparitions. It is the Republican and anti-religious journals that made lots of noise on these affairs and sent their reporters to this site. I am sending you *Ilustracao Portuguesa* with photographs of the principle scenes that occurred. (Gist– She then notes that this journal is anti-religious, but that this article is not.)

But as I was saying, the children arrived at the site where the Virgin appeared to them. This spot [is] marked by a rustic altar with a cross above and two lanterns lit, near an olive tree, or what was an olive tree, only the trunk is left, [because] devout people have pulled off all the leaves and branches, everything.

Father, it is exactly noon, and the rain, which was heavy, stops suddenly, the children are kneeling near the cross and pray. Their little faces, transfigured, are covered with tears. Then suddenly we hear a shout that comes from thousands of mouths. All the people shout: "Miracle, Miracle." "Praised be Jesus Christ." "Praised be the Holy Virgin." And <u>the sun, which one can stare at, resembles a metal disk, without rays. It begins to turn on itself and to ascend and descend several times.</u> That is what people around me say, and what thousands of people affirm that they saw. Me, I did not see it. I could easily stare at the sun and was terribly excited to hear everyone shout that they see extraordinary signs in the sky. I believe Our Lord did not believe me worthy of seeing these phenomena, but my soul did not need to see them to believe in the apparition of the Blessed Virgin to the children. Two of my female cousins, who were next to me, were beside themselves, and affirm that <u>they saw the sun exactly as a fireworks wheel that turned on itself vertiginously. Finally, that lasted some minutes, and again the clouds covered the sun,</u> the children got up and all the people rushed to hear what they would say. I could see from afar one of the children on the arm of a man. I didn't hear what she said, but they say that she said this: "The Holy Virgin blessed the whole world, she wants us to pray, to do penance, and to build a chapel there in honor of Our Lady of the Rosary."

The donations are so great that they are going to begin at once to build a chapel, and this place, unknown a few months ago, has become all at once famous. (Gist– The people departed happy and convinced that Our Lady had appeared. I am sure of it. An old man near us prayed to the Virgin for his son, who presumably was at war. The rest is personal matter.)

Isabel Brandada da Melo

Source: A copy of a letter, in French, from the Marchioness Isabel Brandada de Melo, Lisbon, on vacation in Espinho, to Father Gelase, in Sion, Switzerland. The copy was sent to Father Cruz by Father Gelase in Sept 1941; Doc Crit III book 1 pp 550-556; Jaki, pp 271-273.
Note: Her daughter Gini also apparently saw nothing. See Annex #33.

#70 Oct 31   LETTER OF NASCIMENTO E SOUSA

Oct 31, 1917

My dear friend,

(Gist– It is easy to reply to you, but hard to give a full, detailed description of what I saw.) The many diverse sensations I felt on that unforgettable day do not have an easy explanation, and only one who has experienced them can feel them, and never can completely reproduce them fully and truthfully.

I was one of the first to arrive and the last to leave. I never felt such a great joy nor such a pure satisfaction of soul. From the beginning, and despite the continuous and bothersome rain, I noticed that all of us, in a communion of feelings and ideas, were satisfied and expectant—not a gesture of despair or weakening, nor a word of complaint or impropriety. I am certain, my dear friend, that in rain or the worst possible weather but no one would have moved from there, and despite [the size of] the crowd there, it seemed we already knew each other, were friends and wanted all the best for the others. Next to me, and under our umbrella various people passed [time], sheltering themselves and conversing as if we knew each other for a long time, and were old friends. (Gist– An old man there had walked five leagues. He made an odd statement that required explanation.)

Therefore, and despite all, we expected something, although some of us, and I was among them, were anxious and, to tell the truth, somewhat feared that nothing would happen.

Not all have the deep faith of true believers. I will say more, my companion, Joaquim Sacristao de Turquel, had in his hand a watch set on the sun, and we were fairly worried as time passed.

Now, my friend, let anyone describe it who can. ... It must have been 12:35 to 12:40 on the reliable watch of my friend. I saw with all certainty, because the sunlight allowed us to stare at the sun at will, it and the clouds which surrounded it trembled, hesitatingly, as if obeying a superior will, which at this moment had put forth its hand and obliged it to obey. I had the impression like when someone slaps a person to make him listen. What happened on that occasion? That there was a solar phenomenon, with more or less a display of various colors, don't doubt it. I only saw a very pronounced yellow, and it seemed to me that I saw a black color below the disk, but I don't guarantee this.

But I can't explain what I felt or what I still feel today, and I will never pass such enjoyable moments. Nothing will convey to you our happiness and satisfaction with the events. We interrogated each other, and only a single person said he had not seen [it].

(Gist— The behavior of the people, their happiness at the solar phenomenon, the friendship, and the fact that there was no robbery, disturbance or disaster and especially the solar event convince me that a miracle occurred.)

....

Nacimento

P.S. I saw the children come and leave and went even to the door of the house, where my family entered. There was no discord, no matter how many foolish and insidious questions were made to the poor children by many persons who continually tried and tried. Among them [were] some poorly dressed peasants in their new, flowery clothes.

Source: A letter of 31 Oct from Dr. Nascimento e Sousa to a friend; Doc Crit III book 1 pp 557-559.

Note: The writer was a lawyer from Alcobaca; Jaki, p 108.

#71 October?   LETTER OF LA LANDA

Estemed Senhora D. M. da Piedade Ordaz

(Gist— He intended to write earlier, then thought the addressee had learned all about it, and finally decided to write to her. He heard about Fatima and decided to go there by bicycle, staying the evening before in the house of his sister Maria S. Jose, in Reguenho. On the 13th he went some two leagues from there to the site. He describes the rain, which started about 9:00, says all the people going there got wet. He headed for the little arc and cross, the apparition site. It was said that the apparition would take place between noon and 1:00, solar time.)

The rain did not stop. The sky, completely clouded, led one to think that nothing would happen.

A little before the appointed hour the children arrive, and the rain keeps falling. They go to the site, ask the people to shut their umbrellas and are obeyed. What's more, all the men take off their hats. They start the rosary and the rain stops falling slowly. The very dense clouds began to rarify and the sun began to appear like the moon between one cloud or another. Sometime later the clouds part and the sun shows up in all its splendor. I wanted to look at it, but could not. The clouds continue to cover it, and moments later, break up again, and the sun gives us the most grandiose picture that my eyes have ever seen. It takes on the appearance of the moon, all yellow, but without sending out light, next it changes to celestial blue, followed by a very intense shine, like a spring of bright lights. It takes on a very rapid circular movement and approaches the earth, succeeding in making the impression that all are going to be burned up. But oh, a divine marvel! The sun returns to its place and seemed to say to us: "Don't fear." All, now on their knees, direct their thoughts to God, to Our Lady, and no one remembers this world.

Meanwhile, the miracle having ended, the children stand up from prayer and are carried on the shoulders of various people. The oldest says to the people: "The Lady talked for the last time with me and charged me to say to you: that peace is being made today, and that you should return peacefully to your homes, that the rain won't (Gist– come back) that you should pray to Our Lord, whom you have greatly offended, that the soldiers will shortly return from France, and that she wants us to build a chapel at that place.

During the miracle the objects take on a golden yellow color, having a dazzling effect on the vast enclosure, where 50,000 people were gathered.

Within the luminous globe [the sun] were seen a group of people who moved and which the child said was St. Joseph, announcing peace to the world, his Holy Son blessing them and Our Lady of Sorrows.

The picture is emotional and moving. Tears of emotion and joy are seen in almost all eyes, and from mine some fall too. It is a marvelous scene that my eyes never saw before. During the miracle everything took on a yellowish color, a golden yellow, staying in this state [short unreadable text] for some 30 ... and then ended.

The children get up from prayer and the oldest, carried on the shoulders of a man, said to the people: that Our Lady talked to her for the last time, that peace was made today, that they should pray and go home peacefully, that the rain would not [return], that they should expect their soldiers back shortly from France, and that she was Our Lady of the Rosary and wanted them to build a chapel at that site. [The text ends here.]

Source: A draft of a letter from Professor Antonio La Landa, age unknown, at Reguengo do Fetal, to Mrs. Piedade Ordaz; Doc Crit III book 1 pp 566-569.

Notes: No date is given, but the text clearly suggests a date in late Oct. The signature, and perhaps personal matter, is missing. The draft was given to the archives by the daughter of La Landa.

#72 Nov 1   FATIMA

Continuing the information in our September issue, thanks to the ... collaboration of one of our subscribers, we are transcribing today some parts of a new letter in which a lady adds her conscientious and simple testimony to the narratives which are coming from people of the most different [kinds], which agitate and move opinion since the unforgettable day of 13 Oct. [The letter follows.]

All of us had agreed to meet in Torres Novas, those of us who were going in a truck to Fatima. With what emotion do I pronounce the name of this blessed place. At ten minutes to nine we left, under a continuous rain that accompanied us there, and in my opinion it was the first blessing which Our Holy Mother gave us, after five months of drought. (Gist– She describes her trip and the people going to Fatima, says they stopped to adore the Blessed Sacrament, and to ask Our Lady not to disappoint the people. She did not doubt God's power.)

It was noon, and we ate some lunch, more by reflex than necessity. At 1:00 we left for the site. And you cannot imagine the amount of land occupied by the dense crowd, in the greatest calm and respect, the quantity of automobiles, carriages and vehicles of all kind that filled the road over the length of almost a kilometer, making it difficult for those on foot to pass. We were in a truck, and nothing else was possible.

The time was arriving and I was sure that the weather would lift. And, in effect, a little bit before 2:00 the rain stopped, the sky continuing to be leaden. Suddenly, all the people, full of an indescribable anxiety and part of them possibly discouraged, began to see a little fog at the site of the oak bush, and after some minutes we saw everyone turn toward the sun. I heard later that Our Lady had said to Lucia (one of the children) at this instant: "Order the people to look at the sun."

Suddenly a luminous disk the size of a big host, but which all could stare at, as one stares at the moon, seemed to detach itself from the sun (or got in front of it), lowering visibly, with a continuous rotation, and after a stop, repeated itself. A beautiful cloud, now fire-colored, now purple, now rose, now golden appeared and disappeared successively, reflecting the colors not only on the onlookers but also on all that basin. The yellow color was especially impressive, and it was seen on the other occasions, but less intense. The horizon was marked in a perfect circle by luminous focals, equal in size and distance from one another, giving somewhat the impression of "burns" but in the yellow color that sometimes is seen at sunset. The whole effect was golden and the focals to which I allude kept coming up one after another. Simply marvelous and surprising! ....

I carried a list of people for whom I wanted to pray especially. It seemed that they guessed that I could only shout "Praised be God" and this without stopping. Many (very believable people) saw a beautiful star travel in the direction of the oak bush, like a shine.

I was with the two little ones, who were dressed in white, with very simple veils on their heads. They said to me that Our Lady appeared to them, with St. Joseph and the Child Jesus at his feet, that she said she was Our Lady of the Rosary, that we should pray a lot, that this was one more warning that if they did not repent (and) if they continued to offend her Divine Son, He would order a great punishment for Portugal.

The two little ones, separated, gave a description of the vision in the same form. Lucia, who at her tender age, ought to be crazy, in the middle of that commotion with which she was surrounded, kept saying in a clear voice, and not changing as she kept moving (on the shoulder of her father) what the Lady told her. .... [two lines of dashes]

Awaiting in obedient submission the decision of the Church, let us make ardent prayers and ... prayers that we need so much. (Gist– And may it lead to a revival of faith in Portugal.)

L. de S.

Source: *Raio de Luz*, 1 Nov; Doc Crit III book1 pp 582-584.

Note: The writer is identified only by her or his initials. However, the reference to a new letter in which that lady, etc., suggests that the lady who wrote this letter is the same one who wrote the letter published by *Raio de Luz* in its Sept issue. See #8.

#73 Nov 3   STATEMENT OF ANA MARIA DA CAMARA

About 1:00 on Oct 13, 1917, at the field of Fatima. It is raining torrentially, which does not succeed in indisposing the groups near me. They are saying the rosary, the litany and other prayers. Those who know each other and those who do not unite in their prayers.

A little time after this it stops raining and the sun of every day makes its appearance.

Some minutes pass. It is after 1:30. I feel in my heart a little depressed. I begin the rosary, and in the middle of the second rosary I hear a huge gasp from the crowd and somebody says to me: "Look at the sun." I reply that I see nothing. But seconds later I burst out: "It is the moon." I see a very light silvery blue disk, with no rays, that takes on its natural color and begins to turn vertiginously, and then this disk takes on different colors.

It sends out from itself something like billows of smoke of the color of which it is tinted, but it keeps its perfectly round form, without rays, and can be stared at perfectly. At a certain moment I see the coloring to be vivid rose. Behind every peak rises a gauzy veil of the same color. Both the land and the crowd reflect it. It is grandly beautiful, and in my soul a feeling of fear comes up, unexplainable if I did not have the conviction of something supernatural.

Nobody says aloud what they are seeing, but by the increase in the ardor of invocations to Our Lady on the "culminating" occasions, it is seen that everyone sees more or less the same thing.

The uproar is immense at the moment the sun descends, a movement which I see distinctly, as well as a movement to the right or left, or vice-versa, but at the usual altitude of the sun. These two latter movements were very much less noticeable than the descending movement, and I cannot be sure that they followed immediately after it.

What I have described is what my eyes saw at Fatima. My soul is all with Our Lady.

3 November, 1917

Anna Maria da Camara-Fa [daughter] of Maria [See #11A]

Source: A statement of Ana Maria da Camara, 3 Nov; Doc Crit III book 1 pp 596, 597; Jaki, pp 109,110.

Note: This may be a deposition. For her letter of 19 Oct, see #49. For a letter to her, see #33.

#74 Nov 3   STATEMENT OF ANTONIA DA CAMARA

In the name of the Father, the Son, and the Holy Spirit.

About what I saw marvelous in Fatima, I can affirm with all certainty the rotary movement of the sun, that showed a dark green color. Next to me I kept hearing Our Lady invoked, (and I affirm) that nothing that went on in the sun distracted our attention for anything other than our faith in her presence.

Antonia da Camara daughter of Maria

R. da Junqueira 64-1 [Her street address]

3-11-1917

Source: A statement of Antonia Rafaela da Camara, 3 Nov; Doc Crit III 598 book 1; Jaki, p 110.

Note: Antonia was a sister of Maria da Camara, author of #73 and 11A.

#75 Nov 8   THE MIRACLE OF FATIMA

(Gist– A long article discusses the attitude of modern philosophy to the miraculous. It notes that modern philosophy questions both the eternal existence of matter and the law of preservation of energy and matter. Two key paragraphs follow.)

Contrary to the scientific simplicity of the modern century, Gustave Le Bon demonstrates the appearance and death of matter. Matter decomposes, falls apart, is pulverized and extinguished, a formal denial of the famous law of Lavoisier that nature neither creates nor loses anything and everything is transformed.

The break-up of matter being firm, Gustave Le Bon teaches us that its primordial parts are engendered by something like a condensation of energy. [Since] energy precedes matter, the whole static concept of matter disappears in the air. [A long philosophical discussion follows. It defends the concept of miracles and calls the Fatima phenomenon "truly prodigious."]

Antonio Sardinha

Source: *A Monarquia*, a pro-monarchy, a pro-Catholic journal, Lisbon; Doc Crit III book 1 pp 618-625.

Note: This article is useful for this book chiefly in that it discusses the ideas of Gustave Le Bon, a popularizer of the concept of mass hallucination. See pages 76 and 399. A large majority of this article was quoted in a long pamphlet against Fatima. See #76, which follows.

#76 Nov 8?   THE MIRACLE OF FATIMA

Explanation of the Marvelous Event of 13 Oct 1917

[A Pamphlet by] Helio de Lysia

(Gist– The first two pages are on the theory of miracles. The next two are on the miracles at La Salette, Obermauerbach and Lourdes. It then briefly gives the story of Fatima as follows: three kids, a boy and two girls, say that starting on 13 May of this year a Lady of blinding beauty appears to them, and some signs in the sky coincide with the phenomenon, chiefly in the aurora of the sun. In the next 6 pages it quotes from Pinto Coelho's article in *A Ordem* of 16 Oct, from *Boletim Parochial* of 4 Nov,[10] and from *Illustracao Portuguesa* of 29 Oct. See #34 and #68. Then on the next 7 pages it gives the article from *A Monarquia* of 8 Nov. See #75. Then, in two pages, the author

---

[10] Doc Crit III pp 601, 602.

gives his own conclusions: some Catholics are doubtful, others firm in their belief in the Fatima miracles. The words of the children are not enough.)

For many, perhaps not a majority, there was no miracle. There are however others who believe fervently in it. ... Are the children victims of an illusion, of a hallucination or are they [the seers] being manipulated cleverly for some purpose? Who can say? But what about the signs in the sky? Was it a work of hallucination, a case of collective hallucination, as many psychologists would have us believe, or was it merely a physical phenomenon? The faith of many individuals together is contagious. The believers, praying in ecstasy—and this goes for all religions—create these fantasies in the field of their vision, and this phenomenon, which begins with one individual, is extended to hundreds, and even thousands of them, as it has been proven. History is full of examples of this kind.

An idea or obsession can transmit itself by induction with mysterious conductors, psychological currents through the sky, from individual to individual, and from one to a crowd. Great events which almost always redound in cataclysms for humanity, generally have their origin in the principle I have just explained.

(Gist– Then follows a page about Peter the Hermit, who led people in a Crusade, implying that they were deluded, and about the present Germans who have been deluded by Kant and Nietzsche and other apologist-philosophers into a delirium of mystical madness and German hegemony of the world.)

The delusions resulting from hallucination belong to a unique psychological family.

Can they be created by the force of will of a single person? ... The occultists say yes.

Was Fatima, which many call a miracle, created for given purposes by some cultivator of black or white magic? (Gist– The wise or occult people are best able to explain this extraordinary phenomenon.)

Source: An undated 20-page pamphlet of Eduardo de Lima Metzner, published by Bertran Livraria, Lisbon; Doc Crit III book 1 pp 628-649; Jaki, pp 116, 117. The approximate date was supplied by the Fatima archives, which cited statements in the pamphlet as evidence.

#77 Nov 10   FATIMA

I am asking the director of the newspaper *Correio de Beira* to give me a bit of space for these brief words. Having already seen, in various journals, talk of the extraordinary event at Fatima, since my daughter and I were witnesses, I will only say … what our eyes saw. …

(Gist– She describes her trip from Torres Novas in a rented, enclosed carriage and says she rested at the Fatima rectory. The next day, the 13th, she went to the apparition site. She then describes Fatima, the trip there and the Cova da Iria. By 8:30 the roads were crowded. We went by carriage to the Cova, a huge basin.) The 13th looked like a rainy day, dark and windy.

At 9 or 9:30 it got darker, with more rain, and it seemed it would not get better. As we saw the rain was continuing, at 11:00 we decided to leave our warmth and cover and follow the pilgrims to the site which the 3 astronomers had announced as the theater for extraordinary scenes. At mid-day the three shepherds arrived. (Gist– She names them, gives their ages and dress and says they saw a beautiful lady dressed in white, with a cloud at her feet.)

Some minutes after the arrival of the shepherds the rain stopped, and the sky, dark until then, exactly at the time, (it must have been 1:00) when the three astronomers had forecast the most phenomenal event which could happen, at the forecasted apparition site the sky cleared a bit, which made almost everyone stare at the same spot [in the sky].

It was really an impressive sight, witnessed by 40,000 or 50,000 people, as they were roughly calculated.

I do not claim what I did not see. We did not see Our Lady, nor do we consider ourselves worthy of this. But we saw in the sun alone the confirmation of a phenomenon, of a supernatural event. How it was and where it came from, we cannot say. But it happened, and one can't argue against happenings.

As I said, at 1:30 the clouds opened and the spot where the clouds parted cleared up; and what was our surprise when a silver globe appeared, making a little turn and seeming to be crossed, here and there, by clouds. This [happened] three times, with intervals of, perhaps, three or four minutes.

On this occasion, in back of us, was the scene of the three shepherds at the oak bush. We stayed 7 to 10 meters from the spot to avoid the squeeze of the crowd. At this time the oldest shepherdess ordered silence, and the rest of the scene was for the three. After this nice start, … the sun, as if eclipsed by clouds, but not at all covered, suddenly broke out in all its splendor, very different from usual, a cloud or flame of most brilliant red, which covered it, and after some moments that globe or sphere agitated itself nervously, as if impelled by electricity. It seemed to swell and want to head for, or talk to, the earth, to announce an event of delight and fear.

A golden yellow cloud changed the scenery; and thus this "reality," which seemed a dream to mortals, was disappearing! I would like to be able to describe this unique, marvelous event in chiseled phrases. I limit myself to the simple telling of the truth which we witnessed.

If all of this were forecast by scientists, astronomers, there would be nothing to admire; but no. The innocent and simple voice of children alone aroused the curiosity of thousands of people. Now, it is not natural that these simple children would dare to bring news to the learned; nor claim to teach masters.

Their intention was more modest; just in very simple words they then affirmed that they had seen a very beautiful Lady, hands joined and dressed in white, who told them to have a chapel built at the site, in honor of Our Lady of the Rosary, that they should stop offending God, who was already too much offended! She said the war was ending, that our soldiers would return. Earlier the Lady had told them something which they can't reveal.

When we came by carriage to Torres Novas, the hotel servant ... said to us in mysterious tones: "It seems there is going to be a big noise there." The carriage rolled on. I said to my daughter: "I am used to praying to St. Bartholomew (the patron saint of fear). Since we harm no one, we think that no one will have the right to do it to us. Our Lady will take care of us and all who go there, who will not be at fault if there is no miracle!"

We could have scarcely have said what we would witness at the moment when the nervous sun held its audience in suspense. It seemed to come toward the earth, announcing the miracle and saluting the Queen of heaven and the universe, who in those moments talked through three shepherds, as the children spontaneously and courageously affirm.

(Gist– I believe. But my voice is weak. I hope more authoritative voices will confirm it.)

When the sun returned to normal, everyone retired in great order and silence, quieted by the truth of the events. (Gist– She had gotten very muddy. The oak bush was cut down. Our driver said he had seen nothing of the sun dance. Maybe he was feeding the horses.)

A subscriber of your journal
Aldea Central, 30 Oct 1917

Source: *Correio de Beira*, a Catholic journal, 10 Nov; Doc Crit I pp 297-302; Jaki, pp 107, 108.

Note: The writer was identified by Father Manuel Ferreira in the Parish Inquiry on 18 April 1919, as Maria Jose de Lemos Queiros; Doc Crit I p 297.

#78 Nov 11   THE APPARITION OF FATIMA

Once more the Virgin has appeared to shepherds, this time to kiddies of 7 to 10, showing again her preference for young shepherds, whose sole treasure is the mystic virtues of childish simplicity, of misery … so appropriate to visions and fantasies. In the previous months, to the three children, … the celestial vision promised to return on 13 Oct, perhaps to commemorate the shooting of Ferrer—to explain to the intoxicated faithful the reason for her famous favor.

At the designated time, at the site of the [heavenly] interview—a melancholy moor—there gathered around the visionary shepherds an enormous crowd, who came there by all means of locomotion, already predisposed to the contagious electric shock of mass hallucination.

And then there was the vision and the miracle of Fatima, the new Lourdes, where maybe another pious basilica will stand forth. All these good people, poor for sure, for whom this earth is an inferno, and poor in spirit, those whose kingdom is to be in heaven, all these good people saw, they positively saw <u>the sun, which came out as a silver disk</u> through the clouds on a sad, rainy day, <u>they saw the sun dance, fall and tremble in hysteric convulsions</u>, while, according to what the oldest of the children recited from the shoulders of an individual, the Virgin announced that the war had ended and the soldiers were on their way home.

Reporters described episodes of the impressive and medieval scene. *An old man with a long name, erect and bearded, voiced the Creed as a solemn profession of faith. A lady deplored, with extraordinary fear <u>the blindness of the curious who had seen nothing</u>, of the few who still dared to keep their hat on in view of the evidence of a stupendous miracle.*

If it were possible to be rational with believers and visionaries, one could object with easy logic, too easy even for the troubled souls of mystics, the weakness of a sterile meteorological miracle, that the hardened skepticism, inexplicably allowed by the Almighty, would point out against any atmospheric phenomenon whatever, singularly enlarged and transformed by the over-excited imagination of a religious mob, previously resolved to see with the eyes of faith.

(Gist– It would be better that the mountains and moor pour forth badly needed bread or that the war would really end at the order of the Virgin, as stated by the seers.)

(Gist– The anti-clerical forces attribute the Fatima miracle to a mere clerical hoax.)

Possibly one factor in the case might be a group, operating, if not on the invention or initiation of a miraculous apparition, at least on its encouragement, staging, and on publicity outlays. And if the undertaking is to succeed … a thousand greedy local interests will be entwined. (Gist– A popular pilgrimage site is great for business. When they talked of closing Lourdes even the Masons and free-thinkers objected.)

But today it is worthwhile to consider the root causes for the flare-up in religious faith. Let us leave to meteorologists and experts in psychology the studies of the effects of the sun on rainy days and the explanation of the psychic contagion in mass hallucinations, not considering those who, in the presence of sincere visionaries, are afraid to admit that they see nothing, that they are not in [the state of] grace, as in the tale of the king (Gist– who was naked, but everyone claimed to be richly dressed, not to be thought a fool). On the base of superstition and pre-existing ignorance, which plays the main role in these grand acts of religious faith, is the material misery and moral depression of the tragic current times. (Gist– The needy take consolation in prayer and miracles, if they are afraid to revolt.)

Good grounds, no doubt for maneuvering by selfish interests for sure. But we are not overly afraid. Very mystical, superstitious and ignorant was the great mass of the Russian people ….

Source: *A Aurora*, a liberal journal, Porto, 11 Nov; Doc Crit III book 1 pp 661-663.

Note: The two sentences which I have italicized are clearly a paraphrase of those in the famous article in the major newspaper *O Seculo* on 15 Oct [document #28], except for the phrase which I have underlined.

#79 Nov 13   DEPOSITION OF XAVIER TUNA

13 Nov 1917

(Deposition concerning August and September)
Deposition of Joaquim Xavier Tuna, from Lapas,
Torres Novas county, age 45

"On 13 Aug I saw the sun lower in the sky at the time of the apparition. It never lowered as much as that time, even on Oct 13. All objects around me turned yellow. The people, hearing a noise at the foot of the oak bush, began to flee. Some men, who were on the top of a tree, fell without it doing them any harm. On seeing what was happening, I told the people not to flee, because it was Our Lady who was appearing. Then the crowd stopped fleeing, and almost all took off their hats and many knelt.

On 13 Sep I saw a big cross come out from the sun and head to the side of the east. Its pace was not very hurried. At times it appeared, at others it vanished, until it was out of sight. I saw other things I cannot explain. In Lapas parish there were persons who saw the cross at the same time."

Source: A copy of a deposition of Xavier Tuna, 13 Nov; Doc Crit III book 1 pp 678, 679.

Note: It seems clear that this statement and the next five were gathered by Father Formigao. They are in his handwriting and come from his archives; Doc Crit III book 1 p 678, footnote 1. The depositions are not signed, and it seems likely that these individuals, like most Portuguese at the time, could not write.

#80 Nov 13   DEPOSITION OF JOAQUIM VIEIRA

(Deposition concerning August and September)
Deposition of Joaquim Vieira of Assentiz, Torres Novas county, age 47

"On 13 Aug a little white cloud appeared, which moved from the south to the north in the direction of the east, taking on various beautiful colors. The sun lost its shine completely, being able to be stared at, and changed colors. On 13 Sep I was at the same place, on the side facing north. I was a little upset at not seeing anything extraordinary, like the past month. Persons around me shouted that they had seen [something]. Suddenly I saw something like a soap bubble which children make by blowing with a little straw. When I first saw it, I kept quiet. I saw it a second time and asked out loud: What is that? I can't explain what it was. I lost sight of it a dozen meters above the oak bush. My wife did not see it because she was looking the other way. [Then] I did not look at the sun. The same month I also saw a blue mark in a dark-colored cloud, going away from the sun."

Source: A copy of a statement of Joaquim Vieira, 13 Nov; Doc Crit III book 1 pp 680-681.

#81 Nov 13   DEPOSITION OF ANTONIO RIBEIRO

(Deposition concerning July)
Antonio Ribeiro, from Moita, Fatima parish, age 53

"On July 13 I was near the children. When they arrived, they knelt and began to pray the rosary. When they finished saying it, Lucia said: 'Kneel all who can.' At once I heard her make some questions. Among others she said: 'A person from Pedrogram asks the Lady for a cure or to take her to heaven.' She also asked for a conversion of a family of Athoguia and another from

Fatima. At last I heard her say: "The Lady said that she would work a miracle, so that all would believe.'"

Source: A copy of a statement of Antonio Ribeiro, 13 Nov; Doc Crit III book 1 p 682.

#82 Nov 13   DEPOSITION OF ANTONIO BAPTISTA
(Deposition concerning July)
Antonio Baptista, from Moita, Fatima parish, age 50

"On July 13 I was at the Cova da Iria. I knelt near the children and kept the sun from their heads with an umbrella. Lucia said two or three times: 'Kneel all who can.' She knelt. I seemed to hear a little breeze, a buzz. The little one asked: 'What do you want me to do, my Lady, that I might do.' At once she added: 'There is a person in Pedogram who asks that you convert all of his/her family. There is a woman from Fatima who asks you to convert her whole family. And there is a man from Athoguia who asks Our Lady to take him to heaven as soon as possible. And I ask Our Lady to cure the lame.' She paused a little after each question and petition. Afterwards she said that Our Lady had said that she would make them better, or if not she would give them help to control themselves. When Lucia was listening for a reply, I seemed to hear a buzzing like that of a guitar. When she arose, she said: 'Turn toward there if you want to see her.' I forgot to say that she asked the Lady to make a miracle so that all would believe."

Source: A copy of a deposition of Antonio Baptista, 13 Nov; Doc Crit III book 1 p 683.

#83 Nov 13   DEPOSITION OF MARIA DE JESUS
(Deposition concerning July)
Maria de Jesus, of Boleiros, Fatima parish, age 34

"On 13 July I was at the feet of the children. Lucia brought a basket of flowers and covered the oak bush with them. Afterward she knelt and prayed the rosary, holding in her hand a lighted candle that a lady had given her. She then talked and said that all who could should kneel. At once she asked: 'What does my mother want?' A little later she asked: 'Then you want nothing more of me?' Afterward she made various petitions for persons from Pedrogram, Authoguia and Aljustrel for cures and conversions. She also asked if she could make a miracle so that all the people would believe. After hearing the reply, she said: 'Adios. All look there.' An hour later the child said to me that the Lady had said she would make a miracle on the last day so all would believe."

Source: A copy of a deposition of Maria de Jesus, 13 Nov; Doc Crit III book 1 p 684.

#84 Nov 13   DEPOSITION OF MARIA PEREIRA

Deposition of Maria Rosa Pereira, age 63, from Casal de Fonte, Assentis parish ...

"On 13 Oct I was near the children when the apparition occurred. I saw them well from where I was. When they arrived, they said the rosary, the Confiteor and the act of contrition. Meanwhile, people pressed in more and more, so that the children were in danger of being squashed, despite the efforts of those who surrounded them to hold back the wave [of people]. All wanted to see and hear from close up, which was impossible. Jacinta, distracted and very fearful, cried because of the shoves she felt. Lucia caressed her and asked her not to cry, because nobody would harm her. Francisco also was distracted by the people. Suddenly Lucia said that they should look at the oak bush. The face of the child became more beautiful than it had been, becoming flushed and her lips were compressed. At once I heard her say: 'What do you want? You said that on 13 Oct you would tell me what you wanted.' She was silent for a moment, and then added: 'Yes, but if you do not make some miracle, the people [will] say it is a lie.' After that she was silent for a little. Then she said: 'But what should I ask for? They asked that you save all these people and take them to heaven, and that you cure these sick.' This time there were many people asking. I don't know to whom the little one referred. She said further the following: 'I have come to talk here several times and have never asked your name.' After hearing the response, she said: 'She is the Lady of the Rosary.' Then leaning toward her mother, who was near, but without turning to the people, she said more loudly: 'The Lady said to look at the sun, that she wants to show herself in the stars.' And then Jacinta exclaimed: 'Now my heavenly mother is leaving, look where she is going.' In turn the little boy said: 'I don't see her anymore.' Jacinta turned to him and said: 'She is straight ahead of' ...."

Source: A copy of a deposition of Maria Rosa Pereira, 13 Nov; Doc Crit III book 1 pp 685-686.

Note: In the text I omitted that Father Antonio Lopes Larangeiro, chaplain at Mareiras Grandes, said that he knows Pereira well and she is absolutely worthy of belief.

#85 Nov 18   MIRACLE OF FATIMA

(Gist– In one long type-written page the writer of a letter to this newspaper gives the names and ages of the children and very briefly describes the first five apparitions.)

On 13 Oct it rained very finely in the morning, increasing gradually until it became torrential, impelled by a strong wind. At the apparition site they had built a kind of trapezoid, having a cross at the top and two lighted oil lanterns suspended from it. And on the oak bush there was an arch of flowers, and next to it some small altars. The shepherds arrive. The rain diminishes. The shepherds kneel and pray. The hour arrives and the shepherds order the people to shut their umbrellas and then that they remove their hats. The rain stopped completely. The rapidly moving clouds open clearings, and the sun appears, sending out golden rays, in the normal sense.

But it changed to a dull silver, becoming at once surrounded by scarlet flames and at a given moment it was animated by a rapid movement of rotation, seeming to loosen itself from the sky and to fall toward the earth, and it changed to pale purple. It changed at once to green, and at last to bright yellow that lasted longer and was so intense that it passed the sun color to the earth, with the atmosphere and objects nearby appearing to us to be clothed in the same color.

Our blood ran cold. And to leave no doubt in our minds we looked, after such a stupendous phenomenon, at the sun, to which the least change [from normal] did not return after the end of the yellow color.

One cannot describe the wave of faith which passed over the crowd, which I calculate at 100,000 (the most common calculation is 50,000). Among the crowd which packed the slope, many hands were raised in the air and loud voices called to the Blessed Virgin! A grandiose spectacle!

Lucia was carried on [someone's] shoulders, saying: "That they reform, that the war was ending and that shortly our brave soldiers would return to Portugal from France." The crowd broke up. We went to the shepherds' house and admired the firmness of their replies. Francisco said that he saw the Lady with her hands up, but he heard nothing she said. It is Lucia who talked to the Lady. She said that she was very beautiful, that she came barefooted, with dress and mantle of white, her hands up, where a rosary was hanging, and that she opened her hands when she talked. Jacinta said she saw the Lady in the same form and heard what Lucia heard. I asked this one what she saw in the sun, and she said that it was St. Joseph, giving peace to the world, and that the Lady descended over the oak bush and said: "That she was Our Lady of the Rosary, that the war was going to end and we can expect shortly the return of our soldiers, that men must reform and pray the rosary every day so that God will pardon their sins, that they should make a little chapel at the site where she talked to us, as the people wished, and finally she blessed them.["]

We guarantee the truth of what we have stated.

Joaquim Gregorio Tovares

Source: *Concelho de Macao*, Macao, 18 Nov; Doc Crit I pp 407-409.

Notes: *Concelho de Macao* was a literary and news publication, a bi-monthly. This article is an abridged and edited version of his earlier letter. See Annex #58.

#86 Nov 21 IMPRESSIVE NOTES—(SERRA LETTER)

Fatima

13 Nov 1917

Today is exactly one month since tens of thousands of persons, attracted by the repeated promises of three ignorant peasant children, met on the moor of Fatima.

I was also there; not from a firm conviction that the important events which had been forecast would be realized, but because I was obliged by gratitude for a big favor. The morning of the 13th appeared rainy and threat-ening, but the whirling, impetuous wind, accompanied by a strong down-pour, was not enough to conquer the sincere faith of some and the burning curiosity of others.

(Gist– A paragraph describes the crowds going to Fatima.)

Arriving at the site of the astounding occurrences, I was impressed by the enormous crowd, figured in the many thousands, ... and which gathered together in an orderly, respectful composure, which touched [us].

Not being able to break through to the famous oak bush, ... I remained on the road in a place where everything could be seen well. Up to me came the distant echoes of religious songs, in which the crowd re-iterated the Faith, while thousands of hearts anxiously awaited the solemn hour.

The three children had just arrived, naïve and simple protagonists of the most grandiose and extraordinary spectacle which I ever had the opportu-nity to see. The august moment was arriving. <u>The nasty rain stopped, and toward the north there is seen, in a small opening in the sky, the clear blue, breaking the leaden clouds.</u>

It occurred to my mind, already moved by what I witnessed, that this cloudy morning, with a sky weighed down by dark gray clouds, might be the backdrop to a grandiose spectacle to come. On the watch the hand showed about 2:00, and meanwhile the crowd looked in anxious contemplation for the marvelous event that was to invigorate their faith.

In some candid souls there already arose the fear that the predicted event would not take place, when suddenly, at the voice of the seer, that immense crowd was stirred in a brouhaha indicating fear and surprise; they raised their heads to the sky where thousands of frightened eyes watched the sun in the blue, visible to all, without the intensity of its rays hurting the retina or bothering their vision. It was crowned by various colors, in a fast rotary motion, at times appearing to detach itself from the celestial vault and approach the earth.

The spectators, looking at each other, showed a yellow color to each other, and on the orangish yellow horizon, wherever their eyes fell, they saw beams of pale light, taking an oval form, which seemed to be placed at equal distance apart and reflecting on the earth.

Such was the surprising phenomenon that all had the opportunity to observe, and which from some brought forth a sincere confession of ardent faith, and prompted a benevolent outlook in others, in whom the scorching wind of skepticism singed the flower of faith.

What should one say? It is beyond doubt that we are in the presence of events that deeply moved the crowd, many not hesitating to call it a miracle. Was there one? It would be bold to affirm it. Nevertheless, it is certain that in sound criticism we cannot, and should not, as we appraise the events, separate them from the circumstances that preceded, accompanied and followed them. Assuming that … everything is explained by natural causes, one circumstance is enough to give it the stamp of miraculous—[that] it was forecast for the exact day and time six months ahead of the time and even on the very day.

Coincidence? But would it not be admirable and surprising, the coincidence of the event with such firm and advance notice?

(Gist– The events were public and attracted all kinds of people, including enemies.)

And in sum, if everyone did not confess themselves to be believers, all appeared to be overcome by the Power which produced such a prodigy. (Gist– The majority, unlettered, felt the hand of God was there.)

(Gist– A long paragraph discusses the philosophy of faith and reason, and the next two challenge the men of science to accept what they cannot explain.)

L. S.

Source: *A Ordem*, 21 Nov; Doc Crit III book 1 p 728; Jaki, pp 114, 115.

Note: Although the writer merely identifies himself as L.S., the virtually exact wording of this article and the letter written by Serra to his daughter on 18 Oct makes it clear that the letter in this article was written by Joao Maria Lucia Serra; Doc Crit III book 1 p 690. See #44.

#87 Nov 24   LETTTER OF ADELAIDE GREGO

(Gist– A short personal letter from Adelaide Grego calls the 13 Oct event, which she attended, a great prodigy, where the Virgin showed her power. It is important solely because the writer says: "… what occurred at Fatima was … a great prodigy and here in Torres Novas at the same hour something was also seen in the sun, but that by the description that they make to me it cannot compare.")

Source: A letter of Adelaide Grego of Torres Novas to a friend; Doc Crit III book 1 p 740.

#88 Dec?   TO LIBERAL PORTUGUESE

(A pamphlet published by the Civil Register and
Association of Freethinkers)

(Gist– The first two page gives the reaction of the Church to the new laws which had been imposed against it, and the third discusses what a miracle is. Then it discusses Fatima.)

(Gist– There were those who arranged the event at Fatima. Rich people in cars, humbler ones in carriages and peasants went there to attend) a ridiculous fantasy, in which they inculcated in the naïve people a mass hallucination of the supposed apparition of the Virgin Mother of Jesus of Nazareth. The three children [were] hallucinated or pre-prepared to serve as accomplices in this vile and shameful hoax, profitable and at the same time mercenary and clerical reactionary!

(Gist– Since the childrens' word is not enough and nobody saw the Virgin with the children) they invented those who saw the sun dance the fandango or chifaro with the stars at a certain time on 13 Oct, on the 8th anniversary of the assassination of Francisco Precer, that is in the very 20th century, and not on a similar day and month of 1917!

(Gist– In several paragraphs, it complains of those who gave publicity to the hoax and urges a propaganda campaign and public education for their cause.)

Source: A pamphlet published by the above cited organization in late 1917. It covered five pages in Doc Crit III. It failed to claim that there were people who saw nothing unusual; Doc Crit III book 1 pp 766-770.

#89 Dec 3   GONCALO ALMEIDA GARRETT LETTER

C. Branco 3 11 17
St. Francis' Day
Reverent Father,
Forgive me for the delay in replying to your question, made in a letter to my wife, concerning the extraordinary happenings in Fatima with regard to the mid-day sun.

They were the following:

1. The phenomena lasted some eight to ten minutes.
2. The sun lost its blinding brilliance, taking on the aspect of the moon, being able to be looked at easily.
3. During this period of time, the sun thrice showed a rotary movement on its periphery, sending out sparks of light from its edges, like that of the well-known fireworks wheel.
4. This rotary movement of the edges of the sun, thrice manifested and thrice interrupted, was rapid and lasted 8 to 10 minutes, more or less.
5. Next the sun took on a violet color, then orange, spreading these colors on the earth. Finally, it recovered its brilliance and splendor, impossible to be looked at by the naked eye.
6. It was a little after mid-day and [with the sun] near its zenith (which is of the utmost importance) when these events took place.

I would ask you, Sir, the favor of telling me if this account is confirmed.

The bishop of Portalegre and Mrs. Maria de Jesus Rapozo relate that, being in Torres Novas with others on Oct 20th [a Saturday] at an unstated time, they saw the rotary movement of the sun and the change of colors. The same lady states that these manifestations in the sun were very different from those in Fatima and did not have the greatness of those of Oct 13. It is of utmost importance to know what these differences are, for she was present at both. I would like a clarification of the differences.

The sun is incomparably greater than the earth and has its own slow rotary movement, which does not occur in a few moments or minutes on three [different] times.

In answer to your question, I would say that I do not consider the phenomena seen and observed in the sun to be related to astronomy, properly speaking, but rather to meteorological phenomena of the earth's atmosphere on our image of the sun, as regards the colors and its shine being like that of the moon, and also as regards its apparent rotation.

(Gist– These meteorological effects are weaker at noon than late in the afternoon. The phenomena seen at Fatima were less likely to happen at midday than at dawn or dusk, which gives them more value and importance.) Up to now, nobody had seen the fiery rotation of the sun, and now everyone is seeing them many days and times. A lot of this is imagination.

I want to put some questions to one of the meteorological observatories in the country and perhaps to the astronomical observatory in Coimbra.

(Gist– You did not mention one very important matter, which I understand occurred at the other apparitions—a cloud of smoke rising from the area. It happened six times. At the last apparition my whole family saw it, but were far away and thought it was a fire or incense. You should get witnesses for all six apparitions. I consider it very important and miraculous. I also think you should get testimony to show the difference between the manifestation of the 13th, [and those] which everybody now sees, but did not see before.)

(Gist– I am surprised you did not mention Lucia's prediction about the war ending. It is very important. Was she wrong? Actually, the armistice between Germany and Russia may be the beginning of peace.)

It is essential that the young girl be isolated from so many, many questions. I repeat, it is urgent that so many questions be avoided.

My son, Jose Maria, does not refuse to give a report on what he witnessed at Fatima, as he told me. But a letter directly from you, making the request and not mentioning my suggestion, would have greater weight.

Forgive me this letter with my frank and straightforward observations and declarations, but it was necessary. Please say a Hail Mary for my intentions, I need it.

Yours sincerely, with greatest respect,

Goncalo de Almeida Garrett

Source: A letter of 3 Dec from Goncalo Garrett to Father Manuel Formigao; Doc Crit III book 1 pp 771-774.

Note: The letter was published only sixty years later; Jaki, p 125. Although the text of this letter is not clear, a letter from the writer's wife makes it clear that the writer is stating what he saw at Fatima, not what he had heard and read. Her letter is given here as #89A.

#89A Dec 4   MARIA DE PROENCA GARRETT LETTER

Castillo Branco 4-12-1917

Reverend Sir,

What must you have thought of my silence since you were always so solicitous in answering my letters. But the fault is not mine, I passed on your request at once and both my husband and son were willing to satisfy [your request], but my husband, on account of his affairs, was only able to write (his account) today, and my son, who due to his natural laziness, puts off from day to day what he had to do, has not yet written the description of what he saw. But I won't [let him] put it off and when he has done it, I will send it to you.

I believe he was very impressed by what he saw and perhaps interiorly it did him some good, but what they said to you is unfortunately right. There was no conversion, which I so much want and ask of God, that he act and be a practicing Christian, without fear of human respect. Outwardly he remains the same.

Who can convince me of the proven miracles worked at Fatima, because I would like to believe that Our Lady appeared, and at the same time, last Sunday's gospel impressed [me], and I wonder if all the signs which have been noted could be the beginning of the end.

(Gist– She talks of the archbishop of Braga and Evora and wonders again about the end of the world.)

Excuse all my [writing] faults and accept my respects and those of my sons.

Maria de Joaquina Tovares de Proenca

Source: Letter of Maria de Proenca Garrett to Father Formigao; Doc Crit III book 1 pp 777, 778.

#90 Dec 18   JOSE DE ALMEIDA GARRETT'S ACCOUNT

18-12-1917

I am going to relate, in a brief and concise manner, without any statements that would conceal the truth, what I saw in Fatima on Oct 13, 1917.

(Gist– The times I refer to are the official war time. It is important to note this, since I could not determine exactly when the sun reached its zenith.)

I arrived at mid-day. The rain, which had fallen lightly and persistently all morning, combined with a blustery wind, continued fretfully, as if threatening to drown everyone. The low and heavy sky was gray and its dark clouds, water-laden, predicted abundant rain for a long time to come. I remained on the road, in the shelter of the roof of the car, and somewhat disdainful toward the place where they said the apparition would be seen, not daring to step on the sodden and muddy ground of the freshly plowed fields. I must have been little more than 100 meters from the high wooden posts, topped by a rough cross, seeing distinctly the wide circles of people around them, who, with their umbrellas open, seemed like a vast arena of mushrooms.

A little after 1:00 the children, to whom Our Lady (as they declare) appointed the place, day and hour of the apparition, arrived at the site. Hymns were intoned and sung by the people who encircled them.

At a certain moment this great mass of people, so varied and compact, closed their umbrellas and uncovered their heads, in a gesture which must have been humility or respect, but which left me surprised and admiring, because the rain, with blind persistency, now poured down on their heads and drenched them through. Later I was told that this crowd, which ended up by kneeling in the mud, had obeyed the voice of a child.

It must have been one thirty (14 hours and a half) when there rose up, on the precise spot where the children were, a pillar of smoke, a delicate slender bluish column that went straight up about two meters, perhaps, above their heads and then evaporated. The phenomenon lasted for some seconds and was perfectly visible to the naked eye. Not having noted the time it lasted, I cannot affirm if it was more or less than a minute. The smoke dissipated quickly and, after some time, the phenomenon was repeated a second and third time. On these three occasions, and particularly on the last one, the slender posts stood out distinctly in the dull gray atmosphere.

I looked there with my binoculars. I could see nothing except the columns of smoke, but I was convinced that they were produced by some incense burner, not shaken … Afterward, trustworthy persons told me this used to happen on the 13th of the five months before, and on these days, as on this one, nothing was burned there, nor did anyone make a fire.

While I was looking at the place of the apparitions in a serene and cold expectation, and with diminishing curiosity, because a long time had passed without anything to arouse my attention, I heard a loud brouhaha from thousands of voices, and saw the crowd, which spread out on the big field and reached my feet, or concentrated in small groups around the trees, or on the low terraces which restrained the land, turn their backs away from the point to which up to then it had directed its desires and anxieties and look at the sky on the opposite side.

It was about two o'clock. The sun a few minutes before had broken through the thick layer of clouds which hid it and shone clearly and intensely. I turned to the magnet which was drawing all eyes and I could see it like a disk with a clean-cut rim, the edge alive, luminous and bright, but which did not hurt [the eyes].

I do not agree with the comparison which I have heard made, even in Fatima, that of a dull, silver disc. It was lighter, more alive, richer and with variations, having something of the luster of a pearl. It did not in the least resemble the moon on a clear pure night, because one saw it and felt it to be a living star. It was not spherical, like the moon, nor did it have the same tones nor shadings. It looked like a glazed wheel made of mother-of-pearl. This is not a banal, poetic comparison. My eyes saw it this way. It also could not be confused with the sun seen through fog (for there was no fog at this time), because it was not opaque, diffused or veiled. At Fatima it had light and heat and appeared clean-cut, with a well-defined rim, like [the edge] of a card table.

The arch of the sky was mottled with light cirrus clouds, with slits of blue coming through here and there, but sometimes the sun stood out in patches of clear [blue] sky. The clouds passed lightly from west to east and did not obscure the light of the sun (which did not hurt), giving the impression of passing behind it, easily comprehensible and explainable, but sometimes these flecks, which came as white, seemed to take on tones of pink or diaphanous blue as they passed before the sun.

It was remarkable that over a long time one could fix one's eyes on this day-star, this brazier of heat and light, without any pain or blinding of the retina. This phenomenon, except for two brief interruptions, when the fierce sun sent out more sparkling and refulgent rays, which forced us to look away, must have lasted about ten minutes.

This pearly disk had a vertiginous movement. This was not the sparkling of a heavenly body in full life. It spun on itself with crazy velocity. Then suddenly one heard a clamor, like a cry of anguish, from all the people. The sun, keeping its speed of rotation, loosened itself from the firmament and advanced, terrifying,[11] upon the earth, threatening to crush us with its huge, fiery weight. They were seconds of terrifying impression.

---

[11] *Sanguinio.* This is surely an error for *sanguineo,* meaning "bloodthirsty" or "terrifying."

During the solar event, which I have just described in detail, there were changes in the color of the atmosphere. I cannot be precise about the time, because two months have already passed, and I did not take notes. I recall it was not at the beginning, and I rather think toward the end.

Looking at the sun, I noticed everything around me was becoming darkened. I looked at the nearest objects and [then] extended my glance further afield as far as the horizon. I saw everything an amethyst color. Objects around me, the sky and the atmosphere had the same color. An oak tree nearby threw a dark shadow on the ground. Fearing that I was suffering from an injury of the retina, an improbable hypothesis because, in that case, one could not see things purple-colored, I turned away and shut my eyes, keeping my hands before them to intercept all the light. With my back still turned, I opened my eyes and saw the landscape and the air with the same purple.

The impression was not that of an eclipse. I saw the full eclipse of the sun on the 8th, when I was at Viseu. As the moon progresses to hide the sun, the light keeps graying until everything turns hazy and black. One's sight reaches only a small circle, in which the objects keep getting more and more vague, until they are lost in darkness. The temperature falls considerably and one would say that life on earth is dead. At Fatima the atmosphere, although purple, remained transparent to the edge of the horizon, which could be distinguished and seen clearly. And I did not have the impression of a stopping of the energy of the universe.

Continuing to look at the sun, I noticed that the atmosphere had become lighter. Soon after, I heard a peasant woman who was near me shout out in tones of astonishment: "That lady is yellow." And in fact everything, both far and near, now had changed, taking on the color of old yellow damask. People looked as if they were suffering from yellow jaundice, and I smiled at seeing them look so ugly and unattractive. Laughter was heard. My own hand had the same tone of yellow.

Days later I tried to look at the sun for some short instances. After looking away I saw, after some moments, yellow spots, irregular in shape. I did not see everything of the same color, as if in the air a topaz had been volatilized, but I saw stains or meshes, which moved around with the movement of my eye.

All of the phenomena which I have described were observed by me calmly and serenely, without emotion or fear. It is for others to explain or interpret them. To finish I should affirm that never before nor after 13 Oct did I see similar solar or atmospheric phenomena.

Source: An account by Jose Maria de Proenca de Almeida Garrett for Father Manuel Formigao; De Marchi, pp 137-139; Doc Crit III book 1 pp 793-798; *Fatima: The Great Sign,* pp 60-63.

Note: The date of the account was not given. The date at the top was added by another person, and was undoubtedly derived from a letter from his mother to Father Formigao, which follows as #90A. The eclipse referred to here is surely that of 28 May 1900; Doc Crit II p 326.

Note: His statement that it was 14:30 [14 hours and a half, in text] is clearly in error, since it immediately follows his statement that it was about one thirty and later he says that it was two o'clock or 14:00.

Note: The writer was a lawyer, but not practicing law; Jaki, p 128. I noted earlier that he was surely the same Jose Almeida Garrett who was the director of the newspaper *Beira Baixa.* See #52. This account is the one I referred to in the introduction to this book, pages 1 and 2.

#90A Dec 18   MARIA DE PROENCA GARRETT LETTER

Castillo Branco, 18-12-1917

Reverend Father,

Only today did my no-good son hand me the account that I had asked him to make about what he saw at Fatima. He omitted only one thing, that he saw the rotation of the sun three times.

Does this satisfy you, tell me frankly, since it does not entirely satisfy me? And in regard to the chapel are they thinking about it or not?

If you know anything more, please tell me. It seems to me that what happened on the 8th [of Dec] in Lisbon was already a result of the miracle of Fatima. May Our Lady continue to protect us and the Democrats remain defeated. Compliments, etc.

Maria J. Tavares de Proenca (Garrett)

Source: Letter of Maria de Proenca Garrett to Father Manuel Formigao; Doc Crit III book 1 p 793.

Note: The writer undoubtedly included her son's account of the sun dance (Annex #90) with this letter. Her reference to 8 Dec apparently refers to the coup d'etat of that date which temporarily unseated the anti-clerical government of Portugal. For other letters to or from her, see Annex #24A, #38, and #66. Four of her letters to Father Formigao are not included in this Annex; Doc Crit III book 1 pp 126, 292, 415, 571.

#91 Dec 27   DEPOSITION OF FATHER BRAS DAS NEVES, 27 DEC 1917

Father Francisco Braz das Neves, co-adjutor of the parish of Freixianda .... Declared: that he interviewed on Oct 20, 1917, the two girls of Fatima, to whom it is said that Our Lady has appeared at .... the Cova da Iria .... On the 13th of the month from May to October, inclusive. The oldest, Lucia affirmed to him that when Our Lady appeared to her on October 13 she promised that the war would end on that same day. Further, he declared: that he met her again on December 8 and noted to her that the war did not end on the designated day nor up to that date; she responded that maybe she was mistaken, since her companion, Jacinta, had said that the Lady said in her turn that the war would end, yes, but if the people reformed.

And to be true, I make the present declaration and being required, I swear.

Freixianda, 27 Dec 1917
Father Francisco Braz das Neves

Source: Deposition of Father Neves to the Ourem [inquiry board], 27 Dec 1917; Doc Crit I pp 221, 222.

Note: This inquiry was requested by the bishop of the diocese; Doc Crit I pp 213, 214. This deposition and the two which follow were apparently witnessed by Father Faustino Ferreira, dean of the deanery of Ourem, although he did not sign them. I have chosen to call his inquiry group a board.

#92 Dec 30   DEPOSITION OF VASCONCELLOS

Deposition of Luiz .... Vasconcellos

For months now there have been various versions that Our Blessed Virgin was appearing in the area of Fatima to some little shepherds. I knew of the versions, and that a large number of people from all classes were coming to the spot indicated by the shepherds, chiefly on the 13th of each month ... These rumors began to interest me and thus I tried to learn what was happening. Talking to some people who were there on Sept 13, some said they saw nothing, others that they had seen a star, and others gave fantastic descriptions. Such variations in the testimony convinced me that it was a "joke" with no base. This conviction was strengthened days later when a respected cleric of this county told me that he had learned casually that the little shepherds had at home a book that described the miracles of Our

Lady of Lourdes and Our Lady of La Salette. (Gist– He was like other clerics in the country—cautious. I was little inclined to accept the shepherds' account. Young children have a tendency to imagine things; and it might also be a fraud of some kind.) If it failed it could hurt our religion. Thus, from then on, when the case was mentioned, I was appeared doubtful rather than hopeful.

I was of this inclination when on Oct 13 I went for the first time to the site. I was curious, not a pilgrim. (Gist– A long paragraph describes the people going there.)

(Gist– As I said, I left about 8:00 with my brothers Antonio and Fernando.) Right after leaving it began to rain heavily, turning the road into a continuous quagmire. The wind blew sharply, especially in the Fatima heights. A heavy traffic kept going on the roads. We went through Fatima and continued on the road which connects it with Batalha. The rain continued falling torrentially. At about a kilometer away we saw a crowd of many thousands, who tended to gather on the hills. Were there 30,000 or 50,000? Nobody could say for certain. We stopped. Hundreds of wagons and cars were filling completely the muddy road. At the bottom of the valley within the crowd, I could spot some madeira poles which formed a trapezoid and were topped by a little cross, as I afterward noted from more close up. Now the rain was less heavy. The sun was still hidden behind heavy, dark clouds. Around the trapezoid to which I referred was a numerous group. It was the spot pointed out by the seers, where all attention was concentrated. (Gist– The landscape there had little interest.) I met enough acquaintances, both from Lisbon and other places remote from there. Almost all asked my opinion, perhaps with special interest because I live in this area. To all I replied, smiling incredulously, that it was all a "joke"—that as a Catholic I was not ashamed to admit the possibility of a miracle, but because I am Catholic is why I did not believe, unless this miracle would occur in an obvious and indisputable way; and that even the clergy in the county also doubted, according to what they say. [Gist– He mentions a number of people he met, including Jose Rino, of Alcobaca.]

I tried to get near the spot where the shepherds were ... some 200 meters from the road, but failed, so tight was the circle of people around them. Thus I could neither see nor hear them on this occasion. I could only tell they were praying. I returned to the top of the road and approached Jose Rino and wife, who were near their limousine, talking with various people. These childhood friends asked my opinion, which I expressed as I said earlier. They were almost indignant, and said to me that "for them there was not the least doubt of a miracle, since they were there on Sep 13 and witnessed

in the sun extraordinary lights, exactly at the time and place indicated by
the shepherds, that the clergy was not well informed, and that if I doubted I
should wait." Since it would be touchy to insist, I kept quiet, but remained
absolutely convinced that I would see nothing. I recalled then, as I had
before on various times, the principle of Gustave Le Bon [a French psycholo-
gist] that, in essence, says that an individual in a crowd cannot avoid the
hypnotic current that dominates it. I had to be on guard, not let myself be
influenced. This friend of mine, taking out his watch, told me—there is still
five minutes—look at the sun at one o'clock—that was the time announced
by the shepherds—[and] then you can tell me.

This surprised me, since wherever I looked and where I thought all were
looking was where the shepherds were. I was aware that on this day they
had claimed that something would happen so that afterward no one could
doubt. The sky at this moment was leaden. The rain had stopped. The sun
was not seen, covered by clouds, and nobody would say it would show again
on this day, so rainy and harsh. At 1:00 exactly I heard a great clamor. My
friends shouted to me—Look, look—but at first I only saw that the clouds,
moving lightly, left the sun in the open. Suddenly I saw an intensely rose-
colored edge around the sun, that looked like a dull silver plate, as someone
has already said, at the same time that I had the impression that it had
moved from its original position. Diaphanous vaporous clouds went by, a
little purple, a little orange. In various points of the line of the horizon,
contrasting with the gray of the sky, I also saw yellowish spots. On the landscape and people I also noticed spots of rose and yellow color. The clamor
was all the time greater. This did not last seconds, it lasted perhaps minutes.
On seeing these manifestations, which I did not doubt for a minute were
due to the All-powerful God, an indescribable impression took hold of me.
I know only that I yelled: "I believe, I believe." And tears fell from my eyes,
astounded and ecstatic, in this demonstration of Divine Power. I know also
that I felt no shadow of fear or terror. If I were not Catholic, at this moment
I would have converted. I recall also that I did not kneel, but the majority
of the people knelt, ignoring the great muck. Then did these phenomena
escape the foresight of science but not of the little shepherds of the hills, who
forecast them with truly mathematical precision? [That is] too much, being
so amazing, so marvelous?!

I went to get my brothers, who told me they saw the same thing, like the
other people I met, varying a little in what they saw on the sun. To the persons to whom I had said that it was a "joke," I told them that I saw, and that
now I was absolutely convinced we were looking at a real miracle. The sun
was shining now intensely and did not cease to shine that day and it did not

rain again either. Almost at the moment of leaving I met my friend Emilio Infante da Camara, who said he had gone to see the shepherds and they told him that the war would end shortly or in eight days (I can't be precise). ... The crowd began to break up....

Some weeks later I returned to the apparition site to interview the shepherds. I wanted to know these children. (Gist– He names other people who went with him.) We asked at the church where the shepherd girls could be found. They said they were probably at the apparition site, and that the shepherd boy, who was with them and to whom the Virgin also appeared was near and they would call him. (Gist– He arrived and they invited him to go with them in the car. They asked him questions, but he didn't say much, being so interested in the parts of the car. The writer then describes the site.) We knelt and prayed also. The little Lucia, to whom the Virgin appeared, was talking to strangers. We waited for them to stop and approached her. (He describes her and her dress.) She described the apparition of the Virgin in the way that is well known to all—that the Virgin said to them "that we have offended God much and must mend our ways, that we should build a chapel there in honor of the Lady of the Rosary, that the war would end shortly." My sister asked her what she saw in the sun at the time of the miracle, and she replied "that she saw St. Joseph." I asked her also if she did not fear that if a miracle did not occur the people would kill her, thinking that she had deceived them all. She told me, with some force, "that she knew well that the miracle would happen and therefore she had not thought of such a danger." She also said that before she had heard tell of the miracles of the Lady of Lourdes. A woman, said to be her aunt, helped her on some questions and made various remarks on a secret which they had and would tell to no one, although they already had made various seductive offers and even had threatened to leave them in a well or would burn them if they did not reveal it. They also said that the offerings which they were getting were for the construction of a chapel, and that they were kept with another local lady. They also told us there that the little one was very tired with the constant series of questions that all the people asked. The girl they referred to seemed to me at times to be alert and at times to be distracted. ...

On returning, we stopped again at the Fatima church, and there we were able to talk with the other little one, whose name I forget. She got on the running board of the car which was carrying us, but we did not succeed in getting a word from her, despite our best efforts. She was jovial and had expressive eyes. She must have been eight or nine.

(Gist– He then offers his thoughts on the idea that the events of 13 Oct at Fatima were miraculous and on Lucia's "false prophecy.") Any scientific or philosophic consideration is not appropriate for this deposition, and thus I have limited myself to narrating in detail that which I saw and observed, with all preciseness and impartiality, dispassionately, to which I again swear by my Christian faith and affirm on my honor.

Villa Nova de Ourem, 30 Dec 1917
Luiz Antonio Vieira de Magalhaes e Vasconcellos
Luis de Andrade e Silva, notary

Source: Deposition of Luis Vasconcellos to the Ourem [inquiry board]; Doc Crit I pp 226-237.

Note: Vasconcellos was a lawyer and nobleman, the Baron of Alvaiazere.

#93 Dec 30 DEPOSITION OF FATHER ANDRADE E. SILVA, 30 DEC 1917

I, the undersigned, Luis de Andrade e Silva …. Declare that on 13 Oct 1917 I saw on the moor of Fatima the following:

At the site where they say Our Lady has appeared …. There were more than 50,000 people, 100 cars, innumerable carriages, carts, bicycles and motorcycles who came to Fatima ….

About 12:30, sun time, more or less, the three seers arrived at the apparition site …. Almost everyone uncovered at the order of the seers. They prayed the rosary, intoned religious songs, which reached me at a distance of about 100 meters from the seers. The rain, meanwhile, had stopped. At a certain point I heard repeated exclamations of admiration and amazement, and I saw everyone gazing with naked eye at the sun. Someone at my side called my attention to the sun and I saw in it phenomena which until today I have never [again] seen.

The sun-globe, like a silver disk, turned on an imaginary axis, and at this moment seemed to descend in the atmosphere, heading toward the earth, accompanied at times by an extraordinary bright shine and by an intense heat. The sun's rays showed yellow, green, blue and purple color, according to what they say, but I saw only the yellow color.

After these few minutes, during which these phenomena happened, nobody could stare at the sun anymore, because its rays hurt the retina. Only one who witnessed these phenomena can evaluate what happened then, but cannot describe them exactly.

They tell me that these brusque movements of the sun were forecast by Lucia in August or July and they told me also that before these phenomena began Lucia said these words, whose authenticity I cannot guarantee: "Look at the sun because the Lord is going to give a sign in the sun so that all will believe." Are the phenomena which I saw on the 13th of October miraculous? I can't affirm it without fear of error, but something extraordinary, which I can't explain, occurred and which is further corroborated by the following facts:

1. (Gist— The first and last apparitions were in May and October, the months of Our Lady.)
2. The fact that at each apparition the children always said the rosary and the people accompanied them.
3. The request of the Lady, transmitted by Lucia that the people pray the rosary and do penance.
4. (Gist— The fact that there were no accidents or disorder in that huge crowd.)
5. Of the thousands of people who saw the movement of the sun on that day, as far as I know, none doubted the veracity of the phenomena, although they could not explain them.
6. (Gist— The rapid spread of the news of the apparition and the continuing crowds there.)
7. (Gist— The huge numbers who went to Communion in Fatima, Ourem and others.)

This is my declaration for all the events.
Vila Nova de Ourem
Luis de Andrade e Silva

Source: Statement of Father Andrade e Silva to the Ourem [inquiry board], 30 Dec; Doc Crit I pp 223-225.

#94 Dec 30   STATEMENT OF BARBOSA

Cartaxo, 30 Dec 1917

They asked me to tell how I was cured of the fevers that would not leave me for four months.

I greatly wanted to go to Fatima on 13 Oct, as the last month when Our Lady was to appear to the three children, and also because a miracle had been forecast so that disbelievers would become believers.

(Gist— Even though she was sick, and almost always was lying down, she was able to go to Fatima by truck. It was cold and rainy.)

I won't discuss what happened there, because it is already well known …

I will mention one thing only, because it is not mentioned in any of the descriptions I have read. I am speaking of a kind of smoke that was seen to come from the site, more or less, where the Holy Virgin was to appear. I can't locate the site exactly, because from the truck where I was, I couldn't tell exactly where it came from. It seemed to come from the crowd, but from that part which was closest to the rough arch [the altar]. There were those who noted the smoke and said it was something supernatural, but this idea passed, and it got no more attention, although this kind of smoke was repeated some three times. Later, I thought about the little smoke that no one could explain, and I thought it to be a sign of Our Lady's presence there.

A little after this the miracle occurred, well visible to all, believers and non-believers. (Gist– I felt no big improvement at this blessed time, but the next day the fever was gone. It was miraculous that there were no quarrels or accidents, and no one is known to have gotten sick there, despite the rain and cold.)

I will say that the form of seeing what was in the sky (or rather, between the sky and earth) was truly miraculous, since some saw it in one form, others in another form, and even others in a different manner not equal to any of these. In this I have known extraordinary things.

(Gist– I ask the help of Our Lady.)

Branca de Souza Lobo de Moura de Vilhena Barbosa

Source: Statement of Branca Barbosa, 30 Dec 1917; Doc Crit III book 1 pp 808-810.

Note: This statement was in the archives of Father Formigao and thus may have been given to him by the writer of this statement. Another statement, by the same woman, dated 13 Jan 1919, also in the archives of Father Formigao, describes her recovery, but notes further that at 10:00 that night (13 Oct 1917) her clothes were still wet; Doc Crit III book 1 pp 829, 830.

#95 Dec 30   MY PEREGRINATION—
[Campos pamphlet]
News of the Marvelous Events Occurring in Fatima
on October 13, 1917
By Maria Augusta Saraiva Vieira de Campos

(Gist– The author requested the approval of the bishop of Coimbra for this pamphlet on 19 Oct and received it on Nov 23.)

It was on 7 Sep that a ... lady servant of my family told me that in Fatima ... a miracle was occurring with some shepherds to whom Our Lady has been appearing since 13 May, having promised ... on 13 Oct she would make her last revelations. This promise was not made to the three children, but only to the privileged Lucia, the oldest, and the only one to hear and talk with the Lady. They say that they offered the child gold chains and money to say what she knew, but the little one would not say what she heard, ... even to her pastor, with whom she made her first communion, leaving him amazed by the way that she was prepared for this rite. On the 13th of August the administrator of the county went looking for Lucia and her companions ... who alone receive the grace of seeing the Lady, not hearing and thus not talking to her.

They said more—that many people at that site at noon, sun time, felt something extraordinary, supernatural, kneeling and praying. The same occurred on Aug 13, the day little Lucia was taken prisoner [by] the administrator. On the next Sunday, Aug 19, she asked the Lady not to let her seem to be a liar on Oct 13; and she added that the Lady made her this promise, saying: "Don't worry. All who come here will see a miracle." And thus it happened. The people, and even the pastor, frightened the child, saying if on the 13th the people do not see a miracle, right there she would be cut in pieces. To this she replied, serene and smiling: "They won't do it, no sir, because the Lady does not lie."

Thus I left Coimbra at midnight of the 12th/13th with two friends, Ermolinda Gomes Ribeiro and Mathilde Forjaz de Sampaio, by train, 3rd class [for] Chao de Macas, where we took a carriage to Vila Nova de Ourem. We arrived here at 7:00, went to the pastor to ask for communion, heard Mass with lots of people, and afterwards ate a small breakfast ... We had to walk some 18 kilometers, an uphill road. (Gist– Not disheartened, we prayed the rosary as we went. Traffic was heavy.) It was stifling hot, threatening a storm, since many clouds were stacking up in the sky.

The passengers of a little carriage that passed us ... offered to take our knapsacks, a favor we gratefully accepted ...

After a little time it began to rain, with the rain increasing, pushed by a very cold sharp wind, leaving us in no time as wet and soaked as if we came out of a bath. (Gist– The road was long and winding and people were anxious to get there on time.) At 12:30 we arrived at the apparition site.

(Gist– She describes the site and the crowd and says it was raining and muddy. They joined the crowd and prayed the rosary and sang hymns.)

The rain did not stop for an instant; we shivered from the cold, for the wind was biting. Meanwhile we heard it said: they are carrying in the shepherds. In fact some men were carrying on their shoulders the children, dressed in light blue (Gist– she describes their clothing). ....

I look at my companion Ermolinda Ribeiro and have an impression of great suffering. I ask her what she is the matter, and she says she feels such a sharp twinge that she can scarcely breathe. Her condition pained me—a sick lady, with fever almost every day, quite wet, with feet on the soaking ground, and with no means of transport to take us to a place where she could get care. I remembered to massage her chest, which she accepted. But she was cold, so wet I feared nothing would help.

I confess I had no hope of seeing the miracle. (Gist– We went up to the road to beg for cover in a car or carriage, but no one would help us.)

We were terribly disheartened, when suddenly was heard from all sides: "Miracle! Look at the sun!" The rain stopped as if by charm, people took off their hats, we felt a heat like going into a heated green house, and the disk of the sun began to appear, to be seen clearly on the grayish layer that covered the sky. The heat increased and the sun seemed to descend, to descend each time more, showing new and changing shades. We saw something like a silver veil in round shape, as if it were the full moon. Soon after it passed to a vivid purple, then yellow, then emerald green and finally to the basic color.

Shouts were heard from all sides when something like a snow-white form detached itself from the sun, brilliant, but without hurting the retina, coming toward us, turning again to the sun, and at last hiding itself a third time among the clouds. All cried and from many mouths were heard prayers, petitions, acts of faith.

The little Lucia said that Our Lady asked that they build a chapel there to Our Lady of the Rosary, that the war was coming to an end, that the Portuguese soldiers would return shortly, that the Portuguese should unite and do penance, as God was tired of so many offenses, that they should pray the rosary to avoid the punishment which hung over Portugal if they did not reform.

(Gist– They got a ride back to Ourem with cousins and were lent dry clothes to replace their own, which were still wet, and a priest gave them lodging in an inn, so they could return to Coimbra the next day.) [A prayer to the Sacred Heart follows.]

Source: A pamphlet of Maria Augusta Saraiva Vieira de Campos, published in the magazine *Jornal de Mulher*, 30 Dec 1917; Doc Crit I pp 303-310.

#96 Dec 18, 1918   DEPOSITION OF ALMEIDA LOPES

Deposition of the first witness

Jacinto d' Almeida Lopes, married, 34 years old, property owner, born and residing at Amoreira, Fatima parish, interrogated about what he witnessed concerning events which occurred at the Cova da Iria ... said that on 13 July, 1917, having gone there ahead of time, he stayed near the holm oak, where he was when the children arrived; they arrived, decorated the holm oak, knelt, said the rosary, arose, and then, with a slight delay knelt again, and everyone knelt, and Lucia began talking as if talking to someone, turned to the holm oak where her sight was fixed.

"What do you want of me?"

At this question, she waited a bit, in silence, the time for a brief response. And during this silence he heard a very faint voice, like a bee buzzing, seeming to come from the holm oak, but could not distinguish any words. Then Lucia said: "I have a request here, if you would improve a cripple from Aljustrel, convert a woman and her son from Fatima, and improve [the health] of a man from Athouguia or take him to heaven as quickly as possible."

Having said this, there was a short silence, as if awaiting a reply, and I heard the same faint voice, which I didn't hear when Lucia was talking. Lucia continued: "Could you make all these people be converted?" Silence ... after the time of a brief response, she said, as if confirming what she heard: "Yes, they say the rosary ... that they say the rosary ... yes ... all will be done." And while she said this she accompanied her words with nods of her head.

Lucia continued: "and could you not make it that all these people believe [me]?" Silence ... And at once she said: "Do you want nothing more?" She waited ... and then said: "Neither do I."

Having said this, she got up immediately and turning to the east, said: "Do you want to see Our Lady?" and pointed in the same direction.

On 13 Oct he headed, with so many people, to the apparition site, with the hope of seeing something extraordinary, since he heard that the Lady told Lucia that on the last day she would work a miracle. The rain came down strongly, but did not bother him, since his objective was seeing the extraordinary. As the hour approaches, the crowd increased, [and] he sees little birds flying over and around the holm oak.

He sees, over the crowd which surrounded the holm oak, at times [and] one after another, rise up little clouds of smoke, or what seemed to him to be smoke, like the smoke of an incense burner, when it is shaken, or like cigar smoke. He thinks at first, because he was far from the holm oak, ... that someone was smoking or making a bonfire ...but he learned that there was no fire of any sort there.

The time was near, and then, as if by charm, the rain stopped, <u>the sun broke through the thick, black clouds and showed itself dazzling with its bright rays, which soon took on colors of yellow, scarlet and green, turning objects exposed to it the same color, and then loses its shine and color—</u>being able to be stared at without hurting one's sight—<u>and takes on a rapid rotating movement, seeming to head for the earth.</u>

While he watched these marvels, all the people came out with loud exclamations. This lasted, at most, some five minutes, after which it returned to its normal state.

But he said that on the feast of Purification—2 Feb, 1918—about 3:00 in the afternoon, while at the same site, he noted in the sun the same signs as those on Oct 13, and he had not noted [them] the many other times he was there, and in virtue of what he saw, he is a real believer that it was Our Lady who talked to Lucia, and that the phenomenon that occurred on the days mentioned are supernatural. He said no more, this being his deposition, which was read to him and he confirmed by oath and signed with me.

The Parish (inquiry) of Fatima, 20 Dec, 1918
The Witness—Jacinto d'Almeida Lopes
The Pastor—Manuel Marques Ferreira

Source: Deposition of Jacinto Lopes to the Fatima parish [inquiry board]; Doc Crit I pp 273-276.

#97 Dec 31, 1918 DEPOSITION OF MANUEL GONCALVES, JR.

Deposition of the second witness

Manuel Goncalves, Jr., married, 34 years old, property owner, resident of Montelo of this parish, on being interrogated about what happened at the Cova da Iria, said that on 13 Jul, 1917, he went to the place, where he was at the time indicated by the seers for the apparition, and he noted at this time that the heat, which was extreme, began to diminish. On this occasion the children arrived, said the rosary with the people, led by Lucia, and he did not know if it was on her initiative or someone else asked her. At once he noticed that Lucia, with everyone kneeling—the people and the seers—began to speak toward the holm oak, as if talking with another person, asking questions and awaiting replies, but he was too far away to understand. After a little while she rose quickly and pointed to the east, saying: "Do you want to see Our Lady?!" On this occasion he also noticed that at a certain height over the oak a little cloud formed that rose and went to the east, causing the shine of the sun to lessen, and disappeared.

He said further that on 13 Aug … a little after the time scheduled for the apparition, when the taking of the children was reported, he noticed that there was a strong and unexplainable boom near the holm oak, which frightened all the people, who began to shout with emotion and to flee, and there were even faintings, and that near the sun a cloud formed with all the colors of the rainbow.

He declared, besides this, that on 13 Sep ... he noted that Lucia was talking near the holm oak, as if she were talking with another person, making questions and awaiting replies, and that on this occasion there passed over the holm oak an indescribable something extraordinary, seemingly white flowers, that other persons also noted such a phenomenon, saying they were stars.

"Here I take the occasion to say that on the same 13th, about 3:00 in the afternoon Father Antonio Maria de Figueiredo, esteemed professor at the Patriarchal Seminary in Santarem came to the rectory and said that he saw stars in a region below the stellar region, and that he came to the rectory precisely to tell me this declaration."

He [Goncalves] said further that on 13 Oct ... at the time given by the children for the apparitions, after the rain stopped, he saw there to arise [at] various times from the holm oak a kind of smoke, like incense on the occasion of incensing, and he heard people near him say that it was cigar smoke or a bonfire, but to him it seemed like incensing, since it seemed to him that on that occasion there were no smokers or bonfire of any kind.

With eyes fixed on the oak bush in order to see if something extraordinary would happen, in the direction of the oak, without "deliberately" looking at the sun, he noticed that while the people were shouting loudly and exclaiming about what they saw in the sun, the people as well as the trees and everything in sight took on different colors. He said no more, thus ending his deposition, which, after being read he confirmed it, swearing it to be true and signing it with me.

The Parish [inquiry board] 31 Dec, 1918

The witness—Manuel Goncalves, Jr.

The Pastor—Manuel Marques Ferreira

Source: Deposition of Manuel Goncalves, Jr., to the Fatima parish [inquiry board], 31 Dec 1918; Doc Crit I pp 277-279.

#98 Mar 2, 1919　DEPOSITION OF THERESA DE JESUS (Lucia's sister)

Deposition of the third witness

Theresa de Jesus, married, seamstress, age 24, born in Aljustrel, resident of Lomba of Fatima parish, sister of the seer Lucia, ... on being interrogated by me about what she knew concerning the happening[s] at the Cova da Iria and in her parent's house, about what her sister said about the apparitions of Our Lady, said that on 13 July, 1917, she arrived at the holm oak at the same time as her sister Lucia and her cousin-seers and saw that her sister—

and cousins—without being ordered by anyone knelt, and led the rosary, praying it with the people after telling them to kneel. She rose and stayed on foot for some time, knelt again and said to her cousin Jacinta to look for the flash, because the time was arriving. After some minutes she noted that her sister felt a strong shock, which made her exclaim: "Ay! Our Lady" ... and, turned toward the holm oak, she was talking, asking questions and awaiting responses like when one is talking with another.

She said also that the questions were: 1) What do you want. 2) that there was a cripple to be improved. 3) that she asked for improvement of a woman from Pedrogam. 4) that she asked the conversion of a woman and family of Fatima. 5) that she asked [her] to make a miracle so the people would believe. After asking these questions, [she said that] Lucia rose suddenly and turned to the east, pointed and said: "Turn there if you want to see Our Lady."

She said further that after [error for "before"] Lucia had begun the supposed dialogue with Our Lady, she was told by Jacinta, at her side, to respond to the Lady, saying, "Don't you see the Lady is ready to talk?"

(Gist– She said that Lucia was not taught to lead the rosary by her mother or siblings, as she did at the Cova da Iria, that they said the rosary to themselves at home.)

She said no more, this being her deposition, which was read to her and she swore to its truth and signed with me.

The Parish [inquiry board], 2 March, 1919

The witness—Theresa de Jesus

The Pastor—Manuel Marques Ferreira

Source: Deposition to the Fatima [inquiry board], 2 Mar 1919; Doc Crit I pp 281, 282.

#99 Mar 2, 1919   DEPOSITION OF JOAQUIM VICENTE

Deposition of the fourth witness

Joaquim Ignacia Vicente, married, born and residing in Chainca, in Santa Caterina da Serra parish, ... a trustworthy man, told me that on 13 Aug, having left work at the hour of siesta, ... he went to the Cova da Iria and that a little after the hour set for the apparitions, when the people were already disappointed and ready to leave, he heard two strong explosions similar to the detonation of a bomb or shots, coming from the direction of the holm oak, and at the same instant he saw the great mass of people fleeing, and he fled also, thinking it to be some big disorder in which the

people were involved, and not knowing how or why, on looking back, ...
he saw the people, as if hit by an electric current, running back to surround
the holm oak. This time was for all who were there a time of terror. Some
fainted, others thought it was the last day of their life and their Judgment
Day was on hand, and for some, later, it was a marvel to see the admirable
colors that the clouds were taking on successively, [clouds] which dulled the
sun's rays—colors of bright red, changing to rose and blue, anise-colored, as
it was declared to me minutes after in my home by various people.

The Parish [inquiry board], 2 March, 1919
Father Manuel Marques Ferreira

Source: Deposition to the Parish [inquiry board], 2 Mar 1919; Doc Crit
I pp 283, 284.

Note: For this deposition no signature or statement on swearing was
given.

#100 Nov 22, 1922   STATEMENT OF INACIO MARQUES

(Gist– I heard rumors of the May apparition at Fatima. I went there on
June 13.)

I arrived at 11:45 and found some 12 people waiting at the Cova. I
asked someone: "where are these children who see Our Lady here," and a
voice replies: "wait, it won't be long." And, in effect, in a few minutes they
arrive, accompanied by a small group. They kneel at the famous oak bush
and begin to pray the rosary. I count the people and see that some 40 are
present. When the litany was finished Lucia says: "There she comes" and
orders the people to kneel. She begins asking and responding to someone
whom I can't see or hear. It is the second apparition, and once more she
affirms to the rather small number of spectators—because we can't yet call
them believers—what she is saying—that they come there each month and
that Oct 13 will be the last time and then she will tell them a secret.

Lucia turns and looks into space, as if following with her eyes someone
who is ascending, and as if in ecstasy, keeps pointing out the course that she
takes until she is lost in the Infinite. As a disbeliever, I want to deny what
I am seeing, but looking in the atmosphere I see that everything is cloudy.
It seems that opposing air currents were meeting there and raising a cloud
of dust. The weather darkens, and I seem to hear a subterranean groan.
I feel that the temperature is semi-supernatural, and I am afraid at being
there. (Gist– I returned home and told my mother I didn't know what I saw,
although it was a mystery, it won't be good. I didn't want to believe or deny.)

On June 13 [error for July 13] the crowd is much larger. The same phenomena occur as on the past month. (Gist– The fame of Fatima has grown.)

On Aug 13 the crowd grows, and those who contemplate the Cova, which forms a basin—two small mountains or hills which surround it—see a touching spectacle. Pilgrims come from all over singing … and feeling we are to live through some happy hours. The time passes, the children do not show up, the crowd waits impatiently, when a voice is heard over the mass of the people, [saying] that the administrator of Ourem had taken them away. Protests are heard, and when they begin to disband a shout is heard and a wave of heads turn to the sky, each one affirming what he is seeing. Then I look at the sky and see the clouds changing colors and running in different directions.

On the morning of 13 Sep there was not a cloud in the sky. A blazing heat made us look for shade. Lucia prays the rosary at the indicated time. A conversation with the said Lady follows and then she says "there she goes." The sun darkens to the point of seeing the moon and stars which surround the firmament. The heat lessens and a breeze caresses our faces. Then there is seen, way up above, cutting through the air from east to west, some very small bodies, white as snow. Some say that they are doves, but it can be seen perfectly that they are not birds.

On the hillside to the east was Father Joaquim Goncales, pastor of St. Catherine of Serra, and seeing that he may be looking and seeing nothing, I ask him what he sees. He replies that he sees nothing. I indicate the [right] direction to him, and at once he said that now he is seeing. [More about the priest follows.]

(Gist– He briefly tells of aiding a couple who had no rain protection on Oct 13.) The moment of the apparition comes and there occurs that which all the world knows. The sun turns on itself and all those who were wet appear dry, as I was.

(Gist– He then describes in great detail his rapid cure of pneumonia from his deathbed, after praying to the Virgin of Fatima.)

Inacio Antonio Marques

Source: A letter to the Diocesan Inquiry Board, 23 Nov 1922, published in *Voz de Fatima*, 13 Dec 1922; Doc Crit II pp 149-154.

#101 Oct 13, 1931   DEPOSITION OF FATHER INACIO PEREIRA

I was only nine years old at the time, and I attended the village school. At about mid-day we were surprised by the shouting and cries of some men and women who were passing in the street in front of the school. The teacher, a good pious woman, though nervous and impressionable, was the first to run into the road, with the children after her.

Outside the people were shouting and weeping and pointing to the sun, ignoring the agitated questions of the schoolmistress. It was the great miracle, which one could see distinctly from the top of the hill where my village was located—the miracle of the sun, accompanied by all its extraordinary phenomena.

I feel incapable of describing what I saw and felt. I looked fixedly at the sun, which seemed pale and did not hurt the eyes. Looking like a ball of snow revolving on itself, it suddenly seemed to come down in a zigzag, menacing the earth. Terrified, I ran and hid myself among the people, who were weeping and expecting the end of the world at any moment.

Near us was an unbeliever who had spent the morning mocking the simpletons who had gone off to Fatima just to see an ordinary girl. He now seemed to be paralyzed, his eyes fixed on the sun. Afterwards he trembled from head to foot, and lifting up his arms, fell on his knees in the mud, crying out to Our Lady.

Meanwhile the people continued to cry out and weep, asking God pardon for their sins. We all ran to the two chapels in the village, which were soon filled to overflowing. During those long minutes of the solar prodigy, objects around us turned all colors of the rainbow. We saw ourselves blue, yellow, red, etc. All these strange phenomena increased the fear of the people. After about ten minutes the sun, now dull and pallid, returned to its place. When the people realized that the danger was over, there was an explosion of joy and everyone joined in thanksgiving and praise to Our Lady ...

Source: Deposition of Father Inacio Lourenco Pereira, 13 Oct 1931; De Marchi, p 141.

Note: In 1917 Pereira lived in Alburitel, a small village about eight miles from the Cova da Iria. He was a missionary priest in Madras, India, in 1931 and made this deposition at the urging of his bishop, on 13 July 1931. It was published in the *Catholic Register*, a journal of the diocese of Meliapor [Madras] in July 1931; Jaki, p 208.

#102 1952   STATEMENT OF FATHER INACIO PEREIRA

I attended the elementary school of Alburitel ... On that day of Oct 13, 1917, my parents went to Fatima, as did other people from the area, because it was rumored that Our Lady had announced a miracle for that day. I was a small boy and on the previous evening I did some tricks in the melon patch of a neighbor. For punishment my parents did not take me along.

I was in school and I distinctly remember that it was raining heavily. Suddenly the rain stopped and we heard people shouting outside. The teacher could not contain us. In the street, the crowd, I should say much of the village, pointed at the sky. For a while we saw a sort of very bright glass roof between the black clouds, as it were an opening in the sky. Rays of sun projected through the opening as if so many ribbons falling through that low opening, and in the middle of it, in the very top, much higher, the sun began to lose its brilliance. Yet it was not blinding. It was rather like a firewheel, very large and reddish. A minute later (about a minute, I don't know) "that wheel" began to rotate upon itself at great velocity, pouring out shafts of flame of various colors. Some said: "Its looks like the saw of Verdasca's sawmill." (There was a machine-operated sawmill near Ourem.) The colors from the sky reflected on the faces of the people. Some said: "You are yellow." Others "You are red." (All the colors of the rainbow) and all burst out in cries: "This is the end of the world! May Our Lady save us." Meanwhile many threw away the tools they carried and ran to the chapel to pray aloud.

After a while the sun began to descend zigzag, through the glass roof opening, so that it appeared just above the top of the church tower. It stayed there for two or three minutes. The people knelt in the mud. The sun began to ascend, always up, and rotate. It seemed to be a moment, and then the huge firewheel became the normal sun, and blinded as usual when we tried to look at it.

Source: A statement given to Mr. Barradas de Oliveira in 1952, when Oliveira was in Madras for the Portuguese Ministry of Colonies; Jaki, p 208, 210.

Note: This statement appeared in print in 1953 in Oliveira's *Roteiro de Oriente*, pp 53-55, Agencia Geral do Ultramar, Lisbon, 1953; Jaki, pp 211, 243 [footnote 30].

#103 Oct 29, 1926   TEIXEIRA ARTICLE (TITLE UNKNOWN)

[The first portion of this article gives a detailed summary of the apparitions, says that the writer was on an official mission in the U.S. on Oct 13, 1917, and also says that the report on the sun dance was written a few days after Oct 13 by a member of his family who had witnessed the sun dance.]

Around ten o'clock in the morning of that memorable day it was raining torrentially in the Cova da Iria, a downpour accompanied by a strong wind.

Umbrellas were of little help in protecting anyone from this fury of the elements, but nobody left the place.

Later the rain showers abated somewhat and the black and stormy clouds yielded to lighter clouds with a whitish hue. The sun, in its turn, began to appear as if from behind a curtain, and a little later everybody noticed that the same smallish clouds of light rosy hue, separated from other clouds, passed in front of the sun and disappeared. This repeated itself several times.

The hours went by, the rain stopped, and the sky appeared luminous with clouds.

And that huge crowd of humanity, transfused with devotion, but among whom were many curious, journalists in discharge of their professional duties, and unbelievers, stayed motionless, hoping for something more.

It was announced that the hour specified was at two o'clock in the afternoon. At that exact hour the sun's disk lost its brilliance, turned black; a band of the color of fire began to rotate now in this, now in that direction in front of the sun.

Surrounding the sun, along all its circumference, an enormous splendor, also of the color of fire, a splendor full of majesty and of great dimensions, appeared to many thousands of observers. Then, with all that apparatus [around it], the sun detached itself from its orbit, advancing toward the earth and assuming gradually greater proportions. This phenomenon, never foreseen by any astronomical observatory, produced itself three times in a small interval of time.

And when the sun definitively returned to its normal appearance, all that multitude, now on their knees, implored the protection of the Virgin and shouted "Miracle! Miracle!"

Source: Jaki, pp 175, 176, citing *Jornal de Noticias* Porto, 29 Oct 1926, and *Voz de Fatima*, 13 Feb 1927.

Note: This report obviously gives two accounts of the sun dance, with different details in each. The second account clearly starts with the paragraph beginning: "The hours went by."

#104 Oct 17   DOS SANTOS LETTER

Rua de S. Joao de Malta
Covilha 17-10-17
Distinguished Reverend Father

I was in Fatima on the past 13th and witnessed all the marvelous occurrences which took place at the time of the apparition. I returned home covered with mud and water, but happy, as were the people with me.

(Gist– Please tell me if the seers remembered my petitions during the apparition. I enclose 2,500 (reis) for building the chapel.)

Respectfully Yours,

Maria Rita Dos Santos

Source: A letter of Maria Rita dos Santos of Covilhao, to a priest; Doc
Crit III book 1 p 276.

Note: The text strongly implies that the letter was sent to the pastor of
Fatima.

#105 Oct 21   THE APPARITION OF FATIMA

(Gist– Since May an apparition has appeared each 13th of the month to
three children of Fatima. This has become known and many people attended
the apparitions) .... on 13 Sep more than 20,000 people were there, many
of whom saw nothing which surprised them, but they saw only that the sun
darkened a bit and the air cooled. (Gist– On 13 Oct over 50,000 people
were there, coming by all means of transport. Quotes from *Diario de Noticias* and *O Seculo* of 15 Oct reporting on the Fatima event of 13 Oct are
then given.)

(Gist– The interview of Professor Oom is quoted in full. See #24. The
article then discusses the report of Pinto Coelho in *A Ordem* of 16 Oct. See
#34.)

… Dr. Pinto Coelho affirms that on the following day he saw (in Cascaes) the same phenomenon which was witnessed by 50,000 people on the
moor of Fatima, full of emotion. But it is strange that the famous lawyer
again **saw** the repetition of the phenomenon, (said to be natural) in contradiction with the astronomer Oom, who denies that it is natural and no
one else there gave out this sensational report. [Further comment on this is
made.]

Source: *O Mensageiro*, Leiria, 25 Oct; Doc Crit III book 1 p 442.

Note: The article in *A Ordem* does not say where Pinto Coelho saw the
repetition of the 13 Oct phenomenon and it would seem that *O Mensageiro*
only assumed that he returned to his home in Cascaes, and thus saw the
repetition there. However, as one of the local newspapers serving the Fatima
area, *O Mensageiro* may have determined that Pinto Coelho had not stayed
in the area on 13 Oct. He is known to have come by car, and thus could
easily have returned to Cascaes, in the Estoril, on 13 Oct. See #34.

#107 Dec   THE SUPERNATURAL

(Gist– This long article notes at length the decline of Christianity in Portugal, but sees Fatima as evidence that it was still alive. It notes that the clergy did not get involved in the Fatima events. It then gives a brief account of the sun dance, as follows.)

…. the crowd … almost <u>feared that the sun would fall from its height, where it was oscillating in a rapidity of movements and colors</u>, [and] believed in the miracle.

(Gist– The press and pious people have defended these phenomena as miraculous and created hostility to those who doubt. From this hostility on the part of believers, and that includes nearly all who were at Fatima on Oct 13, Pinto Coelho does not escape. His character is noble, he is a Catholic of undisputed authority and prestige. He is blamed because he faithfully reported what he saw on Oct 14 and explains the Catholic position in such cases: prudence, study, and waiting. Whatever the result of the Church's investigation, Fatima has returned the people to belief in the supernatural.)

Source: *Fe Cristao*, Braga, a Catholic monthly, Dec issue; Doc Crit III book 1 pp 816-819.

#108 Oct?   PEDRO NEVES LETTER

My dear Antonio,

(Gist– Much personal matter is first given.)

There is no news here except the miracle of Fatima. Perhaps you have not heard of it. It is said that in Fatima … three ago months Our Lady appeared to three shepherd girls on the 13th. The miracle gained fame and on the last day over 50,000 people were [there] from all over to see the miracle which had been forecast. From Lisbon alone there were over 400 cars.

At solar noon the shepherds appeared. The rain, which had fallen since morning, stopped suddenly.

Then the child, instructed or not, began to pray. After some minutes of prayer, they clapped their hands and ordered the people to look at the sun, which until then had been covered with clouds. <u>Then the sun, they say, came out of the clouds with a great heat, which dried in a few minutes the soaking clothes [of the people]. And they say it came forth in a mad dance.</u> (Gist– The whole crowd shouted: "Miracle.") Then the children said the war was ending soon.

It would not be bad, if true. I make no comment because I was not there and because it is dangerous to question what these furious people tell us. [Greetings follow.]

Source: A letter of Pedro Botelho Neves of Lisbon, to Antonio Tovar de Lemos, undated; Doc Crit III, book 1 pp 851-853.

Note: No date is given, but the fact that the author wonders if his friend has heard of Fatima suggests that the letter was written quite soon after 13 Oct. Further, at the top of page one there is written in yellow R 1/X1/17 which undoubtedly indicated that it was received (*recebido* in Portuguese), on 1 Nov 1917.

#109 May 30, 1918   THE CURRENT "SHOW"

(The Apparition of a Saint)

(Gist– By curiosity I went to Fatima where they said that a saint appeared on the 13th of each month last year. It is uncontestable that there were thousands of people and vehicles there. I wonder why. A minority came for religious reasons. The rest did not. What happened was mere fantasy. There are thus two hypotheses.)

Either the saint appeared or did not. If she appeared, and said through the mouth of the shepherds that the war was ending on that occasion, she lied, since at present some American republics have announced their participation in the war. If she did not appear, I would say that all the clerics who have been making propaganda from the said miracle have fallen for a trick. In whichever of the hypotheses, the so-called miracle of Fatima can never pass as a fact but as mere fantasy.

It is uncontestable that the sun suffered some kind of alteration (facts cannot be questioned). It was observed not only at Fatima, but also at many other points of the country. But I would ask: did the saint influence this phenomenon? No, because she did not even appear there. [Among] all who was there, who were present none would say; "I saw the saint." They would merely say: "I saw the sun dance." It is sad that in Portugal in the 20th century there are still people who pass as illustrious, who let themselves be embroiled in the said miracle, since all is only a simple phenomenon.

(Gist– I am sure it will long be called a real miracle. The clerics will do anything to keep the Faith in the people. An example occurred in the reign of Manuel I, which clerics said was a miracle, but which was only an optical effect.)

(The author continues to attack the clerics and ridicule the idea of a miracle.)

Source: *A Razao*, Aldegalega, 30 May 1918; Doc Crit III part 2 pp 415, 416. *A Razao (Reason)* was an organ of the Portuguese Republican Party.

Note: The underlining in the third paragraph was not in the article. They were added by me.

ANNEX II

INTRODUCTION

Part II of the Annex is chiefly concerned with the apparitions. Here I give the major interviews of the seers. Because these documents are long, I often gist the less important parts, and I gist more readily those which are available in English, especially those still in print. A number of briefer reports of interviews of the seers have been given in Part I.

Probably the most valuable interviews (which I also refer to as interrogations) are those made by Father Manuel Marques Ferreira, the Fatima pastor, since they were made soon after the reported apparitions. Until 1982 we had only his edited notes on these interviews, dated 6 Aug 1918 and sent to the bishop on 28 Apr 1919, as part of the Parish Inquiry. In 1982 an unedited copy of the pastor's notes was discovered among the effects of Father Jose Ferreira de Lacerda.

The unedited copy had been made on 19 Oct 1917, when he went to the Fatima rectory prior to his interview of the seers.[1] I give both the edited and unedited notes, but for the sake of brevity I gist much of the edited notes when they merely repeat what is given in the unedited notes.

Father Ferreira's notes are not dated, and he does not say whether he made written notes during the interviews. He probably made none during the first, and perhaps the second interview, in view of his doubts and public skepticism. Beginning with the third interview, when the matter had taken much greater importance, he may have begun to make notes during the interviews. If not, he surely transcribed them soon after the interviews, while the details were still sharp in his mind. In this regard, it seems significant that he fails to give us the dates of the first two interviews, but tells us the third was on 14 July, a day after the reported apparition.

---

[1] Doc Crit I, pp 3, 4.

Prior to their interviews, Father Lacerda and Father Manuel Nunes Formigao prepared a long list of questions to ask the seers, and seemingly left
room to record their answers on the same sheet. It thus seems likely that
these two priests made notes on the interviews as they occurred.

To facilitate comparison, I arrange the interviews by apparition, that is
I give together the reports of Father Ferreira and Father Antonio dos Santos
Alves on a given apparition, as well as the statements made by Lucia on the
same apparition in 1922 (her first written report of them), in 1924 (her testimony to the Diocesan Inquiry Board), and in 1941 (her fourth memoir).

A portion of Father Ferreira's reports on his interviews is not oriented
toward specific apparitions. I give this portion separately, after the section
on specific apparitions. Similarly, the interviews of Fathers Lacerda and Formigao are little oriented toward specific apparitions and thus I give them
separately, as the final section of this Annex; since their interviews are long,
I have arbitrarily broken them into segments—A, B, C, etc.—to make it
easier for readers to find the texts indicated by footnotes in the body of this
book.

Finally, I give the testimony of six witnesses made to the Diocesan
Inquiry Board on 23 Sept 1923. This testimony concerns all six apparitions and also unusual phenomena noted at the last five apparitions. However, this testimony gives very little information on the sun dance of 13 Oct
1917. In this part of the Annex, I continue to use parentheses and brackets
as in Part I.

#1 THE FIRST APPARITION, 13 MAY 1917

1A. INTERROGATION BY FATHER FERREIRA, LATE MAY 1917, UNEDITED NOTES

Interrogation made by the pastor of Fatima, Father Manuel Marques Ferreira, of the children who say they saw Our Lady.

First Apparition 13-5-1917. Lucia, 11 years old, daughter of Antonio dos Santos; Francisco and Jacinta, children of Manuel Pedro [Marto] of Aljustrel.

Lucia said they all were walking …. And we all saw a woman. Francisco only saw her when she departed. Lucia said they were seated and the Lady appeared in the direction of Fatima. First they saw a flash of lightning, got up and began to gather the sheep to go, being afraid. Then they saw another flash (and) then they saw a woman on top of an oak bush, dressed in white, white socks on her feet, skirt white, trimmed in gold, white jacket, white mantle, which she wore on her head, the mantle was not gold trimmed, across the skirt was a golden trim, she had a golden cord and very small white earrings, hands folded upward, and she opened her arms and hands when she talked.

This woman said that they should not fear, that she would do them no harm. Lucia asked: "Where are you from?" "I am from heaven." "What have you come into the world to do?" "I have come to ask you to come here for six months and at the end of six months I will tell you what I want." "Can you tell me if the war will last a long time or if it will end soon?" "I cannot tell you yet, while I have not told you what I want." I asked her if I would go to heaven. "Yes you will." "And my cousin [Jacinta]?" "She will go also." "And my cousin [Francisco]?" "He will, but he must say many rosaries." And having said this, she disappeared into the air above. The other two heard the questions and responses, but posed no questions.

Source: Father Ferreira's notes, unedited; Doc Crit I pp 6-9; *Fatima Way of Peace*, p 5.

1B. INTERROGATION BY FATHER FERREIRA, LATE MAY, EDITED

First apparition on 13 May

The children said to be favored by the heavenly vision or apparition of Our Lady are: Lucia, etc. (gives names, age, parents, residence and relationship).

[Statement of Lucia]

When the news began that Our Lady had appeared on 13 May to the above children, and I learned of it, which was about 15 days later, I ordered the mother of the seer Lucia to come to my house, the parish rectory, accompanied by her [Lucia]. The mother came with the daughter, but all upset, as she thought it was all a lie. She ordered her daughter to take back what she had said, that such a lie was a great evil. She threatened, and said she had already threatened the girl with many things that would happen to her if she continued to say that she saw Our Lady and to lie. She said only such things were reserved for her, etc., etc. ...

I was able to quiet the afflicted mother, telling her that if what they said was true, it was a great glory for her whole family. Oh ... if it was true ... but if it was a lie?! ...exclaimed the doubting mother. I counseled her to treat her the same as she had before; and if by chance her daughter was going to the apparition site she should not stop her, and should always bring her to me, and alone, after the day of the apparition, in case that she continues to have the grace of seeing Our Lady. She promised to do all this and even to come with her daughter on the evening or the evening before, so I could indicate to her daughter whatever things she should do or say at the time of the apparition. I dissuaded her from this in order to avoid any bad impression that the impious or bad-intentioned might make, as indeed they did.

After this I proceeded to interrogate the daughter—the supposed seer Lucia—who said that on the 13th of this month of May they were pasturing their sheep with her cousins Jacinta and Francisco at a site called Cova da Iria—two kilometers northwest of the parish church, near the road that leads to Batalha—at about 1:00 in the afternoon—solar time—and that after saying their beads—the rosary—(which she did often) she saw a flash of lightning, which made her fear greatly. She began to gather the sheep and ordered her cousins to gather them to go home, saying that a thunderstorm was coming, but she did not see clouds. Suddenly she saw another flash, and then a Lady of medium height and extraordinary beauty appeared on top of an oak bush—a little oak—and she said: [The words of the Lady and of Lucia are the same as in the unedited notes.] On saying this, the Lady began to rise in the air, going east until she disappeared.

Source: Father Ferreira's edited notes, 6 Aug 1918; Doc Crit I pp 254-257.

1C. INTERROGATION BY FATHER ANTONIO ALVES, 17 SEP 1917, FIRST VERSION

On Sep 17, 1917, I interviewed, at Reixida, Lucia, daughter of Antonio dos Santos Abobara [Abobara was his nickname], 9 years old, and Jacinta,

7 years old, daughter of Manuel dos Santos Marto (from) Aljustrel, Fatima parish, who say they saw Our Lady and they told me the following:

That on 13 May the two were walking with Francisco, pasturing their sheep at a place called Cova da Iria, at the edge of Fatima, that after eating lunch they went to say the rosary to Our Lady, as was their custom, and that a little before finishing it they saw a flash of lightning, which frightened them, at which Lucia asked the others to leave, and that when they were about to leave they saw in front of them a Lady dressed in white, with a mantle on her head, trimmed in gold, that she calmed their fears, saying that she would do them no harm. Lucia asked her what she wanted, to which the Lady replied that she wanted them to come to that site for six months on the same 13th day, and at the last month she would tell them what she wants. At once she began to disappear slowly at her head and thus successively her whole body until her feet were the last to disappear.

Source: Statement of Father Antonio Alves, pastor of Cortes parish; Doc Crit I pp 316, 317.

Note: No date is given for this statement, but comparison of the ink and writing with that of the parish books "leads us [the editors of Doc Crit] to suppose an approximate date of 17 September." Doc Crit I p 315, footnote 2. See my note on the revised version, below.

Note: Lucia and Jacinta were guests of Maria do Carmo Marques da Cruz Meneses for eight days in Rexeida in Sept 1917; Doc Crit I p 313.

1D. INTERROGATION BY FATHER ANTONIO ALVES, 17 SEP 1917, REVISED VERSION

(Gist– This version gives the same information as the first, much of it in the same wording, but adds two statements of interest, as follows:)

"She [the Lady had] a ... shine on her head reminding one of the shine of the sun, but brighter and from her hands hung a white rosary with very beautiful beads."

Source: Statement of Father Antonio Alves, late Sept?; Doc Crit I pp 320, 321.

Note: A comparison of the two versions suggests that this version was made after Father Alves showed the first version to the seers and noted their comments (which referred to this and the other apparitions) and then made this version, incorporating appropriate changes and additions. The seers' hostess, Maria ... Meneses, in an interview with Alfred de Matos, published in 1968 [*Eight Days with the Seers of Cova da Iria*, Alfredo de Matos, pp 42,

43] places the first interview at the nearby church in Cortes and the second in Reixida; Doc Crit I pp 313, 319.

1E. LUCIA'S FIRST WRITTEN ACCOUNT, 5 JAN 1922

May 13, 1917. I was watching the sheep at the Cova da Iria with my cousins Francisco and Jacinta (Gist– playing), and we saw a flash of lightning. I said to Francisco: "Let's leave here, because lightning is starting and there may be a thunder storm." We gathered the sheep to leave. On getting halfway down there was another flash and we saw Our Lady on an oak bush. We were very frightened on seeing the shine which surrounded her. Then she said to us:

"Don't fear, because I will cause you no harm."

"Where do you come from?"

"I am from heaven."

"And what do you want of me?"

"I want you to come here for six months and at the end I will tell you what I want."

I asked her about Maria of Jose das Neves, and she told me, "She is in heaven."

I asked about Amelia, and she told me she is in Purgatory. If she told me something else, I don't remember. And at this she disappeared, rising so high that she arrived at the point that I could not see her anymore.

Source: Lucia's first written account of the apparitions, 5 Jan 1922; Nov Doc, pp 97, 98.

Note: This account was written by Lucia at the request of Father Manuel Pereira, her first spiritual advisor; Nov Doc p 97, footnote 3. Presumably it was given to him and thus kept for eventual publication.

1F. OFFICIAL DIOCESAN INTERROGATION OF LUCIA, 8 JULY 1924

[In this and later interrogations, I use "Q" for "question" and "A" for "answer."]

Q. Did something important happen to you at the Cova da Iria?

A. On May 13, 1917, I was watching the sheep at the Cova … in the company of my cousins … after saying the rosary, as usual, we began to play … when we saw a flash of lightning in the east, and fearing a thunder storm, although the weather was nice, I said to Francisco that it was better that we gather the sheep [and] when we were in the middle of the field, there was another flash, and, two steps in front of us we saw, on an oak bush about a meter high, a very beautiful Lady, seemingly young, perhaps 18 to 22 years old, wrapped in a shine more brilliant than the sun. We were very afraid on seeing the shine which surrounded her, but the Lady said, in a low, but easily understandable, voice: "Don't be afraid, because I won't harm you." I asked her, "Where do you come from?" She replied, "I am from heaven." [I asked]: "What do you want of me?" She replied: "I want you to come here for six months, and at the end I will tell you what I want." I asked her about Maria of Jose das Neves, and she said that she was in heaven; I asked about Amelia, and she said she was in purgatory. If she said anything else this month, I don't remember it. At this, she disappeared, rising very high to the east.

Q. How was the Lady dressed?

A. She was dressed in white, covered from head to the bottom of the dress with a mantle trimmed in gold, held by a golden cord, ending with a tassel, also golden; she had nothing but the mantle on her head, the sleeves of the dress reached her hands, which were folded together at her chest, and from which a white rosary was hanging, ending in a white crucifix; it seems to me she was not barefoot, but I can't say for sure, because she was [standing] over sheets of light and I did not look carefully at her feet. A little of her ears were showing, but I can't say if she had earrings, but it seems to me she had very small gold ones.

[Two questions skipped. Neither is significant for this book.]

Q. Do you remember anything more of what happened that day?

A. Now I remember this: When the Lady said she was from heaven, I asked if I would go to heaven and she said yes, if Jacinta would go, and she said yes, if Francisco would go, and she said yes, but he must pray the rosary. I also remember that after the Lady disappeared, a man came to say that the sheep had gone into the chick pea patch, and that he had already thrown stones at them, but the peas would be eaten, [that] he would tell the owner, and later he said to the owner, Jose Matias, that the sheep had gone into the pea patch, but the peas were not eaten.

[Two questions are skipped, not significant.]

Q. Did the apparition last long? Were you afraid during it? Did you tell someone about it?

A. The apparition was short, and during it I was not afraid. On going home, I arranged with my cousins not to say anything, and on the following days we would go, when we could, with the sheep to the Cova da Iria, watching the sheep and praying an Ave Maria.

Source: Diocesan Inquiry, 8 Jul 1924; Doc Crit II, pp 138-140.

1G. LUCIA'S FOURTH MEMOIR, 1941

High up on the slope in the Cova da Iria, I was playing with Jacinta and Francisco at building a little stone wall … Suddenly we saw what seemed to be a flash of lightning.

"We'd better go home," I said to my cousins, "that's lightning, maybe we'll have a thunder storm."

"Yes indeed," they answered.

We began to go down the slope, hurrying the sheep toward the road. We were more or less halfway down the slope, and almost level with a large holm oak tree that stood there, when we saw another flash. We had gone only a few steps further when, before us on a small holm oak, we beheld a Lady dressed in white. She was more brilliant than the sun, and radiated a light more intense than a crystal glass filled with sparkling water, when the rays of the burning sun shine through it.

We stopped, astounded, before the apparition. We were so close, a few feet from her, that we were bathed in the light which surrounded her or rather which radiated from her. Then Our Lady spoke to us.

"Do not be afraid. I will do you no harm."

"Where are you from?"

"I am from heaven."

"What do you want of me?"

"I have come to ask you to come here for six months in succession, on the 13th day, at this same hour. Later on, I will tell you who I am and what I want. Afterwards I will return here a seventh time."

"Shall I go to heaven too?" "Yes you will." "And Jacinta?" "She will also go."

"And Francisco?" "He will go there too, but he must say many rosaries."

Then I remembered to ask about two girls who had died recently. They were friends of mine and used to come to my house to learn weaving with my eldest sister. "Is Maria das Neves in heaven?" "Yes she is." (I think she was about 16 years old.) "And Amelia?" "She will be in purgatory until the end of time." (It seems to me she was between 16 and 18 years old.)

"Are you willing to offer yourselves to God and bear all the sufferings He wills to send you, as an act of reparation for the sins by which He is offended, and of supplication for the conversion of sinners?" "Yes, we are willing." "Then you are going to have much to suffer, but the grace of God will be your comfort."

As she pronounced these last words—"The grace of God, etc."—Our Lady opened her hands for the first time, communicating to us a light so intense that, as it streamed from her hands, its rays penetrated our hearts and innermost depths of our souls, making us see ourselves in God, who was that light, more clearly than we see ourselves in the best of mirrors. Then, moved by an impulse that was communicated to us, we fell on our knees, repeating in our hearts:

"Oh most Holy Trinity, I adore you! My God, my God, I love you in the most Blessed Sacrament!"

After a few moments, Our Lady spoke again: "Pray the rosary every day, in order to obtain peace for the world and the end of the war."

Then she began to rise serenely, going up towards the east, until she disappeared in the immensity of space. The light that surrounded her seemed to open a path before her in the firmament, and for this reason we sometimes said that we saw heaven opening.

(Gist– We were not afraid of the Lady, but of a thunderstorm.) Besides, the flashes of lightning were not really lightning, but the reflected rays of the light which was approaching. It was because we saw this light, that sometimes we said we saw Our Lady coming; but, properly speaking, we only perceived Our Lady in that light when she was already on the holm oak. The fact that we did not know how to explain this, and that we wished to avoid questions, caused us to say sometimes that we saw her coming, and other times that we did not. When we said we saw her coming, we were referring to the approach of the light, which after all was herself. And when we said we did not see her coming, we were referring to the fact that we really saw Our Lady only when she was on the holm oak.

Source: Lucia's fourth memoir, Lucia's Memoirs, pp 165-167.

#2 THE SECOND APPARITION, 13 JUNE 1917

2A. INTERROGATION BY FATHER FERREIRA, JUNE 1917, UNEDITED NOTES

Second apparition 13-6-1917. Lucia said there was a little wait and during the time she was saying the rosary, and when she was going to say the litany she said that they should not, that there was no time, since there were many people there and she had seen the lightning and headed toward the oak bush with the people who were there. On arriving there she made a genuflection and at the same time the Lady arrived, coming obliquely from the east, and she asked:

"What do you want of me?"

"I want you [singular] to return on each 13th and [singular] to learn to read, so that I can tell you what I want."

"Then you want nothing more?"

"Nothing more."

Her clothing was: a white mantle that went from her head to the bottom of her skirt—it was gold trimmed from the waist down in a cord-like pattern [both] across and up-and-down, and at the edges the gold was closer. The skirt was all white, gold trimmed in a cord-like pattern lengthwise and across, but it only reached her knees; a white jacket without gold trim, having on the cuff only two or three cords; she had no shoes, she had white socks, not gold trimmed; at the neck she had a golden cord with a medal at the bottom; she held her hands together. On her ears she had very small buttons, very close to her ears. She unfolded her hands when she talked. She had dark eyes and medium height.

Source: Father Ferreira's notes, unedited; Doc Crit I pp 11, 12.

Note: The Portuguese language has both a singular and plural form of "you." In this case Lucia is saying that the Lady told <u>her</u> to return and to learn to read. The description of the Lady and her clothing clearly comes from the May interview.

2B. INTERROGATION BY FATHER FERREIRA, JUNE 1917, EDITED NOTES

Soon after June 13 the child Lucia, accompanied by her mother, appeared before me at the rectory. I proceeded to interrogate Lucia. She said that on the 13th of this month, about 1:00 in the afternoon, she went with her cousins Francisco and Jacinta to the Cova da Iria. On arriving they prayed the rosary with the people who were there. After finishing it, the people were ready to start the litany, and she, having seen the flash of lightning, said to them: Don't start it, there isn't time now. [She said] that then they went to the foot of the oak bush and saw the Lady arrive, coming from the east. And she asked her:

"Then what do you want of me?"

The Lady replied: "I want to tell you [singular] to return here on the 13th and learn to read, so I can tell you what I want."

"Then you want nothing more?"

"I want nothing more of you."

And then she began to rise and disappear.

Source: Father Ferreira's edited notes, 6 Aug 1918; Doc Crit I pp 258, 259, 264.

2C. INTERROGATION BY FATHER ANTONIO ALVES, 17 SEP 1917, FIRST VERSION

Second apparition. It was on the 13th of June, and of the same form. This time she said that they should keep going there the following months, that they should learn to read and told them a secret which they should reveal to no one. She said further that in October she would appear to them under the form of Our Lady of the Rosary. (Gist– Days later, on a Friday near the apparition site, they left their flock to pray the rosary and the flock caused no damage.)

Source: A statement of Father Antonio Alves, late Sept?; Doc Crit I p 317.

2D. INTERROGATION BY FATHER ANTONIO ALVES, 17 SEP 1917, REVISED VERSION

Second apparition. On the day of St. Anthony. On this day there was a fiesta in Fatima, which the mother of Lucia (and maybe also that of Francisco and Jacinta) wanted her to attend, but in obedience to what had been asked the month before, they gave up the fiesta and went to the apparition site, where they met some unknown people and scarcely three or four whom they knew. More or less at the same time as the month before, the same vision, in the same form, appeared to them and told them to keep coming there on the following months, that they should learn to read, and she told them a secret which she forbade them to tell to anyone whatsoever. (Gist– A longer account of the sheep straying into the chick peas follows.)

Source: A statement of Father Antonio Alves, late Sept?; Doc Crit I pp 321, 322.

2E. LUCIA'S FIRST WRITTEN ACCOUNT, 5 JAN 1922

June 13, 1917. We were waiting for Our Lady to appear near the oak bush, and then there was a flash of lightning and the Lady appeared over the oak bush. I asked her what she wanted. The reply:

"I want you [plural] to keep coming here all the months and I want you [plural] to learn to read."

I asked her to cure a lame person and some persons who had given me requests: some for sickness, others for the conversion of sinners. The reply:

"Within a year they will be cured."

With this she disappeared, rising to the east and going so high that the clouds and the blue of the sky did not let us see her any more. If she told me something else, I forget it.

Source: Lucia's first written account of the apparitions, 15 Jan 1922; Nov Doc, p 99.

2F. OFFICIAL DIOCESAN INTERROGATION OF LUCIA, 8 JUL 1924

Q. Were you there on the 13th of the next month [June]?

A. June 3 was the feast of St. Anthony and my mother did not much want me to go to the Cova da Iria, because she wanted me to go to the festival of St. Anthony, but some persons who knew of the apparition came to look for me and Jacinta and went with us to the oak bush about mid-day. Jacinta had told her mother that at the Cova da Iria [on May 13] she had seen a very beautiful thing, and at her insistence, told her what it was. I, only after eight days, and on being interrogated by my mother, told her what had happened. That is how she knew.

When we arrived near the oak, we prayed; and when the prayer was finished, I saw a flash of lightning, [although] it was a very hot day, and next the Lady appeared on the top of an oak bush, dressed as before. I asked her: "What do you want of me?" The reply was: "I want you [plural] to keep coming here the other months, that you [plural] pray the rosary every day, and that you [plural] learn to read." As they had requested, I asked the Lady to cure a cripple, and she said if he was converted he would be cured within a year. Then she rose to the east and disappeared among the clouds and blue of the sky.

(Gist– Q. Did anyone else see the Lady? A. I don't know.)

(Gist– Q. After this were you interrogated by anyone about it? A. Yes, many, including priests. My family said I lied and my mother beat me.)

Source: Diocesan Inquiry, 8 Jul 1924; Doc Crit II, pp 140, 141.

2G. LUCIA'S FOURTH MEMOIR, 1941

The 13th of June 1917

As soon as Jacinta, Francisco and I had finished praying the rosary, with a number of people who were present, we saw once more the flash reflecting the light which was approaching (which we called lightning). The next moment Our Lady was there on the holm oak, exactly the same as in May.

"What do you want of me?" I asked.

"I wish you to come here on the 13th of next month, to pray the rosary every day, and to learn to read. Later, I will tell you what I want."

I asked for the cure of a sick person.

"If he is converted, he will be cured during the year."

"I would like to ask you to take us up to heaven."

"Yes. I will take Jacinta and Francisco soon. But you are to stay here some time longer. Jesus wishes to make use of you to make me known and loved. He wants to establish in the world devotion to my Immaculate Heart."

"Am I to stay here alone?" I asked sadly.

"No, my daughter. Are you suffering a great deal? My Immaculate Heart will be your refuge and the way that will lead you to God."

As Our Lady spoke these last words, she opened her hands for the second time, she communicated to us the rays of that same immense light. We saw ourselves in this light, as it were, immersed in God. Jacinta and Francisco seemed to be in that part of the light which rose toward heaven, and I in that which was poured out on the earth. In front of the palm of Our Lady's right hand was a heart encircled by thorns which pierced it. We understood that this was the Immaculate Heart of Mary, outraged by the sins of humanity, and seeking reparation.

You know now, Your Excellency, what we referred to when we said that Our Lady had revealed a secret to us in June. At the time, Our Lady did not tell us to keep it secret, but we felt moved to do so by God.

Source: Lucia's fourth memoir, Lucia's Memoirs, pp 167, 168.

#3 THE THIRD APPARITION, 13 JULY 1917

3A. INTERROGATION BY FATHER FERREIRA, 14 JULY 1917, UNEDITED

Third apparition 13-7-1917. On 14-7-1917 there came into my presence Lucia, 10 yrs old. She said she had left home on the 13th about 11:00, called for Jacinta and reached the new road. We started to run, the people said we should go slowly, that going slowly didn't tire our legs. We arrived and met my sister, and she told me to lead the rosary. I began and they answered. We were there a bit, there was a flash of lightning and the Lady came. I got up, said that they should go back a bit and that those who could should kneel. I knelt again and asked her: "What do you want of me?" "I want you to return on the 13th" and she said more: "Pray the rosary to Our Lady of the Rosary to quiet the war, that only she can help." I said more: "I have a request that you convert a woman from Pedrogam and one from

Fatima and make a boy from Moita better." She said that she would convert them and improve [him] within a year. I said: "Make a miracle so that all will believe." "Three months from now I will make it that all believe." "Do you want nothing more of me?" "No, for now I want nothing more." I told her, "Then I don't want anything more." Then she went toward the east and I said to the people; "Look there to see where she is going." The people turned. She was exactly the same as I saw her the other times.

[Footnote 5 says that the text of the third apparition ended with the words "other times," but in some blank space was added the sentence which follows. "I have a request that you take to heaven a man from Atougia, the sooner the better." "I will take him."]

On 14 July there appeared to me Jacinta, 7 yrs old, daughter of Manuel Pedro Marto; questioned about the vision, she said: that she had seen a small woman four times; once in her house at night, and three times at the Cova da Iria at mid-day. She said that she was the size of Albina, the girl of Antonio Rosa of Casa Velha; at her house she saw her at the side of the attic door and she said nothing. Her mother and brothers were asleep and it was night. At the Cova da Iria she saw her at the foot of an oak bush, on top of it. She came dressed with white stockings and gold-trimmed clothing; she did not have shoes, her skirt was white and trimmed in gold and came to her knees. The gold trim was horizontal gold cords with gold ends.

The jacket was white, all trimmed in gold. She held her hands up at the waist and opened them when she talked to Lucia. She did not hear her say anything. She heard her talk (sometimes she said yes, sometimes no) she did not hear her say how many times she would come there. On leaving, the sky opened, her legs were together and her body already hidden. She heard very pious talk and only remembers hearing that people were going to heaven. She said she had seen the lightning, but sometimes once, sometimes more than once, sometimes before, sometimes after. She carried a white rosary between the thumb and pointer of her two hands; she didn't see earrings; she had a cord of thin gold on her neck.

Source: Father Ferreira's notes, unedited; Doc Crit I pp 13, 16.

Note: The Albina mentioned above was Lucia's cousin, born on 3 Dec 1901, and came from Aljustrel, not Casa Velha. Her father was the brother of the first husband of Jacinta's mother; Doc Crit I p 16, footnote 8.

3B. INTERROGATION BY FATHER FERREIRA, 14 JULY 1917, EDITED

On 14 July the seer Lucia showed up at my rectory. I proceeded to interrogate her. The seer Lucia said that on the 13th of this month of July she went, with her cousins Francisco and Jacinta, at the usual time to the Cova da Iria, and on arriving there led the rosary, praying it with the people (figured at 2,000 persons). When the rosary was over, she waited a bit and then saw the lightning and at once the Lady came. She arose—she was kneeling—and told the people to move back a bit, that those who could and who wanted should kneel, and kneeling again, she asked the Lady: [Questions and answers are the same as in the unedited version, except that Lucia's request for the man from Atougia is part of the regular text, preceding the request for a miracle.] This said, she rose as the other times to the east and disappeared.

Source: Father Ferreira's edited notes, 6 Aug 1918; Doc Crit I pp 259, 260.

3C. INTERROGATION BY FATHER ANTONIO ALVES, 17 SEPT 1917, FIRST VERSION

July 13. This time she asked them to pray the rosary to Our Lady of the Rosary that the war would end, that only she could do [it] and that they continue to come there as before.

Source: Statement of Father Antonio Alves, late Sept?; Doc Crit I p 318.

3D. INTERROGATION BY FATHER ANTONIO ALVES, 17 SEPT 1917, REVISED VERSION

For this month the revised version was virtually the same as the first one.

Source: Interrogation by Father Antonio Alves, Sept?; Doc Crit I p 322.

3E. LUCIA'S FIRST WRITTEN ACCOUNT, 5 JAN 1922

July 13, 1917. Toward mid-day, as the other months, we approached the oak bush to see the Lady. There was a flash of lightning and the Lady appeared on the oak bush. Query:

"What do you want of me?'

"I want you to keep coming the rest of the months. Do you want to learn a prayer?"

"Yes, we want to."

"It is the following: Oh my Jesus, pardon us, save us from the fires of hell, lead all souls to heaven, especially those most in need of it."

At once she confided to us some little words, saying to us:

"Don't say this to anyone. You can tell it only to Francisco."

"I want to ask you for some persons who asked me to ask you for them: some blind, others crippled, others deaf."

"Within a year some will be cured."

And with this she rose to heaven, as the other months.

Source: Lucia's first written account of the apparitions, 5 Jan 1922; Nov Doc p 99.

3F. OFFICIAL DIOCESAN INTERROGATION OF LUCIA, 8 JULY 1924

Q. Did you return to the Cova da Iria in the month of July?

A. I returned on July 13, as the Lady requested; there were plenty of people there; at mid-day we said the rosary at the foot of the oak bush. Upon finishing, [and] while standing, there was a flash of lightning and the Lady appeared on top of the oak bush. I asked her: "What do you want of me today?" the Lady replied: "I want you to keep coming the rest of the months and to continue to say the rosary." Then the Lady said: "Do you want to learn a prayer?" I responded: "Yes, we want to." And the Lady taught us thusly: "Oh my Jesus, pardon us, deliver us from the fire of hell, bring all souls to heaven, especially those most in need."

Next she confided some little words to us, asking that we tell them to no one, except only that we could tell them to Francisco. As they had requested, I asked the Lady for the cure of some persons, some blind, others crippled, and others deaf, and she said that within a year some would be healed.

Source: Diocesan Inquiry, 8 July 1924; Doc Crit II p 141.

3G. LUCIA'S FOURTH MEMOIR, 1941

A few moments after arriving at the Cova da Iria ... we saw the flash of lightning once more, and a moment later Our Lady appeared on the holm oak.

"What do you want of me," I asked.

"I want you to come here on the 13th next month, to continue to pray the rosary every day in honor of Our Lady of the Rosary, in order to obtain peace for the world and an end of the war, because only she can help you."

"I would like to ask you to tell us who you are, and to work a miracle so that everybody will believe that you are appearing to us."

"Continue to come here every month. In October I will tell you who I am and what I want, and I will perform a miracle for all to see and believe."

I then made some requests, but I cannot recall now just what they were. What I do remember is that Our Lady said it was necessary for such people to pray the rosary in order to obtain graces during the year. And she continued:

"Sacrifice yourselves for sinners, and say many times, especially whenever you make some sacrifice: 'Oh Jesus, it is for love of you, for the conversion of sinners and in reparation for the sins committed against the Immaculate Heart of Mary.'"

As Our Lady spoke these last words, she opened her hands once more, as she had done during the two previous months. The rays of light seemed to penetrate the earth, and we saw, as it were, a sea of fire. Plunged in this fire were demons and souls in human form, like transparent burning embers, all blackened or burnished bronze, floating about in the conflagration, now raised in the air by the flames that issued from within themselves together with great clouds of smoke, now falling back on every side like sparks in huge fires, without weight or equilibrium, amid shrieks and groans of pain and despair, which horrified us and made us tremble with fear. (It must have been this sight which made me cry out, as people say they heard me.) The demons could be distinguished by their terrifying and repellent likeness to frightful and unknown animals, black and transparent like burning coals. Terrified and as if to plead for succor, we looked at Our Lady, who said to us so kindly and so sadly:

"You have seen Hell, where the souls of poor sinners go. To save them God wishes to establish in the world devotion to my Immaculate Heart. If what I say to you is done, many souls will be saved and there will be peace. The war is going to end; but if people do not cease to offend God, a worse war will break out during the pontificate of Pius XI. When you see a night illuminated by an unknown light, know that he is about to punish the world for its crimes by means of war, famine, and persecutions of the Church and the Holy Father.

"To prevent this, I shall come to ask for the consecration of Russia to my Immaculate Heart, and the communion of reparation on the First Saturdays. If my requests are heeded, Russia will be converted, and there will be peace; if not, she will spread her errors throughout the world, causing wars and persecutions of the Church. The good will be martyred, the Holy Father will have much to suffer, various nations will be annihilated. In the end, my Immaculate Heart will triumph. The Holy Father will consecrate Russia to me, and she will be converted, and a period of peace will be granted to the world. In Portugal, the dogma of Faith will always be preserved; etc. ... Do not tell this to anybody. Francisco, yes, you may tell him.

"When you pray the rosary, say after each mystery: 'Oh my Jesus, forgive us, save us from the fires of hell. Lead all souls to heaven, especially those who are most in need.'"

After this there was a moment of silence, and then I asked:

"Is there anything more that you want of me?"

"No, I don't want anything more of you today."

Then, as before Our Lady began to ascend toward the east, until she finally disappeared in the immense distance of the firmament.

Source: Lucia's fourth memoir, Lucia's Memoirs, pp 168-170.

Note: The vision of hell and the Lady's words which follow are described also in the third memoir, pages 108 and 109, with almost identical words. But there Lucia adds: "This vision lasted but an instant."

#4 THE ABDUCTION AND FOURTH APPARITION

4A. FATHER FERREIRA'S INTERROGATION, 20 AUG, UNEDITED

Fourth apparition. They were captured. See *Mensageiro #3*.

Lucia said that on the Sunday after the 13th at the place Valinho, she first saw the air as it usually appears. Then she saw Our Lady toward the east, then she set herself on the oak bush.

I bowed and genuflected to her, stood up again and asked her: "What do you want of me?"

"I want you to return to the Cova da Iria; if they had not taken you to Aldea [Aldea da Cruz, the old name of Vila Nova de Ourem] the miracle would have been more widely known. St. Joseph was to come with the Child Jesus to give peace to the world, the Lady of the Rosary was to come with an angel on each side and Our Lady with an arc of flowers around [her]."

I asked her: "The money which you have, what do you want to be done with it?"

"With that money make two little litters; one you are to carry with three little girls like you and go in white; the other Francisco is to carry with three boys like him; they are to wear white capes and take the money to the Lady of the Rosary and use it for her." Then she disappeared in the air above and I said goodbye. I asked her the first and second time who she was, and she said she would tell me on the last day.

Source: Father Ferreira's notes, unedited, late July?; Doc Crit I pp 17-19.

4B. INTERROGATION BY FATHER FERREIRA, 20 AUG, EDITED

On 13 Aug about 10:00, at the rectory where I was with Father Antonio d'Oliveira Reis ... there appeared the administrator of the county, Artur d'Oliveira Santos, bringing in his carriage Father Manuel Carreira Pocas, prior of Porto de Moz. This priest, noting my surprise at seeing him accompanied by the civil authority in a matter of this nature, told me there was nothing surprising, because they had just queried the children at their houses, and that the administrator, as well as he, believed what the children said; that they had no doubt, but came to my house for me to interrogate the children, who were on their way, about a secret (the first time I heard talk of the secret) which they said the Lady told them, but which they do not reveal; and afterward the administrator would take them to the apparition site, where he also wished to go. The administrator said the same thing to me, seeming if not credulous at least curious. About a half hour later the children arrived with their fathers. The administrator asked me to interrogate them, which I did in his presence. When I asked her who it was that taught her to say what she said, she said it was that Lady she saw at the Cova da Iria. When I said that those go to Hell who tell lies that cause such trouble as what she had said, if it was a lie, to have deceived so many people, she replied that if those who lie go to Hell; she is not going to Hell for this reason, because she does not tell lies, but only says what she saw and what the Lady said to her, and that if the people come [to the Cova] it is because they want to, that she has not called anyone. I asked her if the Lady had told her a secret. She replied: yes, that she does not tell it. When I asked her several questions about it, she replied: "Look, if you wish I'll go up there and ask the Lady if she permits me, and if she permits it, then I will tell it." To this the administrator replied: "These are supernatural matters. Let's go, then." He got up, ordered the children to leave my library, where we were, and get in his carriage. This happened in the presence of the parents and the above-mentioned priests. He followed the road to the Cova da Iria for some time, and then turned toward the road to Vila Nova de Ourem, where he took them and where he kept them until the 15th, when he came to return them to their parents. The news of the abduction was carried with lightning speed to the apparition site, where around 15,000 to 18,000 people awaited anxiously for their arrival.

After a few minutes a car and some excited bicycle riders arrived at my door, giving forth the indignation of the big mass of people at the Cova da Iria, who were demanding my lynching as an accomplice in the attempt to take the children. I offered my innocence and even my indignation at such an act. And thanks to the Holy Virgin I was not trampled, if it was not for some improprieties made by a parishioner of this parish.

On the 20th the child Lucia appeared before me and said that on the 13th, when she was taken by the administrator to Vila Nova de Ourem, and where she was, in the house of the same administrator until the 15th, she saw nothing extraordinary. On the 19th, which was a Sunday, she was walking the sheep to pasture at a place called Valhino with her cousin Francisco and his older brother Joao, and upon seeing the air to be like it is when she sees the Virgin, she asked Joao, offering him a *vintem* [a coin] to go call Jacinta, who was at her parents' home. As soon as she arrived, Our Lady appeared on an oak bush; all saw her except cousin Joao, the brother of Jacinta and Francisco.

Then she asked her "What do you want of me?" [The conversation is the same as in the original notes, except that here the text says, "Our Lady of Sorrows was to come with an arc of flowers."]

With this said, she disappeared into the air above. [An unimportant paragraph follows.]

Source: Father Ferreira's edited notes, 6 Aug 1918; Doc Crit I pp 260-264.

4C. INTERROGATION BY FATHER ANTONIO ALVES, 17 SEP 1917, FIRST VERSION

Fourth Apparition. On 18 Aug, at a place called Valinhos: She said that if they had been taken by the administrator, it was so that the miracle would be better known, or instead, if they had not been taken by the administrator, the miracle would not have been so well known. Lucia made various petitions to her that she heal some sick that asked her, to which she replied that she would heal some and other no, because they did not believe [them] or even her Divine Son.

Source: Statement of Father Antonio Alves, late Sept?; Doc Crit I p 318.

4D. INTERROGATION BY FATHER ANTONIO ALVES, 17 SEP, REVISED VERSION

This time she appeared to them at Valhinos on the Sunday after the 13th .... On that day she told them that if they had not been taken by the administrator, the miracle would not have been so well known. (Gist— A repeat of the rest of the first version follows.)

Source: Statement of Father Antonio Alves, late Sept; Doc Crit I p 323.

4E. LUCIA'S FIRST WRITTEN ACCOUNT, 5 JAN 1922

We were going (Gist— to take) the road to the site of the oak bush, and they told us first we had to go to the rectory. We went, thinking he wanted something from us. On arriving we went up onto the porch, awaiting orders on what we were to do. Nobody wanted anything from us. Then they said to us: "Get in the carriage so we can take you quicker to the site."

First my father said we would go on foot; but the administrator again ordered us to get into the carriage, saying that by going in the carriage we would be free from people.

Then, on my father's order, I got into the carriage, and my cousins too. In place of going with us to the Cova da Iria, he went toward Vila Nova de Ourem. I said:

"Its not the way, it's the other way," but the administrator replied that we were going to Ourem to the rectory, and then we would come in a car, that even so we would arrive in time.

And as soon as we got to Ourem, he shut us up in a room, assuring us that we would not get out until we had told the secret the Lady had confided to us. And thus three days passed; he threatened us with various punishments and promised us gold pieces. But he got nothing from us. Then we went to the [Fatima] rectory.

When we arrived home we went to pasture the sheep at a place called Valinho. I went with Francisco and Joao—Jacinta had stayed home. Then I doubted that Our Lady would make us another visit; and then, by the inspiration of Our Lady, I asked Joao to get Jacinta. And since he did not want to, I promised to give him a *vintem* [coin], which I had. Then he went. When Jacinta arrived, there was a lightning flash and the Lady appeared on the oak bush.

"Then what do you want of me today?"

"I want you to continue to come the rest of the months to the Cova da Iria. If they had not taken you, the miracle would be better known."

"The lady who is keeping the money told me to ask what we should do with that money."

"I want you to make two litters for the feast day of Our Lady of the Rosary; Francisco will carry one, with three lads; [you] girls will carry the other, with two other girls."

"I want to ask you for some persons who asked me for a cure from the Lady."

"A year from now some will be cured."

And with this she rose, like all the other months, heading toward the east.

Source: Lucia's first written account of the apparitions; Nov Doc pp 99-100.

4F. OFFICAL DIOCESAN INTERROGATION OF LUCIA, 8 JUL 1924

Q. Did the same thing happen in August?

A. It was different in August. Before 13 Aug I and my cousins were called to the county administration; my uncle did not take his children, but I went with my father. The administrator interrogated me, wanted insistently that I reveal the secret of the Lady, which I did not do, and after writing [notes] ordered me out. On the 13th we were going [to go] to the site of the oak bush, when they told us that first we had to go to the rectory. We went there and got on the porch. After waiting there some time the administrator appeared and ordered us to get into a carriage, saying that thus we would go faster to the Cova da Iria.

My father said we would go on foot, but the administrator insisted that it was better to go by carriage because we would be free of people. Then, on order from my father, I got in the carriage with my cousins. The carriage made a turn and headed toward Vila Nova de Ourem. "Its not that way," I said, but the administrator replied that we were going to the rectory in Ourem and we would still come back on time, because we would come in a car. When we arrived in Ourem, he closed us in a room and said we would not leave until we told the secret which the Lady had confided to us. The next day an elderly lady interrogated us about the secret; then they took us to the administration headquarters, where we were again interrogated, [and] offered pieces of gold to reveal the secret. We returned to the administrator's house, where we had been the night before, and in the afternoon we were again interrogated about the secret. They took us to the jail and threatened to keep us there if we did not talk. We returned to the administration headquarters, and since we had not told the secret, they promised to fry us in oil. The administrator ordered us to leave and told a man to prepare the hot oil. Then they called Jacinta, saying she was the first to be burnt. She left promptly, without saying goodbye. They interrogated her and put her in a room. [Next] they called Francisco, said that Jacinta was already burned and he would suffer the same fate if he did not tell the secret. They interrogated him and ordered him into the same room. Then it was my turn; they told me my cousins were already burned and I would have the same fate if I didn't tell the secret. Although I thought it was certain, I had no fear. They sent me to the feet of my cousins, and a man said it would not be long before we were burned all three. They took us to the administrator's house and we remained there that night in the same room. The next day was almost the same thing: interrogations morning and afternoon, with many promises and threats. On the 16th we went again to the administration headquarters, but they got nothing from us, as the other times. Then the administrator ordered us to get into the carriage and left us at the [Fatima] rectory on the porch.

After we arrived home, Francisco, Joao and I went to a place called Valinho with the sheep. Jacinta stayed home. There was a flash of lightning and I ordered Joao to call his sister, Jacinta. Joao did not want to go, and I promised him two *vintems* [coins] to go. When Jacinta arrived, I told her there had been a flash and probably the Lady was going to appear. We took a short cut down and we saw Our Lady on top of an oak bush. "What do you want of me?" I asked. She said: "I want you to keep coming to the Cova da Iria the rest of the months until October and that you pray the rosary." I asked her further: "What should we do with the money which is at the Cova da Iria?"

Maria of the Rosary, of Moita, had taken charge of it, and neither my parents nor those of my cousins wanted to keep it; she told me to ask the Lady what should be done with the money. The Lady replied: "Make two litters for the feast of the Lady of the Rosary; Francisco, with three other boys is to carry one, and the other is to be carried by you two and two other girls." I asked for the cure of some persons, and she said that within a year they would be cured. I asked her also for a miracle so that the people would believe; she said that at the last month she would make a sign in the sun so that all would believe; that St. Joseph would come with the Child Jesus to bless the world, and Our Lady of the Rosary; [also] Our Lady of Sorrows; [and] that Our Lord would come to give peace to the world. After this she disappeared to the east, like the other months.

Q. Did all see the Lady?

A. I and Jacinta saw and heard. Francisco, like the other times, saw her but did not hear, and Joao saw [and heard] nothing.

Q. Did many people go to your house to ask about the Lady?

A. There were lots of people and even many priests, some of whom treated me as a faker.

Source: Diocesan Inquiry, 8 Jul 1924; Doc Crit II pp 141-143.

4G. LUCIA'S FIRST, SECOND, AND FOURTH MEMOIRS, 1937-1941

[Lucia describes the events of August 1917 in several places in her memoirs. In the first memoir she describes her abduction, in the second a previous attempt by the administrator to obtain the Lady's secret, and in the fourth she describes the apparition.]

Not many days later [in August] our parents were notified that … Jacinta, Francisco and myself, together with our fathers, were to appear at a given hour before the Administration in Vila Nova de Ourem. This meant we had to make a journey of about nine miles, a considerable distance for three small children. The only means of transport in those days were our own two feet or a donkey. My uncle sent word right away that he would appear, but he was not taking his children. ….

My parents thought the very opposite. "My daughter is going. Let her answer for herself. I understand nothing of these things. If she is lying, it's a good thing that she be punished for it."

(Gist– Lucia fell off the donkey three times on the way. She was hurt by the indifference of her parents, especially in contrast with the concern of Francisco's parents.)

At the Administration office I was interrogated by the administrator, in the presence of my father, my uncle and several other gentlemen, who were strangers to me. The administrator was determined to force me to reveal the secret and to promise never again to return to the Cova da Iria. To attain his end he spared neither promises nor even threats. Seeing that he was getting nowhere he dismissed me, protesting, however, that he would achieve his end, even if this meant that he had to take my life. He then strongly reprimanded my uncle for not carrying out his orders and finally let us go home. [From the second memoir.]

When, some time later, we were put into prison, what made Jacinta suffer most was to feel that their parents had abandoned them. (Gist– Lucia and Francisco tried to console her.)

After being separated for a while, we were re-united in one of the other rooms of the prison. When they told us that they were coming soon to take us away to be fried alive, Jacinta went aside and stood by the window … I thought at first that she was trying to distract our thoughts with the view, but I soon realized that she was crying. I went over and drew her close and asked why she was crying. "Because we are going to die," she replied, "without ever seeing our parents again, not even our mother." (Gist– Lucia continued to try to console her, suggesting that she offer her suffering for sinners, and she did so. The prisoners also sought to console her.) "But all you have to do," they said, "is to tell the administrator the secret! What does it matter if the Lady wants you to or not?"

"Never," was Jacinta's vigorous reply, "I'd rather die."

(Gist– They decided to say the rosary and the prisoners joined in. Then one tried to divert their attention by playing the concertina. They started singing, and then one picked up Jacinta and danced with her. Then, further to distract her, Lucia and Francisco danced with her.) [From the first memoir.]

The 13th of August. As I have already said what happened on this day, I will not delay over it here, but pass on to the apparition which, in my opinion, took place on the 15th in the afternoon. As at that time I did not yet know how to reckon the days of the month, I might be mistaken. But I still have the idea that it took place on the very day that we arrived back from Vila Nova de Ourem.

I was accompanied by Francisco and his brother Joao. We were with the sheep in a place called Valinhos, when we felt something supernatural approaching and enveloping us. Suspecting that Our Lady was about to appear to us, and feeling sorry that Jacinta might miss seeing her, we asked her brother to go and call her. As he was unwilling to go, I offered him two small coins, and off he ran.

Meanwhile Francisco and I saw the flash of light, which we called lightning. Jacinta arrived, and a moment later we saw Our Lady on a holm oak bush.

"What do you want of me?"

"I want you to continue going to the Cova da Iria on the 13th, and to continue praying the rosary every day. In the last month I will perform a miracle so that all may believe."

"What do you want done with the money that the people leave in the Cova da Iria?"

"Have two litters made. One is to be carried by you and Jacinta and two other girls dressed in white; the other one is to be carried by Francisco and three other boys. The money from the litter is for the fiesta of Our Lady of the Rosary, and what is left over will help toward the construction of a chapel that is to be built here."

"I would like to ask you to cure some sick persons."

"Yes. I will cure some of them during the year."

Then, looking very sad, Our Lady said: "Pray, pray very much, and make sacrifices for sinners; for many souls go to Hell because there are none to sacrifice themselves and to pray for them." And she began to ascend as usual towards the east.

Sources: First, second, and fourth memoirs, Lucia's Memoirs, pp 35-38, 74, 75, 170, 171.

#5 THE FIFTH APPARITION, 13 SEP 1917

5A. INTERROGATION BY FATHER FERREIRA, 15 SEP 1917, UNEDITED

Fifth apparition 13-9-1[9]17. I called into my presence on the 15th Lucia, who said that on the 13th she saw the same woman dressed in white, that seemed to her to be the same she saw the other times. I saw little more than her face, where I was constantly looking to understand what she was saying. She comes from the east. She said she saw a flash of lightning and then saw the woman arrive on the oak bush, and she said she asked: "What do you want?"

"I want to tell you to keep praying the rosary always to Our Lady of the Rosary, that she slows down the war, that the war end; on the last day St. Joseph is to come to give peace to the world, and Our Lord to bless the people; [and] that you come here on Oct 13."

"There is a boy here who is deaf and dumb, please heal him."

"A year from now you will find him somewhat better."

"I have many requests, some for conversions, others for getting better."

"I will improve some, other no, because Our Lord does not want to believe in them."

"The people would very much like a chapel here."

"Half of the money they have gathered up to now, give it to Our Lady of the Rosary; let the other half be to help the chapel."

I offered her two letters and a vial of perfume.

"They gave me this, if you want it."

"This is of no use up there in heaven."

And she left to the east and I said to the people: if you wish to see her turn toward there.

Source: Father Ferreira's notes, unedited; Doc Crit I pp 21, 22.

5B. INTERROGATION BY FATHER FERREIRA, 15 SEP 1917, EDITED

On 15 Sep there came to my rectory the seer Lucia with her mother. I preceded to the interrogation. She said that on the 13th of the month she went with her cousins Francisco and Jacinta to the site called Cova da Iria, and at the usual time saw the lightning and then saw the Lady arrive, dressed as the other times, that it seemed to her the same white dress, but that she looked at little but her face, to catch the meaning of what she said. She asked her, "What do you want of me?"

The Lady replied: "I want to tell you to continue to pray the rosary, that she lessens the war, that the war is coming to an end, [that] on the last day St. Joseph, or St. Joseph with the Child Jesus, is to come to give peace to the world and Our Lord to bless the people, and that you come here on 13 Oct."

Lucia said: "There is a girl here who is deaf and dumb, please heal her."

And the Lady replied, saying that within a year she would be somewhat better.

"I have here many requests, some for conversions, others for getting better."

And the Lady replied: "I will improve some, others no, because the Lord does not wish to believe in them."

"The people would very much like a chapel here."

The Lady replied to her: "Half the money they have gathered up to now, make litters and take [it] to Our Lady of the Rosary; let the other half be to help the chapel."

Lucia said further that she offered two letters and a vial—a little bottle of perfume—that were presented to her by a man from Olival parish, and when she offered them to her, she said to her:

"They gave me these ... if you want them?"

And the Lady replied: "This is of no use up there in heaven."

Having said this, she rose, going to the east. And then she—Lucia, turned to the people and said: "If you want to see her, turn toward there," and pointed where she was going.

Source: Father Ferreira's edited notes, 6 Aug 1918; Doc Crit I pp 264, 265.

5C. INTERROGATION BY FATHER ANTONIO ALVES, 17 SEP 1917, FIRST VERSION

13 Sep. She said that they should pray the rosary to Our Lady of the Rosary [to ask] that the war would end; that it was about to end; and that on the last day St. Joseph would come with the Child Jesus to give peace to the world and her Divine Son to bless the people.

Source: Statement of Father Antonio Alves, late Sept?; Doc Crit I p 318.

5D. INTERROGATION BY FATHER ANTONIO ALVES, 17 SEP 1917, REVISED VERSION

13 Sep. She said to them that she would appear first under the appearance of Our Lady of Sorrows and then as Our Lady of the Rosary. She asked that they pray the rosary to Our Lady of the Rosary for the end of the war, which was about to end. She told them also that in October St. Joseph would come with the Child Jesus to give peace to the world and her Divine Son to give a blessing to the people.

Source: Statement of Father Antonio Alves, late Sept?; Doc Crit I p 323.

5E. LUCIA'S FIRST WRITTEN ACCOUNT, 5 JAN 1922

Sep 13, 1917. About mid-day we were waiting for the Lady to come. Then there was a flash of lightning and the Lady appeared.

"What do you want of me today?"

"I want you to keep coming here the rest of the months and saying the rosary every day."

"I want to ask you to make a miracle so that all the people believe."

"At the last month I will make a sign in the sun so that they believe, and St. Joseph will come with the Child Jesus to bless the world, and Our Lady of the Rosary; afterwards (will come) Our Lady of Sorrows and Our Lord."

"I want to ask for some people that asked me for a cure from the Lady: some lame, others dumb, others blind, others sick."

"A year from now some will be cured."

If she told me other things this month, I do not remember them.

She arose to the east, as all the other months.

Source: Lucia's first written account of the apparitions, 5 Jan 1922; Nov Doc pp 100, 101.

5F. OFFICIAL DIOCESAN INTERROGATION OF LUCIA, 8 JUL 1924

Q. Did you go the Cova da Iria in September?

A. She replied—I went there many times because people were always asking me to go there and pray the rosary with them. On the 13th I also went there, accompanied by the people. My cousins were already there, with many people. About mid-day a lightning flash occurred and the Lady appeared as usual: I asked: "What do you want of me?" She replied: "I want you to come here next month and keep saying the rosary." At the request of Maria of the Rosary, I asked if she wanted them to build a chapel there; and she said that they should build a chapel in honor of Our Lady of the Rosary. I asked for the cure or conversion of some people and she said that within a year some would be cured, others no.

Q. Nothing more happened in the month of September?

A. She replied—"I asked again that she make a miracle so that the people would believe, because people were saying that I was a swindler and should be imprisoned and burned. The Lady gave me the same reply as the other time, and left as usual."

Source: Diocesan Inquiry, 8 Jul 1924; Doc Crit II pp 143, 144.

5G. LUCIA'S FOURTH MEMOIR, 1941

The 13th of September. As the hour approached, I set out with Jacinta and Francisco, but owing to the crowds around us we could only advance with difficulty. (Gist– A long discussion of the crowds, their efforts to get the seers to petition the Lady for help and her pious reaction to them, follows.)

At last we arrived at the Cova da Iria, and on reaching the holm oak we began to say the rosary with the people. Shortly afterwards we saw the flash of light, and then Our Lady appeared on the holm oak.

"Continue to pray the rosary in order to obtain the end of the war. In October Our Lord will come, as well as Our Lady of Sorrows and Our Lady of Mt. Carmel. St. Joseph will appear with the Child Jesus to bless the world. God is pleased with your sacrifices. He does not want you to sleep with the rope on, but only to wear it during the daytime."

"I was told to ask you many things, the cure of some people, of a deaf mute ..."

"Yes, I will cure some, but not others. In October I will perform a miracle so that all may believe."

Then Our Lady began to rise as usual and disappeared.

Source: Lucia's fourth memoir, Lucia's Memoirs, pp 171, 172.

#6 SIXTH APPARITION, 13 OCT 1917

6A. INTERROGATION BY FATHER FERREIRA, 16 OCT 1917, UNEDITED

Sixth apparition 13-10-1917. On 16 Oct I called Lucia into my presence and interrogated [her]; she said that first she saw the flash, as always; she said to the people: be quiet, the flash was already given; she turned to the east and saw Our Lady come through the air below and told the people: Be quiet, Our Lady is already coming ... Look at her, look at her!

The Lady came and set herself on top of the roses and silk cloth which covered the trunk of the oak bush.

I asked her, "What do you want of me?"

"I want to tell you not to offend Our Lord any more, to pray the rosary to Our Lady, to build a chapel here to Our Lady of the Rosary, ... the war is ending this very day; expect your military back very soon." All of this Lucia said was in answer to the first question.

"I have many petitions, will you grant them all or not?"

"I will grant some, not others." I did not make her any specific petitions, because I was [not] even there to make petitions.

"Do you want anything more of me now?"

"I want nothing more now," said the Lady.

"And I also want nothing more."

Then she [the Lady] left returning by the same way and in the same direction, and she turned and said to the people: "Look, there she goes, there she goes!" The Lady disappeared, but without the clouds that hid her.

Then she said that she looked at the sun and saw St. Joseph and the Child Jesus at the left of the sun; she saw St. Joseph only from the waist up; he came dressed in white and the Child Jesus dressed in red; she saw all of the Child Jesus, and he was seated on the left arm of St. Joseph. St. Joseph was making signs of the cross with his right hand, I think he made it three or four times and then disappeared. After St. Joseph disappeared, all was yellow. [Then] Our Lord arrived, but it seems she could only make out his clothing with a cape; she only saw him from the waist up; he had a small beard and she did not see his hair; she did not get to see his hands, she only saw his torso.

A Lady on foot was at the right side of Our Lord, and Our Lord was on the right side of the sun. Both had a yellow shine, and did not have a child; this Lady was dressed in white and had a blue mantle around her head; she had her hands over her breast, one lower than the other.

Her skirt was white and long and reached to her feet. It seems to her that the white skirt and jacket were not gold-braided; she did not see her in the sun like when she was on the oak bush. Then she disappeared.

Together with St. Joseph she saw another image or Lady who was at the right of the sun. She saw her all dressed in red, her mantle was blue-bordered down to her jacket; She had her hands at her waist, with her fingers interlaced; she had no Child. She had a yellow shine; she disappeared with St. Joseph.

While she was seeing this image, the people were shouting: Look! Look! How beautiful!

And I also looked and said to the people that they should look there, that St. Joseph was there and then Our Lord.

The Lady of the oak bush came dressed exactly like the other times; I saw nothing more or less. I think her skirt was short, like the other times. She said the money was for the chapel, but not all, because some was for the litter; she said she had no idea what the chapel should be made of or who should be in charge.

Source: Father Ferreira's notes, unedited; Doc Crit I pp 23-25.

6B. INTERROGATION BY FATHER FERREIRA, 16 OCT 1917, EDITED

Sixth apparition 13 Oct. On the 16th of this month there appeared before me Lucia with her mother. I proceeded to interrogate Lucia, who said that on the 13th of this month, she went to the site called the Cova da Iria with her cousins Francisco and Jacinta, once there she saw at the same hour as the other times the lightning flash—which always happened since May 13; that she turned to the east, she told the people to be quiet because she had already seen the flash, and then she saw Our Lady descend through the air below; and that she told the people again: Be quiet ... that now Our Lady is coming. Look! ... Do you see her, do you see her? And the Lady came and set herself on top of the silk ribbons and rose flowers which covered the little trunk of the oak bush. Then she asked her:

"What do you want of me?"

And the Lady replied: "I want to tell you that they not offend Our Lord, who is much offended, that you pray the rosary to Our Lady. Make a chapel here to Our Lady of the Rosary (Lucia had doubts whether it was this she had said or if it was: make a chapel here. I am the Lady of the Rosary.) The war is ending, even today, expect the return of your soldiers very soon."

"I have many petitions, if you wish to grant them or no?"

"I will grant some, not others."

"Now do you want anything more of me?"

"Now I want nothing more of you," replied the Lady.

"And I also want nothing more of you." This said, the Lady moved off in the same way and direction as the other times. Then she turned to the people and said:

Look! There she goes, there she goes ... and she rose until she disappeared from sight. Once out of sight she looked at the sun, but not because she ordered her to, and she saw St. Joseph—half body, dressed in white, with the Child Jesus sitting on his left arm. St. Joseph was to the left of the sun and blessed the people with his right hand. It seemed to her that he made three or four signs of the cross over the people. She saw all the child Jesus, dressed in red. And I saw on the right side of the sun Our Lady, full body, dressed in red with a blue mantle on her head wrapped around her at the neck, with her hands interlaced at her waist. This vision disappeared, she said, and all was yellow for some instants, and then she saw Our Lord appear, half body, dressed in white, at the right of the sun; and at the right of Our Lord I saw Our Lady, full body, standing dressed in white with a blue mantle on her head, and her hands over her breast, palms inward, one at the side of the other in a horizontal position. The mantle was not wrapped around [her] like the first vision. Our Lady in none of these visions was seen with the Child. All these visions had a yellow shine, except St. Joseph. While she was seeing these presentations, the people shouted: "Look, look, look. How beautiful!!!" Lucia said further that at this moment she told the people to look there—at the sun—that St. Joseph was there, and then Our Lady. On being queried about what was to be done with the money, she said it was for a chapel, and about who was to make the chapel and take charge of the work, she said she did not know because the Lady did not tell her. And on being asked when Our Lady would appear again, she said she did not expect any more of her because she had promised only six months or six times—and these had now come—and that now she only expected to see her in heaven.

Source: Father Ferreira's edited notes; Doc Crit I pp 266-268.

6C. INTERROGATION BY FATHER ANTONIO ALVES, 17 SEP 1917, FIRST VERSION

[Since the 13 Oct apparition occurred after the 17 Sept interview of the seers by Father Alves, he does not include any reference to the 13 Oct apparition in his first notes on it.]

6D. INTERROGATION OF THE SEERS BY FATHER ANTONIO ALVES, UNDATED

[Father Alves gives a short statement on the sixth apparition at the end of his revised version of his 17 Sept interview with the seers. It is not clear whether this statement is based on a later interview with the seers or if he merely added this statement, based on what he had read.]

Sixth apparition, 13 Oct. She said that she was Our Lady of the Rosary; that the war was ending that day, that our soldiers would return shortly; that they should build a chapel to Our Lady of the Rosary at the site, and that the people should amend their ways, that their sins had greatly offended her Son.

Source: Statement of Father Antonio Alves, Oct 1917?; Doc Crit I p 323.

6E. LUCIA'S FIRST WRITTEN ACCOUNT, 5 JAN 1922

Oct 13, 1917. Like all the other times, we went to the foot of the oak bush to see the Lady. There was a flash of lightning and the Lady appeared.

"What do you want of me?"

"I want to tell you [the people] not to offend Our Lord any more, because he is already much offended, and to continue to pray the rosary every day; and I want you to build a chapel to Our Lady of the Rosary here."

"And how are you called?"

"I am the Lady of the Rosary."

Now I understood that she spoke thusly:

"When I arrive in heaven, the war will end today." But my cousin Jacinta said she had spoken in this manner: "If the world reforms, the war will end today." Therefore I cannot affirm which way she stated these words.

"I would like to ask you for some people who asked that I ask the Lady for cures: some lame, others blind, others deaf, others sick."

"I will cure some, not others."

And with this she rose toward the east like all the other times, going to such a height that the blue of the sky and clouds kept me from seeing her anymore.

When she was hidden, we looked at the sun and we saw, at the right side of the sun, a man from the waist up with a Child around his neck, making crosses with his right hand, holding the child in the other, dressed in white. They had around them a great shine which prevented us from looking [at them] at will. On the left side was Our Lady, as we had seen her when she descended on the oak bush. Upon finishing the crosses, St. Joseph with the Child and Our Lady disappeared.

Immediately after, Our Lord appeared at the right of the sun, being seen only from the waist up. He was dressed in red. On the other side [was] Our Lady of Sorrows, with a purple mantle and still covered with a shine that seemed to blind us.

With this they disappeared and I saw nothing more up to today.

The clothing of the Lady was of these colors: her dress was white; it had twelve stars from the waist down, one after the other; at the neck, a cord, with a ball, which reached down to her waist; her hands were joined and a rosary hung from them; I don't know if it was one of five or of fifteen decades. The rosary was white, as was the crucifix. The mantle covered her from head to the bottom of the dress; it had a gold-trimmed edge. I don't know if she had socks or was barefoot, because I couldn't see her toes. It was because of the light, which did not allow me to stare at them. All around her was such a strong and brilliant light that it did not let me see as I would like, because it blinded me.

It seems that now I have told almost all. If something she said is missing, I do not remember [it]. Please excuse me for writing so badly, I don't know how to do better. I am still learning.

5-1-1922 Lucia of Jesus

Source: Lucia's first written account of the apparitions, 5 Jan 1922; Nov Doc pp 101, 102.

Note: This account was written by Lucia at the request of her spiritual advisor, Mons. Manuel Pereira Lopes; Nov Doc p 97. The last sentence, above, suggests that it was sent to him.

6F. OFFICIAL DIOCESAN INTERROGATION OF LUCIA, 8 JUL 1924

Q. Did you go to the Cova da Iria on 13 Oct? She replied: (Gist– Lucia describes the clothing they wore for the apparition, given to them by "a lady.") It was raining. When we arrived at the Cova da Iria they could not break through the people; the road was full of carriages and cars. At mid-day there was a flash of lightning and the Lady appeared on the oak bush. "What do you want of me?" I asked. She replied: "I want to tell you that they should not offend Our Lord any more, that He is already much offended; continue to say the rosary every day. I want you to make a chapel here to Our Lady of the Rosary."— "Then how should we call you?" She replied: "I am the Lady of the Rosary." It seems to me that she spoke further in this manner: "convert, the war will end today, expect your soldiers back shortly." My cousin told me at home that the Lady spoke thusly: "convert, so that the war ends within a year." As I was thinking about the requests that I wanted to make to the Lady, I did not pay attention well. I gave her the petitions and she gave me the reply like the other times. At this she rose toward the east [and] hid in the clouds. A little before the Lady appeared, it stopped raining; and when she disappeared, we looked at the sun. On one side we saw the form of a man, from waist up, with the Child Jesus in his hands, and on the other side the Lady we had seen at the oak bush. The Child Jesus blessed the people. I had the idea that the man was St. Joseph. There was such a great shine that it did not let us look [at them] at will. They disappeared, and then Our Lord appeared on the right side of the sun, seen only from the waist up, dressed in red, and on the other side Our Lady, dressed in purple, seeming to be Our Lady of Sorrows. Our Lord made several [signs of the] cross. It seems to me that I also saw another figure, which seemed to be our Lady of Mount Carmel, because she had some kind of thing that hung from her right hand. All disappeared, and I have never seen them up to today.

Q. Did your cousins speak anytime to the Lady? She replied: "They never spoke; once we agreed that Jacinta should speak, but when she got there Jacinta said nothing."

Q. Was the Lady smiling? She responded: "She was sad; when she spoke she opened her hands, which were joined and pointed up at her chest."

Q. Where are your cousins. She replied; (Gist– They are dead.)

Q. Are you sure you really saw a Lady on top of the oak bush and were not deceived? She replied: "I am certain I saw her and was not deceived; even if they kill me, I would never say the contrary."

Q. And who was this Lady? She replied: "Before she said she was Our Lady of the Rosary, I did not know who she was. Now I am convinced that she was Our Lady."

When she finished making these declarations, they were read to her by the notary, and she found them all to be true, except the question about her First Communion ...

She swore on the Bible and signed her name in the presence of the president, the defender of the Faith and the notary.

Lucia of Jesus

Father Manuel Nunes Formigao, Jr.

Dean Manuel Pereira Lopes

Source: Diocesan Inquiry, 8 Jul 1924; Doc Crit II pp 144-146.

Note: There are two versions of Lucia's testimony to the Diocesan Inquiry Board, having only minor differences between them. The one I have chosen to use gives both the questions and answers. It was accepted as the official version, and it alone contains the statement that Lucia approved it as accurate. The other [presumably earlier] version states that Our Lady of Sorrows was dressed in blue [rather than purple], and adds that at the end Lucia told the people to look at the Lady, that both St. Joseph and the Child Jesus were dressed in red, and that the Child was barefoot.

Source: Official Diocesan Inquiry of Lucia; Doc Crit II pp 123, 124, 133, 134.

6G. LUCIA'S FOURTH MEMOIR, 1941

The 13th of October, 1917. We left home quite early, expecting to be delayed along the way. Masses of people thronged the road. The rain fell in torrents. My mother, her heart torn with uncertainty as to what was going to happen, and fearing it would be the last day of my life, wanted to accompany me.

(Gist– Lucia describes her trip there.) Once there, moved by an interior impulse, I asked the people to shut their umbrellas and say the rosary. A little later we saw the flash of light, and then Our Lady appeared on the holm oak.

"What do you want of me?"

"I want to tell you that a chapel is to be built here in my honor. I am the Lady of the Rosary. Continue always to pray the rosary every day. The war is going to end, and the soldiers will return soon to their homes."

"I have many things to ask you: the cure of some sick persons, the conversion of sinners, and other things..."

"Some, yes, but not others."

Looking very sad, Our Lady said: "Do not offend the Lord Our God any more, because he is already so much offended."

Then, opening her hands, she made them reflect on the sun, and as she ascended, the reflection of her own light continued to be projected on the sun itself.

Here, your excellency, is the reason why I cried out to the people to look at the sun. My aim was not to call their attention to the sun, because I was not even aware of their presence. I was moved to do so under the guidance of an interior impulse.

After Our Lady had disappeared into the immense distance of the firmament, we beheld St. Joseph with the Child Jesus and Our Lady robed in white, with a blue mantle, beside the sun. St. Joseph and the Child Jesus appeared to bless the world, for they traced the sign of the cross with their hands. When, a little later, this apparition disappeared, I saw Our Lord and Lady. It seemed to me that it was Our Lady of Sorrows. Our Lord appeared to bless the world in the same manner as St. Joseph had done. This apparition also vanished, and I saw Our Lady once more, this time resembling Our Lady of Carmel.

Source: Lucia's fourth memoir, Lucia's Memoirs, pp 172, 173.

OTHER INTERROGATIONS

#7 INTERROGATION OF LUCIA BY FATHER FERREIRA, UNDATED

7A. THE VISION

Lucia said that the Lady which she and her cousins saw was a little more than a meter tall and came dressed in white. Her skirt was white and gold trimmed down and across and was short, that is, it did not reach to her feet. The jacket was white, not gold-trimmed. The mantle was white and went from her head to the edge of her skirt; [it] was trimmed in cord-like gold trim from top to bottom and across, [and] on the edges the gold was closer. The jacket had two or three cord-like gold trimmings at the wrist. She had no belt, band or strip at the waist. She held her hand a little above the waist and from them hung a rosary. Every time that she talked, she separated her hands, more or less, as far as her shoulders. She had dark eyes and was more beautiful than any lady she had seen. Her beauty almost blinded her, and she never tired of looking at her.

It seemed to her that she wore white socks, not gold trimmed, but she was not certain, because she looked a little more at her face. On one occasion, when Jacinta was there, she even turned to her and asked if she wore socks, because she had not noticed.

Source: Father Ferreira's edited notes, 6 Aug 1918; Doc Crit I pp 257, 258.

Note: This description of the Lady is found at the end of Father Ferreira's edited account of his first interrogation of Lucia, in May 1917. But the text ("every time she talked," "She never tired of looking at her," "On one occasion") indicates that the description is derived from his first and other interviews after the apparitions in 1917.

7B. INTERROGATIONS OF JACINTA BY FATHER FERREIRA, UNDATED

Statements of Jacinta

On the various times that I interrogated the seer, Jacinta, she always confirmed that she saw a Lady at the Cova da Iria on the 13th days of May to October, 1917, except for Aug 13, when she was at the house of the administrator of the county, but that in this month she saw her on the following Sunday—at the site called Valinho, to where she was called by her brother Joao, at the request of Lucia.

She said she was a very pretty Lady, all dressed in white, her clothing was trimmed in gold cord, with a veil or mantle on her head; (she was) of the Size of F.—she indicated a girl of average size and some 14 years old—and who carried some beads, very white, hanging from her hands, which she held erect at her waist, and that she opened them more or less when she spoke to Lucia.

When she spoke to Lucia she heard a very saintly voice, but she does not remember her saying, or not, that the persons—the seers—were going to heaven. On the various times that I interviewed her, she never contradicted herself on essentials, although there were some contradictions on non-essential matters, real or apparent. On one occasion—on Aug 21—I went to her parents' house, with five ladies—Mrs. Maria de Jesus Raposo of Torres Novas, and others from Quinta da Cardiga, one of which was some 15 years old and dressed in white. On arriving at the parents' house, Jacinta came in, she was alone, and on seeing the unexpected visitors, was embarrassed, as is normal for a child of the people, and one who had been returned to her parents a few days before, after having been kidnapped. After some warm words, I said to her:

"Look, Jacinta. See if it was one of those ladies you saw at the Cova da Iria, or if one of them here is somewhat like the one you saw."

She raised her little eyes, looked them over from head to toe, and said:

"It was none of these. The other is much more beautiful."

I had her look at one dressed in white, saying: "Then it was not this lady dressed in white, so beautiful, that you saw up there?"

"This lady is very beautiful, but the one I saw there is much more beautiful," she replied.

We went to the house of Lucia's parents, and finding her there, gave her the same question and got an identical response. In regard to the secret, I also did not get her (Jacinta) to reveal it; she only said that it—the secret—was not bad for them—the seers. She said further that that the Lady appeared to her three times more—once on Ascension Day in church during Mass and that she taught her to pray the rosary; another time, at night, over the trap door of the loft, while the family was sleeping; and another time below (or if wrong on top of) it, without saying anything, until she said to her mother: "Look!! .... Don't you see the Lady I saw up there? down there?!!," as her own mother told me.

Source: Father Ferreira's edited notes, 6 Aug 1918; Doc Crit I pp 268-270.

Note: The "F." mentioned above, is for "Fulana," a way of avoiding a statement of the girl's real name; Doc Crit I p 269, footnote 165. She is undoubtedly the Albina, mentioned in Father Ferreira's unedited notes of the July apparition. See 3A. of this Annex. While the date of these interrogations of Jacinta is not given, probably most or all occurred in 1917.

7C. INTERROGATIONS OF FRANCISCO BY FATHER FERREIRA, UNDATED

Statements of Francisco

I interviewed Francisco sometimes in various places and he always told me he saw a very pretty Lady at the Cova da Iria and in Valinho on the same days that his companions had indicated, and that she came dressed in white, but he did not hear her. On the secret, I did not get him to reveal anything. I told him that since he didn't hear the Lady, he had nothing, he had no secret at all. He replied, yes, he had, that Lucia told it to him. I told him he could tell me since Lucia had told it and because it is not a secret nor did the Lady say that he should not tell it. He replied: I won't tell [it] because it is a sin and [because] Lucia said that I should not say it. Here, I recall that Lucia on a certain occasion had told me that the Lady only gave her permission to tell the secret to Francisco and Jacinta.

I did not get such a detailed and timely interrogation with Francisco and Jacinta as I would have liked, and as I did with Lucia, because their father, too believing—if not halucinary—on the first time that I ordered [the seers'] mother to come to the rectory with the children, he came alone in place of their mother with the children, and he said, yes, he would send them, but

[only] if it was to believe them and not to abuse them. I was surprised at hearing such words and others which disheartened me: the true antithesis of the parents of Lucia. In view of this I awaited the developments and did not again invite the parents to bring them to the rectory; I interrogated them only when the opportunity arose, because I thought it my duty to show indifference until there was evident proof or until the Church spoke. (Gist– Then he gives a statement on the number of people at each apparition: 50 at the second, 4 to 5,000 at the third, 15 to 18,000 at the fourth, 25 to 30,000 at the fifth, and 40 to 50,000 at the sixth.)

Source: Father Ferreira's edited notes, 6 Aug 1918; Doc Crit I pp 271, 272.

#8 INTERROGATIONS BY FATHER MANUEL FORMIGAO

Introduction

Father Manuel Nunes Formigao first went to Fatima on 13 Sep 1917. Except for a lessening of sunlight, he saw nothing unusual. A few days later he talked with the bishop, who asked him to "observe and make notes." Father Formigao is considered the unofficial observer of the hierarchy by one author.[2] He interviewed the seers on 27 Sep, and then on five later dates. His notes on these interviews are long, detailed and important. He later was the recording secretary of the Diocesan Inquiry Board and wrote its report to the bishop.[3] And he wrote the earliest books on Fatima. Father Formigao was a doctor of law and theology from the Gregorian Institute in Rome. In 1917 he was a professor at the diocesan seminary in Santarem.[4]

We do not know if Father Formigao made written notes during his first interrogation of the seers on 27 Sep. However, he recorded the interviews in a small notebook before the end of the month.[4] Before the other interviews he prepared questions to ask the seers, leaving room for the answers, which he recorded in pencil. We have, also in a small notebook, a long list of these questions for the Oct 11 interviews, as well as another notebook in which he edited the questions and answers, in ink. We also have his edited notes for all the interviews after Oct 11. However, for these interviews we have the original questions and answers only for Jacinta. In view of the great importance and publicity given to Fatima after the Oct 13 event, it seems likely

---

[2] *Fatima Joie Intime, Evenement Mondial,* p 13.
[3] Doc Crit II pp 9, 18.
[4] Doc Crit pp 37, 38, footnote 2.

that the edited notes of all the interviews were made soon after each these later interviews. However, we have specific information on the date of the edited notes only for September 27. He later wrote, on one occasion, that these notes were written before the end of September, and on another occasion he wrote that they were written on 29 September.

A comparison of the original and edited notes of the interviews for which both are available shows that very little substantive changes were made in editing. For the 11 Oct interviews 19 of the 26 answers of Lucia were virtually identical, as were all seven of Francisco's. And on 13 Oct all 23 of Jacinta's answers were also identical. Some of the other answers were vague or cryptic and required editing for the sake of clarity. And the edited notes contain a few statements not found in the original, apparently not written down by Father Formigao during the interview, but recalled as he wrote the edited notes.

Father Formigao also made notes of his interviews of members of the seers' families and of his local host and of his impressions of the seers and of the credibility of their accounts of the apparitions. I have decided to include these interviews, impressions and analysis.

Source: Doc Crit I, pp 27-29, 37-40, 76, 77, 99, 117-122, 139, 157-161.

#8. FATHER FORMIGAO'S FIRST VISITS, 13 SEP 1917 AND 27 SEP 1917

Father Formigao describes his first visit to Fatima in these words:

"I did not get near the apparition site [on Sep 13]. I stayed on the road about 300 meters away, and I barely noticed the dimming of the sun, which seemed an unimportant phenomenon, due perhaps to the altitude of the hills. I kept, therefore, a prudent, but well-disposed, anticipation, as I had since the events of August, because before then I made a smile of absolute incredulity on hearing any reference to the Fatima apparitions."

Source: *A Guarda*, Lisbon, 5 Sept 1919; Doc Crit I p 27.

8A. FATHER FORMIGAO'S INTERROGATIONS, 27 SEP 1917

(Gist– I went to Fatima to gather more information on the apparitions in order to be able to make a judgment about them. I went to the house of the oldest seer. Lucia was absent and her mother sent for her. While I was waiting, Jacinta arrived. She was tall for her age, modestly dressed and seemed sound of mind and body. Surprised, she acted timidly, answering in a very low voice, and in monosyllables, to my questions. Moments later her brother arrived. He took his hat off and I asked him to sit down. I began my interrogations at once.)

Source: Father Formigao's edited notes; Doc Crit I pp 40-43.

8B. FATHER FORMIGAO'S INTERROGATION OF FRANCISCO, 27 SEP 1917

"What did you see at the Cova da Iria during these months?" "I saw a lady."

"Where does she appear?" "On top of an oak tree."

"Does she appear suddenly or do you see her coming from anywhere?" "I see her coming from the side where the sun rises and stop on an oak bush."

"Does she come slowly or quickly?" "She always comes quickly."

"Do you hear what she says to Lucia?" "No."

"Did you ever speak to the Lady? Has she ever spoken to you?" "No, I have never asked her anything. She speaks only to Lucia."

"Who does she look at? At you and Jacinta or only at Lucia?" "She looks at all three of us, but she looks longer at Lucia."

"Did she ever cry or smile?" "Neither, she is always serious."

"How is she dressed?" "She has a long dress and over it a mantle which covers her head and falls to the edge of her dress."

"What is the color of the dress and mantle?" "It is white and the dress has gold lines."

"What posture does she take?" "Like someone praying. She has her hands joined at the height of her breast."

"Does she carry anything in her hands?" "Around the palm and back of her right hand she carries a rosary. It hangs down over her dress."

"And on her ears?" "You can't see her ears because they are covered by the mantle."

"What color is the rosary?" "It is white."

"Is the Lady beautiful?" "Yes, she is."

"More beautiful than that girl over there?" "Yes."

"But there are ladies who are much more beautiful than that girl." "She was more beautiful than anyone I have ever seen."

Source: Father Formigao's edited notes; Doc Crit I pp 40-47; De Marchi, pp 116, 117.

8C. FATHER FORMIGAO'S INTERROGATION OF JACINTA, 27 SEP 1917

(Gist– I called Jacinta in from play and proceeded to interrogate her.)
"Did you see Our Lady on the 13th of each month?" "Yes."
"Where does she come from?" "She comes from the sky from the side of the sun."
"How is she dressed?" "She has a white dress, decorated with gold, and on her head a mantle, also white. Around her waist is a gold cord which falls to the edge of her dress."
"Does she have boots or shoes?" "She has neither boots nor shoes."
"Then she has only stockings?" "She seems to have stockings, but perhaps her feet are so white that she seems to have stockings."
"What color is her hair?" "You can't see her hair because it is covered by the mantle."
"Does she wear earrings?" "I don't know, because you cannot see her ears."
"How does she hold her hands?" "Her hands are joined at the height of her breast, with the fingers pointing upward."
"Are the beads in the right or left hand?" (Gist– She seemed confused, did not answer.)
"What was the chief thing that the Lady told Lucia?" "She said that we were to say the rosary every day."
"And do you say it?" "I say it every day with Francisco and Lucia."

Source: Father Formigao's edited notes; Doc Crit I pp 48-50; De Marchi, p 117.

8D. FATHER FORMIGAO'S INTERROGATION OF LUCIA, 27 SEP 1917

(Gist– Lucia appeared a half hour later after helping with the vintage.)
Taller and better nourished than the other two, with a clearer skin and healthier appearance, she seemed not to be self-conscious, which contrasted markedly with the shyness and timidity of Jacinta. Simply dressed like the latter, neither her attitude nor her expression denoted a sign of vanity, still less of confusion.
Seating herself on a chair at my side, in response to my gesture, she willingly consented to be questioned on the events to which she was the principle protagonist, in spite of the fact that she was visibly fatigued and

depressed by the incessant visits and the repeated and lengthy questionings to which she was subjected.

(Gist– He gives the names and ages of the members of Lucia's family.)

She was eight when she made her First Communion. Her mother, a good Christian woman, is a good housekeeper, does her domestic chores, tries always to inspire a holy fear of God in her children, and raises them to fulfill all their moral and religious duties. She is greatly worried about the events which at every moment attract thousands of people to her poor home, until then unknown to the world, and since then she has hesitated between a worried anxiety and the hope that her daughter is really privileged with the apparition of the Virgin and the fear that she is the victim of a hallucination which would bring her trouble and cover all her family with ridicule.

At my question about the piety of her Lucia, she replied that she had not noted anything extraordinary in her, she prayed with the same fervor as before the apparitions, as did her sisters.

I began the interrogation of the seer [Lucia].

"Is it true that Our Lady appeared at the Cova da Iria?" "It is true."

"How many times has she already appeared?" "Five times, once each month."

"On what day of the month?" "Always on the 13th except in August, when I was taken to the town by the administrator. In that month I saw her only some days later, on the 19th, at a place called Valinhos."

"They say that the Lady appeared to you also last year. What truth is there in this?" "She never appeared to me last year (nor before May of this year); I never told this to anyone because it is not true."

"Where does she come from? From the area of the east?" "I don't know; I don't see her come from anywhere. She appears over the oak bush, and it is when she leaves that she goes to the east."

"How long does she stay, a little or a lot?" "Little time."

"Enough to say an Our Father and a Hail Mary, or more?" "More, quite a bit more. But not always the same amount (perhaps not enough for a rosary)."

"Were you afraid the first time you saw her?" "I was, so much that I wanted to flee with Jacinta and Francisco, but she told us not to be afraid because she would do us no harm."

"How was she dressed?" "She had a white dress that reached to a little below the middle of her legs, a mantle covered her head, of the same color and of the same length as the dress."

"Did the dress have decorations?" "It had, on the front part, two [lines] of gold braid, which descended from the jacket and was joined by a tassel, also gold, at her waist."

"Is there a belt or ribbon?" "There is none."

"Does she have earrings?" "She has small, yellow ones."

"In which hand does she hold her rosary?" "In her right hand."

"Was it five or fifteen decades?" "I didn't notice well."

"Did it end in a cross?" "Yes, a white cross with white beads. The chain was also white."

"Did you ever ask her who she was?" "I did, but she said she would say only on 13 Oct."

"Did you ask her where she came from?" "I did and she said from heaven."

"When did you ask her this question?" "The second time, on 13 June."

"Does she ever smile or seem sad?" "She never smiles or seems sad, she is always serious."

"Did she propose some prayers for you and your cousins?" "She proposed that we pray the rosary in honor of Our Lady of the Rosary for the peace of the world."

"Did she want many people to be present on the 13th of each month?" "She said nothing in this regard."

"Is it sure that she told you a secret and forbid you to tell it to anyone?" "It is sure."

"Did she say this only to you or also to your companions?" "To all three."

"Could you not reveal it, at least to your confessor?" (Gist– She remained silent, and he did not repeat the question.)

"They say that, in order to free yourself from the bother of the administrator, on the day you were abducted, you told him something as if it were the secret, which it was not, thus deceiving him, and that afterwards you bragged about it. Is it true?" "No. The administrator really wanted me to tell the secret, but as I could tell it to no one, even though he insisted a lot for this purpose, I did not tell it. What I did do was to tell all that the Lady had told me except the secret, and maybe this is why the administrator thought that I had also told the secret. I did not want to deceive him."

"The Lady told you to learn to read?" "Yes. The second time she appeared."

"But if the Lady said she would take you to heaven in October, why should you learn to read?" "That is not true: the Lady never said that she would take me to heaven in October, and I never stated that she told me such a thing."

"What did the Lady say that you were to do with the money which is being offered at the oak bush?" "She said we were to put it on two litters, one of which I and Jacinta were to carry with two other girls, and the other [was to be carried] by Francisco, with three other boys to the parish church. Part of this money was for the feast of Our Lady of the Rosary and the other to help for a new chapel."

"Where does she want this new chapel to be built?" "I don't know. She didn't say."

"Are you glad that Our Lady appeared to you?" "I am."

"On 13 October, will you see only Our Lady?" "St. Joseph will also come with the Child Jesus and peace will be given to the world."

"Did she make any other revelation?" "She said that on the 13th she would make it so that all would believe that she is really appearing."

"Why do you, not infrequently, lower your eyes and stop looking at the Lady?" "It is because she blinds them."

"Did she teach you a prayer?" "Yes. She wants us to say it after each decade of the rosary."

"Do you know this prayer?" "Yes."

"Say it." "Oh my Jesus, forgive us, free us from the fires of Hell, take all souls to heaven, especially those most in need of it, and alleviate the souls in Purgatory, especially those most abandoned."

Source: Father Formigao's edited notes; Doc Crit I pp 51-61; De Marchi, pp 118-121.

8E. FATHER FORMIGAO'S INTERROGATION, 27 SEP 1917, HIS COMMENTS

From the children's responses, and even more from their attitude and way of acting in all the circumstances in which they found themselves, it is clear that it seems to exclude all doubt of their complete and absolute sincerity.

It is not possible that children of such tender age, one of them scarcely seven, coarse and ignorant, would lie and persist in lying for so many months, since they were besieged with questions and interrogations of all kind, and were threatened by representatives of ecclesiastical and civil authorities, persons to whom they owed respect and consideration. No consideration, no fear, is able to stop them from affirming that they see Our Lady. Not even the prison to which they were subjected, after being taken violently from their family nest and taken far from the land where they were born and live, the threats made by elements of the people, which reached the extreme of threatening them with death, if one day they should be caught in a flagrant lie.

The natural and frank way that they express themselves, the simplicity and candor that they display, the indifference and disinterest that they show about whether or not they believe them, the extreme timidity of Jacinta, even the apparent contradictions, easily explainable, into which they fall and which excludes absolutely any agreement between the children, all are signs that the children possess in the highest degree one of the indispensable requirements of a reliable witness: veracity.

But could the children be victims of a hallucination? Could they be deluded, thinking that they [hear] and not hearing, that they see and not seeing. Do we see, in this case, verification of the hypothesis of self-hallucination?

But how, if nothing supports such a supposition, should we accept it gratuitously? It is not a matter of only one witness, there are three. It is not a matter of adults, more subject to hallucinations, but of children. And what children! Children of tender age, gifted with perfect health, and who show not the least sign of hysteria, according to the declaration of a conscientious doctor, who examined them carefully.[5]

Could it be a case ... of diabolical intervention? The devil sometimes transforms himself into an angel of light to deceive believers. Did it happen this time? Jacinta affirms that the dress of the Lady reaches barely to her knees. Lucia and Jacinto (he means Francisco) declare that it goes about to her ankles. Are the children, especially the youngest, confused on this point? If not, this point is difficult to explain and resolve.

(Gist– He speculates further that the children may be deceived or not have noted carefully the lady's dress or that it might be the work of the devil.) But how can we explain the arrival of so many thousands of people, the lively faith and ardent piety, the silence and respect of the crowd, the numerous conversions, resulting from these events, the appearance of extraordinary signs in the sky and on the ground, verified by thousands of witnesses, how to explain, I repeat, all these factors and to reconcile them with Divine Providence and the economy that rules the supernatural world,

---

[5] Fr. Formigao does not state the name of this doctor; he may refer to the doctor that examined the children at the home of the administrator of the county in August. However, no report is known to have been made by him. Doc Crit p 65, footnote 406.

especially since the establishment of Christianity, if the devil is the cause ... of such events?

There remains, then, a single solution. Are the events of Fatima the works of God? It is too soon to reply with certainty to this question. The Church has not yet intervened, naming an inquiry board for it.

When it is made, the mission of this board will be relatively easy to fulfill. On the next October 13, either all will be undone as if by magic, or new proofs, entirely conclusive, will come to confirm those which now exist in favor of the reality of the apparitions of the Virgin.

Sources: The edited notes of Father Formigao; De Marchi, pp 116-121; Doc Crit I pp 62-67.

#9 INTERROGATIONS BY FATHER FORMIGAO, 11 OCT 1917

9A. INTERROGATION OF MANUEL GONCALVES, 11 OCT, UNEDITED NOTES

Manuel Goncalves   clouds white, blue, blood red, rose-colored, yellow one color for each light but weak   the people yellow   [This note was at the top of the page, with no associated question. It is obviously a cryptic note on Goncalves' answer to a question not part of the original list of questions, or an addition to an answer for which Father Formigao had not allowed enough room. See question three of the edited notes.]

Testimony

1. Have the families of the children a good name? Are they decent, respectable people? Do the fathers get drunk? Are the mothers good persons?

The father of Lucia gets drunk, seldom goes to church. Her mother is good and cries because of her husband. In July some bad ones got him drunk to have him do some folly. He ordered the people to leave. He always let his daughter go. A man pushed him and he fell. On the Sunday after the 13th they wanted to leave a tent at his [place]. He wanted to take action against those who put up the tent. The father of Jacinta is very serious, very religious, incapable of deception.

2. What do the people of Fatima think of what the children say? Do they believe them? Do they think they are lying? Or do they think they are victims of a hallucination?

It seems that the children are telling the truth. At first no one wanted to go there. On 13 June—a festival day in the area, St. Anthony's—there were some 60 people there. Another small one went. The parents of Jacinta were not there, they went to the Porto Mos fair, the 13ᵗʰ fair, to buy an ox, their house filled up with people.

3. Did people from here see the extraordinary signs?

There were many. In August almost all.

4. What were the signs?

Hazy air. A cloud lowered to the oak bush. There was no dust in July. A cloud lowered to the oak bush and made the air dusty. The people heard a noise in July also.

5. Do they suspect that anyone induced the children to play a hoax?

No.

6. Have many people come from outside to talk to the children?

Innumerable people came to see the children.

7. Do they accept money that people want to give them?

They have accepted something—some money—when they insist, but not willingly.

8. Are the families poor? Do they live by their work?

They aren't poor. They are fairly comfortable. Jacinta's father does well. The other father does not care for his things well.

9. Do they have property?

Yes.

10. Are there people in Fatima who were close to the children during the apparitions?

In July—Jacinto d'Almeida Lopes from Amoreira; in July Manuel d'Oliveira of Montello.

11. Did you hear her talk?

Some people say they heard the sound of a reply. The child speaks firmly.

12. Does she bless herself and pray?

She prays the rosary. There are people who come to pray at the place at night. Almost every hour of the day, from far and near, and more from afar at the place, especially on Sundays.

Source: Father Formigao's unedited notes, 11 Oct 1917; Doc Crit I pp 81-83.

9B. INTERROGATION OF MANUEL GONCALVES, 11 OCT, EDITED NOTES

(Gist— I went to Fatima on 10 Oct, convinced of the sincerity of the seers, fearing hallucination or demonic inspiration, but expecting the miracle that had been forecast. Fatima might become another Lourdes. I stayed overnight in Montelo, two kilometers from Fatima. I interviewed the son of my host, Manuel Goncalves, Jr., 30 years old.)

1. Have the parents of the children of Aljustrel, who are said to be blessed with the apparition of Our Lady, a good name?

The parents of Jacinta and Francisco are very good people. The father is known as the most serious man of the place. He is incapable of deceiving anyone. Lucia's father sometimes gets drunk and attends church little, but is not a bad man. On the 13th of June some bad-minded companions got him drunk in the hope of getting him to commit some folly at the apparition site. Actually, although he allowed his daughter to go to the site as usual, he ordered the other people to leave. He is the owner of the moor where the oak tree serves as the pedestal for the apparition. The people, seeing that he was drunk, paid no notice to his order and a man pushed him and made him fall. The mother of Lucia is a pious, hard-working woman.

2. What do the inhabitants of Fatima think about the children's statements?

At first people did not want to go to the Cova da Iria. No one believed the children. On June 13, the day of the second apparition, there was a festival in the parish in honor of St. Anthony. At the Cova da Iria there were hardly 70 people at the time of the apparition. The parents of Jacinta and Francisco had gone early in the morning to Porto de Mos for the so-called "fair of the 13th" to buy an ox and return at night. In their absence the house filled up with people who wanted to see the children and question them. At present a large proportion of the people think that they are telling the truth. For my part, I am convinced of it.

3. On the days of the apparitions are there extraordinary signs? Many people claim to have seen them?

The signs are very numerous. In August almost everyone who was present saw them. A cloud came down on the oak bush. In July the same thing was seen. There was no dust in the area. The cloud swept clean the air, which seemed hazy.

4. Is someone suspected of having induced the children into playing a hoax?

No, that is not believable.

5. Did many outsiders come to talk to the children?

Innumerable people from everywhere.

6. Do they accept money which is offered to them?

They have accepted a little something, but don't accept it willingly.

7. Are the families poor? Do they live by their work? Do they own property?

They are not poor and are fairly comfortably situated. If Lucia's family is not better off, it is because her father frequently gets drunk and neglects the care of his properties.

8. Are there people in Fatima who were close to the children during the apparitions?

In July, Jacinto A. Lopes of Amoreira and Manuel d'Oliveira of Montelo were at their feet.

9. What does Lucia do during the apparition?

She says the rosary. When she talks to the Lady she speaks loudly. I myself heard her in June because I was near. Some people say they hear the sound of the replies.

10. Is the apparition site much frequented on other days by the pious and curious?

Many people go there, especially on Sundays. The biggest crowd is at night. People come from far and near, more even from outside the parish. They pray the rosary and sing hymns in honor of the Virgin.

Source: Father Formigao's edited notes, 11 Oct; Doc Crit I pp 102-106.

9C. INTERROGATION OF LUCIA'S MOTHER, 11 OCT, UNEDITED NOTES

Mother of Lucia—Transcript

1. Is your daughter the cousin of Francisco and Jacinta?
Her father is the brother of the mother of Jacinta and Francisco.

2. What is the truth about what happened last year? Where and in what month?

A year ago various little ones (Francisco's brother Joao) stated that a figure, whose face they did not see, wrapped in a white cloth appeared to them at the Cova da Iria and other places, behind the Moinho do Cabeco. Several times. It is the others who said it. It is only later that Lucia said it. The little Teresa of Jose Mathias and Maria of Manuel Pereira. The mother told her she was lying, (and scolded her so much that the first time this year she told Jacinta and Francisco to keep quiet, that her mother would scold them).

3. How did you learn this year about the first time the Lady appeared?
It was her daughter that told her.

4. Did you never scold Lucia for going to the Cova da Iria?
She gave her freedom on these things this year. They asked her if she wanted to go, and she said yes. Other times she said that if they let her she was going. The other children go with their parents.

5. To whom does the flock belong?

The two families. They joined them because they wanted to, as they were going.

6. (Gist– The question and answer concerns how the children were dressed.)

7. Do you have a book called *Short Mission*?

[Father Formigao put here the answer to question #8].

8. Did you used to read it to Lucia?

I read to her about La Salette.

9. And to the other children?

No. Before the other children.

10. Did you think that the reading about La Salette made a great impression on Lucia?

[No answer is given to this question, but it is implied by the next answer.]

11. Did she speak at various timers about the case of La Salette?

She never noticed.

12. Who went to get the abducted children? When? When did the administrator find them?

The administrator, a county official and the mayor, Francisco da Silva of Amoreira. A brother of Jacinta went to talk with the children at the house of the administrator. Her mother was resigned.

13. Did many people come to see your daughter?

Many almost every day.

Many people said they saw signs. Were they deceived? [This seems to be an extra question. If so no answer was recorded.]

Source: Father Formigao's interrogation of Lucia's mother; Doc Crit I pp 83-85.

9D. INTERROGATION OF LUCIA'S MOTHER, 11 OCT, EDITED NOTES

After this interrogation [of Goncalves], I went to Aljustrel, arrived, and went at once to the home of Lucia. ..... Her mother appeared ... and acceded willingly to my request to interrogate her daughter again. [But] first I asked her some questions.

[The first three questions and answers are similar to those in the unedited notes.]

4. Did the children use to go to the apparition site alone or were they with other children?

They went alone. Almost always other children also went, but with their parents and they stayed with them, they did not join with Lucia and her cousins.

5. Did the children guard the flock? To whom did it belong?

Lucia guarded a small flock of sheep and her cousins another. These flocks belonged to the respective families. Sometimes they joined the flocks, but only when they wanted to. I have already sold the sheep which Lucia was guarding.

6. (Gist– The question and answer concerns how the children were dressed.)

7. It seems to me that you have a book called *Short Mission* and that at times you read it to your children. Is that right?

It's true, I have this book and have read it to my children.

8. Did you read the story of La Salette to Lucia and the other children?

Only to Lucia and my other children.

9. Did Lucia talk at times of the story of La Salette and show in any way that this story had made a great impression on her spirit?

I never heard her say anything about this, if I recall well.

10. When the children were abducted by the administrator .... Did anyone demand that they be returned?

A brother of Francisco and Jacinta went to talk to them at the administrator's house. His wife asked if he was looking for the children. To which he replied no. The administrator himself came to return them to Fatima.

11. [The question and answer are the same as question #13 of the unedited notes.]

Source: Father Formigao's interrogation of Lucia's mother; Doc Crit I pp 106-110.

9E. INTERROGATION OF LUCIA, 11 OCT, UNEDITED NOTES

1. Where do you go to get the litters?

To buy the litters. She thinks that she wants a chapel at the Cova da Iria.

2. When will they take the money to the church?

That they make two litters and take them to the festival of Our Lady of the Rosary. She does not explain.

3. On Saturday, besides Our Lady of the Rosary, St. Joseph and the Child, will Our Lady of Sorrows appear, with a bunch of flowers, Our Lord to bless the people and two angels? [The editors of *Documentacao Critica de*

Fatima use three dots to indicate that there was no answer. Presumably the question was not asked.]

4. Will St Joseph and the Child appear to all the people or only to you, Jacinta and Francisco?

… [Not answered.]

5. Who told you that Our Lady would appear on the 13th of each month?

She would make a miracle so that all would believe.

6. Do you feel that something calls or takes you to go there?

I feel a desire to go there. I would be sad if I did not go.

7. When did Our Lady tell you that she would make a miracle on 13 Oct so that everyone would believe that she is appearing?

She said it several times. It was only the last time that I asked her.

8. Are you not afraid that the people will harm you if nothing extraordinary happens on that day?

I am not afraid.

9. Did you see Our Lady pray sometime, pray the rosary or order you to pray?

She ordered us to pray a few times.

10. Did she order you to pray for the conversion of sinners?

She ordered us to pray to Our Lady of the Rosary for the end of the war.

11. Did you see the signs that other people have seen, the star, roses falling from the dress of the Lady?

I saw no star nor extraordinary signs.

12. In July did you hear thunder, roar or the earth shaking?

Never.

13. Can you read? No. Are you learning? No. How are you fulfilling the Lady's order? … [No answer]

14. At times you order the people to kneel and pray. When? When the Lady appears?

She wants it. The Lady does not order it.

15. Do you always kneel when the Lady appears?

Sometimes standing, sometimes kneeling.

16. Does the Lady make the sign of the cross? No. Does she pray? No.

17. Is her voice pleasing? It is pleasing.

18. How old does the Lady seem? How tall is she, a child or a lady?

She seems to be fifteen years old.

19. What color is the rosary chain? The crucifix? Were they gold?

The chain was white. The crucifix white.

20. Did her veil come down to her forehead? It came to her forehead.

21. How was the light, the shine?

A brilliant light, more beautiful than sunlight.

22. Did the Lady ever greet you with her head or arms? Did she ever smile at you?

Nothing.

23. Does the Lady at times look at the crowd? How?

I never saw her look at the people.

24. Do you hear the noise and shouts of the people during the time that you see the Lady?

I don't hear the people talk.

25. Did the Lady ask you in May to return to the Cova da Iria each month until October? Did she say that it was on each thirteenth?

She said it was on the day. On the 13ᵗʰ. From month to month for six months.

Did you hear reading from the *Short Mission*? Did the case of La Salette impress you?

I didn't talk at all, nor think [about it.]

Is the secret for the good of you and your companions? Is it for your spiritual good, for this life? If the people knew, would they be sad? … [No answer.]

Did you say that they would be sad? No.

Tell me the story of your abduction? … [No answer.]

Source: Father Formigao's interrogation of Lucia; Doc Crit I pp 86-91.

9F. INTERROGATION OF LUCIA, 11 OCT, EDITED NOTES

When this interrogation [of Lucia's mother] was over, I asked four trust-worthy persons to attend the interrogation of Lucia, as witnesses: Anastacio da Teresa, Goncalves da Silva and Manuel Henriques, all from Aljustrel, and Francisco Rodrigues from Moita do Martinho. I immediately began the interview of the seer.

[Unlike the interrogations of Lucia's mother and Manuel Goncalves, the interrogations of Lucia are very similar in the edited and unedited versions, although there is some change in the numbering of the questions. Therefore, I give here only those questions where there is a significant difference or where the edited version makes the answer of Lucia clearer. Virtually the entire text of the edited notes is given in *Fatima from the Beginning* pp 123-126.]

1. You told me some days ago that Our Lady wanted the money given by the people to be taken to the parish church in two litters. How are these litters to be obtained and when are they to be taken to the church?

They must be bought with the money which is given, and carried on the feast of Our Lady of the Rosary.

2. Do you know for certain where Our Lady wants the chapel in her honor to be built?

I don't know for certain, but I think she wants the chapel in the Cova da Iria.

3. What did she say she would do in order that people would believe (that she is appearing)?

She said that she would make a miracle.

4. When did she say this?

She said it several times, but only once, on the occasion of the first apparition, did I ask it.

[Questions and answers 5 and 6 and 8 through 14 are similar to those in the unedited notes.]

7. Sometimes do you see the Lady bless herself, pray or move the rosary beads? No.

15. When you tell the people to kneel and pray, is it the Lady who orders it.

I am the one who wants it.

[Questions and answers 17 through 20 are similar to those in the unedited version]

21. Is the shine which envelops her beautiful?

It is more beautiful than sunlight and more brilliant.

[The remaining questions and answers, 21 through 26, are similar to the unedited notes.]

27. Did your mother read [from] the book called *Short Mission*, where it tells the story of the apparition of Our Lady to the boy and girl?

Yes, I heard it.

28. Did you often think of this story and talk of it to other children?

I never thought of this story nor talk of it to other children.

Source: Father Formigao's interrogation of Lucia; Doc Crit I pp 110-114; De Marchi, pp 123-125.

9G. INTERROGATION OF JACINTA, 11 OCT, UNEDITED NOTES

(The answers to seven unanswered questions are given first, as follows.)

The Lady said they should pray the rosary the first time, according to Jacinta.

She heard the secret of the Lady. The second time, on St. Anthony's day. It is for their good and happiness.

It is for all three. It is not so that they get rich. It is not that they go to heaven.

She cannot tell the secret. Our Lady said they should say nothing of the secret.

She held her hands upright. At times she held her hands upturned to the sky.

If the people knew the secret they would be sad.

The Lady said they should be there for six months, from month to month, until she said what she wanted.

[Father Formigao then gives a brief description of the eyes and hair of the seers.]

1. Do you see the feet of the Lady? How are they? ... [No answer.]

2. Does her face have a shine? I can't look [at her] well. It hurts my eyes.

Source: Father Formigao's interrogation of Jacinta; Doc Crit I pp 91, 92.

9H. INTERROGATION OF JACINTA, 11 OCT, EDITED NOTES

When this interview [with Lucia] was finished, I went to the home of the other two seers and proceeded to interview them in the presence of their father and some of their sisters. I interrogated Jacinta first.

1. Did the Lady tell you to say the rosary? Yes.

2. When? When she appeared the first time.

3. Did you hear the secret or was it only Lucia who heard? I heard too.

4. When? At the second apparition, on St. Anthony's day.

5. Is the secret that you will be rich? No.

6. That you will be good and happy? Yes, it is for the good of all three of us.

7. Is it that you will go to heaven? No.

8. Can you tell the secret? I can't.

9. Why? Because the Lady said we were not to tell it to anyone.

10. If the people knew it, would they be sad? Yes.

11. How does the Lady hold her hands? Always upright.

12. Always? Sometimes she turns the palms up toward heaven.

13. In May did she say that she wanted you to go to the Cova again? She said she wanted us to go there for six months running until October when she would say what she wanted.

14. Has she a shine around her head? Yes.

15. Can you look easily at her face? No, because it hurts my eyes.

16. Do you always hear well what the Lady says? Last time I couldn't hear everything because of the noise the people were making.

Source: Father Formigao's interrogation of Lucia; De Marchi, pp 125, 126; Doc Crit I pp 114, 115.

9I. INTERROGATION OF FRANCISCO, 11 OCT, UNEDITED NOTES

1. How old are you? I am nine.

2. Do you hear the Lady or only see her? I only see her, not hear.

3. Do you see the feet of the Lady? How are they? The mantle reaches to her knees, and the dress until the middle of her leg.

4. Does she have a shine on her face? She has a shine, a brightness, around her head.

5. And around her head? I can look there only little because of the light.

6. The money to buy litters? … [No answer.]

7. Would the people be sad if they knew the secret? They would.

Source: Father Formigao's interrogation of Francisco; Doc Crit I p 93.

Note: The edited notes are similar, except that they omit #3 and add that the lady's dress had gold braid, and that her cross and chain were white; De Marchi, p 126; Doc Crit I pp 115, 116.

#10 INTERROGATIONS BY FATHER FORMIGAO, 13 OCT 1917

10A. INTERROGATION OF LUCIA, 13 OCT, EDITED NOTES

13 Oct at 7:00 at night, in the home of the family of Francisco and Jacinta.

Interrogation of Lucia

1. Did Our Lady return again today at the Cova da Iria? She returned.

2. Was she dressed like the other times? She was dressed the same way.

3. Did St. Joseph and the Child Jesus also appear? Yes.

4. Did anyone else appear?

Our Lord also appeared, blessing the people, and the Lady of the two [card] suits.

5. What do you mean by "the Lady of the two suits"?

The Lady appeared dressed like the Lady of Sorrows, but without a sword in her breast, and the Lady dressed like I don't know how, but it seemed to me she was Our Lady of Carmel

6. You saw them all at the same time, did you not?

No, First I saw the Lady of the Rosary, St. Joseph and the Child, then I saw Our Lord alone, then the Lady of Sorrows and lastly the Lady who seemed to me to be the Lady of Carmel.

7. Was the Child Jesus on foot or around the neck of St. Joseph?

Around the neck.

8. Was the Child [fairly] grown up? He was very little.

9. What age did he seem to be? About a year old.

10. Why did you say at one of the times the Lady seemed to be dressed as the Lady of Carmel?

Because she had some things hanging down from her hand.

11. Did she appear on top of the oak bush?

No, she appeared at the foot of the sun after the Lady had disappeared from the foot of the oak bush.

12. Was Our Lord standing? I only saw Him from the waist up.

13. How long did the apparition at the oak bush last? Enough to say a rosary?

We wouldn't finish [one], it seems to me.

14. Did the figures you saw at the sun last very long? A short time.

15. Did the Lady tell you who she was?

She said she was Our Lady of the Rosary.

16. Did you ask what she wanted? I did.

17. And what did she say?

She said the people should amend their lives, not offend Our Lord, who is much offended, ask Our Lord pardon for our sins, that the war is ending today and that we should expect our soldiers back shortly.

18. Did she say anything else?

She said also that she wanted a chapel built at the Cova da Iria.

19. With what money were they to build the chapel?

I think with the money which is gathered there.

20. Did she say anything about our dead soldiers in the war? No.

21. Did she say that you should tell the people to look at the sun? No.

22. Did she say she wanted the people to do penance? Yes.

23. Did she use the word penance?

No, she said we should pray the rosary and amend our lives from our sins and ask pardon of Our Lord, but did not say penance.

24. When did the sign in the sun begin? Was it after the Lady disappeared? Yes.

25. Did you see the Lady come? Yes.

26. Where did she come from? From the east.

27. And the other times? I didn't look the other times.

28. Did you see her leave? Yes.

29. Toward where? To the east.

30. How did she disappear? Little by little.

31. What disappeared first?

It was her head, then her body. The last thing was her legs.

32. When she left, did she back up or did she turn her back to the people?

She left with her back turned to the people.

33. Did she take long to disappear? She wasted little time.

34. Was she wrapped in some brightness?

I saw her in the middle of a shine. This time also it was blinding. From time to time I had to turn my eyes away.

35. Will Our Lady return again?

I don't think she will, but she said nothing.

36. You have no desire to return to the Cova on the 13th? No.

37. Will the Lady make no more miracles, no cures of the sick?

I don't know.

38. Did you ask no petitions of her?

I said that today I have various petitions to be answered, and she said she would answer some, but not others.

39. Did she say when she would answer them? She didn't say.

40. Under what title did she want the chapel to be built?

She said today that she was Our Lady of the Rosary.

41. Did she say she wanted lots of people from everywhere to come there?

She didn't order anyone to come there.

42. Did you see signs in the sun? I saw the sun turning around.

43. Did you also see signs at the oak bush? I saw none.

44. When was the Lady more beautiful, this time or the others?

The same.

45. How long was her dress? It came down to the middle of her legs.

Source: Interrogation of Lucia by Father Formigao, 13 Oct; Doc Crit I pp 127-132.

10B. INTERROGATION OF JACINTA, 13 OCT, EDITED NOTES

[The edited and unedited notes were virtually the same and thus I give only the edited ones, adding in brackets items found only in the unedited notes.]

1. Besides Our Lady, whom did you see today when you were at the Cova da Iria?

I saw St. Joseph and the Child Jesus. [Our Lord was there from the waist up.]

2. Where did you see them? I saw them at the foot of the sun.

3. What did the Lady say?

She said we should pray the rosary to Our Lady every day and that the war is ending today.

4. To whom did she say this? To me and Lucia. Francisco did not hear.

5. Did you hear her say when our soldiers would return? I didn't hear.

6. What else did she say?

She said we should build a chapel at the Cova da Iria. [The other time Jacinta expressed herself thusly: She said the people should build a chapel there.]

7. Did you hear her say this to you or to Lucia? To her.

8. From where did the Lady come? She came from the east.

9. And where did she go when she disappeared? She went to the east.

10. Did she leave turned toward the people? No, she turned her back to them.

11. She didn't say she would return to the Cova da Iria? She said before that it was the last time she would come, and today she also said it.

Did the Lady say nothing more? Today she said that the people should say the rosary every day to Our Lady of the Rosary.

12. Where did she say the people should pray the rosary? She didn't say where.

Did she say we should go to the church to pray? She didn't say that.

13. Do you most prefer to pray the rosary, here in your house or at the Cova da Iria? At the Cova da Iria.

14. Why do you prefer to pray there? For no reason.

15. Did the Lady say with what money the chapel was to be built?

She said they should build a chapel. I didn't want to learn from what money.

16. Did you look at the sun? I did. [No answer.]

17. Did you see signs? I did. [Question and answer not given.]

18. Was it the Lady who told you to look at the sun?

She did not order us to do it.

19. Then how could you see the signs?

I turned my eyes to the side. [They were in front, almost to the north.]

20. Was the Child Jesus to the right or left of St. Joseph?

He was on the right. [At the foot of the sun.]

21. Was he standing or around [St. Joseph's] neck? He was at his side.

22. Did you see the right arm of St. Joseph? No.

How tall was the Child? Did He come to the head or the chest of St. Joseph? He didn't reach up to the waist of St. Joseph.

23. How old did the Child seem to be?

He was like Deolinda of Jose das Neves. [A child some two years old.]

Source: Father Formigao's interrogation of Jacinta, 13 Oct; Doc Crit I pp 123-125, 132-134.

Note: Deolinda was four, almost five, at that time; Doc Crit I p 125, footnote 10.

10C. INTERROGATION OF FRANCISCO, 13 OCT, EDITED NOTES

1. This time also did you see Our Lady? Yes.

2. What Lady was it? It was Our Lady of the Rosary.

3. How was she dressed?

She was dressed in white and had a white rosary.

4. Did you see St. Joseph and the Child Jesus? I did.

5. Where did you see them? At the side of the sun.

6. Was the Child Jesus around the neck of St. Joseph or at his side?

He was at his side.

7. How did the Lady hold her hands? She held them upright.

8. Did you see her only over the oak bush or also at the foot of the sun? I saw her also at the foot of the sun.

9. What was clearer and more brilliant: the sun or the Lady's face?

The Lady's face was clearer; the Lady was white.

10. Did you hear what the Lady said? No, I didn't.

11. Who told you the secret? Was it the Lady? No, it was Lucia.

12. Can you tell it? I don't tell it.

13. You don't tell it because you are afraid of Lucia; you are afraid she will beat you, no? No.

14. Then why don't you tell it? Is it because it is a sin?

I keep quiet; it is a sin to tell the secret.

15. Is the secret for the good of your soul, of Lucia's soul and of Jacinta's? Yes.

16. And for the soul of your pastor? I don't know.

17. Would the people be sad if they knew it? They would be.

18. From what side did the Lady come? She came from the east part.

19. And when she left did she go to the same side?
She also went to the east.

20. Did she go backing up? She left with her back turned toward us.

21. Did she go fast or slowly? She went slowly.

22. Did she walk like us?
She didn't walk; she went straight. She didn't move her feet.

23. What part of the Lady disappeared first? It was her head.

24. Did you see her now as you did the other times?
Now I saw her better than the last month.

25. When was she more beautiful, today or the other times?
She was as beautiful today as last month.

Source: Father Formigao's interrogation of Francisco, 13 Oct; Doc Crit I pp 135-137.

#11 INTERROGATIONS BY FATHER FORMIGAO, 19 OCT, EDITED NOTES

11A. INTERROGATION OF THE CHILDREN, 19 OCT 1917

(Gist– I went by car to Fatima. Many pious women were praying at the Cova da Iria. I went to Jacinta's home, where the three children were being interrogated by Father Lacerda.) The number of visitors of the children is growing day by day. They come at all hours from the most remote points of the country the children are quite worn out. Lucia, especially, is seriously exhausted. One could see that her excessive tiredness caused her to reply to the questions made to her without the attention and consideration which was to be desired. At times she responds almost mechanically. It happened often [that she replied] that she did not recall well the circumstances of the apparition, to the contrary of what occurred before 13 Oct. If care is not taken to spare the children the fatigue of frequent and long interviews, their health may suffer a deep blow.

Source: Father Formigao's interrogation of the seers, 19 Oct; Doc Crit I pp 145-147.

11B. INTERROGATION OF LUCIA, 19 OCT, EDITED NOTES

(Gist– With the permission of Jacinta's parents) I interrogated the three children separately, in the presence of three [women, whose names are given]. I began with Lucia.)

1. On the 13th of this month did Our Lady say that the war was ending on that same day? What were the words she used?

She spoke thus: the war is ending, even today; expect the return of your soldiers very shortly.

2. Did she say "expect your soldiers" or "expect your military"?

She said" "expect your military."

3. But look, the war is still going on! ... The newspapers report that there have been battles after the 13th. How can you explain this, if Our Lady said that the war was ending that day?

I don't know. I only know that I heard her say that the war was ending on the 13th. I know no more.

4. Some people say that they heard you say that day that Our Lady had said that the war was ending shortly. Is that right?

I said it exactly as the Lady had said it.

5. On 27 Sep I went to talk with you at your house, do you recall? Yes.

6. Well, on that day you told me that Our Lady had said that on 13 Oct St. Joseph would also come with the Child Jesus and that after this the war would end soon, not on that day.

I can't recall well now how she said it. Perhaps she may have said this; I don't know. Maybe I didn't understand the Lady well.

7. On this 13th did you order the people to look at the sun?

I don't recall doing it.

8. Did you order [them] to take off their hats?

The other months I ordered it; I don't remember ordering it the last time.

9. Did you know when the sign in the sun was to begin? No.

10. Did you look at it? I looked; it seemed to be the moon.

11. Why did you look at the sun?

I looked because all those people said you should look at the sun.

12. Did Our Lady say that she would ask her Divine Son for the souls of the dead soldiers in the war? No, sir.

13. Did she say the people would be punished if they did not reform from their sins?

I don't remember if she said it. It seems to me [that she did] not.

14. On the 13th you did not have doubts, like today, about what the Lady said. How do you explain your doubts today?

On that day I remembered better. Less time had passed.

15. What did you see about a year ago? Your mother said that you and other children saw a wrapped form, whose face you couldn't see. Why did you tell me last month that there was nothing? !..... [No answer.]

16. That time did you run away? I think I did.

17. On 11 Oct you didn't want to tell me that on the 13th Our Lord was to appear, blessing the people, and Our Lady of Sorrows. Were you afraid that I would make fun of you as other persons had done, saying that it was impossible? Or was it because many strange persons were there and you were shy about saying that before so many people. See, Jacinta has told me all! ..... [No answer.]

18. When did Our Lady tell you that these apparitions were to occur on Oct 13?

It was on the day that she appeared at Valinhos or another 13th. I am not sure.

19. Did you also see Our Lord?

I saw a figure that seemed to be a man; it seemed to be Our Lord.

20. Where was this figure? It was at the side of the sun.

21. Did you see Him bless the people?

I did not see it. But Our Lady had said that Our Lord would come to bless the people.

22. If the people knew the secret which Our Lady revealed to you, would they be sad?

I think they would be as they are; about the same.

Source: Father Formigao's interrogation of Lucia, 19 Oct; Doc Crit I pp 146-151.

11C. INTERROGATION OF FRANCISCO, 19 OCT, EDITED NOTES

(Gist– At once I proceeded to interrogate Francisco.)

1. On the 13th of this month did you see Our Lord blessing the people?

No, I didn't see it; I saw, but it was Our Lady.

2. Did you see Our Lady of Sorrows or Our Lady of Carmel?

I didn't see them. Our Lady appeared like she was down below. She was dressed the same.

3. Did you not look at the sun? I did.

4. Did you not see St. Joseph and the Child Jesus? I did.

5. Were they far or near the sun? Near the sun.

6. On what side of the sun was St. Joseph? He was on the left side.

7. And on what side was Our Lady? On the right side.

8. Where was the Child Jesus? He was at the feet of St. Joseph.

9. On what side? I don't recall on what side.

10. Was the Child big or small? He was very small.

11. Was He the size of Deolinda of Jose das Neves?
He was about like her.

12. When Our Lady was on the oak bush, did you hear what Our Lady said to Lucia?
I did not hear.

13. Did you hear the sound of her voice? I also did not hear it.

14. Did it seem that she was not talking? It seemed so.

15. Did you not see her move her lips? I did not see it.

16. Did you not see her laugh? Also no.

17. Did you see the signs in the sun? What were they?
I looked and saw that the sun was turning around. It seemed like a fire wheel.

18. When did the signs appear, before or after Our Lady disappeared from the oak?
It was when the Lady disappeared.

19. Did you hear Lucia tell the people to look at the sun?
I heard. She gave a shout that the people should look at the sun.

20. Was it the Lady who ordered [her] to tell the people to look at the sun?
It was. The Lady pointed with her finger at the area where the sun was.

21. And when was that? It was when she disappeared.

22. The signs in the sun began then? They did.

23. What were the colors that you saw in the sun?
Very beautiful colors, blue, yellow and others.

Source: Father Formigao's interrogation of Francisco, 19 Oct; Doc Crit I pp 152-154.

11D. INTERROGATION OF JACINTA, 19 OCT, EDITED NOTES

(Gist–The interview of Jacinta took place while they were going from Aljustrel to Fatima, with a specified lady holding her hand, and the other ladies and seers ahead of them.)

1. On Oct 13 did you see Our Lord, the Lady of Sorrows and the Lady of Carmel?

I did not see them.

2. But on the 11th you told me that they were to appear.

Yes. Lucia is the one who saw them, not me.

3. Did you see St. Joseph? I did. Lucia said he was giving peace.

4. Did you look at the sun? I did.

5. And what did you see?

I saw the sun red, green and other colors and I saw it turn around.

6. Did you hear Lucia tell the people to look at the sun?

I did. She said in a very loud voice that they should look at the sun. The sun was already turning.

7. Was it the Lady who ordered her to tell the people?

The Lady said nothing.

8. What did the Lady say this last time?

She said: I come here to tell you not to offend Our Lord any more, that he is very offended, that if the people amend their ways the war would end, if they did not the world would end. Lucia heard better than I what the Lady said.

9. Did the Lady say that the war would end on that day or shortly?

The Lady said that the war would end when she arrived in heaven.

10. But the war has not yet ended.

I think it will end on Sunday.

Source: Father Formigao's interrogation of Jacinta, 19 Oct; Doc Crit I pp 154-156.

11E. INTERROGATION OF JACINTA, 19 OCT, UNEDITED NOTES

1. On the 13th of this month did you see Our Lord blessing the people [and] the Lady of Sorrows and the Lady of Carmel? You said before that they were to appear.

[I saw] St. Joseph and the Child Jesus. I did not see the Lady of Sorrows or the Lady of Carmel. It was Lucia who saw the other Lady, not me. St Joseph was blessing the people.

Did you not look at the sun?

I looked. I saw the sun red, green and many colors, it was turning around.

2. Did you see the signs on this day? .... [The previous question answers this.]

3. Did you hear Lucia tell the people to look at the sun? Was it the Lady who ordered it? Lucia: look at the sun in a very loud voice. Did the signs begin then?

Lucia pointed with her finger to the sun. It was already turning around. The Lady said nothing.

4. What did the Lady say the last time? Say what she said.

I come to tell you not to offend Our Lord, who is much offended, that the people mend their ways, that if the people amend their ways the war will end, if not, the world will end.

5. Did she say the war would end that day or shortly?

Our Lady said that the war would end when she reached heaven.

But the war has not ended!

It will end! It will end! I think it will end on Sunday. Lucia said that St. Joseph was giving peace.

Source: Father Formigao's interrogation of Jacinta, 19 Oct; Doc Crit I pp 141-143.

#12 FATHER FORMIGAO'S INTERROGATIONS, 2 NOV 1917, EDITED NOTES

12A. INTERROGATION OF LUCIA

1. Did the Lady wear stockings? Are you sure of it?

I think they were stockings, but maybe they were not.

2. You once said the Lady wore white stockings. Were they stockings or were they feet?

If they were stockings, they were white. But I am not sure if they were stockings or her feet.

3. Was the dress always the same length?

The last time it seemed longer.

4. You have never told the secret, nor even said the people would be sad if they knew. Francisco and Jacinta say they would be sad. If you can't say this, how can they say it?

I don't now if they should or should not say that the people would be sad. Our Lady said that we were not to say anything to anybody, so I can't say anything.

Source: De Marchi, p 157; Doc Crit I pp 177, 178.

12B. LATER INTERROGATION OF LUCIA, 2 NOV

1. You didn't want to tell me what you saw last year. Probably you think it is an unimportant matter that isn't worth investigating. But I think you are wrong. I need to know what you saw and how the thing happened. Is it certain you saw a white figure?

It is.

2. Where?

I saw this figure at the Cabeco, at Estrumeiras, at the foot of the Cova da Iria.

3. How many times did you see it?

I don't recall how many times.

4. Did you see it on the ground or on top of some tree?

I saw it on top of an oak.

5. What did the figure seem like to you?

It seemed like a figure wrapped in a sheet.

6. Did you talk to it?

I said nothing to it.

7. Were you alone or with other persons?

The first time I was with Theresa of Jose Mathias from Casa Velha and with Manuel Justino Pereira. [An error for Maria of Manuel Justino Pereira. See the interrogation of Lucia's mother, 11 Oct, Annex II #9C.]

8. Did they also see?

They said they also saw.

9. Who was present the second time?

They were Manuel of Jose das Neves of Aljustrel and Manuel of Maria de Jesus from Casa Velha.

10. And the third time? The third time we were alone, I and Joao Marto. He said he saw nothing.

11. The figure was on the same tree every time?

It appeared on more than one tree each time.

12. Who saw the figure first? The others saw first and told me.

13. How long did it stay? It stayed a little time.

14. Did it say anything? It said nothing.

15. Who do you think this figure was? I don't know who it was.

16. Was it Our Lady? I think it was not Our Lady.

17. Is it true that once when you were praying the rosary the animals you were pasturing went into a field where there was wheat and chick peas, but they ate nothing?

It is true.

18. When did this happen?

I don't remember, but it seems it was a Sunday.

19. Did you see the animals eat the wheat or chick peas? No, I didn't.

20. But are you sure they didn't eat?

I know because one of the property owners said that they did no damage.

21. Did you move the animals from this place?

After finishing the rosary we moved them.

22. Whose property was it?

23.(sic) It belonged to Jose Mathias and Francisco Antonio of Casa Velha. They are two adjoining pieces of land.

24. Why didn't you move the animals when you saw them going into a cultivated field?

I didn't move them because I wanted to say the rosary.

25. Didn't you fear they would eat what was planted?

I thought they would eat, but let them go.

26. Didn't you know it was your duty to take them out at once so they would cause no damage?

I confess this fault.

27. I heard it said that you told someone that you would live another 20 years, right?

I don't recall.

28. Before each apparition did you see a stroke of lightning?

At times I saw one, at other times two. The air was clouded, like in a thunderstorm.

29. The first time the Lady appeared were there clouds? I don't recall.

30. What were you doing when the Lady appeared to you the first time? We were praying the rosary before seeing her.

31. At the first apparition, did you kneel or stand? We kept standing.

32. Did the Lady always come wrapped in a shine? Yes.

What color was this shine? It was very light, very white.

33. Did the shine appear before the Lady?

It appeared at almost the same time.

34. At the first time did you ask Francisco and Jacinta not to tell the family anything of what you had seen? Yes.

35. Why? Because last year my mother scolded me when I told her I had seen a white figure, and she said I was lying.

36. Did your mother learn of the apparition from you?

No, it was from Francisco and Jacinta, or from people to whom they told what they saw.

37. Tell me what you heard the Lady say in May.

In May the Lady said not to fear because she would do us no harm. I asked her where she was from, and she said she was from heaven. I asked her what she wanted, and she said that we should come there each month from month to month and at the end of six months she would say what she wanted.

38. From then on why did you go to the apparition site on the 13th and not on another day of the month?

I went on the 13th because that made one month. I understood that I should go on the 13th because the day of the first apparition was the 13th.

39. Did you ask her any questions? I asked her if we would go to heaven and she said yes, but Francisco would have to say the rosary.

40. Did the Lady say anything else? Perhaps, I don't remember.

41. What did the Lady say in June?

She said we should continue to come to the Cova da Iria and we should learn to read.

42. Did she say anything else?

The son of Manuel Carreira was there. He was crippled in the legs and back. I asked the Lady if she would cure him, and she said that within a year he would be cured. And he was cured little by little, in the back. I also asked if she would convert a woman from Moita and she said she would be converted within a year.

43. What else did the Lady say? I recall nothing more.

44. What did she say in July?

She said we should keep coming to the Cova da Iria and pray the rosary for an end to the war, that only she could help. I asked the Lady to cure some sick and convert some sinners who had been recommended to me, and she said she would help some, others no, and that she would convert some, others no.

45. Did she say more? I don't remember if she said any more.

46. What did the Lady say in August? I wasn't there in August.

47. What did she say on Sunday when she appeared to you at Valhinos?

At Valinhos she said that if we weren't taken prisoner the miracle would not be so well known, and St. Joseph would have come with the Infant Jesus to give peace to the world and Our Lord to bless the people.

48. What else did she say?

I asked her what we should do with the money that had been offered, and she said we should carry it in two litters to the Lady of the Rosary on the feast of Our Lady of the Rosary.

49. Were you the one who remembered to make this question?

No, the one who held the money ordered me to ask the question.

50. Did the Lady say anything else?

I asked her again for the sick and sinners recommended to me, and she said some would be better and others converted within a year. That day I didn't ask anything more.

51. What did the Lady say in September?

I don't recall what the Lady said. Perhaps it was this day that she said that on Oct 13 St. Joseph was to come with the Child Jesus to bless the people and Our Lady of the Rosary with a little angel on each side and Our Lady of Sorrows with an arch of flowers.

52. What did the Lady say in October?

I asked her what she wanted. She said we should not offend God anymore, He is already too much offended, that we should say the rosary to Our Lady of the Rosary if we wish to go to heaven, and also said they should build a chapel there to Our Lady of the Rosary or that she was Our Lady of the Rosary. I don't know if she said: "to the Lady of the Rosary" or: "I am the Lady of the Rosary."

53. She didn't say anything more?

I told her I had many requests for cures and conversions, and she said she would improve and convert some, others no.

54. She didn't say anything more?

She said the war was ending today and to expect our military very soon.

55. She didn't say the war would end when she got to heaven?

I don't recall if she said it was when she got to heaven.

56. That day did you tell the people to take off their hats?

I don't remember.

57. Did you let out a shout, telling the people to look at the sun?

I don't remember that I let out a shout.

58. Is it true that the Lady pointed to the sun?

I don't recall what she did.

59. What color was the clothing of the Lady at the foot of the sun?

The mantle was blue, the dress white.

And Our Lord and St. Joseph?

St. Joseph's was scarlet and that of Our Lord and the Child I think were also scarlet.

60. When was it that you asked the Lady to make what was it so that the people would believe that she was appearing to you?

I asked her a few times. The first time I think was in June.

61. When did she tell you the secret? I think it was the second time.

Source: Father Formigao's interrogation of Lucia, 2 Nov 1917; Doc Crit I pp 161-172.

12C. INTERROGATION OF JACINTA BY FATHER FORMIGAO, 2 NOV 1917

1. On which side of the sun did the Child Jesus stand when you saw Him on 13 Oct?

The Child Jesus was in the middle, on the right side of St. Joseph. Our Lady was on the right side of the sun.

2. Was the Lady you saw on the sun different from the one you saw on the holm oak?

The Lady I saw near the sun had a white dress and blue mantle. The one I saw on the holm oak had a white dress and mantle.

3. What color were the feet of the Lady who appeared on the holm oak?

They were white. I think she wore stockings.

4. What color was the clothing of St. Joseph and the Child?

St. Joseph was red and I think the Child was red too.

5. When did the Lady reveal the secret?

I think it was in July.

Source: De Marchi, pp 155, 156; Doc Crit I pp 175, 176.

12D. LATER INTERROGATION OF JACINTA BY FATHER FORMIGAO, 2 NOV 1917

1. What did the Lady say the first time she appeared in May?

Lucia asked what she wanted, and she said we were to go there from month to month, making six months, and that on the last month she would tell us what she wants.

2. Did Lucia ask anything else?

She asked if she would go to heaven and the Lady said yes. Then she asked if I would go to heaven and she said yes. Then she asked if Francisco would go and she said yes, but that he would have to say many rosaries.

3. Did the Lady say anything else?

I don't remember if she said anything else. This was the time the sheep went into the chick peas.

4. What did the Lady say the second time, in June?

Lucia said: "What do you want?" and the Lady replied: "I want you to learn to read."

5. Did Lucia ask anything else?

She asked about sick people and sinners. The Lady said she would make some better and would convert them, but not others.

6. Did the Lady say anything else?

On that day she didn't say anything else.

7. What did the Lady say in August?

In August we didn't go there.

8. You mean that it was the following Sunday at Valinhos that Our Lady spoke? What else did the Lady say?

Lucia asked the Lady if she was to bring Manuel [a brother of Lucia, who was serving in the army at Cabo Verde] and she [the Lady] said that she [Lucia] could bring anybody there.

9. What else did the Lady say?

She said that if they had not taken us to Ourem, St. Joseph with the Child Jesus would come to give peace to the world, and Our Lady, with two angels, one on each side.

10. What else did she say?

She said we were to make two litters and to take them to the feast of the Rosary, I and Lucia with two [other] girls in white, and that Francisco with two other boys were to take the other.

11. Did she say anything else? No.

12. What did the Lady say in September? I don't remember.

13. What did the Lady say in October?

Lucia said: "What do you want?" and she replied: "They should not offend the Lord any more because He is [already] much offended." She said that He would pardon our sins if we wanted to go to heaven. She also said that the people must say the rosary, and that we could expect our soldiers back very soon and that the war would end that day. She said that they were to build a chapel, and I don't remember if she said to the Lady of the Rosary or that she was the Lady of the Rosary.

Source: De Marchi, pp 156, 157; Doc Crit I pp 172-175.

12E. INTERROGATION OF FRANCISCO BY FATHER FORMIGAO, 2 NOV 1917

1. On which side was the Child Jesus when you saw Him near the sun?

He was nearer the sun, on its left side, but on the right side of St. Joseph.

2. Was the Lady you saw near the sun different from the one you saw on the holm oak? The Lady I saw near the sun seemed to be the same as the one I saw below.

3. Did you see Our Lord bless the people? I didn't see Our Lord.

Source: De Marchi, p 157; Doc Crit I pp 176, 177.

12F. INTERROGATION OF LUCIA BY FATHER FORMIGAO, 3 NOV 1917

[Father Formigao made a very short interrogation of Lucia on 3 Nov. It has no value for this book and I do not use it.]

Source: Doc Crit I pp 178, 179.

12G. INTERROGATION OF JOAO, JACINTA'S BROTHER BY FORMIGAO, 2 NOV 1917

(Questions 1 through 8 confirm Lucia's report to Father Formigao on the sign of the approaching apparition on 19 Aug, and his trip to get Jacinta, and her arrival at the Cova.)

9. What did they do then?

Lucia told Jacinta to look where it seemed the Lady was to appear.

10. Did they kneel? No. They all stood.

11. Did you see anything?

I saw nothing. I only heard Lucia talk with the Lady at the foot of the oak bush.

12. Did you hear what Our Lady said? No.

13. What did Lucia say? She asked her what she came there to do.

14. Did you hear the Lady's response?

I didn't, but Lucia stayed waiting a bit.

15. Did Lucia ask any more questions?

Yes, she did, but I don't recall what she said, except the last question, which was if she should bring Manuel there.

16. Lucia didn't tell you what the Lady said?

Yes, the same day at the foot of the oak bush and on the way [back] she told me if she had not been taken to the Town [Vila Nova de Ourem] on the 13th, the miracle would not have been so well known.

17. What was the time when they appeared? It was almost night.

18. Did they stay even longer at the site?

Francisco and Jacinta left, and Lucia and I stayed. Francisco and Jacinta returned and told me later they had gone to pray there, but I stayed a lot to guard the sheep and didn't hear them pray.

Source: Doc Crit I pp 179-181.

#13 INTERROGATION BY FATHER DE LACERDA, 19 OCT 1917

Father Jose Ferreira de Lacerda was pastor of the church in Milagre, but on duty as a military chaplain in France in 1917. He returned on 25 Sep on matters concerning his parish. He did not attend the last apparition at Fatima, but decided to question the seers. He went to Fatima on 19 Oct with a notebook having 36 questions for the pastor, the seers and others. His notes on the seers' replies are in indelible ink, opposite the questions. Not all the questions were asked of the seers, and replies sometimes covered two or more questions. The notebook was found among Father Ferreira's possessions in 1982, some 11 years after his death.

Father de Lacerda edited his notes and published them in his weekly newspaper *O Mensageiro*, of Leiria, on 8, 15, 22 and 29 Nov 1917. A comparison of his original notes with his edited version shows that he was quite loose in editing his notes. However, it is entirely possible that some variations were due to his recollections of parts of the interviews which he was unable to write down during the interviews.

Source: Doc Crit I pp 325-327, 329, 330.

13A. INTERROGATION OF JACINTA BY FATHER DE LACERDA, UNEDITED NOTES

1. How old are you? Whose daughter?

Jacinta de Jesus, 7 years old, daughter of Manuel Pedro Marto and Olimpia de Jesus—She has eight siblings from two marriages.

2. What were you doing when you saw the Lady?

It was mid-day and they were watching the sheep when they saw a Lady dressed in white, hands erect, with beads wound around her arms. Her face was white; she can't compare it with anything. Only on height she says it was equal to Virginia (a twelve-year-old lass); 1 meter 10; she appeared to them on top of an oak bush.

She said that it was her brother who threw a stone and it passed near her.

3. Is it true that the boy threw a stone at the Lady? [Answered in question #2.]

4. What was the vision like? [Answered in question #2.]

5. What clothes did she wear? [Answered in question #2.]

6. Did all hear?

She heard. [She said] that she [the Lady] said that they should come there six times for six months and that she would then say what she wanted and she disappeared.

7. Did they go to Mass the Sunday before? Where?

She goes every Sunday. The day of the apparition was a week day and they did not go to Mass.

8. Where did they usually go to Mass? She goes to Fatima.

9. How was the statue dressed at the chapel where they usually went to Mass?

[She said] that there is a Lady of the Rosary at the church, but it has no rosary beads nor a white dress.

10 Did you hear some sermon on Our Lady of Lourdes or did you play [being her]?

She doesn't know.

11. Did you go to Mass a lot, even on week days?

She goes only on Sunday; because her mother doesn't let her [go on week days].

12. What did you do after seeing the Lady?

It was only at night, when they came home and said that they had seen a Lady from heaven, since that is how she called herself.

13. How was the Lady dressed the first and other times?

Always the same dress.

14. Did she say why she came on the 13th? … [Dots indicate no answer.]

15 Did they always see spots in the sun?

It was only on the last day that they saw at the sun the Child Jesus, St. Joseph and Our Lady. But Lucia saw better.

16. How was she on the oak bush? Did she smile or was sad?

She was serious.

17. What color was her dress and how did she hold her arms?

[She was] dressed all in white, [arms] separated at the bottom, hands erect.

18. Were you afraid when you saw the Lady?

She was afraid the first time; she said not to be afraid, that she would do no harm.

19. To whom did you say what you had seen?

She said to her father and brother that she had seen a Lady.

20. When did you speak to the priest on the matter? She did not say.

21. What did he say? She does not remember.

22. What did Our Lady say the first time? The 2nd, the 3rd, the 4th, the 5th, the 6th?

On St. Anthony's day (the 2nd time) she said they should learn to read. The father says there were 50 to 60 people there.

The last time—Lucia asked what she wanted, and she said—that the war was ending on the 13th when she arrived in heaven; that if the people did not want to amend their ways the world would end; if they did <u>not</u> wish to amend the war would end.

[Note: The word not, which I have underlined, clearly was an error, either by Jacinta or by Father Lacerda; Doc Crit I p 337.]

23. Are they poor or average? ... [No answer.]

24. Do they say the rosary every day? They do.

25. Did she hear sometime that Our Lady would appear to the soldiers? She never heard.

26. Did the pastor ask you to pray the rosary for the soldiers? Yes.

27. Do they know how to read? Did they hear at home or elsewhere about Our Lady's appearance?

She never heard.

28. To whom did she first say that she saw Our Lady?

To her parents and siblings.

29. Who are their parents, their names? How do they make a living? Health, religious feelings, do they say the rosary at home at night or say grace? ... [No answer.]

30. Did they tell you and do you know the story of Lourdes, La Salette or Our Lady of Montserrat? She never heard.

31. Are they alcoholic? What do they say to their sons and daughters? ... [No answer.]

32. (Same as question 22) ... [No answer.]

33. Did the Lady say at what time you should come and the day? <u>She said that we should come at noon.</u>

34. The second time were there people there? What did they say? There were some fifty people.

35. The 2nd, 3rd, 4th, 5th time? ... [No answer.]

36. What did the Lady want? Did she say why she came?

She never heard the Lady say why she came. She spoke slowly [that is, in a low voice].

37. [No question.] She was not afraid to go there.

38. [No question.] Jacinta only went to confession this year.

Source: Father de Lacerda's interrogation of Jacinta, 19 Oct 1917; Doc Crit I pp 334-339.

13B. INTERROGATION OF LUCIA BY FATHER LACERDA, UNEDITED NOTES

1. What is your name, whose daughter are you?

Lucia de Jesus, 10 years, going on 11. Her father—Antonio dos Santos Abobora ("Abobora" = Turnip, a nickname for him), and Maria Rosa. She has 5 siblings.

2. What were you doing when you saw the Lady?

Watching the sheep. There was a flash of lightning and I said: we should leave before we have a thunder storm. There was another flash and I looked at the oak bush and saw a Lady who said: Don't be afraid. I will do you no harm. She was over the oak bush. She was young and had a decent skirt. She doesn't know if the skirt was a *travadinha* skirt, and she has seen ladies with pleated skirts, but the dress of the Lady was not like that. She did not notice if the dress was one piece.

3. Is it true that the boy threw a stone at the vision?

It was the other year that John threw a stone. The mother said that the year before in May another image had appeared and that this one was stoned. It was only a year later that the apparition occurred.

4. What was the vision like? ... [No answer].

5. What dress did she have and what did she say?

The first time that we should not fear, and she would do no harm: that they should come there six times, making six months and then she would say what she wanted. She rose little by little and disappeared.

6. Did all hear? ... [No answer.]

7. Did you go to Mass the Sunday before? Where?

She had gone to Mass because it was Sunday at the first apparition. She appeared at noon.

8. Where do you usually go to Mass? ... [No answer.]

9. What is the statue wearing at the chapel where you usually go to Mass?

[She said] that at the church there is a Lady of the Rosary, but she has a child, a mantle and has no beads, and that one had beads.

10. Did you hear a sermon on Our Lady of Lourdes or play [to be her]?

She didn't know the story of Lourdes, but the pastor has now told her of it.

11. Do you go to Mass often, even week days? Sometimes.

12. What did you do after seeing the Lady?

They saw but she said nothing. She had seen it the other year and told her mother and she scolded her. The first time was at a place called Estru-meiras [near Aljustrel].

13. What clothing did she wear the first time and the other times?

She always wore the same clothing.

14. Did she say why she came on the 13th? [See question #5.]

15. Did you always see spots on the sun?

I never saw anything on the sun, because I always looked at the Lady.

16. How was she on the oak bush? Did she smile or was she sad?

She was serious.

17. What color was the dress? How did she hold her hands?

White. Arms erect.

18. Were you afraid when you saw the Lady?

They were afraid the first time.

19. To whom did you say what you had seen?

I said nothing. It was Jacinta who talked.

20. When did you talk to some priest on the subject?

I didn't talk about it then, but much later, yes.

21. What did he say to you? He asked questions and said nothing.

22. What did the Lady say the 1st time, the 2nd, the 3rd, the 4th, the 5th, the 6th?

The second time they said that they should keep coming there and learn to read; the third time that they keep coming, say the rosary for the ending of the war, because only she could do it; she stayed only a little; there were already lots of people; the fourth time I was captured; the 5th time, she doesn't remember; the 6th time [she said] that people should not offend Our Lord any more, that He is already too much offended, that people say the rosary so that He will forgive our sins, if they want to go to heaven; that they build a chapel there to Our Lady of the Rosary, if they want, that the war was ending that very day and we can expect the return of our soldiers very soon.

[Un-numbered question.] Did you see something in the sun after the Lady disappeared?

First her head disappeared, then her body, then her feet.

I saw near the sun what seemed to be the face of a man and a child.

[Father Lacerda repeated question #20.] Not then, later.

[He repeats question #21.] He said why didn't [we] come to tell her right away.

23. Are you poor or average? ... [Question not asked.]

24. Do you say the rosary every day?

She knows how to say the rosary and said it at times, many times, even with the sheep; now she says it every day.

25. Did you ever hear that Our Lady appeared to the soldiers?

She doesn't remember when, but she had already heard it said.

26. Did the pastor ask to pray the rosary for the soldiers?

She doesn't remember.

27. Were you able to read or hear at home or elsewhere that Our Lady would appear?

She doesn't know how to read.

28. To whom did you first say that you saw Our Lady?

Jacinta talked and she confirmed it.

29. Who are the parents, what are they called, how do they support themselves. Health, religious attitude, do they say the rosary at night at home, and say grace?

The mother can read and has read things about Our Lady, says the pastor, and about Lourdes—the *Short Mission*. [It seems that pastor answered this question, not Lucia.]

30-32. ... [Questions not asked.]

33. Did the Lady say the hours and days you should come?

She never said at what hour we should come, but we came at that [same] hour.

34-36. [Not asked.]

[37.] [No pre-prepared question. #36 was the last one.]

The Lady told her a secret which she will not reveal.

[38.] Lucia has already made her First Communion.

Source: Interrogation of Lucia by Father Lacerda, 19 Oct; Doc Crit I pp 339-345.

13C. INTERROGATION OF FRANCISCO BY FATHER LACERDA, UNEDITED NOTES

1. How old are you, whose son?

Francisco Marto, 9 years old, brother of Jacinta.

2. What were you doing when you saw Our Lady? Watching the cattle.

3. Is it true that a boy threw a stone at the image?

It was (his) brother who threw the stone at the Lady the year before.

4. What was the image like?

5. What clothing did she wear?

6. Did you all hear?

It was sunny, they had moved and he saw a Lady dressed in white. He did not see the lightning. Lucia saw it. The sheep fled into the chick peas and corn, but the Lady said that it didn't matter, that the sheep would not knock them down or eat them. After the apparition they ate.

Lucia said that the Lady said nothing. It was only to Jacinta, because she had already appeared to her.

Francisco saw the image.

She had a mantle on her head and her clothing was all white. [All these replies were given under question #4.]

[Questions 7-12 are not given and obviously were not asked.]

13. What clothing did she wear the first time and other times?

She always wore the same clothing. She was very beautiful.

[Question 14 is not given and again obviously it was not asked.]

15. Did you always see the spots in the sun?

I saw St. Joseph and the Child Jesus in the sun.

[Questions 16-21 are not given and obviously were not asked.]

22. What did the Lady say the first, second third times, etc.?

I never heard her talk.

[Question 23 is not given and obviously was not asked.]

[24.] Did they say the rosary every day?

We said the rosary when we were roaming.

[Questions 25-36 were not given and obviously were not asked.]

Source: Doc Crit I pp 345-348.

#14 INTERROGATION OF SEERS BY FATHER LACERDA, EDITED NOTES

[Father Lacerda published his edited notes on his interrogation of the seers in four issues of his weekly newspaper *O Mensageiro* of Leria, beginning on 8 Nov.]

#14A. THE APPARITIONS OF FATIMA, TALKING WITH THE THREE CHILDREN

It is a rare Portuguese journal, daily or weekly, which has not referred to the occurrences at Fatima, especially the solar phenomena, that the people at the apparition site—let's call it that—witnessed on Oct 13, last.

O Mensageiro will report, little by little, testimony of people who witnessed the event, and which the press has published. We, who are awaiting the Church's verdict on the reality of the apparitions, are scarcely worried by the coincidence of the solar phenomenon, which a person of good faith may deny, with that which the children report. A famous astronomer, queried about whether such a phenomenon is common, said with finality "that no, but if it were natural, astronomic equipment would have registered all the nuances of the sun, however small."

How then can we explain the event witnessed by dozens of thousands of people from all categories, from the most educated to the simplest peasant, from the most fervent Catholic to the skeptic or atheist? By hallucination? But that was not possible in such a large agglomeration of people, and nothing was known before about the phenomenon, and curiously, on seeing the usual time pass, dis-believe and become skeptical. How is hallucination possible in persons of such different categories, and even more in people who did not go to Fatima and witnessed the event in Leria at that time.

Be that as it may, not having gone to Fatima and not having seen the phenomenon, we decided to go and interrogate the children to whom the Lady is said to have appeared. We prepared ourselves with all that our science furnishes us about miracles and apparitions, being aware of the attacks of Zola and others on Lourdes, Paray-le Monial and Loreto, etc.; and we made at home a questionnaire, with no less than 36 different questions, which we would ask the parish priest, the parents, the children, and even the neighbors.

So that our inquiry would satisfy us completely, we would interrogate separately these persons. That we did, and what we heard we will pass on to our dear readers. The first one we got to talk with was Jacinta, but since Lucia, by her age, and being said to be the principle seer, taking the major role in the apparitions, *O Mensageiro* will begin by publishing the replies which she gave.

Source: *O Mensageiro*, 8 Nov; Doc Crit I pp 351-352.

14B. INTERROGATION OF LUCIA BY FATHER LACERDA

(Gist– Father Lacerda describes Fatima and the Cova da Iria.) Not noting anything worth noting at the site, we went to Aljustrel, where the seers live. We talked with Lucia. The fact, that for six months people from everywhere and from all classes have come to interrogate her, must have caused her to lose her air of simple and humble shepherd, and she now expresses herself well and gives to her words a certain tone of conviction. We told her who we are, where we came from and what we are going to do, but it did not bother her at all. She replied to our questions in short responses, and only every once in a while, <u>as we were writing</u>, she said: "Say, are there many people dying in the war? Jacinta has a brother there."

"What is your name? How old are you?"

"I am Lucia de Jesus, I am ten years old, going on eleven. My father is Antonio do Santos Abobora [Abobora is a nickname meaning turnip], and my mother Maria Rosa. I have five siblings."

"What did you do when you saw Our Lady for the first time?"

"We were guarding the sheep. It was sunny. There was a stroke of lightning and I said: 'Francisco, (brother of Jacinta) we should go, since a thunder storm may come.' Another stroke of lightning came and I looked at the holm oak and saw a Lady on top of it, who said: 'Don't fear. I won't harm you'; that we should be there six times, making six months, and then she would say what she wanted."

"What was the Lady like? What clothing did she wear?" [Continued, next issue.]

Source: *O Mensageiro,* 8 Nov; Doc Crit I pp 353, 354.

[The second part of Father Lacerda's notes was published on 15 Nov, with the same headline.]

At the same time that I asked her the question on the description of Our Lady, I asked her to show me how she was, offering her several rosaries. She took a white one, wrapped it around her arm, with the cross hanging down, and straightened her skirt and raised her hands.

"This is how the Lady was. She was the height of Virginia. Her dress was all white, her skirt reached down to her ankles and she had white socks."

Virginia is a 12-year-old neighbor who might be one meter 10 [centimeters].

[A paragraph on the type of skirt worn by the Lady, difficult to translate into English, follows.]

"The Lady was serious and little by little disappeared toward Fatima."

It is only natural that Lucia should know the appearance of the apparition at Lourdes or Paray-le-Monial, and having heard from someone that Francisco threw a rock at the Lady, which occurred at Lourdes, I asked her:

"Do you know that Our Lady appeared at Lourdes to a girl and a little boy threw a stone at her, but did not hit her? Did Francisco throw a stone at the Lady?"

"Francisco threw no stone, and it is only days ago that somebody told me in my house that Our Lady appeared in France, but I don't know how this was."

It is only natural that Lucia should confuse the image[6] which she claims to have seen with one of the statues that are in the church at Fatima or the chapel where she used to go to Mass, and from this I offered the following question:

[Father Lacerda does not state the question, but gives only the answer.]

"The Lady of the Rosary of Fatima and the chapel holds a child and has colored clothing, and the Lady has no child at her neck," Lucia said to me.

"What did you do after seeing and talking with the Lady?"

"I said nothing. Last year I had seen the same Lady in a place called Estrumeiras and I said it to my mother, who scolded me a lot and wanted to beat me, and thus I said nothing. It is Jacinta who told it; then they asked me if it was true and I said yes and told what I had seen."

"Were you afraid when you saw the Lady?"

"I was very afraid, but she said, 'Don't fear.'"

"Do you pray the rosary a lot?"

"Now every day, but before seeing Our Lady I also said it while walking the sheep. My mother ordered me to say it and I said it with the other shepherds."

Source: *O Mensageiro*, 15 Nov; Doc Crit I pp 353-357.

Note: The statement about the Lady being the height of Virginia was made by Jacinta, not Lucia, [Question #2 of #13A] and the estimate of her height as 1.10 meters apparently was made by Father Formigao and seems unlikely for a twelve-year-old girl. See pages 21 and 22.

14C. INTEROGATION OF LUCIA BY FATHER LACERDA, [CONTINUED]

"Did you go back the next month, as the Lady told you the first time? What did she say to you?"[7]

"That we keep going to the Cova da Iria and learn to read. She had the same clothing as the first time. There were people there praying the rosary and starting the litany, when I saw the lightning and told them: 'Don't begin it, since there isn't time,' which was in fact true, since moments after Our Lady arrived, appearing from the east."

"And what did Our Lady tell you the third time, on 13 July?"

---

[6] The Portuguese word *image* can be translated as *image, likeness,* or even *statue,* according to context. In this sentence I translate it first as *image* and then as *statue,* as the context requires.

[7] Beginning with this question, Father Lacerda follows, almost word for word, the interrogation of Lucia by her pastor. Doc Crit p 357, footnote 8.

"When I asked her what she wanted, the Lady said to me: 'I want you to return each 13th; pray the rosary to Our Lady of the Rosary for the end of the war, since only she has the power to help [you].'"

-? [This apparently implies that Father Lacerda asked another question.]

"I said more: 'Make a miracle so that all believe [me]' and she replied: 'Three months from now I will make it that everyone believes.'"

-?! [This apparently expresses surprise and the omission of another question.]

"As they had given me various petitions, I asked the Lady if she would grant them, and she said: [continued in the next issue].

Source: *O Mensageiro*, 15 Nov; Doc Crit I pp 354-357.

[The issue of 22 Nov had the same headline as before.]

"'Some I will grant, others no.' Among the petitions offered were some for conversions and cures of illness."

"What did the Lady say on 13 Aug?"

"I was taken captive by the authorities and was not at the Cova, but they said they had heard a noise at the time the Lady usually appeared."

-? [This seems to indicate that no question was asked for what follows.]

"On that day," Lucia continued, "I did not talk with the Lady, but on the next Sunday I saw the Lady at Valinho, who spoke thusly: 'Return to the Cova da Iria. If they had not abducted you, the miracle would be better known. St. Joseph would come with the Child Jesus.'"

"What did the Lady tell you when she appeared the fifth time?"

"I don't remember well, but it seems to me she said: 'Continue to pray the rosary to Our Lady of the Rosary that the war decrease, that the war is coming to an end; on the last day St. Joseph would come to give peace to the world; return here on 13 Oct.' I offered her two letters, a vial of perfume and made various petitions to her; the Lady told me that she would grant some and others no; and in regard to the things offered, they are not of value in heaven."

"How did the Lady appear on 13 Oct?"

"She came as the other times and wore the same clothing. The lightning had scarcely flashed and I saw her come down from heaven, place herself on top of the arch [of flowers] and I asked her: 'What do you want of me?' She replied: 'That people not offend Our Lord God any more, that he was already much offended; that the people pray the rosary to Our Lady of the Rosary that God pardon us our sins, if the people want to go to heaven; that we should build there a chapel to Our Lady of the Rosary if they wish; that the war was ending that very day and we should expect the return of our soldiers shortly.' I made various petitions to her, as before, and she told me that she would grant some, others no."

"Did you see something in the sun after the Lady had disappeared?"

"I didn't notice well, but it seemed to me that I saw the head of a man and a child."

Source: *O Mensageiro*, 22 Nov; Doc Crit I pp 359-360.

14D. FATHER LACERDA'S COMMENTS

"My interrogation was much more minute; I gave her other questions which would have little interest for our dear readers; I came to know that Lucia prayed the rosary enough times when she was walking and guarding the sheep, that her mother, who knows how to read, is very religious, and that Lucia, simple and ignorant, could not have foreseen what thousands of people observed in the sun on Oct 13. If some have doubts about the words which she put in the mouth of the Lady, or at least in regard to some of the affirmations, in the event which they witnessed only bad-intentioned persons could contest it. Is the phenomenon common or not? If it is, how come the (scientific) machines did not register them? If it is not, how come the children, or better, one child, foresaw it in advance, and without knowing what would come to pass three months from then, said that on the last day 'she would make it so that all would believe.'"

And this question continues to assail us.

Jacinta, the other child who, according to what they tell me, also talked with Our Lady, was the first with whom I talked. Her mother, on seeing us, eyed us with distrust. The question which I asked her, if her daughter was there, and if she would give her permission to talk with her, upset her, and it was only when I told her that I came to tell the soldiers in France that Our Lady had appeared that I got her to look on me better.

Mrs. Olimpia de Jesus—that is the name of Jacinta's mother—had good reason for the reserve she showed on seeing me. There had been so many persons who came to Aljustrel to hear the three children, that they didn't even know what to reply. Some of them had come there with the aim of getting contradictions in the replies of the children—according to what a neighbor told us—and just two days before there came there a demon in human form, the arsonist of the church of Alcanena, to interrogate and threaten the children. The caution and reserve of Jacinta's mother came from this.

If Mrs. Olimpia de Jesus received us in this way, her husband, Mr. Manuel Pedro Marto, had no better an attitude. "What surprises me is to have priests who place doubts on what this child saw and heard!"

Source: *O Mensageiro*, 22 Nov; Doc Crit I pp 360-361.

14E. INTERROGATION OF JACINTA BY FATHER LACERDA

Ignoring whatever advanced opinion [we had], we began to hear the little Jacinta, who was barely 7 years old and had been to confession only once. [Continued in the next issue.]

[The issue of 29 Nov had the same headline as the previous issues.]

The little Jacinta is fairly shy and does not talk to all people. To get her to talk to me I had to give her a rosary, a souvenir I had found in Lourdes, which her mother put next to many others which she already owned. Jacinta replied to me a little more willingly on hearing what was recorded about the apparitions, most times replying unshakably with silence or I don't recall.

Here is what she told me: "It was mid-day and they were watching the sheep when Lucia, Francisco and she saw a Lady dressed in white, hands erect, with some white beads entwined around her arms, and that she appeared over an oak bush. [She said] that the Lady told them to be there six times, making six months, and that after that she would say what she wanted, and then she disappeared." She does not recall what the Lady said each time, but she confirms Lucia's words.

When I make some questions about words which the Lady put forth, Jacinta replies: "I don't recall, Lucia must know." She says the same as Lucia: that in her house they pray the rosary, that she goes to Mass on Sunday. She barely knows her church and a chapel in a place near her. None of the statues there is like the Lady of the Cova da Iria. She said she heard the Lady say that the war was ending on the 13th.

Source: *O Mensageiro*, 29 Nov; Doc Crit I pp 361-364.

14F. INTERROGATION OF FRANCISCO BY FATHER LACERDA

There remained only for us to talk with Francisco, who arrived home from school while I was conversing with Lucia. He is the only one who is complying with what the Lady said the second time she appeared: "that they should learn to read." He is nine years old. He didn't hear the Lady talk, but saw her dressed in white. [He said] that when the Lady was talking, the sheep meanwhile were walking among the wheat and chick peas, [but] caused no damage, knocked none down, nor ate any. To the rest of the questions we posed to him, he was unable to answer.

I forgot to say that the three children told me that the Lady told them a secret and that they would not reveal it to anyone.

My inquiry was over. There remains for me only to await the decision of the Church, which has begun to organize the process. The doubts which assailed me on going there were the same that accompanied me on leaving the three children. Did they really see an image? How can one reconcile the confirmation that the war was ending on 13 Oct, if it is still going on now?

How can we reconcile the forecast of the solar phenomenon, witnessed by such a great number of people?

I don't know. There remains that which I heard.

We await the decision of the Church. As a final explanatory note, I must say that my friend, Father Manuel Marques Ferreira, always remained aloof from all, carrying this practice to the point of not going to the Cova da Iria on the days of the apparition. He went there only the last time, after many requests.

Father Jose Ferreira de Lacerda

Source: *O Mensageiro,* 29 Nov; Doc Crit I pp 364, 365.

Note: Only Francisco could go to school in Fatima, since it was attended only by boys in 1917; Doc Crit I p 364, footnote 5.

#15 OFFICIAL DIOCESAN INQUIRY

15A. [As part of the official Diocesan Inquiry of the Fatima events, sworn testimony was taken between 26 and 30 September 1923. Six depositions are given here. All were signed by Father Manuel Nunes Formigao, as secretary, and Father Manuel Marques dos Santos, as promoter of the Faith. All except one were taken, were also signed by an interrogator, who was different for each deposition. Only one testifier was able to read and write, and he signed his deposition in place of the interrogator.

A seventh document was a signed letter of 23 Nov 1922 of Inacio Marques, previously published in the press and given in Annex I as #100. An eighth was the deposition of Carlos Mendes of 13 Sep 1927, which was substantially the same as his letters of 8 Sep and 13 Oct, which are given in Annex I as #12A and #20. A ninth document is the deposition of the seer Lucia, dated 8 Jul 1924, which is given earlier in this Annex [1F]. The above-mentioned six documents are given here as #15B through #15G. They provide much information on the seers, their families and on the apparitions but little on the sun dance. They are not included in the statistics on the sun dance, but are occasionally cited in the text or footnotes in the chapters on the sun dance.

Frequently the documents say "the testifier said." In most cases I replace "testifier" with the name of the person making the deposition, or merely say "he said" or "she said."]

Source: Official Diocesan Inquiry; Doc Crit II pp 64-157; 7, 8.

15B. DEPOSITION OF MANUEL MARTO

Manuel Pedro Marto, 50, married with Olimpia de Jesus, living in Aljustrel, Fatima parish. (Gist– They had seven children, including the seers Francisco and Jacinta.)

(Gist– He heard about the first two apparitions, says that he and his wife went to the third, and that Lucia asked them to shut their umbrellas, which were open due to the sun. He then briefly says what he heard Lucia say.)

She said that the Lady had said that they should pray the rosary and that the war was going to end shortly. The children were then kneeling. Lucia rose quickly .... And pointing, she said: "Look there if you want to see her" and then added "Now it is too late." She was almost facing the west and turned to the east to show where the Lady went. It was calm and the weather became fresh. (Gist– Many asked questions and took oak leaves. He took Jacinta home.)

(Gist– He describes the kidnapping of the seers in detail and says he then went to the Cova.) At the Cova, after talking with various people, he heard perfectly the boom, followed by the dust and fog. The people fled. Almost all took off their hats, shouted for Our Lady and were happy. ... He saw also a kind of shiny globe turning in the clouds. It seemed that there was a fog around the holm oak after the boom. (Gist– The people were mad at the administrator and the priest, thinking that he was involved in the kidnapping. More discussion of the kidnapping follows.)

(Gist– He briefly describes the apparition of 19 Aug and says that he was at the Cova da Iria on 13 Sep.) He saw nothing and heard nothing, but he heard it said that some people had seen extraordinary things. He heard the seers say that Our Lady was to come in October to say what she wanted and make a miracle so that all would believe. After the 13th the visits to his house were numerous.

(Gist– He was at the Cova on Oct 13.) Lucia said: "Now she is here!" The people affirm that they saw color in the sky and sun. The sun did not bother one's sight. He heard no voice.

Source: Diocesan Inquiry, 28 Sep 1923; Doc Crit II pp 64-69.

15C. DEPOSITION OF OLIMPIA MARTO

Olympia de Jesus, married .... with Manuel Pedro .... is a native and inhabitant of Aljustrel, Fatima parish.

(Gist– She describes hearing about the first apparition from Jacinta and says that she didn't believe her. Then she describes in detail how Jacinta got the family to say the rosary every day.)

Francisco said that he saw the Lady move her lips and open her hands, but didn't hear a word. Jacinta said that the Lady talked only with Lucia. Lucia said that she saw a beautiful Lady with a shine around her head, which blinded her. At the start of the apparition, when she said she saw Our Lady, Francisco saw nothing and advised her to hit her with a stone, and Lucia said: "Then you are from heaven and Francisco does not see you?" The Lady had already said she was from heaven. Our Lady said to Lucia: "Tell him to pray the rosary and he will see me." (Gist– He said seven Hail Marys and then he saw her. A full account of the sheep in the chick peas follows.)

(Gist– She tells of going to the fair on June 13, briefly tells what the seers reported and says she did not go to the first three apparitions. She was afraid they were deceiving her. One day she told them she was going to beat them for deceiving lots of people. The children said the non-believers would be punished. Jacinta told about a secret which Lucia had to tell to Francisco. The seers were offered riches for the secret and they replied that they would not tell it for the entire world. They played exactly as before. She saw no difference in them except that they prayed the rosary. They were more truthful and prayed the rosary several times a day.)

On July 13 they went there and reported that the Lady had appeared as in the earlier months.

(Gist– She briefly describes the kidnapping on Aug 13. She says that she and Lucia's mother stayed home and learned of the kidnapping there. Lucia's mother said: "Good, then they won't lie." Olimpia was worried, but not Lucia's mother. When they heard the crowd shout, she said: "What is going on?" Lucia's mother looked at the sun and said; "The sun is different." The people came and said they had seen signs in the sky and sun.)

(Gist– She tells how her son Joao got Jacinta to go to Valinhos for the apparition of Aug 19.)

(Gist– On Sep 13 the two mothers went furtively to the apparition site and stayed some distance away.) When the crowd shouted that it was seeing signs, they didn't see what it was seeing, but saw a little smoke rise from among the people at the foot of the holm oak.

(Gist– They were happy that the seers were safe. It seems that she heard that Lucia said they were to learn to read. Lots of people queried the seers. Once some rich ladies offered Jacinta their jewels for the secret and she said—not for anything would she tell it. She would only tell her mother that it was good for those who believe.)

On 13 Oct she went again to the Cova and stayed with the seers. After she heard that Our Lady had appeared, Jacinta elbowed Lucia and said: "Talk, Lucia, Our Lady is here now." Lucia breathed twice, like one out of breath. Then she said: "What do you want of me today?" A few moments from then Lucia said more: "They wanted me to get the sick better." Then she said: "Our Lady said she could not make all well, that many were bad." Some moments passed, and she got up quickly and said: "If you want to see her, turn to the east." But following that she said: "Now you don't see her." When she went home Jacinta said to her: "Oh mother, I saw her enter heaven" and she added that it seemed that her legs were separated.

(Gist– A short report on the deaths of Francisco and Jacinta follows.)

Source: The Diocesan Inquiry of 28 Sept 1923; Doc Crit II pp 70-83.

15D. DEPOSITION OF MARIA ROSA DOS SANTOS

(Gist– Personal data is given. She had seven children. Lucia was the youngest.)

In the year before the apparitions, she heard her daughter say that in another place they had seen a person wrapped in a kerchief ....

(Gist– She did not learn of the May 13 apparition until the next day. She questioned Lucia about it.) She said she had seen a very pretty little woman all dressed in white. [She said] that she asked her: "Where are you from?" and she pointed to the sky, saying she was from there. After she asked her if Francisco, Jacinta and Lucia would go to heaven, the apparition replied yes. On hearing this Maria Rosa said: "How lucky you are." The Lady said that they should come there six months and at the last she would tell them what she wants. Maria Rosa refrained from asking the little one many questions.

(Gist– She didn't go to the Cova on June 13, but went to the fiesta instead. On the way she met a group going to the Cova. Each month she worried that the children might be beaten for lying. People said that those who went to the Cova were very satisfied and believed the seers. Lucia led the crowd in the rosary on the way back.)

When later she asked her what she had seen, she replied that she had seen the same little woman as before. Maria Rosa asked what she had said. She said to keep coming there and to learn to read. This made her a dis-believer, because it seemed that Our Lady would not have come to earth to tell her to read.

(Gist– Lucia was as good and humble as ever, with the same happiness. People had given Lucia some coins. She denied getting coins from an elderly lady, so Maria spanked her. She cried and said it was Jacinta who got them. She remained convinced that the seers were lying. She went to the pastor, saying all were lying. The pastor said not to beat the child nor put fear into her.)

She didn't go to the Cova in July because the pastor advised against it. On returning, the house was full of people, asking the girl questions. Almost every day they tried [to do this] so she couldn't go to pasture the flock, and Maria Rosa had to substitute. The little one said that the Lady had told them a secret. …. And that she had asked help for some sick people and it seemed that the Lady said she would help some, others not. ….

(Gist– She briefly reports the kidnapping of the seers. She was not worried and even thought that if they were lying they merited some punishment, and if not the Virgin would protect them.)

Many people came later and tried to comfort her, saying that now they were more believing because it was the first day that signs were seen. The brothers of Jacinta went by bicycle to see what was happening and returned and said that they had seen the children playing on the veranda of the administrator, who was treating them well.

(Gist– The seers returned on the 15th.) The children were as happy and ready to play as before. They said that they had asked them many questions and a doctor came to examine them. The administrator said the people were a pain for having seen signs. ….

On the 19th Lucia came home at night with a little branch of the holm oak and said that Our Lady appeared to them a bit before sunset, around 4:00 …. She took it and noticed that it smelled of perfume very much. She could not compare it with any other perfume.

(Gist– Now she was less an un-believer.) The girl said that the Lady had said to keep coming to the Cova, that there would be a miracle in October, that the soldiers would return from the war, and Our Lady of Sorrows and others would come.

On Sep 13 many people came. Everything went as before.

On Oct 13 she went to the site for the first time, despite the suggestion of the pastor. (Gist– They dressed the seers. She went with the children, but lost them because there were so many people. At the Cova she got through and stayed beside them. Some people had said they would kill them … and [since] on the other hand, it would be sad to have it all end and see nothing, she decided to go. The children told the time the apparitions took place and they wanted to go and be there on time. The last time they had waited a quarter of an hour near the holm oak for the apparition to begin. All three were standing. Jacinta's mother was near.

The people were saying that perhaps there would be nothing because the time was passing and nothing unusual was happening. All three [seers] gave a shout at the same time. "Ay!" Lucia said: "There she comes. Be quiet, there was a flash." It had rained all morning. (Gist– The holm oak was decorated.) Then Lucia said: "She is here." She talked loudly. Maria Rosa saw nothing. She only noticed the same perfume as in the branch from Valinhos, when Lucia said: "There she is."

Lucia asked: "What do you want today." She was silent a little and at once it seemed that she asked for a miracle so all the people would believe. Then she was silent again. A moment later she said she had many petitions of many sick to make to her. (Gist– She describes the posture of the seers.) Lucia, from time to time, raised her eyes and then lowered them. Later, the pastor asked why she did this and she said it was because she was blinded. (Gist– She describes the seers' clothing.) It all lasted a short time. At last Lucia said: "There she goes. Do you see her? Look there," pointing with her hand to the east, toward which she was and had always been the whole time.

Then, naturally, when she lost her from sight, she turned her back to the holm oak and said to the people behind: "Look, Our Lady said to stop offending God, who was already much offended, and that the war was ending." Olimpia said: "Lucia, did you not ask the Lady to make a miracle so that all would believe?" To this Lucia replied: "Do you want a greater miracle than the ending of the war?" She said further that Our Lady had said that they should build a chapel there, that she was Our Lady of the Rosary and that the war would end when she got to heaven.

She turned and said: "There she is. Don't you [think] that she is going to arrive?" (The child does not recall telling the people to look up at the sky, the sun.) It was then that the people began to look up. Maria Rosa saw the sun turn and descend three times, and she could look at it.

She began to fear that the children would be hurt. A doctor of Torres Novas put her on his shoulders and pushed her toward the road. (Gist– She went home. The house was crowded.) One of the things which [had] made her skeptical was that at times in winter evening sessions they talked of the apparition of Our Lady of Ortiga, Our Lady of Fetal, etc. She thought, however, it was good that she would appear now because it would strengthen the Faith.

Source: The Diocesan Inquiry, 28 Sept 1923; Doc Crit II pp 84-95.

15E. DEPOSITION OF JOSE ALVES

Jose Alves, 58 ... resident for 23 years in Moita, Fatima parish. Moita is one kilometer from the Cova da Iria.

(Gist– He heard of the apparitions in May. His nieces have some property there. When he was there in May he didn't see anything unusual. He didn't know the seers or their families before 13 May. After that, he saw them at his nieces.)

He noted that the children were like the other children, perfectly normal, with their head on their shoulders. They seemed serious. He heard a little from them about the apparition, but not much, because they talked of it chiefly to his wife and nieces, especially his wife, who asked lots of questions. What they said was always the same thing, according to what his wife said. They never wanted to retract anything. For this, he held them to be sincere.

While he was not there, but his wife told him [about it] later, his wife asked Jacinta: "Tell me the secret and I will give you my chain." (Gist– Lucia may have been there, but Francisco never came.) Jacinta said: "If you give me that little saint [a statue], I'll tell you." The woman replied: "I can't. It is not mine, it is my niece's." The niece said: "Jacinta, tell me the secret and I'll give it to you." To this she replied: "Not if you give me the entire world."

Once, when his wife was at home asking questions of Lucia, Jacinta entered the conversation and said: "Our Lady comes from there (and pointed to the east) and went away there (and pointed to the Cova da Iria.)" His wife asked Francisco if he had seen Our Lady and he said no, he only saw the shine around her feet. Naturally, he was referring to the start of the first apparition, while he still did not see, before beginning to say the rosary.

One day, at the beginning of the apparitions, his wife went to the Cova and asked Francisco what he [had been] doing. He said they were making a rock wall and Lucia came up with a stone. Then Lucia said: "There was lightning and water [rain] is coming" and they went down the hill, and when they got to the Cova Our Lady appeared to them on a holm oak, which was torn apart by the people. The Lady said: "Don't fear. I am from above, from heaven" and it was then that she told them to come every month and to pray the rosary.

Almost every month he went there on the 13th, since May, and he saw nothing, he only heard that others were seeing things in the sky. He did not hear the boom in August. He heard it said many times that a little smoke showed up.

(Gist– He talks about taking off his hat at the site.) He gave some property for the work [at the Cova] and gave it willingly and never regretted it.

One day the pastor was in his house and said that that was either a very bad or very good thing. I found him to be fairly dis-believing. Alves said to the pastor "not a bad thing because if it was, it would not have ordered [them] to say the rosary nor to pray." The pastor replied: "You are deceived" and he added "the devil uses even the sacraments."

(Gist– A long statement follows on two soldiers or guards who wanted Lucia to ride their horse on her way home.)

Source: The Diocesan Inquiry, 28 Sept 1923; Doc Crit II pp 96-101.

15F. DEPOSITION OF MARIA (CARREIRA) DOS SANTOS

Maria dos Santos, 50, resident of Moita, Fatima parish …

(Gist– She learned of the apparition from her husband and others. On June 13 she went to the apparition site. She did not then know the seers, but knew the family. Before the seers, some women from Boleiros arrived. The seers came with people from Torres Novas.)

Then they went to the shade of a large oak nearby, where they stayed some time, waiting. …. A lass asked them to say a litany, but Lucia said there was no time. Almost at this moment she arose, said the Lady was coming, since there had been a lightning flash. She ran to the foot of the holm oak, knelt, and all did like her. Moments later she asked the apparition: "You ordered me to come here. Please tell me what you want." A buzzing was heard from the holm oak, but not a word of the response was heard. Lucia looked to the holm oak, as did the other two children, all with hands joined. Maria did not hear well what the apparition said, but other persons said that the little one had asked her if she wanted anything more. At once she said: "Look. Do you want to see? There she goes." Then something like the hiss of a rocket, as it gains force, was heard. She looked and saw a smoke cloud rising from the holm oak and heading and rising to the east. And it was seen very high and long. At last it disappeared. The cloud was a light mist. It was warm and sunny, the weather quite clear.

Before the apparition she saw the needles of the holm oak bunched and very straight. After the apparition the needles seemed to be bending toward the east in a circle on top, as if clothing had made them fall in that direction. (Gist– People took branches of it) …. Her husband arrived at the apparition site shortly before the three seers. …..

(Gist– She went to the Cova on three other Sundays before July 13. On that day she brought her sick son Joao. There were lots of people.) When Lucia said that the Lady was coming, her son slipped and fell. He asked them to pray for him, to which she said that the Lady said that he would get better or she would give him the means to control himself, and that he should always say the rosary with his family.

They were all kneeling. Lucia said: "Our Lady is coming now." The same buzzing was heard when she talked and the same hiss of a rocket on her departure. Before the apparition they prayed the rosary. Her husband said that she [Lucia] looked at the Lady and from time to time [looked] to the side, and that he asked her why she did this, to which she replied that her shine blinded her sight. She asked for better health for a person from Pedrogam, for the conversion of a family from Fatima, and for a man from Atouguia, who asked Our Lady to take him to heaven right away. Later Maria heard it said that the Lady had said that there was no hurry, that she knew well he was to be taken.

Lucia also affirmed that the Lady had told them a secret. At the time of the apparition an *ay* was heard, for the little one was frightened. After this many persons tried and asked her for the secret. One day some ladies came and asked her if the secret was good or bad, and she said it was good for some, bad for others, and for her and her cousins it was good.

In August lots of people gathered there. Maria was present, waiting for the children. At noon it was known that the administrator took the children prisoner to .... Ourem. The people were .... indignant. There was a sound at the foot of the holm oak that caused the people such great fright that they seemed to be crazy, shouting loudly and thinking that they were dying.

The people left little by little. Maria saw nothing extraordinary. At the request of the people she took up the offerings to hold them. Nobody, neither the parents of Lucia, to whom the land belonged, nor the parents of Jacinta, nor the pastor wanted to accept the offerings, and he [the pastor] recommended that she hold them until seeing where all this was going.

When the children returned to the Cova da Iria, she asked them to ask the Lady what should be done with the money. At Valinhos, when the apparition occurred there, the little one actually asked this question, and the Lady said that they should make two litters and carry them to the church of Our Lady of the Rosary. Many people were upset that the money was not to be used for something at the site and they said to Lucia to ask permission to make a grotto at the site, a permission which the Lady gave on 13 Sep, with the condition of giving half of the money to Our Lady of the Rosary of Fatima. They gathered 13,540 on 13 Sep and the Lady's order was fulfilled.

On 13 Sep Maria went back to the site again. At Valinhos Lucia [had] asked the Lady, at Maria's request, if Our Lady had appeared anywhere except at the Cova da Iria, and the Lady replied that it was not her, but it was indeed an angel, the form which Caroline, Maria's youngest daughter,

12 years old, and a little one from Espite, saw on 28 July near the holm oak, [an angel] of small size, very pretty, blonde, a form which Caroline later saw on top of the holm oak.

On Oct 13 [clearly an error for Sep 13] when Lucia said, "Now Our Lady is coming," one of her daughters, Maria, ... felt a hit on her face and saw a very beautiful light at her feet and shouted: "*Ay*, Our Lady." The testifier looked and saw a star, a globe, not entirely round, like an egg, very beautiful, rainbow-colored, but livelier, with a tail one and a half meters [long] in brilliant colors. It went by very rapidly, and near the holm oak, and disappeared a hand's length from the ground. She saw the sun descend a lot.

After 13 Sep she told Lucia to ask the Lady who she was. The holm oak shook a lot when she said the Lady was coming. She heard Lucia say: "The Lady permits us to build a chapel, now say under what name we are to <u>adore</u> her." When she arose after the apparition I asked her what name she had said, and the little one said she was Our Lady of the Rosary. On that day Lucia also said: "Now close your umbrellas," that already she sees St. Joseph in the sun and the Child giving a blessing and she [sees] well Our Lady arriving in heaven. After she said this, the sun danced.

From then on the crowd got bigger all the time. .... The people wanted a chapel to be built. They asked the pastor, who allowed it in order to keep the offerings, which were received in species.

Maria talked to a mason and had the chapel built. She ordered a wall to be made last (or next-check) year. Water appeared two years ago.

Source: The Diocesan Inquiry, 28 Sep 1923; Doc Crit II pp 101-111.

Note: The word "adore" in the third to last paragraph was underlined in the Portuguese text. Apparently Father Formigao realized that the word "adore" could not have been spoken by the Lady and wanted to point this out by underlining it.

15G. DEPOSITION OF MANUEL ANTONIO PAULA

Manuel Antonio Paula, 71, native of Boleiros, Fatima parish, living in Lisbon on Santa Maria Street #280, first floor, passed the months September and October, 1917 in his native place. Before this time he knew from letters of trustworthy relatives and from other places in the parish that extraordinary occurrences in the sky had been verified at the time of the apparition of Our Lady to the three children, whom he got to know only in September. He wondered a lot [about this] and tried to find out the truth. (Gist– A friend in Boleiros, Antonio Barralho, said that they were telling the truth.) .....

On 13 Sept he was at the Cova da Iria, but saw nothing. There were lots of people, which many calculated at 50,000. He was more or less seven meters from the children, whom he saw arrive .... He saw them kneel together near the holm oak and pray the rosary. At a certain time persons who were near them said we should remove our hats because the children had indicated that Our Lady was present. (Gist– Near him everyone did.) Almost all knelt when they gave the order. There were people who said they saw a star. Others were sorry they saw nothing. (Gist– He went first to Jacinta's house, which was crowded, so he went to Lucia's. It was crowded too. He asked her mother what had happened.)

The mother replied that she was home at night after the first apparition and she said she had seen Our Lady at the Cova da Iria. She did not want to believe her, because her daughter was not what she would like, meriting to see Our Lady. She wanted to beat her. Lucia, fearful of her, began to tell outside what had happened, but didn't tell anything to her mother. When her mother learned this she said to her: "Then you go telling outside that Our Lady appeared to you, and say nothing to me?" Then she asked the daughter what size the Lady was. She said she was like a [girl] there fifteen years old. She had never seen anyone so beautiful.

(Gist– A priest asked Lucia's father permission to talk with Lucia, who was exhausted. He refused, but later de Paula heard that he allowed it.)

(Gist– De Paula went with Lucia's father to an aunt's house.) The aunt asked him if he had seen anything. He replied that he saw nothing except a white butterfly. .... She asked him what would come of all this. "Why" he asked. "Because people are passing by making their comments and threatening and saying that the little ones and their families should be taken to court because they were deceiving the people."

On 13 Oct when he left Boleiros with other people it began to rain. His sister was afraid she could not return because they said bombs were being thrown, but she quieted down saying if Our Lady was there nothing bad would happen, because she would not allow it. (Gist– He went to a cousin's house in Fatima.) He said to her: "Naturally the children are not going in such a rain." "They are going," she said, "even if it pours." ....

When the rain was over, about 1:00, he headed to the site and near the road met a priest from Pencova[8] who asked him where the apparition site was. He showed him a spot where a mist was seen, a little smoke, fairly thick, which did not seem odd to him, thinking it was incense in honor of Our

---

[8] Presumably Father Cruz Curado. See Annex I, #59.

Lady. He was amazed later when they told him there was no smoke, that no bonfire of any kind was made, nor had a match been lit.

Suddenly the priest looked at the sun and said that the <u>sun was in eclipse</u>, was it not. De Paula also looked at the sun and saw that it did not give any light, a white mist was going over it, it was a moon without shine. The sun was on the left, with the rest of the sky covered. Taking his eyes from the sun <u>he saw the people to be red</u>, very bright and exclaimed: "*Ay* sir, the people are all red." And the priest replied: "They must be red kerchiefs." To which he observed: "How can that be? Then all got together to wear red kerchiefs on their backs?" <u>Later the people appeared gold-colored.</u> He did not see the rotary movement of the sun. The people on this occasion shouted a lot, kneeling, hands raised, shouting for Our Lady, paying no attention to the mud, of which there was a lot, and repeatedly invoking Our Lady. The impression of the people was extraordinary. After the apparitions he had gone to the Cova various times on the 13th and it seems to him that there was various phenomena and miracles, and the crowd was greater each time.

The witness, Manuel Antonio de Paula

[As in all cases, Fathers Formigao and dos Santos also signed.]

Source: The Diocesan Inquiry, 28 Sep 1923; Doc Crit II pp 111-117.

INDEX TO ANNEX I

Document Number	Source (newspaper, unless otherwise stated)	Page in Annex	Date (in 1917, unless otherwise stated)
1	O Seculo	272	23 July
2	A Liberdade	274	25 July
3	O Ouriense	274	29 July
4	Magno letter	274	August ?
5	A Liberdade	276	18 August
6	O Mundo	276	19 August
7	O Mensageiro	278	22 August
8	Raio de Luz (magazine)	279	1 September
9	Brites diary	280	13 September
10	Magno letter	280	10 September
11	Marinhense	282	22 September
11A	Da Camara letter	282	26 September?
12	Correio–Extremadura	283	22 September
12A	Mendes letter	283	8 September
13	R. Grande letter	286	3 October
14	Diario de Noticias	287	13 October
15	O Seculo (Almeida)	287	13 October
16	Basto notes	289	13 October
17	Brite's diary	292	13 October
18	Fr. da Silva letter	292	13 October
19	Coelho letter	293	13 October
20	Mendes letter	294	13 October

Document Number	Source (newspaper, unless otherwise stated)	Page in Annex	Date (in 1917, unless otherwise stated)
21	Bento Statement	296	13 October
22	de Castro letter	297	15 October
23	Correia statement	298	13 October?
24	Jornal de Leiria	299	14 October
24A	Garrett letter	299	14 October
25	Coutinho letter	300	15 October
26	Sampaio letter	302	15 October
27	Diario de Noticias	303	15 October
28	O Seculo (Almeida)	304	15 October
29	O Portugal	308	15 October
30	Pinto letter	309	15 October
31	Holstein letter	310	16 October
32	Parente letter	310	16 October
33	Manoel letter	312	16 October
34	A Orden (Coelho)	315	16 October
35	A Patria	318	16 October
36	O Primeiro de Janeiro	318	16 October
37	Basto letter	319	17 October
38	Rapozo letter	319	16 October
39	De Melo letter	320	17 October
40	O Portugal	322	17 October
41	O Portugal	323	17 October
42	A Republica	324	17 October
43	Pena letter	325	18 October
44	Serra letter	326	18 October
45	Democracia de Sul	328	18 October
46	A Lucta	329	18 October
47	O Mensageiro (Silva)	331	18 October
48	O Seculo (Oom)	333	18 October
49	da Camara letter	333	19 October
50	O Dia (Patricio)	335	19 October

Document Number	Source (newspaper, unless otherwise stated)	Page in Annex	Date (in 1917, unless otherwise stated)
51	Constanca statement	336	20 October
52	Beira Beixa	341	20 October
53	Correio de Beira	342	20 October
54	Gazeta de Familacao	342	20 October
55	Caminho letter	343	20 October
56	A Guarda	345	20 October
57	A Defesa	345	20 October
58	Tovares statement	346	21 October?
59	A Liberdade	349	23 October
60	O Seculo	350	24 October
61	A Ordem (Romana)	351	25 October
61A	Porto da Mos depositions	352	25 October
61 B	Mira deposition	353	25 October
61C	Mira deposition	353	25 October
61D	Carvalho deposition	354	25 October
61E	Menitra deposition	354	25 October
61F	Dos Santos deposition	354	25 October
61G	Da Rosa deposition	354	25 October
61H	Joao deposition	355	25 October
61I	De Matos deposition	355	25 October
61J	Amado deposition	355	25 October
61K	Gomes deposition	356	25 October
61L	Caravalho deposition	356	25 October
61M	Pedro deposition	356	25 October
62	O Democrata	357	26 October
63	A Republica	357	26 October
64	Anita letter (Grojean)	359	27 October
65	Camara letter	362	27 October
66	Rapozo letter	363	27 October
67	Voz de Paroco	365	27 October

Document Number	Source (newspaper, unless otherwise stated)	Page in Annex	Date (in 1917, unless otherwise stated)
68	Ilustracao Portugesa	366	29 October
68A	A Verdade	367	31 October
69	de Melo letter	368	31 October
70	Nascemiento e Sousa letter	371	31 October
71	La Landa letter	372	October?
72	Raio de Luz (letter)	374	1 November
73	Camara statement	375	3 November
74	Camara statement	376	3 November
75	A Monarquia	377	8 November
76	Helio de Lys (pamphlet)	377	10 November
77	Coreio de Beira (Queiros)	378	10 November
78	A Aurora	381	11 November
79	Tuna statement	382	11 November
80	Vieira statement	383	11 November
81	Ribeiro statement	383	11 November
82	Baptista statement	384	11 November
83	de Jesus statement	384	11 November
84	Pereira statement	385	11 November
85	Concelho de Maio	386	18 November
86	A Ordem	387	21 November
87	Grego letter	389	24 November
88	The Reaction (a pamphlet)	389	December?
89	G. Garrett letter	390	3 December
89A	M. Garrett letter	392	4 November
90	J. Garrett letter	392	18 December
90A	M. Garrett letter	396	18 December
91	Neves deposition	397	27 December
92	Vasconcellos deposition	397	30 December

Document Number	Source (newspaper, unless otherwise stated)	Page in Annex	Date (in 1917, unless otherwise stated)
93	Silva deposition	401	30 December
94	Barbarosa statement	402	30 December
95	Jornal de Mulher (Campos)	403	30 December
96	Lopes deposition	405	18 December, 1918
97	Goncales deposition	407	31 December, 1918
98	De Jesus deposition	408	2 March, 1919
99	Vincente statement	409	2 March, 1919
100	Marques statement	410	23 November, 1922
101	Pereira statement	411	1931
102	Pereira statement	412	1952
103	Jornal de Noticias (Teixera article)	413	1926
104	Dos Santos letter	414	17 October
105	Portugal; Madeira	415	27 October
106	O Mensageiro	416	25 October
107	Fe Cristao (magazine)	416	December
108	Neves letter	416	1 November
109	A Razao	417	30 May, 1918

INDEX TO ANNEX II

Document Number	Source	Page in Annex II
	FORMIGAO QUERIES IN SEPTEMBER	
	Introduction	458
8A	First queries, September 17	459
8B	Queries of Francisco, September 27	460
8C	Queries of Jacinta, September 27	461
8D	Queries of Lucia, September 27	461
8E	Formigao comments	464
	FORMIGAO QUERIES, OCTOBER 11	
9A	Queries of Goncalves–unedited	466
9B	Queries of Goncalves–edited	467
9C	Queries of Lucia's mother–unedited	469
9D	Queries of Lucia's mother–edited	470
9E	Queries of Lucia–unedited	471
9F	Queries of Lucia–edited	473
9G	Queries of Jacinta–unedited	474
9H	Queries of Jacinta–edited	475
9I	Queries of Francisco–edited	476
	FORMIGAO QUERIES, OCTOBER 13	
10A	Queries of Lucia–edited	476
10B	Queries of Jacinta–edited	479
10C	Queries of Francisco–edited	480
	FORMIGAO QUERIES, OCTOBER 19	
11A	Queries of seers–edited	481
11B	Queries of Lucia–edited	482
11C	Queries of Francisco–edited	483
11D	Queries of Jacinta–edited	484
11E	Queries of Jacinta–unedited	485

THE SUN DANCE: INDEX OF THE SECTIONS

About Leonine Publishers

Leonine Publishers LLC makes fine Catholic literature available to Catholics throughout the English-speaking world. Leonine Publishers offers an innovative "hybrid" approach to book publication that helps authors as well as readers. Please visit our web site at www.leoninepublishers.com to learn more about us. Browse our online bookstore to find more solid Catholic titles to uplift, challenge, and inspire.

Our patron and namesake is Pope Leo XIII, a prudent, yet uncompromising pope during the stormy years at the close of the 19th century. Please join us as we ask his intercession for our family of readers and authors.

Do you have a book inside you? Visit our web site today. Leonine Publishers accepts manuscripts from Catholic authors like you. If your book is selected for publication, you will have an active part in the production process. This book is an example of our growing selection of literature for the busy Catholic reader of the 21st century.

www.leoninepublishers.com

CPSIA information can be obtained
at www.ICGtesting.com
Printed in the USA
FFOW02n0133190717
37840FF